Greek Letters and the
Latin Middle Ages

HIC·TITVLVS·EST·
LIBRI·HVIS·DISPVTA
TIO·ABBATIS·THEODORI·
GENERE·GRECI·ARTE·
PHILOSOPHI·CV·IOHE·VIRO·
ERVDITISSIMO·ROMANE·
ECCLESIE·ARCHIDIACO
DO·GENERE·SCOTHO·

Walter Berschin

Greek Letters and the Latin Middle Ages

From Jerome to Nicholas of Cusa

REVISED AND EXPANDED EDITION

Translated by Jerold C. Frakes

The Catholic University of America Press
Washington, D. C.

Originally published as *Griechisch-lateinisches Mittelalter. Von Hieronymus zu Nikolaus von Kues*, © 1980 A. Francke Verlag, Bern und München

LIBRARY OF CONGRESS CATALOGING-IN-PUBLICATION DATA
Berschin, Walter
  Greek letters and the Latin Middle Ages.

  Translation of: Griechisch-lateinisches Mittelalter.
  Bibliography: p.
  Includes index.
    1. Greek language—Study and teaching—History.
  2. Greek language—Influence on Latin (Medieval and
  modern) 3. Civilization, Medieval—Greek influences.
  4. Education, Medieval—History. 5. Learning and
  scholarship—History—Medieval, 500–1500. 6. Hellenism.
  7. Humanists. 8. Greek philology, Medieval and late.
  I. Title
  PA55.B4713 1987   480.'7'04   86-9762
  ISBN 0-8132-0606-5

Contents

v

Translator's Preface

The topic of the Greek tradition in the medieval West is not a new one to medievalists, as the bibliography to the present volume amply illustrates. But as Professor Berschin shows in his introductory chapter, there has been a long-standing need for an in-depth survey of the wide-ranging topic. According to the numerous reviews of the original (German) edition of Professor Berschin's study, the book has in large part satisfied that need and has moreover struck a resounding chord among scholars, for it provides not simply a lucid survey of this immense and complex field of study, taking into account both primary manuscript sources and the mass of scholarly publications of the past *several* centuries, but also a synthesis of this material and integration of it into a comprehensible intellectual and historical context, such that it can serve as both a reference volume for the specialist and an introductory manual for the student or general reader interested in medieval culture and its relations with classical antiquity. Perhaps its greatest virtue is indeed its quality as synthesis and integration, for in the face of the overwhelming mass of material, the easiest path to take would be to allow the book to become a mere catalogue, a *Handbuch* in the traditional sense. Berschin has religiously avoided this avenue.

It seems only appropriate that in the course of the preface to the original edition the author refers to E. R. Curtius *en passant*. In very different contexts, numerous reviewers of the first edition have also mentioned Curtius—most often in comparing Curtius' monumental work on the Latin literary tradition in the medieval West to Berschin's present study of the corresponding Greek tradition. One reviewer (Hans-Joachim Zimmermann, *Archiv für das Studium der neueren Sprachen* 133 [1981], 374) formulates his comparison thus: coupled with Curtius' study, Berschin's completes the "Greco-Latin diptych" of the antique tradition in the medieval West. In any case, it is certainly true that the two works have in common their comprehensive scope and astounding mastery of both primary and secondary research materials.

As generally characteristic of Berschin's study, one may take Bernard of Chartres' oft-cited (also by Berschin) metaphor of "modern" scholars as dwarfs on the shoulders of giants. As he notes in his introductory chapter, previous studies of the present topic have in general been grossly inadequate. But having said as much, one must immediately admit (and

Berschin does) that this statement is possible only as the result of the work of precisely those earlier pioneers—Bentley, Jourdain, Renan, Eggers, Rose, Gardthausen, and later Manitius, Sandys, Traube, etc. Standing on their shoulders means to *use* them in the best sense, to learn from them—not only to look forward, but also to look backward, to see how these giants intellectually came to be, and to learn in general *how* to look, to discover their methods and those of their forebears. He notes in his preface that it is sometimes surprising how much in the older handbooks is not inaccurate or superseded. But one can only know that if one has already taken the measure of these giants and mounted their shoulders in order to look back—back to the materials with which they worked, and the only materials on which such study can legitimately be based—the manuscripts, and this again teaches us a valuable lesson in the old way of seeing, now made new again.

One might generally compare the problem of the modern scholar of the Greek tradition in the medieval West to the one faced by modern textual criticism in its confrontation with the humanistic *lectio recepta* of ancient authors. There one needed to fight one's way back through the *editiones principes* and the ideology underlying the notion of the authority of *editiones principes* and *lectio recepta*—all the while learning as much from their virtues and the immense erudition of those pioneering giants as we dwarves are capable of doing—in order to gain access to the material, theory, and practice necessary to prepare critical editions. Here one must contend with ideology as well: the *lectio recepta* of the prejudices and preconceptions, both positive and negative, concerning the knowledge of Greek at various times and places in the medieval West, usually based at best on very narrow examinations of primary material. Here also, the struggle back through the field of now-dead giants leads to the manuscripts, and this is Berschin's goal, his method, his ultimate ground, and the point of the study itself. Alongside its virtue as a consummate synthesis, Berschin's study thus distinguishes itself most through the author's comprehensive knowledge of the manuscript tradition and his ability to render that tradition, in its various historical contexts, accessible to the reader.

Even with the publication of the original edition, Berschin's study did not reach its greatest possible audience, nor even all those who could profit from it, especially outside the field of specialized medieval studies. For despite all graduate language requirements and good intentions, many students and scholars (not just in the U.S.) who might profit from Berschin's research can summon the will perhaps to read a pertinent article-length study in German, but hardly to read an entire book in that language, especially if it is of the detail and density of the present volume. In both style and method of presentation, however, Berschin's study is indeed intended not just, or not even primarily, as a reference volume to be "consulted," but as a book to be read. Thus one can justify the English translation, if such justification be necessary, by thinking of it in terms of one of the recurring metaphors of the study: as a *translatio studii*, albeit on a modest scale.

For much the same reason as that for translating the book as a whole, it seemed expedient to translate all substantive citations in the book (which was not the case in the original edition). The original texts of the ancient and medieval citations are with few exceptions also printed; citations from modern scholarship are generally given in the original language only if that original formulation is itself noteworthy. While the practice of translating citations has increased the volume of the book somewhat, it is nonetheless of value, since the author makes such great use of both manuscript material and modern scholarship in the development of his argumentation.

As the title page indicates, the present edition is more than a mere translation of the original German edition. Soon after its publication, when I first approached Professor Berschin about the possibility of preparing an English translation of the book, he had already been at work for some time on a revision of the German text. In the ensuing years, this revision has been carried out, and the additions and corrections have been incorporated into the present text. In addition to the thorough revision of the text in general, the bibliography has been expanded; a chronological table has been added; and the final chapters, especially Chapter XII, have been reworked to the extent that they are essentially new. Thus the present edition is a fully revised and expanded version of the original German edition.

I have striven both for accuracy in rendering the sense of the original and for a stylistic level corresponding to it. I hope to have achieved the former goal in terms of Jerome's principles of *ad sensum* translation. About the latter I have no illusions: rarely has a reviewer failed to note and praise the unusual (for philological treatises) lucidity, liveliness, precision, and literary quality of Berschin's fine style. I must humbly take my place with those medieval translators, treated in the pages that follow, whose aspirations to the rendering of both the sense and the style of their exemplars had to remain content with the former.

In the course of the past five years of sporadic periods of intensive work on the translation, many colleagues and friends have offered suggestions and criticism for the improvement of the English version. I thank them all. The University of Southern California Faculty Research Fund has kindly provided partial financial support for the project. Finally, my thanks are due the author, whom I have consulted at every stage of the work and who has shown extraordinary interest and patience throughout.

A note on proper names:

The proper names of hundreds of authors—Greek, Latin, Spanish, Italian, French, Catalan, Arabic, Hebrew, German, Flemish, English and Gothic, from antiquity to the Renaissance—who wrote and received names in one or more of the languages associated with those cultures, constantly threaten to turn the present work into a mere annotated catalogue. In the German original the author dealt with this labyrinth by means of an intricate system that is, however, not adaptable to use in English. In the translation I have normally substituted the dominant English form of the name for all personages for whom such a form exists (whether that form is Anglicized or not); otherwise the 'original' (usually Latin) form is given preference. The index of names includes variant forms and cross-references and should provide some further aid.

J.C.F.

Author's Preface

There is a constant murmur of Greek behind Latin.
D. J. R. Bruckner, rev. of the *Oxford Latin Dictionary*,
The New York Times Book Review (9 Oct. 1983), p. 27

The aim of this book is to interpret the Latin literature of the Middle Ages from a particular point of view and with a specific approach—from the perspective of the Greek East and with an inquiry into the importance of Greek script, language, and literature in the Latin West during a thousand-year period. It is conceived as a literary history of the Latin Middle Ages *sub specie graecitatis*.

This perspective is not altogether common in medieval studies. The lack of a survey of this subject has, however, long been lamented, and such a study has been labeled a desideratum for research. This deficiency was felt perhaps even more strongly in the nineteenth than in the twentieth century.[1] Our picture of the Middle Ages seems in this regard to have become more one-sided, and it is centered "in the western and southern (not northern or eastern!) cultural tradition,"[2] according to the most widely read book on medieval Latin literature.

The first task of such a study is to investigate the quite widely scattered secondary literature in order to take into account the broad spectrum of the medieval Greco-Latin tradition. I have striven for a comprehensive knowledge of the material. The fact that, for example, the specialist in the Graecolatina of the thirteenth century remains relatively unacquainted with the work of the experts on the twelfth, and that scholars of the fourteenth century neglect important works on the thirteenth, made this attempt at completeness indispensable, even though such completeness is scarcely possible, considering the profusion and diffusion of the publications. Older and rarely cited research literature was taken into account wherever possible. In reading these older works it became clear how rarely they have actually been superseded in all respects, and how frequently an advance in one field has been paid for by a step backward in another.

During and after the primary research, the question arose as to how the material might be offered to the reader in a manageable form: by which methodological criteria could the relevant details of literary history be

xiii

separated from the less important, the accessible from the still inaccessible? I had to keep well clear of the catalogue form—that old, convenient model of literary history, which has accompanied us, with various modifications, right down to the present day. This form is useful as a first step in the examination of the subject and is a legitimate guide through complex traditions. It is not suitable as literary history, however, since it is not selective in its inclusion of material and does not inquire into the cultural context of literary works, which forms the very substance of literary history. The principle of selection employed was that in every case the material had to yield meaningful units which could be presented in a clearly defined historical progression. It seemed more important to correctly fix the caesurae in the sequence of Greek spheres of influence in the Latin West and to identify in each case their essential elements than to include every detail of the tradition. In this respect, the present treatment adheres to the principles of "period history."

The term "literature" is understood in the older, comprehensive sense. Thus the so-called technical literature is incorporated into the study, since it is a focal point of medieval Hellenism. On the other hand, the book presents no history of the schools, the education, the culture, in fact no history of any kind, nor indeed an apology, although aspects of each of these categories have been included in the work where the explication of the literary context admits or requires them.

Even when I had to be selective, I attempted to maintain a balance. In the treatment of the "borders of the Middle Ages" I was somewhat more selective, while I allowed myself a greater latitude in dealing with the central periods. This is especially the case in the treatment of the Greek tradition in the monasteries of the Lake Constance area, which could be understood as a methodological model: based on similar manuscript research, it would have been possible to examine in their cultural contexts the Graecolatina of Fleury, Monte Cassino, and Verona.

Thus, after the method and scope of the primary research and the epochal-historical principle in the selection of the material, the third principle of this literary history must be addressed: as far as possible I have subjected the manuscripts to a detailed examination, through which I discovered time and again how complicated problems are simplified in an unexpected fashion as soon as one returns to these documents of the textual tradition. Thus the study has ultimately become a book which attempts to present literary history *based on the manuscripts*.

I hope to demonstrate that this genre of literary history is the appropriate one for the Latin Middle Ages. I can scarcely hope to set a precedent, however, since Horace's principle *nonum prematur in annum* would then become the minimum requirement for every attempt at literary history. Yet I would like this study to encourage a more concrete and realistic consideration of medieval literature, based on the manuscript tradition: the essence of this literature lies in the manuscripts, and it is there that it lives on among us.

This topic was treated in survey form in the *Reallexikon der Byzantinistik*.[3] The fact that this literary history could develop from that study is due to the aid, advice, and active assistance of many. Many of the libraries listed in the manuscript index have supported the work through permission to examine their codices. For information and microfilms of manuscripts, special thanks are due to the Badische Landesbibliothek in Karlsruhe, the Stiftsbibliothek in St. Gall, the Österreichische Nationalbibliothek in Vienna, the University Library in Leiden, the Bibliothèque Nationale in Paris, the city libraries of Laon and Metz, and the Vatican Library. Finally, I would like to thank the staff of the university libraries in Freiburg and Heidelberg (most of whom have remained unknown to me), who, over a period of six years each, have procured in great volume the literature for this book.

I would like to express my gratitude to them all here. In addition, there are many friends, colleagues, and fellow students to be thanked for their helpfulness, above all my dear wife, who has shared the burden of this book also. In memory of my courageous mother (d. 24 Jan. 1972, in Günzburg), the book is dedicated to my son, Wulfila.

W. B.

Greek Letters and the
Latin Middle Ages

FORMAE LITTERARVM SECVNDVM GRECOS

	alpha			o uelu		
ṗa	A	mia	i	O	ebdenta	Lxx
	bita			pi		
ṗb	B	dia	ii	Π	ogdenta	Lxxx
	gamma			co pin		
ṗg	Γ	tria	iii	nola Ϙ	emnenta	xc
	dilta			ro		
ṗd	Δ	tessera	iiii	P	ecaton	c
	e			simma		
ṗe	Є	penta	v	C	diacusin	cc
	episinon			thau		
nota	Ϛ	exa	vi	T	triacusin	ccc
	zita			eu uel ui	tetracusin	cccc
ṗz	Z	ebda	vii	Y fi		
	hita				pentecusin	d
ṗe	H	ogda	viii	Φ o		
	thita			hi		
ṗth	Θ	nia	viiii	phi X	exacusin	dc
	iota			psi ꞇꞇ psi		
ṗi	I	deca	x	Ψ Ψ	eptacusin	dcc
	cappa			o longil		
ṗc	K	ecusi	xx	po ꞆꞆ	ogdacusin	dccc
	lauta			sincope		
ṗl	Λ	trinta	xxx	notul ∧	niacusin	dcccc
	mi ts mi					
ṗm	ꟽ Ж	serenta	xL			
	ni					
ṗn	N	pennenta	L			
	xi ꞇ xi xi si xi					
ṗx	Ꝫ Ꝫ Ꝫ Ꝫ	exenta	Lx		

Review of the Research Literature

The Humanistic Prejudice. We have adopted the concepts of the "revival," "rebirth," and "rediscovery" of classical antiquity, as descriptive formulae for an epoch, into our historical consciousness directly from their axiomatic use by the Humanists. It has long been known that there was no direct "line of connection between the Renaissance and antiquity," that "not a single Roman writer was newly discovered,"[1] that the script which was revived at that time, on models presumed to be ancient, was the Carolingian (in its Italian form of the high Middle Ages), and that the manuscripts of ancient works, freed from the "gloomy dungeons" of the monasteries into the glorious freedom of humanistic private ownership and the printing offices, had their origin almost without exception in medieval, primarily Carolingian, scriptoria.

The concept of continuity was not the strong point of humanistic consciousness. No Humanist would have accepted the notion that he was a dwarf who could see more and farther only because he sat "on the shoulders of giants."[2] The independent self-assurance of the era considered itself as little obligated to the immediate past as to the still unknown future. The history of text transmission records how endangered every medieval manuscript was as soon as it had passed into the hands of the Humanists: "Wie viel handschriften sind verschwunden, erst nachdem die schützenden klostermauern gefallen oder schwach geworden waren. und dann nicht bloss *zwischen* kloster und officin, grade *in* der officin, wie viele sind zerstört worden, oft unwiederfindliche unica, durch die unvorsichtige nachlässigkeit der begehrlichen liebhaber selbst, denen mit der ersten drucklegung alle zukunft abgefunden schien" ("How many manuscripts have disappeared, only after the protecting walls of the monastery had fallen or become weak. And then not only *between* the monastery and printing office, but precisely *in* the printing office, how many have been destroyed, often irrecoverable unica, as a result of the incautious negligence of their grasping admirers themselves, for whom the initial publication apparently satisfied all obligations to the future").[3]

Humanistic Greek studies were more original, pioneering, and attentive to preservation than Latin studies. Humanists had made the survival of the intellectual life of the Greeks possible, even after the fall of the imperial city of Constantinople in 1453. They welcomed the scholarly

Greeks with open arms, and after the death of the generation of emigrants, the Humanists passed the torch of Greek scholarship on to the schools and universities—admittedly with all the alterations which an intellectual world undergoes when it survives only in the schools and at the scholar's desk (for example, the change of Greek phonetics from the living "iotacism" to Erasmus' stillborn pronunciation). It was, however, a true *translatio studii* which was accomplished in the fifteenth century, a politico-intellectual event of universal significance.

Humanism could point to its originality in Greek studies more legitimately than in Latin. This the Humanists frequently did, and the humanistic judgment that "the Middle Ages knew no Greek" lingers on as a *communis opinio* even to the present day. In general it is justified; but *as* a generalization, it is misleading. There is a "dotted line," so to speak, of concern with and knowledge of Greek which runs though the whole of the Latin Middle Ages, and early Humanism continued precisely this tradition of medieval Greek studies.

Bilingual Bibles and "Critica Sacra." The continuity between medieval and modern Greek studies becomes evident especially in regard to the bilinguals, the numerous Greco-Latin manuscripts of the Psalter, the Gospels, the Pauline epistles, and even the Acts of the Apostles preserved from late antiquity and the Middle Ages as an aid in the individual study of Greek.[4] They were sometimes consulted at synods, and from the sixteenth century on, the "Critica Sacra" made use of these codices, which promised easy access to the Greek Scriptures by means of the Latin text.[5]

The bilingual which was first used for an edition of the Bible seems to have been the "Codex Bezae," a fifth-century Greco-Latin uncial manuscript of the Gospels and Acts, which has been in Lyon since the second third of the ninth century at the latest. At that time, Deacon Florus and Ado, later bishop of Vienne, worked on and with the manuscript. In 1546 at the Council of Trent, Bishop Guillaume Duprat of Clermont quoted from the manuscript; four years later Robert Estienne (Stephanus) had it collated. During the Huguenot disturbances, Théodore de Bèze (Beza) "discovered" the codex and later presented it to the University of Cambridge. The text of the codex has been published in full three times: first in 1793 by Kipling as a facsimile script not altogether free from errors, then in 1864 by F. H. Scrivener in a diplomatic edition, and finally in 1899 in photographic facsimile.[6]

After the "Codex Bezae," the "Codex Laudianus" of the Acts was probably the bilingual which was studied earliest and most intensively in biblical criticism. This Greco-Latin uncial manuscript, probably written in Sardinia ca. 600, has served both medieval and modern biblical studies, for according to an early conjecture which more recent scholarship has confirmed, the Venerable Bede studied Greek and wrote a commentary on Acts using this bilingual. This manuscript came to the monastery of St. Pirmin at Hornbach in the Palatinate probably in the eighth century and thereafter most likely to the cathedral library in Würzburg. In the Thirty Years' War, Archbishop Laud acquired the manuscript for Oxford. John Fell incorporated the variants of the codex into the Oxford Greek New Testament in 1675; and Thomas Hearne published the entire text of the manuscript in Oxford in 1715. In 1870 Constantin von Tischendorf made arrangements for a new edition in Leipzig and had a Greek uncial typeface cut for the purpose, which has since repeatedly served as a model for the accurate reproduction in print of late antique and medieval Greek majuscule.[7]

A third Greco-Latin manuscript often referred to was the ninth-century "Codex Boernerianus" of the Pauline epistles, which was the property of Christian Friedrich Boerner, later professor of theology at Leipzig; it became known when Ludwig Küster incorporated its variant readings into the second edition of John Mill's Greek New Testament. In the seventeenth century, the manuscript belonged to Paulus Junius in Leiden; its medieval repository was St. Gall. This bilingual was also edited more than once: the Wittenberg professor Christian Friedrich Matthaei published a line-for-line edition in 1791 in Meißen; there was even a second edition of this painstaking book. In 1909, on the five hundredth anniversary of the University of Leipzig, a facsimile appeared which may be considered the most beautiful reproduction of any Greco-Latin manuscript of the Middle Ages.[8]

The "Codex Paulinus Augiensis," the Reichenau counterpart of the "Codex Boernerianus" formerly of St. Gall, and likewise of the ninth century, had a typical fate. At the time of the Council of Basel, the manuscript was borrowed by one of the jurists at the council and most likely never returned; the manuscript later came into private collections, first in Schaffhausen, then in Heidelberg, where Richard Bentley, Regius Professor of Theology at Cambridge, acquired it in 1718 for a projected new edition of the New Testament. In the following year he borrowed the aforementioned Greco-Latin Paulus manuscript from his Leipzig colleague Boerner, so that the closely related Pauline bilinguals of Reichenau and St. Gall were together for several years with Bentley in Cambridge —and would have remained together there, had Boerner not done everything in his power to bring about the return of his manuscript. A diplomatic edition of the Cambridge "Codex Paulinus Augiensis" also appeared.[9]

The theologico-editorial occupation with the bilingual biblical manuscripts generally yielded information concerning medieval Greek studies only incidentally. The theologians sought the original text or an early stage of the tradition in these manuscripts. After it became clear that the bilinguals were completely unsuited to that purpose, the interest in them, at least in regard to textual criticism, generally waned.[10] Yet for more than two centuries theologians brought the bilinguals great publicity. Their editions, line-for-line reproductions, and facsimiles of Greco-Latin manuscripts, produced with a view to the "Critica Sacra," remain philologically valuable.

A place of honor in the history of scholarship on medieval bilinguals is due to the theologian Heinrich Christian Michael Rettig of Gießen. Among scriptural text critics, he advanced farthest toward a medieval philological understanding of a Greco-Latin biblical manuscript when he devoted the few years granted to him as a teacher in Zurich to editing (1836) the Evangelium graecolatinum of the St. Gall Stiftsbibliothek (Cod. 48). When he recognized that even the complete printing of a codex would not clear a path through the tangle of the vast multitude of variant readings, but rather only the *vividae quasi imagines* of the manuscripts and their pages could be of aid, he had the codex copied onto tracing paper ("Strohpapier") in order to eliminate to the extent possible all arbitrary influence in the reproduction of the text. This tracing was then mechanically transferred to stone plates and reproduced as a photograph before photography, as it were. In his valuable preface, Rettig described almost all characteristics of the codex necessary for its evaluation. He also recognized the St. Gall evangelary and the Dresden Paulus ("Boernerianus") as *fratres gemellos* (Rettig, *Codex Sangallensis Graeco-Latinus interlinearis*, p. xix).

Paleography. At the beginning of the eighteenth century, the new science of paleography was also occupied with the Graecolatina of the western European libraries. In his *Palaeographia Graeca* (1708), the Maurist Bernard de Montfaucon adduces "Specimina Codicum Graecorum septimi circiter saeculi, qui apud Latinos scripti sunt," "Specimen Graecum noni saeculi apud Latinos, ex Psalterio Monasterii S. Michaëlis in Lotharingia, quod Sedulii Scotti manu exaratum fuit," "Specimen ex Glossario Laudunensi Graeco-Latino. . . ."[11] Herewith the founder of Greek paleography directed attention to the old bilinguals; in the "Sedulian Psalter" he made known an exceptional example of a purely Greek manuscript written in the West, and in the glossary of Laon, the most important pedagogical manuscript of the Greek language from the Carolingian period.

Literary History. At the same time, the collector's zeal of the era brought much to light in the field of literary history with respect to the Graecolatina. For example, Burgundio's major translator's prologues were published in 1724 by the Maurists Edmond Martène and Ursin Durand in *Veterum Scriptorum . . . Amplissima Collectio*; this edition is in some respects valuable even now.[12] Ludovico Antonio Muratori was the first to refer to the Italian Greek scholars and translators of the high Middle Ages, when he wrote in the third volume of his *Antiquitates Italicae Medii Aevi*, "De literarum fortuna in Italia post annum Christi MC."[13] Gian Girolamo Gradenigo included medieval Greek studies as an independent topic of literary history in his *Lettera all 'Emin^{mo} . . . card^{le} Angelo Mª Querini, . . . intorno agl 'Italiani, che dal secolo XI. insin verso alla fine del XIV. seppero di greco*, published in 1743 in Venice, which seems to agree essentially with the *Ragionamento istorico-critico intorno alla letteratura greco-italiana*, published in 1759 in Brescia.[14] The scholarly Theatine took as his point of departure the fact that many contemporary literary histories—true to humanistic propaganda—saw the beginning of Greek studies in the West no earlier than Chrysoloras, or at the earliest in the era of Petrarch and Boccaccio. In order to oppose the ignorance concerning medieval Greek studies and make amends for this injustice, inflicted primarily on the Italian Hellenists, Gradenigo wrote his very distinguished and specialized study. Girolamo Tiraboschi profited from these studies and, in his *Storia della Letteratura Italiana* (1772–81), evaluated "non pochi Italiani . . . che furon dotti del greco" ("not a few Italians . . . who were educated in Greek").[15]

In the nineteenth century, leadership in the literary historical treatment of the Graecolatina shifted from Italy to France. In his *Recherches sur les anciennes traductions latines d'Aristote* (1817), the Orientalist Amable Jourdain responded to the problem set for an essay competition of the Académie des Inscriptions et Belles-Lettres concerning the appearance and influence in the West of the translation of Aristotle from *Arabic*.[16] In this study, Jourdain of course also encountered the long line of translators of Aristotle from *Greek*—Jacobus of Venice, Robert Grosseteste, William of Moerbeke, and others. Jourdain's method of research was such that he did not depend exclusively on the well-known—whether true or false—literary historical data, but rather scrutinized the works of the Scholastics for citations from Aristotle. Moreover he also took it upon himself to analyze the manuscripts. One chapter of his book is devoted to the "Examen des anciennes versions latines d'Aristote conservées à la Bibliothèque du Roi." Of these manuscripts, Jourdain edited "Spécimens" of some thirty Greco-Latin and fifteen Arabo-Latin translations of Aristotle. In the proportion of Greco-Latin to Arabo-Latin translation in the Paris library, it became clear that the traditional notion—that the Middle Ages in the West owed its Aristotle primarily to the Arabs—was indefensible. Jourdain did not yet dare to draw the radical conclusions from the manuscript tradition which were unavoidable after the comprehensive examination of the Latin Aristotle tradition conducted for the *Aristoteles latinus*. Minio-Paluello was the first to reverse the old prejudice—ultimately also of humanistic origin—concerning the transmission of the Aristotelian texts: "tutto il Corpus aristotelico, ad eccezione del De Caelo, de parte dei Meteorologica e della zoologia, è giunto alle scuole di lingua latina dal greco prima che dall'arabo" ("with the exception of *De Caelo*, and part of the *Meteorology* and the *Zoology*, the entire Aristotelian corpus reached the Latin schools from Greek before it did from Arabic").[17]

The Académie des Inscriptions et Belles-Lettres was somewhat less fortunate in awarding its 1848 prize to Ernest Renan for his "Histoire de l'étude de la langue grecque dans l'Occident de l'Europe depuis la fin du Ve siècle jusqu'à celle du XIVe siècle." Renan judged his work even more severely than did the Académie and never allowed it to be published.[18] In Stralsund at the same time, Friedrich Cramer wrote *De Graecis medii aevi studiis* in the archaic style of the learned *dissertatio* and published the first part of it in 1849: *inde a primo medio aevo usque ad Carolum Magnum.* The second part, which was to treat the period from the Crusades to Humanism, was never published.[19]

Cramer made especial use of the possibilities offered by the editions of the *Monumenta Germaniae Historica*, which had been appearing in rapid succession since 1826. He gathered information on his topic from these volumes and from older, primarily historical, literature. The controlling idea of his study was that the papacy was to be seen as the true enemy of both vernacular and Greek studies in the Middle Ages: "Quo maior enim erat papalis potentia, eo magis una latina regnabat lingua" ("for the greater the papal power, the greater the exclusive rule of the Latin language"). Gregory the Great provided Cramer with evidence here; Cramer considered Nicholas V an exception to the rule; and he did not take Eugenius III, a patron of the high Middle Ages, into account. More pertinent than his main thesis were his incidental observations—for example, that it means very little when a person is said to be *utriusque linguae peritus* in a medieval document,[20] or that an author's occasional use of a Greek word does not indicate that he knew Greek. Yet Cramer not only failed to observe these restrictions himself, but even went so far as to interpolate vigorously when it seemed to him necessary for rounding out his presentation. Thus he concluded, on the basis of the exchange of envoys between the Frankish and Byzantine Empires in Charlemagne's time, that there must have been men throughout the Frankish Empire who knew Greek. From the report that Abbot Heito of Reichenau wrote a "hodoeporicon" about his embassy to Constantinople, Cramer inferred that, since it had a Greek title, the travelogue must have been written in Greek—Jerome was simply no longer read in the Prussian secondary schools![21] Cramer drew from obscure sources the claim that Homer was read in the monasteries of Benediktbeuren and Wessobrunn during the Middle Ages, and he inferred from such lines in Waltharius as "dic,

homo, quisnam / Sis aut unde venis, quo pergere tendis?" (ll. 587–88:
"Tell, sir, who you are, where you come from, and where you are going")
that Homer was also known in St. Gall.

Nothing is more characteristic of the misplaced Neohumanistic perspective—
from which medieval Greek studies were viewed—than the search for traces of a
familiarity with Homer. "In the considerably large number of common features"
in the *Iliad* and *Waltharius*, G. Finsler (*Homer in der Neuzeit* [Leipzig/Berlin
1912], p. 2) "is tempted" to see "a direct influence of Homer" on the *Waltharius*
poet. The same book also contains a compilation of the most remarkable legends of
"Homer in the Middle Ages" which the nineteenth century produced: "By means
of laborious study," Walafrid Strabo in Reichenau was supposed to have "advanced to the point of reading Homer" and spent "long winter evenings" with his
teacher, Wetti, over a Homer codex, which "had been bought in Aachen from a
Greek from Constantinople." "An Exemplaren Homers wäre auch sonst kein
Mangel gewesen, da Abt Hatto [Heito] und Erlebald mehrere gekauft hätten, als
sie als Gesandte Kaiser Karls beim griechischen Kaiser in Konstantinopel weil-
ten" ("Nor was there as a rule any shortage of Homer codices, since Abbot Hatto
[Heito] and Erlebald are to have bought several while they lingered in Constantinople as Emperor Charles' ambassadors to the Greek Emperor"). This scholarly
legend originated in a literary supplement to the 1856–57 annual school report of
the monastery at Einsiedeln, in which an unnamed enthusiast of things medieval
(M. Marti), published an "autobiography" of Walafrid Strabo, in the manner of
Scheffel's *Ekkehard* (1855), with the title "Wie man vor tausend Jahren lehrte und
lernte." As a result of various errors which were neither intended nor occasioned
by the author, the little "novelette" soon came to regarded as a historical source—
even long after J. König ("Walafried Strabo und sein vermeintliches Tagebuch,"
Freiburger Diöcesan-Archiv 15 [1882], 185–200) had set the matter straight.

Literary historical studies of the Graecolatina were frequently conducted during the nineteenth century by means of Cramer's method of
collection and more or less critical appraisal of literary documents. Émile
Egger published his lectures *L'hellénisme en France* in 1869. While he
presents a valuable outline of Greek studies in late antique Gaul and in
sixteenth-century France, his exposition of the French Middle Ages is too
general. Egger regarded the manuscript tradition too skeptically: "Je ne
sais pas, à vrai dire, si, depuis le sixième jusqu'au commencement du
quinzième, il a été écrit en France une seule copie d'un auteur grec, soit
sacré, soit profane" ("In truth I do not know if a single copy of a Greek
author, whether religious or secular, was made in France from the sixth to
the beginning of the fifteenth century").[22] Montfaucon's *Palaeographia
Graeca* could have helped him here. Egger nevertheless renounced interpolation as a means of bridging the gaps in the text tradition. He mentioned that there was scarcely anything known of the "Collegium Constantinopolitanum," which had given such wings to Jourdain's historical
fantasy, allegedly founded in 1204 by Latins under King Philip II Augustus and Pope Innocent III after the conquest of Constantinople.[23] Yet he

still naively believed in the Greek "interpreters' school," supposedly founded in 804 in Osnabrück by Charlemagne, that had played a similarly important role in the older literature.

A "bellum diplomaticum" was fanned into flame in the early eighteenth century by a document attributed to Charlemagne, according to which Greek and Latin schools were to be established in the newly created bishopric of Osnabrück, in order to prepare the bishops of that see to function as envoys in the case of dynastic alliances between the Western and Eastern Empires. This "battle of the documents" was not settled until the beginning of this century, when the documents became verifiable and were finally recognized by diplomatics as eleventh-century forgeries (of Bishop Benno of Osnabrück [1068–88]?); cf. *MGH Diplomata Karolinorum* (Hanover 1906), I, no. 273, pp. 404 f., and M. Tangl, "Die Osnabrücker Fälschungen," *Archiv für Urkundenforschung* 2 (1909), 186–326, esp. pp. 258 ff.

In his extensive treatise "Les études grecques en Europe" (1878), Charles Gidel proposed to close the wide gaps left by Egger in his treatment of the Middle Ages. This exposition is distinguished by its careful use of older literature: the conclusions of Gradenigo, Jourdain, and Cramer were reproduced in great detail. Rarely, however, did Gidel deviate from the opinions expressed by his authorities. Thus, for example, in his account of Greek studies among the Irish in the early Middle Ages, he could not free himself from Ozanam's *La civilisation au cinquième siècle* (1855) and Hauréau's *Singularités historiques et littéraires* (1861). As a consequence, he interpreted Columban's adonics (*Fidolio fratri suo*)

> Femina saepe
> Perdit ob aurum
> Casta pudorem.
> Non Iovis auri
> Fluxit in imbre,
> Sed quod adulter
> Obtulit aurum,
> Aureus ille
> Fingitur imber.

[A chaste woman often gives up her honor in return for money. Jove did not flow in the shower of gold, but because the paramour did offer gold, this golden shower was invented.]

as evidence for the wandering Irish monk's having read Greek: "Ces souvenirs de la mythologie antique, si curieux dans les vers de l'apôtre irlandais, peuvent avoir passé par le latin pour venir jusqu'à lui; mais nous ne savons pas s'ils auraient cette précision, cette justesse, cet air d'invention originale et neuve, s'ils n'étaient qu'un reflet d'Horace ou d'Ovide" ("These reminders of ancient mythology, so curious in the verse of the Irish apostle, could have been transmitted to him through Latin;

but we are not sure whether they would have this precision, this appropriateness, this air of new and original invention, if they were no more than reflections of Horace or Ovid").[24] In general, Gidel's work remains an outstanding accomplishment in literary history, even if the critique of the material presented is not of great depth.[25]

One may regard Charles Cuissard's *L'étude du grec à Orléans depuis le IXe siècle jusqu'au milieu du XVIIIe siècle* (Orléans 1883) as a second echo of the interest evoked by Egger's *Hellénisme en France*. Cuissard understood "à Orléans" in the broad sense: in his view, Fleury (Saint-Benoît-sur-Loire) also belongs to this category, and, insofar as the Middle Ages are concerned, the presentation deals almost exclusively with this great monastery. Cuissard lapses into typical errors of judgment concerning traces of Greek in the Middle Ages: ". . . Théodulfe savait le grec. Il se glisse parfois quelques hellénismes dans ses vers; ses *Capitulaires* nous offrent le mot *gastrimargia* pour indiquer sa gourmandise" ("Theodulf knew Greek. Hellenisms sometimes creep into his verses; his *Capitularies* use the word *gastrimargia* to signify his gluttony," p. 21). The incipit of the famous *Ilias latina* is cited as evidence for a Greek text of Homer at Fleury (p. 40): "Dans un manuscrit de cette époque [Bern 286] nous avons trouvé les deux vers suivants:

> Iram pande mihi pelide, diua, superbi,
> Tristia qui miseris iniecit funera ⟨Grais⟩.

Comment expliquer cette traduction parfaitement correcte, si l'auteur n'avait pas eu sous les yeux le texte grec d'Homère. . . . Il y a donc tout lieu de croire que Fleury possédait sinon l'Iliade entière, du moins une partie, et le souvenir de Troie vivait dans les coeurs" ("We have found the following two lines in a manuscript of the period [Bern 286]: . . . . How can one explain this perfectly correct translation, unless the author had Homer's Greek text before him. . . . Thus there are sufficient grounds for believing that Fleury possessed at least part of the *Iliad*, if not the entire work, and the memory of Troy lived on in their hearts"). Despite all inadequacies, however, Cuissard broke new methodological ground by restricting his study to one region and one monastery and by taking his material from manuscripts and library catalogues.

One can also regard the book by Abbé A. Tougard, published in a limited edition in Rouen, as a supplement to Egger's *Hellénisme en France*: *L'Hellénisme dans les écrivains du moyen-âge du septième au douzième siècle* (1886). Without taking Gidel's exposition or any other important earlier work into account, Tougard held to the notion that one could get a general survey of the Greek studies of medieval authors by means of an examination of the relevant volumes of Migne's *Patrologia Latina*. A sort of Index Graecitatis of the *Patrologia Latina*, from volume 80 to volume 217, was the result.

With that the nineteenth-century attempts at a comprehensive literary historical treatment of the topic cease. With one exception (Cramer), the authors wrote in France; the Académie des Inscriptions et Belles-Lettres played a major role in this special interest of French scholarship in the mutual relationships of the Greek East and the Latin West: not only Jourdain and Renan, but Gidel as well, were ultimately led to their studies by essay competitions of the Académie, which also administered the *Recueil des Historiens des Croisades*. In the course of the nineteenth century, to be sure, the connection between literary history and manuscript research—the latter of which was resumed on the basis of the accomplishments of the Maurists by Léopold Delisle and Henri Omont—was lost.

Specialized Studies in the Nineteenth Century. Literary historical treatments of the Graecolatina are generally lacking in nineteenth-century German scholarship; but its contribution to research on special problems was nevertheless significant. Among the first to again work in the centralized libraries, which had also appeared in Germany as a result of secularization, and work as extensively and thoroughly as the eighteenth-century Benedictine scholars, was Franz Josef Mone, a progeny of Heidelberg romanticism, who, as director of the Karlsruhe archives, published his manuscript studies and discoveries in a series of epoch-making compilations. One of these was *Lateinische und griechische Messen* (1850), in which Mone published, among other things, the liturgical translations of Leo Tuscus and Nicholas-Nectarius of Otranto from an Ettenheimmünster manuscript. Through his study of Latin manuscripts which contained Irish glosses, Johann Kaspar Zeuß founded Celtic philology (*Grammatica Celtica* 1853), which thereafter made important contributions to the investigation of Greek studies in the early Middle Ages. In his *Anecdota Graeca et Graecolatina* (1864 and 1870), the Berlin librarian Valentin Rose presented the booty of a learned, fifteen-year-long "ars venatoria" in European manuscript libraries; his ϑηράματα fill one volume of discoveries pertaining to the history of ancient and medieval Greek science. The developments in the cataloguing of manuscripts were also significant. When manuscript libraries with outstanding collections had expert cataloguers, such as Hermann Hagen in the Bibliotheca Bongarsiana in Bern, Montague Rhodes James in the Cambridge libraries, or again, Valentin Rose in Berlin, then research in the area of the Graecolatina profited directly.

In his *Griechische Paläographie*, which appeared in two editions, Viktor Gardthausen concentrated his attention, as did Montfaucon, on the western bilinguals and the Greek script in the West.[26] Friedrich Maassen thoroughly examined the canonistic manuscripts with their numerous translations from Greek for his *Geschichte der Quellen und der Literatur des canonischen Rechts* (1870). Georg Goetz made the tradition of ancient and early medieval Greek-Latin and Latin-Greek dictionaries available in his *Corpus Glossariorum Latinorum*. By means of manuscript research, C. P. Caspari came to one of the first solidly based treatments of the "gottesdienstlichen Gebrauchs des Griechischen im Abendlande während des früheren Mittelalters" ("liturgical use of Greek in the West during the earlier Middle Ages").

Medieval Latin Philology. In Germany the foundation, as university disciplines, of the medieval philology of both classical languages—Byzantine studies and medieval Latin philology—made possible the integration of all these already highly specialized studies. Ludwig Traube, who was a pioneer in many areas of medieval Latin philology, addressed the problem of the Graecolatina on many occasions and from diverse perspectives. During his ten years of work on the third *Poetae* volume of *MGH* (1886–96), he published, among other things, "Von Sedulius und seinen irischen Genossen geschriebene Handschriften" and "Kenntnis des Griechischen bei den Iren zur Zeit Karl's des Kahlen" (in "O Roma nobilis" in the transactions of the Munich Academy).

Traube's point of departure for the section concerning the Sedulius manuscripts was the Greek Psalter of Sedulius Scottus, which Montfaucon had found in Verdun and evaluated in detail in *Palaeographia Graeca* (the manuscript has been in the Arsenal Library in Paris since the French Revolution). Traube collated the text with two Greco-Latin manuscripts: the Codex Boernerianus, which C. F. Matthaei, in the epilogue to his edition, had already characterized as closely related to Sedulius' Psalter (on the basis of a comparison of engraved reproductions!); and the evangelary of St. Gall 48, which Rettig had recognized as quite closely related to the Boernerianus. Traube associated these three Bible manuscripts, as well as the poetic and grammatical manuscript Bern 363 (the "Bernese Horace"), as the key to the whole, with the Irish Priscian manuscript St. Gall 904. He not only observed paleographical relationships among the latter four manuscripts, but also discovered interesting mutual relationships among the names in the diplomatic notes. Thus, since the time that Traube published his tabular comparison of names in "O Roma nobilis," it has been certain that the "Codex Boernerianus," the evangelary of St. Gall 48, the Priscian of St. Gall 904, and the "Horace" of Bern 363 are all evidence of the intellectual life of one and the same group of Irish scholars; Traube's mistake was to "affix" this group to the famous Sedulian manuscript and abruptly to designate this Irish group as that of Sedulius.

Rettig had incidentally alluded to the Greco-Latin Psalter Basel A. VII. 3 in 1836 (p. xliii). He had not seen the Basel bilingual; otherwise the shrewd manuscript expert would have certainly noticed even then that the third text of this Greco-Latin compilation of Irish execution, the evangelary of St. Gall 48 and the Pauline epistles ("Codex Boernerianus"), was not the Sedulian Psalter, but rather the Basel Psalter. Thus this discovery was left for Samuel Berger (or rather, for the Basel librarian Sieber, who gave it over to Berger for publication; *Histoire de la*

Vulgate [1893], pp. 115 f.). Traube noticed his error; this may be inferred from the organizational method of the "biblical corpus" in *MGH Poetae* (1896), III, 821, where he places the Basel Psalter directly next to the St. Gall 48 and the "Codex Boernerianus," as did Berger. In the first fascicle of "Quellen und Unter-suchungen zur lateinischen Philologie des Mittelalters," which he edited, Traube also had to endure the determined opposition voiced against the text-critical aspect of his attribution of the "Codex Boernerianus" to Sedulius Scottus: S. Hell-mann, *Sedulius Scottus* (Munich 1906), p. 148, n. 5. Traube never responded to the issue (d. 1907).

The section on Sedulius and the manuscripts of his circle was followed in Traube's "O Roma nobilis" by another section on the "Kenntnis des Griechischen bei den Iren zur Zeit Karl's des Kahlen." Methodologically, these pages have become fundamental for the study of the knowledge of Greek in the early Middle Ages. Traube's critical maxim is as valid now as it was then: "Es wird im Allgemeinen noch viel zu viel auf mittelalterliche Zeugnisse gegeben, wenn sie von irgend Jemand behaupten: er habe Griechisch gekonnt. Auszugehen ist . . . von den damals zur Erlernung der Sprache vorhanden gewesenen Hilfsmitteln"[27] ("In general, far too much credence is still given medieval testimony when it maintains of someone: he knew Greek. One must begin . . . with the resources which were available at that time for learning the language").

In the same passage, Traube opposes the editorial method which "die Graeca ad amussim optimorum scriptorum wortlos abkorrigiert" ("silently corrects the Graeca [Greek terms] ad amussim optimorum scriptorum"). In the third fascicle of the third *Poetae* volume of *MGH* (1896), Traube demonstrated how such texts may be edited without trampling the textual tradition. Under the rubric "Carmina Scottorum Latina et Graecanica," he collected a series of Greco-Latin poems of the ninth century (pp. 685–701). He edited the Greek passages in majuscule, the Latin in minus-cule—just as the Graecolatina almost always appeared in the Middle Ages. In the Greek majuscule script used for this last fascicle of his edi-tion, Traube replaced the letters E Ξ Σ Ω with the forms in common use since the Augustan age: Є Ꙅ C ꙍ. He placed interlinear and marginal versions of the Graeca in a separate section, *Glossae*, of the critical appa-ratus. He used the greatest of care in the appended plates and his com-mentary. Plates 5–7 of the volume and the notes to them are concealed but significant contributions to the understanding of Greek studies in the Middle Ages.

Traube dealt with the Graecolatina a third time in his *Einleitung in die lateinische Philologie des Mittelalters*. There he gave in broad strokes an overview of the literary historical aspect of Greek in the Middle Ages. What Paul Lehmann edited and published on the basis of both Traube's and his students' notes (1911) was, however, no more than a rough draft.[28]

Eduard Norden pointed out in his work *Die antike Kunstprosa* (first published in 1898) that he collected his evidence "über die Schicksale der griechischen Sprache im Westen vom Beginn der Berührung Griechenlands mit Rom bis zu dem Zeitpunkt, in dem Petrarca durch Vermittlung des Barlaam aus Kalabrien sich eine notdürftige Kenntnis der griechischen Sprache erwarb" ("concerning the fortunes of the Greek language in the West from the period of the first contacts of Greece with Rome to the time at which Petrarch acquired his scanty knowledge of the Greek language through Barlaam of Calabria"); to be sure, "das zu verarbeitende Material ist so ungeheuer groß und z.T. auf Gebieten verstreut, die meinen Studien und Interessen fern liegen, daß ich zu seiner völligen Sammlung und Verarbeitung noch Jahre gebrauchen werde" ("the material to be assimilated is so enormous and in part so scattered through domains which are distant from my own studies and interests that I will still require years for its complete collection and assimilation"; 2nd ed., p. 666, n. 1). In addition, Norden wanted to provide the complement to this study, on "die Schicksale der lateinischen Sprache im Osten bis auf die Übersetzungstätigkeit des Maximos Planudes und Demetrios Kydones" ("the fortunes of the Latin language in the East, up to the translation work of Maximos Planudes and Demetrios Kydones"). Norden gave up the latter plan in the addendum to the third edition, and the comprehensive treatment ("zusammenfassende Behandlung") of Greek in the West was not realized either. While Norden succeeded in *Die antike Kunstprosa* in presenting the continuous stylistic development through antiquity and the Middle Ages, the circumstances of the ancient and medieval textual traditions differed so greatly with respect to this area of literary and cultural history that the topic (which must be based on manuscript study) was one which classical philology could scarcely manage.

The Contemporary Situation. In the last three-quarters of a century, many specialists have investigated the topic of Greek in the Middle Ages in their own areas—to a certain extent with the insights provided by Traube's work—and they have increased our understanding of the subject: scholars of theological history (Martin Grabmann and Berthold Altaner for patristic and late medieval studies, Arthur Allgeier for medieval psalters); historians of philosophy (Raymund Klibansky for the *Plato latinus* and Lorenzo Minio-Paluello for the *Aristoteles latinus*); musicologists (Michael Huglo, Egon Wellesz, Jacques Handschin); historians of the liturgy (A. Baumstark and L. Brou); historians of canon law (Eduard Schwartz and Cuthbert Hamilton Turner). The historian Harold Steinacker wished to evaluate the knowledge of Greek in early medieval Rome on the basis of conciliar acts and papal letters.[29] Numerous investigations of Greco-Latin translations, especially from the patristic period, have appeared in the *Revue Bénédictine* (Germain Morin, André Wilmart); and studies of Greco-Latin hagiography have been published in the *Analecta Bollandiana*. The *Archives d'Histoire Doctrinale et Littéraire du Moyen Âge*, founded by Étienne Gilson and Gabriel Théry, have also published new texts fom the translation literature of the high Middle Ages. Developments in the history of science in the area of the Graecolatina have been made available through the works of George Sarton and Lynn Thorndike; and the manuscripts of pre-Salernian medicine were published by Augusto Beccaria. Research on Humanism has made manifold contributions, from the classic works of Remigio Sabbadini to the exceedingly well documented treatises of Roberto Weiss, to the *Catalogus Translationum et Commentariorum* of Paul Oskar Kristeller.

And here one, in fact, again enters the area of literary scholarship, where the most important advance was achieved in Max Manitius' *Geschichte der lateinischen Literatur des Mittelalters*, which appeared as part of the *Handbuch der Altertumswissenschaft*. The first volume appeared in 1911, and the second (1923) and third (1931) brought the coverage up to around the year 1200. At the same time Gustav Krüger completed the *Geschichte der römischen Litteratur* of Schanz-Hosius with the volume "Die Litteratur des fünften und sechsten Jahrhunderts" (1920). These two literary histories are quoted without further citation in the present study; only in exceptional cases will attention again be drawn to specific sections of the handbooks.

On more specialized topics: the understanding of the reception of Dionysius the Areopagite was greatly advanced by the epoch-making research of Gabriel Théry, Maïeul Cappuyn's book on John Scottus, and the splendid collection of the *Dionysiaca* by P. Chevallier. In numerous studies, Max Ludwig Wolfram Laistner has investigated the Greek element in early medieval thought and letters, primarily among the Anglo-Saxons and Irish. Charles Homer Haskins has presented the Italian translations of the high Middle Ages in new contexts.

For decades (mainly) French philologists have concentrated their research on late antiquity, and as a result also on that period's Graecolatina (Henri-Irenée Marrou, Gustave Bardy, Jacques Fontaine). Étienne Delaruelle undertook to write a comprehensive treatment in his 1946 essay "La connaissance du grec en occident du Ve au IXe siècle." Just as Tougard had done, Delaruelle restricted himself essentially to a "dépouillement" of Migne's *Patrologia Latina* and overlooked modern editions as well as important secondary literature. The omission of Italy from the analysis is methodologically also hardly defensible, since it was precisely there that the primary zone of contact was to be found between Greeks and Latins in the early and high Middle Ages. Even so, Delaruelle knew well the works with which he dealt.

In his *Les lettres grecques en occident*, Pierre Courcelle presented a broad analysis of the Greek element in Latin literature from the end of the fourth to the end of the sixth century; it is of great aid in the analysis of the medieval situation. This book, written according to the classic philological methods—text comparison and source study—scarcely made use of Elias Avery Lowe's great paleographical opus, *Codices Latini Antiquiores*, in whose twelve folio volumes Lowe, responding to Ludwig

Traube's postulate, made available all Latin (and Latino-Greek) manuscripts up to 800. Lowe's "Paleographic Guide" made possible a new comprehensiveness and precision in philological work with manuscripts; the determinaton of the date and provenance of Greco-Latin glossaries and bilinguals makes new contributions, as well as calling to mind little-noticed older contributions, even in the field of literary history.

The present book could not have been written without two works from its own field of medieval Latin philology and without the impetus of Byzantine studies. Albert Siegmund provided a guide through ecclesiastical translation literature in his book *Die Überlieferung der griechischen christlichen Literatur in der lateinischen Kirche bis zum zwölften Jahrhundert*, which grew out of his dissertation written under Paul Lehmann. Even when he does not illuminate the darkest recesses of the subject, he is always reliable and indispensable, since he always refers to the manuscript tradition. Such is even more the case with Bernhard Bischoff's dense essay, provided with numerous references to new material, "Das griechische Element in der abendländischen Bildung des Mittelalters," which primarily follows the often convoluted trail of the Irish in Greek studies of the medieval West (up to 1200 and omitting Italy and Spain). The essay is elucidated and supplemented by a series of further treatises by the same scholar, noted here in the bibliography.

Since 1968 the article "Abendland und Byzanz" has been appearing in the *Reallexikon der Byzantinistik*,[30] of which the section "Griechisches im lateinischen Mittelalter" was the nucleus from which the present book developed. The study concentrated on the period between 500 and 1400 A.D.; with a view to the research of specialized disciplines, the late antique and humanistic epochs are presented only in the form of "dotted lines" ("punktierte Linien"), which are taken up again in the topics of the central chapters. It would not have been appropriate to omit late antiquity and Humanism: Jerome, as the point of departure of medieval philology, and Nicholas of Cusa, as the rallying point of medieval philosophico-theological Graecolatina, had to define the borders. A narrow conception of "literature" was also inadmissible. It was precisely in the domain of technical literature—philosophy, medicine, natural sciences—that the Greco-Latin exchange of ideas was so brisk in the medieval period. The characteristic shift from a predominantly scholarly interest in Greek to the interest in belles-lettres, under humanistic influence, would lose its significance if the presentation were to concentrate on the latter from the outset. Even when abbreviation in the area of technical literature and in the boundary epochs of the study was unavoidable, I endeavored to make use of proportion and arrangement as a means to writing literary history.

[II]

Valuation and Knowledge of Greek

. . . adsolent Latini homines Graece cantare oblectati sono verborum nescientes tamen quid dicant. [The Latins are accustomed to singing in Greek, delighted by the sounds of the words, but not knowing what they are saying.]

The "Ambrosiaster" (saec. IV) on 1 Cor. 14:14; CSEL 81, 2, p. 153, 6

Sex lectiones ab antiquis Romanis grece et latine legebantur; qui mos apud Constantinopolim hodieque servatur, ni fallor, propter duas causas: unam quia aderant Greci, quibus incognita erat latina lingua, aderantque Latini quibus incognita erat greca; alteram, propter unanimitatem utriusque populi. [Six texts were read by the ancient Romans in Greek and Latin; this custom is observed even today in Constantinople for two reasons, if I am not mistaken: first, because Greeks were present, to whom Latin was an unknown language, and Latins were also present, to whom Greek was unknown; secondly, for the sake of concord of both peoples.]

Amalar of Metz (saec. IX), Liber officialis II 1, 1, ed. I. M. Hanssens, Amalarii episcopi opera liturgica omnia (Rome 1948), II, 197

1. "Sacred Languages"

Ekkehart IV of St. Gall tells of a pupil in the monastic school who was taken to the Hohentwiel to Duchess Hadwig so that he might learn some Greek from her. He expressed his wish in the hexameter[1]

Esse velim Grecus, cum sim vix, domna, Latinus.

[I would like to be Greek, my lady, although I am scarcely a Latin.]

This is the most concise formulation of the aporia in which the Latin West found itself during the Middle Ages in relation to Greek. Latin was enough of a problem by itself: it was no longer anyone's native language, but it was nevertheless indispensable as the language of the liturgy, political administration, scholarship, and most arts, and almost all energy expended on language learning was concentrated on Latin.[2] Greek could at best be one's "second foreign language"—and thus only a very few medieval Westerners acquired the ability to understand a Greek text with unfamiliar content. Nevertheless, Greek held an important place in the medieval consciousness. In several periods of the Latin Middle Ages, Greek was held in remarkably high regard—measured by the knowledge of Greek that one could acquire over and above Latin.

18

The valuation of Greek in the Latin Middle Ages has its origin primarily in the position of prominence which the Greek language enjoyed in the early history of Christianity. In scriptural study and to a great extent also in medieval exegesis, it was never forgotten that Greek was one of the original languages of the Scriptures (the New Testament). The untranslated symbolism of the threefold "Ego sum ⋏ et ⲱ" of the Apocalypse, for example, referred the reader of the Latin Bible to the Greek original.[3] If, for Christians of late antiquity, Greek was the second of the *tres linguae praecipuae*[4]—those languages in which Pilate, as a blind instrument of divine providence, had the inscription written on the Cross[5]

> Pilatus iubet ignorans: I, scriba, tripictis
> digere versiculis, quae sit subfixa potestas,
> fronte crucis titulus sit triplex, triplice lingua
> agnoscat Iudaea legens et Graecia norit
> et venerata deum percenseat aurea Roma

[Unknowing, Pilate ordered: "Go, compose and arrange in thrice-written lines what kind of ruler is hung below, let the legend on the front of the cross be threefold; in three languages let Judaea read and recognize, Greece know, and golden Rome the revered regard God"]

—the notion of the special dignity of the three languages of the Cross acquired its specifically medieval character from Isidore of Seville, who first wrote of the *tres linguae sacrae*.[6] Here the essence of medieval language acquisition and especially the medieval study of Greek is already expressed with the greatest concision: the three sacred languages were cult languages; the veneration of which they were the instruments came to be directed to them also. Thus Greek was more honored than studied in the Middle Ages, even if Jerome (the *vir trilinguis*) in his letter to the Goths Sunnja and Friþila concerning the translation of Psalms (*epist.* 106) "kept alive the conviction of the utility and necessity of knowing Greek,"[7] and at the same time asserted the final authority of the *hebraica veritas* in Old Testament textual criticism. In the early Middle Ages, the Irish followed in Jerome's footsteps;[8] in the twelfth and thirteenth centuries, it was the Englishmen Andrew of St. Victor,[9] Robert Grosseteste, and Roger Bacon, and in the fourteenth century, Simon Atumanus; Erasmus of Rotterdam and Johannes Reuchlin rise above the late antique-medieval horizon.

During the Middle Ages the writings of Dionysius the Areopagite were closely associated with the Scriptures. The confrontation with the great Syro-Greek theologian of symbolism runs through the Latin Middle Ages in an unbroken line; even when his apophatic theology was unintelligible or too contemplative for the West, at least his doctrine concerning angels had an influence—from Gregory the Great to Dante, who otherwise had almost no knowledge of Greek matters.[10]

For the Latin Middle Ages Greek was also an "original language of the

liturgy"; after all, the Latin liturgy contained Greek in prominent positions—whether as a remnant of the ancient Roman use of Greek as the
liturgical language, or as an ornament of ecumenical intent added at a
later date to the Latin liturgy.[11] No exclamation appealed to the Germanic
peoples as strongly as the liturgical ΚΥΡΙΕ ΕΛΕΗCΟΝ;[12] it is also to be
found as a battle cry, as well as the last line of stanzas in vernacular songs.
Next to the kyrie, the trishagion was the most popular Greek element in
the Western liturgy:

ΑΓΙΟC Ο ΘΕΟC · ΑΓΙΟC ΙCΧΥΡΟC · ΑΓΙΟC

ΑΘΑΝΑΤΟC ΕΛΕΗCΟΝ ΗΜΑC.

The Old Spanish ("Mozarabic") and Old Gallic ("Gallican") liturgies
adopted the Greek chant, which in these liturgies took the place of the
gloria in the Roman mass. From the ninth century—first in the Frankish
Empire—the trishagion was incorporated into the Roman rite, in the *im-
properia* sung on Good Friday.[13]

Greco-Latin readings from the Old and New Testaments were also introduced into the Roman rite; the Greek and Latin reading from the Epistles and the Gospels in the solemn papal mass is a relic of an originally
more general practice; it is not certain whether the practice was native to
Rome or had been brought there from the North.[14] The bilingual readings
and the readings of the Greek prologue to the Gospel of St. John on
Easter night were especially remarkable liturgical usages in the Latin
Middle Ages.

In the ninth century, the Order of St. Amand, for example, prescribes for
Easter night: "Deinde secuntur lectiones et cantica seu orationes, tam grece quam
latine" ("then readings and songs or prayers follow, Greek as well as Latin"); *Les
Ordines Romani du haut moyen âge*, ed. M. Andrieu (Louvain 1951), III, Ordo
XXX B, p. 472. Clear evidence for this liturgical usage is contained in the famous
Oxford manuscript Bodleian Library Auct. F. 4. 32, a facsimile of which R. W.
Hunt published under the title *Saint Dunstan's Classbook from Glastonbury*
(Amsterdam 1961). The third section of the manuscript, "the patriarch of all
Welsh books known" (Henry Bradshaw), written around 817 in Wales, is a brief
scholarly collection of computational and Greco-Latin texts (and a runic alphabet).
The Graeca are written partly in Greek majuscules, as the *pauca testimonia de
prophetarum libris per grecam linguam*, fols. 24ʳ–28ᵛ. The scribe attached a
Greco-Latin alphabet as an aid to reading. In the subsequent readings for Easter
night, *tam per latinam quam per grecam linguam*, he wrote the Greek column of
the text in Latin minuscules. The variation in the system of rendering the
Graeca—between the texts of the prophets and the readings for Easter night—
may be explained thus: the former were seen as material for study, the latter as
liturgical texts, which were to be read fluently and were therefore transcribed. On
liturgical classification, see Schneider, *Cantica*, pp. 67 ff., and Fischer, in *Colligere Fragmenta*, Festschrift Alban Dold (Beuron 1952).

The Greek prologue to the Gospel of St. John is found at the end of the Greek

Psalter Vat. Reg. gr. 13, which is thought to have originated in the West (more likely in the twelfth than in the tenth century); see H. Stevenson, *Codices Manuscripti Graeci Reginae Svecorum* (Rome 1888), p. 9. Schneider (in *Biblica* 30 [1949], 490 f.) sees a magical significance therein: "Regin. 13 endet mit dem Johannesprolog, diesem alten christlichen Abwehrmittel gegen die bösen Geister. So übernimmt der Psalter noch eine neue Aufgabe: Er ersetzt die Zauberbücher der Heiden" ("Regin. 13 ends with the prologue to John, the ancient Christian protective device against evil spirits. Thus the Psalter assumes yet an additional purpose: it replaces the heathens' magical books"). This conclusion is, however, based too exclusively on late medieval circumstances; in the "Evangeliarium Spalatense" (Split, Chapter Library, s.n.), after all, there is the example of an appended Greek prologue to John, which plainly served liturgical purposes. Such an interpretation proceeds from the prefatory liturgical acclamation: *HIRINI PASI . . . DOXA SI KYRIE* (cf. facsimile in Lowe, *CLA*, XI, 1669). In recent years the prologue to John in this codex has been repeatedly interpreted as evidence for the knowledge of Greek in early medieval Dalmatia. After Lowe, in his paleographical description, located the half-uncial evangelary and its appendix (also half-uncial) in the vicinity of the North Italian Greco-Latin Psalter of the Chapter Library in Verona (Cod. I), it became open to question whether V. Novak's interpretations are based on an accurate determination of the manuscript's provenance (in the bibliography to *CLA*, XI, 1669; see also P. Diels, "Zur Kenntnis des Griechischen im Kroatien des VIII. Jahrhunderts," *BZ* 51 [1958], 41 f.).

The bilingual credo, which was sung in the catechumenal liturgy on the Wednesday after the fourth Sunday of Lent ("Mittfasten"), was widespread. In a tenth-century sacramentary from Fulda, the Greek credo is thus embedded in the liturgical order:[15]

> . . . accipiens accolitus unum ex ipsis infantibus masculum et tenens eum in sinistro brachio ponit manum super eum.
> Et interrogat eum presbiter dicens: Qua lingua confitentur dominum nostrum Iesum Christum?
> Respondit accolitus: Greca.
> Iterum dicit presbiter: Annuntia fidem ipsorum qualiter credant.
> Et tenens accolitus manum dexteram super infantis ⟨caput⟩ dicit symbolum decantando grece: Pysteu . . .

> [. . . taking a male child from these children and holding it on his left arm, the acolyte places his hand above it.
> And the priest asks him, saying: "In what language do they confess our Lord Jesus Christ?"
> The acolyte responds: "In Greek."
> The priest speaks again: "Proclaim their faith, just as they believe."
> And holding his right hand above ⟨the head⟩ of the child, the acolyte recites the *symbolum*, singing in Greek: "Pysteu . . ."]

In this *ordo scrutinii* the credo was spoken in Latin by another acolyte for the girls. In the baptismal scrutiny, there were many variant possibilities, as there were generally in the Latin liturgy before the Council of

Trent. The sentences which preceded the Greek credo could, for example, also have been said in Greek, as in the following tradition, which clearly indicates that the text was copied without being understood:[16]

> Et interrogat eum presbiter graece. Dicit: ⟨P⟩ya glossa omologesin ton kirion ymon iesun christon?
> Respondit acolutus: Ellenistin.
> Iterum dicit presbiter: Anangilon tin pistin auton ton os pisteugesin.
> Et dicit acolutus simbolum graece decantando his verbis: Pysteugon . . .

The bilingual baptismal scrutiny is perhaps the germ of the "missa graeca," the most significant medieval expression of liturgical Hellenism, which is a liturgy of the mass in which the gloria and credo, as well as the paternoster, agnus dei,[17] and other parts of the mass, can be sung or read in Greek.

Up until recently, the development of the "missa graeca" has been studied mainly for *St. Denis*, primarily through the work of Omont, "La messe grecque de Saint Denys," in *Études d'Histoire du moyen âge dédiées à G. Monod*, which is supplemented in details by Delisle in *Journal des Savants* (1900); H. Leclercq, in *Dictionnaire d'Archéologie Chrétienne et de Liturgie* (s.v. "Grecque, Messe"); Weiss, in *Rivista di Storia della Chiesa in Italia* 6; Handschin, in *Annales Musicologiques* 2; and Huglo, "Les chants de la missa graeca de Saint-Denis," in *Essays Presented to E. Wellesz*. The principal (and most splendid specimen of the Carolingian "missa graeca" in St. Denis is contained in Paris, BN lat. 2290 (saec. IX², fols. 7ᵛ–8ᵛ; although probably a later addition to the codex), which includes, in a liberal format and with an interlinear Latin translation, the *Doxa en ipsistis, Pisteugo, Agios,* and *O amnos tu theu*. Based on the emphasis given to the patron of St. Denis in the form ΔΙΟΝΙΟΙΙ, previous scholars held the origin of the manuscript in St. Denis to be certain (Delisle, "Mémoire sur d'anciens sacramentaires," pp. 102–5; Omont, "La messe grecque," p. 178), although it clearly exhibits the "Franco-Saxon" style of painting (cf. the facsimile in V. Leroquais, *Les Sacramentaires et les Missels Manuscrits des bibliothèques publiques de France* [Paris 1924], pl. 10), which has been associated with the Abbey of *St. Amand* since Delisle's study. The manuscript was written in "St. Amand for St. Denis" (K. Gamber, *Codices Liturgici Latini Antiquiores*, 2nd ed. [Fribourg 1968], p. 356, no. 760). Two additional Carolingian manuscripts containing texts of the "missa graeca" are—as has long been known—traceable to St. Amand: Paris, BN lat. 2291 (with "paleofranconian" neums; cf. J. Handschin, in *Acta Musicologica* 22 [1950], 69 ff., and E. Jammers, in *Scriptorium* 7 [1953], 235 ff.) and Stockholm A 136 (cf. Gamber, *Codices Liturgici*, pp. 413 f., no. 925, and p. 356, no. 763). Thus the interest in the origin of the "missa graeca" should concentrate much more on St. Amand than St. Denis. Cf. the table of "Handschriften, die griechische Ordinariumsstücke enthalten," in C. M. Atkinson, "Zur Entstehung und Überlieferung der 'Missa Graeca,'" *Archiv für Musikwissenschaft* 39 (1982), 113–45, here pp. 120 ff. Atkinson assumes that the origin of the "missa graeca" was linked with the first translation of the works of Dionysius the Areopagite by Hilduin of St. Denis. He dates the origin to ca. 827–35. But the valuable list of manuscripts published by Atkinson points to the last third of the ninth century and to the monastery of St. Amand.

The "missa graeca" in *St. Gall* may well date from the end of the ninth century as well, the texts of which are transmitted in numerous manuscripts of the tenth and eleventh centuries (see Chapter VIII). The texts of the "Minden Troper" (which belong to the Berlin library, but are now in Cracow), written for Bishop Sigebert of *Minden* (1022–36), probably also come from St. Gall: "ΚΥΡΙЄ o theos, Δoxa en ipsistis, Πisteuuo, Πatir imon, Λgyos" and the agnus dei, all in Greek and Latin, in part with variant possibilities (cf. V. Rose, *Verzeichniss der lateinischen Handschriften* [of the Königliche Bibliothek in Berlin] [Berlin 1903], II/2, theol. qu. 11 = no. 694, pp. 684 ff.). MS Vienna 1888 (saec. X), which includes texts of the "missa graeca" (in part with neums), comes from *St. Alban's* in Mainz, the most important abbey of the Ottonian period in terms of liturgical history (H. J. Hermann, *Beschreibendes Verzeichnis der illuminierten Handschriften in Öster-reich* [Leipzig 1923], VIII/1, 185 ff.). A unique and splendidly designed "missa graeca" is found in the MS Dusseldorf D 2 (saec. X–XI), from the convent at *Essen*, which contains melodies (in part new) and a new interfusion of the Latin mass with Greek chant (Jammers, *Die Essener Neumenhandschriften*, esp. pp. 19–21 and pls. 8–9); I. Opelt, in *Jahrbuch der Österreichischen Byzantinistik 23* (1974), 77–88. In this manuscript, the "Cherubicon"—as an offertory—appears for the first time: *I ta cherubin mysticos Iconizontes.* . . . In England there are also traces of the "missa graeca"; cf. W. H. Frere, *The Winchester Troper* (London 1894), pp. xxvi f. (bibliog.), and E. Bishop, *Liturgica Historica* (Oxford 1918), pp. 140 ff. One peculiarity here is a Greek litany, which, according to Bishop, goes back to the Byzantine era of Rome; the most important manuscript is the "Psalter of King Æthelstan" (d. 941) from Winchester, now London, BL Cotton Galba A XVIII: fols. 199^v–200^r, the aforementioned litany; fol. 200^rv, a Greek paternoster, credo, and sanctus (incomplete). On the manuscript, see also Caspari, "Über den gottesdienstlichen Gebrauch," pp. 5 f.

This selection from several of the manuscript sources important in the history of the "missa graeca" demonstrates clearly that the "missa graeca" had its high point from the ninth to the eleventh centuries. Up to the present, evidence from the late Middle Ages has come only from St. Denis, where, in the Renaissance, Guillaume Budé was set to revising the texts and where the "missa graeca" survived until the Revolution—in a revived, Baroque form. The later history of the "missa graeca" is, however, not entirely restricted to St. Denis: around 1500 this form of the liturgy again appeared in Germany—in Würzburg, for example, where it attracted the attention of Conrad Celtis and served him as evidence of an unbroken Greek tradition in Germany:

> Graecorum linguam gensque hodierna tenet.
> Nam faciunt lingua Graecorum sacra quotannis
> Et templum Argolicis personat omne modis . . .

[And the people of our day hold fast the language of the Greeks. For they carry out their religious services in the language of the Greeks, and the entire church resounds with Argolian melody]

Conrad Celtis, *Amores* I 12, 42–44, ed. F. Pindter (Leipzig 1934), p. 24. On this subject, see also Pralle, *Würzburger Diözesangeschichtsblätter* 16/17 (1954/55), 360, and M. Hoffmann, "Nachlese zum Problem des 'Missa Graeca' in Würzburg und Bamberg," *Würzburger Diözesangeschichtsblätter* 26 (1964), 140–47. Hoffman took the erroneous designation of a baptismal scrutiny (in a Bamberg manuscript of the fifteenth/sixteenth century) as *Officium Missae Graecae* to be just cause for regarding the "missa graeca" collectively as a late mystification of the Graeca in the catechumenal liturgy: "The Greek of the 'missa graeca' is due to the Greek credo, which was occasionally used, and to several other linguistic scraps, laboriously learned for the sake of the *traditio symboli* [the catechumenal liturgy]. To see in them a version of the mass entirely in Greek—such an assumption is based on no liturgical manuscripts and no credible evidence and remains the postulation of an excessive Philhellenism" (p. 147). This erroneous judgment (which neglects the manuscript tradition and the research literature) and the omission of the "missa graeca" from J. A. Jungmann's *Missarum Sollemnia* illustrate the need for a clarifying and comprehensive treatment of the "missa graeca," which would have as its task the differentiation of the baptismal scrutiny and "missa graeca," scholarly and liturgical traditions, precursors, fundamental form and later developments. The U.S. musicologist Charles M. Atkinson has published lists of sixty manuscripts of the "missa graeca" and related texts, which now provide the basis of such research (in "'O amnos tu theu': The Greek Agnus dei in the Roman Liturgy from the Eighth to the Eleventh Century," 7–30, and "Zur Entstehung und Überlieferung," pp. 113–45).

Many liturgical texts survived in the West exclusively in Latin translation; it is often difficult to prove that they are translations from Greek, if no clear indication of Greek origin, such as the incipit with *Hodie* (CHMEPON), is present.[18] The Marian antiphon *Sub tuum praesidium confugimus*, which leads to the pictorial image of the Madonna of Mercy and which circulated in the West from the ninth century on at the latest, is an example of a famous Latin text which was recognized as a translation from Greek only after a fourth-century papyrus with the Greek text was found:[19]

> Sub tuum praesidium confugimus sancta dei genitrix
> nostras deprecationes ne despicias in necessitatibus
> sed a periculis libera nos semper
> virgo gloriosa et benedicta.

[We take refuge in your protection, holy mother of God, that you might not disregard our prayers in times of need, but free us from danger always, glorious and blessed virgin.]

The *Alleluia* of the Roman mass, with versicle, is of Greek origin and was most likely introduced in the second half of the seventh century under the Eastern popes via Constantinople or Syria;[20] the famous *Alleluia* versicle of the third Christmas mass, *Dies sanctificatus*, is translated from Greek:[21]

Dies sanctificatus illuxit nobis
venite gentes et adorate Dominum
quia hodie descendit lux magna super terram.

[The holy day has dawned for us. Come all peoples and praise the
Lord, for today the great light has descended to earth.]

This *Alleluia* was sung in Latin, in Greek (*Ymera agiasmeni*), in both languages, and with Gregorian and Greek melodies, with the greatest of
variety.

There were also hymns and tropes translated from Greek, such as the
Hymnos Akathistos (perhaps translated in St. Denis), an ode composed by
Romanos Melodos—which, as the Latin *Grates nunc omnes*, became the
most famous Christmas sequence of the Middle Ages—and the *O quando
in cruce* of the Beneventan liturgy.[22]

The most conspicuous evidence of the medieval effort to incorporate
Greek into the Latin liturgy is to be found in the ceremony for the dedication of a church, in which the bishop drew with his staff the Greek and
Roman alphabets in the form of a reclining cross (X) on the floor of the
church. This rite is first documented in an eighth-century *ordo*, according
to which the Latin alphabet is inscribed.[23] Even the *Tractatus de dedican-
dis ecclesiis*, attributed to Remigius of Auxerre (d. ca. 908), bases its interpretation on the Latin alphabet.[24]

> What it signifies, that the bishop writes the alphabet on the floor.
> Having duly finished these things, the bishop should begin to
> write the alphabet on the floor with his staff, beginning in the left
> corner in the east and proceeding to the right corner in the west, and
> begin again there in the same manner. . . . This might seem a child-
> ish game, if it were not believed that it was established by great and
> saintly men, that is, the Apostles. . . . What else is to be understood
> in the alphabet than the first principles and rudiments of sacred doc-
> trine [*initia et rudimenta doctrinae sacrae*]. Thus even Paul says re-
> provingly to the Hebrews: For you who should be teachers for the
> time again need to be taught what the elements of the world and the
> first principles of God's word are . . . [*elementa mundi et exordia ser-
> monum dei*; cf. Heb. 5:12: *elementa exordii sermonum dei* (Vulgate);
> τὰ στοιχεῖα τῆς ἀρχῆς τῶν λογίων τοῦ θεοῦ (Septuagint)].

Hence it follows that the subject here is more than a "learned and yet
naive" ceremony ("gelehrte und doch naive," Gardthausen), for the
ancient στοιχεῖα doctrine lives on here—the alphabet as symbol of the
world,[25] which, through the form X of the dedication symbol, also represented Plato's symbol of the cosmos "chi," which the Latin Middle Ages
also knew from the *Timaeus*.[26]

Since two crossed rows of letters had to be drawn, it was only natural to provide the doubled sign of the cosmos with still a third symbol—the "ecumenical symbol" of multilingualism. The use of the Roman *and* the Greek alphabets in the dedication rite is first documented in the "Pontificale Romano-Germanicum" (probably produced in the second half of the tenth century at St. Alban's in Mainz).[27]

2. Hierarchical and Political Conflicts between East and West

Greek was not held in the same regard throughout the Latin Middle Ages. In some eras and cultural circles of the period, its authority was especially great: in Gothic Italy of the sixth century, among the Irish of the early Middle Ages, in the Carolingian ninth and Ottonian tenth century, among the Normans of Southern Italy, in England of the thirteenth century, and—on the threshold of the modern period—in fifteenth-century Florence. With its ancient Greek monastic colonies, Rome was a metropolis of Greco-Latin intercourse until the eleventh century. The hierarchical conflict between the bishops of the older Latin and the younger Greek imperial cities quite early proved to be a negative factor in the valuation of Greek: "In the political domain, it was the West that struggled for autonomy against the inherited priority and universality of the Byzantine Empire. In ecclesiastical matters, on the other hand, Constantinople was the younger partner that claimed autonomy and equality vis-à-vis the Roman priority and universality."[28]

Pope Gregory the Great once failed to respond to the letter of a noble lady in Constantinople "because she wrote to me in Greek, although she is a Latin."[29] Pope Nicholas I (858–67) and Photius, patriarch of Constantinople (858–67 and 877–86), were the first ecclesiastical leaders of West and East to confront one another with unrestrained severity; the argument between East and West even led to dispute about the Latin and Greek languages. Emperor Michael III had called Latin a "barbarian and Scythian language," whereupon the pope defiantly suggested that he not only give up the title "Emperor of the Romans" but also expurgate the Latin readings from the liturgy of the stational masses at Constantinople.[30] Pope Nicholas requested the advice of West Frankish scholars concerning the errors of the Greeks. Bishop Aeneas of Paris wrote a *Liber adversus Graecos* for the archbishops of Sens; Ratramnus of Corbie wrote a *Contra Graecorum opposita* for Reims. But for the time being, the dispute retained a simple episodic character.

The tenth century arrived, a time of amicable relations with the Greeks, and Greek monasticism in Rome again grew strong. Its influence was to be felt up to the middle of the eleventh century—when the dynasty of popes from the house of Count Gregory I of Tusculum, the founder of Grottaferrata, came to an end. The fourth abbot of Grottaferrata, Bartholomew the Younger, a Calabrian and student of Nilus of Rossano, was the last of the Greeks in Rome to exercise influence on a pope—Benedict IX (1032–44). Soon thereafter, Cardinal Humbert the Lotharingian laid a papal bull of excommunication on the altar in Hagia Sophia (1054); with surprising abruptness, the ecclesiastical ties between East and West were severed. A self-assured and expansive West, henceforth led by Rome and directed by a hierarchy which became increasingly characterized by law instead of liturgy, glanced without admiration to the Greek East and acknowledged the Greeks as little as the Jews as preeminent because of their close association with the world of Christ's life. Yet even after the events of 1054, there were popes who were interested in Greek studies: Eugenius III (1145–53), the patron of Burgundio and many other twelfth-century writers, Alexander V (1409–10), and Nicholas V (1447–55), the contemporary of Nicholas of Cusa. Beginning with the Council of Lyons (1274), many popes of the late Middle Ages supported, even if they did not highly esteem, the now weak Byzantine Empire and its emperor.

Compared with the hierarchical conflict between East and West, the political one—the problem of the two emperors ("Zweikaiserproblem," Ohnsorge)—had less influence on the valuation of Greek in the medieval West. On the eve of the Frankish Empire, it was more the political rivalry than the theological examination of the *Libri Carolini* that produced the very problematic attitude toward the Greek doctrine of the icons. Pope Hadrian I denied the request for the sanction of the Frankish treatise, however, so that it remained no more than a scholarly curiosity. Much more volatile was the issue of the *filioque* addition to the credo (*et in spiritum sanctum . . . qui ex patre* filioque *procedit*), which, having first come into use (probably) in Spain, soon spread through Charlemagne's empire. The conflict concerning this addition broke out at the Christmas service in 808, in the place where the two versions of the credo came into liturgical contact with one another—in Jerusalem, where the Frankish monks of the monastery on the Mount of Olives sang the *symbolum* with the new *filioque*, which especially the Greeks of St. Saba's would not tolerate. As had his predecessor, Hadrian, Pope Leo III took the ecumenical position with regard to the Frankish zeal in cultivating their own self-image. He rejected the addition and had the Greek and Latin creeds, written in the authentic forms—without the *filioque*—on silver tablets, put up in St. Peter's. But that did not suffice to do away with the infelicitous addendum: when the credo, which originally formed a part of the baptismal liturgy, was introduced into the Roman mass in the eleventh century after the manner of Spanish, English, French, and German practice, the *filioque* was also admitted. "The most serious and most protracted doctrinal controversy between the Greeks and Latins was due to a Frankish, not a Roman, decision."[31]

Political relations between the Eastern and Western emperors were often dramatic, but never dangerous. The diplomatic intercourse between the old Byzantine Empire and its younger counterpart in the West frequently gave occasion for reciprocal attempts at humiliation and deception, as the accounts of Notker I of St. Gall and Liudprand of Cremona illustrate for the time of Charlemagne and Otto the Great, respectively; this did not, however, lead to any lasting Western enmity toward the Greeks that would have detracted from the regard in which the Greek language and literature were held. Even the military conflicts between the Eastern and Western Empires in Italy caused no irreconcilable antagonism; and even in the ninth century they occasionally cooperated in a joint defense against the Arabs. The Ottonian period brought the closest relations between the Greeks and Latins, due to the Emperors Otto II and III. In the twelfth century, the universal claims of both empires once more came into vehement conflict when Emperor Manuel I exploited the strained relations between the Western Imperium and the pope and again tried to gain a foothold in Italy. In reality, however, the conflict consisted only of reciprocal demands. The expansive attitude which the Latin West adopted toward the Greek East in the late Middle Ages was not influenced by the political conflict between the Eastern and Western Empires: the existence of both was threatened in the thirteenth century, and they struggled in part against the same adversaries. The lesser powers were the more serious enemies of the universal power of Constantinople. The Venetian Republic diverted the fourth Crusade to Constantinople; Charles I (of Anjou), who had obliterated the Hohenstaufen dynasty, was deterred from an attack on Constantinople only by the Union of 1274 and then the Sicilian Vespers. A counselor of King Philip VI of France formulated the most malicious suggestions for dealing with the Greeks that history has preserved. Due only to his respect for the three "sacred languages" was he willing to forgo the plan to deprive the Greeks of their script and language. He recommended that Constantinople be captured and that six directives be implemented:[32]

> The third directive is that whoever has more than one son must send the second to school for Latin instruction. And if Greek were not one of the three primary languages in which the *titulus* of our crucified Lord was trebly written, I would make the beneficial and intelligent suggestion, as I think, that this language be exterminated altogether.

3. Greek Alphabets

In the Greek alphabet, Christianity of late antiquity and the Latin Middle Ages found allusions to mysteries which the Roman alphabet lacks. All Greek letters are numerals, and five are *litterae mysticae*: Λ—beginning; ω—end; Λω—the symbol of history, which "runs from Λ to ω and then is unrolled again from ω to Λ"; θ—the sign of death; Τ—the figure of the cross; Υ—the Pythagorean symbol of the course of human life.[33] The Greek alphabet is no rarity in Western libraries of the Middle Ages, not only in works in which a Greek alphabet is germane to the text anyway, such as Isidore's *Etymologiae*, Bede's *De temporum ratione*, and Hrabanus' *De computo*, but also as an additional entry in various kinds of other manuscripts. The spectrum of possibilities extends from a simple series of the characters to an alphabetical table, such as the one in Cod. Vindob. 795 (ca. 800), with script variants, phonetic transcription, and Latin equivalents and numerical values of the Greek letters. A table such as this one certainly found use as an instructional tool, an ancestor of the *Alphabeta Graeca* which were still widely used in language instruction of the humanistic era.[34]

A great number of uses were found for the Greek alphabet, which in part seem fanciful to us today.[35] The spelling of the *nomina sacra* "Jesus" and "Christus" as IHC and XPC, which appeared quite early among the Irish, originated in the notion of Greek as one of the "sacred languages."[36] One could also impart an exotic aura to one's own name by writing it in Greek letters; this practice was fashionable especially in the tenth century.[37] This method could be used to encode Latin texts in general, and the use of Greek letters was especially popular for signatures.[38] The transcription in the Greek alphabet of vernacular texts, as in a Sardinian document of 1100 and Sicilian and Calabrian manuscripts of the fourteenth/ sixteenth centuries,[39] was an interesting and exceptional case of this usage. A knowledge of the numerical values of the Greek letters was necessary if a scriptorium labeled its parchment quires in Greek,[40] or if, for instance, the author of a formulary tried his hand at the *epistola formata*. The rite for the dedication of a church, mentioned above, required a knowledge of the Greek alphabet (or at least a text of the alphabetic table), which was inscribed on the floor of the church to be dedicated.[41]

Although majuscule script was replaced by the minuscule in the Greek East, as well as in the Latin West during the eighth and ninth centuries, Greek letters were consistently written in majuscules in the West. Minuscule alphabets, such as those which occur in individual manuscripts of the ninth to eleventh centuries in Laon, Murbach, and Flavigny, are rare;[42] also quite exceptional is the use of Greek minuscules by Liudprand of Cremona. Roger Bacon's *Grammar*, which teaches both alphabets, already belongs to the period when new lines of communication, opened by the mendicant orders, existed between the East and the West in the Mediterranean area.

In the Greek majuscule of the Western tradition, there are a number of peculiarities to be noted. The letters Σ and Ω, not reintroduced until the modern era, were, of course, unknown in the West during the Middle Ages; they were represented by C and ⲱ. In most cases E and Ξ also had the uncial form (Є Ꙃ). Up to this point, the Western usage corresponds to the development of the script in the East. The confusion of Θ and Τ, Η and Є, Υ and Ι, ⲱ and Ο is typically Western: more precisely, there was a preference for the seemingly "more Greek" letters Θ, Η, Υ, and ⲱ at the expense of Τ, Є, Ι, and Ο. Thus it was a widespread custom in music manuscripts of southwest Germany, for example, to estrange the *nomen sacrum* "Christus" with Greek letters, leading to hyper-Greek forms, such as ΧΡΥϹΘΙ (*Christi*). The use of Ͻϲ for Μ was a very popular Grecistic spelling in the West; the former character was used in the late antique Christian schools of Syria as a siglum for ΜΑΘΗΤΗϹ, then in early medieval England (Aldhelm) for *magister*; and from that time on, the letter was regarded in the West as a Greek Μ. This "M siglum" in Greek majuscule manuscripts is an identifying feature of the Western provenance of the script.[43] The symbol Ͱ in medieval manuscripts, the "spiritus asper," which simply stands for *h*, was often misunderstood.[44]

4. Glossaries and Other Sources of Greek Vocabulary—Greek Influence on the Medieval Latin Vocabulary

A considerable amount of Greek vocabulary was accessible to the Latin Middle Ages through the bilingual glossaries which had been handed down from the schools of antiquity and which even contained some idioms. The most important such *Latin-Greek* glossary which came down to the Middle Ages was that of "Philoxenus." Only one Carolingian manuscript has been preserved. In the sixteenth century, a second manuscript was at St. Germain-des-Prés in Paris, which was used for the Stephanus edition of 1573 before disappearing.[45] A *Greek-Latin* counterpart is extant in the "Cyrillus glossary" of an eighth-century uncial manuscript, which came to its present repository—London—via the library of Nicholas of Cusa.

London, BL Harl. 5792, ed. G. Goetz and G. Gundermann, *Corpus Glossarium Latinorum*, II, 215–483 (glossae graeco-latinae) and 487–506 (idiomata). In their description of the manuscript (pp. xx ff.), the editors date the codex "saec. VII"; in the first edition of *CLA* II, Lowe dates it "saec. VII–VIII"; B. Bischoff ("Panorama der Handschriftenüberlieferung aus der Zeit Karls des Großen," in *Karl der Große* [Dusseldorf 1965], II, p. 249, no. 124) dates it "saec. VIII ex." Cf.

Lowe in the second edition of *CLA* (1972), II, no. 203. The problem of the date of the codex, as well as the as yet unsolved problem of its provenance—Italy or Gaul—is important for its epochal classification: does this monument of Greek studies belong to the "Byzantine" or "Lombard" culture of Italy, in the "Merovingian" or "Carolingian" period? These four cultural spheres are temporally and spatially quite near one another in the eighth century. On the "Cyrillus glossary" and related dictionaries, see most recently J. Gribomont, "Saint Bède et ses dictionaires grecs," *RB* 89 (1979), 271–80.

The glossary of MS Laon 444, the famous textbook manuscript written by Irishmen in Laon during the second half of the ninth century, is closely related to the "Cyrillus glossary." Text witnesses for the large old glossaries are conspicuously lacking from the high and late Middle Ages.

The textual tradition of the "Hermeneumata," a language textbook existing in many versions and consisting of three parts—a glossary, a terminological index organized according to topic (animals, plants, medicine, etc.), and reading and conversation passages—also extends essentially no further back than the Carolingian period; various passages were handed down to the high Middle Ages in trivialized form.[46]

The works of Latin lexicography, flourishing since the eleventh century, incorporated Greek material, but the knowledge and pseudo-knowledge of Greek possessed by these authors served only to further disorient Greek studies. Greek terms were used by the lexicographers in the definition of words and were themselves "etymologically" interpreted. Throughout the high Middle Ages, beginning with the *Elementarium doctrinae erudimentum* (ca. 1050) of the Lombard Papias, one can follow a constantly deteriorating "lexicographer Greek," in which Greek nouns usually end in *-os* and *-on*, verbs in *-in* and *-on*; Greek compounds are dismembered for the sake of etymological explanation, and the elements of the compounds then go their own separate ways as independent "Greek" words.[47] Through the *Derivationes* of Hugh of Pisa, the *Grecismus* of Eberhard of Béthune, and the *Cornutus* of John Garland, this form of Greek also asserted itself in the late medieval schools and universities, although the reaction against the corrupted "school Greek" began even in the thirteenth century: a comprehensive Greek-Latin lexicon, with declensional and conjugational information on the Greek words, was produced in England, where Bishop Robert Grosseteste fostered Greek studies (London, College of Arms, MS Arundel 9).

Glossaries were, however, neither the sole sources for Greek and pseudo-Greek words during the Middle Ages nor the ones most often used. Numerous Graeca were found in the works of Quintilian, Lactantius, Jerome, Macrobius, and Priscian, the majority of whom were "school authors" of the Middle Ages; some of these words were exceedingly corrupt, while others were intelligibly transmitted and even passed into the active vocabulary of the Latin Middle Ages.

The false paths occasionally traveled by scholarship before a medieval Graeco-latinum of this kind was correctly understood and its origin ascertained may be illustrated by *foronimus*. The term occurs in a Reichenau Mauritius sequence of the tenth century:

> Innocentius
> deo carus et foronimus
> cunctae militiae praefuit.

Clemens Blume read *Foronimus* without hesitation in his edition, *Analecta Hymnica* (vol. 53, p. 304), and thus created a saint who exists neither in the Theban legend nor anywhere else. Von den Steinen (*Notker*, I, 611) remarks that *foronimus* stands for ⲫⲉⲣⲱⲛⲩⲙⲟⲥ = "der seinen Namen ('der Unschuldige') mit Recht trägt" ("who bears his name ['the innocent one'] legitimately"). He also notes a parallel: "The rare word also occurs at the same time in Ruotger's vita of Brun of Cologne, written soon after 965 ['. . . quibus abbatem preposuit nomine Christianum, suę videlicet professionis foronomum"; ed. I. Schmale-Ott (Cologne/Graz 1952), c. 28, pp. 28 f.]. Did Ruotger know the sequence; or was he in the chancery with its poet around 950? It is indeed a small world. . . ." More probable than such a relationship is the independent discovery of the word by the poet of the Reichenau sequence and the Cologne biographer—either in John the Deacon's widely read vita of Gregory the Great (c. I 2: *Quod* ⲫⲉⲣⲱⲛⲩⲙⲟⲥ *fuerit*) or directly in Jerome's *epist.* 47: "Gratulor tibi et sanctae atque uenerabili sorori tuae Serenillae, quae ⲫⲉⲣⲱⲛⲩⲙⲱⲥ calcatis fluctibus saeculi ad Christi tranquilla peruenit" ("I congratulate you and Serenilla, your holy and reverend sister, who in terms of her own name has reached the peace of Christ through the trampling storms of the world"); *CSEL* 54, 345 f.

The technical language of the *VII artes liberales* was and continued to be imbued with Greek and Grecisms, especially conspicuous in rhetoric,[48] dialectic, and astronomy, but certainly most extensively in music. Since the *VII artes liberales* were the determining factors in the school system until the high Middle Ages, the tradition of the late antique Grecistic technical language was thus guaranteed, and not merely as scholarly ballast, but even as an influential part of poetic vocabulary. The technical language of medicine also made extensive use of Grecisms—as it still does today. The Christian theology of the West had felt the pervasive influence of Greek since late antiquity, and, in the course of the centuries, the Greek elements had been integrated rather than eliminated.[49]

The ease with which Greek terms and terminological elements were incorporated into the Medieval Latin vocabulary is surprising. Many Medieval Latin Grecisms came about by more complicated means than did *anthropus*, perhaps introduced by Alcuin, in which only the ending was latinized.[50] Thus, the technical compound *chirotheca*, for a bishop's glove, was invented in the tenth century from the syllable *chir-*, familiar from numerous compounds (cf. *chirurgia*, etc.) and *theca*; the word became a fashionable "Greek" term which simply did not exist in Constantinople.[51] The useful word *biblia* was apparently not invented

before the twelfth century, perhaps as a shortened form of the old designation for a manuscript of the complete Bible—*bibliotheca*.[52] The prefix *archi-* was much used in Medieval Latin;[53] word formations with *anti-*
and *pseudo-* "received an impetus in the Investiture Controversy."[54]
Compounds with *poly-* (*poli-*) had publicity value as book titles, in
which a tendency toward Grecisms is in general to be found: *Brachylo-
gus, Catholicon, Dragmaticon, Geronticon, Gnotosolitos* (from ΓΝѠΘΙ
ϹΕΑΥΤΟΝ !), *Hypognosticon, Metalogicon, Micrologus, Pancrisis, Pan-
theon, Policratus, Polipticum* (ΠΟΛΥΠΤΥΧΟΝ 'many-paged book'),
Proslogion, . . .[55] An ancient tendency lives on here in the Latin Middle
Ages: six Greek and only one Latin title occur in the works of Prudentius
(*Cathemerinon, Apotheosis, Hamartigenia, Psychomachia, Peristepha-
non, Dittochaeum—Contra Symmachum*). Such models called forth
emulation, and just as Prudentius' Greek titles should actually be written
in Greek—Gennadius explicitly *cites* ΑΠΟΘΕѠϹΙϹ, ΨΥΧΟΜΑΧΙΑ,
ΑΜΑΡΤΙΓΕΝΕΙΑ (*De viris illustribus*, c. 13)—it would comply with the
intentions of the authors to render many of the Grecistic medieval Latin
titles with Greek script. That certainly holds true for the ΑΝΤΙΚΕΙΜΕ-
ΝΟΝ of Julian of Toledo, and probably also for his ΠΡΟΓΝѠϹΤΙΚΟΝ,
certainly for John Scottus' ΠΕΡΙ ΦΥϹΕѠϹ ΜΕΡΙϹΜΟΥ or *Liber* ΠΕΡΙ
ΦΥϹΕѠΝ and Liudprand's *Liber* ΑΝΤΑΠΟΔΟϹΕѠϹ or ΑΝΤΑΠΟ-
ΔΟϹΙϹ, probably also for Anselm of Havelberg's ΑΝΤΙΚΕΙΜΕΝΟΝ— or
Liber ΑΝΤΙΚΕΙΜΕΝѠΝ, in which the German of the twelfth century
appropriated the title from a Spaniard of the seventh century.

Many Greek words and Grecisms entered the Latin language through
the adoption by the West of material objects, techniques and crafts, and
modes of behavior from the East—in the domains of philosophy (*analysis*
for the first time in Albertus Magnus), medicine (*argalia* 'catheter' first in
Constantinus Africanus), astronomy (*astrolabium* or *astrolapsus*, for instance, in Hermannus Contractus), seafaring (*chelandium* 'warship' in
Agnellus of Ravenna and Liudprand of Cremona), etc.[56] The Latin vocabulary of "common usage" was not "expanded to any great degree" ("der
usuelle Wortschatz [hat] keinen nennenswerten Zuwachs erhalten")[57]
through the adoption of Greek words or neologisms on Greek models;
even so, the Greek coloring of Medieval Latin cannot be ignored. The
creative freedom to adapt Greek words to Latin usage was an opportunity
consciously exploited by many authors to render their Latin richer and
more colorful. In the later Middle Ages, Greek asserted itself as a component of the Medieval Latin scientific language, which—then as now—
oftentimes brutally dismembers the language in forming its technical
terms.

5. Greek Grammar in the Middle Ages

There was no textbook in the early and high Middle Ages from which anyone in the West could learn grammatical Greek, as one could learn grammatical Latin from the works of Donatus and Priscian. The ancient grammar of Dositheus, originally intended for Greeks learning Latin, existed
at various places in an at least partially Greco-Latin parallel version. Yet
only a small portion of the grammatical system of the Greek language was
dealt with in the work, and there was almost nothing concerning acci-
dence. The Irish made excerpts from Macrobius' difficult work "On the
Distinguishing and Common Properties of the Greek and Latin Verb";
only these excerpts of the text have survived.[58] Here one can see what late
antiquity could recognize as a Grecistic tendency in Latin[59]—whether it
was actually interpreted and utilized in this respect is questionable. The
oldest surviving medieval attempt at a Greek textbook is the brief bilingual text ΤΙ ΕСΤΙΝ *doctus* (perhaps from St. Denis).[60] The Irish associates
of Martin of Laon (d. 875) sketched a rough outline of a Greek grammar
which circulated in continental Irish circles during the ninth century.[61] In
the Ottonian period, Froumund of Tegernsee, who had perhaps learned
some Greek in the Pantaleon monastery in Cologne, attempted at least
the beginning of a Greek grammar.[62] Not until the thirteenth century
were there again attempts at Greek grammars. The Englishman John of
Basingstoke (d. 1252), a friend of Robert Grosseteste, is supposed to have
translated a *Donatus Graecorum* from Greek—the title suggests that the
book is a Greek grammar.[63] The work is, however, not preserved. The
case is different with the grammar of Grosseteste's younger countryman
Roger Bacon. His grammar (which has survived) was suitable for use as an
introduction to reading Greek. He also began to write a Hebrew
grammar.

As the early Humanists gave spirited expression to their yearning for
the original Greek sources, the time had come as well for the widespread
need for and acceptance of a Greek grammar. Manuel Chrysoloras, who
began to teach Greek in Florence in 1397, wrote the Ἐρωτήματα τῆς
ἑλληνικῆς γλώσσης as an aid to his instruction, a grammar written completely in Greek, in question-answer form. It became the first widely
circulated textbook of Greek in the Latin West, especially after Chrysoloras' student Guarino Veronese adapted the work into Latin, so that it
could also be used without a Greek teacher.

The Γραμματικὴ εἰσαγωγή of Theodore of Gaza (d. 1475) was prized
by the Humanists even more than Chrysoloras' grammar; Aldus Manutius
printed the work for the first time in 1495. The Ἐπιτομὴ τῶν ὀκτὼ τοῦ
λόγου μερῶν of Constantine Lascaris, the first book printed in the Greek
language in Italy (Milan 1476), was dependent on Theodore of Gaza.

The new grammatical resources only gradually displaced the medieval methods of learning Greek. Thus Ambrogio Traversari (d. 1439), Humanist, minister general of the Camaldolese Order, and later translator of Diogenes Laertius and Dionysius the Areopagite, still learned Greek through the comparison of biblical texts, progressing from the familiar Psalter to more difficult texts. He recommended the method without hesitation:[64]

> But since you say that you have discovered that I learned Greek without the aid of a teacher . . . I will disclose to you how I came to my moderate knowledge of this language. I had a Greek Psalter, quite familiar to me through religious education. I thus began to compare it with the Latin Psalter, to note first the verbs, then nouns, then the remaining parts of speech, and to commit the meaning of each to memory and, to the extent possible, to remember the signification of all the words. Thus I made a beginning. I then passed on to the Gospels, the Pauline epistles, and the Acts of the Apostles, and made myself intimately acquainted with them; for they contain a very great number of words and are all translated faithfully, diligently, and not without elegance. Soon I indeed wished to see the books of the heathen and understood them easily.

6. Greek Manuscripts in Western Libraries

Not before the fifteenth century were there large collections of Greek manuscripts assembled in the West, and only from the sixteenth century on were they used by a substantial number of Western scholars and other interested parties.[65] The greater portion of the Greek inventory of the Dominican Library in Basel, the Laurentiana in Florence, the Marciana in Venice, the Vaticana in Rome, the Hapsburg Hofbibliothek in Vienna, and the Bibliothèque du Roi in Paris was first brought together through the combined efforts of Greek emigrants, Latin Humanists, and bibliophile princes. Yet ancient Greek book collections were not inaccessible to the Latin Middle Ages. Greek monasteries, none of which could have been completely without books, flourished in Rome from the seventh to the eleventh century. Grottaferrata has preserved parts of its ancient hoard of Greek books even up to the present day. There were populous Latin districts in Constantinople during the high Middle Ages, and in this period a great number of Italian scholars lived in the Christian metropolis on the Bosporus and made use of the rare-book libraries of the city. Moses of Bergamo was one of these scholarly Italians in twelfth-century Constantinople; he is the first Westerner known to have collected Greek manuscripts in great volume. If his own testimony is true,[66] then the hunt for Greek manuscripts began two centuries before Guarino of Verona and

Giovanni Aurispa. The Greek libraries of southern Italy were even closer to the Latins than those in Constantinople. Casole in Apulia, Carbone in the Basilicata, Stilo in Calabria, and Messina in Sicily had the most notable monastic libraries of the Italo-Greeks; the Cathedral Library of Rossano is still in possession of its cimelia, the famous sixth-century Greek purple evangelary ("Codex purpureus Rossanensis"), which was not "rediscovered" there by scholars until 1879 and which recalls the significance of southern Italy for the transmission of Greek texts.[67] Not before the manuscript research of recent years has the astonishing volume and the high quality (manuscripts of the classics!) of Italo-Greek book production and transmission come to light.[68] Manuscript by manuscript, a "translatio studii" from Byzantium to the West appears, whose line of textual transmission threads its way directly from the Macedonian Renaissance in tenth-century Constantinople, to the court library of the Norman and Hohenstaufen rulers of southern Italy, to the papal library of 1300; the Italian Renaissance picked up this thread as its starting point.

This hoard of Greek books first appears in 1295 at the end of a catalogue of the papal library: "Item Dyonisius super celesticam [!] Ierarchicam [!] in greco. Item Simplicius super phisicam Aristotilis . . ." With the exception of Dionysius the Areopagite (characteristically placed at the beginning of the list) and one other work, the twenty-three volumes all contain works of natural science and philosophy—a remarkable collection for the papacy (ed. A. Pelzer, *Addenda et emendanda ad Francisci Ehrle Historiae Bibliothecae Romanorum Pontificum . . . tomum I* [Rome 1947], pp. 23 f.).

A catalogue of the papal library from 1311 lists the same stock of Greek books: "Item libri, qui sequuntur scripti in greco: primo scripsimus comentum Procli Permenidem Platonis ˙And˙ et est in papiro . . ." There have been several changes. In all there are now thirty-three Greek codices; ed. F. Ehrle, *Historia Bibliothecae Romanorum Pontificum tum Bonifatianae tum Avenionensis* (Rome 1890), I, 95–99. In nineteen of these books one finds this remarkable ˙And˙, for which Ehrle provides the hardly convincing resolution *antiquus*. We learn from an inventory of 1327 that the thirty-three Greek codices were kept in two crates; ed. Pelzer, *Addenda et emendanda*, p. 34. In 1339 they (all of them?) are found in a single crate together with Hebrew books (ibid., p. 64); in 1369 there are still seven Greek books in the papal library (cf. Ehrle, *Historia Bibliothecae*, pp. 376 [no. 1183], 398 [no. 1512], 429 [no. 2007]. The popes obviously managed to carelessly lose their small but fine Greek collection during their Avignon adventures.

The enigma of the notation *And* in the catalogue of 1311 has been solved by August Pelzer in a striking way (*Addenda et emendanda*, pp. 92 f.): it is to be resolved *Andegavensis* = Anjou!—that is, these books came to the papal library "from Anjou." When did the house of Anjou have cause and opportunity to present the papacy with a collection of Greek books? Pelzer answers: after the battle near Benevento (1266), when Charles of Anjou, whom the papacy had summoned to southern Italy, had disposed of the hated Hohenstaufen King Manfred. Thus the core of the Greek collection of the Norman-Staufer court library came into the possession of the papacy in 1266 in a similar way to that by which the Heidelberg Bibliotheca Palatina did in 1623.

Codicological research has confirmed Pelzer's brilliant conclusions. Nine of the thirty-three Greek books of the 1311 catalogue have now again been identified, and the findings demonstrate clearly that this could not have been a casual acquisition by the popes or by Anjou, nor was it plunder from the conquest of Constantinople in 1204; rather the collection came from the court in Constantinople to the court in Palermo around the middle of the twelfth century: "Ces volumes sont de magnifiques produits des ateliers constantinopolitains au moment de la renaissance scientifique et philosophique des IXe et Xe siècles" ("These volumes are the magnificent products of the ateliers in Constantinople at the moment of the scientific and philosophical renaissance of the ninth and tenth centuries;" P. Canart, "Le livre grec," p. 149). Almost half of all known scientific "classical manuscripts" of the Byzantine Renaissance of the ninth/tenth century have been preserved via the Norman-Staufer court library (G. Derenzini, "All 'origine della traduzione di opere scientifiche classiche: vicende di testi et di codici tra Bisanzio e Palermo," *Physis* 18 [1976], 87–103). Thus the history of the Greek court library in the West extends back into the twelfth century, and the Greek collections in Renaissance court libraries in the West were then not altogether without precedents.

In the outstanding monastic and cathedral libraries of the Middle Ages, there were, however, at most only scattered Greek manuscripts. The Abbey of St. Martin in Tours possessed, at least in fragments, a Greek papyrus codex from Egypt, which contained a homily of Ephraem Syrus on "Fair Joseph."[69] An illuminated Greek copy of the ΧΡΙСΤΙΑΝΙΚΗ ΤΟΠΟΓΡΑΦΙΑ of Cosmas Indicopleustes has been traced to the collection of the early medieval Cathedral Library in York.[70] Reichenau had a precious Greek Psalter from the eighth to the sixteenth century.[71] The Abbey of St. Denis tended the splendid uncial manuscript of the works of Dionysius the Areopagite which Louis the Pious had obtained from Constantinople;[72] various other Greek manuscripts were added in the high and late Middle Ages.[73] In the monastery of St. Simeon, established in the Porta Nigra in Trier, there was a Greek lectionary of the tenth/eleventh century.[74] In the midst of the Investiture Controversy, the wealthy and ostentatious canons of St. Gereon in Cologne procured a magnificent Greek Psalter, which was written and illuminated around 1077 in a scriptorium closely connected with the Greek emperor.[75] The first illumination, by a Greek artist, shows

Ο ΑΓΙΟϹ ΜΑΡΤΥϹ ΤΟΥ ΧΡΙϹΤΟΥ ΓΕΡΕШΝ.

Many other large libraries of the Middle Ages also had their Greek showpieces to exhibit. Occasionally, the Latin West also produced manuscripts entirely in Greek. In the ninth century, as Montfaucon has noted, Sedulius Scottus was capable of writing a Greek Psalter with odes.[76] From the Ottonian period on, Greco-Italian southern Italy offered the opportunity to obtain scribes who were acquainted with the Greek alphabet. A lectionary written in 1021 by an Italo-Greek Ἐν χόρα Φραγκίας κάστρο δὲ Κολονίας (= Cologne?) later made its way to St. Denis.[77] In England even Western scribes ventured to produce various Greek *minuscule* manuscripts. According to M. R. James, the Greek Psalter of Cambridge, Emmanuel College III. 3. 22 is of English origin.[78] In the thirteenth century, Bishop Robert Grosseteste commissioned a large-scale Corpus Dionysiacum in Greek minuscules.[79] Grosseteste, his students, and his assistants brought together, by means of purchasing and copying, a significant collection of Greek manuscripts in England, so that it is true, at least for this country, that interest in Greek books had already arisen in the late Middle Ages;[80] to be sure, it was a narrow circle until Humanism created a broader audience for the purely Greek book.

The typical medieval form of the Greek codex was the *bilingual* manuscript. It was an inheritance from late antiquity and the Middle Ages in part made good use of it. The Mediterranean cultural symbiosis of the late Roman Empire had brought forth many such bilinguals—Latino-Greek and Greco-Latin. The most famous examples of late antique Latino-Greek editions are the remnants of the bilingual Vergil codices, recovered from the Egyptian sand; thus far, no less than nine such bilinguals of the champion of the imperial Roman cause have been brought to light.[81] During Justinian's time, it was certainly still possible to write codices in both imperial languages in Constantinople; the Florentine digest codex ("Codex Pisanus," soon after 533) bears impressive witness to this fact. It seems, however, that the Byzantine Empire of the medieval period proper no longer fostered bilingual editions of Roman authors,[82] and—if southern Italy is excluded—produced no Latino-Greek manuscripts at all.

A Greco-Latin Homer, the counterpart of a Latino-Greek Vergil, apparently did not exist in late antiquity. The West was interested in Christian bilinguals, in Greco-Latin editions of portions of the Bible; a Greco-Latin anthology of canon law may have also existed during late antiquity, at least in one copy.[83] The Latin Middle Ages carried on the tradition of assorted scriptural bilinguals: the Psalter, Gospels, Pauline epistles, and Acts of the Apostles (in fact those four books of the Bible whose comparative study Ambrogio Traversari recommended for self-instruction in Greek!). It would have been easy for the bilingual tradition of the Acts of the Apostles to have disappeared, as other bilingual scriptural texts must have: the tradition has only two witnesses—the "Codex Bezae" in Cambridge and the "Codex Laudianus" in Oxford.[84] The Carolingian period transmitted only the Psalter, Gospels, and Pauline epistles, to some extent in the new interlinear bilingual form, which was especially cultivated by the Irish. In the Ottonian period, the bilingual tradition of the Pauline epistles dies out. The fragmentary "Codex Waldeccensis" (saec. X ex.) completes the circle of this bilingual tradition of the Middle Ages, in which the beginning and end are joined; for this bilingual manuscript, the last of the Pauline epistles known from the Middle Ages, is an exact copy of the earliest manuscript—the "Codex Claromontanus."[85] The production of bilingual texts of the Gospels is extraordinarily rare in the high and late Middle Ages. Yet a bilingual edition of the Apocalypse curiously surfaces at that period.[86] The Greco-Latin Psalter reached the age of Humanism, however, in an unbroken tradition. This Greco-Latin text outlasted all else because it was the text with which the Latin Middle Ages was doubtless most intimately familiar and was thus better suited than any other text to introduce the Latins to a basic study of Greek. This tradition of the Greco-Latin Psalter manuscripts, which span the entire Middle Ages, from the Cod. Verona I (saec. VI–VII) to the Cod. Plut. XVII 13 of the Biblioteca Laurenziana (which was "erst wenige Jahre alt, als in Florenz das große Unionskonzil begann" ["only a few years old as the great Union Council began in Florence"]),[87] and to the great trilingual (Hebreo-Greco-Latin) Psalter produced for Duke Federigo of Urbino in Florence in 1473,[88] presents scarcely touched material for the further investigation of Greek studies in the Latin Middle Ages.[89]

The Greek text is presented in various manners in these Psalters: in Greek script (generally majuscule) or in Roman transcription; the Greek and Latin texts on facing pages, in parallel columns, or arranged interlinearly. The base text (left page, left column, or principal line in interlinear versions) is generally Greek. The Psalters in which the Greek text is presented only in Roman transcription must have originally served primarily liturgical purposes: Greek *liturgica* were always written in the Roman alphabet in the West, since they were to be read or sung aloud and were not intended to be studied. On the other hand, manuscripts with the Greek text written in Greek script were textbooks or even showpieces. The possibilities for combination are numerous and the distinctions between them fluid: even such an obvious example of a textbook as the St. Gall *psalterium quadrupartitum* presented the Greek text only in Roman transcription. In general, each of the numerous bilingual Psalters of the Middle Ages requires its own particular historico-philological interpretation.

The other Greco-Latin books of the Middle Ages may be regarded as offshoots from the main trunk of bilingual biblical texts: in the sixth century, bilinguals of the first four ecumenical councils by Dionysius Exiguus; in the eleventh century, Gregory's *Dialogi*;[90] in the thirteenth century, the liturgical and polemical bilinguals of Abbot Nicholas-Nectarius of Otranto. The Dominican mission in the "Orient" continued this latter tradition and produced its controversial theological tracts in bilingual editions ("Bartholomaeus," *Contra Graecos*; Buonaccorsi, *Thesaurus veritatis fidei*). Leontius Pilatus' translations of Homer and Euripides for the early Florentine Humanists were designed as interlinear bilinguals. Finally, one must not forget the striking bilingualism of the imperial correspondence from Constantinople, of which a number of splendid examples from the twelfth to the fifteenth centuries have been preserved in Italian archives.[91] When the corpus of manuscripts has finally been fully catalogued, the history of the Greco-Latin bilinguals will open one of the most informative perspectives on the ever-shifting interest in Greek texts that has persisted through the ages.

III

Philosophical and Theological Hellenism in Latin Late Antiquity

Graeca leguntur in omnibus fere gentibus, Latina suis finibus, exiguis sane, continentur.
[Greek literature is read in almost all countries, while Latin is confined within its own rather narrow borders.]

Cicero, *Pro Archia* 23

Graecia capta ferum victorem cepit et artis / intulit agresti Latio. . . .
[When Greece had been conquered, she enslaved the uncivilized victor and attacked boorish Rome with her arts.]

Horace, *epist.* II 1, 156

Ancient Latin literature and culture were in constant contact with the older Greek literature and culture; imitation, reaction, and assimilation alternated with each other. Livius Andronicus of Taranto, a Greek prisoner of war from Magna Graecia in southern Italy, translated Homer's *Odyssey* and Greek dramas: a *translator* is considered the founder of Latin literature. The earliest Roman historians published in Greek; Cato wrote in Latin on principle. The Roman assimilation of Greek philosophy began in Scipio's learned circle of friends.

The classical formulation of *translatio studii* as a deed of conquest may be traced to Cicero:[1]

The philosophy of Greece would never have become so important had it not matured in the discussions of the most learned men on various points of view; therefore, I exhort all those who can to snatch the glory of this genre from the already ailing Greece and to transmit it to this city, just as our forefathers, by their zeal and diligence, did with all other forms of glory which could be won.

He created a Latin technical language for philosophy, modeled on the Greek, and with extensive direct borrowing of Greek concepts and expressions. He translated Aratus' ΦΑΙΝΟΜΕΝΑ and Plato's ΤΙΜΑΙΟC and ΠΡWΤΑΓΟΡΑC; his *Laelius* was a counterpart to Theophrastus' ΠΕΡΙ ΦΙΛΙΑC, as was his *De re publica* to Plato's ΠΟΛΙΤΕΙΑ. The *Somnium Scipionis*, from the sixth book of *De re publica*, fascinated readers for centuries through its union of Roman historical lore [*Geschichtserin-*

nerung], Hellenistic astrology, and the desire for immortality; after the loss of the *Hortensius*, the work became another Ciceronian *protrepticon* to philosophy.

In his *Instituta Oratoria*, Quintilian produced the Roman textbook of and lifelong guide to verbal culture: only with constant reference to Greek—*unde et nostrae* [*disciplinae*] *fluxerunt*—could Latin gain full powers of expression and comprehensibility.[2]

Around the time of Christ's birth and in the first centuries of the Christian era, there were *utriusque linguae docti* in great numbers.[3] Augustus wrote letters in which there were almost as many Greek words and idioms as Latin.[4] It was primarily Africa, the *terra bilinguis*, that produced authors who made use of Greek and Latin with the same facility.[5] Apuleius and Tertullian, the first and the most eloquent of all Christian apologists of the Latin West, forged the possibility of theological expression in Latin through neologisms and loanwords from Greek.

The Latin of the early Christians teemed with Greek terms: *agape, anathema, angelus, anti-christus, apocalypsis*, etc.[6] The attempt was often made to imbue a common Latin word with a secondary, Christian sense by means of "connotation," and thus avoid the direct borrowing of a Greek (or Hebrew) term—until it was finally realized that the practice was not effective, whereupon a neologism was coined. ϹШΖЄΙΝ 'redeem' was initially translated with *sanare* and *liberare*. Tertullian experimented with *salvum facere* and *salutificator* (or *salvificator*) for the related noun ϹШΤΗΡ, until finally the redeeming words appear in Cyprian of Carthage: *salvare* and *salvator*.[7] Augustine interpreted and remarked on this silent Grecization of Latin quite accurately: "*salvare* and *salvator* were not Latin words before the Salvator came; when he came to the Latins, he also made the terms into Latin words."[8] The transformation of Latin under the influence of the new faith from the East is so striking that scholars have even spoken of an "altchristliche Sondersprache."[9]

1. Pagan Neoplatonism

During the third century, vitality returned to Greek philosophy: in Alexandria and, for a quarter of a century (245–70), also in Rome, Plotinus taught a revived Platonism. His student Porphyry (d. 305) arranged the writings of his master in *Enneads*, "group of nine," and systematized his teachings, which—as Neoplatonism—had great influence on late antiquity and—in the Christian adaptation of Dionysius the Areopagite—on the Greek and Latin Middle Ages.

Neoplatonism brought a new incentive to Greek studies among the educated classes of all persuasions. The principal defenders of the ancient religion saw in Neoplatonism an alternative to the victoriously advancing

Christianity: Emperor Julian ("Apostata," d. 363) and the Roman senatorial circles of the Symmachi, Nicomachi, and those associated with Vettius Agorius Praetextatus, whom Macrobius depicts in his *Saturnalia*, gathered for a philosophical banquet. Vergil was their heritage and Neoplatonism their contemporary endowment—thus one could briefly summarize the topics which occupied these *nobiles* and *docti* in their symposia. That Hellenism and Latinity belonged together was also demonstrated by Macrobius in his philosophical treatise "On the Distinguishing and Common Properties of the Greek and Latin Verb." Finally, he wrote a commentary on Cicero's *Somnium Scipionis*, and thus presented an introduction to Neoplatonism which, along with Chalcidius' commentary on the *Timaeus* and Boethius' *Consolation of Philosophy*, remained a basic philosophical text until the rise of Aristotelianism in the high Middle Ages.[10]

Praetextatus (d. 384), the central figure in Macrobius' *Saturnalia*, had close relations to the Greek East; he translated the commentaries on Aristotle written by the philosopher Themistius (d. 338), who taught in Constantinople; it was probably in the circle of Themistius and Praetextatus that the paraphrase of Aristotle's *Categories* originated which Alcuin recommended to Charlemagne as a work of Augustine's.[11] Among the participants in the symposium of the *Saturnalia* was Rufus Festus Avienus, whose didactic poem on geography and cosmology transmitted both Hellenistic science and Hellenistic beliefs. In *Orbis terrae* he adapted the ΠΕΡΙΗΓΗCΙC of Dionysius ("Periegetes"); in *Ora maritima* he compiled Greek descriptions of coastlines. Avienus produced an enlarged Latin adaptation of Aratus' ΦΑΙΝΟΜΕΝΑ and thus entered into competition with Cicero and Germanicus, both of whom had already rendered this famous Hellenistic didactic poem, with its astrological lore, into Latin.

Since Aratus' ΦΑΙΝΟΜΕΝΑ is one of the very few literary works cited in the canonical writings of the New Testament (Acts 17:28; Paul on the Areopagus), Jerome mentions all three translations of the ΦΑΙΝΟΜΕΝΑ in his *Comm. in epist. ad Titum* I, on v. 12 (*Migne PL* 26, col. 572). Jerome says that in addition to Cicero, Germanicus, and Avienus, *multi, quos enumerare longum est*, had translated the work. One translation, considered a work of the early medieval period and bearing the barbarous title *Arati ea quae videntur* (= ΑΡΑΤΟΥ ΦΑΙΝΟΜΕΝΑ!) has been edited by E. Maass, *Commentariorum in Aratum reliquiae* (Berlin 1898), pp. 102 ff. M. Manitius, "Lateinische Übersetzungen aus der Aratusliteratur," *Rheinisches Museum*, n.s., 52 (1897), 305–32, is still useful for orientation in the topic.

The *Verzeichnis astrologischer und mythologischer illustrierter Handschriften des lateinischen Mittelalters*, vol. I: Rome (Heidelberg 1915), vol. II: Vienna (Heidelberg 1927), vol. III: England (London 1953), vol. IV: Italy (London 1966), begun by Fritz Saxl and continued by the Warburg Institute, contains abundant material on the medieval transmission of the "Aratea." The two finest Carolingian copies of ancient "Aratea" manuscripts have recently been published by W. Koehler and F. Mütherich, *Die karolingischen Miniaturen*, vol. IV (Berlin 1971):

London, Harley 647 (Aratea of Cicero with Hyginus' annotations) and Leiden, Voss. lat. Q. 79 (Aratea of Germanicus, with the verses of Avienus). Concerning the Aratea on the "constellation mantle of Henry II," see Chapter X.

The *Nuptiae Mercurii et Philologiae* of Martianus Capella is no less important for the literary and intellectual history of late antiquity, in terms of Graecolatina, than the three preserved works of Macrobius. This encyclopedia of the *VII artes liberales*—grammar, rhetoric, dialectic, arithmetic, geometry, astronomy, and music—woven into the fable of the deification of Philology and her marriage to Mercury, is written in a kind of Latino-Greek style: Greek names, Greek terms (declined as in Greek) in a Latin context, aphorisms, and fashionable Greek customs, such as the minutely explained computation of the sum of the numerical values of the letters of names. . . .[12] The *Nuptiae* were a perennial object of study in the medieval West, especially in the monastic and cathedral schools from the ninth to the eleventh century.

2. "Interpretatio christiana"

ΤΟΥ ΓΑΡ ΚΑΙ ΓΕΝΟC ΕCΜΕΝ 'for we are of his race'—with this half-line from Aratus' ΦΑΙΝΟΜΕΝΑ, used in his "Hellenistic address" on the Areopagus, Paul reminded the Greeks of their poets' and philosophers' lofty conception of divinity.[13] This biblical citation (and two others) served Jerome as principal witnesses in his defense of the continuity of pagan and Christian literature.[14]

Greek philosophy, which had erected an altar to the "unknown god," and Christian theology were not born as feuding brothers. The Stoics taught much which seemed to Christians worthy of consideration; in late antiquity, Paul and Seneca were thought to have carried on a friendly correspondence, and, on the basis of this widely read fictional correspondence, Jerome included Seneca as the only pagan in his *De viris illustribus*.[15]

In his *Divinae Institutiones*, Lactantius reflects the dependence even of the Christians on the religious undercurrents of the time; "the Sibylline Oracles and Hermes Trismegistus had more authority for him than did the great geniuses of ancient Greece."[16] In the fourth and fifth centuries, the Neoplatonism of Plotinus and Porphyry influenced the thought of Christians such as the Roman rhetor Marius Victorinus and Manlius Theodorus, rhetor in Milan.[17] Recently, Chalcidius, the translator of and commentator on the first half of Plato's *Timaeus*—and a Christian—has also been sought in the sphere of Milan Platonism around 400. While the older translations of Plato by Cicero and Apuleius sank into oblivion,

Chalcidius' *Timaeus* became the basic text in the medieval study of Plato; until the mid-twelfth century, it was the only Platonic dialogue which was widely circulated in the West in Latin translation.[18]

The great synthesis of Neoplatonism and Christian theology was a work of the fifth or sixth century; the unknown author of this work judiciously concealed himself behind the name of the sage of the Areopagus, who, according to Acts, was the only one not to desert Paul in Athens, as he spoke of the resurrection of the dead. Official heathen Neoplatonism ended with the closing of the Athenian Academy by Emperor Justinian in 529; the philosophico-theological work of the Areopagite took its place and allowed Neoplatonism in Christian interpretation to survive another thousand years. In terms of the Medieval Latin school curriculum, this author "turned stones to bread": in order to read and understand him, again and again one actually turned to a study of Greek; his works were sought in the original Greek even in the West. For the Latin Middle Ages, it was not Homer but Dionysius who was the "seer" for whose sake it was thought worthwhile to undertake the study of Greek.

3. Jerome and Rufinus

During late antiquity, there was also a completely different kind of Hellenism, which could be characterized by the key words *Bible* and *exegesis, Christian ecclesiastical history* and *monasticism.*

The original language of the New Testament was for the most part Greek; the Septuagint was the Greek translation of the Hebrew Old Testament which was regarded as authoritative, even inspired. Exegesis and theology initially developed more extensively in the Greek East than in the Latin West. Among the ancient exegetical schools, the Alexandrine school aroused the greatest interest, especially through Origen (d. 254), its head and chief proponent. In the exegesis of the Old Testament, every critical work had to make use of Origen. In his ΕΞΑΠΛΑ, he produced the basis for the literal interpretation of the Old Testament: the work was an edition of the Old Testament in six parallel columns—original Hebrew with transcription in Greek alphabet, and four Greek translations, among them the Septuagint.

In Christian hymnody and ecclesiastical history, the Greek East was also further advanced than the Latin West. Additionally, during the third century, first in Egypt and then in Syria, there arose in monasticism a way of life which quickly became a model in the West.

The Gaul Hilary of Poitiers (d. ca. 367) was the first Western author to devote himself fully to Greco-Christian culture.[19] In his exegetical writings, he practiced the allegorical method of the Alexandrine school. According to Jerome, Hilary's *Homiliae in Iob* and several of his *In psalmos tractatus* conformed so closely to the works of Origen that they could be regarded as free translations.[20] In his major work, *De trinitate*, Hilary made use of Greek theological terminology. Most likely during his exile in Asia Minor, he became acquainted with Greco-Christian hymnody, and stimulated by it, he composed Latin hymns—the first of this poetic genre, which came to be so important in the Middle Ages.[21]

In the final third of the fourth century, two prominent mediators of Greco-Christian literature appeared: the clerics Rufinus of Aquileia (d. 410) and Jerome of Stridon (d. 420), who had been friends since their youth. Both became inspired by Eastern monasticism, sought an acquaintanceship with it in the East, and founded monastic establishments in Palestine; both wanted to make Origen's works accessible to the Latins, which led to a quarrel between them. Rufinus did little more than translate; Jerome was more ambitious, especially in his later years, and made use of his knowledge of Greek theology in his own theological writings.[22]

The most important of Rufinus' translations are Eusebius' *Ecclesiastical History* and Origen's principal work of dogma, ΠΕΡΙ ΑΡΧWΝ.[23] In each work, Rufinus was both translator and editor. He compressed, altered, and expanded Eusebius' *Ecclesiastical History*, which extended up to the year 324.[24] His most valuable addition was the continuation of the history up to the death of Theodosius the Great (395). In the context of the fierce controversy over Origen's orthodoxy, which broke out toward the end of the fourth century, Rufinus thought it well advised to render the controversial passages of ΠΕΡΙ ΑΡΧWΝ in such a way as to avoid further offense. Jerome, the philologist and partisan of the anti-Origen faction, reacted sharply against this practice. After the year 400, Rufinus translated the Adamantine dialogue ascribed to Origen, in order to emphasize his orthodoxy.[25] Rufinus propagandized for Eastern monasticism with the translations of Basil's monastic rule[26] and the "History of the Egyptian Monks," which had been written as a travel novel.[27] He also translated some homilies of Basil and Gregory Nazianzus, the other prominent Cappadocian theologian of the fourth century.[28] Finally, he was also the translator of the pseudo-Clementine *Recognitiones*, the voluminous "first Christian novel."[29]

In his capacity as author of monastic biographies and translator of the "Pachomiana," Jerome also propagandized for monasticism.[30] In his younger years, he devoted himself to the transmission of the works of Eusebius and Origen.[31] Around 380 he translated and edited Eusebius' *Chronicle* and continued it up to the year 378. At about the same time, he responded to the great demand for texts of Origen by translating fourteen homilies each on Jeremiah and Ezekiel, and he announced that he would translate a great part of Origen's work into Latin. Subsequently he translated two homilies on the Song of Songs, which he presented to his patron, Pope Damasus (d. 384). Then his translation of Origen's homilies on Luke appeared—perhaps also as a reaction against the commentary on Luke which Ambrose of Milan published in 387. The series of homilies on Isaiah also appears to have been translated before the outbreak of the Origen controversy. The translation of a work on the Holy Spirit written by Didymus of Alexandria (d. ca. 398), completed by Jerome before 392, is also to be seen in the context of Jerome's initial veneration of Origen and his school. After Origen's doctrine had been condemned (after about 394), Jerome translated only one other work of the discredited theologian: ΠЄΡΙ ΑΡΧѠΝ, as a counter-translation to Rufinus' rendering, in order to give the "heretical" passages their due.

Jerome did not forgo exegesis of Origen, even after he was no longer well disposed toward his doctrine. Yet he now preferred to present the exegetical works, which were based on Origen, under his own name.[32] Besides the polemic against Origen and his own theological ambition, a third circumstance deterred Jerome from presenting the West with the greatly desired "Origenes latinus": Pope Damasus gave the student of Donatus a more distinguished exercise in translation—the revision of the Latin Bible.

In many of his polemical works, exegetical treatises, translator's prologues, and even letters, Jerome ornamented his Latin style, modeled on Cicero and Suetonius, with Greek elements (which G. Grützmacher criticizes as a "bad habit" that "grew worse over the years"; *Hieronymus* [Berlin 1906], II, 142). This was his practice not just in those passages where Greek was necessary for philological explanation (as in *epist*. 106, *Ad Sunniam et Fretelam*). An example of Jerome's Latin, interspersed with Greek, which was of great importance for medieval Greek studies, is *De viris illustribus*, c. 80:

> Firmianus, qui et Lactantius, Arnobii discipulus, sub Diocletiano principe accitus cum Flavio grammatico . . . Nicomediae rhetoricam docuit ac penuria discipulorum ob Graecam videlicet civitatem ad scribendum se contulit. Habemus eius *Symposium*, quod adulescentulus scripsit Africae et Ὁδοιπορικόν *de Africa usque Nicomediam* . . . et *Institutionum divinarum adversus gentes* libros septem et Ἐπιτομήν eiusdem operis in libro uno ἀκεφάλῳ . . .

In his edition (Leipzig 1896), Richardson printed three of the four Greek literary terms in Greek type (not *Symposium*), certainly more accurately than C. A. Bernoulli (Freiburg/Leipzig 1895), who printed them all except ἐπιτομήν in Roman type.

The example demonstrates how Jerome's Graeca still pose problems even for modern editors. For the medieval scribe, the crux of such texts was how he should copy the words of his source, most of which were unfamiliar to him. The modern editorial problem is to uncover an originally Greek form, which has been obscured in the text tradition by Latin glosses.

4. "Vetus latina" and "Vulgata"

For the Middle Ages, the most important but also the most peculiar Greco-Latin translation of antiquity was the Septuagint. While translation was viewed as a "patriotic deed" in antiquity[33]—the subjugation of a foreign subject to the rules of one's own language and its rhetoric—the dominant principle for the anonymous early Christian translators was that of literalness—of a kind which could only break with the tradition of the linguistic norm. In their tendency toward expressiveness, these translators elevated subliterary vocabulary to the heights of solemn discourse, as, for example, *manducare*, the "berüchtigte Schibboleth echt biblischer Texte, das nun vollends in seiner Anwendung auf das Abendmahl: *Accipite et manducate* allein schon Spott und Übelkeit der kultivierten Welt herausfordern mußte" ("the infamous shibboleth of genuine early biblical texts, which now in its application to the Last Supper—*Accipite et manducate*—by itself provoked scorn and disgust in cultivated readers").[34]

Some works of Greco-Christian writers were also translated into Latin in the literal style of the early translations of the Bible,[35] for instance, the first letter of Clement, the "Shepherd" of Hermas,[36] and the *Adversus haereses* of Irenaeus of Lyon.[37] Even Chalcidius' translation of the *Timaeus* is strictly literal; a comparison to the fragments of Cicero's translation illustrates the differences between the ancient classical and Christian biblical methods of translation.[38]

In the course of the fourth century, the linguistic tastes of Christians became differentiated; they accepted rhetoric and classicism into their cultural domain. The two Latin translations of the Greek vita of St. Anthony—the first literal, the second, which followed immediately, freer—illustrate most clearly the problem of form at that time. The *bios* of the monastic father Anthony (d. 356) written by Athanasius the Great was rendered in a crudely literal Latin translation shortly after its composition (ca. 365). Scholars conjecture that the work was translated in Rome (the question remains open), the only place where the translation has been preserved.[39] Evagrius of Antioch supplanted this translation with a newer version, completed around 370 according to classical principles of translation.[40]

> Presbyter Evagrius Innocentio charissimo filio in domino salutem.
> Ex alia in aliam linguam ad verbum expressa translatio sensus operit et veluti laetum gramen sata strangulat. Dum enim casibus et figuris servit oratio, quod brevi poterat indicari sermone, longo ambitu circumacta vix explicat. Hoc igitur ego vitans vitam beati Antonii te petente ita transposui ut nihil desit ex sensu cum aliquid desit ex verbis. Alii syllabas aucupentur et litteras, tu quaere sententiam.

[Greetings from the priest Evagrius to Innocent, his dearest son in the lord.

Literal translation from one language into another conceals the sense and strangles the seeds, just as does the luxuriant grass. For when the style is a slave to the grammatical cases and figures of speech, it can scarcely explain even by involved circumlocution what could have been expounded briefly. I have avoided that and translated the life of St. Anthony, which you requested, in such a way that none of the meaning, even if some of the words, is lacking. Others may have an eye for syllables and letters, you seek the meaning.]

Without mentioning the older translation of the vita of St. Anthony, Evagrius vigorously distanced himself from it. Jerome cites Evagrius' prologue in his famous *epist.* 57 (*Ad Pammachium de optimo genere interpretandi*) as a plan for free, sense-oriented translation.

Roman provenance has also been established for the brief but important translation *Admonitio S. Basilii episcopi ad monachos,* Inc. *Stude, monache, diligenter* (*Clavis PG* 2890; ed. A. Wilmart, in *RB* 27 [1910], 226–33), which, as "une règle monastique avant la lettre," Wilmart dates to the pre-Benedictine period or contemporary with Benedict (saec. V–VI). The *Admonitio S. Basilii ad filium spiritualem,* Inc. *Audi, fili, admonitionem,* which is easy to confuse with the former text, is regarded by P. Lehmann (*Die Admonitio S. Basilii ad filium spiritualem,* SB Munich [1955]) as a translation of a lost Greek text by Basil the Great, and the translation as the work of Rufinus. The linguistic parallels adduced by Lehmann leave too many questions unanswered, however, to definitively ascribe the translation to Rufinus.

The translator of the *Passio SS. Machabaeorum,* the fourth book of Maccabees from the Septuagint, endeavored "to write fine, even elegant, Latin,"[41] while at the same time (ca. 400), Eustathius translated Basil's homilies on the Hexaemeron in a strictly literal fashion.[42]

The interest in a new Latin text of the Bible must be seen against this background. The literal method of translation had been abandoned only in part. For texts which could claim authoritative status, the principle of literal translation—with some restrictions—retained its validity. In general, Jerome professed the principles of free translation; for the Scriptures, however, *ubi et verborum ordo mysterium est,* he wished to restrict the freedom of translation more than elsewhere.[43] Under the pontificate of Pope Damasus, Jerome first revised the New Testament.

Considerable remnants of a fifth-century manuscript are preserved in St. Gall Cod. 1395, which can give an idea of the appearance of Jerome's first biblical work when it was complete: a manageable format (ca. 23 × 18.5 cm.); two columns in half uncial, the newly developed script of late antiquity, which was often used in Christian literature; very fine parchment. It is noteworthy that this oldest copy of the Gospels in Jerome's version, later called "Vulgata," was provided with Greek notations. Previously, these annotations were thought to be additions by later biblical scholars.[44] Now it is thought possible that they stem from Jerome himself.[45]

After the New Testament, Jerome revised the Psalter (*Psalterium Roma-num*); he compared the Latin text with the Greek, and in doing so, he did not on principle discard the nonclassical form of the language, which was in part due to literal translation, but rather emended it only where such change seemed to be demanded by the sense. Later in Caesarea, when Jerome had become acquainted with Origen's ΕΞΑΠΛΑ, he also began to revise the Old Testament and translated it anew, now no longer from the Greek text of the Septuagint, but from the Hebrew original (e.g., the *Psalterium iuxta Hebraeos*).

It was neither the *Psalterium Romanum* nor the *Psalterium iuxta Hebraeos* that gained acceptance in the Middle Ages, but rather Jerome's *Psalterium Gallica-num*, which is methodologically intermediate between those two translations. The *Psalterium Gallicanum* is the closest of the three versions of the Psalms to the Septuagint. According to Allgeier (*Die Psalmen*, pp. 302 ff.), the *Psalterium Galli-canum* represents the "compromise" version of the text, which Jerome produced at the end of his scholarly work on the Psalter. This version, as the one which most nearly satisfied the various requirements, was thus justly preferred in the subse-quent ages.

In his review of Sandys' *History of Classical Scholarship*, Traube out-lined the extraordinary significance of the multiple Latin translations of the Psalter for the history of philology and for intellectual history in general: "Scarcely any facts of textual tradition which confronted the Western Middle Ages contributed as much to the awakening of critical thought and widening of the intellectual horizon as the existence of Jerome's three Psalters, their deviations from each other, their rela-tionship to the Hebrew original and to the Septuagint translation, Jerome's extensive commentary on specific passages, with reference to still other Greek translations, and the concise but eloquent style which his critical notations incorporate into the text of the Psalterium Gallica-num. . . ." "If one maintains that the Middle Ages lacked the faculty of critical thought in general, it must on the contrary still be strongly emphasized that the period occasionally produced excellent philological works, certainly as a result of Jerome's work."[46]

The three translations of the Psalms were not infrequently combined in textbooks during the Middle Ages, so that the three columns could be compared line-by-line ("Psalterium triplex," "Psalterium tripartitum"). Occasionally it was even thought that this arrangement of this philological tool could be traced back to Jerome himself.

[Jerome] translated the Psalter into Latin from the corrected Greek translation of the Septuagint and delivered it to all churches of Gaul and some of Germania for the purpose of [liturgical] song. For this reason, he called it the "Psalterium Gallicanum," while the Romans still sang the Psalms from the widely circulated and incorrect edition, according to which they composed the songs and passed the practice on to us. Thus it happens that the words which are sung in the offices of the day and night [according to the Psalterium Romanum] are mixed [with the text of the Psalterium Gallicanum] and confusingly inserted into our Psalms in such a way that those who are less well informed can scarcely distinguish any more what corresponds to our edition and what to the Roman. As Jerome, the sacred father and experienced teacher, saw this, he placed the three translations *into one volume*; and the Psalterium Gallicanum, which we sing, he placed in the first column, the Romanum in the second, the Hebraeum in the third. (Bern of Reichenau, *De varia psalmorum atque cantuum modulatione*, ed. M. Gerbert, *Scriptores Ecclestiastici de Musica* [St. Blasien 1784], II, 93)

"Novum testamentum graecae fidei reddidi, vetus iuxta hebraicum transtuli" ("I translated the New Testament from the Greek original, the Old Testament from Hebrew")—thus Jerome honored himself at the end of his literary history *De viris illustribus*. Not all his contemporaries were as convinced of his accomplishment. Augustine was not; he prized the Septuagint, liked using the Old Latin translations, and would have preferred to see Jerome translate patristic writings; particularly he wished to have an "Origenes latinus." Jerome's Latin Bible ("Vulgata") prevailed over the various versions of the Old Latin Bible ("Vetus Latina," formerly "Itala") only little by little in the course of the Middle Ages. The Latin of the Vetus Latina, characterized by its literal translation of the Greek, was repressed in, but did not completely disappear from, the Vulgata.

Jerome's Hellenism is essentially circumscribed by the Bible and biblical exegesis. He knew Greek patristics and only as much of other writers as was useful for the study of the Scriptures. He had no understanding of the Platonism of his contemporaries: he wondered what Aristotle had in common with Paul, and Plato with Peter, imagined how Jupiter and Plato "with his ignorant students" would stand before the Last Judgment,[47] and characterized the prematurely deceased Vettius Agorius Praetextatus as a heathen, "abandoned and naked in filthy darkness"—not (as Praetextatus' wife, with reference to Neoplatonic astrology, had inscribed on his tomb) *in lacteo palatio*.[48]

5. Augustine

Augustine (d. 430) earned no great reputation as a Hellenist,[49] but his theological work was one of the most important links to Greek thought which Latin Christendom of the Middle Ages possessed. In his youth, he had the usual Greek instruction with a *grammaticus*; but he thought Homer without substance, and Greek did not interest him. Later, in

Cicero's *Hortensius* and the translations by Marius Victorinus, he was confronted by Greek philosophy in Latin dress. He was under the spell of Platonism as he came to know something of the life of St. Anthony (as described by Athanasius), which came to him in Milan via Trier, and which moved him to be baptized.[50] His Platonism seemed no hindrance in this course of action; he never renounced it. As a Christian, bishop, and theologian, he again approached the Greek language; he wished to make use of the Septuagint and examine the Latin translations, and he was able to do so.

Augustine eagerly took up the Greek mode of symbolic interpretation, as in the explanation of Adam's name as deriving from the Greek names for the four quarters of the earth: from the first Adam, mankind had been scattered throughout the world; the second Adam brought them back into a unity.

In his ninth homily on the Gospel of John, he spoke about the wedding at Cana and wanted to describe the six ages of the world to his audience in amusing fashion—*ut emineat iucundius*—through the metaphor of the six jars:[51]

> Who does not know that all people originate in him and that in the four letters of his name, the four quarters of the earth are signified by the Greek names? For when East, West, North, and South are said in Greek, as the Holy Scriptures mention in many places, you find Adam at the beginning; for the aforementioned four quarters of the earth are called namely, ΑΝΑΤΟΛΗ, ΔΥCΙC, ΑΡΚΤΟC, ΜΕCΗΜΒΡΙΑ. If you write these four names one beneath the other, as in verse, Adam is read at the beginning.

In the immediately following homily, Augustine again returned to the topic, this time with a variation. The subject was the forty-six years needed to build the temple in Jerusalem:[52]

> What does the number forty-six signify? You heard yesterday, in the four Greek letters of the four Greek words, that Adam is [scattered] throughout the whole world. . . . How do we find the number forty-six even here? Because Christ's flesh was of Adam. For the Greeks count with letters. Where we have the letter *A*, they have alpha, and alpha is one. When they write beta, which is their *B*, as a number, numerically it is two. When they write gamma, numerically it is three. Where they write delta, it is numerically four; and thus they have numbers through the entire alphabet. What we call *M*, they call *mu*, and it signifies forty; for they say ΜΥ ΤΕCCΕΡΑΚΟΝΤΑ. Consider what number those letters produce, and there you will find the temple, built in forty-six years. For ΛΔΛΜ contains Λ which is one, Δ which is four, so you have five; again Λ which is one; that makes six; it also contains Μ which is forty; that is forty-six.

Augustine took up the playful thought a third time and gave it an eccle-siological turn:[53]

"He shall judge the world with righteousness" [Ps. 95:13]—not a portion, for he did not buy a portion. He must judge the whole, for he gave the price of the whole. . . . Adam signifies the earth accord-ing to the Greek language—I have already spoken of this. There are, namely, four letters: ΛΔΛΜ. According to the language of the Greeks, the four quarters of the earth have these four letters at their beginning: they call the East ΑΝΑΤΟΛΗ, the West ΔΥCIC, the North ΑΡΚΤΟC, the South ΜΕCΗΜΒΡΙΑ; thus you have ΛΔΛΜ. Adam is thus scattered through the whole earth. He was at one place and fell; dashed to pieces, as it were, he filled up the whole earth, but God's mercy collected the pieces from all sides. . . .

For propaedeutic reasons, Augustine was also interested in the "Oracu-la Sibyllina," as the Christian rhetor Lactantius, who had incorporated the Greek text into his *Divinae Institutiones*,[54] had been a century earlier. Augustine included the Latin translation of the famous Song of the Sibyl in his *De civitate dei*; the acrostic of the work ΙΗCΟΥC ΧΡΕΙCΤΟC ΘΕΟΥ ΥΙΟC CΩΤΗΡ —proclaimed the name of the Savior and also, in the first letters of the words of the acrostic, his symbol, ΙΧΘΥC:[55]

Ι	Iudicii signum tellus sudore madescet.
Η	E caelo rex adueniet per saecla futurus,
C	Scilicet ut carnem praesens, ut iudicet orbem.
Ο	Unde Deum cernent incredulus adque fidelis
Υ	Celsum cum sanctis aeui iam termino in ipso.
C	Sic animae cum carne aderunt, quas iudicat ipse.
Χ	Cum iacet incultus densis in uepribus orbis,
Ρ	Reicient simulacra uiri, cunctam quoque gazam,
Ε	Exuret terras ignis pontumque polumque
Ι	Inquirens taetri portas effringet Auerni.
C	Sanctorum sed enim cunctae lux libera carni
Τ	Tradetur, sontes aeterna flamma cremabit.
Ο	Occultos actus retegens tunc quisque loquetur
C	Secreta, adque Deus reserabit pectora luci.
Θ	Tunc erit et luctus, stridebunt dentibus omnes.
Ε	Eripitur solis iubar et chorus interit astris.
Ο	Voluetur caelum, lunaris splendor obibit;
Υ	Deiciet colles, ualles extollet ab imo.
Υ	Non erit in rebus hominum sublime uel altum.
Ι	Iam aequantur campis montes et caerula ponti
Ο	Omnia cessabunt, tellus confracta peribit:
C	Sic pariter fontes torrentur fluminaque igni.

C   Sed tuba tum sonitum tristem demittet ab alto
ω   Orbe, gemens facinus miserum uariosque labores,
τ   Tartareumque chaos monstrabit terra dehiscens.
н   Et coram hic Domino reges sistentur ad unum.
ρ   Reccidet e caelo ignisque et sulphuris amnis.

Judgment day shall be signaled by the sweat of Earth's fear.
Eternal the King, come from the heavens,
So that he might judge the world, present in flesh.
On God the believers and faithless shall look,
Uplifted with saints at the end of the ages.
So he shall judge them, their souls with their bodies.

CHoked by dense brambles, the Earth lies untended;
Rejected are man's idols and all of his treasures;
Earth blazes up, the heavens and seas all consumed;
Invading even Hell, the fire bursts its gates.
Saints in their bodies gain freedom and light,
The wicked are damned to fire everlasting.
Openly all men their most secret deeds then confess;
Searching, God opens their hearts to the light.

THen resounds mourning and gnashing of teeth.
Eclipsed is the sun and the harmony of spheres;
Obliterated is heaven and consumed the moon's splendor;
Uplifted the valleys and cast down the hills.

Undone the distinction between high and low,
Into plains fall the mountains and the waves of the sea;
Of the Earth remain fragments, all things shall cease;
Streams and fountains alike are consumed by the flames.

Sorrowful the trumpet peals from on high,
Over the wretched, who moan in their sin and their grief;
Torn open, the Earth shall reveal both chaos and Hell.
Eminent rulers stand in the judgment of God.
Rivers of fire and brimstone shall fall from the heavens.

In order to become acquainted with Greek exegesis, Augustine had to wait for translations, as did most of the Latins of his time. In 394, he still hoped to deter Jerome from the translation of the Bible in favor of translations of Greek theologians, especially Origen: "I beseech you, and with me the whole fellowship of African churches entreats you, to spare no pain or effort in translating the works of those who have dealt with our Holy Scriptures in such excellent fashion. For you can bring it about that we also have these great men, above all the one whom you so enthusiastically celebrate in your writings [Origen]. *I would not wish you to trouble yourself with a translation of the sacred canonical Scriptures into Latin,* unless it be done in the manner of your translation of Job, so that the differences between your translation and the Septuagint, which is of the highest authority, are made manifest by the notations employed."[56] Toward the end of this life, Augustine had a sufficient mastery of Greek to be moved to undertake the translation of an excerpt from Epiphanius' *Panarion*, since he held the work to be important and since no one else in the African Church could be found for the translation of the work.[57] Augustine translated excerpts from the works of John Chrysostom (d. 407), as he needed them for his own works,[58] and insofar as there were no translations already at hand of those which Deacon Anianus of Celeda had executed in order to support the doctrine of Pelagius, opposed by Jerome, Origen, and Augustine. However, this activity is not the most crucial in defining Augustine's importance as a mediator between Greek and Latin. It is rather a combination of three elements that already made Augustine, with his interests in Greek, a characteristic author of the Middle Ages: (1) the direct knowledge of Greek texts is restricted to only a few (although in Augustine quite significant) works; (2) otherwise he is dependent on translations;[59] (3) even so his thought is allied to and participates in the Platonic tradition of Greek thought.[60] In its dominant Augustinianism, the early Middle Ages in the West was ruled by Platonism—up to the Scholastic period, which in turn embraced Aristotelianism as a philosophy more closely related to its fundamental character.

To be sure, the Greek undercurrent of Augustinianism rarely came to the surface; but the Latin Middle Ages repeatedly referred to Augustine's interpretation of Adam, according to the Greek ΑΔΑΜ, as dispersed to the four corners of the earth; and the song of the Cumaean Sibyl attained immortality through Augustine's *City of God*. She is the Sibyl to whom the poet of the *Dies irae* appeals:[61]

> Dies irae, dies illa
> Solvet saeclum in favilla
> Teste David cum Sibylla.

IV

"Ecumene": Monasticism, Pilgrimage, Secular and Ecclesiastical Law in the Roman Empire

Necnon et collationes patrum et instituta et uitas eorum, sed et regula sancti patris nostri Basilii quid aliud sunt nisi bene uiuentium et obedientium monachorum instrumenta uirtutum? [And not just the *collationes* of the Fathers, but also their precepts and biographies and even the rule of our Holy Father Basil—what are they except the means to a proper way of life, monastic obedience and moral excellence? Benedicti Regula LXXIII 5–6

Within the Borders of the Greco-Latin Ecumene and Beyond

An extensive movement toward harmonization took place within the Christianized Roman Empire of late antiquity. In philosophy and theology, the Greek East influenced the Latin West; in law and military matters, the opposite was the case. Through Christianity, Palestine, Syria, and Egypt also entered into the cultural symbiosis of Christian late antiquity. The "griechisch-orientalische[r] Schimmer" ("Greco-oriental lustre," Traube) of the Latin Middle Ages stems primarily from this circumstance. The tendency of the period toward harmonization extended even into the script: the form of the uncial script is essentially the same in Latin, Greek, and Coptic, so that one may speak of it as the "ecumenical" script of late antiquity.

The Christian ecumenical community of the late Roman Empire did not, however, include all of Christendom of that period. The disputed border between the Roman and Persian Empires divided the Syrian nation; the Christians in eastern Syria were usually Persian subjects. Even before Nestorius was condemned as a heretic at the Council of Ephesus (431), the eastern Syrian Church had begun to dissociate itself from Antioch, which was nearby, but still in the Roman Empire; Nestorianism provided these Christians who were not part of the Roman Empire with a doctrinal identity. The gravitational center of Nestorianism shifted via Edessa and Nisibis toward the East, farther into the Persian Empire.

Soon the Nestorians held respected positions as physicians, teachers, and translators among the Persians, Arabs, Indians, Chinese, and Mongolians; and, as a scattered minority in the expanses of Asia, they also constituted a kind of universal church, which had a very different existence from that of the Imperial Byzantine Church and the Western Church of the bishops and pope; little information concerning the Nestorians made its way to the West. Not until the twelfth century, as Western Europe had its first experiences with the harshness of the Moslems on the eastern shores of the Mediterranean (conquest of Jerusalem in 1095, fall of Edessa in 1144) did the West begin to hope for miracles from the Christians "behind" the Moslems; the legendary reports about John the priest-king took concrete form in a letter allegedly from John the presbyter to the Greek emperor Manuel, the Latin emperor Frederick, and the pope. Christian of Mainz, Emperor Frederick's governor in Italy, is supposed to have translated the letter from Greek. Pope Alexander III answered the letter and sent Philip, his physician, from Venice into this Oriental fairy tale—which was, nevertheless, true, to the extent that it brought information concerning the distant world of the Nestorian Christians that lay beyond the realm of Greco-Latin Christianity.[1]

By way of the translators' school in Baghdad, which flourished in the ninth century, the Nestorians became mediating agents for Greek during the Latin Middle Ages, even if only as links in the long chain of the tradition Greek—(Syrian)—Arabic—(Hebrew)—Latin, by which Greek thought was passed on across the lands south of the Mediterranean, until it was received by the Latin West in twelfth-century Spain.[2]

1. *Vitas patrum*

The monasteries in the mountains were like tents full of heavenly choirs, singing Psalms and zealously studying, fasting and praying, rejoicing in hope for the future, toiling in deeds of mercy, joined in love and harmony among themselves. In truth it was all to be regarded as a land unto itself, full of piety and justice. No one there did wrong or was wronged; nothing was known of the tax collector's chiding; but rather it was a host of ascetics, and all thoughts were concentrated on one thing alone—virtue. When one saw the monasteries and the conduct of the monks, one could but cry out and say: "How goodly are thy tents, O Jacob, and thy tabernacles, O Israel! As the valleys are they spread forth, as gardens by the river's side, as tents that the Lord hath pitched and as cedar trees beside the waters."[3]

Thus Athanasius, in his vita of St. Anthony, described the magical spell which emanated from the first monasteries. Soon after the death of the monastic father in 356, Athanasius wrote his *bios* and dedicated it ΠΡΟС

ΤΟΥΣ ΕΝ ΤΗ ΞΕΝΗ ΜΟΝΑΧΟΥΣ .⁴ The book was immediately translated very literally into Latin. This rough translation, in the manner of the
"Vetus Latina," was immediately supplanted by the more elegant free
translation of Evagrius of Antioch (see above, Chapter III).

In Evagrius' translation, the Latin vita spread as quickly through the
Western half of the empire as did the Greek original in the East. The vita
was already being read in Trier during the reign of Emperor Gratian
(375–83). As Augustine reports, four court officials went for a walk in the
garden northeast of the city (later the district of the Abbey of St. Maximin)
while the emperor was at the circus games. Two of them came upon a
monk's cell in which the vita of Anthony lay open; they read from the
book and were so moved by it that they immediately abandoned their
offices and became monks. One of the others, who could not make such a
decision so quickly, the African Ponticianus, related this occurrence and
much about Anthony and the desert monks to his countryman Augustine
while on a visit to Milan. It was a crucial discussion in Augustine's con-
version.⁵

Jerome gave a literary reaction to the vita of Anthony; with his *Vita S.
Pauli primi eremitae*, he wanted to deprive Anthony at least of the fame of
having been the first of the Desert Fathers. In his *Vita S. Hilarionis*, he
also competed with the biography of Anthony: he called Hilarion *successor S. Antonii* and had him travel through Sicily, Dalmatia, and Cyprus,
fleeing before his fame, before he found peace and quiet in inaccessible
mountains, just as had Anthony. In his *Vita S. Malchi monachi captivi*,
Jerome gave in completely to his delight in a well-written, fantastic story.

The vita of Anthony translated by Evagrius and the three Latin vitae by
Jerome became fundamental texts of the widely disseminated genre of the
Latin Middle Ages—the *Vitas patrum*.⁶ The *Vita S. Symeonis Stylitae*,
translated from Greek into the "kreatürliche Sprache des alten Kirchenla-
tein" ("natural language of old Church Latin," Hugo Ball), was a basic element of the biographical portion of the collection; the work acquainted
the West with the mode of life of the stylites, which nevertheless continued to seem scandalous in the West. Dionysius Exiguus contributed
the *Vita S. Pachomii* and the *Paenitentia Thaisis* to the genre. Probably in
the sixth/seventh century, numerous biographies of female penitents, in
the manner of the last-named text, were added to the lives of the monastic
fathers; among them were the *Vita S. Mariae meretricis neptis Abrahae
eremitae* and the famous *Vita S. Mariae Aegyptiacae*. The *Vita S. Iohannis Eleemosynarii* by Leontius of Neapolis translated by Anastasius Bibliothecarius in the ninth century was still included in the manuscripts of
the *Vitas patrum*, as were some of the works of the Neapolitan translation
school. Original biographies in Latin were, however, no longer added to
the collection after Jerome.

In addition to biography, the collections of aphorisms characteristic of the East, the *Apopthegmata*[7] (*Verba seniorum, Adhortationes sanctorum patrum*), also belonged to the *Vitas patrum*; these works were translated primarily in the sixth century. The last great work of this genre, the ΛΕΙΜШΝ of John Moschus (d. 619 in Rome), was, however, not fully translated until 1423 by Ambrogio Traversari (*Pratum spirituale*). The West made no contributions in this alien literary form.

A third genre of the *Vitas patrum*, and perhaps their "ältester, ursprünglichster Kern" ("most ancient, original core form," Batlle), are the travelogues and descriptions of personal experience written by Eastern monks: the *Historia monachorum in Aegypto*, translated by Rufinus, and the *Historia Lausiaca* of Bishop Palladius of Helenopolis in Bithynia, which was translated into Latin soon after publication (419–20). The meager Latin contribution to the genre of travel literature in the *Vitas patrum* consisted of excerpts from the first of Sulpicius Severus' dialogues on St. Martin, and from Cassian's *Instituta* and *Conlationes*. Thus even with all the expansion and supplements which came during the course of the Middle Ages, the *Vitas patrum*, considered as a whole, remained almost exclusively a collection of Greek authors of the fourth and fifth centuries, which kept the memory of early monasticism alive in the West and often brought about a surprising reawakening of the monastic spirit.

The history of the collection has not yet been written; important comments on its early stages are contained in the introductory pages of Batlle's *Die "Adhortationes."* On the whole, the edition of the Jesuit Heribert Rosweyde (*Vitae Patrum* [Antwerp 1615; 2nd ed., 1628] = *Migne PL* 73 and 74, to col. 516) has not yet been superseded. On the one hand this edition demonstrated the renewed interest of the Counter-Reformation in a medieval work which was considered as important then as ever before (of which Martin Luther nevertheless induced his friend Georg Maier [Maior] to prepare a "gereinigte Ausgabe" ["purified version"], Wittenberg 1544); on the other hand, it was the beginning of critical editions in the field of hagiography (before the *Acta Sanctorum* of Jean Bolland). Rosweyde followed late medieval manuscripts and incunabula, and thus presented the work in the form which it had attained in the late Middle Ages—including Traversari's translation of Moschus (*Pratum spirituale*). It is inaccurate when Siegmund (*Die Überlieferung*, p. 136) writes that "Rosweyde first introduced the collective term 'Vitae Patrum,' although he compiled the material from the most varied sources in which it circulated in the M[iddle] A[ges]." Rosweyde in fact merely produced an arrangement and harmonization of the various late medieval collections. He did, however, assist in the triumph of the form "Vitae Patrum" over the late antique title *vitas patrum*—a concession on his part to the linguistic sensibilities of his time, since he of course knew from his study of the manuscripts that the ancient and commonly used form was *Vitas patrum* (cf. Rosweyde's *Prolegomenon* I: Quae horum librorum inscriptio). When his purpose was to explain to a librarian what it was that he sought, he also favored the nonclassical form: *"Est autem liber, quem desidero, qui ŭulgo Vitas-Patrum inscribitur . . ."*; cited in *AB* 83 (1965), 51.

2. Sulpicius Severus and Cassian

In late antiquity, Gaul had already become the classic land of Western monasticism. The Pannonian Martin, who founded the first Gallic monastery in Ligugé near Poitiers in 360, found in Sulpicius Severus a biographer, who, in the course of a decade (395–404), wrote a vita, three letters, and three dialogues about his hero, and whose *Vita S. Martini* began to compete in renown with the vita of Anthony:[8]

> But now I will give you a full report of this book's circulation and how there is almost no place on earth where the substance of this salubrious story is not already generally known. Your zealous disciple Paulinus was the first to bring the book to Rome; then, as the book was being eagerly sought throughout the city, I saw the book dealers rejoice, because there was nothing in greater demand from them, nothing sold more quickly or expensively. When I arrived in Africa, the book had already long preceded my passage; it was already being read in all of Carthage. Only a priest in the Cyrenaica did not yet have it, but I allowed him to transcribe my copy. What should I say of Alexandria, where almost everyone knows the book better than you do? It has made its way through Egypt, the Nitrian Desert, the Thebaid, and all domains of Memphis. I saw how an old man in the wilderness read the book.

According to Sulpicius Severus, all miracles of which one heard from the East were also to be found in Martin's vita: he surpassed all hermits and anchorites. Sulpicius maintained that when his book of *Dialogi* came to Egypt, then that land, although it was arrogant because of the great numbers of its saints' miracles, should not disdain to hear how through Martin alone Europe was not inferior to Egypt and all of Asia.[9]

Besides Sulpicius Severus, a monastic writer of very different orientation appeared in Gaul—the "Scythian" John Cassian.[10] He had lived in Bethlehem even before Jerome, toured the Egyptian hermitages from there, especially the famous ones of the Desert of Sketis, was ordained deacon in Constantinople by John Chrysostom (ca. 399), had been in Rome (ca. 405), and finally founded the monastery of St. Victor outside of Marseilles and a nunnery in that city.

In his *De institutis coenobiorum et de octo principalium uitiorum remediis* he dealt with the external arrangement of the monasteries in Palestine and Egypt, as well as the eight principal vices against which monks struggle: *gastrimargia* (intemperance), *fornicatio*, *philargyria* (avarice), *ira*, *tristitia*, *acedia* (indolence), *cenodoxia* (vanity), *superbia*. In his *Conlationes*, he went "from the external and visible disposition of the monks . . . to the invisible essence of the inner man" (preface). The work consisted first of all of ten lectures by masters of the spiritual life, which Cassian wrote down from memory and composed in dialogue form; following this section came two supplements to each of seven of the *conlationes*, so that the work contained twenty-four of them.

Cassian presented the material, which was not unproblematic for the Western mentality, with great care. He allowed much of the material to retain its Greek character, took over Greek philosophical, psychological, and ethical concepts, and included biblical passages and even philosophical maxims in Greek, when he thought it an aid to comprehension. One passage, which also incidentally shows how Cassian came to terms with ancient philosophy, may serve as an example:[11]

> primum philosophos nequaquam credendum est talem animi castitatem qualis a nobis exigitur adsecutos, quibus iniungitur ut non solum fornicatio, sed ne inmunditia quidem nominetur in nobis. habuerunt autem illi quandam μερικήν, hoc est portiunculam castitatis, id est abstinentiam carnis, ut tantum a coitu libidinem cohercerent: hanc autem internam mentis ac perpetuam corporis puritatem non dicam opere adsequi, sed nec cogitatione potuerunt. denique famosissimus ille ipsorum Socrates hoc, ut ipsi concelebrant, de se non erubuit profiteri, nam cum intuens eum quidam φυσιογνώμων dixisset: ὄμματα παιδεραστοῦ hoc est oculi corruptoris puerorum, et inruentes in eum discipuli inlatum magistro uellent ultum ire conuicium, indignationem eorum hac dicitur conpressisse sententia: παύσασθε, ἑταῖροι· εἰμὶ γάρ, ἐπέχω δέ, id est: quiescite, o sodales: etenim sum, sed contineo.

[First of all one should not think that the philosophers have attained such a chastity of spirit as is demanded of us, for we are forbidden even to say not only fornication, but even impurity. Yet they have a certain small portion of chastity, namely, abstinence of the flesh, so that they at least control their sexual desire: as to the inner purity of mind and the continuous purity of body, I do not wish to say that they can achieve them in fact but not even in thought. For is it not so, as they themselves admit, that Socrates, the most famous of them, was not ashamed to openly confess this? For once, as a physiognomist looked at him and said, "He has the eyes of a pederast," his disciples rushed at the man and wanted to revenge the insult to their master; it is said that he held their indignation in check with the words: "Calm yourselves, friends, for I am indeed so, but I control myself."]

Sulpicius Severus and John Cassian had quite different attitudes toward Eastern monasticism. The former was concerned with outdoing the East, the latter with transmitting the inner and outer forms of Eastern monasticism. Sulpicius separated himself and his heroes from all things Greek: he wrote polemically not only against Hector and Socrates, but even against Eastern monasticism, when his purpose was to praise Martin's deeds. Cassian, "taught by experience, wrote in a balanced style" and "invented words"[12] in order to render monasticism, which was itself foreign, accessible to the West.

Cassian's work had further influence on monasticism in Lérins and on the movement which emanated from there up the Rhone. The two addressees of the second book of the *Conlationes* (XI–XVII), Abbot Honoratus of Lérins (archbishop of Arles, 426) and Eucherius (later bishop of Lyon), passed on his intellectual heritage.[13] The widely read introduction to biblical study which Eucherius published under the title *Instructiones* ended with a list *De graecis nominibus*. This list is a kind of basic Greek vocabulary of late antique ecclesiastical Latin:

theos: deus . . .
omousion: unius substantiae
omooeusion: similis substantiae
Christus: unctus
spiritus paraclitus: spiritus con-
    solator sive advocatus
hagios: sanctus
angelus: nuntius
thronus: sedis vel solium
apostolus: missus . . .
propheta: praedictor
martyres: testes
episcopus: superinspector . . .
presbyter: senior
diaconus: minister
clerus: sors
ecclesia: evocatio uel collectio
catholica: universalis ΑΠΟ
    ΤΟΥ ΚΑΘΟΛΟΝ
synagoga: conventus uel congre-
    gatio
ethnicus: gentilis
hypocrita: simulator
heresis: secta
monachus: solitarius
heremus: desertum
paroecia: adiacens domus, id est
    dei
dioecesis: gubernatio . . .
laicus: popularis ΑΠΟ ΤΟΥ
    ΛΑΟΥ
catechumenus: instructus sive
    audiens

neophytus: novella plantatio
baptisterium: tinctorium
chrisma: unctio
eucharistia: gratia
holocaustum: totum combus-
    tum . . .
symbolus: conlatio aut pactum
    vel conplacitum, quod sit
    homini cum deo
hymnus: carmen in laudem dei
antiphona: vox reciproca
pentateuchus: quinque volu-
    mina . . .
exodus: exitus vel egressus . . .
deuteronomium: secunda
    lex . . .
paralipomenon: praetermisso-
    rum vel reliquorum . . .
evangelium: bona adnuntiatio
    sive bonum nuntium
apocalypsis: revelatio
gazophylacium: divitiarum cus-
    todem, conpositum de lingua
    Persica et Graeca
synodus: comitatus vel coetus
canon: regula
teuchos: volumen . . .
apocrypha: recondita vel occulta
hexapla: sexsimplicia
apologia: excusatio . . .
anagoge: superior sensus
tropologia: moralis intellegentia
parabola: similitudo

(Eucherius, *Instructiones* II 15, ed. K. Wotke, *CSEL* 31/1 [1894], 159–61, abbreviated here; older edition, *Migne PL* 50, cols. 821 f.)

Not all later Gallic monks who, like Cassian, looked to the light from the East did so with the necessary powers of discrimination. For Lent, a hermit near Nice had roots brought from Egypt, which the hermits there were accustomed to eat. A deacon built a pillar for himself near Trier in order to imitate Symeon the Stylite; he lost his toenails in the cold and froze his beard to icicles; bishops came, took him down from the pillar, and had it destroyed.[14] This deacon had begun his ascetic career at the grave of St. Martin; the Fathers of the Jura, Romanus, Lupicinus, and Eugendus most likely also found inspiration there, and by virtue of their *natura gallicana*, they surpassed the Eastern ascetics.[15]

The West found a balance of East and West and thus its own "disciplined" form of monasticism in Benedict and his Rule. He recommended the study of the Vitas patrum, *instituta*, and *conlationes*.[16] For both simple and learned monks, the "lives of the Fathers" remained a guide to the origins of monasticism, while Cassian's *Conlationes* provided higher training in the spiritual form of life.[17] But works dealing with Martin also gained great renown, not as a book of ascetic readings in the East, as Sulpicius Severus vainly imagined,[18] but rather as a saintly *libellus* of the national saint of the Franks (*Martinellus*), which the scriptorium at Tours exported, primarily in the Carolingian period.

3. Late Roman Palestine

The influence of Palestine and its neighbor Syria on the world of the early Middle Ages cannot be stressed strongly enough. Both simpletons and men of learning went on pilgrimages to Palestine, the "Holy Land." As an early theological school, Syrian Antioch—"after Jerusalem, the second home of Christianity"[19]—had the highest reputation except for Alexandria in Egypt. Since the days of Hellenism, Palestine and Syria had been seats of Greek culture—not exclusively, for even after the destruction of Jerusalem in 70 A.D., Jews lived in Palestine, and in Nisibis and Edessa, the fame of the Syrian tongue arose in the fourth century with the great Ephraem Syrus.

Around 400, the pilgrim Etheria described in her *Itinerarium* her three-year journey to the holy places of the Old and New Testaments and the apostolic period. In an appendix to her report, which was intended for her nunnery in Spain or southern France, she described the liturgy in Jerusalem, which was multilingual in a remarkable way: the principal language of the liturgy was Greek, from which the readings were translated into Syrian as a matter of course, "because of the people, so that they may always learn. To be sure there are also some Latins here who understand neither Syrian nor Greek, and lest they be distressed, a translation is also made for them, for there are Greco-Latin brothers and sisters here. . . ."[20]

Thus the conditions in Palestine in late antiquity were extremely favorable for a theologian interested in languages and history. Jerome was the most important but not the only Latin to take advantage of them. He, "whose eloquence the whole Occident awaited as the dew on the fleece,"[21] had settled in Bethlehem in 386; Palestine offered him more advantages in his revision of the Latin Bible than did any other country. At the same time, Jerome developed "an active program of propaganda"[22] ("eine rührige Propaganda") for the *peregrinatio* to the Holy Land, which drew pious Roman ladies such as the widow Paula, whose *hodoeporicon* Jerome wrote in his famous *epist.* 108, and the younger Melania, whose beneficence, asceticism, and studies remained in the memory of both Greeks and Latins.[23]

But there was also the self-willed British theologian Pelagius, whose doctrines met with more approval (or tolerance) in the East than in the West. One of his disciples, the deacon Anianus (Annianus) of Celeda, tried to support his doctrines through translations of works of the celebrated Antiochian John Chrysostom (patriarch of Constantinople, 398–407).[24] Anianus translated (ca. 415–20) John's seven discourses on the apostle Paul, *De laudibus S. Pauli*—as a supplement to the commentary on Paul by Pelagius?—and perhaps the discourse *Ad neophytos*. It is doubtful that Anianus was also the early translator of John Chrysostom's *De sacerdotio*.

Only the first twenty-five of the ninety homilies on Matthew are preserved in Anianus' Latin translation; even in the high Middle Ages, the Latin series must have been incomplete (see Chapter XI, under "Pisa"). Despite the text tradition, patristic research assumes, however, that Anianus translated all ninety homilies on Matthew: Altaner, *TU* 83, 416–23; H. Musurillo, "John Chrysostom's Homilies on Matthew and the Version of Annianus," *Kyriakon* (Münster 1970), I, 452–60.

The discourse *Ad neophytos* played a role in the Pelagian controversy of the time: S. Haidacher, "Eine unbeachtete Rede des hl. Chrysostomos an Neugetaufte," *Zeitschrift für katholische Theologie* 28 (1904), 168–93; J. P. Bouhot, "Version inédite du sermon 'Ad neophytos' de S. Jean Chrysostome, utilisée par S. Augustin," *Revue des Études Augustiniennes* 17 (1971), 27–41. On the text tradition, see also A. Wilmart, "La collection des 38 homilies de saint Jean Chrysostome," *The Journal of Theological Studies* 19 (1918), 305–27. Altaner (*TU* 83, 418 f.) notes how weak the evidence is for the ascription of the translation to Anianus. His caution is also valid for many of the new and most recent attributions of Latin Chrysostom homilies to Anianus. One must bear in mind that the translation school in Vivarium was also actively interested in John Chrysostom.

With respect to the *De sacerdotio*, Siegmund (*Die Überlieferung*, p. 92, n. 1) draws attention to the fact that in a Breslau library catalogue of the late Middle Ages, the translation is ascribed to Germanus of Auxerre, which is, however, the only evidence of Germanus' activity as a translator.

We do not know where or under what conditions Anianus produced his important translations, which apparently concentrate on his contemporary John Chrysostom. An obvious conjecture is that Anianus, who also wrote a polemic against Jerome (cf. Jerome, *epist*. 143, 2) worked in the vicinity of Jerusalem or Antioch. Pelagius, whom Anianus respected, lived in Jerusalem at least from 412 to 415; the translator could have found John Chrysostom's writings most easily in Antioch, where John worked as presbyter until 398, and where he was well remembered by everyone. Even in the twelfth century Antioch possessed a hoard of John Chrysostom's works, from which Burgundio obtained the Greek text for his new translation of the homilies on Matthew.

Besides the prologues and letters of Jerome, a hagiographic tale also records the East-West literary life in Palestine in the early fifth century—the so-called apocalypse of Stephen, *Revelatio S. Stephani*.[25] The burial places of the first martyr, Stephen, the teacher of law Gamaliel, Gamaliel's son, and Nicodemus were revealed in dreams to the priest Lucianus of Kaphar-Gamala, near Jerusalem. Patriarch John II of Jerusalem opened the graves in December 415. The presbyter Avitus of Braga, a learned correspondent of Jerome's, who had been in the Holy Land since 409 and did not dare return to his Galician homeland because of the Germanic invasions,[26] asked Lucianus to write an account of his vision and the exhumation of the bodily remains. Lucianus composed the report in the form of a detailed letter, written in Greek; Avitus immediately translated the letter into Latin, and in doing so he followed the method of learned late Latin writers, by including individual Greek words in the Latin context. Before the second interment of St. Stephen's remains, Avitus obtained some of the relics. Avitus wanted to send both, the Latin *Revelatio S. Stephani* and the relics, to Braga with Orosius, a countryman and student of Augustine's, who had appeared in Jerusalem as a plaintiff against Pelagius (who had been supported by Patriarch John II). Avitus had served as his interpreter, and he—more confident than Avitus—still hoped to return to Braga in spite of the Vandals, Suevi, and Alans. But Orosius got no farther than the Balearic Islands and then went to North Africa; thus a part of the relics of Stephen, which were intended for Braga and Spain, remained in Minorca, others in the North African cities of Uzalis and Calama. In Minorca and Uzalis, local accounts of miracles were immediately added to the *Revelatio*, demonstrating the increased receptivity for the miraculous during that troubled period.

Epistola Severi ad omnem ecclesiam de virtutibus ad Iudaeorum conversionem in Minorcensi insula factis in praesentia reliquiarum S. Stephani and *De miraculis S. Stephani* [Uzali factis] *libri II*, both in the appendix to vol. VII of the Maurist edition of Augustine (= *Migne PL* 41, cols. 821–32 and 833–54); a new edition of the *Epistola Severi* by G. Seguí Vidal, *La carta encíclica del Obispo Severo* (Palma de Mallorca 1937), pp. 149–85. B. Blumenkranz, *Les auteurs chrétiens latins du moyen âge sur les juifs et le judaïsme* (Paris/The Hague 1963), pp. 106–10, considers the letter a forgery of the seventh century, since "cette prétendue encyclique s'insère très naturellement dans cette littérature d'Espagne du VIIe siècle qui, d'une part, connut une foison de faux littéraires, et, d'autre part, vit le problème juif prendre une acuité rarement atteinte ailleurs" ("this alleged encyclical may be inserted quite naturally into the Spanish literature of the seventh century, in which, on the one hand, literary forgeries abound, and where, on the other hand, the Jewish problem took on an acuteness rarely attained elsewhere"; p. 107). One may object, however, that the literary historical relationships between the *Epistola Severi* and *Miracula* of Uzalis on the one hand (quotation of the *Epistola* in the *Miracula* I 2; cf. Seguí Vidal, pp. 35–38) and the *Miracula* of Uzalis and Augustine's *De civitate dei* on the other (XXII 8, 21) are so close that the forger must have been not only a consummate literary scholar—better in fact than most modern scholars who work with this complex—but also an exceedingly influential interpolator, so that he could falsify the relevant references in all copies of the texts in circulation. That is quite unlikely.

Even Augustine did not remain aloof from these events which had moved so many people.[27] Lucian's letter circulated through the *orbis christianus* of late antiquity: in addition to the Latin version, it was also translated into Syrian, Armenian, Georgian, and even Ethiopian; late antique literary historical writing contributed to the fame of the text.[28] It was incorporated into many homilaries and passionals in the West in Avitus' translation; the letter was often read as an appropriate text for the "Inventio S. Stephani" (3 Aug.) or for the actual St. Stephen's day (26 Dec.); good scriptoria transmitted the Graeca of Avitus' text in the same manner as they included the Graeca of Jerome or Priscian in their texts, so that due to its sprinkling of Greek words, the text became a conspicuous component of medieval homilaries. It was not forgotten that the name of Augustine was also marginally connected with the events depicted in the work.

4. The Translation Principles of the Digests of the *Corpus Iuris Civilis*—Conciliar Acts—*Epistola formata*

From the point of view of the modern legal system, one can hardly imagine how much material of literary historical value was included in the civil and especially ecclesiastical legal codes of late antiquity. For example, the Digests of Justinian's *Corpus Iuris Civilis* contain Greek quotations from Homer to Plutarch, and, in an introductory *constitutio*, the famous prohibition of commentaries. Regulations on translation are connected to that prohibition which help to illuminate the context of the literal method of translation employed in the Latin Middle Ages:[29]

Hoc autem, quod et ab initio nobis visum est, cum hoc opus fieri deo adnuente mandabamus, tempestivum nobis videtur et in praesenti sancire, ut nemo neque eorum, qui in praesenti iuris peritiam habent nec qui postea fuerit, audeat commentarios isdem legibus adnectere: nisi tantum si velit eas in Graecam vocem transformare sub eodem ordine eaque consequentia, sub qua et voces Romanae positae sunt (hoc quod Graeci κατὰ πόδα dicunt), et si qui forsitan per titulorum suptilitatem adnotare maluerint et ea quae παράτιτλα nuncupantur componere.

[But that which seemed proper to us from the beginning, when we ordered this work, with God's approval, appears timely to decree at the present, that no one experienced in the law either now or later dare to add commentaries to these laws; unless he wish to translate them into Greek in the same arrangement and order in which the Latin words are placed (which the Greeks call "by the foot") or if he would perhaps wish to note the exact titles and compose what are called "explanatory annotations."]

Ecclesiastical or canon law was established at the church councils, and important writers of the patristic period participated in the preparation for them and in carrying them out. The conciliar acts, which explain the development of the decrees (canones) in the council, are not merely the minutes of the debates, but often also contain a rich collection of other material, including letters, treatises, and even hagiographic texts.

The imperial councils of late antiquity took place without exception on Greek soil: Nicaea (325), Constantinople (381), Ephesus (431), and Chalcedon (451); the basic dogma of the church was formulated in these four councils. The four subsequent councils, which gained "ecumenical" authority, were much more councils of the Imperial Byzantine Church than councils of the Ecumene. With one exception they took place in the imperial capital, Constantinople: Constantinople II (553), Constantinople III (680–81), Nicaea II (787), Constantinople IV (869–70). The Latin participation in these four councils was much less significant than in the first four; yet the councils from 553 to 870 were of great importance for the West and its relationship to the East. After a long interruption, the series of councils called by the pope during the high Middle Ages recommenced, beginning with the Lateran Council of 1123; these councils brought about no further meetings of note between Latins and Greeks. At the second Council of Lyon (1274), however, a Greek legation appeared in order to participate in the negotiations for a reunion of the Church, and this occurrence was repeated in 1438–39 in Ferrara, shortly before the fall of Constantinople.

The language of debate in the councils of late antiquity was Greek, since they were held in Greek-speaking territory. The second language of the empire was, however, not excluded for this reason: "Official Latin documents were read in Latin; the Roman legates spoke Latin. A Greek translation followed immediately, executed by a bishop proficient in both languages . . . or by a secretarius of the Imperial Consistory, whose office required that he know both languages. Emperor Marcian held his official address at the Council of Chalcedon in Latin, which at that time was still the language of the court and the army; he appended a Greek allocution himself. . . ." Thus there are many traces of "Zweisprachigkeit in den Konzilsakten" ("bilingualism in the conciliar acts").[30] Essentially, however, the conciliar acts and decrees were Greek texts.

The Latin West developed no fixed practice in the reception of conciliar acts and canons.[31] There is no collection of the acts of the first ecumenical council (Nicaea 325); only the *Canones* (guiding principles, *regulae*) are preserved. Bishop Caecilian of Carthage took a Latin translation of the *Canones* home with him from the council. This translation gained currency in North Africa, while a book of laws was produced in Rome under the name *Canones Nicaeni*, in which the translation of the original *canones* was combined with the canons of the Synod of Sardica (Sophia) from 342, where the papal see was granted certain prerogatives. In Augustine's time, the African Church had difficulty maintaining its Nicaean conciliar acts against the Roman *Canones Nicaeni*.[32] The second imperial council, which met in Constantinople in 381 and from which there is also no collection of acts, "did not take Rome and the West into consideration at all,"[33] and as a consequence, was not heeded by the Roman Church, which, through Pope Damasus, Jerome, and Ambrose, was gaining self-confidence; nor was it even acknowledged until the sixth century. At the third ecumenical council in Ephesus (431), the West was represented by Patriarch Cyril of Alexandria; in Constantinople soon after the council, Marius Mercator translated the acts (in part) and various supplements, such as Cyril's letters.[34] Not until the sixth century was a complete translation of the Ephesian acts executed, which was then revised in the Akoimetan monastery (with its extensive library) in Constantinople by Rusticus the Roman deacon and nephew of Pope Virgilius.[35] Bishop Julian of Cos represented the papal see at the Council of Chalcedon (451); at the request of Pope Leo I, he translated the acts of this fourth imperial council.[36] In Constantinople, Deacon Rusticus also published these conciliar acts in a new Latin version (564–65).[37]

The imperial councils of 325–451 and the many "local" synods of the era produced a great number of doctrinal and ecclesiastical texts which had need of compilation and ordered arrangement. Additionally, there were episcopal decrees, especially those of the bishops of Rome (Decretals), which laid claim to authority quite early and were valued in the West second only to the conciliar canons. The "Kanonessammlungen der alten Reichskirche" ("collections of canons of the ancient Imperial Church") included some texts from each of these categories.[38] The Greek collections preceded the Latin; among the Latin collections, those of the African Church proved the most reliable. In Rome (perhaps around 500) an imprecisely translated collection was produced in the so-called Prisca.[39] But

Rome also produced the collection which served as a model in the Middle Ages: that was due to the Scythian monk, Dionysius Exiguus, who had been in the service of the Roman Church for more than a quarter of a century, since the days of Pope Anastasius II (496–98), and who had an expert knowledge of Greek. He published the conciliar canons in two editions[40] and compiled the papal Decretals separately. The second edition of Dionysius' *Codex canonum*, together with his *Codex decretalium*, became known in the compilation *Collectio Dionysiana*; in the form sent to Charlemagne by Pope Hadrian, the collection, under the name *Diony-sio-Hadriana*, came to be of great importance for the Latin Middle Ages.

The first translation of Dionysius' conciliar canons has been edited by A. Strewe, *Die Canonessammlung des Dionysius Exiguus in der ersten Redaktion* (Berlin 1931), according to MS Vat. Pal. lat. 577, saec. VIII–IX, from the Anglo-Saxon zone of influence in Germany. At the same time K. Christ pointed out "Eine unbekannte Handschrift der ersten Fassung der Dionysiana," in *Festschrift Georg Leidinger* (Munich 1931), pp. 25–36: Cassel, Hess. Landesbibliothek theol. qu. 1, from the same cultural sphere as the Palatinus MS. On the paleographic localization of both manuscripts, see B. Bischoff, "Panorama der Handschriften-überlieferung aus der Zeit Karls des Großen," in *Karl der Große* (Düsseldorf 1965), II, 248 and nn. 117 and 119. This work by Dionysius appears to have been part of that great current of early medieval text transmission: Rome—England—Germany.

Dionysius' collection of canons overshadowed all other works of the kind in the Latin West, not only because he worked more carefully and translated better than his predecessors, but also because he was able to produce a well-ordered book from the rather difficult material without compromising the text. That Dionysius himself viewed the work in this light is shown by his addition of dedicatory prefaces to his collection of canons, whereby he transferred a characteristic feature of literary works to the collection.[41] This transference of literary models onto this book of common use, a collection of canons, is even more evident in the third edition than in the first and second:[42]

Domino beatissimo papae Hormisdae Dionysius Exiguus.
Sanctorum pontificum regulas, quas ad verbum digerere vestra beatitudo de Greco me compellit eloquio, iam dudum parvitatis meae nonnullo studio absolutas esse cognosco. Sed quorundam su-percilium, qui se Grecorum canonum peritissimos esse iactitant qui-que sciscitati de quolibet ecclesiastico constituto respondere se velut ex occulto videntur oraculo, veneratio vestra non sustinens imperare dignata est potestate, qua supra ceteros excellit antistites, ut, qua possum diligentia, nitar a Grecis Latina minime discrepare atque in unaquaque pagina aequo divisa tramite utraque e regione subnec-tam. . . .

[Dionysius Exiguus to Pope Hormisdas, my blessed master.

The literal translation of holy bishops' canons from the Greek, which your Holiness requested of me, was completed some time ago through the efforts of your humble servant. But your Reverence could not tolerate the raised eyebrows of certain people, who boast of their expert knowledge of the Greek canons, and who, if you ask them about any church doctrine, seem to respond as if with an obscure oracle, and thus by the power which surpasses that of other bishops, you considered it worthy to order me to take great pains not to let the Latin text differ from the Greek, and to place both texts on each page, facing each other in opposite columns. . . .]

Thus Dionysius described his bilingual collection of canons for Pope Hormisdas (514–23). Its use in the East-West controversies of the time is well known; in difficult passages, the parallel columns offered convenient recourse to the *veritas graecorum canonum*; by this method, even a pope who knew no Greek could find his way around in the Greek text. In this collection, Dionysius restricted the content strictly to the canons of the Councils of Nicaea, Constantinople, Ephesus, and Chalcedon; neither the so-called *Canones Apostolorum* nor the original Latin Canons of the Synod of Sardica nor those of the African synods, which he included in his earlier collections, were included in this third compilation, whose purpose it was to present that which was most specifically relevant for the Greco-Latin Imperial Church in its entirety (*universitas*).[43]

The significance of this book was not limited to its intended use. The format of the bilingual text resembled the late antique bilinguals of the most important scriptural books too closely: Psalters, Gospels, Acts of the Apostles, Pauline epistles. These books were, however, showpieces at least as much as they were aids to scholarly study: they presented the authority of the Scriptures in both languages of the imperium. With his Greco-Latin editions of the canons of the four imperial councils, prepared for the pope, Dionysius associated these texts of ecclesiastical law with the biblical texts presented in bilingual editions: this precisely reflects the process by which the canons developed within the many councils and synods of late antiquity. The same Pope Hormisdas for whom Dionysius prepared the unique bilingual edition of the canons was the first pope to acknowledge (in a *professio fidei*) the "four holy synods," the four "ecumenical" councils, including the first council of Constantinople (381), which up until then had not been recognized in Rome.[44] Subsequently, this profession was often made by popes, patriarchs, and bishops. Gregory the Great formulated the idea that the four imperial councils could be compared in authority to the four Gospels: ". . . sicut sancti evangelii quattuor libros, sic quattuor concilia suscipere et venerari me fateor, tota devotione complector, integerrima approbatione custodio, quia in his velut in quadrato lapide sanctae fidei structura surgit . . ." ("Just as the four books of the holy Gospels, so I confess to accept and revere the four councils; I embrace them with complete devotion; I keep them with the purest approbation, because the building of the holy faith rises up from them as from a squared stone").[45] Thus the concept of the four Gospels, which was revered in the liturgy, is transferred to the book of canons of the "four councils."

Among the early conciliar acts there is one text which was of great importance for early medieval Greek studies, the *regula formatarum*. These instructions—in the form of an *epistola formata*—for the encoding of ecclesiastical letters of safe-conduct and introduction are transmitted in many manuscripts as an appendix to the canons of the Council of Nicaea. The rubrics of several manuscripts demonstrate clearly that the *regula* made its way into the Western collections of canons through Patriarch Atticus of Constantinople (406–25) via the African Church of Augustine's time.

As noted above, Carthage was in possession of an authentic translation of the canons of the first ecumenical council, while in Rome, the *Canones Nicaeni*, a contamination of the canons from the Council of Nicaea with those of the Synod of Sardica, was in use. At a synod in Carthage in 419, the question was raised whether the *Canones Nicaeni*, submitted by the Roman legates, were actually the canons of Nicaea. It was decided to send to the patriarchal sees of Constantinople, Alexandria, and Antioch for authentic copies so that they might be compared. The African Church received a translation with the addendum of the *regula formatarum* from Constantinople.[46]

The question whether the *regula* was actually sanctioned in any manner by the Council of Nicaea, or whether the text is rather to be considered a scholarly frivolity of the fourth century, can be left aside here. In the tradition, it became the most important canonistic text for Greek studies, next to the "linguistic canon" of the Council of Vienne (1312). It was transmitted not only in collections of canons, but also in collections of formulae; *epistolae formatae* were in fact written—whether this art served *vitae, non scholae*, is open to question, however. The *regula formatarum* nevertheless provided an incentive to study the numerical values of the Greek letters.[47] The text reads:[48]

> Greca elementa litterarum numeros etiam exprimere, nullus qui uel tenuiter greci sermonis noticiam habet ignorat. Ne igitur in faciendis epistolis canonicis, quas mos latinus formatas uocat, aliqua fraus falsitatis temere agi praesumeretur, hoc a patribus CCCXVIII Nicea constitutis saluberrime inuentum est et constitutum, ut formatae epistolae hanc calculationis seu supputationis habeant rationem, id est ⟨ut⟩ adsumantur in supputationem prima greca elementa Patris et Filii et Spiritus sancti, hoc est Π Υ Λ, quae elementa octogenarium, quadringentesimum et primum significant numeros. Petri quoque

apostoli prima littera id est Π, qui numerus octuaginta significat; eius
qui scribit epistolam prima littera; cui scribitur secunda littera; ac-
cipientis tertia littera, ciuitatis quoque de qua scribitur quarta et in-
dictionis quaecumque est id temporis, id est qui fuerit numerus ad-
sumatur. Atque ita his omnibus litteris grecis, quae ut diximus
numeros exprimunt, in unum ductis unam, quaecumque collecta
fuerit, summam epistola teneat. Hanc qui suscipit omni cum cautela
requirat expressam. Addat praeterea separatim in epistola etiam
nonagenarium et nonum numeros, qui secundum greca elementa
significant ΛΜΗΝ.

[Everyone who has the slightest knowledge of Greek knows that the
letters of the Greek alphabet also have numerical value. Lest by
chance any false deception occur in the issuance of canonistic letters,
which are called *formatae* in Latin, it was found advantageous and
decided upon by the 318 fathers gathered at Nicaea that the *epistolae
formatae* be reckoned or computed in this manner: the first Greek
letters of the words for Father and Son and Holy Spirit are added,
that is, Π Υ Λ, which signify the numbers eighty, four hundred, and
one. Take also the first letter of the apostle Peter, that is Π, which
signifies the number eighty; the first letter of the one who writes the
epistle; the second letter of the one addressed; the third of the
bearer; the fourth of the city where the epistle is written; and the
number of the current indiction. That is, add their numerical values.
And thus all these Greek letters, which as we said have numerical
values, are to be added, and the sum is to be noted in the epistle.
The recipient should examine it very carefully. Further, the number ninety-nine, which according to the Greek values is signified by
ΛΜΗΝ , is also to be added in the epistle separately.]

In the Carolingian period, the *epistolae formatae* and their key often
occur in collections of "formulae" and canons;[49] in the tenth and eleventh
centuries, they are rare. In the end, they survive only as an interpolation
in Gratian's *Decretum*.[50]

[v]

Gothic Italy

The Goths—are they to be considered otherwise than the Vandals? After this people had conquered Rome, having poured into Italy a first and a second time, we accepted their rule and, as many believe, also their language, and are to a considerable degree descended from them. Proof thereof are the manuscripts in Gothic script, of which there is a multitude: if this people could so spoil the Roman script, what is to be expected of the language. . . ? Behold how far Roman literature has now fallen. The ancients mixed the Greek language into their own; now these do the same with Gothic.

Lorenzo Valla, *De linguae latinae elegantia* III[1]

The Gothic epoch in Italy served the Humanists only to the extent that it explained numerous developments which were disagreeable to them, such as the decline of Roman literature, the rise of the "Gothic script," the development of the Italian from the Latin language. The curious inaccuracies on the part of the Humanists concerning the Goths have long since been corrected: they had nothing to do with the development of the Romance idiom from Latin, nor with vaulted arches and broken-shafted letter forms, nor did the history of Roman literature end with the onset of their reign. Moreover, Greek studies in Italy managed to survive the political downfall of the Western Roman Empire and flourished anew under Theodoric the Great (493–526).

1. The Bible among the Goths

For historical reasons the Goths were more deeply rooted in the Greek than in the Latin world. They had come into contact with the Greek half of the empire first; it was Greek-speaking Christians who converted them; and their liturgy retained its Greek character. The Goths became involved in the christological disputes of late antique theology and were branded "Arians"; yet they also took part in the late antique philological work on the text of the Bible. By means of the scriptural language which Wulfila (d. 383) created in the process of grappling with the Greek and Latin, the Goths set up a memorial for themselves of a permanence equal to their foundation of empires.[2]

Even after Wulfila there seem to have been Goths who, in addition to their own language, knew both of the world languages of antiquity and, for purposes of philological study, even made the effort to learn Hebrew. In his famous letter on the translation of the Psalms, which was read in the medieval schools as an *exercitium* in scriptural criticism (and is studied as such even today in theological textual criticism), Jerome wrote to the Goths Sunnja and Friþila:

> Truly the apostolic and prophetic creed has been fulfilled in you: "their words go out over the whole world; their speech to the ends of the earth." Who would have believed that the barbaric speech of the Goths would seek the Hebraic truth, and, while the Greeks sleep and squabble, Germania conducts research on the words of the Holy Spirit.[3]

Was the writer of the *Opus imperfectum in Matthaeum* also to be found among these learned barbarians?[4] Under the false but successful banner of John Chrysostom, this Arian philological commentary made its way through the Middle Ages—from Paulus Diaconus and Charlemagne to Claudius of Turin and Pope Nicholas I, to Abelard and Thomas Aquinas—cutting a wide swath of rationalism through the undergrowth of allegorical and mystical interpretations of the Bible.[5]

It is not clear whether Gothic-Greek-Latin biblical scholarship in the tradition of Wulfila still existed in Theodoric's empire. Ostrogothic Northern Italy has nonetheless transmitted the remains of the Gothic Bible in magnificent form as cimelia.

> The "Codex argenteus Brixianus" (Brescia, Biblioteca Queriniana, s.n., saec. VI[1]), from the Lombard royal monastery of S. Giulia (S. Salvatore) near Brescia, is of particular importance among the showpiece manuscripts preserved from Gothic Italy (facsimile in *CLA*, III, 281). It is a Latin evangeliarum, written with silver ink on purple parchment, containing the beginning of a proem to a *Gothic* Bible in which textual notes were to be included: the siglum GR was to indicate that the text followed the Greek, LA that it followed the Latin text. It is evident that this double sheet with the proem could not have been initially intended for inclusion in the (unannotated) Latin evangeliarum in which it is now found; it is, however, vexing that the proem is not a foreign body in the codex, but is in fact paleographically identical to it (purple parchment, silver ink, page format, script, number of lines per page and letters per line). One might conclude from this identity that the lost (or incomplete) Gothic text was planned as a parallel version to the Latin "Codex argenteus Brixianus." A new study by Henss, *Leitbilder der Bibelübersetzung* (bibliog.).

2. Boethius, Symmachus, Priscian

During Italy's Ostrogothic period there appeared once more, in the person of Boethius, a major representative of philosophical Hellenism in the tradition of Vettius Praetextatus and Macrobius. Boethius still adhered to the old idea of conquest through translation, that is, the concept of translation as a patriotic deed. He was possessed of the ambition to consummate the Roman domination of the world by transmitting the "arts of Greek wisdom" to his fellow Roman citizens.[6] To this end he planned to translate into Latin and provide with commentary first the complete works of Aristotle and then the dialogues of Plato, and finally to harmonize the two into a *concordia*.[7]

Of this grand design, Boethius was able to realize only a fragment. But it now seems that in the mass of "Boethius" manuscripts there are in fact more original Boethius texts preserved than was earlier believed. The work on the *Aristoteles latinus* in recent decades has brought to light almost all of the Boethian translations of the Aristotelian "Organon":

> *Categoriae*—Boethius' translation edited in *Aristoteles latinus*, I/1
> *De interpretatione*—Boethius' translation edited in *Aristoteles latinus*, II/1
> *Analytica priora*—Boethius' translation edited in *Aristoteles latinus*, III/1–2
> (two recensions)
> *Analytica posteriora*—no Boethian translation
> *Topica*—Boethius' translation edited in *Aristoteles latinus*, V/1
> *Sophistici elenchi*—Boethius' translation edited in *Aristoteles latinus*, VI/1

"If some future Lefèvre or Rota or Lorit plans a new Opera Omnia of Boethius thanks to Aristoteles Latinus, he will now have at his disposal, for the first time since antiquity, the original texts of the Boethian Organon"; J. Shiel, *Vivarium* 20 (1982), 139. Boethius' commentaries on his translations of Aristotle were not as entombed by the textual tradition as were the translations themselves. Printed editions of the commentaries *In Categorias Aristotelis (Migne PL* 64, cols. 159–294) and *In librum Aristotelis De interpretatione* (two versions, *Migne PL* 64, cols. 293–640) have been on hand for quite some time. In these commentaries there is, however, also an abundance of material that was translated from Greek; cf. J. Shiel, "Boethius' Commentaries on Aristotle," *Mediaeval and Renaissance Studies* 4 (1958), 217–44. Shiel now maintains that the commentary on *Analytica priora*, printed by L. Minio-Paluello in *Aristoteles latinus*, III/4, with the title "Ps.-Philoponi aliorumque scholia," may also be attributed to Boethius; cf. "A Recent Discovery: Boethius' Notes on the Prior Analytics," *Vivarium* 20 (1982), 128–41.

In addition to his work on the Aristotelian texts themselves, Boethius also concerned himself with the introductions to Aristotelian thought current at the time. He wrote a commentary on Porphyry's *Isagoge* (an introduction to Aristotle's *Categoriae*), based on the translation by Marius Victorinus; later he wrote a second commentary on the same work, basing it this time on his own translation.[8] As a foundation for philosophical studies, the young Boethius designed a *quadruvium* of arithmetic, music, geometry, and astronomy, which he initially promoted by means of translation. King Theodoric had Cassiodorus write to Boethius that, as a result of his translations, "the musician Pythagoras and the astronomer Ptolemy are read as if they were members of the Italic race, the mathematician

Nicomachus and the geometrician Euclid are heard as if they were Ausonians."[9] The Latin adaptation of the ΑΡΙΘΜΗΤΙΚΗ ΕΙCΑΓΩΓΗ of Nicomachus of Gerasa is contained in Boethius' *Institutio arithmetica* and is dedicated to Symmachus.[10] A translation of Euclid dating from the time of Boethius, preserved in a fragment and palimpsest discovered in a Veronese codex at the beginning of the last century, appears to be the remains of the translation praised by Theodoric.[11] The translation of "Pythagoras" is lost, unless Cassiodorus is here referring to Boethius' *De institutione musica*. No translation by Boethius of Ptolemy's astronomical writings has survived, though Gerbert d'Aurillac possibly still knew it in the tenth century.[12] The high Middle Ages did not become reacquainted with Ptolemaic astronomy before the Sicilian translation of the ΜΕΓΙCΤΗ CΥΝΤΑΞΙC.

In the long run, Boethius unquestionably achieved one of his goals: to awaken the logical-dialectical spirit in the Latin West. His competent translations and commentaries, especially his commentary on Porphyry's *Isagoge*, in which he considerably expanded the Latin philosophical vocabulary, had great influence on the early Middle Ages and contributed to the rise of Scholasticism in the high Middle Ages. Thanks to Boethius' efforts, Greek thought and science, as well as elements of the Greek language—especially prominent in the *De musica*—survived in some small degree in the Latin West.

This second blossoming of ancient philosophical Hellenism in Italy was only possible because of the good relations which senatorial circles in the old capital had with the Greek East, especially with Constantinople. Symmachus, Boethius' father-in-law, was the most important Roman patron of East-West relations. He was in contact with the grammarian Priscian, who taught in Constantinople and who dedicated three of his shorter treatises to Symmachus, all of which treat Greco-Latin topics.[13] In the eighteen books of his *Institutiones artis grammaticae*, Priscian translated into Latin the teachings of the Greek grammarians Apollonius and Herodian and thus established the extensive system of Latin grammar. He also rendered into Latin hexameters the ΠΕΡΙΗΓΗCΙC of Dionysius, which Avienus had already adapted into Latin in the fourth century.[14]

The mistrust that was beginning to arise between Constantinople and Ravenna, between Catholics and Arians (ca. 523), was catastrophic for this transmission of Greek ideas into Italy, depending as it did on scholarly interests. Theodoric had Boethius (524) and Symmachus (525) executed as traitors. While in prison, Boethius crowned his endeavors in philosophical transmission not with a reconciliation of the Aristotelian and Platonic systems, but instead with the evocation of Philosophy in the *De consolatione Philosophiae*, a work which stamped the philosophical imagination of the Middle Ages as scarcely any other work was to do.[15]

3. Cassiodorus

While philosophical and secular Hellenism disappeared for a long time from the Latin West after Boethius and Symmachus, the subsequent fate of Italy turned Cassiodorus (d. after 580), the great stylist of the official correspondence of the Gothic rulers, into the guardian and continuator of the historico-theological interest in Greek which Jerome and Rufinus in particular had championed in late antiquity. In their concern for the preservation of that which still existed and for the restoration of that which was threatened with decay, the letters of Cassiodorus written while still at the Gothic court reveal his conserving spirit. After retirement from his post at the Gothic court in 537, Cassiodorus dedicated himself completely to the preservation of the intellectual legacy which he had inherited. When his plan (with Pope Agapetus I) to establish a Christian academy in Rome had failed, he took the ever-growing ascetic movement into the service of his preservation project. On his estates in Calabria he founded Vivarium, a monastery and hermitage. As a new Ezras, he made the major task for himself and his monks the transmission and accurate interpretation of the Scriptures.[16] In his *Institutiones divinarum litterarum* he wrote an introduction to this study; the liberal arts, on which Cassiodorus wrote his own *Institutiones saecularium litterarum*, were also to be of service. Greek had no small place in the *Institutiones*:

> When one finds anything in them [sc. the Latin interpreters] to have been poorly explained, then those who know the language should eagerly seek out what is of value in the Greek commentators; let living knowledge be sought with a passionate spirit, so that negligent tepidity among the disciples of Christ is eliminated.[17]

Cassiodorus did, however, take the disappearance of Greek education into account:

> We wish, with God's help, to deal primarily with the Latin writers; since we are writing for Italians, it would be most suitable to publish Latin commentators. One grasps most readily what is said in one's own native language.[18]

He collected translations of Greek exegetical works and enlarged the holdings of the library in Vivarium by means of new translations, prepared by a whole school of translators: Epiphanius translated Didymus, Bellator some of Origen, and Mutianus some of John Chrysostom.[19] Anonymous "friends" translated a Greek excerpt from the ΥΠΟΤΥΠѠCEIC of Clement of Alexandria, the "first Christian scholar,"[20] and the fifty-five homilies on the Acts of the Apostles by John

Chrysostom.[21] Cassiodorus' view of Greek exegesis as a supplement to Latin can clearly be seen from his remarks concerning the commentaries on the Pauline epistles, a number of which he lacked. He believed that Jerome had written commentaries on them, and he still hoped to acquire these works; in any case, however, he brought together in the eighth bookcase of his library, the case for Greek works in the original, a collection of *Greek* commentaries by John Chrysostom on the Pauline epistles in question. Should the desired commentaries not be found, and other Latin commentaries also prove untraceable, then the Greek "Chrysostoman reserve" was to be translated into Latin without delay, so that authentic commentaries on all books of Scripture would be available at Vivarium.[22]

The translators of Vivarium also made a significant contribution to historical studies. Cassiodorus had been the historian of the Goths in his younger days, and he saw to it that the Latin West, which had little in the way of ecclesiastical history in the beginning (except Jerome's and Rufinus' adaptations of Eusebius' great historical work), obtained a more complete historical picture. With the help of Epiphanius, he combined the Greek ecclesiastical historians Theodoret, Sozomen, and Socrates, who continued the work of Eusebius, into the Latin *Historia tripartita*.[23] Flavius Josephus appealed to him particularly:

> We had his works rendered by our friends with great care—since he is exceedingly subtle and varied—into twenty books of Latin. He also wrote seven additional books on the Jewish captivity with astounding finesse, the translation of which some attribute to Jerome, some to Ambrosius or Rufinus.[24]

The translation of the seven books of *De bello Iudaico* already existed, therefore, in Cassiodorus' time.[25] His friends translated the twenty books of *Antiquitates*[26] and *Contra Apionem*. Both historical works of the translation school at Vivarium, the *Historia tripartita* and the *Antiquitates*, became basic historical texts in the Latin Middle Ages. More than once Cassiodorus refers to the translators of Vivarium as "friends." Unfortunately, almost no historical information has survived concerning this realm of the harmonious spirit of preservation, as we would like to envisage Cassiodorus' Vivarium. But it seems to be no accident of the textual tradition that none of the translations from Vivarium has a translator's prologue, a matter of course for Jerome, Rufinus, and Dionysius Exiguus: "L'absence de prologue fait la marque propre des humbles amis de Cassiodore" ("The absence of a prologue is the identifying mark of the humble friends of Cassiodorus").[27]

4. Dionysius Exiguus

Cassiodorus held scarcely any of his contemporaries in as high regard as the Scythian monk Dionysius, who took for himself the humble surname "Exiguus."[28] He dedicated an elogium to Dionysius in his *Institutiones*, where, among other things concerning him, it is mentioned that he "had such a command of Latin as well as Greek that he could render every Greek book which came into his hands into impeccable Latin, and by the same token, he could read forth a Latin book in Greek, so that one believed the words which flowed smoothly and swiftly from his mouth were written in the text."[29]

He "ist als Findelkind von skythischen, d.h. gotischen Mönchen aufgezogen [worden] und hatte, sei es von diesen, sei es in Konstantinopel, eine gute Ausbildung erhalten, zu der auch eine solide Kenntnis des Griechischen gehörte" ("was a foundling, who had been reared by Scythian, i.e., Gothic, monks, and had received, either from them or in Constantinople, a good education, to which a solid knowledge of Greek also belonged"); Schwartz, *Zeitschrift für Rechtsgeschichte* Kan. Abt. 25 (1936), 108. Schwartz gave excessive rein to his historical fantasy here, for the dedication to Bishop Petrus (from Tomi, on the Black Sea?) does not yield this interpretation: "Beneficiorum vestrorum memor . . . semperque ante oculos mentis adponens sancta nutrimentorum vestrorum studia parvulo mihi dependsa . . ." (*Epistola Cyrilli synodica interprete Dionysio*, praef., ed. Schwartz, *Acta Conciliorum* I 5, 2, p. 235; *Migne PL* 67, col. 10). It says no more than that Dionysius came under the spiritual guardianship (*sancta nutrimentorum studia*: the shift in meaning of *nutrire* 'nurture' to 'raise', already documented in antiquity, was common in monastic literature) of Bishop Petrus as a child (in keeping with the monastic predilection for the diminutive, *parvulus* need not necessarily have meant 'infant').

An explanation of Dionysius' Greco-Latin bilingual upbringing requires no novelistic interpretation of his youth: his native *Scythia* (to which he and others bear witness) was a part of the bilingual province of Moesia Inferior. Dionysius came from one of those overlapping linguistic zones which have provided born translators in every era; Cassian was, for example, also *natione Scytha*. On further conjectures concerning Dionysius' biography by Schwartz, Caspar, and Peitz, see the legitimate critique by Steinacker, in *Mitteilungen des Österreichischen Instituts für Geschichtsforschung* 62 (1954), 51–55.

Unlike Boethius, Symmachus, and Cassiodorus, Dionysius stood altogether aloof from the Gotho-Roman government. His milieu, partially revealed in his prologues, was that defined by a more secluded religious life, with a strong inclination to monasticism and Eastern asceticism. Sixth-century Rome had already moved so far from the center of the political stage that this spirit could evolve there; in Rome at the end of this century, Pope Gregory the Great became the consummate representative of this ideal and thus served the Middle Ages as an ever-present exemplum.[30]

As already noted, Dionysius performed invaluable services for the Roman Church as a translator and collector of canonistic material. In his works on chronography, his mastery of the Greek language enabled him to settle the old conflict between the Eastern and Western methods of determining the date of Easter. In his *Liber de paschate*, he recognized the superiority of the Alexandrine calculation and contributed to its displacement of the Roman method, albeit with one significant modification: while it had been customary since Eusebius' ecclesiastical history to count the years since the Diocletian era (called *aera martyrum*), in his Easter table commencing with the year 532, Dionysius introduced the method of calculating from the birth of Christ. Through his own works on chronography, the Venerable Bede helped this method of calculating from the year of the Incarnation to gain general acceptance; the founder of the "Christian Era" was, however, Dionysius.[31]

Dionysius' most extensive translation project, besides the collections of conciliar canons, was the ΠЄΡΙ ΚΑΤΑϹΚЄΥΗϹ ΑΝΘΡШΠΟΥ, *De conditione hominis* (*De opificio hominis, De imagine*), of Gregory of Nyssa,[32] which he dedicated to the presbyter Eugippius, abbot of Lucullanum near Naples.[33] Dionysius writes that he had great difficulties with the translation, since Gregory analyzed philosophical problems in great detail and "omitted practically nothing which those learned but idle spirits have dealt with, in involved disputation on the topic."[34] The dispute with the *docti et otiosi ingenii* of ancient philosophy concerning the human condition was more of an annoyance than a pleasure for Dionysius, who attests to the estrangement from ancient philosophy felt among those circles in Rome (contemporary with Boethius) that were coming into prominence, and he makes clear in the same preface that they found dogmatic dispute tiresome. He countered possible criticism of his translations in this regard with the explanation that he worked not as a censor, but as a translator. In his troubled times, to which he gave vivid expression, Dionysius hoped only for inner peace through intellectual pursuits, and thus it must have been the contemplative aspect of Gregory of Nyssa's anthropology which prompted Dionysius' intense concentration on the translation. While he imposed an increasingly strict literalism on himself in his canonistic translations, he followed the traditional method of *fides sententiarum* in his translation of Gregory. The fact that he translated the author's prologue also corresponds to the spirit of literary translation: the reader of the Latin version of Gregory knew that the work was conceived as a continuation of Basil the Great's discourses on the creation, and thus the literary historical context was preserved. Basil did not get to the exegesis of the sixth day, and his brother Gregory completed the unfinished work.[35]

Dionysius' translation of the vita of Pachomius is of considerable literary historical importance.[36] His preface, addressed to his high-ranking patroness, contains a declaration of his devotion to hagiographic literature and voices the hope that the exemplary life of her father might be given expression in that genre.

Heribert Rosweyde demonstrated some 370 years ago that the father of the patroness could be none other than Symmachus, himself a patron of Greco-Latin studies who was brutally executed in 525 (*Vitae Patrum*, 2nd ed. [Antwerp 1628], p. 138 = *Migne PL* 73, cols. 271 ff.). Not until the new edition of the vita of Pachomius by van Cranenburgh and Mähler was this reference again taken into account and confirmed. In comparison with this identification, it is of secondary importance whether the daughter of Symmachus who commissioned the translation by Dionysius was Galla, as Rosweyde believed, or Proba, as Mähler now suggests (in van Cranenburgh, *La vie latine*, pp. 37–42). It is not known whether the plan for a biography of Symmachus was realized; for our purposes, it suffices to recognize that the translation of the vita of Pachomius was closely associated with the Christian biographical literature which was in its initial stages of development in early sixth-century Rome. The *Commemoratorium vitae S. Severini*, dedicated by Eugippius to the Roman deacon Paschasius in 511, belongs in this context, as do the papal biographies of the *Liber Pontificalis*, which were written in the early sixth century. The biographical writings of Jerome often set a precedent, especially clear in the work of Dionysius, who, more than anyone else, could claim to be the new Jerome of the Roman Church.

Dionysius again translated freely—he says *fide translatoris*—and produced a work with an impeccably Latin character. In this way he continued the tradition of Jerome, who had translated Pachomius' didactic works and written three anchorite biographies as companion pieces to the vita of St. Anthony. Now Dionysius added the vita of the founder of cenobitic monasticism to them.

He produced two additional hagiographic translations: the *Historia inventionis capitis S. Iohannis Baptistae*[37] and the *Paenitentia S. Taysi (Thaisis).*[38] It is again Egyptian themes (particularly from Greek Alexandria) which predominate, as is often the case in Dionysius' work.[39]

What significance the school of Ammonius of Alexandria had for Boethius' Greco-Latin work has been shown by Pierre Courcelle.[40] The Athenian Academy had been in decline since the death of Proclus in 485; under the direction of his student Ammonius, Alexandria became the center of Greek intellectual endeavor. As the ecclesiastical focal point of Egypt, Alexandria was also the transmitter of Egyptian Christian spirituality and asceticism. The one Alexandria is mirrored in Boethius, the other in Dionysius Exiguus. In this respect these two very different "mediators," Boethius and Dionysius, resemble one another: it is a Greek light of oriental tint that falls on these portal figures of the Middle Ages.

5. The End of Antiquity: Translated and Untranslated Material

Wenn wir das Zeitalter betrachten, in dessen Mittelpunkt Cassiodor steht, gewinnen wir den Eindruck, als sähe die antike Gesellschaft das Schiff ihrer Kultur dem Untergang geweiht und suchte von ihren geistigen Schätzen zu retten, was zu retten ist, in möglichst kleine, tragbare Bündel verpackt. [When we consider the epoch in the center of which Cassiodorus was active, we get the impression that ancient society saw its culture doomed to extinction, as a galley to shipwreck, and it sought to save that portion of its intellectual treasures which was salvageable, packed in the smallest and most easily transportable bundles possible.]

T. Zielinski, Cicero im Wandel der Jahrhunderte, 3rd ed. (Leipzig 1912), p. 131

Waren von jeher die Römer in wissenschaftlicher hinsicht auf die Griechen angewiesen, so bestand gradezu die ganze wissenschaftliche (philosophische im weiteren sinne und besonders medicinische) litteratur des 4. bis 6. jahrhunderts, in den absterbenden ausgängen des lateinischen altertums, in übertragung griechischer bücher. [While the Romans had always been dependent on the Greeks in intellectual matters, almost the entire body of scientific literature (in the broad sense of philosophical and especially medical literature) of the fourth to the sixth centuries, i.e., in the declining stages of Latin antiquity, consisted of translations of Greek words.]

Rose, Anecdota, II, 167.

The stock of Greek literature in the Latin West consisted for a long time of those Latin translations which existed at the end of the Gothic epoch in Italy. Not until the ninth century were substantially new translations added, and only in the twelfth and thirteenth centuries did translations in any number again appear. Until the age of Humanism, late antique translations remained the basic stock of Greek literature in the Latin West.

Despite the efforts of Boethius, Latin versions of the Greek philosophers were rather scarce; most conspicuously, the works of Plato were lacking, except for the *Timaeus*, which was of great importance for the early Middle Ages.

In addition to the canonical Scriptures, the theological literature of late antiquity contained a profusion of so-called Apocrypha,[41] not all of which were so absurd and fantastic as the Acts of Andreas and Matthew among the Cannibals.[42] The *Liber de ortu B. Mariae virginis et infantia salvatoris*,[43] for example, contains poetic accounts of the childhood of Mary and Jesus, which were with good reason highly valued throughout the Middle Ages. Mary's death was also described in the early Apocrypha, and this treatment was later adopted into the liturgy and the arts (*Transitus Mariae*).[44] One may assume that most of the Greek Apocrypha were rendered into Latin, many of them more than once. The so-called *Decretum Gelasianum de libris recipiendis et non recipiendis* gives an idea of the quantity of such works available at the end of antiquity.[45] Even now the compass of the Latin tradition can scarcely be defined, and such an important medieval genre as the *Passiones apostolorum*, with its series of (apocryphal) biographies of the Apostles, is much more poorly researched than the comparable genre of the *Vitas patrum*.

Many theological works of the Alexandrine school of Origen were translated by Rufinus; but a complete "Origenes latinus," which Augustine wished to have, never materialized. Numerous works of John Chrysostom also existed in Latin versions: the Pelagian controversy had contributed to this end. Basil the Great was somewhat less well known, and the name of his brother, Gregory of Nyssa, was almost unknown in the Latin Middle Ages, since his only work available in Latin translation, the ΠЄΡΙ ΚΑΤΑCΚЄΥΗC ΑΝΘΡѠΠΟΥ, was ascribed to the other, more familiar Cappadocian Gregory (Nazianzus). Athanasius remained surprisingly unknown, despite his long sojourn in the West and despite the fact that his *Vita B. Antonii* enjoyed tremendous popularity. Except for this vita, however, probably only "scattered fragments" ("versprengte Stücke") of Athanasius found Latin translators.[46] The commentary on Psalms byTheodore of Mopsuestia, from the Antiochene school of exegesis, was translated into Latin by Julian of Aeclanum.[47] The principles of the Antiochene school became somewhat familiar in the West, especially during the early medieval period, through the *Instituta regularia divinae legis* of Iunilius Africanus, a student of Paulus of Nisibis.[48] On the whole, however, the exegetical works of the Antiochene school, which stressed the concrete and historical in opposition to the allegorical method of the Alexandrine school, was little disseminated: "the failure of Antiochene exegesis to penetrate the Latin has as much significance, in a negative way, as the success of the Alexandrians."[49]

Greco-Christian historiography was well known through the mediation of Jerome, Rufinus, and Cassiodorus. The fact that Eusebius' *bios* of Constantine the Great was not translated into Latin was significant in the development of the imperial concept in the medieval West. The *Actus Silvestri*,[50] which probably originated in fifth-century Rome, changed the historical image of the first Christian emperor and founder of the new Christian Rome to that of a disciple of Pope Silvester, who abandoned the ancient imperial city out of respect for the Roman bishop and left the pope in a semi-imperial position in the West. The "Donation of Constantine" (*Constitutum Constantini*) was fabricated on this basis, probably in the eighth century. Only through Western ignorance of Eusebius' biography of Constantine was this biased Roman Christian image able to remain almost unchallenged until the fifteenth century.[51]

Greek mythology was well known and remained so, primarily due to Ovid's *Metamorphoses*; Orpheus was, for example, an invariably familiar heroic figure in the Middle Ages.[52] Late antique interpretations of myth, already allegorical to a certain degree, were also important in the medieval period. One such work was the *Mitologiarum libri III* of the African

Fulgentius, whose identity with Bishop Fulgentius of Ruspe (d. 533) in the Vandal Kingdom of Africa, praised by his biographers as a scholar of Greek, is disputed.[53]

The Latin Middle Ages possessed no translation of Greek heroic poetry. The Homeric heroes were known from the *Ilias latina* of the first century and from the translations of the Greek "eyewitness accounts" of the Trojan War, which circulated under the names Dictys and Dares. By contrast, it was the pride of the Humanists to again know the "true Homer." For the Middle Ages, Alexander the Great was more important than Hector and Achilles. The most important ancient source for the Alexander romances of the Middle Ages was the (probably) fourth-century *Res gestae Alexandri Macedonis*, translated by Julius Valerius from the Greek romance of Pseudo-Callisthenes.

The Latin Middle Ages became acquainted with a typical novel of late antiquity in the *Historia Apollonii Regis Tyri*.[54] The text tradition of the work does not begin before the ninth century in the West, but the cultural milieu (thermal baths, memorial statues, etc.) refers so clearly to antiquity that no doubt of the ancient origin of the novel remains. It has not been proven, but is generally accepted, that the novel was translated from Greek.[55] In its fundamental motif of "recognition" and many other details, the *Historia Apollonii Regis Tyri* resembles the pseudo-Clementine *Recognitiones*, mentioned above as the "first Christian novel."

The West became acquainted with Greek natural science of Christian orientation through the *Hexaemeron* homilies of Basil the Great, which Eustathius translated around 400, and through the *Physiologus*, the principal work of Greco-Christian nature symbolism. Medieval man was fascinated by the fantastic and mythical properties of the forty-eight animals, plants, and stones described in the book, from the lion to the oriental sycamore, as well as by their more esoteric significance; the work was translated into Latin for the first time in the fifth century at the latest, and from there it passed into almost all European vernaculars, first into Old English (in the eighth century), then into Old High German, Old French, Flemish, Icelandic, Provençal, and Italian. The beastiaries of the high and late Middle Ages also had their origins in the *Physiologus*.[56] Although the manuscript tradition reaches back no further than the high Middle Ages, the masterful Latin adaptation of Greek physiognomical writings, the *De physiognomonia liber*, is dated to late antiquity, due to its superb style of free translation.[57]

"The art of medicine, as distinct from pure science, alone continued to flourish and even to advance during the early medieval centuries."[58] This fact is also revealed in the translations and adaptations of Greek medical literature, which became more abundant in the fifth and sixth centuries.[59] Both of the excerpts which Oribasius, the personal physician of the

emperor Julian, prepared from his own standard work, CYNAΓWΓAI
IATPIKAI, were probably translated in sixth-century Gothic Ravenna.[60]
The chief work of Greek pharmacology, the ΠЄPI YΛHC IATPIKHC of
Dioscorides (first century A.D.), apparently did not arouse interest until
the end of the antiquity: Cassiodorus knew an excerpt, the *Herbarium
Dioscoridis*, concerning medicinal plants;[61] then, probably still in the
sixth century, the complete text of Dioscorides' *De materia medica* was
rendered in a very literal translation. An alphabetically arranged adaptation was produced in the school of Salerno in the ninth century. Petrus of
Abano (Padua) published this version in a newly revised form around
1300. The "rhythm" of this textual tradition and its assimilation in the
Middle Ages is thus quite different from those characteristic of Greek philosophy, theology, history, epic, and natural science, each of which was
defined by the various "Renaissances."[62]

VI

Early Byzantine Italy and the Maritime Lands of the West

1. The "Byzantine" Era of the Papacy and Italy

The deep caesura between "antiquity" and "the Middle Ages" in Italy was brought about not by the substitution of the Gothic monarchy for the Western Roman Empire, but rather by the Byzantine succession to Gothic dominion and by the invasion of the Langobards in an Italy which had been again brought under Byzantine rule only shortly before (568). The ancient character of Rome fell into decay; the city "verpuppte sich zugleich und verklösterte sich auf seltsame Weise" ("retired into its shell at the same time and became monasticized in an unusual manner"; Gregorovius).

The last Goths were defeated by Byzantines on Mt. Vesuvius in 553, but Constantinople had already exercised great influence in Italy long before that—in Rome since 537. The catalogue-like *Liber Pontificalis*, which had been kept by the papal administration since the beginning of the sixth century, described the changeover from Gothic to Byzantine rule in a scene of impressive perspicuity:[1]

> He [Belisarius] sent for the holy Pope Silverius to come to him in the Pincio Palace and had all the clergy detained at the second and third curtain. Silverius entered the inner chamber with Vigilius alone [his successor, chosen by Constantinople], where the Patricia, Antonina, lay on a couch, and the Patrician, Belisarius, sat at her feet. And as Antonina saw him, she said to him: "Tell me, sir Pope Silverius, what have we done to you and the Romans, that you wish to deliver us into the hands of the Goths?" While she still spoke, John, the subdeacon of the first district, came in, took the pallium from his neck, and led him into another chamber; he undressed him, clothed him in a monk's habit, and had him led away. Then, seeing him to be a monk already, Xystus, the subdeacon of the sixth district, came forth and announced to the clergy that the lord pope had been deposed and made a monk. When they heard this, they all fled.

Everything that Westerners both admired and abhorred for centuries as "Byzantine" is contained in this scene: Caesaro-papism, court intrigue,

rule by females and eunuchs, theatrical politics, and calculated ceremony. Liudprand of Cremona, as ambassador of Otto the Great, wrote his
colorful commentary on this topic in the tenth century.

Pope Vigilius (537–55), the first of the bishops of Rome appointed by
Constantinople, suffered a fate scarcely better than that of his predecessor, Silverius, who had been friendly to the Goths. When he withheld
assent to Justinian's "Three-Chapter Edict," in which the emperor sought
a doctrinal compromise with the "Monophysites" who remained in the
empire, he was brought to the imperial capital (545–47) at the order of the
empress Theodora. A council summoned by Justinian to Constantinople
in 553, which is designated the fifth ecumenical and second Constantinopolitan council, discussed the "Three Chapters"; Vigilius followed the
council's debate from nearby Chalcedon, to which he had been able to
escape from Constantinople. Vigilius knew no Greek, but some members
of his retinue were proficient in both languages, as, for instance, Rusticus,
the pope's nephew, who was occupied with conciliar acts long after the
council of 553, and who, in the Akoimetan monastery in Constantinople,
reedited the Latin Acts of Ephesus (431) and Chalcedon (451) according to
Greek copies.[2]

It characterizes the new era that Pope Pelagius I (555–61), Emperor
Justinian's appointee as successor to Vigilius, was the first bishop in the
ancient Western capital to know Greek since the transition from Greek to
Latin as the liturgical language. It is not without significance that he dedicated himself to the translation of ascetico-mystical aphoristic literature of
Eastern monasticism. He thus continued the great work whose foundation had been laid by Athanasius in his *bios* of Anthony, the father of
monasticism, and whose foundation walls had been raised by Jerome with
his three vitae of monastic fathers, and by Rufinus with his *Historia
monachorum*. In Rome, the first well-known author to work with hagiographic material was Dionysius Exiguus, in the early sixth century; by the
middle of the century, the leading ecclesiastical circles were at last working intensively with monastic literature. While Pelagius was deacon, i.e.,
at the time when he was playing an important role beside and against
Pope Vigilius, he translated a series of *Verba seniorum*[3] (*Adhortationes
sanctorum patrum*); the translation was completed by John, a subdeacon,
who later as John III became Pelagius' successor in the highest ecclesiastical office in the West.[4] Thus the construction of the *Vitas patrum* gradually drew to a close; in the Latin West, the work was regarded as a treasure house of spiritual instruction and exemplary biography for a
thousand years.

With his *Dialogi*, Pope Gregory I, the Great (590–604), produced the
Latin complement to the Eastern lives of the fathers: henceforth Italy and
the entire Latin West had its *Vitae patrum italicorum*. Soon they also became famous in the East as a continuation of the ancient monastic fathers

which was itself worthy of study. Gregory was consciously a Latin who had little interest in or knowledge of Greek, despite his service for several years as papal apocrisarius in Constantinople; the vocation of the *consul dei* was an eminently Roman one.[5] In the middle of the "Byzantine era of the papacy," he won Britannia for the *orbis latinus* and thus took the first and most important step toward a new ecclesiastical Roman Empire of the Middle Ages.

Under Gregory's successors, Rome became "more Byzantine" than before, especially as a result of the Greek monasteries in Rome, which became places of refuge for orthodox Greek monasticism during the Monothelitic dispute of the seventh century and the iconoclastic conflict of the eighth and early ninth century. In addition, the Arabs in the Eastern Mediterranean, advancing under the banners of Mohammed, drove Christians from the Levant to Rome. Theodore of Tarsus, one of the most famous Greeks in seventh-century Rome, may well have come to Rome as a refugee, for his Cilician homeland fell to the Arabs in 645. The monastery of St. Anastasius *ad aquas Salvias*, in the southern district of Rome, between S. Paulo Fuori le Mura and the catacombs of the Via Appia, is the oldest Greek monastery in Rome.

Today it is the monastery of SS. Vincentius and Anastasius, near Tre Fontane. The sources of the history of the monastery until A.D. 1000 are assembled in clear order by Ferrari, *Early Roman Monasteries*, pp. 33 f. See also Michel, *Ostkirchliche Studien* 1 (1952), 41 f., and J.-M. Sansterre, *Les moines grecs et orientaux à Rome aux époques byzantines et carolingiennes* (Brussels 1983), I, 13 ff. The monastery seems to have initially been occupied by Cilician monks. Theodore of Tarsus in Cilicia, sent from Rome in 668 to be archbishop of Canterbury, possibly came from the monastery of St. Anastasius; in any case, one could thus explain the uncommon interest which one of Theodore's "student's students" ("Enkel-Schüler"), the Venerable Bede, showed for the *Passio S. Anastasii Persae*, the patron of the Greek monastery in Rome: ". . . librum uitae et passionis sancti Anastasii male de Greco translatum et peius a quodam imperito emendatum, prout potui, ad sensum correxi" ("To the best of my abilities, I corrected for meaning the book of the life and passion of St. Anastasius, which was poorly translated from Greek and even less favorably emended by an unskilled [editor]")—thus Bede wrote in the list of his *Historia ecclesiastica gentis Anglorum* (V 24). The Persian Anastasius became a martyr in 628 under Chosroes II. It is possible that Bede's edition of the *Passio S. Anastasii Persae* is still extant among the numerous versions of the Latin text tradition; cf. C. Vircillo Franklin and P. Meyvaert, "Has Bede's Version of the *Passio S. Anastasii* Come Down to Us in BHL 408?" *AB* 100 (1982), 373–400.

The Greek monastery in Rome is first attested to in the Acts of the Lateran Synod of 649, where Monothelitism (which had the support of the emperor) was debated, with Pope Martin presiding (649–53; d. 655 in exile at Chersonesus in the Crimea). This last great christological controversy of the early Christian period was intellectually borne by the

Greeks in Rome, led by Maximus the Confessor (d. 662); the Greek monks not only collected evidence for the debate, but also, according to Rudolf Riedinger, composed the speeches of the council fathers, which were then translated from Greek into Latin. Thus the synodal acts came into being even before the synod as a kind of "Textbuch austauschbarer Rollen"[6] ("libretto of interchangeable roles")—a strange historical situation in which the genre of conciliar acts came close to dramatic literature. Pope Martin I, during whose reign the Lateran Synod of 649 took place, knew no Greek; his predecessor, Theodore I (642–49), under whom preparations for the synod were made, was, however, a Palestinian Greek.[7] After Theodore I, numerous other Greeks or Greek-speaking Sicilians mounted the *cathedra Petri* up to the middle of the eighth century. At the end of the seventh century there was a lengthy sequence of such Greek popes: Conon (686–87), Sergius I (687–701), John VI (701–5), John VII (705–7), Sisinnius (708), Constantine I (708–15).[8] The most important among them was no doubt the Syrian Sergius, "who was born in Palermo, whose family came from the vicinity of Antioch" (*Liber Pontificalis*), and who, because of his refusal to acknowledge the ecumenical validity of Eastern ecclesiastical customs, only just escaped the fate of Vigilius and Martin I;[9] he did, nevertheless, enrich the Western Church with very important elements of Greek piety.

The long processions from the Forum (St. Adriano) to St. Maria Maggiore, on the four great Eastern feasts of the Blessed Virgin, were introduced in Rome under Sergius I: Candelmas (*Ypapanti*), Annunciation, Assumption (*Dormitio*), and nativity: "Constituit autem ut diebus Adnuntiationis Domini, Dormitionis et Nativitatis sanctae dei genetricis semperque virginis Mariae ac sancti Symeonis, quod Ypapanti Greci appellant, letania exeat a sancto Hadriano et ad sanctam Mariam populus occurrat" ("It was established that on the days of the annunciation of the Lord, the assumption and holy birth of the eternal virgin and mother of God, Mary, and St. Simeon's, which is called *Ypapanti* in Greek, the procession should proceed from St. Adrian's, and the people should advance to St. Mary's"; Duchesne, *Liber Pontificalis*, I, 376). Cf. Frenaud, "Le culte de Notre Dame dans l'ancienne liturgie latine," in H. du Manoir, *Maria* (Paris 1961), VI, 157–211, esp. p. 184. It is assumed that the translation of several processional antiphons for feasts of the Virgin go back to this period. The pre-Carolingian antiphonary of Mont Blandin (Brussels, Bibliothèque Royale 10127–10144, *CLA*, X, 1548) clearly indicates that such translations were originally used in a bilingual liturgy; e.g., the famous processional antiphon *Adorna thalamum tuum* for Candelmas, ed. R. J. Hesbert, *Antiphonarium Missarum Sextuplex* (Brussels 1935), p. 38; cf. Wellesz, *Eastern Elements*, p. 61, and Hesbert, *Corpus Antiphonalium*, IV, no. 6051.

> Chatacosmyso thon ninphona su Sion
> Adorna thalamum tuum Sion
> coe ipodexe ton basileon Christon
> et suscipe regem Christum
> aspase thyn Marian
> amplectere Mariam

thyn epuranion phylyn
que est celestis porta
authy bastazi thon Basileon thys doxis
ipsa enim portat Regem glorię
nephyli photos yparchy parthenos
novo luminis subsistit Virgo
ferusa en chersin Yon proeosforu
adducens in manibus Filium ante luciferum
on labon Symeon en anchales autu
quem accipiens Symeon in ulnis suis
ekyrixen lais
predicavit populis
despotyn authon ene
Dominum eum esse
Zois ce thanatu
vite et mortis
cę Sothyra tu chosmu
et Salvatorem mundi

[Adorn your bridal chamber, O Zion, and receive Christ the King; embrace
Maria, who is the gate of Heaven, for it is she who bears the King of glory;
the Virgin stands in the freshness of light, bearing forth the Son in her arms
into the light, whom Simeon received into his arms and prophesied to the
people that he was the Lord of life and death, the Savior of the world.]

According to the *Liber Pontificalis*, the feast of the Exaltation of the Cross,
which celebrated the history of the rood—its legendary discovery by Helena, the
mother of Constantine, theft by the Persians in 614 from the Anastasis Basilica,
and triumphant return by Emperor Heraclius in 628—was introduced in Rome by
Pope Sergius I. E. Bishop is responsible for the discovery that the bilingual litany
for All Saints' Day which, along with a "Missa graeca," is contained in the "Æthelstan Psalter" (London, BL Cotton Galba A XVIII, saec. IX and X, from Winchester) and several other, chiefly English, manuscripts was produced in Rome during
the Papacy of Sergius I and came to England from Rome: *Liturgica Historica*, pp.
140 ff.; Brou, in *Sacris Erudiri*, I, p. 170; Bischoff, *Mittelalterliche Studien*, II,
263, n. 92.

Under Sergius a translation was also made of the acts of the sixth
ecumenical council in Constantinople (Constantinople III, 680–81);[10]
Pope Leo II (682–83), who came from Sicily and whose bilingualism is
extolled in the *Liber Pontificalis*, began the translation during his brief
pontificate.[11] At least the name of one of the translators of that period is
known: Bonifatius Consiliarius.[12]

Pope Zacharias (741–52), the last of the Greek popes of the seventh and
eighth centuries, translated the most famous work of Gregory the Great,
the *Dialogi*, into Greek, whereby Gregory, who so strongly resisted
speaking Greek, became known as ΓΡΗΓΟΡΙΟC ΔΙΑΛΟΓΟC to the
Greeks.[13] With the same pope, the "Byzantine" era of the papacy also
came to an end: he made the momentous statement to Pepin, the Frankish majordomo, that "it is better that he who has the power be called king
than he who no longer has any royal power," and thus he cleared the path

to the throne for the distant parvenu, in whose protection he could then immediately take refuge from the dangerously close Greeks and Lombards.

The "Chronicon Palatinum" (Cod. Vat. Pal. lat. 277; *CLA*, I, 91) was written in the eighth century in Italy (perhaps Rome) by an author who used the Greek chronicle of Johannes Malalas or a Latin epitome of it; T. Mommsen, ed., *MGH Auctores antiquissimi* (Berlin 1898), XIII, 427 ff.; L. Traube, "Chronicon Palatinum," *Vorlesungen und Abhandlungen* (Munich 1920), III, 201 ff.

In the second half of the seventh or first half of the eighth century, a monk named Petrus translated the revelations of a Syrian, which are known under the name "Pseudomethodius"; several of the manuscripts of the translation belong to the eighth century (cf. Siegmund, *Die Überlieferung*, pp. 172 ff.). According to the editor, E. Sackur (*Sibyllinische Texte und Forschungen* [Halle 1898], p. 56), the text was certainly translated in Gaul, as the "Eigentümlichkeiten des fränkischen Vulgärlateins der Merovingerperiode" ("peculiarities of the Frankish Vulgar Latin of the Merovingian period") and "Syrisch-gallische[r] Verkehr" ("Syro-Gallic intercourse") suggest. But since no Greco-Latin translation or translator can be established for the time period in question, Sackur's conjectures lead to no probable determination of provenance. "Pseudomethodius" became important for the concept of the imperium in the East and West; cf. G. Podskalsky, *Byzantinische Reichseschatologie* (Munich 1972), pp. 54 f.

The numerous hagiographic translations from Italy are difficult to date, but many seem to go back to the Byzantine era in Italy, such as the oldest translations of the vitae of SS. Anastasius the Persian, Bonifatius of Tarsus, Eustathius, Adrian and Natalia, Nicholas, Sergius and Bacchus, Theodore; the cult of these saints in Rome serves as a basic point of departure for dating the texts; cf. Siegmund, *Die Überlieferung*, pp. 226–54, under their names. After the ΛΕΙΜΩΝ of John Moschos (d. 619) there were again authors in Rome who wrote in Greek. The vita of the martyred pope Martin I (d. 655) was probably written by a Greek in Rome; but it was not until the ninth century that a Latin translator for the work was to be found (Anastasius Bibliothecarius; see below, Chapter IX). The passion of St. Tatiana seems also to have been a text written by the Greeks of Rome; cf. F. Halkin, "Sainte Tatiana, Légende grecque d'une martyre romaine," *AB* 89 (1971), 265–309. There is a Latin translation of the work which has survived in only a handful of Roman manuscripts (the oldest of which is Rome, Vat. Archivio di S. Pietro A 2, saec. X–XI)—an indication of the Roman origin of the translation?

Ravenna, the residence of the Exarch from the sixth to the eighth century, must also be considered a site of Greco-Latin translation. In the ninth century, Agnellus of Ravenna speaks of his bilingually educated ancestor Johannicius (*Liber pontificalis ecclesiae Ravennatensis*, c. 146: "Et rogatus a pontifice, ut omnes antiphonas, quas canimus modo dominicis diebus ad crucem sive sanctorum apostolorum aut martirum sive cunfessorum necnon et virginum, ipse exponeret non solum Latinis eloquiis, sed etiam Grecis verbis, quia in utraque lingua fuit maximus orator" [*MGH Scriptores rerum Langobardicarum*, p. 373]. L. M. Hartmann, "Johannicius von Ravenna," in *Festschrift Theodor Gomperz* (Vienna 1902), p. 322, interpreted the passage thus: "Auf Wunsch des Erzbischofs erklärte er die in der Kirche von Ravenna üblichen Antiphonien in lateinischer sowohl wie in griechischer Sprache" ("At the request of the archbishop he explained in both Latin and Greek the antiphonies common in the church of Ravenna"). But is it not rather a matter of the composition of bilingual antiphons?

In addition to the hagiographic material, medical texts may also have been translated in some number in Byzantine Italy. The ΘΕΡΑΠΕΥΤΙΚΑ of Alexander Trallianus (d. 605 in Rome), the youngest brother of the architect of Hagia Sophia, were translated into Latin perhaps even during the author's lifetime; Thorndike, *History of Magic and Experimental Science*, I, 579–84. The codex Milan, Bibl. Ambrosiana G 108 inf., saec IX, is a copy of an old medical miscellany manuscript with translations of and commentaries on Hippocrates and Galen, which the "physician Simplicius read, collated, and wrote in Ravenna according to the words of the court physician, Agnellus": "ex vocem [sic] Agnello archiatro, deo iuvante, ego Simplicius medicus legi, contuli et scripsi in Ravenna feliciter"; cf. Beccaria, *I Codici di Medicina*, no. 92, here p. 290.

The history of Greek studies and translations in Lombard Italy is even more obscure than in Italy's Byzantine period. Yet even here Greek must have been of interest in the eighth century—the knowledge of Greek among the Italo-Lombardic grammarians at Charlemagne's court did not come about by chance. Duke Arichis II of Benevento (758–87), friend of Paulus Diaconus, understood how to maintain his duchy between the Greeks and Carolingians, and founded a Sophia church in Benevento on the model of Hagia Sophia, into which he transferred the relics of St. Mercurius (among others) from Aeclanum in 768. The Greek *passio* of the soldier-saint originally venerated in Cappadocia—"le plus effacé . . . dans le glorieuse phalange des saints militaires" ("the most effaced . . . in the glorious phalanx of military saints," St. Binon)—circulated in an expanded Latin version under Arichis; the duke may have ordered the translation.[14]

2. Spain

One of the most ambitious plans of the Eastern Emperor Justinian (527–65) was to rescue Spain from the Visigoths and Suevi, Italy from the Ostrogoths, and Africa from the Vandals; Emperor Heraclius (610–41) finally gave up the entire plan. The relationship between the Greek East and Spain was multifaceted and intimate, especially during the sixth century.[15] Surprisingly, it was not in Byzantino-Visigothic Spain, but rather in the distant northwest of Spain, inhabited by the Suevi, that translation literature arose. At the same time as, or soon after, the Roman translations of the *Apopthegmata*, similar compilations were collected there: by order of the Suevian apostle, Martin of Braga (d. ca. 580), a certain Paschasius translated parts of a codex called *vitas patrum grecorum* given to him for this purpose; the translation is called *Liber Geronticon*;[16] Martin himself, who had been in Palestine before he founded the monastery Dumio among the Suevi and become archbishop in the Suevian royal city of Braga, undertook a collection of *Sententiae patrum Aegyptiorum*.[17] A translation of a collection of Greek canons is also ascribed to him.

In the second half of the seventh century, as the Suevian kingdom was incorporated into the Visigothic monarchy, Abbot Valerius of Bierzo in

Galicia produced an edition of the *Vitas patrum* which contained transla-
tions of Greek saints' lives; it is not clear whether they are the work of the
Galician translators' school founded by Martin of Braga or came from
Italy.[18]

The Catholic Romanic populace and the Arian Goths of the Visigothic
kingdom were reconciled by Bishop Leander of Seville (578–99), who
came from Byzantine Cartagena. The successor to the bishopric of Seville
was Leander's younger brother, Isidore (599–636), who, all things considered, was Spain's most famous Latin author.

His short treatise *De ortu et obitu patrum* (*Migne PL* 83, cols. 129–59) contains
a core of prophets' lives, translated from Greek, within the series of eighty-six
brief biographical sketches of figures from the Old and New Testaments; see
T. Schermann, *Prophetarum vitae fabulosae* (Leipzig 1907), and *Propheten- und
Apostellegenden nebst Jüngerkatalogen des Dorotheus und verwandter Texte, TU*
31/3 (Leipzig 1907); A Vaccari, "Una fonte del 'de ortu et obitu Patrum' di S. Isi-
doro," in *Miscellanea Isidoriana* (Rome 1936), pp. 165–75.

Isidore's principal work is the *Etymologiae* (*Origines*), which served the
West for centuries. As a second Varro, he attempted, in twenty brief
books, to summarize conceptually the trivium, quadrivium, medicine,
law, theology, history, philosophy, zoology, geography, book production,
architecture, mineralogy, metallurgy, agriculture, military matters, public and private games, shipbuilding, and other areas of knowledge and
technology. As was generally the case in antiquity, the knowledge transmitted by Isidore was primarily Greek; via the Latin mediators from
whom he derived his information, numerous Graeca are preserved in Isidore's work. He uses Greek words, which are written in Greek script and
incorporated into the Latin text according to ancient practice.[19] The Greek
alphabet is explained historically—after the manner of ancient models—
at the beginning of the works; in addition he includes the important doctrine of the *litterae mysticae*, which was characteristic of the medieval
valuation of Greek:[20]

Cadmus, the son of Agenor, first brought seventeen Greek letters
to Greece from Phoenicia: Λ Β Γ Δ Ε Ζ Ι Κ Λ Μ Ν Ο Π Ρ C Τ
Φ. Palamedes added three more during the Trojan War: Η Χ Ω.
Thereafter, the lyric poet Simonides added three more letters: Ψ Ξ
Θ. Pythagoras of Samos first developed the letter Υ on the model of
human life: its lower stroke signifies the younger years, the still uncertain ones, which have not yet given themselves up to either vice
or virtue. The bifurcation, however, which remains begins in
adolescence: its right arm is steep, yet leads to the blessed life; the
left is easier; it leads to disaster and destruction. Persius says of this
letter: "And the letter which extends the Samian branches / showed
you the ascending path on the right hand" [III 56].

The Greeks have five letters of mystery. The first is Υ, which signifies human life, of which we have just spoken. The second is Θ,
which signifies death, since judges place this letter Θ by the names
of those whom they condemn to execution. And theta signifies ΑΠΟ
ΤΟΥ ΘΑΝΑΤΟΥ, i.e., "from death." For this reason, it also has a
shaft through the middle, which is the sign of death. A certain one
says of this: "Theta, you are far more wretched than all other letters."
The third, Τ , signifies the cross of the Lord; therefore it is translated
into Hebrew as "sign." Concerning this letter, the angel in Ezekiel
[9:4] is told: "Go through the middle of Jerusalem and trace a tau on
the forehead of the sighing and lamenting men." The remaining two
letters are, however, claimed as the first and last by Christ for himself. At the beginning and end, he says: "I am the λ and ω." When
these two letters move toward each other, λ rolls to ω and ω in
turn rolls up again to λ ; so that the Lord showed that the course
from the beginning to the end and the return from the end to the
beginning is in him. But all Greek letters form words and numbers.
For the letter called alpha signifies one, the one called beta two;
where they write gamma, it is called three, and delta four; and thus
all their letters have numerical values. The Latins do not use letters
for numbers, but form only words from them, except for *I* and *X*,
which figure also signifies the cross and has the numerical value ten.

In another passage of the work, Isidore designated the Greek language as
one of the *tres linguae sacrae*:[21]

There are three sacred languages: Hebrew, Greek, and Latin, which
are the most distinguished throughout the whole earth. For it was in
these languages that Pilate wrote the Lord's legal case on the cross.
Thence, it is also because of the obscurity of the Holy Scriptures that
a knowledge of these three languages is necessary, so that one can
refer to the others when the text of one language gives rise to doubt
about a name or a translation. Yet Greek is considered an especially
splendid language among the rest of the nations. For it is more resonant than Latin and all other languages. Its variety is divided into
five components: first, the ΚΟΙΝΗ, i.e., "mixed" or "common,"
which everyone uses; second, the Attic, namely, the language of
Athens, which all Greek authors have used; third, the Doric, which
the Egyptians and Syrians have; fourth, the Ionic; and fifth, the
Aeolic. . . . There are several distinguishing characteristics in the
observation of the Greek languages; their language is thus divided.

The greater part of this explanation is derived from older works, as is
generally the case in the *Etymologiae*: Isidore praises the beauty of the
Greek language after the manner of Quintilian; the doctrine of the *linguae
sacrae* is developed from Augustine's statement concerning the *linguae
principales*, etc.[22] Yet whoever not only uses but also reads Isidore will

observe that there is an "inner line . . . which connects all these apparently thoughtless excerpts" ("innere Linie . . . die sich durch alle diese
scheinbar gedankenlosen Excerpte zieht").[23] Isidore's achievement with
respect to the medieval knowledge of Greek lies in his concentration on
fundamental and clearly organized material: the *litterae mysticae* and
linguae sacrae were schemata of a new archaism which well suited the
newly Christianized nations of the West.

3. Ireland

One of the most tenacious of modern legends concerning the Middle Ages
is that classical studies escaped from Gaul to Ireland during the collapse of
late antiquity, and that Greek was studied and known in Ireland during
the early medieval "Dark Ages": "L'hellénisme banni du continent
Occidental alla se réfugier plus loin dans cette île qui avait échappé à la
conquête romaine: l'Irlande.—L'état des lettres y était alors florissant depuis des siècles, grâce au zèle intelligent des Druides qui avaient importé
leurs lumières des Gaules. Convertis au christianisme, ils n'en con-
tinuaient pas moins à cultiver la littérature ancienne. . . . Le mysticisme
qui constituait le fond du caractère irlandais, les rendit enclins aux rêv-
eries philosophiques, ce qui explique leur ardeur pour les doctrines de
Platon. L'étude de la langue grecque formait donc l'une des bases de leur
enseignement." ("Hellenism, banned from the western reaches of the
Continent, sought refuge further away on the island which had escaped
the Roman conquest: Ireland. At that time, literary studies had been
flourishing for centuries, thanks to the intelligent zeal of the Druides, who
had imported their cultural lights from Gaul. After their conversion to
Christianity, they did not lessen their cultivation of the study of ancient
literature. . . . The mysticism which constitutes the basis of the Irish character disposed them to philosophical reveries, which explains their ardor
for the doctrines of Plato. The study of the Greek language was thus one
of the foundations of their education.") Here, in his *Alde Manuce et l'Hellénisme à Venise* (p. xvii), the book collector and learned amateur
Ambroise Firmin-Didot formulated especially well and imaginatively
what others before him had already written about "le miracle irlandais" in
cultural history.[24] Already in 1905, Maurice Roger correctly readjusted
the standards on the basis of his manuscript studies, and in 1912, Mario
Esposito came to very negative conclusions after a critical analysis of all
sources cited up to that time on which the high opinion of Greek studies
in Ireland had been based: "During the earlier period, from the sixth to
the end of the eighth century, serious evidence of Greek or classical
knowledge in Ireland is slight and almost non-existent."[25]

The Irish question has nevertheless persisted. From the relative and period-specific, historical point of view, many traces of Greek among the Irish are significant simply because they appear almost nowhere else: Greek letters as display script in the Schaffhausen Adamnan codex, written before 713 on the island of Iona—ϕΙΝΙΤΥϷ CHKYNΔYC ΛΙΒΕϷ (*finitur secundus liber*); and on the last page, the Greek paternoster in Greek majuscules (in part already with ƆC for M).[26] Esposito correctly notes, "The orthography is not suggestive of any accurate knowledge of Greek grammar," but orthography and grammar should not be the only standards of scholarly interest in these early traces, so typical of the medieval reception of Greek; nor may they be considered in isolation. Along with the Adamnan codex from Iona, one must also take into account the early Northumbrian fragment of an evangelary which includes a display page on which the Greek paternoster is written in the Roman alphabet;[27] in addition, one must consider the "Book of Lindisfarne," written by Bishop Eadfriծ of Lindisfarne (698–721), with the illumination titles *O AGIOS MATTHEUS O AGIUS MARCUS O AGIOS LUCAS O AGIOS IOHANNES*, which should not be understood as an awkward copy of Greek illumination titles: there is a design of embellishment and encoding involved in this use of Greek words and letters.[28] Thus there was certainly an "ornamental" and perhaps even a liturgical interest in Greek in the Irish-Northumbrian culture domain around 700. The "Book of Armagh," Ireland's oldest "historical work" (ca. 807), presents a kind of compilation of these uses of Greek: page titles, subscriptions, and even a name are written in Greek: ΔΙΚΤΑΝΤΕ ΤΟϷΒΑΚϷ (*dictante Torbach*) with "spiritus asper" Ϝ for *h*![29] The Latin paternoster is also written in Greek majuscules in the "Book of Armagh." If one considers Ireland and Northumbria together, one can itemize a brief series of "Greek" paternosters:

> before 700, Durham, Greek in the Roman alphabet
> after 700, Iona, Greek in the Greek alphabet
> after 800, Armagh, Latin in the Greek alphabet

All variations on the Greco-Latin mode are thus represented. Coincidence or conscious variation? Similarly the Trier-Echternach illumination school "fully declined" in Latin the phenomenology of the Greek word and letter in the tenth/eleventh century.

This ornamental Greek of the Irish frequently radiated out to the Continent, although without tangible and demonstrable evidence for direct Irish influence in each particular case. B. Bischoff, *Die südostdeutschen Schreibschulen der Karolingerzeit*, 3rd ed. (Wiesbaden 1974), describes ninth-century southern German manuscripts with such Graeca; among them is the manuscript of Gregory's *Dialogi*, Augsburg Ordinariatsarchiv 10 (from Füssen, St. Mang), saec. IX in., with ΛƆCHX (*amen*: ƆC for M as in many Western documents; X for N, "wohl aus der Rune für N zu erklären" ["most likely to be explained on the basis of the rune for

N"]; Bischoff, p. 50) and EXΡLIСIθ. In spite of the Continental minuscule and Old High German glosses (in the vowel cipher attributed to Boniface and explained in the *De inventione linguarum*, *Migne PL* 112, cols. 1581–82), the insular influence in the lively ornamentation is unmistakable, and the Grecistic method of writing *Amen Explicit* also belongs to this insular "ornamentation."

Greek words occur occasionally in the poetry and prose of the Irish; for example, in the antiphonary of Bangor, Ireland's oldest "book of poetry," one finds *proto, agie, agius, pantes ta erga, zoen*.[30]

The glosses in the *Hisperica famina* ("Occidental Orations"), a work which has often been associated with Irish erudition, abound in rare terms, with a sprinkling of Greek and Hebrew words:[31]

> Titaneus olimphium: inflamat arotus tabulatum,
> thalasicum: illustrat uapore flustrum . . .

[The titanian star inflames the edifice of the heavens, lights up the calm of the sea with fire.]

"These documents prove very little beyond a slight acquaintance with Greek vocabulary, such as could easily be derived from the textbooks and glossaries then in circulation" (Esposito); seen in the context of its time, however, this "slight acquaintance" with Greek is not inconsiderable. Just such an interest is often attributed to the *filid*, that Irish caste which particularly cultivated language and poetry; *Auraicept*, their textbook, which is thought to go back to the seventh century, contains the Greek alphabet (with numerical values) after the Hebrew.[32]

Without question the Irish of the early Middle Ages were intensively occupied with script, language, and grammar. That is shown not only by the triad of splendid Irish Priscian manuscripts of the ninth century, in Karlsruhe, St. Gall, and Leiden, but perhaps also by the tradition of the enigmatic Virgilius Maro, whose abstruse grammar was transmitted by the Irish.[33] Through grammatical texts of late antiquity, the Irish came into direct contact with Greek; the same is true of exegesis, to which the Irish were particularly devoted.[34] A typical Irish endeavor in the fields of grammar and exegesis seems to have been to determine what the equivalents of a given word were in the "three sacred languages." Even St. Columban (d. 615) gave a solemn trilingual flourish to his letter to Pope Boniface IV: ". . . mihi Ionae hebraice, Peristerae graece, Columbae latine . . ."[35] To be sure, the search for the equivalents in the three sacred languages was not always successful. The Irish *Liber de numeris*, "eine Fundgrube für ausgefallenes Wissen" ("a storehouse of obscure information"), contains a good example thereof: ". . . *Pater, Filius*, and *Spiritus sanctus*, in Hebrew these three persons are called *Abba, Ben*, and *Ruha*; and in Greek *Pater, Bar* [!], but I have not found the Greek for 'spirit.'"

Migne PL 83, cols. 1293–1302 (in the appendices to Isidore of Seville), here col. 1302. The passage was first excerpted by Bischoff (*Mittelalterliche Studien*, II, 249), then by R. E. McNally, "Der irische Liber de numeris" (diss., Munich, 1957), p. 51, and idem, in *Theological Studies* 19 (New York 1958). McNally (diss., p. 156) proposes that the *Liber de numeris* originated in southern Germany in the late eighth century—more specifically, among the associates of Virgil the Irish bishop of Salzburg (745 or 767–84). H. Löwe treats the problem cautiously in "Salzburg als Zentrum literarischen Schaffens im 8. Jahrhundert," *Mitteilungen der Gesellschaft für Salzburger Landeskunde* 115 (1975), 99–143, here pp. 104 f.

Even in the field of epigraphy, fragments of Greek have been brought to light in modern times from early medieval Ireland: an inscription on the slab of Fahan Mura on the northern Irish coast, held to be illegible, was deciphered by R. A. S. Macalister ("The Inscription on the Slab at Fahan Mura," *The Journal of the R. Society of Antiquaries of Ireland* 59 [1929], 89–98) as a Greek doxology:

ΔΟΞΑ ΚΑΙ ΤΙΜΕ ΠΑΤΡΙ ΚΑΙ ΥΙΩ
ΚΑΙ ΠΝΕΥΜΑΤΙ ΑΓΙΩ

(corresponds to *Gloria et honor patri et filio et spiritui sancto*). The discoverer associated the formulation of the text with a Toledo Synod of 633; cf. Macalister, *Corpus inscriptionum insularum Celticarum* (Dublin 1949), II, 118 ff., pl. XLVII. Macalister's reading is confirmed by F. Henry, *Irish Art in the Early Christian Period*, 3rd ed. (London 1965), p. 126 and pl. VII. One must nevertheless voice some misgivings concerning the early dating of the inscription. It would be unique in seventh-century Ireland. According to our knowledge of Greek studies among the Irish, the inscription belongs more probably to the eighth century. Here one may compare the dating of the stone to "around 800"—on the basis of evidence from art history and style—by P. Harbison, in P. Harbison, H. Potterton, and J. Sheehy, *Irish Art and Architecture from Prehistory to Present* (London 1978), p. 65.

Thus it can be said that the Irish were in any case remarkably interested in Greek during the seventh and eighth centuries. On their green island and in the monasteries of Irish character on the northern English coasts, they did not read Homer or Plato, but rather learned the Greek alphabet wholly or in part, excerpted Greek words from late antique sources—Jerome, Macrobius, Boethius, Priscian, Isidore, and others—and probably even participated in the transmission of glossaries; as for complete texts, only short liturgical pieces were evidently known. With a knowledge of Greek acquired in this manner, they could not understand or translate longer Greek texts with which they were unacquainted. But on the Continent, the *Scotti peregrini* had a scholarly advantage simply because of their greater receptiveness for languages, especially Greek; and in the ninth-century cultural realm of the Carolingians, with its better resources, it was again possible for an *Irishman* to translate texts into Latin from Greek.

4. England

The most important of the emissaries whom the papacy dispatched to England with Augustine and his companions came from the Greek monasteries in Rome; in 668 Pope Vitalian (657–72) sent the North African Hadrian and the Cilician Theodore to the island missionized by Gregory the Great. Bede reports in his *Historia ecclesiastica gentis Anglorum* (731) that Hadrian and Archbishop Theodore taught Greek in Canterbury; their accomplishment was still seen in the fact that "even today there are still students of theirs who know Latin and Greek as well as their native language."[36] All too often this sentence has simply been accepted, without checking whether the historian's statement was based more on hearsay and the veneration of Hadrian and Theodore than on personal experience. At another place in his *Ecclesiastical History*, Bede mentions two of Hadrian's and Theodore's alleged trilingual students by name: Tobias (V 8 and 23) and Albinus (V 20); we know nothing further of their knowledge of Greek.[37]

Two splendid manuscripts from the scriptorium of Wearmouth and Jarrow, Bede's monastery, nevertheless attest to the fact that Greek was held in high regard there: the "Codex Amiatinus" contains a much-discussed scribal inscription in Greek,[38] and ornaments the double-page illustration of Solomon's temple in Jerusalem (fol. 2ᵛ/IIIʳ) with the Greek names of the four cardinal points of the compass: ANATOL⟨E⟩ DYSIS ARCTOS MESEMBRIA.[39] In the fragmentary evangelary, now bound with the "Utrecht Psalter" and paleographically similar to the "Codex Amiatinus," the following inscription appears in the margin (which has been marked out with compasses) of one of the title pages:[40]

† ΑΓΙΑ ΜΑΡΙΑ ΒΟΗΘΗCΟΝ ΤѠ ΓΡΑΨΑΝΤΙ

[Blessed Mary, be of aid to the scribe]

Their most important student was Aldhelm of Malmesbury, "Englands ältester Klassiker" ("England's earliest classical scholar," Manitius), who occasionally flourishes Greek terms, which, however, by no means proves that his Greek was "comme sa langue maternelle" ("like his native language").[41] One of Aldhelm's Grecisms which is especially appropriate and had important consequences was his use of sigla to mark questions and answers in *De metris et enigmatibus*: "so that no confusion may arise through the negligence of the scribe, as usually happens, I have placed the Greek letter ϽC before the teacher's words, a Δ before the student's, so that by means of the foreign letters, which differ from Roman script, all possibility of error is removed."[42] As Aldhelm himself notes, he took this device from Iunilius' *Instituta regularia divinae legis* (saec. VI med.), although with one modification, which clearly shows that he was not ac-

quainted with the system as conceived in Greek: while Iunilius designated the "teacher" (διδάσκαλος) with Δ and the "student" (μαθητής)
with Μ, Aldhelm has Δ for "student" (*discipulus*) and Ↄ (= *M*) for
"teacher" (*magister*). Yet since, according to the tradition, Δ questioned
and Μ answered, it happened that, due to the reversal of the sigla, the
student always questions the teacher in Aldhelm's treatise, and not the
other way around. Bede, Alcuin, Hrabanus Maurus, and many others followed Aldhelm's practice, "und der Wahnsinn hat mit der Zeit Methode
bekommen" ("and in time this madness acquired method").[43] Aldhelm
took over the siglum Μ in the form Ↄc. Along with the Schaffhausen
Adamnan codex, Aldhelm's *De metris* contains the earliest manuscript
witness of this "M siglum," which can be traced through the steps of the
tradition Aldhelm—Iunilius—Paul of Nisibis (Theodore of Mopsuestia?)
back to its supposed origin in one of the Syrian schools of late antiquity.[44]

Two new traces of Greek in the *instruction* at the school of Canterbury have
been uncovered by recent research in Medieval Latin: Walther Bulst has shown
that a translation of the Sibyl's song, improved over Augustine's version (*De civitate dei* XVIII 23) and containing the acrostic

IHCOYC XPEICTOC ΘEOY YIOC CⲰΤΗР CTAYPOC

originated in England "around 700"; Aldhelm (d. 709) was the first, and for a long
time the only, person to use the translation; it belongs to the circle of the Canterbury school: Bulst, "Eine anglo-lateinische Übersetzung aus dem Griechischen
um 700," *Zeitschrift für deutsches Altertum* 75 (1938), 105–11. Bischoff (*Mittelalterliche Studien*, I, 155) proposes Constantine's "Oration to the Congregation of
the Saints" (Eusebius) as the Greek source of this translation.
    Bernhard Bischoff has found direct evidence in biblical glosses that the two Ro-
man ambassadors taught in England; the glosses follow the Antiochene method of
literal exegesis and objective commentary; the great Alexandrine allegorist,
Origen, is not to be found in them. "What a piece of biblical cultural information
is contained in the commentary on John 10:3, *Et vocem meam audient*, 'Mos est
orientalium pastorum praecedere et cantare gregibus suis.'" The hyrax (*choero-
gryllus*) in Lev. 11:5 is described: it resembles a pig, but is smaller; it inhabits the
craggy crevices of the Sinai. The *pepones*, mentioned in Num. 11:5, a species of
large melon, attains such a size in Edessa that a camel can barely carry two of
them"; *Mittelalterliche Studien*, I, 208.

The Venerable Bede (d. 735) is the first "medieval scholar" in the sense
that he immersed himself in Latin as a thoroughly foreign language without direct contact with the Mediterranean world—the environment of the
greatest teacher of the eighth century extended geographically scarcely
more than a few dozen miles around Jarrow into Northumbria. The beginnings of the artificial Latin of the Middle Ages and the modern period are
found here; for while lexical, morphological, and syntactic changes were
taking place in literary Latin on the Continent at this time due to its contact with the developing Romance languages, on their island the Angles

and Saxons learned the language from books, among them splendid codices of late antiquity, which they were able to acquire on their many pilgrimages and embassies to Rome. They learned the literary language of late antiquity, which then through Anglo-Saxon missionary work and the "Carolingian Renaissance" in essence also became the scholarly language of the Middle Ages.

This turning point in the study of the Latin language, which is only sketched in broad outline here, was also a turning point in Greek studies. Bede was probably also the first to have approached the Greek language in what became the typical medieval manner[45]—through the study of bilinguals. In addition to an increase in the number of Graeca used, the study of a Greco-Latin manuscript of the Bible also introduced a deeper literal understanding of the Holy Scriptures. It was Bede's concern with this latter aspect that brought him, in his later years, and now dissatisfied with his *Expositio actuum apostolorum*, to write a second commentary on the Acts, *Retractatio in actus apostolorum*.[46] In this work, Bede used a Greco-Latin manuscript of the Acts;[47] one of the main purposes of the new commentary was to compare the Greek and the Latin texts of the Bible. It seems that Bede had no other bilingual books of the Bible at his disposal. Even so, he presented in his *Retractatio* an example of the value of a Greco-Latin textual comparison—insofar as it was still needed after the interpretations of the text by Jerome and Augustine. Additionally, in his explanation of the Greek system of numerals in *De temporum ratione*, Bede also performed a small service for Greek studies in the Middle Ages.[48]

VII

Merovingian Gaul and the Carolingian Courts

Luget hoc Graecia novis invidiae aculeis lacessita: quam sui quondam incolae iamdudum cum Asianis opibus aspernantur, vestra potius magnanimitate delectati, studiis allecti, liberalitate confisi; dolet inquam se olim singulariter mirabilem ac mirabiliter singularem a suis destitui; dolet certe sua illa privilegia (quod numquam hactenus verita est) ad climata nostra transferri. Quid Hiberniam memorem contempto pelagi discrimine paene totam cum grege philosophorum ad littora nostra migrantem? Quorum quisquis peritior est, ultro sibi indicit exilium, ut Salomoni sapientissimo famuletur ad votum. [Irritated by new stings of envy, Greece laments this: that its own former inhabitants despised it, along with its Asian riches, for a long time, delighted more by your magnanimity, attracted to learning, confident in liberality; I say it grieves Greece that it, once singularly wondrous and wondrously singular, has lost them; certainly it grieves that its own privileges are transferred to our climes (since it never before feared this). What is to be said of Ireland, which, with its flocks of philosophers, has almost completely migrated to our shores, having despised the dangers of the sea? Whoever is more knowledgeable among them orders himself away into exile, so that he might serve the wishes of the most wise Solomon.]

Heiric of Auxerre to Charles the Bald, *MGH Poetae*, III, 429

1. Late Roman and Merovingian Gaul

As in all more highly cultivated regions of the Roman Empire, Greek and Latin existed alongside one another in late antique Gaul. Ausonius of Bordeaux, who taught Gratian (later to become emperor) in Trier (364) and was consul in 379, is our chief witness of Greco-Latin education in fourth-century Gaul. He was inspired by both the Latin and the Greek muses, and once they even met and confronted each other in a macaronic poem:[1]

ΕΛΛΑΔΙΚΗC ΜΕΤΟΧΟΝ ΜΟΥCΗC Latiaeque Camenae
ΑΞΙΟΝ ΑΥΓΟΝΙΟC sermone adludo bilingui.
Musae quid facimus? . . .

[I, Ausonius, chatter with Axius, who is divided between the Greek and Latin muses, in bilingual conversation. Muses, what am I to do?]

Ultimately the muses even dispute syllables, and Ausonius reconciles them by adding Greek endings to Latin words.

The Gallic arch-mannerist included a poem, *De litteris monosyllabis Graecis ac Latinus*, in his *Technopaegnion* with comments on form, history, and signification of the Greek and Latin letters:[2]

Pythagorae biuium ramis pateo ambiguis	Y
Vocibus in Grais numquam ultima conspicior	M
Zeta iacens, si surgat, erit nota quae legitur	N
Maeandrum flexusque uagos imitata uagor	ʒ

[As the double path of Pythagoras, I stand here open with branches spreading in two directions Y. In Greek words I am never seen at the end M. Z lying down, when stood up, is a sign to be read N. I roam about, imitating the Meander and wandering movements ʒ.]

This passage already shows clear signs of the playful use of Greek which was characteristic of the Middle Ages. Yet in fourth-century Gaul, the Greek *grammaticus* was still present. In Trier, Bordeaux, Toulouse, and Narbonne, for example, Greek teachers could be found during this period. Of course Ausonius' evaluation of the *Grammatici Graeci Burdigalenses*, contained in his *Commemoratio professorum Burdigalensium*, is scarcely complimentary:[3]

> Sedulum cunctis studium docendi,
> Fructus exilis tenuisque sermo.
> Sed quia nostro docuere aevo,
> Commemorandi.

[Diligent zeal for teaching among all, but meager fruit and feeble speech. Only because they taught in *our* time, are they to be mentioned.]

Ausonius' heathen, or at least not primarily Christian, Hellenism was carried on in the Platonism of the *De statu animae* of Mamertus Claudianus and in the philosophical and historical reminiscences of Sidonius Apollinaris, who in addition provides typical examples of Late Latin Grecistic style.[4] Courcelle sees a connection between their reading of Greek and the rule of the Greek Anthemius in the West (467–72); in a novel concept, from the literary historical point of view, he deals with Claudian and Sidonius under the rubric "La renaissance de 470."[5] Sidonius came from Lyon, Claudian was a priest in Vienne: thus it is in the Rhone district that the last vestiges of Platonism in Gaul are found.

The territories along the Rhone were also the scenes of the Christian Hellenism of late antique Gaul. Cassian, an important authority on Greek and the Greek monastic life, was at work in early fifth-century Marseille. The monastery in Lérins had absorbed much of the Greek spirit through Cassian, but the study of Greek was scarcely to be found there any longer.[6] On the other hand, a scholar of Greek literature again stepped forth toward the end of the fifth century in the old Greek establishment of ΜΑCCIΛIΛ (Marseille)—the priest Gennadius. He wrote an important continuation of Jerome's authors' catalogue, *De viris illustribus*; it may be concluded from his article on Greek authors that he read Greek literature. According to his own testimony, he also translated from Greek (*De viris illustribus*, c. 11). The introduction of Greco-Latin hymns by Caesarius of Arles (502–42) may be considered the last of the branches of Christian Hellenism in the Rhone area; the motivation which the authors of the *Vita S. Caesarii* give for this innovation cautions against extensive interpretation in terms of the level of Greek culture in Arles: the bishop wished to deter the faithful from chatting in church.[7]

While vestiges of the imperial bilingualism had survived in the Visigothic and Burgundian kingdoms of Gaul, even they disappeared with the expansion of Frankish dominion throughout Gaul. Yet even then not all traces of Greek are lacking, especially in the early Merovingian period: in 508 Clovis, king of the Franks, is supposed to have received honorary appointment as consul and the royal vestments with diadem and purple mantle from the ambassadors of Emperor Anastasius I.[8] A Greek physician in the service of Theodoric the Great dedicated a work on the correct use of food (especially bacon, of which the Franks were so fond) to Clovis' son Theodoric.[9] Gregory of Tours reports of King Chilperic (murdered 584) that "he added [new] letters to ours, ω as the Greeks have, *ae, the, uui*, whose forms are

ω ae the uui

⊙ ω z ρ

And he sent epistles to all the cities of his kingdom, so that the boys might be taught in this manner and that the books written in the old style be erased with pumice and written anew."[10]

It seems that the use of Greek was reduced to the level of curiosities in Merovingian Gaul. Here the transfer of power to the Teutons signified a break with the tradition of antiquity. The new France was separated from antiquity by a deeper chasm than was Byzantine Lombardic Italy or Visigothic Spain, and it is not without reason that the "Romance" language, French, has strayed further from "Roman" than any other language of the family except the very distant and isolated Romanian language. Only in the liturgy was the presence of Greek maintained and perhaps even strengthened. The Synod of Vaison introduced the "Kyrie" into the Gallic liturgy in 529, and made a remarkable reference to the practice not only of Rome and Italy, but also of the Christian East:[11]

And because the agreeable and exceedingly beneficial custom of saying the "kyrie eleison" more frequently and with great devotion and penitence has been introduced in the Apostolic See and throughout all the provinces of Asia and Italy, it has also pleased us by the grace of God to introduce this so holy custom in all our churches at matins, in the mass, and at vespers.

Soon thereafter (according to its own testimony), the only surviving commentary on the liturgy from Merovingian Gaul was written, the "Expositio Brevis Antiquae Liturgiae Gallicanae," so called by the Maurist Martène. The work identifies its author as Bishop Germanus of Paris (555–76);[12] liturgical scholars assume a late, although still Merovingian, origin for the work.[13] The significance of the trishagion is explained in this work:

ΑΓΙΟC Ο ΘΕΟC · ΑΓΙΟC ΙCΧΥΡΟC ·
ΑΓΙΟC ΑΘΑΝΑΤΟC ΕΛΕΗCΟΝ ΗΜΑC

sanctus deus sanctus fortis sanctus immortalis miserere nobis

and the text is concisely labelled *Aius* in the "Expositio":[14]

But the *Aius* is thus sung in Greek before the reading from the prophets, because the proclamation of the New Testament in the world was made in Greek. . . . The honor of the language in which the gospel of Christ was first conceived in symbols and taught in letters is preserved when the church sings the first song, *Aius*, begun by the bishop, in both Latin and Greek. And, so that the connection of the Old and New Testaments is shown, "amen" is said in Hebrew, corresponding to the *titulus* which Pilate placed on the cross in a trinity of languages, according to God's plan. . . .

The trishagion was sung both before the reading and before the gospel. The first trishagion corresponded to the usage of Constantinople, the second to that of Egypt; the Gallic liturgy combined the two.[15]

This example demonstrates that Greek influence in the West at this time need not be the same as Byzantine influence. It is possible that traces of the much-discussed "Syrians in the West" are evident here. Gregory of Tours mentions Syrians in Gaul at many points in his *Historiae*. Even if one may not speak of an "occupation de l'Occident par les Orientaux" ("occupation of the west by Orientals"),[16] there were certainly anchorites from the Christian East, and here and there probably even exclusively Syrian or Oriental groups.[17] Did they contribute to literary exchange between the Greek and Latin world, i.e., beyond general cultural, artistic, and liturgical influences?

The only report of a translation in Merovingian Gaul mentions a Syrian as interpreter. In his *Liber de gloria martyrum*, Gregory of Tours gives an epitome of the legend of the Seven Sleepers of Ephesus and closes with: "Quod passio eorum, quam Siro quodam interpretante in Latino transtulimus, plenius pandit" ("that describes the account of their deaths much more extensively, which I have presented in Latin from the translation of a certain Syrian").[18] It is, however, not clear that this lost work was a translation from *Greek*. Research has more or less determined the provenance of many translations from Greek to be in Merovingian Gaul— Pseudo-Methodius,[19] the early medieval Aratus translation,[20] the "Excerpta Barbari."[21] But until at least *one* of the translations is proven to be from the Merovingian period, all such ascriptions remain doubtful. The first reliable evidence of Greek studies in the Merovingian period is found in the grammatical manuscript Wolfenbüttel, Weiss. 86, which contains, among other material, *Esidori . . . grammaticae artis nomina grega et latina notata*, as well as a prayer, gloria, credo, magnificat, and benedictus in Greek uncial and in part with a Latin interlinear version in Tironian notes.[22] The manuscript comes from St. Martin's in Tours and probably belongs to the mid-eighth century.[23] Without the testimony of this Weissenburg manuscript, one would not imagine that Graeca existed during the Merovingian period in association with grammatical material and ancient shorthand.

2. Three Generations of Carolingian Monarchs

. . . magnanimus Karolus, cum legati regis Bizantini venirent ad se et de domino suo illi suggererent, quia fidelis ipsi amicus esse voluisset et, si viciniores essent, eum filii loco nutrire et paupertatem illius relevare decrevisset, ferventissimo igne se intra pectus retinere non valens in hęc verba prorupit: "O utinam non esset ille gurgitulus inter nos! Forsitan divitias orientales aut partiremur aut pariter participando communiter haberemus." [When the ambassadors of the Byzantine ruler came to Charlemagne, the magnanimous, and let it be known that their lord wished to be a faithful friend to him [i.e., Charlemagne], and if the two became more intimate, he [i.e., the Byzantine ruler] would deign to support him as a son and relieve him of his poverty, Charlemagne was not able to contain the raging fire in his breast and burst out with the following words: "Oh, if this little stream did not separate us, we would either divide the oriental riches among ourselves, or, sharing them equally, have them in common!"]
Notker Balbulus, *Gesta Karoli* I 26.

Greek played an important role in the culture of the Carolingian court for a hundred years—under Charlemagne, his successor, Louis "the Pious," and the West Frankish Carolingian Charles (II, "the Bald"). According to a very obscure account, the Greek aspirations of the Carolingians go back to the beginnings of their rule: Pepin, who forced the Merovingian king into a monastery in 751 and had himself anointed king by Boniface, is sup-

posed to have received a packet of "books written in Greek" from Pope
Paul I (757–67).[24]

In addition to his prodigious deeds in war, Pepin's son, Charles, was
not only concerned with acquiring a good command of Latin, but also interested in Greek; "he could understand Greek better than he could
speak it," reports the emperor's biographer, Einhart.[25] Topoi of Suetonius' *De vita Caesarum* are obviously behind this statement.[26] And an entirely different tradition is responsible when Thegan, the biographer of
Louis the Pious, says of Charlemagne that "at the end, before the day of
his death, he, along with Greeks and Syrians, made an excellent revision
of the four Gospels of Christ."[27] With reference to Louis' knowledge of
Greek, Thegan again used Einhart's telling formulation.[28]

The panegyric to Charles the Bald has another tone: "You not only ex-
plored the greatest and most holy authors of the language of Latium, but
even learned to consult the Greek fathers,"[29] writes John Scottus in the
dedication of his translation of Dionysius. Heiric of Auxerre wrote to
Charles the Bald: "You made this your singular concern, that wherever
famous masters of the arts were to be found on earth, . . . your Eminence
brought them together from everywhere for public instruction"—followed by the famous lines quoted at the beginning of the present
chapter.[30]

Despite its high tone, the panegyric to Charles the Bald corresponds
more closely to reality than those to his father and grandfather: the ruler
stood in the background, offered encouragement and inspiration, and
attracted scholars to his court. Louis the Pious is nevertheless also deserv-
ing of praise as a patron of Greek studies; the culture of his court is now
seen in a different light due to the discovery of Hilduin's translation of
Dionysius. The same is true of Charlemagne, concerning whose "court
Greek" Traube once expressed the opinion:

Noch bleibt der grosse Name Athen und Homer auch für diese Epi-
gonen, noch übt er einen gewissen romantischen Reiz; aber sein Inhalt hat sich verflüchtigt. Der Dichter Angilbert, den seine Genossen Homerus nannten, hat keinen griechischen Buchstaben zu
malen vermocht, und in der kaiserlichen Pfalz, die man beginnt, mit
Athen zu vergleichen, hat man Griechisch nur etwan getrieben, um
sich mit dem oströmischen Kaiser zu verständigen. Aber die alten
griechischen Flicken, die man aus Glossarien und Commentaren
trennte, um sein Buch damit zu zieren, und die wir heute verwün-
schen, waren der Purpur des damaligen Dichtergewandes und sind
in ihrer Häßlichkeit doch rührend.

[Even for these epigones, the great names still remained Athens and
Homer, and they still occasioned a certain romantic fascination; but
their content had evaporated. The poet Angilbert, whose compan-

ions called him Homerus, was not able to write a single Greek letter, and in the imperial palace, which had begun to be compared with Athens, Greek was used only occasionally in order to communicate with the Eastern emperor. But the old Greek scraps which were taken from glossaries and commentaries in order to ornament one's own books, and which we curse today, were the imperial purple of the poets' robes at that time, and even in their ugliness they are touching.][31]

Traube still viewed the beginning of Greek studies as an event which appeared rather suddenly around 840, an inundation of Irish influence. We now see that the level of these studies at court continually rose through three successive generations. The opinion about the "old Greek scraps" is most appopriate for the first period of courtly culture under Charlemagne, defined by the Italian grammarians (ca. 780–95). The second, Anglo-Saxon period, with Alcuin, abbot of St. Martin at Tours, as its leading representative (796–804), still produced the instructive alphabetical table which Arn, abbot of St. Amand and archbishop of Salzburg, ordered to be written along with Alcuin's *Orthographia* (pl. 2). We can no longer be so certain that Angilbert, abbot of St. Riquier, was not "able to write" the Greek alphabet from such a table (which would of course still not justify the name "Homer," nor would Traube's sarcasm concerning the excessive self-esteem of the period be defused). In the third cultural period, as it were, at Charlemagne's court, which derived its impetus from native talents during the last decade of the emperor's life, translations of liturgical texts were probably already produced (see section 5, below). The first major translation came during the reign of Louis the Pious: Hilduin's *Dionysiaca*. Charles the Bald could continue the "traditions propres du Palais" ("the court's own traditions," Cappuyns); during his reign the high point of Carolingian Greek studies was reached. And not only that: this West Frankish Carolingian came to be the most important patron of Greco-Latin translations in the entire Middle Ages.

3. Italian Grammarians at Charlemagne's Court

A marriage plan most likely provided the external incentive for the first efforts to learn Greek at Charlemagne's court: Hruodtrud, Charlemagne's oldest daughter, was to marry Basileus Constantine VI. The betrothal was contracted in 781; two years later the grammarian Petrus Diaconus of Pisa, a teacher at Charlemagne's court, presented a poem in the king's name to the Lombard scholar Paulus Diaconus, who was crossing the Alps as a petitioner in another matter; the poem entreated Paul to remain in the Frankish Kingdom and teach Greek to the clerics who had been chosen to accompany the imperial bride. Paul did not value his own competence in this area very highly:[32]

> Graiam nescio loquellam, ignoro Hebraicam;
> Tres aut quattuor in scolis quas didici syllabas
> Ex his mihi est ferendus maniplus ad aream . . .

[I do not know the Greek language, I am ignorant of Hebrew; I learned three or four syllables in school; from them I must now bear the sheaves to the threshing floor . . .]

And he was accordingly skeptical of the success to be expected from his efforts:

> Si non amplius in illa regione clerici
> Graecae proferent loquellae quam a me didicerint
> Vestri, mutis similati deridentur statuis.

[If the clerics of this region produce no more Greek than they learn from me, they will be ridiculed as if they were mute statues.]

This self-critical statement by Paulus Diaconus was qualified, however, in the last stanza of the poem:

> Sed omnino ne linguarum dicar esse nescius,
> Pauca, mihi quae fuerunt tradita puerulo
> Dicam; cetera fugerunt iam gravante senio.

[But lest I be said to know nothing at all of languages, I will say a few things which were taught to me as a young boy; the rest have fled now that I am burdened by old age.]

What follows is a skillful Latin translation of a Greek original from the *Anthologia Palatina* (VII 542). The grotesque poem is very much after the manner of late Hellenistic tastes:

> De puero qui in glacie extinctus est.
> Trax puer adstricto glacie dum ludit in Hebro,
>   Frigore concretas pondere rupit aquas.
> Dumque imae partes rapido traherentur ab amni,
>   Praesecuit tenerum lubrica testa caput.
> Orba quod inventum mater dum conderet urna,
>   "Hoc peperi flammis, cetera," dixit, "aquis."

[On the boy who died in the ice. While playing on the frozen Hebrus, a Thracian boy broke through the frozen waters with his weight. And as his lower body was grasped by the fierce stream, an ice floe sliced off his youthful head. The deserted mother found it, put it in an urn, and said, "I bore this for the flames, the rest for the waters."]

Paulus Diaconus was still aware that this was a translation from Greek. Was Paul himself the translator? This opinion first appeared when it was discovered that Paul cited a translation from Greek.[33] On the other hand, it has been objected that the Latin translation was only quoted by Paul and was not his own work.[34] Conclusions drawn from manuscript evidence about the knowledge of Greek among Italian grammarians at Charlemagne's court support the latter interpretation.

We do not know what results came from Charlemagne's plan for Greek instruction. But Paulus Diaconus was certainly correct in his opinion that the Graeca in the school satchel of an Italian grammarian would scarcely suffice for an education in the language.

Ludwig Traube noted that one "could write a book" about the grammatical manuscript Diez. B. Sant. 66 of the Staatsbibliothek Berlin (Stiftung Preuß. Kulturbesitz), which he had discovered (*Einleitung*, p. 51). The manuscript gives an idea of what knowledge of the Greek language was to be found at the Carolingian court of the early period, which was characterized by the Italian scholars (facsimile edition by Bischoff, Graz 1973). A northern Italian, who may be identified by the content and arrangement of the volume as a grammar teacher at Charlemagne's court ca. 790, entered the following Graeca in the manuscript: the antiphon for Good Friday in Latin and Greek (in the Roman alphabet, p. 116): *crucem tuam adoramus—ton stauron su proskinomen*; then, the magnificat in Greek (in the Roman alphabet). The subsequent treatise on the alphabet contains the Greek majuscule alphabet in the historical presentation taken from Isidore's *Etymologiae* I 2. Further on in the treatise, the Greek numerals are dealt with, followed by a "list of the Greek names for nineteen rhetorical figures, most in corrupted form, with brief commentary"; Bischoff, introduction to the facsimile, p. 37. The most important Greco-Latin text in the codex is surely the *Grammatice artis nomina grece et latine praenotata* (p. 349; incomplete due to loss of quires). Except for the incorrect majuscule subscription to Servius' *De centum metris*—ΕΚΑΤΟΜΕΤΡΩΝ · ΚΑΤΑ ϹΕΡΒΩΝ ΤΕΛΩΝ (p. 277)—all Graeca in the manuscript are written in the Roman alphabet. Obviously the Italian grammarian made an effort to collect Graeca; it is interesting that as a result of this concern, he even included liturgical material, although the codex did not otherwise contain such material.

In 787 Paulus Diaconus returned to Italy; in the same year, at the second council of Nicaea (designated the seventh ecumenical council), Empress Eirene brought an end to the iconoclastic dispute. As a result of the political tensions between East and West caused by the council, the betrothal of Hruodtrud and Constantine VI, the son of the empress Eirene, was broken off. The response of the Carolingian court to the council of Nicaea was the "Libri Carolini."

4. Iconoclasm and the "Libri Carolini"

OPUS INLUSTRISSIMI ET EXCELLENTISSIMI SEU SPECTABI-
LIS VIRI CAROLI NUTU DEI REGIS FRANCORUM GALLIAS
GERMANIAM ITALIAMQUE SIVE HARUM FINITIMAS PROVIN-
TIAS DOMINO OPITULANTE REGENTIS CONTRA SYNODUM
QUE IN PARTIBUS GRAETIAE PRO ADORANDIS IMAGINIBUS
STOLIDE SIVE ARROGANTER GESTA EST.

Under this pretentious title, Charlemagne had the response to the second council of Nicaea (787) published in his name;[35] he had read through the text and added many comments in agreement with it;[36] the actual author was the Visigoth Theodulf, bishop of Orléans.[37] The cited title of the work reveals at once the basic error which undermined the Frankish position: it assumed that the council of the empress Eirene had sanctioned the *adoratio* of images (*pro adorandis imaginibus*). In the Greek conciliar acts, however, the veneration of images (ΠΡΟCΚΥΝΗCΙC) was sharply distinguished from the worship of God (ΛΑΤΡΕΙΑ). Charlemagne's court was not aware of this distinction; the council was "refuted" at this point on the basis of a Roman translation of the conciliar acts,[38] which rendered both concepts as *adoratio*. The Carolingian response ignored the theological foundation of the veneration of images through God's incarnation and concentrated on polemical comparisons between the value of images on the one hand and the eucharist, the Holy Scriptures, even the Ark of the Covenant and relics on the other:[39]

> You who say that you preserve the purity of your faith in images, stand humbly before them and commemorate with incense; we examine eagerly and with skillful investigations the Lord's commandments in the books of divine law. You survey the images in the light; we concentrate on the Holy Scriptures!

The Scriptures themselves and that which they designated holy are considered sacred by the "Libri Carolini"; and since some value is attributed to the remains of the Old Testament patriarchs, relics are valued by the Franks much more highly than images, about which it seemed to the Frankish theologians that there was nothing in the Bible.[40] The ambitious undertaking shows on the one hand how poorly equipped the Western theologians were in regard to Greek studies; on the other hand, the Western voluntarism is so extremely pronounced in the "Libri Carolini"[41] that there no longer seemed to be any means of communication with the contemplative theology of the East.

The "Libri Carolini" are more a manifesto of Western self-conceit than an actual serious dispute with Greek theology. Just how easily one capitulated to difficulties and took flight to cheap arguments is shown by the words "Quod gregorii niseni episcopi, ex quo illi ad suum errorem adstruendum testimonia trahunt, et uita nobis et praedicatio sit incognita" ("That the life and writings of Gregory, bishop of Nyssa, from whom they drew their evidence in constructing their erroneous arguments, are unknown to us"). (A facsimile of the corresponding page from Vat. Lat. 7207 is printed in *Karl der Große*, vol. II: *Das geistige Leben* [Düsseldorf 1965], p. 53.) The text explains that Gregory of Nyssa is unknown and thus it is not appropriate to adduce evidence from his works in controversial matters. In addition, only the prophets, the Gospels, and the Latin Fathers were to be admitted; the Greek Fathers could also be considered if they were *catholici* and had been translated into Latin *a catholicis*. The Westerners could not have more openly displayed the limitations of their own capabilities. Gregory of Nyssa's ΠЄΡΙ ΚΑΤΑϹΚЄΥΗϹ ΑΝΘΡѠΠΟΥ had been translated by Dionysius Exiguus, and in the second half of the eighth century this translation was also copied in Corbie: Paris, BN lat. 12134 (*CLA*, V, 621), with the colophon on fol. 212ᵛ *Explicit sancti Gregori Nyseni episcopi De imagine sub sequentia eorum que a fratre eius beato Basilio in Exahemero sunt relicta* ("Here ends the *De imagine* of St. Gregory of Nyssa, which is a continuation of the *Hexaemeron* of his blessed brother, Basil"); despite this remark, a note was added in the ninth century on the flyleaf—. . . *Gregorii Nazianzeni . . .* , which was then again corrected (at the earliest in the tenth century) to *Niseni*.

At an imperial synod in Frankfurt in 794, it was announced that the participants at the Council of Nicaea seven years before had pronounced a sentence of excommunication on all those "who do not offer service and worship to the images of the saints just as they do to the deified Trinity."[42] At this, Charlemagne's bishops unanimously rejected the Greek council. The abyss which had opened was deepened both theologically by Frankish efforts to dogmatize the Augustinian *filioque* by accepting it into the credo, and politically through the foundation of a Western Empire in 800.

The problem of images played an important role in the intellectual life far into the ninth century; for even though the second Council of Nicaea made the decisive step toward ending iconoclasm, which the Orthodox Church has since celebrated annually on the "Sunday of the Holy Fathers" in October, the iconoclastic dispute lasted for more than a hundred years thereafter before it was settled in 843; it was maintained that the iconoclastic principle was based on the Old Testament, but it also offers a striking parallel to the hostility toward images which the rising power of the time—the Arabs—exhibited. The Synod of Constantinople, which convened in 843 and put an end to the devastating inner dispute, has also become part of the liturgical memory of the East—the "Sunday of Orthodoxy" (first Sunday of Lent), on which a liturgical text is read which summarizes with the greatest of concision the Eastern theology of icons:[43]

The uncircumscribable word of God has circumscribed itself in his incarnation through you, Holy Mother of God. And by reestablishing the defiled image in its original form, it permeates the image with divine beauty. But confessing salvation, we portray this in word and deed.

The West reflected upon the development in the East. In the early years of the reign of Louis the Pious (814–40), the bishops Claudius of Turin and Agobard of Lyon took the field against the veneration of relics, saints, and images[44]—remarkably, these theologians also came from the area of Latino-Arabic contact in Spain, just as did Theodulf. But unlike Theodulf's "Libri," the corresponding works of Claudius and Agobard were no longer circulated under the emperor's name. Dissenting voices were raised against this "Carolingian Rationalism" (which, with respect to the images, was rather a Carolingian "Arabism"): Jonas of Orléans, the successor to Theodulf's episcopate (Theodulf was removed from office in 817), wrote De cultu imaginum against Claudius. The acts of a Parisian synod in 825 show the beginnings of a more discriminating view of the Eastern theology of icons than Theodulf's "Libri Carolini" and the acts of the Frankfurt Synod in 794.

To be sure, those in the West still used the poor translation of the conciliar acts which rendered both "veneration of images" and "worship of God" undifferentiated with adoratio, but now there was an attempt to distinguish between different forms of adoratio. At least the usefulness of the images was recognized;[45] the Byzantine conception of the testimonial value of the images could be approached through quotations from the Church Fathers. This change was influenced to a considerable degree by the Byzantine embassies sent to the West, by means of which the West was also to become acquainted with the Greek author who took precisely the opposite theological path from that of the positive "Libri Carolini"— Dionysius the Areopagite, the teacher of apophasis and theologia negativa.

5. Diplomatic Missions—Louis the Pious and Hilduin of St. Denis

After Charlemagne had conquered the Lombard King Desiderius (774) and made himself king of the Lombards, Frankish rule in Italy bordered on Greek territory. The plan of marrying a Frankish princess to the successor to the Greek throne was not thought of as a distant adventure, but rather its purpose was to bring two neighboring kingdoms into closer association. According to the Byzantine historian Theophanes, Charlemagne himself is supposed to have considered marrying the empress Eirene; of course this report does not harmonize very well with our conception of the great Charles.[46] Since 800 the Frankish Kingdom had been an Empire, and thus arose the "problem of the two emperors" ("Zweikaiserproblem").[47] An understanding between East and West was reached relatively quickly. Diplomatic missions were sent between Empress Eirene and Charlemagne (Byzantine missions in 799 and 802), and after

Emperor Nicephorus I (802–11) had, with the Greek fleet, restricted the limits of Frankish power to the land and retaken Venetia and Dalmatia from the Franks, ambassadors went back and forth annually between 811 and 815. This practice continues with greater intervals under Louis the Pious (Byzantine missions in 824, 827, 831, 833, 839), and even under his sons the connection was never completely broken. This link was of great importance for the development of Carolingian self-confidence; the literary echo was correspondingly polyphonic.

For the presentation copy of his "best seller" *De laudibus S. crucis*, intended for Emperor Louis the Pious, Hrabanus Maurus designed the famous figural poem that depicted the emperor himself and noted the xenial gifts of the Greeks with great honor:[48]

> En regna Graium omne per aevum munera donant
> Et Persa dat, sicque eius sobolis latus ambit.

> [Behold! Greece bestows gifts through all time, and the Persian too gives and thus draws nigh to his (Louis the Pious') son.]

The creator of the "Lotharpsalter" emulated Hrabanus when he recorded Emperor Lothar's reception of a Greek embassy in Trier in 842 with the following *titulus* next to the portrait of the emperor:[49]

> Hunc oriens recolit mittens ueneranter Achiuos
> Qui ueniam curui poscant et foedera pacis.

> [The East comes to visit again, and honorably sends Greeks who, bowing, seek your favor and covenants of peace.]

The Greeks found Frankish efficiency uncanny: ΤΟΝ ΦΡΑΝΚΟΝ ΦΙΛΟΝ ΕΧΙϹ · ΓΙΤΟΝΑ ΟΥΚ ΕΧΙϹ —"Francum amicum habeas, vicinum non habeas" ("May you have Franks as friends but not neighbors").[50] While the Greek ambassadors made a good impression in the West with their gifts, instruments, and liturgical chant, the Western legates had to tolerate many an insult on the Bosporus: the traditional method in Oriental politics came into play—the humiliating treatment of ambassadors, to which the Westerners did not always respond as shrewdly as in Notker's story (in the *Gesta Karoli*) of the turned-over fish.[51] It may be taken as reliable historical information that the embassy to Constantinople in 811, led by Abbot Heito of Reichenau (also bishop of Basel), was poorly treated.[52] Archbishop Amalar of Trier reports in the *Versus marini* on the embassy of 813, which he and Abbot Petrus of Nonantola led: the Westerners waited eighty days before they were allowed to appear and speak at court; the waiting time resembled imprisonment—this practice never changed.[53] On the other hand, the Byzantine embassy that came to Aachen in 812 in response to Heito's previous mission, also had insults to tolerate, if one can believe Notker's report. Notwithstanding, the Greeks are supposed to have provoked great admiration with their *organa*, which Charlemagne immediately ordered to be copied and built. Delighted by the Greek legate's singing of antiphons on the octave of Epiphany, Charles is also supposed to have commanded a translation of the antiphon series, and, Notker adds maliciously, he demanded such a speedy execution of his order that the clerics, who had not yet had breakfast, allowed the barbarism *conteruit* instead of *contrivit* to slip into the translation! In fact a series of antiphons for the octave of Epiphany does exist (Inc. *Veterem hominem*) which can be shown to be a contrafactum of a Greek series of antiphons; part of the tradition even contains the *conteruit* which Notker ridicules.

The story of the Heito whom Charles avenged is in Notker's *Gesta Karoli* II 6, ed. H. F. Haefele, 2nd ed., pp. 55 ff. The story about the translation of the antiphons follows (II 7, ed. Haefele, p. 58, with variant reading g). The edition by P. Jaffé, *Bibliotheca rerum Germanicarum* (1867), IV, 631–700, here 673, is based on the text of a group of manuscripts which Haefele (p. xxxviii) considers a revision of Notker's *Gesta Karoli* from the high Middle Ages. The verification of Notker's account and the determination of Greek models and even the melodies is due to research in musicology: Handschin, in *Annales Musicologiques* 2 (1954), 27–44; J. Lemarié, "Les antiennes 'Veterem hominem' du jour octave de l'épiphanie et les antiennes d'origine grecque de l'épiphanie," *Ephemerides Liturgicae* 72 (1958), 3–38; O. Strunk, "The Latin Antiphons for the Octave of the Epiphany," *Mélanges G. Ostrogorsky* (Belgrade 1964), II, 417–26. The antiphons are printed in seventeen pieces by Lemarié, pp. 6 f., according to the antiphonary of Compiègne (Paris, BN lat. 17436); cf. also Hesbert's *Corpus Antiphonalium Officii*, III. (The research is conducted without much coordination of effort: the editor Haefele does not take Handschin, Lemarié, or Hesbert into account; Strunk ignores the new edition of the *Gesta Karoli*, etc.)

The cited articles from musicology show that the series of antiphons had an early and extensive circulation; thus it must also be the case that the translation was disseminated from a Carolingian court. The *terminus ante quem* here is the antiphonary of Compiègne (Paris, BN lat. 17436) from the palace school of Charles the Bald.

The *Annales regni Francorum* report on the same Greek ambassadors of 812: "In Aachen, where they came to see the emperor, they received the contractual documents from him in the church and offered *laudes* in their fashion, that is, in Greek, by calling him Emperor and Basileus." There are a number of apparently contradictory concepts in this account. How could both titles *imperator* and ΒΑCΙΛΕΥC occur in Greek *laudes*? How could the Greeks do homage to Charlemagne *more suo* and at the same time offer him *laudes*, i.e., a quite specifically Western form of acclamation which begins "Christus vincit, Christus regnat, Christus imperat" ("Christ conquers, Christ rules, Christ governs")?

Or is it conceivable that the *laudes regiae* were translated from Latin into Greek? Remarkably a royal acclamation from the late Carolingian period, translated from Latin into Greek, has been preserved in Metz. This Carolingian city honored King Louis III (876–82), the son of Louis the German, with the acclamation. The text tradition indicates that even at that time the text already had a long history.

"Nam Aquisgrani, ubi ad imperatorem venerunt, scriptum pacti ab eo in ecclesia suscipientes more suo id est Greca lingua laudes ei dixerunt, imperatorem eum et basileum appellantes"; *Annales regni Francorum*, a. 812, ed. F. Kurze (Hannover 1895), p. 136. A Metz codex of the ninth century, edited by Prost in 1886, contains *laudes* translated into Greek:[54]

Metz, Bibl.	*uincit*		*regnat*	*superlaudabilis*
Munic.	Christos[a] nicha ·		Christos Uasileuge ·	Christos epenos ·
Cod. 351,				
fol. 78[r]	*nos serui regis*			
	Ẹmis duli ton uasileon ·			
			multi anni	
	E⟨xacuson Christe⟩		R̄P Iohanni apostolicu papa polla ta eti ·	
			servua illum	
	⟨Litrota⟩[b]		R̄P Filaxon autu ·	
			regi	*et eius potestati*
	E⟨xacuson Christe⟩[c]		R̄P Polla ta ethi[d] · Ludouuicu uasileon	ke aptukratoron ·
			multi anni	
			polla ta eti[e] . . .	

---

[a]Xp̄s, *ter scrib. Cod.*   [b]λ *Cod.*   [c]Ei *Cod.*   [d]*ex* ehi *corr. Cod.*   [e]*ex* egti *corr. Cod.*

The gaps in the tradition of the invocations are conspicuous. Metz 351 is evidently an incomplete copy of another tradition. The translation of the *laudes* is of not inconsiderable quality: compare how the translator solved the problem of the beginning acclamation which results from the two significations of ΒΑCΙΛΕΥΕΙ = *regnat* and *imperat* (cf. E. K. Kantorowicz, *Laudes Regiae* [Berkeley/Los Angeles 1958], pp. 27 f.). It is puzzling that Louis III, who was never emperor and is not known for having imperial aspirations, was called "Emperor and Autocrat"— ΒΑCΙΛΕΥC ΚΑΙ ΑΥΤΟΚΡΑΤΩΡ (the gloss *eius potestati* is incorrect). This discrepancy was already noted by Prost, who believed that he had found the solution to the problem in a letter of Pope John VIII, in which the son of Louis the German was encouraged to make an expedition to Rome (pp. 242 ff.). Kantorowicz thought, quite generally, "This translation, most likely, should be linked to the intellectual interests prevailing at the court of Charles the Bald" (pp. 27 f.). On the other hand, it should be noted how exactly ΒΑCΙΛΕΥC ΚΑΙ ΑΥΤΟΚΡΑΤΩΡ corresponds to the description of the imperial *laudes* of 812: "imperatorem eum et basileum appellantes." Even if the Metz tradition (from the Arnulf monastery, the home of the cult of the sacred progenitor of the Carolingian dynasty) is not itself the *laudes* translated into Greek in 812 (in a form adapted to a later Carolingian ruler), the preserved text at least gives an idea of the Greek *laudes* of that memorable embassy; and the address of the Western ruler as ΒΑCΙΛΕΥC ΚΑΙ ΑΥΤΟΚΡΑΤΩΡ is quite certainly the form of address mentioned in the imperial annals, with which Charlemagne was granted a rank similar to that which the

Eastern emperor possessed. The fact that a Greek embassy offered the *laudes* and that it did so in Greek has a symbolic importance even beyond its political significance. For the symbolic purpose of reviving the bilingualism of the ancient Roman Empire, the emperors in Constantinople also had themselves eulogized in Greek *and Latin* even in the tenth century; cf. Handschin, *Das Zeremonienwerk Kaiser Konstantins*, pp. 34 ff.: "Gotenspiel"; and pp. 49 ff.: "Was von den Cancellariis quaestoris bei den kaiserlichen Prozessionen zur Hauptkirche auf römisch gesungen wird." A new discussion of the Metz imperial *laudes* and their background by O. G. Oexle, "Die Karolinger und die Stadt des heiligen Arnulf," *Frühmittelalterliche Studien* 1 (1967), 250–364, here p. 302, and K.-U. Jäschke, "Zu Metzer Geschichtsquellen der Karolingerzeit," *Rheinische Vierteljahresblätter* 33 (1969), 1–13.

The decisive intellectual event of ninth-century Greco-Latin relations was set in motion by the Greek ambassadors of 827, who, while in Compiègne, presented Louis the Pious with the gift of Emperor Michael II: the four theological treatises and ten letters of Dionysius the Areopagite. The reception of the works of the Corpus Dionysiacum—as "a kind of sacred relic of Greek studies extending throughout the Middle Ages"[55]— begins with this uncial codex presented at that time and preserved up to the present.[56] Through Dionysius' works the apophatic element of Eastern thought, the consciousness of the unknowability of God, was opened up to the West. Hilduin, Alcuin's student and Emperor Louis' archchaplain and abbot of the monastery of St. Dionysius outside of Paris, was called upon by Emperor Louis to compose a *passio* on Dionysius;[57] Hilduin certainly also obtained the precious Greek codex so that he could write the biography of the patron saint of the monastery on the basis of Dionysius' works—for the martyr venerated in St. Denis was held to be the great Greek teacher.

While it was earlier believed that Hilduin translated only a few passages of the Greek codex for his *Passio S. Dionysii*,[58] it has been recognized since the research of Théry that Hilduin had a translation of the entire codex executed (ca. 831–35); Théry assumes that Greeks assisted in the translation.

Edition of Hilduin's translation by Théry, in *Études dionysiennes*, II (1937); preparatory study in *Études dionysiennes*, I (1932). According to Théry, the translation was produced "phonetically": taking part were a "lecteur," who read the Greek uncials aloud, a "traducteur," and a "scribe transcrivant sous la dictée et transcrivant par inadvertance les hésitations même de ce traducteur" ("a scribe transcribing from dictation and transcribing inadvertently even the hesitations of the translator"; *Études*, I [1932], 137). To Siegmund, "scheint der ganze Apparat des Übersetzens möglichst kompliziert aufgezogen" ("the entire translation apparatus seems to have been made as complicated as possible"); thus he explains the doublets of the translation (such as *divina ac dealis* for ΘΕΙΚΟC), from which Théry drew his own conclusions, on the basis of a working copy of the text, "in which either the translator himself or the corrector entered corrections either in the margin or even above the relevant word, which a scribe then copied side by side in the running text"; *Die Überlieferung*, pp. 183 f.

To be sure, Hilduin and his assistants were not successful in transposing Dionysius' basic theological principles into Latin in clearly recognizable form. The point in question is the contrast between affirmative and negative theology, ΚΑΤΑϕΑϹΙϹ and ΑΠΟϕΑϹΙϹ. While ΚΑΤΑϕΑϹΙϹ and ΚΑΤΑϕΑϹΚѠ are suitably translated with *professio/affirmatio* and *affirmare/praedicare*, ΑΠΟϕΑϹΙϹ and ΑΠΟϕΑϹΚѠ are rendered with *sententia* and *dicere*. These latter translations are of course not incorrect according to Byzantine and modern Greek semantics, but they do not convey what Dionysius intended—negation, absence, denial.[59] Because of this basic flaw, Hilduin's remarkable and pioneering translation could be no more than a preparatory work—preparatory to a translation which was the intellectual equal of the Greek text.

6. Charles the Bald and John Scottus

Although his elder half-brothers surpassed him in martial proficiency, Charles the Bald (840–77), son of Louis the Pious and his second wife, Judith, far surpassed them all as patron of the arts and literature. He was the actual successor to Charlemagne and Louis the Pious for only a few years as emperor (875–77); from the very beginning of his reign, however, he resolutely and successfully supported the intellectual heritage of the Carolingian palace schools. Approximately fifty literary works were dedicated to him,[60] among which there are not a few translations and adaptations from Greek.

The most important Carolingian schools were in the domain of Charles the Bald; they guaranteed the West Franks an intellectual importance even if their political significance was lacking. This fact becomes clear in the dispute between Pope Nicholas I and Patriarch Photius of Constantinople. Whereas the initiative in the conflict about images and the second council of Nicaea came from Charlemagne's court, and the papacy stood by patiently, two generations later the new controversy concerning the *filioque* and the papal primacy was carried on by Rome. But Nicholas did not want to do without the West Frankish scholars. He requested the judgments of the archbishops against the errors of the Greeks. Bishop Aeneas of Paris wrote a *Liber adversus Graecos* for the archbishopric of Sens in 868; Ratramnus of Corbie wrote a *Contra Graecorum opposita* for the archbishopric of Reims.[61] These works again played an important role at the beginning of the investiture controversy.[62]

Above all others, there was one at the court of Charles the Bald who wrote and translated to the glory of his patron—John Scottus, an Irishman without ecclesiastical rank who had been at the West Frankish court since 845 and who designated himself with the resonant name *Eriugena*, "Irish offspring," in his works.[63] Because of his own abilities, he was alone as valuable as many others together and soon brought renown to the ambitious court. It is generally assumed that he taught at the court school of Charles the Bald—wherever it may have resided—and that he introduced Martianus Capella's *Nuptiae Mercurii et Philologiae*, which was of great importance in the Middle Ages, into the educational system. In any case, he wrote *Annotationes ad Marcianum*.[64] The glosses to the ninth book of Martianus Capella, *De harmonia*, became especially important. John Scottus was the first to again understand the Greek terminology of this book, and thus he provided the basis on which musical theory could further develop and reach its zenith in the *Musica Enchiriadis* at the end of the Carolingian period.[65]

In an earlier work directed against the Saxon Gottschalk, *De praedestinatione*, John showed that he was theologically interested in Greek. He acquired a profound understanding of Greek only in the course of many years, most likely for the initial purpose of satisfying the pressing desire of his royal patron for a new and improved translation of the Dionysian codex which the aforementioned Greek embassy had presented to his patron's father, Louis. John was intensively occupied with the *Corpus Dionysiacum* in the period 850–60, and toward the end of the decade, as "still quite an unskilled beginner in Greek studies" (*rudis admodum tiro adhuc helladicorum studiorum*), he dedicated the completed translation to Charles the Bald.[66] At the same time, however, the dedicatory epistle makes clear that John had found pleasure in the well-nigh arcane theology of the Areopagite: "In my opinion it is a highly complex work which is quite remote from modern sensibilities, impenetrable for many, intelligible to few, not only because of its age, but also because of the profundity of its heavenly mysteries." John would not have been an Irish scholar if it were not precisely the remote and difficult aspects of the text that particularly excited him.

Thus he wrote an explanatory commentary on the translation of Dionysius' *Hierarchia caelestis*[67] and accepted another translation commission from Charles the Bald for a further major work of early Byzantine theology, the *Ambigua* of Maximus Homologetes (the Confessor), in which the author explained difficult passages of Gregory of Nazianzus and in doing so referred often to Dionysius the Areopagite. John wrote to King Charles:[68]

A very difficult task indeed, most orthodox of kings, you have imposed upon your humble servant, who is indeed very weak in Latin, and how much more so in Greek! Moreover, you have ordered me, as if learned in both languages [*veluti erudito utriusque linguae*] to expedite the work and hasten to its completion. But by the strength of my feeble intellect, I have both made haste and, guided and aided by grace, finished the work. Perhaps I would not have ventured into such dense obscurity and would have defended myself with some excuse, had I not seen that the aforementioned most blessed Maximus often introduces and elucidates in a wondrous manner in the course of his work the most obscure sentences of that most holy theologian, Dionysius the Areopagite, whose symbolic and theological interpretation I recently translated in like manner by your order.

The translations of Dionysius and Maximus comprise John's actual accomplishments for the court, which were celebrated even in poems as the patron's claim to renown.[69] At the same time or somewhat later John also executed other translations, which are thought to have come about in the course of his own philosophico-theological work, as preparatory work for his own writings. John seems to have been as little acquainted with Dionysius Exiguus' translation of the ΠΕΡΙ ΚΑΤΑCΚΕΥΗC ΑΝΘΡΩΠΟΥ of Gregory of Nyssa as were Theodulf and his assistants in the composition of the "Libri Carolini"; he translated the work again in his literal fashion.[70] A translation of Maximus' *Quaestiones ad Thalassium* has also been discovered,[71] and it has also been inferred from John's speculative works, which are to be dealt with presently, that he translated the *Ancoratus* of Epiphanius of Salamis for his own use.[72]

John Scottus translated word for word in the medieval manner. If one compares his translation of ΠΕΡΙ ΚΑΤΑCΚΕΥΗC ΑΝΘΡΩΠΟΥ with that of Dionysius Exiguus, it becomes clear how awkwardly the ninth-century Irish translator deals with the languages, in comparison with the Greco-Latin monk of the sixth century. Yet the literal mode of translation did have its advantages, precisely when dealing with a text as difficult as that of Dionysius. It reflected the Greek syntax with photographic exactitude in the Latin, and attempted to achieve precise accuracy at the expense of stylistic quality. John dealt with the Latin vocabulary with remarkable freedom; many Greco-Latin neologisms originated in his works.[73]

The knowledge gained through his activities as a translator imbued John with no slight measure of self-confidence. Eventually he had enough faith in his knowledge of Greek to try his hand, as a kind of Ausonius *redivivus*, at playful Greek and Greco-Latin verse:[74]

CΤΙΧΟΙ ΙΩΑΝΝΙC GLORIOSO REGI KAROLO

uiuas nunc	uiuas rex		plures	in	a͞r	annos
ΖΕC ΝΥΝ	ΖΗC ΒΑCΙΛΗC	ΠΛΙCΤΟΥC	ΕΙC	ΤΟΙC	ΕΝΙΑΥΤΟΥC	
futurus		x͞p͞o	congregare in	multa	saecula	
ΜΕΛΛΟΜΕΝΟC	Χ͞Ω	CΥΝΖΗΝ	ΕΙC	ΠΟΛΛΑC	ΑΙΩΝΑC	
salua			cui	a͞r	regnum	dedisti
X͞P͞E COCON	ΚΑΡΟΛΟΝ ΤΟ		ΤΗΝ	ΒΑCΙΛΕΙΑΝ	ΕΔΟΚΑC	

To be sure, the Irishman did not always write such ceremonial verse; from his reading of Ausonius and his knowledge of Greek, he also wrote the most biting epigram of his time:[75]

> Hic iacet Hincmarus cleptes vehementer avarus
> hoc solum gessit nobile, quod periit.

[Here lies Hincmar, an exceedingly greedy thief; the only good thing he ever did was die.]

His work with the very difficult Greek theological texts gave John the courage to write a commentary on the Gospel of John[76] and a homily on the prologue to that Gospel;[77] even in the twelfth century (when Rupert of Deutz wrote his commentary on John) such an undertaking was considered daring, since Augustine himself had already written a commentary on the fourth Gospel. Finally, John wrote a speculative work based on his knowledge of early Byzantine theology, which was itself unique in the West; he gave the book the Greek title ΠΕΡΙ ΦΥCΕШC ΜΕΡΙCΜΟΥ (*De divisione naturae*).[78] In the work he dealt with the order of creation, which was understood to represent the possibility of man's intellectual and spiritual ascent: body—vital movement—sense perception—reason—spirit. Thereafter come

> the three remaining steps of the ascent, one of which is the passage of the spirit into knowledge of all things which are near to God; the second is the passage of knowledge into wisdom, i.e., a fervent contemplation of truth, to the extent possible for a created being; the third and highest step is the miraculous submersion of the purest spirits into God himself, as if into the darkness of the most inconceivable and inaccessible light, in which the origin of all things is concealed, and then the night will give light just as the day. . . .[79]

For a long time it has been thought that the *Solutiones ad Chosroem* of a certain Priscianus Lydus were translated by John Scottus or one of his associates; see C. B. Schmitt, in *Catalogus Translationum*, III, 80 ff., and the bibliographical references there; also the article by M.-T. D'Alverny, in *Jean Scot Érigène et l'histoire de la philosophie*, pp. 145 ff.

Manitius suggests that "in this context, another of John's works is perhaps relevant, one which was still in Michelsberg in the fifteenth century—*Disputatio Theodori Graeci cum Johanne Scotto*."[80] This work would evoke our greatest interest, since it would put us on the trail of a Greek whom John could have consulted; it is, however, not one of John's works, but rather one by Honorius Augustodunensis—*Clavis physicae*[81]—the oldest copy of which displays on its title page (pl. 1):[82]

DISPVTATIO ABBATIS THEODORI GENERE GRECI ARTE PHI-
LOSOPHI CVM IOHANNE VIRO ERVDITISSIMO ROMANE EC-
CLESIE ARCHIDIACONO GENERE SCOTHO.

In the twin arch of a Romanesque building, the Greek THEODORVS, with the typical facial features of a Greek apostle type (Paul), and IOHANNES, in the style of a Roman philosopher, sit in disputation. The unshod Greek abbot and philosopher, wearing an open robe, holds a text band in his hand, on which a leonine hexameter appears:

> Dogmatis is lumen pandit per mentis acumen.

[He reveals the light of doctrine through the sharpness of his intellect.]

The Irishman, whom the patron or the artist held to be a Roman archdeacon, and who perhaps for that reason is represented with finely stitched shoes, is characterized by the text band:

> Inuolucrum rerum petit is fieri sibi clarum.

[He strives that the significance of things be revealed to him.]

Discussion between East and West, a Greek and an Irishman, revelation (*Dogmatis lumen*) and perception of significance behind the concealing veil of things (*Inuolucrum rerum*)—the title page, which the great symbolist Honorius Augustodunensis or an intelligent reader added to his *Clavis physicae*, is itself replete with symbols. It is unusual but understandable that John Scottus and not the author of the work is portrayed there, since Honorius Augustodunensis assimilated so much of John's ΠΕΡΙ ΦΥCΕWC ΜΕΡΙCΜΟΥ in his *Clavis physicae* that he labeled his book a *liber excerptus*. Honorius Augustodunensis thus considered John as his teacher or authority. But how does the Greek, Theodore, come into the picture? M.-T. D'Alverny, who published the illustrations of the Paris manuscript (formerly Bamberg?), understood *abbas Theodorus, genere Grecus, arte philosophus* to be Theodore of Tarsus, the first archbishop of Canterbury, and "évoquant la mémoire vénérée de Théodore, le dessinateur a voulu incarner l'autorité reconnue à l'*Orientale Lumen*"[83] ("by evoking the venerated memory of Theodore, the illustrator wished to incarnate the recognized authority of the *Orientale Lumen*").

A Greek named Theodore who debates with a Western scholar can in fact hardly be anyone else but Theodore of Tarsus. But is one not becoming involved in "confusions chronologiques" or demanding too much of twelfth-century symbolism if one explains the illustration as though the illustrator were trying to represent a historically authentic debate scene or a symbolic East-West intellectual encounter? In its representation of groups of people, the Middle Ages regarded as unimportant the verism of their actual contemporaneity; it allowed the Evangelists to sit on the shoulders of the prophets, prophets of various eras to converse with each other, John the Baptist to stand next to the Cross, etc. Yet the associations harmonize, are often symbolic, but are never as vague as in the interpretation noted above. A source would have to be postulated which associates Theodore of Tarsus and John Scottus—that is, if such a work did not already exist in the outline of the filiation of the great Western grammarians and their students; the work is practically unknown, but is nevertheless important in the history of the schools and education of the early Middle Ages; it has been given the appropriate name *Grammaticorum* διαδοχή. The text is transmitted in a manuscript of Ademar of Chabannes (d. 1034), an important writer from the Abbey of St. Martial in Limoges, and is traceable to the grammarian Gautbert (of Auxerre?) in the tenth century.[84] According to the *Grammaticorum* διαδοχή, Theodore of Tarsus was at the top of the genealogical tree of medieval erudition and grammatical knowledge. The illustrator of the Bamberg manuscript could reasonably link him with John Scottus in conversation—in a dialogue between Oriental teacher and Occidental student, which the unbroken tradition in the schools preserved for several generations, a "west-östlicher Divan" of scholars.

Since a considerable number of the names recorded in the *Grammaticorum* διαδοχή are also important for the study of Graecolatina, the text is edited here once again:[85]

Theodorus monacus quidam a tharso cilitię atque adrianus abbas scolę grecorum romę quondam positi · simulque grecis ac latinis litteris liberalibus quoque artibus instituti a papa romano britanniarum insulę sunt directi · ac eandem tam salubrirus fidei documentis quam eciam secularis philosofię inlustrarunt disciplinis · Quorum discipulatui Aldelemus quidam uir uenerandus inhęrens · Bedam dinoscitur habuisse successorem · Ex cuius fonte quidam cuius nomen excidit fluenta hauriens doctrinę · rhabanum cognomento Maurum eruditorem proprię reliquit scolę · Qui ab episcopis gallicanis siue a regibus francorum transmarinis a partibus docendi causa accitus · ac postmodum episcopatus honore ditatus · alchuini cognomento albini institutione est dotatus · Qui susceptę scolę eruditioni nauiter inseruiens[a] · doctrinę philosoficę smaragdo reliquit gimnica campestria · Quę ille theodulfo postmodo aurelianensi episcopo constituto · contradidisse uisus agnoscitur · Qui[b] iohannem scotigenam heliam ęque eiusdem gentis patriotam uirum undecumque doctissimum philosoficis artibus expoliuit · At helias heiricum informans · sapientię merito egolismensi[c] donatus est throno · Heiricus porro remigium sancti germani autricę urbis monacum alium quoque sancti amandi eiusdem ordinis edocens hubaldum · alterum litteris alterum praefecit musis · Remigii porro cum plurimi extiterint successores hi fuerunt

Leid. Voss. lat. O. 15 fol. 147ᵛ

cf. Ter. Maur. v. 2846 et Aug. *De civ. dei* XVIII 2 (ambo de Varrone); Beda V 18 (de Aldhelmo), Einhart, *Vita Karoli*, c. 25 (de Alcuino)

eminentiores ˙ Gerlannus senonum archiepiscopus ˙ vuido Autisioderensium presul ˙ gauzbertus quoque ipsius germanus never-
nensium pontifex ˙ daoch quoque brittigena ˙ qui omnes gallias doctrinę suę radiis inlustrarunt ˙ Ambrosius quoque hisraelis preceptor
auditoris[c'] ˙ egroalis ˙ Gontio[d] nihilominus ˙ quorum alter britanniam
alter italiam septemplici minerva celebrem reddidit ˙ E quorum fon-

fol. 148[r] tibus hi qui hodieque studere dinoscuntur ˙ eruditio/nis eorum
riuulos exhauriunt ac sitibundis doctrinę pocula refundunt ˙ Quorum
ciatos quia fialas nequaquam[e] assequi ualet quidam non modo opere
uerum monacus gautbertus[f] sola professione guttatim sitiens exsor-
bet ˙ Scutellarum nihilominus mensis illorum sublatarum reliquias
lingendo adlambit ˙ Infelix prorsus qui sensus acumine hebetatus ex-
saturari nequit famelicus ˙

Recapitulatio nominum ˙ Theodorus monacus et abbas adrianus ˙
aldelmo instituerunt grammaticam artem ˙ Aldelmus ˙ bedam ˙ Beda ˙
rhabanum ˙ Rhabbanus ˙ alcuinum[g] ˙ Alchuinus ˙ smaragdum ˙ Smaragdus ˙ theodulfum ˙ Theodulfus ˙ iohannem et heliam reliquit set
non imbuit ˙ Elias ˙ heiricum ˙ Heiricus ˙ hucbaldum et remigium ˙
Remigius gerlannum episcopum ˙ Gerlannus[h] ˙ guidonem episcopum
autisioderensium ˙

---

[a]uel insistens *supr. lin.* [b]Qui per *Cod.* [c]egolismensis *Cod.* [c']*lectio* Bethmann, *valde incerta.*
[d]*Gonno legit* Delisle. [e]nequat qui *Cod.* [f]*gau/b̄/, manus altera primo loco/scripsit z, secundo*
inus, *an nomen* Gauzlinus *substituere intendens?* [g]*Nomina Hrabani et Alcuini signis invertit*
aliquis. [h]*littera* l *super aliam, incertam, ducta.*

[A certain monk named Theodore, from Tarsus in Cilicia, and
Hadrian, abbot of the schola of the Greeks, both previously in Rome
and educated in both Greek and Latin and also in the liberal arts,
were sent by the Roman pope to the island of the Britons, which they
illuminated with the healing documents of the faith and also the disciplines of secular philosophy [668 A.D.]. The honorable Aldhelm
clung to them as a student [Aldhelm of Malmesbury, d. 709] and is
known to have had Bede as successor [the Venerable Bede, d. 735].
A certain person, whose name has passed from memory, drank the
streams of learning from Bede's spring [the anonymous teacher is
elsewhere identified as Simplicius; Ademar, *Histor.* III 5; *Migne PL*
141, col. 30] and left behind Hrabanus, called Maurus, as the head of
his own school [Hrabanus Maurus, d. 856]. He was summoned as a
teacher by the Gallic bishops, or rather the kings of the Franks, from
across the sea and afterwards endowed with episcopal office and entrusted with the education of Alcuin, called Albinus [Alcuin, d. 804].
He diligently served the erudition of the school which he had taken
over and left the field of philosophical learning to Smaragdus [Sma-
ragdus of St. Mihiel, d. ca. 830]. He seems to have later given it over
to Theodulf, later bishop of Orléans [Theodulf of Orléans, d. 821].
He trained in the arts of philosophy John the Irishman [John Scottus,
d. ca. 880] and Elias, of the same country and an all around learned

man, [Elias, bishop of Angoulême 861–75]. And Elias trained Heiric [Heiric of Auxerre, d. 876] and was by reason of his wisdom endowed with the see of Angoulême. Next Heiric taught Remigius, a monk of St. Germanus in Auxerre, and Hucbald, another monk of St. Amand from the same order. The former he set up over scholarship [Remigius of Auxerre, d. ca. 908], the latter over the muses [Hucbald of St. Amand, d. 930]. And, since there were many descendants of Remigius, only the most prominent will be mentioned here: Gerlannus, archbishop of Sens [d. 954]; Wido, bishop of Auxerre [d. 961]; his brother Gauzbertus, bishop of Nevers [d. after 958]; the Briton Daoch [*Daocius Reuvisii seu Ruyensis in Armorica monasterii abbas*? (d. after 917; Mabillon, *Annales OSB*, III, 357)]; they illuminated all of Gaul with the rays of their learning. Also Ambrosius [?], teacher of his hearer [?] Israel [Israel of St. Maximin in Trier, d. after 947], Egroalis [?], and also Gontio [Gunzo of Novara? (d. after 956)], of whom the former made Britannia famous through the sevenfold Minerva; the latter did the same for Italy. Those who study today drink from their fountains, the brooks of their erudition, and they serve up cups of knowledge to the thirsty. One of them, Gautbertus [of Auxerre?], who is a monk only by vow and not by works, sips thirstily, drop by drop, from their goblets, since he can by no means reach their saucers; he licks the remains from the dishes placed on their table; utterly miserable, he cannot be satiated, though famished, since his intellect is so dull.

A recapitulation of the names: the monk Theodore and Abbot Hadrian taught Aldhelm the art of grammar; Aldhelm taught Bede; Bede Hrabanus; Hrabanus Alcuin; Alcuin Smaragdus; Smaragdus Theodulf; Theodulf left John and Elias, but did not initiate them; Elias taught Heiric, Heiric Hucbald and Remigius; Remigius Bishop Gerlannus; Gerlannus Bishop Wido of Auxerre.]

In the same century that the illustration of John Scottus in debate with Theodore the Greek was executed, William of Malmesbury wrote that toward the end of John's life, as his orthodoxy began to be questioned in France, he went to the court of Alfred the Great of Wessex; he then taught in Malmesbury and was murdered by his students there: "a pueris quos docebat grafiis foratus animam exuit" ("He died, stabbed by his students with their styli").[86] The martyrdom of St. Cassian, which was known from Prudentius, provided the basis of this legend. An unidentified person also discovered the students' motive for the murder of their teacher: he apparently compelled them to think.[87]

VIII

Carolingian Monasteries

Monastic Schools and Cathedral Schools

The Carolingian realms were centralized, agrarian, and monastic. Counts, cities, and bishops played subordinate roles to the royal courts and monasteries. Artisans and intellectual activity were found primarily in the large monasteries. The "Plan of the St. Gall Monastery" expresses most clearly the full range of activities found in a Carolingian monastery: agriculture, stock-raising, horticulture, brewing, the trades of the blacksmith, gold smith, armorer, harness-maker, and many others necessary for day-to-day needs, care of the ill, lodging, and service to the king, school, and library . . . and everything in the rhythm of the *divinum officium*.[1] The idea of the "great monastery" was not a Carolingian innovation, nor was this the kind of monastery founded by Benedict of Nursia. It developed during the "Dark Ages": Visigothic Spain in the time of Leander and Isidore of Seville developed the highly organized, culturally active monastery, "rich in gold, jewels, servants, land, and livestock."[2]

Monastic schools and libraries were superior to cathedral schools and libraries in the ninth century, but the monasteries were not the only centers of intellectual life. In at least two episcopal cities of the Carolingian realm, there are, now as then, ancient book collections which reach far back into late antiquity: in Verona and Lyon. In the ninth century, there were librarians and scholars in those cities who could appreciate and use these treasures. Archdeacon Pacificus of Verona, whose name is immortalized in the Cathedral of Verona in the three sacred languages—

> Pacificus Salomon mihi nomen atque Irenaeus
> Pro quo funde preces mente legens titulum[3]

[Pacificus, Salomon, and Irenaeus are my names; by reading this inscription, may you remember me in your prayers.]

—was at least interested in Greek.[4] Many entries in the Greco-Latin psalter of the cathedral library in Verona show that the codex was not merely a showpiece.[5]

In the mid-ninth century, Deacon Florus in Lyon studied the bilinguals of the Gospels and Acts, now called "Codex Bezae," and Archbishop

Ado of Vienne made use of some texts in the manuscript for his martyrology.[6]

Rome was the most notable exception to the rule of monastic preeminence over episcopal cities in the ninth century; its intellectual strength grew rapidly in the second half of the ninth century, only to deteriorate so much the more in the tenth century. Throughout the Latin Middle Ages, however, Rome, the only ancient metropolis in the West, had its own unique development. In general, it was not until the tenth century that the episcopal cities, cathedral schools, and cathedral libraries began their rise and gradually surpassed the monastic establishments.

1. Greek in the Monastic Schools? Tours, Fulda, Corbie

Formerly, scholars too readily overestimated the possibility of Greek studies in Carolingian monasteries and drew far-reaching conclusions from the presence of a few Greek terms in the works of Carolingian authors; yet these Graeca often signify no more than that the Carolingians had studied earlier authors with great attention and had learned the Greek alphabet. In Tours there was a tradition of interest in Greek which went back to the Merovingian period. At least one Greek manuscript was to be found there (see above, Chapter II, n. 69). A grammarian's manuscript from mid-eighth-century Tours (Wolfenbüttel, Weiss. 86) shows traces of Greek studies. In another manuscript of the same period, Greek letters are used as numerals.[7] During Alcuin's abbacy in Tours (796–804), Jerome's *epist*. 106, the famous model of biblical textual criticism, addressed to the Goths Sunnja and Friþila, was added to a manuscript containing Jerome's Psalterium iuxta Hebraeos.[8] Thus one had to come to terms with the Greek words with which Jerome had seasoned his letter. In a Tours evangelary, which dates to the time 800–810, the scribe Adalbald asked God's help in the following manner:[9]

ΔC ΛΔHCΘω CKϝIBHNΘH ΛΔΛΛBΛΛΔω
[deus adesto scribenti Adalbaldo]

Around 840, the oldest preserved codex of Suetonius' *Caesares* was written.[10] This text is one of those works of Latin antiquity which are quite thoroughly permeated with Graeca. One can recognize that painstaking care, but also helplessness with word division and doubtful readings or mistakes in the source manuscript, attended the copying of the text. The Greek passages were generally copied without having been understood, which indicates that there was no Greek instruction in Tours, even on a very elementary level. As abbot, Alcuin did not usher in a renaissance in this regard.

There are no indications in Alcuin's works that he had learned Greek. Still, one can give him credit for studies of the kind shown in the fine Greek alphabetic and numerical table of Cod. Vindobonensis 795 (see pl. 2). This pedagogical page with the title "Formae litterarum secundum grecos" contains the Greek alphabet in majuscule, in part with variants (e.g., the M siglum appears as a variant). The names of the letters are written above them (*alpha, bita,* in Byzantine iotacism). The Latin equivalent is given at the left (*pro a, pro b . . .*); at the right, the name of the letter, when it is read as a numeral (*mia, dia*) and the numerical value in Roman numerals. The manuscript was written around 799 for Alcuin's friend Arn of Salzburg and contains Alcuin's letters, in addition to other material.[11] The circumstances make it appear probable that we have a work of Alcuin's school before us in this instructive alphabetical table. At the very least, it enabled the scribe and reader to copy the Greek letters and understand their phonetic value correctly.

Alcuin's most famous student was Hrabanus Maurus, who, while still a young man, became well known for his figural poem *De laudibus sanctae crucis* (ca. 810). Some of these poems take the form of Greek letters.[12] The twelfth poem, for example, yields the following figure:

The accompanying heading reads "De nomine Adam protoplasti, quomodo secundum Adam significet et eius passionem demonstret." Hrabanus undoubtedly took this interpretation of the name Adam as an anagram of the four points of the compass from Augustine (see Chapter III):

Λ   ΝΑΤΟΛΗ
Δ   ΥCΙC
Λ   ΡΚΤΟC
Μ   ΕCΗΜΒΡΙΑ

He then arranged the tetragram in the form of a cross, whereby he created additional opportunities for exegesis, without detracting from the Augustinian symbolism; the explanation of the numerical value of ΛΔΛΜ = 46 in terms of the temple in Jerusalem, which was built in the same number of years, is also found in Hrabanus' commentary on the figural poem. The fourteenth poem represents in Greek letters the numeral 5,231 as "the number of years from the creation of the world to the year of the passion and resurrection of the Lord"![13] The twenty-second figural poem is even more clearly Grecized; it seems to be strewn with Greek letters. The letters produce Greek words (not always entirely correct)— Ο CΟΤΗΡ ΙΗCΥC ΛΛΗΘΙΛ . . .—and the whole merges into the figure of a "monogram" of the name of Christ: ☧ .

What Alcuin was for the school in Tours, Hrabanus was for the one in Fulda. Under Hrabanus the monastery of Fulda, located in the far eastern reaches of the Frankish kingdom, became an intellectual focal point that drew students from all points of the compass, even from the West, which had an abundance of schools of its own. During the Thirty Years' War, however, Fulda's ancient monastic library (still intact at that point) was in large part destroyed, so that it is especially difficult to reconstruct the state of Greek studies in early medieval Fulda. The usual traces of evidence from manuscripts, necessary for composing a picture of the elements of Greek studies, are generally lacking, since the manuscripts themselves have been lost.

At any rate the school had access to the Greek alphabet; in emulation of Bede's *De temporum ratione*, Hrabanus included it in his *Computus*.[14] Undoubtedly there were also Greco-Latin books of the Bible in Fulda. A library catalogue, compiled during Hrabanus' abbacy (822–47), lists a typical inventory of bilinguals:

Item euangelium iohannis et lucae grecolatinum˙
Item psalterium grecolatinum˙
Item epistolae pauli grecolatinae˙

Cod. Vat. Pal. lat. 1877, fol. 36ᵛ; cf. Becker, *Catalogi*, no. 128. The library catalogue was not compiled in the twelfth century (Becker), but rather around 830 in Fulda (B. Bischoff, *Lorsch im Spiegel seiner Handschriften* [Munich 1974], p. 10). The bilingual Psalter appears to have still been in Fulda in the sixteenth century; cf. the late catalogue (I 6) printed by Falk in *Beiträge zur Rekonstruktion der alten Bibliotheca fuldensis* (Leipzig 1902), p. 89.

After A. Allgeier's *Bruchstücke eines altlateinischen Psalters aus St. Gallen*, SB Heidelberg (1929), p. 56, n. 1, the conjecture that the inter-linearly glossed bilingual Psalter of the Würzburg seminary came from Fulda is found in the scholarly literature on the subject. There is no reason to accept this supposition, however, especially since the ninth-century library catalogue of the Würzburg Salvatorstift lists a *Grecum psalterium* (Becker, *Catalogi*, no. 18, 88). The codex, whose text was closely related to the "Basel Psalter" (Allgeier, "Exegetische Beiträge," pp. 268 f.), was evidently of Irish origin, as had already been noted by F. Delitzsch, "Über iroscotische Bibelhandschriften," *Zeitschrift für luther. Theologie und Kirche* 25 (1864), 217–23. The codex burned in 1945.

These bilinguals are no longer extant; but a descendant of the group is perhaps preserved in the Psalter Kues, Cod. 10.[15] Traces of other material relevant to the topic of Greek studies are identifiable in several scattered ninth- and tenth-century manuscripts from Fulda.[16] In general, however, the researcher has little evidence beyond the Graeca found through an examination of the Fulda authors. Here one must mention Hrabanus' student Bruun Candidus, whose *Vita Eigilis* (ca. 840) includes several examples of "ornamental Greek."[17] His contemporary Ermenrich of Ellwangen went still further in his *Vita B. Soli*, where he begins to experiment with a Greco-Latin macaronic style: instead of *Valde mirabilem*, he calls St.

Solus of Solnhofen *Sfodra mirabilem*,[18] because he needed the *s* for the acrostic of the name! Later, while a guest in St. Gall, he demonstrated that he could elegantly transform a Greek glossary or a bilingual into a macaronic poem:[19]

> Hoc ipse exponat posco problema tibi:
>
> *vinum butyrum bibe   lac   oleum*
> Oenon paleon   pimelin gallan eleon,
>
> Et non miraris dulcia nosse tua.
>
> *Novum vide loquor verbum move sorbeo prandium*
> Neon ide lalo   rema   sison ripho ariston,
>
> Vescere qui poteris tuque poeta tuis.
>
> *curator   sapiens   sufflat studium   mortuus*
> Phrontistes phronimos phisa philoponia nechros,
>
> Hoc fecit Christus primus in orbe deus.

Artistically, the poem is of little significance, but quite the opposite is true from the perspective of literary history, for Ermenrich's wit shows that John Scottus did not invent the Greco-Latin linguistic mannerism that was so common in the late Carolingian period, but rather that there was such a tendency much earlier.

Only with some reservations can Walafrid Strabo, Einhart, and Lupus of Ferrières be counted as members of Hrabanus' school. They are all associated with it, but there is no conclusive evidence that Fulda was the primary source of their education. Walafrid Strabo took an interest in the relations of language and history and in one passage betrays a surprising insight into the relationship between Greek and Gothic.[20] Einhart was able to quote a Greek proverb about the Franks.[21] Lupus of Ferrières occasionally consulted him about Greek words in Boethius and Servius.[22] Lupus, who is considered the most distinguished of Carolingian humanists, also left traces of an interest in Greek studies in his notebooks. Thus, for example, in his fine, broad-margined copy of Cicero's *De natura deorum*,[23] he especially emphasizes the Graeca. The situation was the same for many scholars during the earlier Carolingian period; they could find their way relatively well when it was a question of isolated words or a simple sentence, or where the corresponding Latin text was familiar, as in liturgical texts. The motivation was lacking for in-depth studies; the re-formed and revived form of Latin was already enough of a task to learn.

Among the exegetes of the ninth century, Paschasius Radbertus of Corbie and Christian of Stablo are considered the most knowledgeable of the Greek traditions. Paschasius Radbertus used an ancient translation of Origen's commentary on Matthew in writing his own commentary on the work.[24] He also seems to have had recourse to the Greek text of the gospel.[25] The same is true of Christian of Stablo, who also wrote a commentary on the first gospel around the year 865.[26] He was able to differentiate between ΟCΙΟC and ΑΓΙΟC, ΕΠΙΦΑΝΕΙΑ and ΘΕΟΦΑΝΕΙΑ, and especially ΔΟΥΛΕΥCΙC and ΛΑΤΡΕΥCΙC:[27]

'Dominum Deum adorabis.' Adorare est autem tota fide Dominum   Matt. 4:10
credere et ex totis praecordiis diligere, remissionem peccatorum petere, et omnia bona ab illo sperare praesentia et futura. Graece autem differentius hoc dicitur, ubi adorare quod ad Deum pertinet proscynesai dicitur ΠΡΟCΚΥΝΗCΑΙ adorare quod ad hominem pertinet ΚΑΙΝΕΙΝ dicitur: 'Et illi soli servies.' Quid est hoc quod dicit   Matt. 4:10
Dominus, 'Illi soli servies,' cum Paulus apostolus dicat 'per charitatem servire invicem'? Nunquid aliud dominus praecepit, et aliud   Gal. 5:13
Paulus? . . . In Graeco quoque sermone similiter est differentia de hac re. Siquidem servitium quod ad hominem pertinet douleusis, ΔΟΥΛΕΥCΙC, dicitur, et servus doulos, ΔΟΥΛΟC, dicitur. Illud vero servitium quod ad solum Deum pertinet ΛΑΤΡΕΥCΙC vocatur. Unde in cantico Zachariae non dicitur douleusate, ΔΟΥΛΕΥCΑΤΕ,   Luke 1:74.
sed latreuein, ΛΑΤΡΕΥΕΙΝ ΑΥΤΩ serviamus illi. Has discretiones debemus scire inter creaturam et creatorem, ut a nullo sancto petamus remissionem peccatorum, sed per eos studeamus impetrare, ut detur nobis a Deo; neque credamus in aliquem, nisi in Deum, quia credimus sanctos, sed non credimus in sanctos.

["You will worship the Lord God." Now to worship is to believe in the Lord with all your faith and to love him with all your heart, to seek the remission of sins, and to place your hope in him for all good things, present and future. This is said differently in Greek, however, where *adorare* is called *proscynesai* when it refers to God, but *klinein* when it refers to man. "And you will serve him alone." What does this mean, that the Lord says "You will serve him alone," while the apostle Paul says "serve one another through love"? Is it that the Lord teaches one thing and Paul another? . . . In this matter also, Greek differs in a similar manner. If the service is rendered to man, it is called *douleusis*, and the servant *doulos*. But the service rendered to God is called *latreusis*. Thus in the canticle of Zacharius, it is not *douleusate* but *latreuein auto*, "let us serve him," that is said. We ought to be aware of these distinctions between the created and the creator, so that we do not seek the remission of sins from a saint, but strive to attain through them that God grant it to us. And let us not believe in anyone except it be God, since we believe there to be saints but do not believe in the saints.]

Through this realization the inaccurate tendencies of the "Libri Carolini," which had arisen from a lack of differentiation between the various Greek terms, were also overcome: all were rendered in the translator's Latin of the time with *adorare*.

Christian of Stablo also understood Greek orthography to some extent and had surprising insight into the nature of the abbreviations of the "nomina sacra."[28] It is assumed that he consulted the Greek text of the Gospel of Matthew; perhaps he even had a bilingual evangelary. He mentioned that he had seen "a book of the Gospels written in Greek which was said to have belonged to Hilary, in which Matthew and John came first, and the other two thereafter. I then asked Euphemus the Greek why this was so. He said to me: 'after the model of a good farmer, who yokes his stronger oxen in front.'"[29]

This is one of the passages which makes Christian of Stablo an interesting—in the literary historical sense—exegete of the ninth century. It was thus evidently possible for Christian to consult with a Greek in the Frankish Kingdom. With this information, a new historical perspective appears to open up, and the *Graecus quidam* with whom Lupus of Ferrières consults[30] takes his place beside Christian's informant. An expert in this area of study informs us, however, that the "Greek Euphemus" could also have been an Irishman: "This Euphemus may of course have been a Greek, as his name, if genuine, suggests; but the fact that he is called 'Graecus' need not by itself mean more than that he knew some Greek. For 'Graecus' is a sobriquet applied to Irishmen who had some acquaintance with that language";[31] and Lupus' *Graecus quidam* was "probably an Irishman with a little Greek rather than a Greek."[32] This daring interpretation is a reflex of Ludwig Traube's "Irish thesis."

2. The "Irish Thesis": *Graeci* and *Scotti*

"Anyone on the Continent who knew Greek during the time of Charles the Bald was either an Irishman or without question had acquired this knowledge from an Irishman, or else the report which surrounded the person with such renown was a fraud. The entire development is characterized by the fact that the copy of Dionysius the Areopagite which Paul I once sent to King Pepin was first understood and translated for Charles the Bald by the Irishman John Scottus."[33] These sentences, from Traube's 1892 treatise "O Roma nobilis," became the new "Irish thesis" which replaced the older opinion of the survival of classical studies in Ireland during the Dark Ages: there was no profound study of Greek during the seventh and eighth centuries, while in the ninth century, the subject was to a certain extent the exclusive domain of the Irish.

Traube's "Irish thesis" is so exceptionally accurate—as will be shown here also—that in the few instances in which it does not account for the facts of the case, it has had a coercive influence on other research toward an accommodation to its principles. An imaginary "insular impact" was

seen, for example, in the Reichenau Pauline bilingual in order to subsume the text under this thesis,[34] and *Graeci* were interpreted to be Grecizing *Scotti*.

But there were Greeks even in the Carolingian realm. Alcuin mentions
a question "cuiusdam sapientis Greci," which this person, who is called
"Atheniensis sophista ex achademica scola" at another place, had posed
"quibusdam catholicae eruditionis filiis in palatio."[35] (The question with
which the Greek upset the "Palace school" was what sort of price is meant
in 1 Cor 6:20: "Empti enim estis pretio magno.")

In his *Translatio SS. Marcellini et Petri*, Einhard tells of a "iuvenis inter
cubicularios regis, natione Graecus, nomine Drogo," who was healed in
Einhard's *oratorium* in Aachen in 828, while a portion of Marcellinus' relics, returned by Hilduin, was there.[36] Was this chamberlain of Louis the
Pious possibly an assistant of Hilduin in the translation of Dionysius? At
any rate, Einhard's miracle story—as was so often the case in the genre of
miracula in the Middle Ages—transmits valuable historical details; and
the presence of at least *one* native Greek at the court of Louis the Pious is
guaranteed.

Around the middle of the ninth century, a Greek named Jacob lived in
Bourges; he is supposed to have led a glorious life in Constantinople at
the court of Leo V (813–20; the Armenian known as the reviver of iconoclasm), and then after a pilgrimage to Palestine to have come to Bourges.[37]
One would like to be able to trace the reply of Euphemus the Greek to
Christian of Stablo back to such an anchorite, since his account of the
ancient Christian arrangement of the Gospels, "after the model of a good
farmer, who yokes the stronger oxen in front," is quite characteristic of an
apopthegm.

3. St. Denis: The *Hymnos Akathistos*

The first major translation from Greek in medieval Europe north of the
Alps is accounted for through the presence of Greeks in St. Denis. It is
conjectured that they assisted in the first translation of Dionysius, since it
is difficult to imagine how a translation—even one as slavishly literal as
Hilduin's—could have been produced with the resources available:
glossaries, bilinguals, late antique grammatical treatises. Recently the
conjecture has been advanced that the first Western attempt at a Greek
grammar is also to be attributed to these "deduced" Greeks in St. Denis.[38]

In a methodologically interesting study, Michel Huglo has ascribed the
ancient Latin translation of the *Hymnos Akathistos*, discovered by Paul
von Winterfeld,[39] to Hilduin's translators in St. Denis.[40] The Greek *Hymnos Akathistos* may go back to Romanos Melodos.[41] It was not later than

the end of the iconological conflict that the officium of the hymn ("during which one was not seated") was included in the Byzantine liturgy on Saturday before the fifth Sunday of Lent. The occasion became a festival of thanksgiving to Mary for the deliverance of Constantinople from its great afflictions—the siege of the Persians and Avars in 626 and the sieges of the Arabs in 677 and 717. It became the festival in celebration of the events of the Dark Ages, which were seen as miraculous by the religiously sensitive (and as astounding by the historical scholar), and which made Constantinople into the bulwark of Christianity without whose protection even the West would not have been able to develop as it has. This was understood by very few during the Middle Ages. Perhaps the patron or translator of the Latin version of the *Akathistos* was among those who did understand; but its translation could have just as well been motivated by the profusion of metaphorical language and symbolism of the Virgin Mary or even by the fame of the text in general. The *Hymnos Akathistos* was after all practically *the* hymn of the Byzantine Empire.[42]

Thus begins the victory-bearing and healing hymn of the holy mother of God, Mary, which was rhythmically composed by the holy Patriarch Germanus of Constantinople and whose individual sections begin in alphabetical order, and which originated thus:

In the days of Theodosius [III; 715–17], the predecessor of Leo [III], the father of Constantine who is called *Calvus* [Constantine V; 741–75], at the time when Chilperic ruled the Franks, Maslamah, the ruler of the Saracens, heard of the splendor and wealth of the city of Constantinople, assembled an infinite military force on land and sea, and led them to the city and laid siege to it. While he sorely afflicted the city with daily attacks, one morning, at the beginning of his address to the troops . . . he saw a woman of unimaginable brightness, clothed in purple, with a powerful host of white-robed men, descend from Heaven, proceed around the walls of the city, and hold up a pallium toward the walls; in its protection, under God's sign, the city remained safe and the enemies' strength dissipated. Thence it happened that this Maslamah perceived the divine miracle and requested that he be allowed to enter the city with only one thousand men; he was granted his request, brought many gifts, worshiped the Lord and the holy Virgin, gave his hand on an alliance, and returned to his lands.

Theodosius, however, although he performed his duties valiantly, was shorn as a cleric within a short time and agreed to Leo [III; 717–41] as his successor to the throne. Leo cruelly and unjustly drove the aforementioned holy man, Germanus, . . . who was already over ninety years old, from his see into a *diaconia* which is called *Istabiru* [εἰς τὰ βήρου?] in Greek, and—oh woe!—had him treacherously killed. He is buried in the monastery called Istaromeus [εἰς τα Ῥωμαίου?], where to the honor of our Lord Jesus Christ he is revered with appropriate veneration, befitting the glory of the martyrs.

And as a result of these things, the praiseworthy and exemplary custom was established by this distinguished man and his successors and came to be accepted practice, that every year at the festival of the Annunciation, . . . as if in unison the city sang the triumph which the 318 Fathers of the Nicaean Council under Constantine the Great had commended to the Virgin, at the public station of the aforementioned festival, which is called "In the Open Fields" [*ad Blachernas*], and in all catholic churches of Greece.

After every OIKOC "in response to the preceptor," the people then sang Germanus' ephymnion in which the city thanks its patroness for its deliverance and entreats:

> Sed sicut habens imperium inexpugnabile
> de omnibus periculis me libera
> ut clamo tibi:
> Ave sponsa insponsata!

[But just as you hold the empire impregnable, free me from all dangers as I cry out to you: Hail to the bride unwedded!]

Then follows the rhythmically varying abecedarian hymn with its unprecedented wealth of Mary's attributes, translated so literally, to be sure, that the St. Gall scribe of MS Zurich C 78 stops while still in "house A" with the remark, ". . . propterea pretermissus est a nobis quia male de greco in latinum versus nihil habuit veritatis" ("therefore we pass over it, since it is so poorly translated from Greek into Latin that no truth remains in it").

The prologue, which attained a certain circulation independent of the *Hymnos*,[43] is informative about Byzantine history and imperial theology. The author appears to be well informed about the history of Byzantine rulers; the erroneous surname given to Constantine V may well be attributed to a scribe: he wrote *Calvus* instead of *Cavallinus* ('horse breeder', the less vulgar of the emperor's two nicknames, the other being KONPONYMOC 'dung-boy'). A second imprecision was most likely intended by the author. It was not Emperor Theodosius III but rather his successor Leo III who broke the one-year blockade of the city in August 718. But Leo the Isaurian was the iconoclast, and the author of the prologue did not want him to have the glory of the great victory, especially since Germanus of Constantinople, who introduced the *Akathistos* officium on 25 March 719, was also a victim of iconoclasm. The author generally seems to have had detailed information concerning Germanus.[44] It is not yet fully decided whether the prologue was originally a Latin text or was a translation from Greek.[45]

According to Huglo, the Greek original of the hymn belonged to the Italian branch of the text tradition.[46] Accordingly, the translator and author of the prologue should be sought first in early ninth-century Italy. Was Methodius, who had fled the iconoclasm of Leo the Armenian, not among the Greeks in Rome ca. 815–20, and did he not possess all prerequisites for composing the prologue and translating the hymn? He was a Sicilian by birth, a monk in Constantinople, a partisan of the iconodule faction, a hagiographer, hymnographer, and mediator between East and West.[47] But there is also the conspicuous mention of the Frankish King *Hildricus*, by which Chilperic II (715–21) is meant. This induced Huglo to conjecture that the prologue originated in the Frankish Kingdom. He also found a further argument for the Frankish as opposed to the Italian origin of the translation in the comparison of word parallels in the *Hymnos Akathistos* and the Dionysiaca of both Hilduin and John Scottus. A brief chart led to his conclusion of the "utilisation d'un glossaire semblable à celui qu' Hilduin emploiera pour traduire les oeuvres de l'Aréopagite" ("utilization of a glossary similar to the one used by Hilduin in translating the Areopagite's works"),[48] and thus of the origin of the work in St. Denis around 825, as the veneration of images was also rehabilitated in the West at the Paris Synod of Louis the Pious, and at the same time as Germanus was also quoted.

The argumentation is problematic, and it is not out of the question that a new investigation would point to Italy as the place of origin after all[49]— just as in general all links between Carolingian Greek studies and St. Denis have been based to a considerable degree on scholarly conjecture. With respect to one area of Carolingian Hellenism, however, the traditional fame of St. Denis no longer seems supportable: the "Missa graeca" comes from St. Amand rather than St. Denis.[50]

4. The Schools of Laon and Auxerre, Abbo of St. Germain-des-Prés, and the "Beginning of a New Era (ca. 870)"

Despite the necessary correction of the "Irish thesis," it remains true that the Irish *peregrini* were especially important in ninth-century Greek studies north of the Alps. After about 840 it seems that they fled to the Continent in great numbers from the Danes and Vikings who were wreaking havoc in their homeland. The most famous of these exiles, John Scottus, found his lifework in close association with Charles the Bald's palace school in Compiègne, Reims, Soisson, or Laon. He was connected with a group of Irishmen in Laon,[51] led by the Irishman Martin (d. 875) and under the patronage of Bishops Pardulus (848–57) and Hincmar of Laon (858–78). The latter, nephew of the all-powerful (in the West Frankish Kingdom) Archbishop Hincmar of Reims, seems especially to have identified himself with the foreigners of his episcopal city and with their studies. Around 870, however, his uncle and metropolitan issued an angry and, in its extreme severity, all the more remarkable document concerning the stylistic taste of his nephew and suffragan, whom he initially supported, later hated, and finally removed from office and had blinded:[52]

Verba quoque obstrusa et undecunque per glossulas collecta et sine ratione posita, quae in hoc scripto tuo posuisti . . . redarguunt te typo iactantiae, cum dicat apostolus: 'Vocum novitates devita' et: 'Malo quinque verba loqui in ecclesia ad aedificationem quam decem milia verborum in lingua.' Qui enim linguam, in qua natus es, non solum non loqui, verum nec intelligere nisi per interpretem potes, cum suppeterent sufficienter verba latina, quae in his locis ponere poteras, ubi graeca et obstrusa et interdum scottica et alia barbara, ut tibi visum fuit nothata atque corrupta posuisti, paret quia non ex humilitate vel ad manifestationem ea, quae dicere voluisti, graeca verba, quae ipse non intelligis, inconvenientissime posuisti, sed ad ostentationem illa insipientissime inseruisti, ut omnes qui illa legerint intelligere possint, te illa velle vomere quae non glutiisti. Hunc namque morem etiam a pueritia habuisti in his, quae te dictare rogabam, maxime autem in versibus et praecipue in figuris porphyriacis; in quibus verba linguae alienae atque obstrusa, impropria et utilitate sensus carentia, quae nec ipse intelligebas, studiose ponebas. Quod mente percipiebam et mihi admodum displicebat: Sed cum viderem te per iactantiam amore laudis flagrare et me non posse sentirem in aetatis adolescentia te ad tantum robur mentis accendere, ut ad discendi ac versificandi studium te provocarem et iactantiae a te pravitatem eraderem, ne acriore correptione fractus revocareris ab studio, permisi te interim, tantum ut studio litterali incumberes, de scientia iactitare, donec in maturiore aetate ab illo etiam vitio possem compescere. . . . Quoniam sancti et sapientes ac magnae auctoritatis viri et etiam utriusque linguae, graecae videlicet et latinae, periti suis scriptis verba graeca nisi ea, quae in scripturis vel canonibus sive legibus sine interpretatione sunt posita et veluti latina in usu habita, verum et obstrusa suis dictis immittere ad ostentationem noluerunt. De hebraea vero lingua Alleluia et Osanna atque Amen propter auctoritatem primae linguae et reverentiam sensus sine interpretatione usi fuerunt. Nos etiam moderni glossarios graecos quos suatim lexicos vocari audivimus, sed et sapientum scripta de nominibus obstrusis habemus et adeo sensatuli sumus, ut nostras dictatiunculas eo usque circumducere et producere possimus, quatenus verba graeca vel obstrusa de glossariis adsumpta in admirationem vel stuporem nescientibus seu scalpentes aures habentibus proferre possimus, cui vanitati obviat scriptura dicens: 'Vanitas vanitatum, et omnia vanitas.'

cf. 1 Tim. 6:20

and

1 Cor. 14:19

Eccles. 1:2

[And also the abstruse words, which you have collected from everywhere out of glosses and used without understanding in this text of yours . . . , convict you of arrogant ostentation, since the apostle says: "Avoid novel words" and "In church I would prefer to speak five

words for edification than ten thousand words in tongues." Since
you, who not only cannot speak your native language, but cannot
even understand it without an interpreter, since sufficient Latin
words exist which you could have used where you placed Greek, abstruse, and sometimes even Irish and other barbaric words, abbreviated and corrupted as you thought good: thus it appears that it was
not out of humility or for clarification of what you wanted to say that
you most unbefittingly used the Greek words which even you do not
understand, but most foolishly introduced for vain ostentation, so
that all who read the work will see that you only spew out what you
cannot swallow. You have had this manner ever since your youth in
those things which I asked you to compose, most especially in verses
and particularly in figural poems, in which you diligently used foreign, abstruse, inappropriate, and senseless words which even you
did not understand. I perceived this in my heart and it displeased me
greatly. But when I saw that because of vanity you burned with a
desire for praise, and realized that I could not incite you to any
strength of mind in your youth, so that I could rouse you to study and
poetic composition and eradicate your perverse ostentation, lest, dis-
couraged by sharper reproof, you be deterred from study, I allowed
you to boast of your knowledge for the time being, just so that you
would remain in literary studies until I could suppress even this vice
at a more mature age. . . . For the holy and wise men of great authority who also knew both languages, namely, Greek and Latin, used
only those Greek words in their writings which occur without translation in the Scriptures or canons or laws and are used as Latin
words; but they did not want to introduce abstruse words into their
writing for ostentation. But the Hebrew *Alleluia* and *Hosanna* and
Amen were used without translation because of the authority of the
first language and the veneration of the sense. We moderns have
Greek glossaries, which we have heard called "lexica" in the manner
of the Greeks, and scholarly works on the abstruse words, and we are
so very clever that we can expand and elaborate on our little
speeches so that we can bring forth Greek words or abstruse words,
collected from glossaries, to the admiration and wonderment of the
ignorant or those having ticklish ears, which vanity the Scriptures
oppose, saying: "Vanity of vanities, and all is vanity."]

The most important evidence of scholarly studies in Laon at the time of
Bishop Hincmar is codex 444 of the Bibliothèque Municipale in Laon,
which goes back primarily to Martin the Irishman; the codex was "a true
Thesaurus linguae Graecae in its century."[53] In essence, the manuscript
contains a large Greek-Latin lexicon, which is rather directly dependent
on the "Cyrillus glossary" of Cod. Harl. 5792,[54] and a smaller Latin-Greek
dictionary, compiled according to comparative linguistic criteria—nouns
which are masculine in Latin and whose Greek equivalents are feminine

or neuter, etc.[55] Of the numerous brief components of the manuscript, an attempt at a Greek grammar is especially noteworthy.[56] Various *Graeca collecta* are informative about the method of Greek studies in Laon.[57] These "collections" are Greek words that have been systematically excerpted from literary works and translated: from Priscian's grammar; from the paraphrase of Aristotle's *Categoriae decem*, mentioned above, that was ascribed to Augustine;[58] from Jerome's letters; and even from the Grecistic poems of John Scottus: *graeca quae sunt in versibus Iohannis Scotti*! The codex or a part thereof was addressed to an "Abbot S" by "M⟨artinus⟩";[59] after the glossary, the following dedication is written in Tironian notes:[60]

> Graecarum glossas domino donante peregit
> H tibimet frater servire paratus
> Namque geris vittas longo quo tempore felix
> Pontificale decus . . .

[By the gift of the Lord and for you, H, the brother prepared to serve has completed these glosses of Greek words; for you, O fortunate pontifical glory, wear the fillets for a long time.]

"H" is to be resolved as "H⟨incmaro⟩" and interpreted as a reference to Bishop Hincmar of Laon.

In addition to Laudunensis 444, Martin of Laon also seems to have been the author of a Hebrew-Greek-Latin glossary with barely 200 lemmata,[61] and the brief dictionary *Scolica Graecarum glossarum*, containing approximately 450 lemmata.[62] Martin wrote Greek verses just as did John Scottus.[63] Recently a commentary on Martianus Capella has also been attributed to him.[64] The research on the school of Laon is, however, not yet complete.[65] John Scottus was the model of the school; among his works, the commentary on the Gospel of John was preserved and transmitted only in Laon, and during the revival of the school under Anselm of Laon (d. 1117), the text was again studied and was even incorporated into early scholastic exegesis via the "Glossa ordinaria."[66]

Further manuscripts from Laon that contain traces of Greek studies are Laon, Bibl. Municipale 252 (lectionary), "in which the epistle on the feast of St. Thomas (= Eph. 2:19 ff.) is written in Greek, in Roman transcription" (Siegmund, *Die Überlieferung*, p. 31, n.); Cod. 403 bis (*Hegesippus*), fol. 141^v. Deacon Atpertus recorded his name in Greek letters (Contreni, *The Cathedral School of Laon*, p. 52); Cod. 424, explanations of Greek terms from Oribasius (ibid., pp. 123 f.); Cod. 445 ("Glossarium Ansileubi"), fol. 96^v—Greek alphabet, fol. 97^r—*Christus vincit* . . . in Greek majuscules (Contreni, personal communication). In addition, one must note the sacramentary from St. Denis Laon, Bibl. Municipale 118, with a Greek *Gloria* in Latin transcription; cf. V. Leroquais, *Les sacramentaires et les missels manuscrits* (Paris 1924), I, 64 ff.

The school in the monastery of St. Germain of Auxerre is usually associated with Laon;[67] in the former, Heiric of Auxerre displayed a knowledge of Greek in his metrical *Vita S. Germani*. It is certain that Heiric borrowed the Greek ornaments for the poem, presented to Charles the Bald around 875, largely from John Scottus; it is not so certain, however, whether he "in regione Laudunensi, ubi Scotti morabantur, Graecam linguam et Dionysii qui dicitur Areopagitae theosophiam addidicit."[68] The tenth-century *Grammaticorum* διαδοχή of the grammarian Gautbert (of Auxerre?) identifies Heiric's teacher as the Irishman Elias, who became bishop of Angoulême around 862. In any case, Heiric's Hellenism leads—altogether in Traube's sense—to an Irish trail. Remigius of Auxerre (d. 908) in his turn drew on the Greek expertise of his teacher, Heiric; through the works of this prolific writer, many Graeca entered into the scholarship of the time. Bishop Christian's "Greek signature" at a synod in 864 rounds out the picture:[69]

CHRISTIANUS AUTISIDORENSIS EPISCOPUS egrapsi.

In this atmosphere of Greek studies in the West Frankish Kingdom, Abbo, a monk in St. Germain-des-Prés in Paris, also made an interesting attempt to experiment with the Latin poetic language. Around 888 he wrote two slender "books" in hexameters describing the Norman siege of Paris in 885–86, followed by an addendum on the events up to 896, i.e., above all, the transfer of power from the last, incompetent Carolingians to the local authorities, in this case Count Odo of Paris. But even he did not seem to Abbo to present adequate material for a heroic poem; thus he concluded the second book of his *Bella Parisiacae urbis* with an appeal to his countrymen to give up their three principal vices—pride, sensual pleasure, and extravagance in dress—and composed the third book as a *regula* for clerics. Abbo illustrated this less original topic with rare and unique words which were then interpreted in glosses. Here he linguistically surpassed his first two books, where to be sure he made use of obscure terms often enough, but did not Grecize as obstinately as in the third book:[70]

> *birrum undique villosum*   *inberbis, sine barba*
> Inque thoro   amphyballum   habeas, effebus et absit
>
> *equ⟨u⟩s*   *qui ob turpitudinem amatur*
> Canterus adsit habunde tibi, sed   amasius absit.

Abbo wrote his Graeca with pedagogical purpose: not only did he gloss them, but he also conceived a system of marking gender and declensional class: "super greca nomina graecas quere figuras; super vero latina latinas;

verbi gratia: quocumque enim Φ et Π femininum nomen et primae declinationis scias . . . M et Π masculina et prime declinationis significant
nomina" ("Look for Greek symbols above the Greek nouns, but Latin
above the Latin. For example, wherever you find a Φ and Π, you know
the noun to be feminine and of the first declension . . . , while M and Π
signify masculine nouns of the first declension"). It seems, however, that
the notations of this system in the poem are no longer completely preserved in the text tradition. The entire poem was thus also a vocabulary
exercise:[71]

> Φ *pugna*   *sacer principatus non ·i· fossa Tartari*
>   Machia sit tibi, quo ierarchia, neque cloaca.
>
>   *pecunia   convivium   lucida*
> Non enteca nec alogia,   verum absida tecum
>
>   *vigor animi et corporis industria*
> Conmaneant, mentes, acrimonia, non quia mordet.

In the second half of this brief book, the number of Grecizing words
increases for the letters *A, B,* and *C* to such a degree that one has the
impression that Abbo was now depending primarily on the first few quires
of a glossary. But Abbo's method of working cannot of course be explained
so directly; according to Laistner, Abbo rather made principal use of a
glossary which contained an especially great number of lemmata under *A,
B,* and *C*: the aforementioned *Scolica Graecarum glossarum.* Abbo's
work is rich in curiosities; but even so, his phraseology is quite often successful—though not for classical tastes, except perhaps in the context of
"macaronic" tolerance:[72]

>   *lutum totum convivia   via*
> Sperne platon olon, sinposia, quatinus odon
>
>   *medius sons*
> Te lustret. Temeson   vigeas, si non potes insons.

Laistner reports that "modern historians, with some justification, have
lamented over the eccentric latinity that Abbo affects, which makes his
poem difficult and tedious to read,"[73] and Löwe warns in *Deutschlands
Geschichtsquellen,* "nicht gerade sehr angenehm zu lesen" ("not exactly
very pleasant to read").[74] If Hincmar of Reims could have seen the book,
he would have passed even more severe judgment. It was from just such
"Graeca et obstrusa . . . et alia barbara," which had annoyed him to no
end in his nephew Hincmar of Laon, that someone now composed a
didactic poem and had success with "this manner"; for numerous copies of
the particularly stilted third book of Abbo's *Bella* have been transmitted

separately. While Abbo's style is hermetically impenetrable, the glosses
again render it accessible; through the glosses, the style becomes
"hermeneutic."[75] A more moderate imitator of this style was the North
Italian author of the *Gesta Berengarii imperatoris*, completed between
915 and 924.[76] He also gave access to his text through glosses.

Even during the period of Carolingian rule, the forces were developing
which were to overcome the classicism associated with the dynasty and its
era and lead to the new stylistic ideal of the tenth century. The anti-
classical movement, manifested in book illumination by the "Franco-
Saxon style," also had its parallels in literature. Around 870 lies a border-
line between two periods in Western intellectual history, and the poems
of John Scottus, the school of Laon, the stylistic conflict of the two Hinc-
mars, Heiric's *Vita S. Germani*, and Abbo's *Bella* are prominent land-
marks along this border. In the most advanced West Frankish centers,
the macaronic style, which Carolingian classicism had considered long
since outmoded, again became fashionable—e. g., Greco-Latin macaronic
verse and fanciful lexical creations in the style of the "Hisperica famina."
The reappearance of this "ornamental Greek" is as little the "création" of
an individual[77] as the ostentatious ornamental style of the school of illumination in St. Amand and its "Franco-Saxon branch academies," which
revert in an almost radical manner to the graphic and stylistic tendencies
of the pre-Carolingian insular art of book illumination: "pre-Carolingian
forms in the representation of the human figure," avoidance "of all motifs
of ancient origin," "not the slightest influence of the ornamentation of the
'Renaissance' schools, . . ." "Around 870, the Carolingian movement in
France is obviously dead."[78]

5. Sedulius in Liège—Dubthach's Cryptogram—
Adespota Scottorum

Tunc oriente magi venerunt dona ferentes,
    Ad Christum properant tunc oriente magi.
Partibus occiduis Scotti veniuntque sophistae,
    Sophica dona ferunt partibus occiduis.

[Then Magi came from the Orient bearing gifts, to Christ hastened the Magi from the
Orient. And from the Occident came Irish sophists, who bore sophistical gifts from the
Occident.]

Sedulius Scottus, Carm. 11, 29–32

What John Scottus had been to the West Frankish Kingdom, Sedulius
Scottus, the "Vergil of Liège," was to the central realm of Lotharingia.[79]
In the fifth decade of the ninth century, he and his two companions were
welcomed by Bishop Hartgar of Liège; Sedulius' presence in Liège is
documented up to 858. He wrote a Greek Psalter which, through its

bilingual supplementary material, "Cantica," and "Oracula Sibyllina" (from Lactantius), attests to the author's acumen in textual criticism. Sedulius certified this work as his own with the Greek phrase:

$$\text{CH}\Delta\dot{\text{Y}}\text{ΛIOC . CK}\dot{\text{O}}\text{TTOC. EΓ}\dot{\omega}. \acute{\text{E}}\Gamma\text{PA}\psi\text{A.}$$

Paris, Bibliothèque de l'Arsenal 8407, fol. 55ʳ; a facsimile of this page and a description of the manuscript in H. Omont, "Inventaire sommaire des manuscrits grecs des bibliothèques Mazarine, de l'Arsenal et de Sainte-Geneviève à Paris," *Mélanges Graux* (Paris 1884), pp. 305–20. On the "Cantica," see Schneider, *Die altlateinischen biblischen Cantica,*" pp. 172–77, and "Die biblischen Oden im Mittelalter," *Biblica* 30 (1949), 487 f. According to Schneider, the "Song of the Vineyard" (Isa. 5) was translated from Latin back into Greek for a bilingual liturgy on Easter night; on this topic and on the approximation of the Greek to the Latin in the liturgical bilinguals in general, see Fischer, in *Festschrift Dold*, pp. 150 and 154 ff. On the "particularly thorough" revision of the "Oracula Sibyllina," see Bischoff, *Mittelalterliche Studien*, I, 151.

With its Greco-Latin supplementary material, the "Sedulian Psalter" is such an outstanding witness to Greek studies in the ninth century that only with great reluctance can scholars be brought to consider it an out-of-place erratum of intellectual history. There has been no dearth of attempts to place the work in a larger context. Traces of an interest in Greek may certainly be found in Sedulius' grammatical work;[80] yet a relationship between the "Sedulian Psalter" and the "Codex Boernerianus," which C. F. Matthaei and later Ludwig Traube had maintained, was no longer tenable once the originals or photographs of them were compared.[81] And with this revision of scholarly opinion, the supposed connection between the Sedulian Psalter and a series of further manuscripts, which formed a group with the "Boernerianus" (St. Gall 48, the "Basel Psalter," the "Bernese Horace," the "St. Gall Priscian"), also became untenable. Thus Sedulius Scottus could no longer be considered the center of a circle of Irish scholars which spread in a broad and shifting zone from the Channel coast through Lotharingia and southern Germany to northern Italy, as had previously been thought. Some relationships remain of course: over two hundred glosses in the "Bernese Horace," marked sed⟨ulius⟩, and the presence of the "Sedulius" gloss even in Codex St. Gall 48, bear witness to Sedulius Scottus' importance in the scholarly *peregrinatio* of the Irish in the Frankish Kingdoms.[82]

Sedulius' poems allow one to plot lines of communication; three of the poems (*Carm.* 27, 34, 35) address Sedulius' Irish countrymen. It is uncertain whether the Marcus mentioned in *Carm.* 34 is Bishop Marcus, who settled at St. Gall around the middle of the ninth century and who must be regarded as the central figure in the production of the "Codex Boernerianus" and related manuscripts:[83]

Egregios fratres, Fergum Blandumque saluta,
Marcum, Beuchellem, cartula, dulce sonans.

[Sing sweetly and greet, little poem, the distinguished brothers,
Fergus, Blandus, Marcus, and Beuchell.]

The head of the Irish *quadriga* is Fergus, whom Sedulius praised in
Carm. 35 for a (now lost) poem to Charles (the Bald? or the son of Emperor Lothar I?); at least a few Greco-Latin glosses written by this Irishman and close associate of Sedulius have come to light.[84]
Fergus also appears with another Irish "four in hand" in a text of a Bamberg manuscript; the principal item of the text is—once again—transmitted in a manuscript from Liège (now Brussels).[85] One may draw several inferences from this concerning the routes of Irish scholars (Ireland—Wales—the Continent), their cryptic style of scholarship, and their delight in competition:

> This is the inscription which Dubthach left in the fortress of Mermin, king of the Britons, in order to test the Irish sages, since he thought himself the most eminent man of all the Irish and Britons. For he thought that none of the Irish and still fewer of the British scholars could read and understand this script in the presence of King Mermin. But with God's help, that script was not a secret to us, Caunchobrach, Fergus, Dominnach, and Suadbar, since we interpreted the inscription by means of a Greek book of annals and the alphabet [*per annalem Grecorum libellum atque alphabeti*].

IB Є IZ IB Є IΓ. IZ Є KΛ. Γ IΔ IΓ Γ H IΓ.
IH λ IΛ K IΘ Є IB.

> The inscription reads: "Mermin rex Conchen salutem." Thus if you want to understand this inscription, pay close attention to the aforementioned series of Greek computations of the years [*Grecorum annalis compoti seriem*] and the Latin letters which are arranged according to the Greek alphabetic symbols, and recognize that the Latin letters are in accord with the Greek alphabetic symbols in the corresponding lines. . . . Thus when you see the Greek letters IB in Dubthach's aforementioned text, look at the series of Greek [numerical] letters, . . . and since they come in twelfth place there, they must signify the twelfth letter of the Latin alphabet [i.e., *M*]. And since Є takes the fifth place in Greek computational series [*in ipsa greca calculi serie*], the fifth letter of the Latin alphabet, *E*, is correctly signified, and progressing in this way, you will understand the entire meaning of this or a similar text.
>
> Let it also be known to your prudence, good Colgu, our most learned master, that we do not send this explanation to you as if to someone ignorant; rather, we implore you, in your benevolent love, to pass this explanation on to our ignorant and simpler Irish brothers

who want to sail across the Irish sea, so that they do not blush before
Mermin, the illustrious king of the Britons, because they do not
understand that text. . . .

The scribe immediately availed himself of the decoded cipher in order
to add his signature to this *expositio*: *Suadbar scripsit*. Then the cryptog-
rapher Dubthach received yet another sarcastic cut for writing the Welsh
name *Concen* with the second *c* aspirated (*Conchen*). The signature of
another person in cipher is then also appended.

The intellectual adventure on which this Irish group reported in its
"forfanterie naive" ("naive boasting," L. Gougaud) thus proceeded mod-
estly but also romantically. The Irish recognized the symbols put before
them as Greek letters, or rather numerical symbols; they were further
aided by a *computus* with Greek numerals, perhaps an "Easter table" for
the determination of the date of Easter according to Dionysius Exiguus,
where the Greek numerals are often employed and explained. Mermin
was king in Wales in the second quarter of the ninth century. Concen was
also a king; he died on a pilgrimage to Rome in 854 or 855. A certain
Dubthach copied part of the "Leiden Priscian";[86] his name is also found in
the St. Gall evangelary St. Gall 48, the "Codex Boernerianus" (Dresden A
145[b]), and the Codex Bernensis 363, which was written by Irish scholars
on the Continent.[87]

A number of anonymous works (*Adespota*) may be mentioned at this
point. The Greco-Latin "Murbach Psalter"[88] (Gotha mbr. I 17), saec.
IX–X, contains a Greek prayer, ΥΨΥΛΟC ΚΥΡΙΟC ΔΥΝΑΤΟC, a
ΟΡΟΘΕCΙΑ ΚΑΙ ΕΚΘΕCΙC ΓΡΑΜΜΑΤΟΝ ΕΒΡΑΕΙΚΟΝ, and a
ΚΑΤΑΛΟΓΟC ΓΡΑΜΜΑΤΟΝ ΕΛΛΗΝΩΝ, all in hexameters. Traube
printed these poems, whose somewhat affected trilingual erudition does
in fact give the impression of an Irish origin, in the "Carmina Scottorum
Latina et Graecanica."[89]

The "Versus cuiusdam Scotti de alphabeto," which attained a considerable circulation,[90] may be compared with both alphabet poems of the
"Murbach Psalter." Traube did not include them in his collection of "Carmina Scottorum Latina et Graecanica," since he held them to be pre-
Carolingian; but they seem to belong to the ninth century.[91]

6. St. Gall

In the time when the canon Grimald was abbot and Hartmut was
deputy abbot, as it were, Marcus, a bishop of Irish origin, came to
visit Gallus, his countryman, while on the way back from Rome. He
was accompanied by Moengal, his sister's son, whom our brothers
later called Marcellus, after his uncle, in the diminutive form. Mar-

cellus was well educated in the divine and human sciences. The bishop was asked to remain with us for a while, after his nephew had already been approached on the subject. After lengthy deliberation, they consented, and, on the appointed day, Marcellus distributed many of his uncle's gold pieces through the window and in so doing feared that he was going to be torn to pieces by them [i.e., his attendants]; for they raged against him, since they thought that he had convinced the bishop to remain behind. The bishop gave the horses and mules to those, singled out by name, to whom he wished to give them; the books, however, the gold, and the vestments, he retained for himself and St. Gallus. . . . Some time later, the schools of the cloister were given over to Marcellus, along with Notker, who later bore the nickname "the Stammerer". . . . It is delightful to recall how the cell of St. Gallus began to grow and finally bloomed under these signs. . . .[92]

Thus around the middle of the eleventh century the abbey of St. Gall recalled the arrival two hundred years before of the two important Irishmen who were without question epoch-making in the educational history of St. Gall. The more significant Greek studies in St. Gall also begin with this event,[93] for the group of Greco-Latin biblical manuscripts already mentioned is owed to these Irishmen: the St. Gall evangelary St. Gall 48, the manuscript of the Pauline epistles Dresden, Sächsische Landesbibliothek A. 145[b] ("Codex Boernerianus"), and the "Basel Psalter" (Universitätsbibliothek A. VII. 3).[94] The manuscripts pose many problems in details, and the history of their origin is still obscure; yet it is certain that the manuscripts were designed according to a firm plan as a small corpus of the most important and most familiar biblical books, by the Irish; and it can also be regarded as certain that all three manuscripts were added to the books of St. Gall as an inheritance from the Irish bishop Marcus.

These three bilinguals depart from the traditional double-column format by presenting the text interlinearly. The Greek text in majuscules is the principal text in this format, with the smaller Latin text in minuscule written between the lines of the Greek text. The initial letters are filled in with color, which, along with the well-balanced graphic layout of the script, produces an artistic impression, no matter where the codex is opened. It is possible that an illumination was originally planned at least for the evangelary: at the end of the Gospel of Matthew in St. Gall 48, one finds a plan for a series of miniatures for the Gospels, in which the legends to the illuminations are written in Greek, the instructions for the illuminator in Latin. Thus, for example, for the Gospel of John:[95]

> . . . dominus coccinea ueste indutus arun
> dinem in dextera tenens per aurem sinistram

uide uel ecce rex
adprehenditur ЄΙΔЄ Ο ΒΛϹΙΛЄΥϹ
iudęorum
ΤШΝ ΙΟΥΔΔΙШΝ · ΛΟΝΓΙΝΟϹ
cum lancia . . .

It seems that two further bilinguals were soon added to Bishop Marcus' corpus of Graecolatina in St. Gall—two Psalters written by native scribes in the traditional double-column style. One of the manuscripts, which has been dated to the end of the ninth century, still has the Greek column in Greek script,[96] while the other (perhaps already saec. X), has the Greek text in Roman transcription[97]—just as the Psalterium quadrupartitum of Salomo III from 909.

Notker Balbulus, the student of Moengal-Marcellus, is supposed to have copied the seven catholic epistles in Greek around 880; they should be understood as a complement to Marcus' collection of bilinguals.[98] The monks in St. Gall also copied Dositheus' grammar, which, originally written as a Latin grammar for Greeks, was still more interesting than Priscian's *Institutiones*, of which St. Gall possessed an outstanding Irish copy.[99] Despite numerous further traces in St. Gall manuscripts of an occupation with Greek,[100] it appears that the monks of St. Gall were interested in neither intensive grammatical studies nor translations.[101] Compared with the grammatical studies of the Irish in Laon or John Scottus' work as a translator, or even with Sedulius Scottus' exegetically oriented works, the Greek studies in St. Gall at first glance give the impression of having no purpose, as if they were only a "frivolous Hellenism."

When one writes ΚΥΡΙЄ ЄΛЄΗϹΟΝ and ЄΡΙΤΑΦΙUΜ[102] and enters the title-lines of biblical books in a Latin–Old High German biblical glossary (in part) in the Greek alphabet,[103] when the stag in an initial capital thirsts for a spring marked ΦШΝϹ, when the patron saints of the establishment are invoked as ΑΓΙЄ ΓΑΛΛЄ and ΑΓΙЄ ΟΤΜΑΡЄ in a Greek litany,[104] then one is reminded of the "ornamental Greek" of Irish and Irish-influenced manuscripts of the eighth and early ninth centuries, which were certainly also known in a St. Gall rich in *libris scottice scriptis*.[105]

The liturgical bilingualism of the "Missa graeca" corresponds to this paleographical Greek ornamentation in the texts; it neither required nor provided an extensive knowledge of Greek and actually represented nothing alien, but rather only alienated the native material. This latter seemed to be the main concern of the *ellinici fratres* of St. Gall.[106]

The key manuscript among the numerous St. Gall manuscripts with liturgical Graeca seems to be Stiftsbibliothek 381. The first text contained in this "St. Gall book of poems," written in the tenth century,[107] is Notker the Stammerer's letter to Lantpert on the meaning of the tone letters; it is

here that Notker speaks of the "Hellenistic brothers." Following the letter come *Doxa en ipsistis* ("gloria"), *Symbolum apostolicum grece: Pis-
teuuo is theon*, *Carmen angelicum grece et latine*, *Oratio dominica grece
et latine*, and, at the end of the Greco-Latin section, the Greek and Latin
creeds (Nicaeno-Constantinopolitanum), divided into semantic units. The
third section of the manuscript consists of five liturgical poems by Hartmann of St. Gall, of which the last, "ad processionem diebus dominicis,"
closes stirringly:[108]

> Agne dei patris qui mundi crimina tollis
> Optatae pacis munera dona tuis
> ΚΥΡΡΙΕ pantocrator ysos sodisse te pantes
> Su basyleos ymon ΧΡΙΣΤΕ eleyson ymas.

[O Lamb of God the Father, who takes away the sins of the world,
grant to your own the gifts of longed-for-peace; Lord and omnipotent
one, save us all together; have mercy on us, Christ, our king.]

The first three sections of St. Gall 381 do not seem to have come
together by accident; all three document the Greek element in St. Gall's
"Golden Age," which delighted in poetry and the liturgy. We may be able
to identify two of the enigmatic *ellinici fratres* by name: Notker Balbulus,
the master of the sequence, and Hartmann.[109] It is scarcely accidental that
the splendid Greco-Latin liturgy is situated between the works of these
two Hellenists.

The liturgical Graecolatina are transmitted in not a few St. Gall manuscripts of the tenth and eleventh centuries.[110] They also met with approval
beyond St. Gall. In the early eleventh century, for example, as the art
lover Bishop Sigebert of Minden commissioned the monasteries in the
Lake Constance area to write and illuminate a unique collection of books
for his cathedral church, the Greco-Latin liturgy necessarily also had to
be included in the troper ornamented with ivory portraits of the poets of
St. Gall.[111]

The "Psalterium quadrupartitum" is another work of lasting importance
from among St. Gall's Greek studies; in this work, as in Origen's
ΕΞΑΠΛΑ , the individual recensions of the Psalter are juxtaposed in parallel columns; of course the texts which were relevant and accessible in the
Latin Middle Ages were different from and fewer in number than those
included by Origen. The "Psalterium tripartitum," a copy of which was in
Reichenau, was widely disseminated in the Carolingian period and contained the three versions of the Psalter which went back to Jerome: "Psalterium Gallicanum," "Psalterium Romanum," and "Psalterium iuxta
Hebraeos." This form was now "surpassed" through the addition of a
fourth column with the text of the Septuagint in Roman transcription. The
oldest preserved manuscript identifies itself as a work commissioned by

Bishop Salomo III of Constance and dates from 909. Salomo III, Notker the Stammerer's student, may be considered the first to have turned the idea of a "Psalterium quadrupartitum" into a reality; the fertility of the idea is attested to in a series of copies and further developments of the text.

Bamberg, Staatl. Bibliothek Bibl. 44 (A.I.14) contains letters of Jerome on the translation of the Psalms, the dedicatory poem of Salomo III, *Nongentis pariterque novem* and other *Versiculi*, then the actual "Psalterium quadruplex," and at the end (for the most part bilingual), the cantica, paternoster, "Symbolum apostolorum," "Te deum," litany, gloria, "Symbolum Nicenum," "Symbolum Athanasianum"; cf. F. Leitschuh, *Katalog der Handschriften der K. Bibliothek Bamberg* (Bamberg 1895), I, 36–39; a paleographic description in Chroust, *Monumenta Palaeographica*, Ser. I, Lief, 16, 3–4. According to the detailed study by Allgeier (in *Jahresbericht der Görresgesellschaft* [1938], 102 ff., and in *Biblica* 24 [1943], 270 ff.), the St. Gall work had as its models the Reichenau "Psalterium triplex" with Jerome's three Psalters (Karlsruhe, Aug. XXXVIII, saec. IX[1]) on the one hand, and, with respect to the Greek text, the bilingual Psalter of the Milanese monk Symeon on the other. On the cantica in the "Psalterium quadrupartitum," see Schneider, in *Biblica* 30 (1949), 485.

At the end of the tenth century and the beginning of the eleventh, two copies were made of the St. Gall–Bamberg text of 909; even in terms of medieval copying habits, they were both exceptionally accurate reproductions of the original: it seems that both copies conform page for page and line for line to the Bambergensis and even reproduce the scribal errors and format of the parchment leaves. Even the mention of King Louis the Child (d. 911) in the bilingual litany attached to the Psalter is accurately transmitted (ed. Cagin, *Te Deum*, p. 545):

ΙΝΑ ΤΟΝ ΚΥΡΙΝ ΛΟΥΔΟΒΙΚΟ	Ut domnum hludouuicum regem
ΡΙΓΑ ΚΑΙ ΤΟΝ ϹΤΡΑΤΟΝ ΤΟΝ	et exercitum christianorum
ΧΡΙϹΤΙΑΝΟΝ ΔΙΑΦΙΛΑΞΕ ΚΑΤΑ-	conseruare digneris:
ΖΙΩϹΙϹ ϹΕ ΠΑΡΑΚΑΛΟΥΜΕΝ	te rogamus audi nos

[That you might deem it worthy to save Lord Louis the King and the army of Christians, we entreat you to hear us.]

The ancient repository of the one copy is the Cologne Dombibliothek (Cod. 8), that of the other is the Essen Convent (now in the cathedral treasury, s.n.).

Two leaves of a twelfth-century copy of especially expensive design are preserved in MS 629 of the Universitätsbibliothek in Freiburg: while the St. Gall–Bamberg original has forty-line pages and measures 40.1 × 30.8 cm., the Freiburg pages contain fifty lines, and the text format itself measures 42 × 30 cm. A folio volume such as this could be ascribed to the monastery in Prüfening (cf. *MBK* IV/1 [1977], p. 420, line 139, and p. 422, line 62). In comparison to the Bamberg text, the "Psalteria quadrupartita" of Paris, BN nouv. acq. lat. 2195 (48-line, written in 1105 for St. Martin in Tournai, under Abbot Odo) and Valenciennes, Bibliothèque Municipale 14 (B.1.37), saec. XII, from St. Amand, have been slightly modified. (These two manuscripts are closely related to one another.)

In the works of Ekkehard I (d. 973) and Ekkehard IV (d. ca. 1060), St. Gall Hellenism fades and disappears. A distinguishing mark of Ekkehard I's meager but important corpus of sequences is the attempt to integrate declined Greek words into the Latin text: "agio pneumati se vas exhibuit; physin per fidem superans; partenu casta genitum; Odon ad antropon/ corda parat deo; pneumati to agio/ nitidum vas exhibet et electum."[112] Ekkehard IV, the compiler of the St. Gall traditions, offers Graeca of diverse kinds in his poems,[113] for example, the verse in the manner of Hartmann's processional:

> *Uirgo mater dei salua nos omnes˙*
> Partenu matira theu sodisse te pantes˙
>
> [Virgin, mother of God, save us all.]

or containing nothing but familiar components:

> *omnicreator noster tu rex   miserere˙*
> pantocrator imon   su basileos eleison˙
>
> [Almighty, have mercy, you our king.]

or in the ancient Irish manner of "trilingual" erudition:

> *grece˙ neutrum˙ Ebraice femininum˙ latine masculinum˙*
> *in uirtute pari uiget˙*
> Pneuma Ruha Flatus˙ Viget omnigenis vocitatus˙

[The spirit is possessed of the same strength, no matter how signified: in Greek, a neuter—*pneuma*; in Hebrew, a feminine—*ruha*; in Latin, a masculine—*flatus*.]

The poetic tales of Greek lessons from the beautiful Duchess Hadwig in Castle Hohentwiel also originate with Ekkehard IV.[114] She is supposed to have once been engaged to "a Greek King Constantine," who had her "excellently trained in Greek" by a eunuch whom he sent to Germany, while a second eunuch, whose task it was to paint a portrait of the bride, was less successful, since the maid "contorted her mouth and eyes because of her hatred of the marriage." At a later time—still according to Ekkehard IV—she was more gracious, especially once when Ekkehard II ("Palatinus") came to visit at Hohentwiel with Purchart, a student from the monastery school:

And when she had sat down, she asked, among other things, why this boy, who was himself standing near them, had come along. "On account of Greek, my lady," said he [Ekkehard]. "I have brought the boy, who already knows much else, so that he might catch something from your mouth." The boy himself, who was handsome in appearance, spoke up thus, since he was well versed in metrics:

Esse velim Grecus, cum sim vix, domna, Latinus.

["I would like to be a Greek, my lady, although I am scarcely a Latin."]

And she was so delighted by this, just as she was always eager for new things, that she drew him to her and kissed him and set him on a footstool closer to her. Curious, she asked that he compose more impromptu verses for her. The boy, however, looked at both teachers, as if unaccustomed to such a kiss, and said:

Non possum prorsus dignos componere versus;
nam nimis expavi, duce me libante suavi.

["I cannot compose worthy verses straight away, for I took great fright from the Duchess' sweet kiss."]

She, however, far from her accustomed severity, burst into laughter and then finally stood the boy before her and taught him to sing the antiphon *Maria et flumina*, which she herself had translated into Greek, in this manner:

Thalassi ke potami, eulogi ton kyrion;
Ymnite pigon ton kyrion alleluja.

["Seas and rivers, praise the Lord; fountains, sing alleluia to the Lord."]

And later she often summoned him in free moments and wanted to hear impromptu verses from him; she taught him to speak Greek and became especially fond of him. Finally, when he left, she also presented him with a Horace and several other books which our library contains today.

Was there in fact a eunuch who taught Greek in tenth-century Swabia? The duchess or the narrator of her story could well have come across a form of the cited translation in a bilingual Psalter, in whose common appendix of cantica the ΕΥΛΟΓΕΙΤΕ ΘΑΛΑCCΑΙ ΚΑΙ ΠΟΤΑΜΟΙ was also contained in the "Hymn of the Three Youths" (Dan. 3:77–78).

One of the last important writers of the monastery in St. Gall was the monk Herimannus, who wrote a *Vita S. Wiboradae* around 1075. He gave his own name an unfamiliar form, as was frequently done in the Middle Ages: for *R* he wrote a Greek Ρ and for *M* the ↃϹ siglum: HEΡIↃϹAN-

NUS.[115] By the fifteenth century at the latest, the name was no longer understood correctly and was copied as "Hepidannus." The error has continued even into the modern period: this phantom author "Hepidannus" is still found in Manitius' literary history.

7. Reichenau

The local lines of tradition in St. Gall are much easier to trace than in neighboring Reichenau—the "Augia felix," which was more highly favored in the initial stages by nature and the goodwill of the ruling powers, but where only a fraction of the manuscript collection is still preserved as a complete corpus. In a period of about seventy years (ca. 850–920), there were three generations that cultivated Greek studies in St. Gall: that of the Irishmen associated with Marcus and Marcellus-Moengal, with its bilinguals; that of Moengal's student Notker Balbulus, with its liturgical poetry (ellinici fratres); and finally Notker's student Bishop Salomo III, with the compilation of the four-part Psalter. In Reichenau the traces of Greek are distributed over a much longer period of time—they extend from Abbot Petrus in the eighth to Abbot Alawich I in the tenth century—but their coherence is less evident than in St. Gall.

Abbot Petrus of Reichenau (782–86) is supposed to have brought a valuable Greek Psalter from Rome back to the island monastery in Lake Constance.[116] Abbot Heito of Reichenau led the embassy of 811 to Constantinople; but this fact does not entitle him to be counted as one of the Greek scholars of the Latin Middle Ages. His odoporicum is lost.

In the time of Reginbert (d. 846), the renowned librarian of the island monastery, a "Psalterium tripartitum" was produced which contained Jerome's three recensions in parallel columns; Jerome's epist. 106 ("Ad Sunniam et Fretelam"), with Reginbert's textual notes on several Greek concepts, is prefaced to the work.[117] A manuscript of Jerome's Adversus Iovinianum, copied in Reichenau ca. 840 for Archbishop Otgar of Mainz, displays some understanding of the Greek majuscule script.[118]

Walafrid Strabo, teacher of Charles the Bald and later abbot of Reichenau (842–49), expounded the relationships between German and Greek words with remarkable historico-philological acumen in his work De exordiis et incrementis and explained these relationships, quite accurately, on the basis of the Gothic translation of the Bible:[119]

> I would now like to speak of how our barbaric German language [secundum nostram barbariem, quae est theotisca] designates the house of God—at the risk of appearing ridiculous to the Latins (if they were perhaps to read these words), as though I wished to equate

unsightly sons of apes with the children of Augustus. . . . Just as the house of God is called *basilica*, i.e., 'house of the king', so also is it called *kyrica*, i.e., 'house of the lord', since we serve the Lord of Lords and King of Kings there. But if someone asks us how these scraps of Greek came to us, the answer is that barbarians also served as soldiers in the Roman army. Many preachers of God's word, familiar with both Greek and Latin, ventured among these wild beasts in order to do battle with their heathen errors; they taught our tribal cousins many useful things which they did not know before. We know that especially from the Goths or Getae, who, when they were won for the Christian faith—even if indirectly—were living in the Greek provinces. Those tribes spoke our German language [*nostrum id est theotiscum sermonem*]. As history shows, zealous men of those tribes translated the holy books into their own language, of which scattered memorials are extant even today. We have learned from reports of trustworthy brothers that certain Scythian peoples, especially those from Tomi [on the Black Sea], celebrate the holy offering in that language even today.

The wandering Irishmen also came to Reichenau, and with their manuscripts came evidence of their interests in Greek. The finest of them is the "Reichenau Notebook," now at St. Paul in Lavanttal, which contains materials for Greek study among its poetic (the famous Old Irish poem on the white cat Pangur), scientific, and grammatical texts—a list of the Greek articles with Latin translation and a Greek-Latin glossary.[120]

The "Codex Paulinus Augiensis," Reichenau's counterpart to the "Codex Boernerianus," formerly at St. Gall, exhibits no Irish influence. A native scribe wrote the manuscript of the Pauline epistles with Greek majuscules and Carolingian minuscules in two columns.[121] Was this the only bilingual text at Reichenau? Or may one assume that the much more accessible bilinguals of the Psalter and Gospels were already present at Reichenau when an interest was taken in the rare bilingual Paulus?

Not only did Irishmen come to Reichenau (as also to the more remote St. Gall), but Greeks as well. Reichenau, which was closely associated with the Carolingian rulers from the beginning and once again under Charles III (876–87; d. 888 and buried in Reichenau-Mittelzell) occupied an important position in the political life of the Frankish Kingdom, has documented several visits from Greek countries in its "Liber confraternitatum"—for example, around 837, an embassy of the Patriarchs Basil of Jerusalem and Christopher of Alexandria, which counted among its members a recluse from St. Sabas and one from the monastery on the Mt. of Olives.[122] Later it appears that Methodius, the great missionary to the Slavs, stayed at Reichenau for a time; a Greek wrote in the "Liber confraternitatum":[123]

ΜΕΘΟΔΙΟC
ΛΕΟΝ
ΙΓΝΑΤΙΟC
ΙΟΑΚΙΝ
CΥΜΕΟΝ
ΔΡΑΓΑΙC

Around 934 the *Miracula S. Marci* tell of a Greek Bishop Constantine and the monk Symeon from Jerusalem, to whom the monks at Reichenau give credit for bringing the "Pitcher of the Wedding at Cana," which is still there today. The adventurous biography of this Greek, *Vita Symeonis Achivi*, was written before the end of the century.[124] At the end of the tenth century, Johannes Philagathos of Rossano, who was influential under Theophan, and for whose sake Piacenza was made an archbishopric, entered his name in the Reichenau confraternal book; this entry puts the final seal, as it were, on the succession of distinguished Greek visitors to Reichenau: "IOHANNES grecus ˙ Placentinę civitatis ARCHIEPIS-COPUS."[125]

It is fitting, in this context of the active relations between Reichenau and individual Greeks, that one finds a Latin letter in a formulary that is addressed to the abbot of Reichenau and that ends with a cosmopolitan flourish: "Kere, kyri agapite!" ("Greetings, dear sir!").[126]

It seems clear that neither the Irish nor the Greeks transplanted to Reichenau Greek studies that then led to translation work; the famous "Reichenau Corpus" of sermons on Mary, which was translated from Greek, had a different origin.

Karlsruhe, Bad. Landesbibliothek Aug. LXXX, saec. IX ex., described by A. Holder, *Die Reichenauer Handschriften*, 2nd ed. (Wiesbaden 1970), I, 220–22 and 659 f. The manuscript contains Latin translations of the most important homilies on Mary written by Greek theologians of the eighth century: two homilies by Andrew of Crete on the feast of Mary's birth; a "sermo de uirginitate sanctae Mariae seu super Anna et Simeone habitus in die Ypopantis," by Amphilochius of Iconium (for Candlemas); three further homilies by Andrew of Crete for *dormitio* (Assumption of the Blessed Virgin); four homilies by Cosmas Bestetor (Vestitor) for the same feast; and another by Germanus I of Constantinople and two by John of Damascus, likewise for *dormitio*. The manuscript closes with an appended original Latin text, *De assumptione*, in which the preceding ten translations of Greek homilies for *dormitio* are in a certain sense summarized. According to a parallel manuscript tradition that has recently surfaced, the author was Bishop John of Arezzo (G. Philippart, in *AB* 92 [1974], 345 f.) who was of some importance at the splendid court of Pope John VIII (872–82); cf. *MGH Epistolae*, VII, passim.

The identity of the translator or translators of the "Reichenau Corpus" and of the author of the final text in the collection, and the determination of the time and place of composition of these works, have great literary historical significance. Wenger's response (*L'Assomption*, p. 148) to these problems cannot stand up to critical examination: ". . . en l'absence d'apocryphes et à défaut d'homélies explicites, quelqu'un songea, sans doute à Reichenau même, car on y enseignait le grec, à se procurer les textes grecs sur la Dormition. Ce que la littérature byzantine a produit de meilleur sur le sujet fut recueilli et traduit. Le résultat de cette entreprise est le codex Augiensis LXXX, . . . qui sur 14 homélies mariales, en contient dix sur l'Assomption. Une onzième homélie est une sorte de synthèse, faite probablement par le traducteur, de tout le matériel traduit." (". . . in the absence of apocryphal works and lacking homilies, someone proposed to procure the Greek texts on *dormitio*, without doubt in Reichenau itself, since Greek was taught there. The better Byzantine treatments of the subject were collected and translated. The result of this undertaking is the Codex Augiensis LXXX, . . . which contains ten homilies on the Assumption among its fourteen on the Virgin. An eleventh homily is a kind of synthesis, probably written by the translator of the other texts.")

The manuscript is certainly not a collection of the usual kind; instead, it is a well-ordered compilation in which a plan is at work which could be linked to the *patrocinium* of the Assumption of the Blessed Virgin in Reichenau. The paleographical evidence points in a completely different direction, however. The manuscript of the translations was dated a century too late by Holder ("saec. X ex." instead of saec. IX ex.); it came from Italy (B. Bischoff), as did these translations. Significant literary historical evidence is given for this argument in Anastasius Bibliothecarius' statement that he translated the "sermonem . . . de virginitate super Anna et Symeone" of Amphilochius of Iconium (*MGH Epistolae*, VII, 428; cf. Siegmund, *Die Überlieferung*, p. 178; parallel tradition of the sermons in MS Orléans 175 [152] from Fleury).

It was the achievement of Reichenau to transmit the collection which introduced the eighth-century Byzantine theological position, especially on the *assumptio*, and which stood in direct opposition to the "rationalistic" and critical interpretation of the Assumption of the Blessed Virgin proposed by a Carolingian theologian in the guise of Jerome (and further feigned to be such by Archbishop Hincmar of Reims).[127] The original Latin summary, *De assumptione beate Marie*, appended to Aug. LXXX, was widely disseminated in southern Germany; in the twelfth century, Gerhoh of Reichersberg republished it and defended it against the Carolingian Pseudo-Jerome.[128]

In the eleventh century at Reichenau, a famous teacher and author again came forward in Hermannus Contractus. This master of the quadrivium was certainly no Greek scholar, but in his poems he gave the finest expression to the Greco-Latin macaronic style of the late Ottonian–early Salian period—not in *Salve regina*, which the monastic tradition later attributed to him, but in his authentic sequences, e.g., the one on Mary Magdalene, which begins:[129]

> Exsurgat totus almiphonus
> supercaelestium chorus
> citharoedorum
> omnifarie deo
> eulogizans cum Alleluia.

[May the whole arise, sweetly sounding, the super-celestial chorus of the cithera players eulogizing God with alleluia in all languages.]

The Grecisms in Hermann's sequence on the Cross are so numerous that Guido Maria Dreves partially transposed the text into Greek minuscule:[130]

(6a) Tu totus desiderium,
  boni totius genus
  generalissimum,
  gaudimonium
  tu quam verissime
  hyperbolicum
  solaque tu soteria,
  clemens tui nos intima
  pasce theoria!

Θεὸς πάντα ἐλεήμων,
ἄφεσις benignula
tu τῶν ἁμαρτιῶν,
sanctimonium
dulce, iucundulae
tu deliciae
portus quietis unicae,
ἀρχὸς patrum et optimas
ἐλέησον ἡμᾶς!

[You, all desire, the
most comprehensive order
of all good; you, most
truly the highest joy
and you alone our sal-
vation, nourish us, O
gentle one, with your
inmost philosophy!]

[God, merciful to everything,
you, beneficent for-
giveness of sins,
sweet sanctity,
you, pleasant
delight, haven of unique
repose, first and best
among the fathers, have mercy on us!]

Hermannus Contractus certainly did not write the sequence using these letters, but, to put it bluntly, that was his intent. A traditional precept of liturgical language, observed especially in the Ottonian–early Salian period (i.e., in Hermann's time) prescribed candor in dealing with foreign material. The ceremonial liturgical style readily admitted the "Pentecostal" union of Latin with Greek, the older "sacred language."

IX

Italy in the Ninth and Tenth Centuries

1. Frankish, Lombardic, Arabic, and Greek Rule

At the moment when Lombard rule was about to take hold throughout the entirety of Italy, it was replaced by Frankish dominion. Adelchis, the son of the conquered and captured Lombard King Desiderius, fled to Constantinople in the vain hope of reconquering his kingdom with Byzantine aid. The Lombard Duke Arichis II of Benevento (758–87) was more fortunate in maintaining his position: "au sud de la péninsule, la nation vaincue par Charlemagne garde son indépendance" ("in the southern region of the peninsula, the nation conquered by Charlemagne retained its independence").[1]

King Charles, who by right of conquest had been a *rex Langobardorum* since 774, was rarely in Italy during the following forty years. On Christmas Day 800 he received the imperial crown there; he had columns brought to Aachen from Rome and Ravenna, and from Ravenna also the equestrian statue of Theodoric the Great. Franks (and in northern Italy also Alemanni) occupied monasteries and episcopal sees; learned Lombards earned the favor of their new lord through teaching and service at the court north of the Alps. Italy contributed to the "Carolingian Renaissance."[2]

The Franks seemed to favor the metropolitan see of Milan—the city of St. Ambrose—over the old Lombard royal city of Pavia. The Carolingians chose Ambrose as their patron when they founded the large-scale new monastery of S. Ambrogio near Milan in 789. Both of the Carolingian rulers who died in Italy, King Pepin (810) and Emperor Louis II (875), were buried in this new foundation and not in the long-distinguished S. Pietro in Ciel d'Oro at Pavia, where Boethius and Augustine were entombed; the same is true of the Lombard King Liudprand, who had the remains of St. Augustine brought to Pavia from his "exile" burial site in Sardinia! Some traces of Greek studies also point to the Carolingian "great monastery" of S. Ambrogio: the ordained monk Symeon produced a bilingual Psalter here in the mid-ninth century.

Berlin, Stiftung Preuß. Kulturbesitz, Staatsbibliothek Ham. 552, described by H. Boese, *Die lateinischen Handschriften der Sammlung Hamilton zu Berlin*

(Wiesbaden 1966), pp. 269 f.; cf. N. A. Bees, "Zum Psalter 552 der Hamilton-Sammlung," *Byzantinisch-Neugriechische Jahrbücher* 12 (1936), 119–28, with a photograph of the note (on fol. 1[r]) concerning the author and the scribe: ΚΥΡΙΕ ΒΟΕΙΘΙ ΤΟΝ ΔΟΥΛΟΝ ΣΟΥ ΣΥΜΕΟΝ ΜΟΝΑΧΟΥΣ ΠΡΕΣΒΙΤΕΡΟΥ . . .

The Psalter contains the Greek text (in the Roman alphabet) on the left and a Latin version ("Symeon's Recension") on the right, and a Greco-Latin cantica and credo in the appendix. Research on the text of the manuscript has taken the appendix as its point of departure: Schneider, *Cantica*, pp. 107–19, and "Die biblischen Oden im Mittelalter," *Biblica* 30 (1949), 485, and in *Biblische Zeitschrift*, n.s., 4 (1960), 281. Allgeier has dealt with the actual text of the Psalms (*Das Psalmenbuch*, pp. 116–18, and in *Biblica* 24 [1943], 271 f.). The most reliable result (in a relative sense) of these exegetical studies seems to be the determination that a relationship exists between the Milanese double Psalter and Salomon III's *Psalterium quadrupartitum*. (Is it then necessary to draw the conclusion that the Milanese manuscript was lent to St. Gall, or that it even remained there? Do the few terminological parallels [Schneider, *Cantica*, p. 112, n. 65] establish a strong enough connection between Symeon's Psalter and Sedulius' Psalter that one may conclude "daß auch die Arbeit des Simeon der irischen Schule ihre Anregung verdankt" ["that Symeon's work also owes its stimulus to the Irish school"]?)

Due to the *inscriptio* in the Milanese double Psalter, we are on rather solid ground historically: the work was produced by the ordained monk Symeon under Abbot Peter I (854–58) or Peter II (858–99) in the monastery of St. Ambrogio; the scribe's name was Magnus. The "Litterae de psalterio transferendo," which prefaced an edition of the Milanese Psalter provided with text-critical symbols, offer a much greater opportunity for historical interpolation. Here a ninth-century biblical scholar made no use of Jerome's famous critical symbols ÷ (*obelus*) and ·⁜· (*asteriscus*) but rather constructed a new system of symbols primarily from Isidore's *Etymologiae*:[3]

> De notis. Quinque sunt notae, quas in hoc psalterio depinximus, id est I. Θ Theta. II. Ψ Psi. III. ⳩ Chrismon. IV. ⁊ Et. V. Ͻ Diastole.
>
> I. De nota Θ Theta. Haec quidem nota mortem significat, quam Graeci theta hoc est apo tu thanatu, id est a morte vocant. . . . Hac autem littera ego usus sum in his locis, ubi superfluum esse videtur. . . .
>
> II. De nota Ψ Psi. . . . Per hanc autem literam Graeci ΨΕΥΔΟΝ, hoc est falsum, scribunt . . . ita et haec nota falsitatem significet in his locis, ubi aliud sonat in Latino, aliud vero in Graeco.
>
> III. De nota ⳩ Chrismon. . . . Haec quidem ex voluntate scriptoris ad aliquid notandum ponitur. Ego quippe ea usus sum in his locis, ubi in Latino minus habetur quam in Graeco consonanti Hieronimo. . . .
>
> IV. De nota ⁊ Et. . . . in his locis usus sum, ubi ΚΑΙ, id est Et apud Graecos et sanctum Hieronimum habetur.
>
> V. De nota Ͻ Diastole. . . . Qua vero nota utuntur grammatici . . . ad discernenda verba, quae male sibi cohaerentia esse videntur.

Ego autem ea usus sum in his locis, quae a duabus praefatis notis, id est ·Ө theta et ѱ psi, notantur, ut discernat ea verba usque ad quae loca superflua aut mutata esse notantur. . . .

[On symbols. There are five symbols which we employ in this Psalter, i.e., I. Ө theta; II. ѱ psi; III. ₣ chrismon; IV. 7 et; V. Ɔ diastole.

I. On the symbol Ө theta. This symbol signifies death; it is called theta, i.e., 'from death', by the Greeks [cf. *Etym.* I 3, 8]. . . . I employ this letter, however, in those passages which seem superfluous. . . .

II. On the symbol ѱ psi. . . . The Greeks use this letter in writing ѰЄΥΛОΝ, i.e., 'false'. . . . Thus this symbol signifies falsity in those passages which say one thing in Latin but another in Greek.

III. On the symbol ₣ chrismon. . . . This was used by the scribe when he wished to note something [cf. *Etym.* I 21, 22]. But I employ it in those passages in which the Latin text agrees less with Jerome than does the Greek. . . .

IV. On the symbol 7 et. . . . I employ it in those passages where ΚΛΙ, used by the Greeks and St. Jerome for 'et', is found.

V. On the symbol Ɔ diastole. . . . Philologists use this symbol to distinguish words which seem to have little coherence. [cf. *Etym.* I 19, 7]. But I use it in those passages marked with two of the aforementioned symbols, i.e., Ө theta and ѱ psi, so that one can distinguish these words in all passages where they are marked as superfluous or emended. . . .]

The Carolingian philologist wanted to elucidate "the relationship of the Milanese text to the Greek original and Jerome's Psalterium Gallicanum."[4] Almost nothing in the text of the Milanese Psalter was changed in his revision; whether our Carolingian Jerome intended to do more than just devote himself to a scholarly task must remain undecided, despite theological concern with the problem.[5]

The attempt to identify the author more closely is also problematic. In 1893 Morin, who reported "Une révision du psautier sur le texte grec par un anonyme du neuvième siècle," conjectured (certainly under the influence of Traube's "O Roma nobilis," 1891) that Sedulius Scottus was the author.[6] Rahlfs on the other hand not only rejected Sedulius as author, but also called all Irish participation in the composition of the work into question. In his opinion the reviser was an Italian, since he says in his preface, "*meae provinciae consuetudo, mos priorum meorum* . . . und [meint] damit die Gewohnheit der mailändischen Kirche"[7] ("'the usage of my province, the customs of my ancestors,' and with these phrases [means] the custom of the Milanese church"). Without coming to terms with this argument, Schneider again wished to assign the reviser to "a group of Iro-Scottish monks";[8] this interpretation has since become the received opinion.[9]

It must be pointed out how slight the evidence is on which such conjectures rest: it consists of a group of eight poems in the Codex Bernensis 363 (of unquestionably Irish origin) to Emperor Lothar (d. 855), a Duke Leodfrid, Bishop Sofrid of Piacenza (ca. 852), and especially Archbishop Tado of Milan (860–68). The last-named is addressed quite clearly on the subject of hospitality for the Irish:

> Collige Scottigenas, speculator, collige sophos.
> Te legat omnipotens; collige Scottigenas.

[Assemble the Irish, Bishop, assemble the sages. May the Omnipotent choose you; assemble the Irish.]

(*MGH Poetae*, III, 236). According to Ernst Dümmler, Milan is "to be regarded as the place of residence of the poet," whose verses betray "a remarkable similarity to Sedulius' poetic progeny." One can concur thus far; but that Sedulius Scottus himself was the poet ("just as his countryman Dungal, whom we first find in St. Denis and subsequently in Pavia [and Bobbio], so Sedulius could have also moved from Liège to Milan, especially since his patron, Emperor Lothar, ruled both cities" [Dümmler, p. 319]) is less certain. Traube did not wish to go so far as to draw this conclusion; he assumed that there was an Irish colony in Milan (cf. "O Roma nobilis," p. 349, and the edition of the poems of Codex Bernensis in *MGH Poetae*, III, 232–37). Hermann Hagen expressed no opinion on the historical and literary questions in his preface to the facsimile edition of Codex Bernensis 363; in Hagen's index of "nomina propria codicis marginibus adspersa," Sedulius' name is strikingly prominent, followed by the name "Johannes," who was certainly Johannes Scottus. Bieler's facsimile edition of the Basel Psalter has again demonstrated that the scribe of Cod. Bernensis was also associated with the "St. Gall group of bilinguals" ("sanktgallischen Bilinguengruppe"; cf. Bieler, p. xix): the relationships are thus much more complex than they were thought to be in the older research literature, and there seem to have been relations among all Irish groups on the Continent.

Works of translation have not yet been traced with any certainty to the Carolingian region of Italy. One could imagine them most easily in hagiographic literature. There were polyglots in Italy at all times, and even the Italian *grammaticus* of Charlemagne's time, for example, had a few Graeca immediately at hand, as the Berlin MS Diez. B. Sant. 66, dealt with above, demonstrates.

Perhaps one can progress further by means of the *Vita S. Donati episcopi*, translated from Greek (*BHL* 2304). In a skillful prologue, the translation is dedicated to Anastasia, a *famula dei*. The *Vita* was already widely circulated north of the Alps in the first third of the ninth century.[10] This same St. Donatus, bishop of Arezzo, was the subject of a poem entered in Berlin, Diez. B.66 by the Italian grammarian—the only hagiographical material in the manuscript.

In general, translations were more commonly produced in Italy along the borders between East and West and in the overlapping cultural zones around those borders. The Venetian territories formed such a zone: while Ravenna, the Byzantine exarchate's capital, was lost to the Lombards even in the eighth century, the Byzantine fleet was able to keep the city of Venice free from Lombard and Frankish rule. The city formally belonged to the Greek Empire, but soon had no more than a very loose association with Constantinople.

In deference to the papacy, which had brought them into the country to oppose the Lombards, the Franks were restricted in their expansion to the south. Thus the Lombard Duchy of Benevento could remain as a kind of buffer state between the Frankish and Greek relams. The duchy, which in the monastery of Monte Cassino possessed a cultural focal point of great importance, thus became the heir of Lombard independence: Benevento was even able to ward off that most successful product of the Carolingian Renaissance, the Carolingian minuscule. The use of the Beneventan script remained the dominant script there into the twelfth century. Duke Arichis II of Benevento (758–87), Bishop Aio (870–85), and the lector Ademar of Benevento are mentioned as translators or patrons of translators.[11]

From the ninth century on, the Greek Empire waged an unsuccessful war against the Arabs in Sicily. In 878 Syracuse fell; in 962 with the fall of Taormina, all of Sicily was lost. Not before the arrival of the Normans was Sicily again to be wrenched from Arab control and gloriously reintegrated into the intellectual life of the West. But the loss of Sicily strengthened the Greek will to assert itself in southern Italy. In 876 the Greeks took over Bari from the Lombards, and in 880 Saracen Tarento was reconquered. The Byzantines divided the land into sections called "Calabria" and "Langobardia." With the latter, they claimed that their rule was a continuation of the Lombard principality of Benevento.[12] Bari was the most important Byzantine naval station in Langobardia, Reggio was its counterpart in Calabria. In 915 the Greeks, accompanied by troops from Benevento and Spoleto and troops of Pope John X, won a victory over the Saracens on the Garigliano, thus strengthening the Byzantine position in Campania. The coastal cities of Campania, especially Naples, which played a particularly important role in the cultural life of the ninth and tenth centuries, were loosely dependent on the Byzantine Empire in a manner similar to that of Venice. This sovereignty in southern Italy, newly established under the first Macedonian emperor, Basil I (867–85), endured almost two centuries;[13] it ended with the Norman victory of Robert Guiscard over the Byzantine katepan of Bari in 1071.

Sixteen years later, Robert Guiscard presented the archbishop of Bari with the courtyard of the Byzantine katepan's palace to build a house for a new Greek master, whose influence would soon reach regions of which the Byzantines had hardly any clear conception! St. Nicholas, whom sailors from Bari brought to their home city from Myra in Asia Minor in 1087, was the new and permanent resident.[14]

2. Rome and Anastasius Bibliothecarius

When the papacy exchanged Byzantine rule in Rome for Frankish patronage, the Greco-Latin relations were by no means interrupted in Rome. On the contrary, Greek monasticism in Rome grew in great numbers time and again in the eighth and ninth centuries due to the iconoclastic conflict; and no longer did the exarch hasten from Ravenna to Rome, no longer did a dromone land at Ostia to deport to Constantinople or the Black Sea a monk who had fled to Rome, or even an unobliging pope! In the early ninth century there were at least nine fully or partially Greek monasteries at Rome: S. Anastasius ad Aquas Salvias, S. Caesarius in Palatio, S. Erasmus, S. Gregorius in Clivo Scauri, S. Praxedis, S. Saba, S. Silvester in Capite, and the two establishments belonging to S. Lorenzo fuori le Mura, S. Cassianus and S. Stephanus.[15] Most likely it was in one of these monasteries that the splendid Greek manuscript of the *Dialogues* of Gregory the Great was written, in Pope Zacharias' translation and dating precisely from the year 800; one of the scribes takes his leave with the following multiply encoded Greco-Latin subscription:[16]

$$
\begin{array}{c c c}
 & \text{MH} & \\
\text{KOYN} & \text{NI} & \text{B}\lambda \\
\text{NE} \quad \overline{\text{IC}} & \Delta\omega & \overline{\text{XC}} \ \text{BOY} \\
\text{ME} & \text{K}\lambda & \text{CE}\rho \\
 & \text{C}\lambda\lambda &
\end{array}
$$

IHCOYC XPICTOC NI-Kλ. $\Delta\omega$-MH-NE C$\lambda\lambda$-BOY KOYN-CEρ-Bλ ME:

DOMINE SALVUM CONSERVA ME

During the iconoclasm of Emperor Leo V the Armenian (813–20), the Syracusan Methodius, later patriarch of Constantinople (843–47), was among the Greeks in Rome; he was actively engaged in copying and collecting texts while exiled in Rome.[17] In the ninth and tenth centuries Rome was still "une place où l'on possède, d'où l'on expédie et où l'on fait des manuscrits grecs" ("a place where Greek manuscripts were owned, exported, and produced").[18]

In this milieu, the talent of Anastasius of S. Maria in Trastevere developed, a most proficient translator who was hardly less well versed in the Greek literature of the time than in the Latin literature. He felt himself called to be pope, but was then satisfied with the role of the most trusted adviser to several popes in Byzantine and southeast European matters and administered the library at the illustrious papal court of John VIII (Anastasius "Bibliothecarius," d. 878/79).

Arthur Lapôtre's rare monograph *De Anastasio bibliothecario sedis apostolicae* (Paris 1885) purports to portray *hominem, non scriptorem* (p. 4), but includes in the appendix a useful list of Anastasius' works (pp. 329–38), which can still be of great assistance in the search for Anastasius' translations. E. Perels, *Papst Nikolaus I. und Anastasius Bibliothecarius* (Berlin 1920) is concerned with the authorship of papal letters; the detailed "Geschichte des Anastasius" (pp. 185–241) deals with Anastasius' translations only marginally. The best overview of the translations which can be attributed to him with some certainty is given by G. Laehr, in *NA* 47 (1927/28), 416–18. The letters and translator's prefaces are edited by Perels and Laehr in *MGH Epistolae*, VII, 395–442; with few exceptions, the translations themselves must still be read in *Migne PL* 129. A new bibliographical overview by G. Arnaldi, "Anastasio Bibliotecario," *Dizionario Biografico degli Italiani* (Rome 1961), III, 25–37. C. Leonardi, "L'agiografia romana nel secolo IX," in *Hagiographie, cultures et sociétés* (Paris 1981), 471–89, here pp. 474 ff.: "L'agiografia di Anastasio Bibliotecario"; P. Devos, "Anastase le bibliothécaire: Sa contribution à la correspondance pontificale. La date de sa mort," *Byzantion* 32 (1962), 97–115.

At the beginning of Anastasius' work as a translator there was a great work of seventh-century Byzantine hagiography, the *Vita S. Iohannis Eleemosynarii* of Bishop Leontius of Neapolis in Cyprus; through his work, Anastasius became reconciled with Pope Nicholas I (858–67).[19] This vita, significant in the context of medieval biographical literature, was actually a supplement. In the foreword, Anastasius translates Leontius' title as *De vitae residius Iohannis Alexandrini antistitis*, "On that which is left over of the life of Bishop John of Alexandria." It is a matter here of the third biography of John the Merciful. It was supposed to include only what was "left over." But in the hands of Leontius, the most important Greek hagiographer of the seventh century, these gleanings became the biography that eclipsed all its predecessors.

It is a collection of stories about John the Merciful and the great theme of his life—compassion and an infinite willingness to help his fellow men. This patriarch of Alexandria is a kind of St. Francis of the early Middle Ages. Leontius makes great use of the technique of the frame story, without its becoming so closed a construction as it became, for example, in the *Thousand and One Nights*. Both this form and the radically ascetic content of the vita must have seemed decidedly oriental to the Western reader of the ninth century. In his translation Anastasius strengthened this impression, in that his text is strewn with Graecolatina: *philochristus* 'lover of Christ', *xenodochium* 'hospice', *nosocomium* 'hospital', *gerontocomium* 'home for the aged', etc. The translation is not without error and often awkward, when Anastasius translates too literally from the Greek text:[20]

ἐφοβοῦντο γὰρ μὴ	timebant enim, ne iterum idip-
πάλιν τὸ αὐτὸ σχῆμα ποιήσῃ	sum *schema* faceret eis ille sem-
αὐτοὺς ὁ ἀείμνηστος.	per memorandus.

In general, however, Anastasius was able to produce a readable and understandable text. The Roman translator had chosen his first major translation project with a great understanding of literature and history. He continued the old Roman interest in ascetic literature from the Alexandrian cultural circle. On the basis of this translation, he found a deserved place in the literary history of the Middle Ages.[21]

Anastasius dedicated his translation of the *Vita S. Basilii* attributed to Amphilochius of Iconium to Subdeacon Ursus, the court physician of Pope Nicholas I.[22] Anastasius had also chosen this Greek text with great care. He sought out possible preliminary studies and did not neglect to include the preface of the Greek author in Latin translation, in addition to his own prologue; this had been Dionysius Exiguus' method in former times.

In his prologue to the *Vita S. Basilii* (*MGH Epistolae*, VII, 399 f.), Anastasius reports that although he thought a translation of the vita already existed, he decided to undertake this project—appealing to Jerome's translation of the Bible! Upon closer examination, he determined to his relief that only two *miracula* from the vita had been translated up to that time (*Vita S. Basilii* 8 and 10, each a complete narrative unit in itself, the first of which Hrotsvitha of Gandersheim adapted as one of her "dramas," *Basilius*). Was Anastasius referring to the translation by the Greek Euphemius, of which he could have had some knowledge through the doctrinal report of Bishop Aeneas of Paris *Adversus Graecos* (see Chapter VIII, sec. 1, above)? The two chapters mentioned by Anastasius are, however, not the same two which were inserted in *Adversus Graecos*.

Further hagiographic translations followed: around 868 the *Vita S. Iohannis Calybitae*, dedicated to Bishop Formosus of Porto, who had just returned from Bulgaria (one of the Romans' greatest goals was to win this country for the Roman church);[23] in 875, the *Passio SS. Cyri et Iohannis* of Sophronius of Jerusalem, which can be seen as a supplement to the vita of John the Merciful;[24] at about the same time, the *Translatio S. Stephani*, which is dedicated to Bishop Landulf of Capua;[25] a *Passio S. Petri Alexandrini episcopi* and the *Passio SS. MCCCCLXXX martyrum* for Bishop Peter of Gabii.[26] Around 875, Anastasius also dedicated an account of the discovery of the relics of St. Clemens of Rome to Bishop Gauderich of Velletri, who was himself engaged in literary activity; the work was written by the "philosopher" Constantine of Thessalonica, later apostle to the Slavs and called Cyril, who was also held in high esteem in Rome.[27] For Bishop Aio of Benevento, Anastasius translated a homily by Theodorus Studites on the Apostle Bartholomew.[28] When Charles the Bald went to Rome for the imperial coronation (875), Anastasius also joined the group of scholars who paid homage to him. He dedicated to the emperor in the first year of his reign the translation of the *Passio et miracula S. Demetrii*[29] and—as an appendix, as it were, to John Scottus' translation of Dionysius, which Anastasius had revised—a *Passio S. Dionysii*, translated from Greek with a preface which not only is well founded historically and literarily, as are most of Anastasius' other translator's prologues, but also provides insight into the development of Anastasius' own Greek culture. The original Greek text, which Anastasius still remembered from his youth, was discovered in a Roman monastery. The author was Methodius of Syracuse, the most important of the "Greeks" who from time to time dwelled in Rome. In the discussion of Dionysius' surname, which Hilduin had reported, Anastasius refers to Greek copies of the Gospels and Psalms: just as was the case north of the Alps, the comparison of biblical books must have been the most important aid in language study in Italy as well. Of course the Italians had the incomparable advantage of greater ease in coming into contact with speakers of Greek:[30]

> Anastasius, humble librarian of the Apostolic See, to the most august lord and most benevolent Emperor Charles, the ever noble worshiper of the true God, an eternal empire with Christ in the Lord.
> Behold, most ingenious and most Christian of emperors, who unearths and investigates the truth as if a treasure, . . . the *Passio* of the holy, godly martyr Dionysius, once the Areopagite, then bishop of Athens, which I read in Rome during my childhood, which I heard from envoys from Constantinople, and which by your order was long sought and finally found in the greatest of monasteries at Rome. With God's help I have translated it into Latin as best as I can by gathering up my strength (from much weakness) for a translation contest; even if the translation is not word-for-word, I have striven to draw out the entire meaning. Thus the opinion of certain people may change, who do not think Dionysius the Areopagite the same one whose body and virtuous works emit a pleasant scent in Paris, since the Greek language, in which he was in fact born and wrote his sublime works, now certifies and proclaims this in agreement with the Latin language. We are well aware of the fact that the prominent exegetes of the Church who wrote in Latin immediately consulted the Greek text of the Holy Scriptures when they encountered passages of uncertain meaning; and according to its sense, they warded off every cloud of ambiguity without further delay. . . . I could say much about that, with God's instruction, if I were writing an apology and not a preface. Receive therefore, most august Emperor, this Dionysius, who comes on the wing from Greece anew, and since you rejoice to have [his vita] in Latin, rejoice also that you receive it rendered from the Greek language. Since, however, some say that the blessed Dionysius is called "pinnacle of Heaven" (πτερύγιον τοῦ οὐρανοῦ) by the Greeks [cf. Hilduin's *Passio* of Dionysius], it is to be noted that the blessed John Chrysostom describes him in the last of his sermons as "bird of heaven" (πετεινὸν τοῦ οὐρανοῦ). The difference between the two names is to be understood from the sacred books of the Gospels and Psalms written in Greek. For on the one hand, a Latin codex translates the Greek πτερύγιον not by *ala*, but by *pinnaculum*

[Matt. 4:5]; on the other hand, πετεινὸν is often translated into Latin as *volucris*. The text of this *Passio* was written by the blessed Methodius, who was sent by the Apostolic See to Constantinople as a priest and took over the pontifical office of that city; and from that time on, all reckoned him among the saints and honored him as such because of his confession and struggle; he published little that he had gleaned from the many preceding works. . . .

In the month of June, in the ninth indiction, in the fourth pontifical year of our blessed lord, Pope John VIII, and in the first imperial year of our most generous lord, the ever merciful Charles.

The majority of the hagiographical translations which came about in the eighth decade of the ninth century are to be seen as occasional works (as opposed to the two vitae named first), for Anastasius had meanwhile turned to great works of ecclesiastical law, history, and theology. On behalf of Emperor Louis II (855–75) and Pope Hadrian II (867–72), Anastasius was in Constantinople in 869–70, where he participated in the eighth ecumenical council which took place during those years; he brought the conciliar acts back to Rome and translated them. Thereafter he thought it necessary to replace the poor translation of the acts of the seventh council from 787 with a better one, which he dedicated to Pope John VIII (872–82).

The dedicatory texts for the translation of the acts of the seventh council are included, with much historical information, in *MGH Epistolae*, VII, 403–15. Leonardi confirmed the old hypothesis, which goes back to Caesar Baronius, that Cod. Vat. lat. 4965 with Anastasius' preface and translation may be traced back to Anastasius himself (Leonardi, in *Studi Medievali* III/8 [1967], 59–192; see also Lohrmann, in *Quellen und Forschungen aus italienischen Archiven und Bibliotheken* 50 [1971], 420 ff.); this manuscript, written by several scribes, most likely of the papal scriptorium (870–71), was the working copy into which Anastasius entered his corrections. The manuscript was already in Verona by the tenth century; Bishop Rather wrote glosses in the manuscript. It may well be the oldest Western manuscript which allows a direct glimpse into the "translators' workshop."

Anastasius also accomplished important work in the field of historiography. Here he continued the translation work of Cassiodorus, as the title of the *Chronographia tripartita* itself expresses; in this work he translated parts of the *Chronography* of Patriarch Nicephorus I of Constantinople (d. 829), parts of the *Chronicle* of George the Syncellus (d. after 810), and especially parts of the continuation of the latter work by Theophanes Homologetes (the Confessor, d. 818).[31] The *Collectanea* are connected to this great work. In the former, Anastasius translated and compiled important Greek sources from the dramatic periods of the "Byzantine eras of the Papacy"—documents concerning Pope Honorius I and especially Pope Martin I and Maximus the Confessor, the champions and sufferers of that dark and, for the Romans of the ninth century, notable period when old and feeble Rome became the refuge of orthodox Greek monasticism, fleeing a monothelitism which was promoted by the state's executive power.[32] Among the documents here assembled by Anastasius' excellent historical sense, one finds the unique eyewitness account of the arrest of Pope Martin I in 653 while in the Lateran Basilica, his staged mock trial in Constantinople, and his disappearance in barbarous exile on the Black Sea.[33]

Both of the historical translations are dedicated to Johannes Diaconus, the great historiographer at the papal court of John VIII, and are generally considered mere preparatory work for an ecclesiastical history planned by John, just as they characterize themselves in the prologues.

Most recently on this topic, see Löwe, in Wattenbach and Levison, *Deutschlands Geschichtsquellen*, H. 4, p. 466. Laehr had nonetheless already shown that much of the material in Anastasius' prologues must be attributed to courtesy and conventional modesty—for example, when Anastasius assures Bishop Martin of Narni that he was motivated to undertake the translation of the *Commemoratio* on the fate of Pope Martin I only through the bishop's efforts, which even Anastasius himself halfway contradicts when he explains that he is working on the *Acta Maximi Confessoris*, i.e., just that collection from which the bishop received an advance sample. Cf. Laehr, in *NA* 47 (1927/28), 434, on the independent character of the *Chronographia tripartita*: "Wenn Anastasius seinen Freund [Johannes Diaconus] ermahnt, im Anschluß an dieses frühere kirchengeschichtliche Werk [die *Historia tripartita* des Cassiodor] sein Buch möglichst umfassend zu gestalten, so mag der Leser Empfindung haben, daß diese Aufgabe zum guten Teil schon von Anastasius gelöst ist, zumal er am Schluß ausdrücklich hervorhebt, daß er nicht karge Auszüge aus den griechischen Autoren bringt, sondern fast alles übersetzt, was nicht bei Eusebius oder in der Historia tripartita schon erzählt ist . . ." ("When Anastasius exhorts his friend [Johannes Diaconus], by referring to this earlier work of ecclesiastical history [Cassiodorus' *Historia tripartita*], to cast his book in the most comprehensive possible form, the reader may sense that Anastasius has already completed a good part of the task, especially since he expressly emphasizes at the end that he has not presented miserly excerpts from the Greek authors, but rather translated almost everything which had not already been included in Eusebius' work or in the *Historia tripartita*").

In truth these translations by Anastasius have a value in themselves, independent of their actual or pretended cause, and must be regarded as the third, and for several centuries the last, great Western attempt to assimilate Greco-Christian historiography. Just as Jerome and Rufinus provided a Latin audience for Eusebius, as Cassiodorus and Epiphanius did for Sozomenus, Theodoret, and Socrates, so did Anastasius again give a Latin voice to Theophanes in particular, the historian of Greek monasticism of the seventh and eighth centuries.

The epochs of the seventh and eighth centuries, with which Anastasius' historical work was concerned, also occupied the translator (as a successor to Dionysius the Areopagite) with its best and most difficult material—its theology of mysteries. It seems that Anastasius first became acquainted with the *Areopagitica* itself as a reviewer of John Scottus. Pope Nicholas I had requested Charles the Bald to send John Scottus' translation to Rome.[34]

It was not until 875, eight years after Nicholas' death, that Anastasius returned the translation with his supplements. In his accompanying letter to Charles the Bald, the Roman librarian shows his astonishment that a *vir barbarus* was able to intellectually grasp such an author as Dionysius and translate his works into another language. Anastasius criticized the translation—quite legitimately—as too literal and so difficult to understand that John Scottus, "quem interpretaturus susceperat, adhuc redderet interpretandum"[35] ("who had undertaken to explain (translate) Dionysius, had now rendered his works in need of explanation"). In order to offer something besides criticism, Anastasius added annotations on Dionysius from Johannes Scythopolis and Maximus the Confessor to the copy of the text which he returned; he had become acquainted with these scholia during his stay in Constantinople.[36]

His work on Dionysius and above all the impressive personality of Constantine-Cyril of Thessalonica led Anastasius deeper into the early Byzantine theology of the mysteries. He translated the ΙϹΤΟΡΙΑ ΕΚΚΛΗϹΙΑϹΤΙΚΗ, attributed to Patriarch Germanus of Constantinople (d. 730), and a Greek summary of the ΜΥϹΤΑΓΩΓΙΑ of Maximus the Confessor.[37] He sent both translations to Charles the Bald.[38]

A comprehensive evaluation of Anastasius Bibliothecarius' work, the most significant achievement in translation between Dionysius Exiguus in the sixth century and Burgundio of Pisa in the twelfth, is still to be written. Deliberately associating himself with the Scythian translator in the Rome of the Gothic period, this Roman translator of the ninth century liked to call himself ANASTASIUS EXIGUUS, and it is in this perspective that his work must be assessed.

Laehr's study, cited frequently in the foregoing analysis, closes with the judgment: "Wenn auch einem Photios oder einem Johannes Scottus nicht ebenbürtig, repräsentiert Anastasius doch nicht unwürdig die römische Bildung, kurz bevor sich die Nacht der Barbarei über die ewige Stadt senkte" ("Even if not of the stature of a Photius or John Scottus, Anastasius is not an undeserving representative of Roman culture shortly before the night of barbarity descended on the eternal city"; *NA* 47 [1927/28], 468). Remarkably, the "historian" among the translators of the Latin Middle Ages is judged by modern historians according to standards which do not belong to his (or their) domain. For the translator Anastasius can scarcely be compared with the theologian Photius; in order to compare John Scottus and Anastasius as translators, it would be necessary to determine what material in the Dionysius translations that go under John's name is due to Hilduin, what to John himself, and what to Anastasius' revision. The fact that John exhibited other qualities as a theologico-philosophical writer cannot be played off against Anastasius' achievement as a translator. It is quite characteristic of this

long-established prejudice that both of the John Scottus colloquia of recent years
(*The Mind of Eriugena*, 1973; *Jean Scot Érigène et l'histoire de la philosophie*,
1977) ignored the Carolingian translator's Italian counterpart.

3. The Translation School of Naples

In the second half of the ninth century, Naples emerged as the focal point
of literary culture in Italy. While the impulse for translation diminished in
Rome after Anastasius,[39] Naples opened up to Greek culture and was in
general one of the few places in the West where a cultural continuity was
preserved throughout the late ninth and early tenth century.[40] The
famous marble calendar of S. Giovanni Maggiore in Naples functioned as
a symbol of, or plan for, this continuity;[41] the calendar names Latin and
Greek saints together and, according to the will of the bishop who had it
set up—most likely Athanasius I (849–72)—was to promote the veneration of the saints of the city, where there was a special fondness for combining Latin and Greek harmoniously in the liturgy.[42]

With its translations from Greek, the Neapolitan translators' school
served, almost without exception, the cult of the saints. At the beginning
there are two accounts in which the Virgin quite obviously intercedes for
sinful men, the *Vita S. Mariae Aegyptiacae* and the *Paenitentia Theophili*.
A certain deacon named Paul had compiled them and dedicated them
Domino gloriosissimo ac praestantissimo regi Carolo.[43] Maria Aegyptiaca
came to be one of the most famous of the choir of pentitents in all of Western literature.[44] As a result of its motif of a pact with the devil, the
Paenitentia Theophili became associated with the life of Basil that Anastasius had translated.[45] What was extraordinary about Theophilus is that he
was able to extract himself from his entanglements with the devil due to
the intercession of the Virgin. This devotion of the sinner to Mary is also a
motif in the *Vita S. Mariae Aegyptiacae*. Thus a common intention in the
first two Neapolitan translations of the ninth century has been proposed,
since they are "the first two texts through which the idea of Mary's saving
intercession took form in the West."[46]

Deacon John, famous as the historian of the Church of Naples,[47] gave
the West a still more famous work of Greek hagiography in 880, when he
published a free adaptation into Latin of a work by the Patriarch Methodius on St. Nicholas[48] (*Vita S. Nicolai*).[49] With this work, this Byzantine
saint of the common people made his appearance in the West and began
his triumphant march through western Europe, an advance to be compared only with St. Martin's. Further translations by Johannes Diaconus
worthy of mention are the *Passio XL martyrum Sebastenorum*[50] and a *Vita
S. Euthimii*,[51] both of which were commissioned by Abbot John of St.
Severin near Naples. On behalf of Bishop Athanasius II of Naples (ca.

876–98), who was himself active as a translator,[52] a certain Guarimpotus worked as a translator and, in his prefaces, demanded the ancient freedom to translate "plurimis additis, plurimis ademptis, mutatis et transmutatis dictionibus aliisque pro aliis positis," without, however, making great use of this freedom himself.

P. Devos, "L'oeuvre de Guarimpotus, hagiographe napolitain," *AB* 76 (1958), 151–78. The method of comparing topoi found in the prefaces does not lead to a reliable determination of authorship, as it might appear in Devos' work. Guarimpotus (Warimpotus) is certainly the translator of the *Passio S. Eustratii et IV sociorum in Armenia (BHL* 2778), which was produced by order of Bishop Anastasius II and in which Guarimpotus explains that he will append a *Passio beatissimi Guari* to it. Devos' identification of Guari with Blasii is quite daring (". . . la déformation de *Blasii* en *Guari,* si bizarre qu'elle soit, pèse peu dans la balance" ["the deformation of *Blasii* to *Guari,* as bizarre as it may be, does not weigh heavily in the balance"; p. 162]). It is known that the *Passio S. Febroniae* was a work commissioned by Bishop Athanasius II of Naples; one may suppose that Guarimpotus was the translator. A note in P. Rabbow, "Zur Geschichte des urkundlichen Sinns," *Historische Zeitschrift* 126 (1922), 76, points to another translator, however: "Codex Cavensis 15, a late paper manuscript (which is, however, according to the subscriptio, a copy from a *passionarium* from Monte Cassino written in Lombardic script), gives evidence that the translation of the *passio Febroniae* is the work of a certain *Petrus coelestis*: 'prologus in passionem s. Febroniae virginis de graeco in latinum translatum per Petrum coelestem iussu Athanasii iunioris' ['the prologue to the passion of St. Febronia the virgin was translated from Greek into Latin by Petrus coelestis at the order of Athanasius II].'" Except for the prologue (*AB* 76 [1958], pp. 165 f.), the *Passio S. Febroniae* is still unedited. According to the preface to the *Passio,* the same Bishop Athanasius II of Naples also occasioned a translation of the *Passio S. Petri Alexandrini episcopi;* Devos would now like to deprive Anastasius Bibliothecarius of that very text (*BHL* 6692–93) which the *communis opinio* from A. Mai to G. Laehr (in *NA* 47 [1927/28], 445–48) has attributed to him on solid grounds, and add it to the oeuvre of the Neapolitan Guarimpotus. Devos' confident publication of an *anonymous translation of the Passio S. Petri Alexandrini (BHL* 6698b) in *AB* 83 (1965), under the title "Une passion grecque inédite de S. Pierre d'Alexandrie et sa traductions par Anastase le Bibliothécaire," does not make his other attribution any more convincing. Only a full analysis of the manuscripts of all Neapolitan translations will make possible a carefully balanced judgment of each translator's part in these works, up until now labeled "anonymous." The passage in the prologue to the *Passio S. Eustratii* which concerns free translation is also found almost word for word in the prologue to the *Passio S. Febroniae* (ed. Devos, in *AB* 76 [1958], 155 and 166, respectively). In the latter prologue, the translator invokes the liberties which the Greek translators of the Septuagint took with the Hebrew original; the Neapolitan translator could infer this from the critical notes in Jerome's *Psalterium iuxta LXX* ("Gallicanum"): "Porro septuaginta interpretes quanta addiderint vel quanta omiserint, testes sunt asterisci et obeli etiam et doctissimi Hieronimi editio" ("Furthermore, the asterisks and obelisks, and even the edition by the most learned Jerome, are witnesses to how much the seventy translators may have added or omitted").

For one of the two Athanasii of the episcopal see in Naples, a certain Gregorius, who called himself *clericorum infimus,* revised the *Passio*

Anastasii Persae, the Latin translation of which had once so offended Bede.[53] In his preface, Gregory the cleric also mentions a "Nicolaus prelustris archipresbyter, Achivos quidem luculente, Latinos vero ex parte apices eruditus"; if this archpriest, educated more in Greek than in Latin, is identical with the later "dominus Nicolaus praesul peritissimus grecorum atque philosophus," whom Ursus (the translator to be dealt with next) once asked for advice, then we have come to the turn of the century.

In the tenth century, the dukes of Naples (or rather Campania) became prominent patrons of translation. The priest Ursus translated Pseudo-Amphilochius' *bios* of Basil (the third translation of the work) for the *loci servator* Gregory II of Naples (d. 915–16);[54] the subdeacon Bonitus revised a *Passio S. Theodori* and additionally reported in the preface that the pious people of Naples occasionally ridiculed saints' lives.[55] Subdeacon Peter of Naples (d. after 960) also began his extensive hagiographic work under Duke Gregory II.[56] Peter based his Latin adaptations of Greek saints' lives in part on older translations, which he recast in a playful sequence of rhyme and verse.

Many of the translators named wrote prefaces to their works which present a lively picture of the Greco-Latin life in and around Naples and also make clear that in Naples it was last but not least Campania's ducal house that so eagerly read Greek narrative literature in Latin. Elements of literary culture among the laity are also seen in the prologue which Archpriest Leo wrote for his translation of the Alexander novel by Pseudo-Callisthenes. Leo became acquainted with this work while serving as the ambassador of Duke John III (928–68/69) in Constantinople around the middle of the tenth century; he copied the narrative and brought it to the duchess; later he prepared a translation.[57] This was not the first translation of the Greek Alexander novel. Julius Valerius had already translated it in the early fourth century, and this translation was rather widely circulated in an epitome.[58] It has, however, not from there but from the Neapolitan translation that the rich and multiform Alexander romances of the high Middle Ages developed.[59]

[x]

The Ottonian Era

Vultus adest domini, cui totus sternitur orbis,
  Signo iudicii vultus adest domini.
Ergo fremit populus, nec cessant tundere pectus
  Matres cum senibus, ergo fremit populus.
Sistitur in solio domini spectabile signum,
  Theotocosque suo sistitur in solio.
Hinc thimiama dabunt, hinc balsama prima reponunt,
  Thus myrramque ferunt, hinc thimiama dabunt.
Dat scola Greca melos et plebs Romana susurros,
  Et variis modulis dat scola Greca melos.
Kyrie centuplicant et pugnis pectora pulsant
  Christe faveto! tonant, Kyrie centuplicant.

[The face of the Lord is present, to whom the entire world bows down; in a sign of judgment, the face of the Lord is present. Therefore the people tremble; neither mothers nor the elderly cease to strike their breasts; therefore the people tremble. A visible sign is placed on the throne of the Lord, and the mother of God is placed on her throne. Hence they will give incense, hence they will store up prime balsam and bear forth frankincense amd myrrh, hence they will give incense. The Greek school will sing and the Roman people hum, and the Greek school will sing in various melodies. They raise the Kyrie a hundred times and strike their breasts with blows. Christ be with us! they thunder, they raise the Kyrie a hundred times.]

"Carmen in assumptione sanctae Mariae in nocte quando tabula portatur" (Rome, A.D. 1000), MGH Poetae, V, 467.

1. "Ottonian Style"

The romance of Alexander in Naples has already led far into the tenth century in more than just a chronological sense: in its fantastic diversity and profusion of material, its origin at a ducal *court* (in connection with which a *lady* took special interest in the romanticism of the great Macedonian's heroic life), in its form, which was little concerned with classical models, the Neapolitan romance was a typical work of the tenth century.

The Latin literature of the *saeculum ferreum* cannot compare with the preceding era in quantity and, in general, also not in linguistic quality; but it is surprisingly well endowed with inventiveness, new points of departure, and talented authors.

The period is called the "Ottonian" after the ruling dynasty of the time; in the strict sense, the period comprises the sixty-six year reign of Otto I

(936–73), Otto II (973–83), and Otto III (983–1002), and in the broader sense it also includes the reign of the founder of the Saxon line, Henry I (919–36), and also that of Henry II (1002–24). Art historians calmly speak of "Ottonian style" which they allow to extend far into the eleventh century. "The great caesura in German art history of the eleventh century does not lie between the Ottonian and 'Salian,' but rather falls in the time of Henry IV. It cuts through the middle of the 'Salian' period. . . . The Romance countries had no 'Ottonian' art, but rather a 'premier art roman,' whose style lasted until around 1070, and thus also up to the Investiture controversy."[1] Such statements from art history are worth taking into account in a literary consideration of the Latin Middle Ages that is based on stylistic analysis, which is, to be sure, a method that is only in its developmental stages.[2]

One element of the "Ottonian style" is the conscious use of Greek in Latin contexts. Rather of Verona (d. 974), the early medieval genius of self-ironical prose, entitled one of his works ΦρΕΝΕϹΙϹ 'madness'. He called one or more of his other works ΧΡΟΝΟΓΡΑΦΙΑ, and, in mentioning this title, he considered the author (himself):[3]

Graecizando vanus, cum non sit saltem Latinus.

[Vain in his Grecizing, since he is not even a Latin.]

It was, however, in the blossoming genre of the sequence, the first new poetic form developed in "Medieval Latin," that the newly awakened delight in Greek was shown. The first master of this poetic genre, Notker I of St. Gall (d. 912), had a great and varied interest in Greek and wrote ΥΠΟΔΙΑΚΟΝΙϹϹΑ above some of his sequences as the title of the melody; but otherwise he usually avoided Greek words in his sequences. Macaronic verse is displeasing in every "classical" epoch. The situation is quite different in the sequences of Ekkehard I of St. Gall (d. 973), who says that John the Baptist "prepared the way of the Lord into the hearts of men" in this manner:[4]

Odon ad antropon
corda parat deo . . .

These passages are still not evidence of Greek studies, but they are signs of the prevailing fashion. And this fashion could certainly develop in the direction of polyglot poetry,[5] as is, quite surprisingly, the case in the *tri*lingual versicles of the *Historia de S. Willibaldo* of Bishop Reginold of Eichstätt (966–91). Here one finds verses in the manner of the sequence, with the succession of languages Latin—Greek—Hebrew—Greek—Latin as a representation of Willibald's pilgrimage from "Latin" through "Greek" and into "Hebrew" territory and back!

St. Willibald of Eichstätt is known to posterity primarily through the autobiographical travelogue of his pilgrimage to the Holy Land, which the nun Hugeburc of Heidenheim wrote down for him (*MGH Scriptores*, XV, 86–106). This suggested to Reginold the idea of presenting the saint's pilgrimage to Palestine as a path through Latin, Greek, and Hebrew "linguistic landscapes"—as a journey through the "three holy languages." We would, to be sure, hardly dare interpret this remarkable work in this way if the eleventh century Eichstätt tradition did not formulate it in precisely such terms. "For as our most holy pilgrim journeyed from Italy to Greece, from Greece to Judaea, and from Judaea back to Greece, from Greece to Italy and from there back here to us, so our very ingenious *musicus* composed first Latin, then Greek, then Hebrew, and again Greek and finally Latin versicles" ("Anonymous Haserensis," *De episcopis Eichstetensibus*, 12, *MGH Scriptores*, VII, 257). No edition of the entire *officium* yet exists. All essential information may be found in B. Bischoff, "Reginold," in Stammler and Langosch, *Verfasserlexikon*, V, 943–45.

2. Otto the Great and Liudprand of Cremona

Three political events of the mid-tenth century defined the relationship between the Greeks and the empire of the Ottonians and their successors in the high Middle Ages: the renewed alliance of the Western Empire with Italy (since 951), the victory of Otto the Great over the Hungarians (955), and his coronation as emperor in Rome (Candlemas 962). In Italy the Ottonians, who took advantage of their rule in Italy by residing there for long periods of time, soon came into conflict with the Greeks; the imperial coronation of Otto I again made the Western Empire into a power to be taken seriously; and finally, the victory over the Hungarians—Otto the Great's crucial deed in the development of his power—had the greatest significance for East-West relations in the long run, since it prepared for the opening of the overland route from the West to Constantinople.[6]

Scholars from the old Lombard cities followed Otto the Great out of Italy in order to improve education and scholarship north of the Alps. In this sense the Ottonian "Renaissance" repeated the Carolingian on a smaller scale. The *magistri* Stephan and Gunzo of Novara were certainly not of the stature of Peter of Pisa, Paulinus of Aquileia, and Paulus Diaconus at Charlemagne's court in earlier times. In Otto the Great's retinue there was, however, such a unique figure as Liudprand of Cremona, who not only had an unusually extensive knowledge of Greek, but was also an excellent Latin scholar, and in addition had the ability to turn both to good literary use.

Born in Pavia, he received the name of the Lombard king buried in S. Pietro in Ciel d'Oro. His family played an important role in the Italian Kingdom: in 927 his father was the ambassador to Constantinople of King Hugh of Provence, who resided in Pavia; he died soon after his return.

Liudprand's stepfather was also one of King Hugh's legates in Constanti-nople (941). When Berengar of Ivrea took control of the Italian Kingdom, the influence of Liudprand's family continued unabated: young Liud-prand was entrusted with an embassy in 949: "What should I tell you first—with what ease he will absorb the Greek lessons, since he has already drained the Latin goblet to its dregs, even in his youth?" With these words, King Berengar is supposed to have made the financial sup-port for Liudprand's embassy palatable for his ambitious stepfather.[7]

The description of his reception by Constantine VII Porphyrogeni-tus, published by Liudprand ten years later, belongs to the realm of "Weltliteratur."[8]

> Before the imperial throne stood a bronze, but gilded, tree, the limbs of which were full of diverse kinds of birds, also of gilded bronze, which all sang at the same time each according to its specific song. The emperor's throne was, however, so artfully built that at one moment it seemed low, in the next higher, and immediately thereafter quite lofty. Lions of enormous size, I do not know whether of metal or of wood, but in any case gilded, stood as if guards of the throne, in that they raised a great roar with their movable tongues, their tails beating the floor and their jaws open. Thus in this hall, supported by two eunuchs, I was led before the face of the emperor. At my entrance the lions roared and the birds chirped, each in its own way; I was, however, seized by neither fear nor astonishment, since I had sought out detailed information about all these things from people who knew them well. When I had fallen to the floor be-fore the emperor for the third time and raised my head, I caught sight of him, whom I had seen sitting at a moderate height before, raised almost to the ceiling of the hall and dressed in other clothes than before. How this happened, I cannot comprehend, unless it was in the same way as the beams of winepresses are raised. The emperor said nothing with his own mouth at this moment, since even if he had wished to do so, it would not have been proper, due to the great dis-tance between us; through his logothete, however, or his chancellor, he informed himself concerning Berengar's life and well-being. After I had answered in fitting manner, I withdrew, at a sign from the translator, and was led to my assigned quarters.

This is one of the magnificent concluding scenes of the ΑΝ-ΤΑΠΟΔΟCΙC, which is, as far as is known, Liudprand's first literary work and is at the same time one of the first works of "Ottonian literature." Liudprand certainly recognized soon after Otto's first Italian expedition (951) who was to control Italy's future. He was at Otto's court by 956 at the latest, and there he made the acquaintance of the Spanish bishop Re-cemund, the ambassador of the caliph ʿAbd ar-Raḥmān III to Otto the Great. This bishop from Arabic Spain called upon the worldly-wise deacon from Pavia to describe "the deeds of the emperors and kings of all Europe as one who knows them, not through doubtful hearsay, but through his own observation." Two years later in Frankfurt, Liudprand began the task; he continued to work on it "en route": he even worked on the text while on the island of Paxoi in the Ionian Sea.[9]

Liudprand surrounded his work with a colorful history of its origin, but one should not allow that to divert attention from the fact that the book was intended for the court, where literature again came to be of interest after the paralysis of intellectual life had receded with the victory over the Hungarians in 955. Under the Ottonians many a talented cleric soon earned a bishopric for himself with a virtuoso literary accomplishment— as had Reginold of Eichstätt, mentioned above.

Ottonian relations to Spain were as difficult and exciting as those with Constantinople: the marvels of which one heard from Spain[10] were comparable to those from the Byzantine East, and thus it must have seemed quite appropriate to Liudprand to dedicate a book to the Christian bishop at the Spanish caliph's court, since the book contained so much novel material from the Byzantine East. On the other hand, he was to have great difficulty in sending the work to its addressee.

Thus an unheard-of (in various senses) history of the troubled period between 888 and 950 in the three arenas Constantinople, Germany, and Italy came about; Liudprand is "the first medieval writer whose works show a broad horizon and give a lively portrayal to the most diverse scenes."[11] If he had been a baroque author, he could have called his history "Theatrum Europaeum." Liudprand nevertheless gave his history quite a surprising and personal title—ΛΝΤΛΠΟΔΟCΙC, 'recompense', which is, however, precise and expressive, just as Rather's ΦΡΕΝΕCΙC, 'book of recompense', in the good as well as the bad sense, means that the author acknowledges his work as a subjective report, which he then also presents in the subjective form of anecdotes, invective, interspersed poems. . . . The most personal, formal element of the book is the Greek material which was incorporated into some passages. Most likely it was not even legible, since it was originally written by Liudprand in minuscule script: in the West it was only in majuscule, if at all, that Greek texts could be dealt with. If the reader had succeeded in deciphering Liudprand's minuscule, then he confronted another difficulty: Liudprand's Graeca are not always those which were familiar from Latin ecclesiastical language and exegesis, but rather they are in part quite unusual. Whoever wanted to read the entire book would have required an interpreter for the glosses to the Graeca, as for example in the following tale of a lion hunt of the emperor-to-be Romanus I Lecapenus:[12]

De leone ferocissimo, quem Ρομανος interfecit. Imperante Leone, Constantini huius genitore, Ρομανος imperator iste, quam-

quam πτοχος, ab omnibus tamen χρησιμος habebatur. Erat autem ex mediocribus ipsis, qui navali pugna stipendia ab imperatore acceperant. Qui cum saepius et iterum εις την μαχην nonnulla χρησιμοτατα faceret, a sibi praeposito adeo ετιμηθη, οπως προτοκαραβος fieri mereretur.

Quadam autem nocte dum exploratum Saracenos abiret, essetque eodem in loco palus atque arundinetum non modicum, contigit leonem ferocissimum ex arundineto prosilire cervorumque multitudinem in paludem dimergere unumque eorum capere sicque ventris rabiem mitigare. Ρομανος δε τον αυτων ψοφον ακουων εδειλασεν σφοδρα. Putavit enim Saracenorum multitudinem esse, qui se conspectum fraude aliqua vellent perhimere.

Ορθρου δε βαθεως exurgens, cum diligentissime cuncta consideraret, conspectis vestigiis ευθεως, quid hoc esset agnovit. Leone itaque in arundineto commorante Ρομανος Grecum ignem, qui nullo praeter aceti liquore extinguitur, undique per arundinetum iactare praecepit. Erat autem in arundineto acervus arundinibus plenus, in quem leo confugiens illo est ab igne salvatus; ventus quippe contraria ex parte flans ignem, ne ad acervum usque perveniret, amovit. Ρομανος praeterea post ignis extinctionem uno tantum cum assecula, ensem solum dextra, sinistra autem pallium gestans, locum omnem peragrans lustrat, si forte os ex eo vel signum aliquod repperiret. Iam vero cum in eo esset, ut nichil inveniens repedaret, quid hoc monstri esset, quod acervus ille sit ab igne salvatus, studuit visere. Cumque duo propter assisterent secumque rebus ex nonnullis confabularent, leo eos tantum audivit, quoniam quidem ob caligantes oculos παρα τω καπνω videre non potuit. Volens igitur leo animi sui furorem, quem ab igne conceperat, in hos evomere, saltu rapidissimo, qua illorum voces audierat, eos inter prosiliit. Ρομανος vero, non ut suus assecula pavitans, sed ea potius mente consistens, ut, etsi fractus caderet orbis, inpavidum ruinae ferirent, pallium, quod manu gestabat, leonis inter brachia misit. Quod dum pro homine leo discerperet, Ρομανος totis hunc a tergo viribus inter clunium iuncturas ense percussit. Qui dissotiatis divisisque cruribus quia stare non potuit, poenitus cecidit. Leone igitur interfecto Ρομανος seminecem assecula suum solo stratum eminus vidit, quem et vocare voce praecipua coepit. Sed cum nullum daret omnino responsum, isdem Ρομανος propter eum adstitit pedeque pulsans: εγειρε, ειπεν, αθλιε και ταλεπορε, μη φοβου! Qui consurgens prae admiratione, dum leonis immanitatem conspiceret, non habuit ultra spiritum. Εξεπλισσοντο δε παντες περι του Ρομανου ταυτα ακουσαντες. Unde factus est, ut tam pro ceteris quamque pro praeclaro praesenti hoc facinore non multo post a Leone imperatore tanto donaretur honore, οπως παντα τα πλοια suis essent in manibus eiusque iussionibus oboedirent.

Glosses: πτοχος ptochos ˙i˙ pauper; χρησιμος chrisimos ˙i˙ utilis; εις την μαχην is tin machin ˙i˙ in pugna; χρησιμοτατα chrisimotata ˙i˙

Horace, *Carm.* III 3, 7–8

utilia; ετιμηϑη οπως προτοκαραβος etimithi opos protocaravos ˙i˙
honoratus est, ut (quatinus *Exc. Mett.*) primus navium; Ρομανος δε
τον αυτων ψοφον ακουων εδειλιασεν σφοδρα Romanos de ton auton
psofon acuon ediliasen sfodra ⟨˙i˙⟩ nomen proprium—autem—articulus—eorum sonitum audiens timuit valde; Ορϑρου δε βαϑεως
orthru de vatheos ˙i˙ mane autem primo (profundo *Exc. Mett.*!);
ευϑεως eutheos ˙i˙ statim; Ρομανος nomen proprium; παρα τω
καπνω para to capno quod est ob fumum; εγειρε ειπεν αϑλιε και
ταλεπορε μη φοβου egire ipen athlie ke talepore mi fobu ˙i˙ Surge,
dixit, miser noli timere (ne timeas *Exc. Mett.*); εξεπλισσοντο δε
παντες περι του Ρομανου ταυτα ακουσαντες exeplissonto de pantes
peri tu Romanu tauta acusantes ˙i˙ stupebant autem omnes de—articulus—Romano haec audientes; οπως παντα τα πλοια opos
panta—articulus—ta plia ˙i˙ ut omnes naves.

[On the ferocious lion which Romanus killed.

During the reign of Emperor Leo [VI, 886–912], the father of the
current Emperor Constantine [VII, 945–59], Emperor Romanus [I,
920–44] was considered by all to be capable, although poor. He belonged to that ordinary class of men who received a soldier's pay from
the emperor for their participation in naval battles. After repeated
and frequent demonstrations of his ability in battle, he was honored
by his commander by being given command of the ships.

One night as he went out to reconnoiter the Saracen positions and
came upon a swamp and thick reeds, it happened that a ferocious lion
sprang forth from the reeds and drove a herd of deer into the swamp,
seized one of them, and thus allayed its hunger. But Romanus was
very frightened by this noise, for he thought that it was a troop of
Saracens who had discovered him and now wanted to destroy him by
means of some trick.

He rose early in the morning, and when he had carefully considered the entire matter and had seen the tracks, he knew immediately
what this was. And thus, since the lion was still lying among the
reeds, Romanus ordered Greek fire, which can be extinguished by
no other liquid besides vinegar, to be cast into the thicket from all
sides. In the thicket there was, however, a heap of reeds, into which
the lion had fled and thus remained unharmed by the fire. For the
wind, which was blowing from the other direction, prevented the
fire from reaching the heap. After the flames had died away, Romanus went through the entire area with only one attendant, in his right
hand his sword, in his left his mantle, looking closely for a bone or
any other sign of the lion. But when he had found nothing and was
prepared to return, he wanted to see how that wonder could have
occurred that the heap had remained untouched by fire. And while
the two stood nearby and talked about various things, the lion heard
them but could not see them, since its eyes were clouded because of
the smoke. Wishing to vent its rage, caused by the fire, on the men,
the lion sprang forth in a ferocious leap to the place where he heard

their voices, between the men. Romanus, however, was not afraid, as was his attendant, but rather held the notion in his mind that even if the world were to fall, dashed to pieces, the falling ruins would strike dead a fearless man; he cast his mantle, which he held in his hand, between the paws of the lion. And while the lion tore it to pieces as if it were a man, from behind Romanus struck down with his sword between the hind parts with all of his strength. And since the lion could no longer stand with severed and separated legs, it collapsed completely. After he had thus killed the lion, Romanus saw his attendant lying half-dead on the ground at some distance, and he began to call him in a loud voice. But when he gave no response whatsoever, Romanus went and stood next to him and struck him with his foot: "Rise up," he said, "you miserable and wretched one, fear not!" When he had arisen and seen the savage lion, he was struck breathless. And everyone was astonished when they heard these things from Romanus. And thus it happened that not long afterwards he was honored by Emperor Leo for this remarkable deed, as well as for others, in that all ships were given into his hands and obeyed his orders.]

The theme of the tale is clearly aristocratic; from earliest times the lion hunt had been the pastime of the ruling class in the East; both Greek and Hebrew mythology know the lion-conquering hero; Christ himself triumphs over dragons and lions in the pictorial imagination of late antiquity and the Middle Ages: "conculcabis leonem et draconem" (Ps. 89:13). Thus the lion, which very few Westerners had ever seen, always actively occupied their imagination.

The tale is, however, also typical for its time. There were no more powerful lions depicted in the Middle Ages than those on imperial silk products from tenth-century Constantinople; imperial silk fabric of this kind, with almost life-sized lion figures, has been found in the graves of Archbishops Heribert and Anno of Cologne.[13] They were not originally made for the purpose of shrouding the remains of Western clergymen, but rather belonged to the characteristic depiction of a monarch of the Byzantine heroic age, in which the lionhearted warrior was the most beloved sovereign of the era; in the tenth century, this is also true in the West, in Scandinavia, Russia, Syria, and Persia.[14] Thus one may regard Liudprand's tale as typical of the monarchial image in tenth-century Constantinople, Western Europe, and many other countries; and Liudprand could count on arousing special interest, since he had rather adeptly interwoven the topical motif of the Saracens into the tale.

Liudprand provided this chapter of his book with an especially sumptuous Greek decor. Here he had produced a Greco-Latin museum piece for the tastes of the times, so receptive to stylistic mixtures—comparable to Ottonian bookbinding, in which "Latin" goldsmiths framed Greek ivories with their work, or comparable to the books and deluxe documents in which Ottonian painters imitated Byzantine fabric patterns on parchment as the backgrounds of their paintings.

One must go back to antiquity in order to find Greco-Latin prose comparable to Liudprand's. Scattered Greek words had been a common feature of "scholarly literature"—exegesis and *artes liberales*—since late antiquity, and their pristine legitimacy was reaffirmed in the Carolingian era; in addition, Graeca were again used in Latin verse in the later ninth century (expressing chiefly theological concepts). Liudprand was, however, the first and only medieval author to link Latin and Greek in narrative prose.

It is difficult to identify the principles according to which Liudprand interspersed Greek in the text. The use of Greek for names, titles, and direct speech lends a Byzantine color to the tale and strengthens the impression of its authenticity. Liudprand strove for and achieved a comic effect in his explanation of the conditions which had enraged the lion: "quoniam quidem ob caligantes oculos παρα τω καπνω . . ." There are many biblical echoes in the text: "εδειλιασεν σφοδρα, ορθρου δε βαθεως, εγειρε, Εξεπλισσοντο δε παντες . . . ακουσαντες," and above all, "μη φοβου" (cf. Luke 24:1, Matt. 17:6 f. and 22:33).

Liudprand certainly had some understanding of the effect of his Graeca. For instance, when he narrated the story of Zeus' famous quarrel with Hera about whether man or woman feels more pleasure in love, and his account was entirely in Greek, he could be certain that the court would spare no pains to decipher the text.[15] His book obviously came into circulation very quickly, with the court as its starting point, and its Graeca were carefully studied.

The episcopal cities of Freising and Metz are early sites of the transmission of Liudprand's *Liber* ΛΝΤΛΠΟΔΟCΕWC. Bishop Abraham of Freising (957–93) acquired a manuscript of the text for his cathedral library, now Munich Clm 6388, while in Italy (see the new paleographical description by N. Daniel, *Handschriften des zehnten Jahrhunderts aus der Freisinger Dombibliothek* [Munich 1973], pp. 105 f.). Since the Greek passages were entered into this manuscript in empty spaces left for them in the text, earlier editors regarded the manuscript as the original copy, completed by the author (Pertz, *MGH Scriptores* [1839], III; Dümmler, *MGH Scriptores in usum scholarum* [1877]). The manuscript is intended for readers who have absolutely no understanding of Greek; the Graeca are first written in Greek majuscules, above which there is a phonetic (iotacistic) transcription, and after which there is a Latin translation: "INCIPIT LIBER ΛΝΤΛΠΟΔΟCΕWC, ANTAPODOSEOS, RETRIBUTIONIS . . . ΕΝ ΤΗ ΕΧΜΛΛΟCΙΛ ΛΥΤΟΥ, EN TI ECHMALOSIA AUTU, IN PEREGRINATIONE EIUS . . . EDITUS." According to Pertz and Dümmler, this was Liudprand's intention; with respect to the delicate area of Graeca and their embedding in the Latin text, it was very convenient for the editors to follow the manuscript of Bishop Abraham of Freising.

F. Koehler, however, showed that Bishop Abraham's manuscript could not possibly be Liudprand's autograph and published tenth-century excerpts of Greco-Latin passages from the ΛΝΤΛΠΟΔΟCΙC in Metz, Stadtbibliothek 145, from which one can clearly infer that Liudprand's Graeca were written in minuscules, not given in Roman transcription, and also not translated in full ("Beiträge zur Textkritik Liudprands von Cremona," *NA* 8 [1883], 49–88). Koehler saw these excerpts, most likely quite accurately, as the reflex of a very good manuscript of the ΛΝΤΑΠΟΔΟCΙC, which Bishop Dietrich I of Metz (965–84), who was closely associated with the Ottonians, may have brought to his episcopal city.

In his *Textgeschichte Liudprands von Cremona*, which appeared in 1908 in the series "Quellen und Untersuchungen zur lateinischen Philologie des Mittelalters," founded by Ludwig Traube, J. Becker emphasized the critical significance of the Metz excerpts[16] and concurred with Koehler's opinion with regard to the Graeca: "If it is improbable, even to some extent impossible, that the glosses and transcription were not originally from Liudprand, and if, furthermore, a direct branch of the tradition shows no sign of them, then we may assume that the glosses and transcription do not in fact go back to the original, but flowed into the main stream of the tradition at a later point in its course" (p. 37).

Scarcely any of these notions were taken into account in Becker's edition, which appeared seven years later. Becker accepted MS Clm 6388 as the standard manuscript with respect to the presentation of the Graeca, as had his two editorial predecessors at *MGH*; just as in their editions, Becker detracts from the visual impact of the Freising-Munich manuscript in that the "superscript Roman transcription is printed behind the Greek words" (ed. of 1915, p. xxxvi). Thus the three *MGH* editions are very similar in their treatment of the Graeca, with respect to which they present a text which never in fact existed in this form. Becker drew the justification for the return to Koehler's conclusions (and those of his own dissertation) from the view, presented in *NA* 36 (1910), 209–11, that the version of the Graeca in "usum scholarum," as they were presented in the Munich manuscript, went back to Liudprand, "perhaps to facilitate reading." This ill-founded notion "facilitated" above all Becker's edition, so much so in fact that it no longer even seemed necessary to include all of the "Metz Excerpts" in the apparatus of the *MGH* edition, despite the fact that they are invaluable for the determination of the Greek element in Liudprand's work.

In 968 Liudprand led the Western emperor's embassy to Nicephorus II Phocas (963–69), which was supposed to win a bride for Otto I's son and co-emperor (since 967), Otto II, from the Byzantine imperial family. It was not an opportune moment for a matchmaking expedition, since both Ottos had designs on southern Italy. Capua and Benevento had paid homage to Otto the Great (967); the Greek naval base at Bari barely escaped capture (968). And so Liudprand suffered the standard Byzantine treatment: he was delayed for a long time, poorly provided for, and generally humiliated. Liudprand, bishop and imperial legate, was all the more taken aback by this treatment, since he had received quite a favorable impression when he was in Constantinople twenty years before, as a deacon and ambassador of a less important king. Emperor Constantine, the author of the famous book on courtly ceremony ΕΚΘΕCΙC ΤΗC ΒΑCΙΛΕΙΟΥ ΤΑΖΕWC, had impressed the Western barbarian at that time with his refined throne ceremony, designed especially for foreign diplomats.

Nicephorus (963–69), the general and ascetic, obviously thought little of such theatrical receptions. In the *Relatio de legatione Constantinopoli-tana*, Liudprand had to report to both Ottos and Empress Adelheid not only about the insulting treatment, but also about the savage arguments which occurred at some banquets: "The warriors of your lord can neither ride nor fight on foot; their large shields, heavy armor, long swords, and the weight of their helmets do not allow them to fight anyway. Their glut-tony also hinders them in this. . . . Your lord also has no fleet. . . ." "You are not Romans at all, you are Lombards." "The dumb, foolish Pope [John XIII] apparently does not know that St. Constantine brought the imperial scepter, the entire senate, and all of Roman knighthood over here with him; he left behind in Rome only common servants, name-ly, fisherman, secondhand dealers, bird-catchers, bastards, rabble, and slaves." The theologically well-versed emperor inquired ironically whether Westerners counted Charlemagne's Frankfurt synod concerning icons (*Saxonica synodus*) as a Council.[17]

Liudprand still had his pen as a means of revenge for the dishonor suf-fered, and he used his mixed Greco-Latin prose for this purpose, as in the ΛΝΤΛΠΟΔΟCIC . The indignant Bishop of Cremona found the appropri-ate background for his own imperial acclamation in an imperial procession with the multitude's cries of homage:[18]

Cumque quasi reptans monstrum illud procederet, clamabant adula-tores psaltae: "Ecce venit stella matutina, surgit Eous, reverberat obtutu solis radios, pallida Saracenorum mors, Nicephorus μεδων!" Unde et cantabatur: "μεδοντι Nicephoro πολλα ετη! Gentes, hunc adorate, hunc colite, huic tanto colla subdite." Quanto tunc verius canerent: "Carbo extincte veni, μελλε anus incessu Sylvanus vultu rustice lustrivage capripes cornute bimembris setiger indocilis agres-tis barbare dure villose rebellis Cappadox!" Igitur falsidicis illis in-flatus naeniis Sanctam Sophiam ingreditur. . . .

Glosses: μεδων ῗ princeps; μεδοντι ῗ principi; πολλα ετη ῗ plures anni sint; μελλε without translation; according to Koehler, to be read as μελε; according to Kresten, *Römische Historische Mit-teilungen* 17 (1975), pp. 36 f., it should be μελας 'black'.

[And now as he proceeded like a creeping monster, the musicians called out their flattery: "Behold, here comes the morning star, Lucifer rises, his gaze drives back the rays of the sun, the pale death of the Saracens, Nicephorus the emperor!" And another chant is: "Long live Emperor Nicephorus! Peoples, honor him, reverence him, submit to such a ruler as this." How much more true would it have been, had they sung: "Come, you burned-out coal, fool, creep-ing like an old woman, ugly as a wood-sprite, boor, swamp-rat, goat-foot, horned one, half-beast, bristly one, rude, rustic, barbaric, harsh, shaggy, rebellious Cappadocian!" Puffed up by such deceitful songs, he enters S. Sophia. . . .]

3. Otto II and Theophano—Otto III and Gerbert d'Aurillac— The Emperors of the Early Eleventh Century

The Saxon rulers in the West and the Macedonians in the East were fundamentally rather similar: earnest, warlike dynasties, filled with their religious missions, had come to power in the East and West. Perhaps the conflict between Otto and Nicephorus was so intense because they were simply too similar.[19] After the ignominious murder of Nicephorus (969) and after further consolidation of Ottonian power in Italy, an embassy led by Archbishop Gero of Cologne again sought the hand of the Byzantine bride from John I Tzimisces. The imperial court put on no more airs: on Low Sunday 972 Emperor Otto II and Theophano were married in St. Peter's Cathedral.

The magnificent marriage document, written in gold ink on parchment onto which designs had been painted with purple ink, was one of the first monuments of Ottonian Byzantinism; it came into the possession of the nunnery at Gandersheim from the property of the Empress Theophano; Sophia, the daughter of Theophano and Otto II, was educated there under Abbess Gerberga (d. 1002), who also belonged to the Ottonian family, and later became Gerberga's successor as abbess (1002–39). On this document (now Wolfenbüttel, Niedersächsisches Staatsarchiv, 6 Urk 11), see the exhibition catalogue *Die Heiratsurkunde der Kaiserin Theophanu* (Göttingen 1972) (bibliog.) and the essays by W. Deeters and W. Ohnsorge in *Braunschweigisches Jahrbuch* 54 (1973). An ivory panel from a book binding also exists which depicts the coronation of Otto II and Theophano by Christ (Paris, Musée Cluny) and is in an even more strikingly Byzantinistic style. Christ is designated by Greek ĪC X̄C; the titles written above the crowned couple are executed partially in Latin and partially in Greek: OTTO ĪM̄P P̄MAN X̄C + ΘΕΟΦΑΝΩ ĪM̄P X̄C (OTTO IMPERATOR ROMANORUM ΑΥΓΟΥCTOC + ΘΕΟΦΑΝΩ IMPERATRIX ΑΥΓΟΥCTOC). The small kneeling figure at Otto's feet, probably the donor of the ivory, is designated with the Greek prayer: K̄Ε ΒΟΗΘ Τ C Δ ̊ ΙΩ ά AMEN = KYPIE ΒΟΗΘΕΙ TON CON ΔΟΥΛΟΝ ΙΩΑΝΝΗΝ MONAXON AMEN 'Lord, help your servant John the monk, amen', according to F. Dölger's reading (not yet the definitive reading), "Die Ottonenkaiser und Byzanz," in *Karolingische und ottonische Kunst* (Wiesbaden 1957), pp. 49–59, here pp. 56 ff. (bibliog.). It is supposed that the figure represents Johannes Philagathos of Rossano (cf. Schramm and Mütherich, *Denkmale der deutschen Könige und Kaiser*, p. 144, no. 73).

It is difficult to overestimate the significance of the fact that a Greek ruled as *imperatrix* in the West. It was possible then, for a short time, that Latin bishoprics and monasteries could be ruled by Greeks: Johannes Philagathos of Rossano received the Lombard imperial abbey of Nonantola and later also the see of Piacenza, which had been elevated to an archbishopric at his wish (988). Around 980 a Greek monk named Gregory founded a *cella Salvatoris* in Rome; Otto III later entrusted the newly founded monastery of Burtscheid near Aachen to him.[20] Now it was possible not only for Patriarch Sergius of Damascus, "who left his church out of love of Christ and arrived in Rome as a pilgrim,"[21] to take over an important Roman monastery in 977, but also for Greek Basilians and Latin Benedictines to live together, each order according to its own rule. This monastery, SS. Boniface and Alexius on the Aventine, soon became a center of a new Roman mission in Poland, Bohemia, and Hungary, whose symbolic figure and martyr was Emperor Otto III's friend Adalbert of Prague (d. 997).

Emperor Otto II (973–83) risked the peace of his empire for the sake of southern Italy, which the Eastern Empire could no longer effectively defend against the Saracens who were advancing from Sicily. The battles of Cotrone and Stilo in Calabria (982), which proceeded well initially but later proved disastrous, brought the young emperor into mortal danger from the Saracens and Byzantines; he was saved through several adventurous turns of fortune and finally also by his own daring and that of Bishop Dietrich of Metz, who was guarding the imperial family in Rossano. For all that, the Arab advance was checked, albeit at great cost.

In 980 Otto III was born to Theophano and Otto II. When he was sixteen and crowned emperor, Otto III drew Gerbert d'Aurillac to himself as teacher and friend. Gerbert had long been associated with the Ottonian dynasty and was considered a marvel of his time, due to his knowledge of the quadrivium; Otto III, who felt himself to be as much a Saxon as a Greek, wanted Gerbert to ignite the "spark of Greek intellectual activity." Gerbert's answer to the emperor was: "I do not know what divine things are expressed when a man who is Greek by birth and Roman by empire demands the treasures of Greek and Roman wisdom as if it were his inheritance."[22] At Otto III's wish, he wrote *De rationali et ratione uti* in 998, "lest Greece boast that it be alone in imperial philosophy and Roman power."[23] Under the emperor who was both Roman and Greek, the wish was to excel in both. And thus Boethius' Greco-Latin contest was again taken up, to which Gerbert dedicated the epitaph:[24]

. . .

Infundis lucem studiis et cedere nescis
Grecorum ingeniis, sed mens divina coercet
Imperium mundi. Gladio bachante Gothorum
Libertas Romana perit, tu consul et exul
Insignes titulos praeclara morte relinquis.
Nunc decus imperii summas qui praegravat artes
Tertius Otto sua dignum te iudicat aula

. . .

Hor. *epist.* II, 1, 13

[You give light to our studies and do not yield to the Greek genius, but a divine mind rules the empire of the world. Under the raging sword of the Goths, the freedom of Rome perishes. You, consul and exile, leave behind a distinguished honor through your noble death. Now the glory of the empire, Otto III, who excels in the highest arts, has judged you worthy of his palace.]

In Rome, where Otto III and Gerbert ruled together as emperor and pope (Silvester II, 999–1003), there must have also been intellectual exchange between Greeks and Romans. The Latino-Greek monastery of SS. Boniface and Alexius on the Aventine was quite closely associated with Otto. The emperor's administrative organization in Rome was related to Greek offices and titles.[25] The singing of the Roman *scola Greca* accompanied the nocturnal procession in the vigil of the Assumption of the Blessed Virgin in the year 1000, in which the most sacred icon of Rome, the pantocrator tablet of the Lateran's Capella Sancta Sanctorum, considered an *acheiropoieton*, was carried the long way through streets, illuminated with torches, to the Forum and from there to S. Maria Maggiore and then back to the Lateran:[26]

> Dat scola Greca melos et plebs Romana susurros,
> Et variis modulis dat scola Greca melos.
> Kyrie centuplicant et pugnis pectora pulsant
> Christe faveto! tonant, Kyrie centuplicant.

During his short life, Otto III was unable to establish a secure bridge between Greek and Latin. While the emperor could attract Latin scholars from beyond the borders of his empire, he could not win the leading Italo-Greeks for himself and his cause. Johannes Philagathos set himself up as antipope in Rome in 997; his exceedingly severe punishment caused the great monastic father Nilus of Rossano, who was perhaps already prepared to revive the ancient Greek monastery of St. Anastasius in Rome's southern precincts, to draw back from the emperor. The news of the emperor's death on 24 January 1002, when he was only twenty-two years old, was waiting for his bride from the Macedonian imperial family when Archbishop Arnulf of Milan brought her across the sea to Italy.

By no means was it the case that "Ottonian Hellenism" ceased with the death of Otto III; but it was indeed no more than an echo when Otto III's Byzantinistic ceremonies survived in the literature,[27] and Nilus of Rossano (d. 1004) remained in the Roman sphere of influence and founded the monastery Grottaferrata in the Albanian mountains. Under the emperors Henry II (1002–24), Conrad II (1024–39), and Henry III (1039–56), the Greek element at court again diminished, until the point at which it disappeared completely in the reign of Henry IV (1056–1105). The vestiges which testify to the lasting influence of Greek are primarily artistic in nature.

Henry II's constellation mantle, in the Bamberg Domschatz, is a unique example of the cult of the sovereign in the oriental and Hellenistic traditions: DESCRIP-CIO TOCIUS ORBIS 'description of the universe'. The constellations are from Aratus' ΦΑΙΝΟΜΕΝΑ, as Ernst Maass discovered ("Inschriften und Bilder des Mantels Kaiser Heinrichs II.," *Zeitschrift für christliche Kunst* 12 [!] [1899], 321 ff., 361 ff.). PAX ISMAHELI QUI HOC ORDINAVIT 'peace be with Ishmael, who designed this'): this Ishmael is hardly "ein Musterzeichner des sarazenischen Gewandhauses" ("a pattern-maker from the Saracen clothiers' market," Maass), but rather Ishmael or Melus of Bari, the "duke of Apulia," who fled to Emperor Henry in Bamberg in 1019–20 and died there; see R. Eisler, *Weltenmantel und Himmelszelt* (Munich 1910), I, 15 ff. The work is now attributed to the "Regens-burg artists' group"; Messerer, *Der Bamberger Domschatz*, pp. 54–57.

Conrad II, the first Salian emperor, once again made an attempt to arrange a marriage between his imperial heir and a Byzantine princess. In the *Gesta Chuonradi*, Wipo reports about the embassy of Bishop Werner of Strasbourg in 1027–28; at the same time, the report illustrated the dif-ficulties which could confront such an embassy even after the opening of the land route:[28]

At this time, the emperor sent Bishop Werner of Strasbourg as the ambassador to Constantinople. He was impeded to an extraordinary degree in this undertaking—in my opinion because he pretended that he wanted to go to Jerusalem to pray—by the judgment of God, whom none can deceive! For since he brought with him a great ret-inue of men and a still larger one of dumb beasts, horses, oxen, sheep, swine and an immense number of valuable objects of this world, when he came to Hungary, he was forbidden passage by King Stephan [the saint!], which at this time did not happen to any pil-grims. Then he turned around and proceeded with his entire retinue through Bavaria, entered Italy, and was held up for a long time on the Veronese border; with the greatest difficulty he finally reached the Adriatic Sea via Venice and after a calamitious voyage arrived in Constantinople. Since he was honorably received by the Greek emperor [Constantine VIII, 1025–28] and came to be on rather familiar terms with him, he expressed the desire to visit Jerusalem with the emperor's aid. . . . He died soon thereafter, however, and was buried in the same city [Constantinopole]. . . . With respect to the purpose of the embassy, the Greek emperor [Romanus III, 1028–34] later answered in a letter to Emperor Conrad, written in golden letters.

Bishop Werner of Strasbourg had taken on the toils of the embassy in vain. But even without a Greek consort for Henry III, one could not omit Greek where the divine appeared in the *saeculum*. In the "Golden Evangelary of Henry III," which was written around 1045 in Echternach for the cathedral at Speyer, CVONRADVS IMPERATOR and GISELA

IMPERATRIX were portrayed underneath the *Majestas Domini*; in the text which frames the illumination, they profess the "Ottonian proskynesis":

+ ANTE TVI VVLTVM MEA DEFLEO CRIMINA MVLTVM
DA VENIAM MEREAR CVIVS SVM MVNERE CAESAR

[I sincerely lament my sins before your face. Grant forgiveness, may I deserve it, you through whose grace I am emperor.]

Latin words are also written in the mandorla, but, in the proximity of the *pantocrator*, they have been transformed and have taken of the form of the second sacred language—the one closer to the original source:

+ BHNHΔIKΘVM NOMHN MΔIHCΘΛΘIC HIVC IN ΛHΘHPNVM
ΕΘ PHПΛHBIΘVP MΔIHCΘΛΘ⟨Ε HIVC⟩ OMNIC ΘHPPΛ

+ BENEDICTUM NOMEN MAIESTATIS EIUS IN AETERNUM
ET REPLEBITUR MAIESTATE EIUS OMNIS TERRA

[Blessed is the name of his majesty forever, and all the earth will be filled with his majesty.]

Remarkably, this change from Latin to Greek at the midpoint is also found in the illumination: the head, the raised right hand, the feet, and the medallion of the angel at the foot of the *majestas* were all added to the painting later by a Greek artist. Could it be only by chance that Greek and Latin are united in both word and image on the display page of this book?[29] Or is it not rather more of a commentary on Emperor Henry III's reply to Emperor Constantine IX Monomachus: ". . . he was a descendant of Greek stock, among others, through Theophano and most valiant Otto; thus it was not surprising that he loved the Greeks and wished to imitate them in character and custom. . . ."[30]

Occasionally Henry III's court style Grecizes even in official documents. An imperial document from 1053 contains the following as the signature of the chancellor:[31]

ΥΔΕΛ	CΛN
ΥΥΥ̇	CΕΛ
NΥ̇ΘΕ	ΛΛ
PΥ̇Υ̇	PΥ̇Υ̇

IDEA VVINITHERII CANCELLARII.

4. Greek *Anachoresis* in the West

The topic of the Greek *anachoresis* in the Latin West had already been raised in the seventh through the ninth century: there were Greek monks in Byzantine and post-Byzantine Rome, "Syrians" in Merovingian Gaul, and time and again during the Carolingian period there was a "Greek" at court or somewhere else in the realm. And whatever the meaning of "Graecus"—someone from southern Italy, Palestine, or Constantinople— it was in every case surely someone who came from a Greek environment, and hardly a Grecizing *Scottus*, as Laistner would like to imagine.

In the tenth century, reports of Greeks in the West increase. Initially this fact may cause surprise, since there were no longer monothelitist or iconoclastic conflicts in Constantinople, to escape which a person would have to flee, if he did not feel called to be a confessor or martyr but also did not wish to share the prevailing doctrinal view. There were more hospitable places than the northern reaches of Western Europe for Greeks who wished to retire from the world for the sake of their salvation; and the attraction of the Ottonian court does not suffice (despite Theophano) as an explanation of the phenomenon. The Ottonian era was probably more open in a general sense to the Greeks, especially to Greek monasticism, than any other period in the Western Middle Ages; this positive attitude was so strong that many Greeks felt it to be an invitation to remain in the West.

This new receptiveness for things Greek was basically founded on a new consciousness which had developed in Western monasticism. The vita of John of Gorze, the reviver of Lotharingian monastic life, shows clearly what effect the search for new directions in monasticism had. In 933 John made a pilgrimage to the grotto of St. Michael on Mt. Gargano in Apulia; deeply impressed by the idea of again living "labore manuum ad exemplar antiquorum sanctorum" ("by the labor of one's hands, on the model of the ancient saints"), he wanted to settle in Beneventan Italy (in close proximity to Italo-Greek monasticism) with his companions, who were weary of transalpine monasticism. It was with great difficulty that the bishop of Metz kept John and his followers in his domain.[32] Monks "from Greece" had to compensate for the abandoned nearness to the Greeks in Italy; they lived in Gorze among the Latins.[33] Thus the spirit of this monasticism was no longer so much that of the cultural missionary of the great Carolingian monasteries as it was that of the asceticism of more ancient monastic practice, which had survived more intact in the East than in the West and was gloriously revived in the tenth century on Mt. Athos by the monastic father Athanasius.

Bishop Gerard of Toul (963–94) "assembled a considerable group of

Greeks and Irishmen and supported the mixed assemblage of diverse languages with his own funds. He established the rule that they come together daily at separate altars in the oratory, where they, humbly supplicating, were to praise God in the manner of their own countries."[34] In 1011 an Archbishop Macarius of Antioch is supposed to have made a pilgrimage to Ghent and died there in a holy manner a year later;[35] in 1016 Symeon the Armenian died in his hermit's cell near the Benedictine monastery of Polirone near Mantua. The vita, written in the form of a travel-aretalogy, with which the monastery celebrated the honored monk as a saint soon after his death, reported long journeys to Santiago de Compostela and St. Martin's of Tours which he was supposed to have made earlier in his life.[36] In the imperial monastery of Nonantola, the southern Italian (probably of Greek culture) Cosmas of Matera, who assumed the ancient surname "Jagipus," wrote an affected Latin poem in honor of SS. Senesius and Theopomp, *graeco de fonte*, as he maintains.[37] Around the year 1030, a Greek monk or perhaps even bishop, named Constantine, even arrived in England; William of Malmesbury reported that he stayed in Malmesbury and lived for his spiritual exercise and for the vineyard which he had planted.[38]

In this Greek *peregrinatio*, as in the Latin movement of the early Middle Ages, there were of course more than merely ascetic motives involved. In addition to the Greek Symeon, who came to Reichenau and to whose memory the monks there dedicated a vita, there were also embassies from the Greek East which came to the island monastery.[39] *Greci operarii* built the Chapel of St. Bartholomew next to the Paderborn Cathedral for Bishop Meinwerk of Paderborn (1009–36).[40] An oriental cleric named Alagrecus (= *ala grecus* 'the Greek'?) is supposed to have appeared in Maastricht; he identified the local patron saint, St. Servatius, as a relative of the Holy Virgin.[41]

As one of the last Greek pilgrims in the West, St. Symeon of Trier stands brightly illumined by history's light. The joyous charity of Duke Richard II of Normandy and the friendship of Richard of St. Vanne (Verdun),[42] the leader of a great pilgrimage by the land route from Verdun, Trier, Limoges, and Angoulême to Palestine (1026–27), had attracted Symeon, who had been born in Syracuse and was living in Jerusalem, to the West; Archbishop Poppo prevailed upon Symeon to stay in his episcopal city, Trier, for which he was praised by his city in one of the "Cambridge Songs":[43]

> O quam felix tu fueras,   quod hunc uirum adduxeras,
> qui me fuscam illuminat   et me fractam resolidat.

[O how fortunate you were that you brought this man who illuminates me in darkness and refortifies me in my weakness.]

In a strange way Symeon did indeed fortify the city: He had himself locked up in the Porta Nigra and died there as a recluse on 1 June 1035. Soon after his death, Abbot Eberwin of St. Martin's in Trier wrote an accurate account of his life,[44] and in his memory the monastery of St. Symeon was founded in the expanded and transformed gate of the Roman citadel. Protectively integrated into the Romanesque monastery, the Roman monument survived through its second millenium, up until the early nineteenth century, when the former was demolished in order to excise—in neo-humanistic manner—the ruins of antiquity from their historical context.

Nilus of Rossano had the greatest influence on the West. When the monastic father withdrew into the ancient Lombard duchy of Benevento to escape the advancing Saracens in the year 980, he was received with great honor by Duke Pandulph Ironhead; and when the band of Italo-Greek monks proceeded up Monte Cassino, it seemed to one of Nilus' students as if the Latin monks, with their Abbot Aligern, greeted the great Greek ascetic as if he were the monastic father Anthony or the resurrected Benedict. Vallelucio was granted to the Greeks for the erection of a monastery; they were asked to sing the Greek office in the main Latin monastery—which seemed to the biographer of St. Nilus as if it were the fulfillment of the promise "the lion and the ox graze together and their young are together" (Isa. 11:6–7 and 65:25); Nilus was asked for instruction on the character and substance of monasticism, which he then gave in Latin: "Monachus est angelus . . ."[45]

Nilus went further north with great hesitation; his path stops near Rome. But Westerners sought his companionship; Emperor Otto II, Adalbert of Prague, and Romuald of Salerno sought his counsel, and Emperor Otto III followed him just as his relative Nicephorus Phocas had followed Athanasius the Athonite.[46] Nilus' foundation, Grottaferrata, in the Albanian mountains, was the only Italo-Greek monastery to survive the era.[47]

Thus there is a Greek ΞΕΝΙΤΕΙΑ ('life abroad') in the West, whose focal point was in the tenth century; it is comparable to the Irish *peregrinatio* of the seventh and eighth centuries and is almost a complementary counterpart to it, since the Greek migration took place in approximately the same "Lotharingian" zone as had the Irish; they came from opposite directions, and occasionally the pilgrims coming toward each other actually met—in Toul, perhaps in Trier—despite the displacement in time.

"Irishmen and Greeks"—during the late Carolingian and Ottonian eras, these words most likely expressed both the concept of learning which came "from afar" and also that of the extreme representatives of the Christian family of nations, in each case from the western European, Con-

tinental perspective. Yet it seems that the late Carolingians were more
interested in the foreigners' learning, while the Ottonians saw them
rather as agents of transmission for the foreign liturgical and ascetic forms;
here one might compare what Heiric says about the Irish and the Greeks
at the court of Charles the Bald with Bishop Gerard of Toul's request of
his foreign guests. Thus it would be inappropriate to be concerned with
the profit of the Greek ΧΕΝΙΤΕΙΑ in the West for Greek studies of the
post-Carolingian period. The Westerners of the tenth and eleventh centuries, who so eagerly took the Greeks in, did not seek their knowledge
and scholarship, but rather the image of ancient monasticism, "the an-
gelic life."

5. Ottonian Centers: Trier-Echternach—Metz— Cologne-Essen—Regensburg—Bamberg

The traces of Greek studies in the Ottonian era are scattered and do not
clearly illuminate the cultural contexts. The Carolingian cultural traditions were preserved in only a few places after the dissolution of the enormous empire of the Carolingians, and after the assaults of the Normans,
Saracens, and Hungarians. Added to this is also the shift of cultural focus
and of political as well as economic importance from the large monasteries
to the episcopal cities: thus the monarch of the Ottonian period and high
Middle Ages who became a prebendary (as, for example, Henry II in
Bamberg, Magdeburg, Strasbourg, and elsewhere)[48] corresponds in a certain sense to the Carolingian monarch who became the abbot of a large
monastery (for instance, Charles the Bald in St. Denis).

In the Ottonian Empire, bishops became administrators of parts of the
imperial territory. On the other hand, these bishops and their cities,
which had been taken into the imperial service in this manner, were filled
with monastic ideals; many bishops of the following two or three generations regarded as their ideal to live and die as monks, although they lived
in the midst of worldly affairs, just as Otto the Great's brother Brun of
Cologne and Ulrich of Augsburg had done. Thus it was especially the
monastery on the *edge* of the episcopal city that flourished during this
transitional period, for it most successfully embodied and made possible
that Ottonian *intra et extra*: St. Maximin in Trier, St. Pantaleon in Cologne, St. Alban in Mainz, St. Emmeram in Regensburg, Kloster
Michelsberg above Bamberg.

One of the most important bridges between the Carolingian cultural
traditions and the tenth century was Reims, where Flodoard wrote the
annals of the years 919–66 and the "History of the Church of Reims."[49]
There was an initial attempt made to establish in *Trier* under Archbishop

Robert (931–56, a relative by marriage of the Ottonian dynasty) a kind of court school for the new Saxon dynasty. It was probably there that the Irishman Israel, "l'ultimo dei maestri palatini scoti" ("the last Irish teacher at court"),[50] gave the young Brun lessons. Greeks are also supposed to have participated:[51]

> The Irish Bishop Israel, in whose school the very famous man about whom we are speaking declares that he learned the most, was once asked about the conduct [of Brun] . . . and answered that he was a very holy man. . . . Greeks, whom he also had as teachers, were astounded by so much mercy, and without doubt took worthy questions posed by Brun home to their fellow citizens, whose endeavors at an earlier time are supposed to have been constantly directed toward hearing or inventing something new.

It can no longer be critically determined to what extent these Greeks, who admired the wisdom of the little Saxon, are a reality or only a literary *contrapposto* to the (historically attested) Irish teacher—somewhat on the model of Heiric's homage to Charles the Bald in the preface to the vita of St. Germanus. There are, nevertheless, further indications of an interest in Greek in Ottonian Trier. A small interlinear Latino-Greek Psalter was probably produced there and has been associated with the oeuvre of the "Master of the Registrum Gregorii."[52] This is accurate in so far as the same calligrapher who wrote the famous "Codex Egberti" (Trier, Stadtbibliothek Cod. 24; at the beginning illuminated by the "Registrum Master") also wrote at least part of the Latin base text in the Latino-Greek Psalter. Curiously, the base text is Latin and the interlinear version Greek, so that the bilingual book "was appropriate for a male or female reader who had had training in Greek and wanted an introduction to the use of Latin."[53] The traditional designation as the "Psalter of Theophano" is justified in this manner, although it was obviously the Trier Archbishop Egbert (977–93) and not the Greco-German empress who was the *spiritus rector* of this unusually beautiful work.

Two further bilingual Psalters are found in the vicinity of Trier, in the Hospitalbibliothek in Cusa, which was collected by Nicholas of Cusa. The conventionally designed Psalter Cusa 10 was mentioned above (Chapter VIII, sec. 1). Cod. Cusa 9, with Psalms 109–50 written in three narrow columns, is more interesting: Greek text in Roman minuscule, Latin Vulgate, Greek text in Greek uncial. Allgeier has examined the manuscript thoroughly and come to the conclusion that this Psalter was not only used as an introduction to Greek, but also designed as such from the very beginning.[54] Not only is the threefold presentation of the text an indication of school use (cf. the presentation of Liudprand's Graeca in Abraham of Freising's copy), but also the partial absence of the Greek articles (for the purpose of achieving verbal symmetry) is a clear indication that the

Psalter, which was of no liturgical use, was designed as an elementary textbook of Greek vocabulary:[55]

Eulogísise	Benedicat tibi	ЄΥΛΟΓΙCЄCЄ
Kírios	dominus	K̄C̄
Ek sýon	ex syon	ЄK CΥΟΝ
ke idýs	et uideas	KΑΙ ΙΔΥC
agathá	bona	ΑΓΑΘΑ
hierusalem	hierusalem	H̄Λ̄M
pásin	omnibus	ΠΑCΙΝ
imeras	diebus	ΙΜЄΡΑC
zoís su	uitae tuae	ΖΟΙC CΟΥ

The Psalter as a vocabulary book—in late antiquity Vergil was adapted in a similar manner for the use of Greek-speaking students.[56]

MS Cusa 9, fol. 61ᵛ, contains "in addition to various practice strokes with a pen" (Siegmund, *Die Überlieferung*, p. 26), the copyist's entry "Iohanes grecus costantinopoleos orfanos et peregrinos scripsit" ("John, a Greek from Constantinople and an orphan and pilgrim, wrote this"); the script is, however, Western in character (Gardthausen, *Griechische Paläographie*, 2nd ed. [1913], II, 258), which caused Siegmund to remark: "the subscription could well have been copied from the source text." Hamann's opinion (n. 55 above) that the manuscript was written in Italy is paleographically indefensible; it was written north of the Alps and in the ninth/tenth century rather than the tenth (B. Bischoff). The *tres linguae sacrae* are presented at the end of the manuscript in an alphabet and the paternoster.

The extraordinary framing of the *majestas domini* of the "Evangelary of Sainte-Chapelle" leads back to the Trier "Master of the Registrum," the artistic genius of the tenth century; in the mandorla, which surrounds the enthroned Christ, the following Greek text is written:

H BΑCΙΛЄΙΑ COΥ KΥΡΙЄ BΑCΙΛЄΙΑ ΠΑΝΤШΝ ΤШΝ ΑΙШΝΟΝ
KΑΙ ΔΙCΠΟΤЄΙΛ COΥ ЄΝ ΠΑCЄ ΓЄΝЄΑ KΑΙ ΓЄΝЄΑ

Paris, BN lat. 8851, fol. 1ᵛ, Trier "ca. 984," a photograph and description in Schramm and Mütherich, *Denkmale*, no. 83. The inscription is of Ps. 144:13—without question the result of the study of a bilingual Psalter. It is not a random text, but rather one which presents Christ as *monarch*: "regnum tuum regnum omnium saeculorum et dominatio tua in omni generatione et progenie."

The gold-lettered manuscript was intended for a monarch of the Ottonian dynasty. It was a model for another gold-lettered, and still more famous, manuscript, the "Codex Aureus Epternacensis," written for Emperor Henry III. The *Echternach* master, who painted the *majestas domini* in this codex, not only imitated the device of the Trier "Master of the Registrum," but even surpassed it, in that he wrote (or had someone else write) the mandorla in Greek *minuscule*:

ο ϑρονος ⟨σου ο ϑεος εις τον⟩ εονα του εονος
ραυδος ευϑιτιτος η ραυδος τις βασιλιας σου

Nuremburg, Germ. Nat. Museum MS 2° 156142, fol. 3ᵛ, Echternach 1020–30, facsimile in W. Berschin, "Drei griechische Majestas-Tituli in der Trier-Echternacher Buchmalerei," *Frühmittelalterliche Studien* 14 (1980), 299–309, here p. 304. The Echternach atelier made use of a verse from the Psalms, just as had the artist in Trier:

sedes tua deus in saeculum saeculi virga directionis virga regni tui (Ps. 44:7).

What is the source of this acquaintance with Greek minuscule? And what is the source of the "Byzantine" phonetics (εονα, ραυδος, ευϑιτιτος, etc.)? The script is the most sensational aspect of this discovery; for with it, a major manuscript from the imperial library is added to the (up until now) rather modest ranks of documents written in Greek minuscule in the West during the high Middle Ages.[57]

A direct line leads from the "Codex Aureus Epternacensis" to the "Golden Evangelary of Speyer" in the Escorial, in which the earthly ruler is now depicted at the feet of the heavenly monarch: Greek letters are again used in the mandorla, once again in a different form, as a cipher of the Latin text (see above, sec. 3, ad fin.):

+ BHNHΔIKΘVM NOMHN MAIHCΘΛΘIC HIVC IN ΛHΘHPNVM
EΘ PHΠΛHBIΘVP MAIHCΘΛΘ⟨E HIVC⟩ OMNIC ΘHPPΛ

With these three *majestas tituli* from the Trier-Echternach school of manuscript illumination, an entire series of possibilities for the representation of Greek in a Latin context again passes in review (much as with the Greek paternoster among the Irish):

　ca. 984　Trier—Greek in Greek majuscule
　1020–30 Echternach—Greek in Greek minuscule
　ca. 1045 Echternach—Latin in Greek majuscule

Additional, less important evidence for Greek in Trier and Echternach includes the school manuscript Trier, Stadtbibliothek 120, saec. X–XI, which contains "Versuche in griechischer Schrift" on the *Expositio S. Ambrosii in psalmum CXVIII*, M. Keuffer, *Beschreibendes Verzeichnis der Handschriften der Stadt-bibliothek*, vol. II (Trier 1891), p. 12. A manuscript of book I of John Scottus' ΠEPI ΦYCEWC MEPICMOY was written in the eleventh century in the monastery of S. Eucharius at Trier; a metrical adaptation follows in the manuscript, *Depressus usquequaque Omnis pondere noxae*, which contains Greek words, some of which are written in Greek majuscule, some in Greek minuscule.[58] At one time this manuscript also belonged to the library of Nicholas of Cusa.

In Paris, BN lat. 9345, fol. 96ᵛ and Trier Stadtbibliothek 1093/1694, fol, 115ʳ, an Echternach scholar of the mid-eleventh century (Thiofrid of Echternach?) wrote the Greek majuscule alphabet above the Easter tables; and in the manuscript now in Trier, there is also a list of *greca nomina signorum* ('constellations'); see J. Schroeder, *Bibliothek und Schule der Abtei Echternach um die Jahrtausendwende*, diss., Freiburg 1975 (Luxembourg 1977), pp. 40, 46, 104. Cf. the catalogue "Griechische Wörter bei Thiofrid gebraucht," in W. Lampen, *Thiofrid von Echternach* (Breslau 1920), pp. 70–78.

J.-C. Muller has provided a complement to our knowledge of Graeca in Echternach manuscripts in "Linguistisches aus der Echternacher Klosterbibliothek," *Hémecht* 3 (1983), 381–403, here pp. 394 f.: Paris, BN lat. 9530 contains the *ex libris* "Biblion Agiou Willobrordi," written in Roman script (fol. 57ᵛ); BN lat. 9534 contains a Greek majuscule alphabet (not minuscule) on fol. 73ᵛ; in BN lat. 9666, on fol. 1ʳ, a Latin paternoster in Greek majuscules begins ΠΛΘΕΡ ΝΟϹΤΕΡ; it was once classified as "essai de poème incompréhensible"!

Metz, with its ring of monasteries that once encircled the episcopal city, was certainly the most famous site of liturgical culture north of the Alps in which Graeca were present during the early Middle Ages and of some importance in all periods. According to a tradition from St. Arnulf outside of Metz, Louis III, the son of Louis the German, was honored with Greek *laudes*, and a tenth-century glossator interpreted the text, even if not entirely without error. Bishop Dietrich of Metz (965–84) could obviously continue even older Greek traditions in Metz. He presented a manuscript to the monastery of St. Vincent, near Metz, which contained texts of the "missa graeca,"[59] and he was probably also the one to bring the Liudprand manuscript, to which the excerpts of the ΛΝΤΛΠΟΔΟϹΙϹ in Metz Cod. 145 can be traced, from Italy. Bischoff noted traces of late tenth-century Greek studies in Metz, Cod. 179 (Isidore) and 215 (Jerome), both now destroyed.[60]

In *Cologne*, one could expect to find Greek studies especially in St. Pantaleon, the monastery founded by Archbishop Brun (953–65) where Empress Theophano (d. 991) is buried. Froumund, a monk from southern Germany, was in St. Pantaleon around 990 for his studies; while there he designed and executed an important Boethius manuscript,[61] which was well stocked with lines of verse which, "characteristically for him, luxuriated in Greek vocabulary":[62]

> *Ave   mvndi*
> Chere salus cosmoy Splendens super aethra Sophya
>   *diuini sermonis quę sunt amara ad intellegendum*
> Quęque theologię caput es amarugmata pandens,
> *annus perpettuus   virtus   divinitatis*
> Chronos perpetuum, dynamis praeclara theosi,
>   *compositrix sermonis christi*
> Tu Christi logotheta manes, tu cuncta creasti.

[Hail, savior of the world, he who shines above the heavens, wisdom, you are the summit of all theology and you reveal its bitter truths,

time in perpetuity, excellent strength of divinity, you remain
Christ's logothete, you the creator of all.]

The same "Maihingen Boethius manuscript" also shows how Froumund
came by his Greco-Latin vocabulary.[63] In the course of his readings he
collected rare and especially Greek-sounding words and noted them in
the margins of the manuscript. One of the sources of his vocabulary exercises was the *Gesta Apollonii*,[64] a Carolingian poetic version of the Apollonius novel of late antiquity. Later Froumund's excerpted words found
their way into the editions of the "Glossarium Salomonis" that appeared
in the high and late Middle Ages.

Froumund's interest in Greek becomes even clearer in a second manuscript that he designed in part "in monasterio sancti pantaleymonis"
(probably St. Pantaleon in Cologne); in these quaternions written there,
one finds the only Ottonian attempt at a Greek grammar.[65] Froumund
noted the Greek alphabet, the numerals, the Greek articles, examples of
nominal declensions, and a vocabulary of approximately two hundred
words. The grammatical text offers no evidence of firsthand lessons given
by Greeks; it seems rather to be a witness of a continued interest in grammar in the manner of the Irishman who wrote the "Reichenau Notebook"
in the ninth century.

In Cologne, the "Ottonian school of painting" came into prominence
under the archbishops Evergerus (984–99) and especially Heribert (999–
1021), the friend of Otto III; its greatest works are also of literary historical value, since, in a peculiar way, they develop the genre of the *titulus*
into a theology of icons. In its full-page *tituli*, the "Sacramentary of St.
Gereon" contains splendid rhythmic annotations to the illustrations, each
of which refers to the symbolic character of the illustration.[66] The core
vocabulary of these illustration titles consists in part of neologisms:

HVIUS PICTI *IMAGINATIUO* FIGVRATVR . . . (title for the
Annunciation)

HOC MATERIALE *INSPECTIUUM* . . . (title for Christ's birth)

GREGORVS DEI SERVVS ˙ CVIUS STATVA ˙ EX MATERIA ET
FORMA ˙ FVLGET IN HOC *SIGNATIVO* COMPOSITA . . .
ISTUD *OPERATIUUM* ˙ SIMULAT ASCENSUM DOMINI . . .
(title for the Ascension)

The designation of each illustration with a noun ending with the suffix
-ivus points to a method of word formation based on Greek—more specifically, based on John Scottus' translation of Dionysius, in which the Greek
adjectives in -IKOC, -IKH, -IKON were rendered with often quite auda-
cious neologisms in *-ivus, -iva, -ivum*.[67] It appears as if the anonymous
author of the Cologne *tituli* had studied John Scottus' *Dionysiaca* and for-

mulated his theology of images on the model of the language of John's translation.

The *tituli* of the "Sacramentary of St. Gereon" served as models within this artistic school. Much of that same material reappears in the "Hitda Codex" in abbreviated and concentrated form; in the *majestas domini* of this work, the school's figural interpretation of images is most concisely formulated:[68]

> Hoc uisibile imaginatum ˙
> figurat illud inuisibile uerum ˙
> cuius splendor penetrat mundum ˙
> cum bis binis candelabris ˙
> ipsius noui sermonis ˙

[This visible product of the imagination is the figure of that invisible truth, whose brilliance penetrates the world with the two binary candelabra of its new discourse.]

This is the Ottonian counterpart to the barren attitude toward icons which one finds in the "Libri Carolini." The scribe wrote this poetic prose in gold ink on purple parchment in the court hand—as a Western chrysobull of the theology of images.

P. Bloch and H. Schnitzler maintain in several passages of their book *Die ottonische Kölner Malerschule* that the school of painters was located in St. Pantaleon (cf. also Bloch in the afterword to the facsimile edition of *Der Darmstädter Hitda-Codex*, pp. 106 f.), which in itself seems to fit the image of intellectual life in this important monastery.

The manuscripts themselves, however, do not point to St. Pantaleon in any way. On the contrary, much evidence from the text tradition points to St. Gereon. See Chapter II, above, on the lectionary (Paris, BN gr. 375) written by a Greek in Cologne (?) in 1021 and on the Greek Psalter (Vienna, Österreichische National-bibliothek theol. gr. 336) written in Constantinople around 1077 for St. Gereon in Cologne.

The transmission of Greek material in the nunnery in *Essen* may be taken as representative for the convents which were closely associated with the Ottonian dynasty. Abbess Hadwig (before 947–before 971) had a "Codex domesticus" (of patron saints of the convent) ornamented with illustrations, some of which received Greek captions:[69]

ΚΕΡΟΥΒΥΝ	ΘΕΟΤΕΚΟC	CΕΡΑΦΥΝ
ΑΓΙΟC ΚΟCϽCΑC	ΒΑCΙΛΕΟC	ΑΓΙΟC ΔΑϽCΙΑΝΟC
	ΒΑCΙΛΕШΝ	

Appropriately, the abbess's epitaph also contains the ornament of a few Greek words.[70] A Greek Paternoster was entered in one sacramentary,[71] a "missa graeca" in another.[72] The Marsus shrine, destroyed in 1794, was produced under the Abbess Mathilde (d. 1011); Abbess Theophanu (1039–57) was responsible for its final form. According to a publication from the year 1639, it bore a Greek inscription, which was to have had the following form:[73]

Domina		*Me fieri*
Mathildt		*iussit*
+		ΑΥ
ΜΙΑ	Effigies	ΤΟ
ΕΝ	Ottonis II	ΚΡΑ
Χ͞Ω	imperatoris	ΤΩΡ
ΠΙ⟨C⟩ΤΟC		ΡΩΜ
ΚΑC		ΑΙΩΝ
ΙΑ		Ε. Ο.

The seventeenth-century editor resolved the "E.O." at the end as "εὔδοξος Otto" and translated as

Una in Christo   Imperator Romanorum
firma germanitas   gloriosus Otto

Is it thus a memorial for Emperor Otto II from the granddaughter of Otto the Great (Abbess Mathilde of Essen)? W. Ohnsorge has suggested another solution to the riddle:[74] it is a question of the inscription of a Byzantine chrysobull with the text ΜΙΧ⟨ΑΗΛ⟩ ΕΝ Χ͞Ω ΠΙCΤΟC ΒΑCΙΛ⟨ΕΥC⟩ . . . 'Michael, the emperor who believes in God . . .'. The enigmatic "E.O." would thus be a scribal error for "O N⟨εοc⟩," that is, Emperor Michael VI (1056–57) was meant. The round picture in the center does not depict an Ottonian, but rather just this Emperor Michael VI, and the whole is to be understood as the chrysobull of a Byzantine state display document that has been detached and inserted as an ornament in the Marsus shrine.[75]

In the early eleventh century Essen acquired a *psaltarium quadrupartitum* that is still in the Essen cathedral treasury; and Abbess Swanhild (ca. 1058–after 1085) had herself depicted on the title page of an evangelary at the feet of the Virgin; in the accompanying hexameter, there was an attempt at encipherment akin to that of the "Golden Evangelary of Henry III":[76]

C͞ΧΑ	ΜΑΡΥΑ
ΛΑ ΠΡΩ	ΠΡΥΜ
ΝΑΤ͞Υ	ΦΕΡ
ΝΡ͞Μ	ΥΥΡΓΩ
ΠΡΕ	ΧΑΤ͞Υ

SANCTA MARIA
AD PROPRIUM NATUM FER NOSTRUM VIRGO PRECATUM.

[Holy Mary, Virgin, bear our prayer to your son]

The traces of Greek in *Regensburg* are few, but conspicuous. Scholarship associated itself with a school of painters here, and produced illustrations which were as magnificent as they were enciphered, especially in the "Uta codex."

Munich, Clm 13601; on fol. 2ʳ, among the titles to a representation of the Virgin, one finds the inaccurate and "hyper-Grecizing" ΘΗΕΟ – ΘΟΚΟC; on fol. 4ʳ is the so-called Erhard portrait; according to Ewald M. Vetter, the original portrait of Christ as a high priest was "changed" into a portrait of St. Erhard with the later addition of a title identifying it as such. The inscriptions on the depicted priest's pallium are ΙΗΡΑΡΧΗΙΑ and SACER PRINCIPATUS, which refer to Dionysius' "hierarchies," or rather to the dedicatory epistle of the translator, John Scottus, to Charles the Bald (*MGH Epistolae*, VI, 158 ff.). Cf. G. Swarzenski, *Die Regensburger Buchmalerei des X. und XI. Jahrhunderts* (Leipzig 1901), pp. 93 and 98; A. Boeckler, "Das Erhardbild im Utacodex," *Studies in Art and Literature for Belle de Costa Greene* (Princeton 1954), pp. 219–30; B. Bischoff, "Hartwic von St. Emmeram," in Stammler and Langosch, *Verfasserlexikon*, V, 335–37.
One might compare these titles with those on the crucifixion in "The Sacramentary of Henry II" (Clm 4456), which was most likely written in Regensburg for the Bamberg cathedral treasury: Η CTΑΘ-ΦΡΩCIC. According to G. Swarzenski, *Die Regensburger Buchmalerei*, p. 65, the title is "a distortion of the usual Greek term for the crucifixion, ἡ σταύρωσις; at the same time it is evidence for the fact that Greek was actually *heard* ("stafrosis") and phonetically written in Regensburg. In the same codex one finds the Byzantine motif of Christ's coronation of the emperor. The *titulus* ingeniously gives reverence to Emperor Henry II with the words (in the Greek alphabet) ΧΡΙCΤΟ 'the one anointed (in the Greek manner)'; see Messerer, *Der Bamberger Domschatz*, pl. 3.

Around 1049, the Abbey of St. Emmeram claimed to be in possession of the genuine relics of Dionysius the Areopagite. Otloh of St. Emmeram, one of the most zealous promoters of the venture to outdo St. Denis, copied John Scottus' Dionysius translation in his calligraphic hand.[77] A sculpture of this great new saint was placed in the vestibule at St. Emmeram, and the name was ornamented with a Greco-Latin epithet: "MACHARII DIONYSII." The most magnificent romanesque statue in Regensburg, the so-called Astrolabium of St. Emmeram (ca. 1070), also belongs to this realm of the imagination devoted to Dionysius and Paul on the Areopagus. The Astrolabium depicts Aratus ("SIDEREOS MOTUS RADIO PERCURRIT ARATUS"), from whom the words derive with which Paul seeks to win over the philosophers on the Areopagus: "For we are also his offspring." A St. Emmeram trope and sequence manuscript of the eleventh century contains texts of the "missa graeca."[78] In Arnold of St. Emmeram, there was an author around the middle of the century in Regensburg who made use of a Grecistic vocabulary, just as did, for instance, his contemporary Ekkehart IV of St. Gall.[79]

Through Emperor Henry II, the cathedral library in *Bamberg* became the repository of the Ottonian court library. The St. Gall *psalterium quadrupartitum* found its home here.[80] The Neapolitan Alexander novel, translated from Greek, is only one of many other literary works of the Ottonian period which are preserved complete nowhere else. No less than four manuscripts of Boethius' *Arithmetic* demonstrate how important this text was for the "Ottonian Renaissance."[81] It was the guide to the quadrivium—MUSICA, ARITHMETICA, GEOMETRIA, ASTRONO-MIA—as an illustration in Cod. Class. 5 (HJ.IV.12) shows.[82] This Boethius manuscript, the most distinguished of those in Bamberg, had been written in Tours for Charles the Bald, and arrived in Bamberg's cathedral library, the youngest of its day (founded 1007), most likely via Otto III's court library by way of Henry II.

One of the manuscripts of ΠЄΡΙ ΦΥϹЄѠϹ ΜЄΡΙϹΜΟΥ that came from John Scottus' workshop came into Otto III's possession, probably via Reims and Gerbert's library, and thence into the Bamberg library.[83] In the twelfth century it was in Kloster Michelsberg above the city. There was also a *Clavis physicae* there, with the title page on which the Greek Theodore is disputing with the Irishman John;[84] the Michelsberg library catalogue from the end of the twelfth century lists a *psalterium graecum*.[85] Wolfger of Prüfening came from the school in Michelsberg; in 1158, in his enormous compilation of glossaries (now Clm 13002), he transmitted yet again a late antique *hermeneumata* tradition in an impressive and influential form.[86]

XI

The High Middle Ages: From the Middle of the Eleventh Century to the Latin Conquest of Constantinople (1204)

. . . regni uestri partes etsi oppugnari, nunquam tamen expugnari [sc. deus] permisit, sed in uos magni illius Romani imperii gloriam nomenque transfudit. Voluit, ut sicut potestas sic et uocabulum ad uos transmigraret, ac religione mutata, imperio translato, sicut a pagano Romulo Roma dicebatur, sic a Christiano reparatore Constantino uestra urbs Constantinopolis uocaretur. Hanc ut dixi uelut metam intransmeabilem, uelut inuictum obicem, uelut praefixum quem nunquam liceat transgredi terminum, omnia prouidens supernus oculus paganis regibus, barbaris gentibus posuit, quo oriens terreatur, boreas subdatur, occidens defendatur. [. . . even if [God] allows some of your realm to be attacked, he has never suffered it to be conquered; but he transferred the glory and name of this great Roman Empire to you. He wished that just as the power migrated over to you, so should the name as well; and since the religion had been changed and the power transferred, so also, just as Rome had been named after the pagan Romulus, so your city of Constantinople was named after the Christian renovator Constantine. The all-seeing celestial eye has imposed, as I said, something like an impassable boundary, an unbreachable barrier, a fixed line which can never be crossed, on the pagan kings and barbarian nations, whereby the East is feared, the North subdued, the West defended.]

Abbot Peter the Venerable of Cluny, *epist.* 75, to Emperor John II Comnenus

1. The Schism of 1054

The idea that epochs are not necessarily defined by round numbers, battles, and genealogical accidents certainly holds true in medieval studies for the turning point which took place around the middle of the eleventh century. The Western Imperium, which still had a powerful presence under Henry III, ran into a serious crisis under his son, Henry IV; the papacy, on the other hand, experienced an unprecedented increase in power. The "Romanesque" style in architecture arose. Book illumination of the old artistic schools degenerated; it arose anew at other places, but never regained the significance it had during the "Ottonian" period. The liturgy no longer took as central and dominant a role as it had formerly; the "politically gifted" forced their way up the ladder: even under Henry III, an Adalbert of Bremen and an Anno of Cologne obtained their archbishoprics. Ecclesiastical law soon became the discipline in which the cleric who was called to lead distinguished himself; no longer could one obtain an episcopal see on the basis of one's artistic ability, no matter what that talent might be. The missionary impulse was exhausted; the new borders established by the *orbis latinus* in the early eleventh century— in Hungary, Bohemia, Poland, Sweden, Norway, and Iceland—were scarcely extended any further in the East and North. The "concept of the Crusades" arose, perhaps the most important phenomenon of this eleventh-century turn of the era.[1]

The large, well-organized pilgrimages of the early eleventh century, which took the overland route through Hungary, Bulgaria, and Constantinople to the Mediterranean coast and on to the Holy Land, were precursors of the crusades. The foundation of the Christian Kingdom of Hungary on the model of the Western Imperium (King Stephan I, 997–1038) and the firm ties between the Bulgars and the Greek Empire, due to Emperor Basil II Bulgaroctonus, had opened this route between the East and the West; the route came to have great historical significance. The most famous of the pilgrimages of the eleventh century was certainly that of the year 1064, which included in its number Archbishops Siegfried of Mainz and Thiemo of Salzburg, and Bishops Gunther of Bamberg and Altmann of Passau; in spite of occasional military entanglements, this pilgrimage was still of an entirely religious character—the "Ezzolied" bears witness to this fact:

> o crux salvatoris,
> du unser segelgerte bist.
> disiu werlt elliu ist daz meri,
> min trehtin segel unte vere,
> diu rehten werch unser segelseil,
> di rihtent uns di vart heim.
> der segel de ist der ware geloube,
> der hilfet uns der wole zuo.
> der heilige atem ist der wint,
> der vuoret unsih an den rehten sint.
> himelriche ist unser heimuot,
> da sculen wir lenten, gote lob.

[O cross of the savior, you who are our mast. All this world is the sea, my Lord the sail and ferryman; goods works are the lines of our sails, which direct our course home. The sail is the true faith, which helps us toward salvation. The wind is the Holy Spirit, which leads us to the right way. Heaven is our homeland, there we shall land, God be praised.]

Ezzo, *Cantilena de miraculis Christi* 33, ed. F. Maurer, *Die religiösen Dichtungen des 11. und 12. Jahrhunderts* (Tübingen 1964), I, 300. The *Vita Altmanni* reports that Ezzo composed the song on the journey to Jerusalem in 1065 (c. 3,

MGH Scriptores, XII, 230). Bishop Gunther of Bamberg, who commissioned the song, died during the return trip from Constantinople. His body was wrapped in a large Byzantine curtain of silk which depicted the emperor of the East on horseback between two crowned female figures (the "Günthertuch" is now in the Bamberg Domschatz).

Somewhat more than thirty years later, the Latins thought that they had to ensure the safety of the last portion of the route on a permanent basis: the crusader states of Antioch, Edessa, Tripoli, and Jerusalem (1099) were thus founded. The readiness for a solution won by force had obviously increased.

It was an act of violence in the style of the new era when Cardinal Humbert of Silva Candida excommunicated Patriarch Michael Cerullarius of Constantinople by laying a bull on the main altar of Hagia Sophia on 16 July 1054. This reformed monk from Lotharingia had attained great influence at the court of the German Pope Leo IX (1048–54); he was named archbishop of Sicily, which was at that time still under Saracen control and offered him no possibility of action. He led the embassy which sealed the schism between the Greek and Latin churches that was to last for centuries.

Humbert is to be remembered for his work in that typically eleventh-century genre, the polemical treatise. A number of Greco-Latin polemical treatises in Codex Bernensis 292 are associated with him. At the beginning of the codex, in the Latino-Greek polemic, attributable to the cardinal, one finds the translation of a letter from the Bulgarian Archbishop Leo of Achrida to Bishop John of Trani, which takes a position against the Saturday fasts and azyme (unleavened bread) of the Latin Church. Perhaps Humbert magnified the importance of the controversy between East and West with the translation of this letter. In answer to this letter, Humbert wrote a Latin dialogue between a Roman and a Constantinopolitan (from the year 1054), about which it is noted in the Codex Bernensis that the text was translated into Greek by order of Emperor Constantine IX Monomachus. Thereafter a treatise against the Latins (in Latin translation) by Nicetas Stethatus appeared and was followed by Humbert's refutation. The dossier was rounded out by the embassy's report and the text of the fateful bull of excommunication.

The best overview of this literary complex is found in the description of the manuscript Bern 292 in H. Hagen, *Catalogus Codicum Bernensium* (Bern 1875), pp. 311–13. H. Hoesch gives a new description and evaluation of the section of the manuscript relevant here, in *Die kanonischen Quellen im Werk Humberts von Moyenmoutier* (Cologne/Vienna 1970), pp. 11–16. The texts mentioned are edited by C. Will, *Acta et scripta quae de controversiis ecclesiae graecae et latinae saec. XI compositae extant* (Leipzig/Marburg 1861). A. Michel followed up his two-volume work *Humbert und Kerullarios* (Paderborn 1924 and 1930) with numerous other studies, in which he attributed a whole series of works to Humbert, whom he had raised to the level of a universal thinker and author on the basis of parallel passages in the various works (even the beast epic, *Ecbasis cuiusdam captivi per tropologiam!*). But the *indigesta moles* of Michel's Humbert studies scarcely concerned the Greco-Latin portion of Humbert's oeuvre.

It is open to question whether the translations of the Greek polemical treatises, which offered the cardinal such a welcomed motivation for his own polemics, were executed by Humbert himself, or whether he only had them prepared.[2] It is mentioned in the vita of Pope Leo IX that the pope "learned to read the Holy Scriptures in Greek"[3]—could this be an indication of how Humbert also worked with Greek? In Humbert's sphere of ecclesiastico-political activity in southern Italy, interpreters and translators were not hard to find. But Humbert also takes an important place in Greco-Latin literary history as a patron: he was the first to be interested exclusively in the controversy between East and West.

One of the southern Italian opponents to the Roman claims has become more distinct through a study by C. Giannelli: "Reliquie dell'attività 'letteraria' di uno scrittore italo-greco del sec. XI med. (Nicola arcivescovo di Reggio Calabria?)," *Atti dello VIII Congresso Internazionale di Studi Bizantini* (Rome 1953), I, 93–119. The concern here is a glossator who writes Greek and Latin; in pl. 10, Giannelli gives samples of the "scrittura latina originalissima" (with scattered Greek letters) from Cod. Vat. gr. 1667. The glossator, who was, according to Giannelli, Archbishop Nicholas of Reggio in Calabria or an Italo-Greek from among his associates, formulated critical opinions about Rome and the Latins.

The Western attitude toward the Greeks changed around the middle of the eleventh century—not everywhere nor simultaneously, but at any rate in the movement of "Reform monasticism," which was dominant for about three generations and through Gregory VII even attained to the papacy. The movement wished forcibly to impose and enforce the Kingdom of God on Earth; and it was to be a Latin Kingdom of God. From this perspective, Greek was of secondary importance. This new situation is clearly illustrated by the actions of a reform monk and enemy of the emperor, who made use of just that encoding and transposing device with which the Ottonian and early Salian emperors represented themselves as learned, universal, and exalted in the "second sacred language"—namely, by writing Latin words in the Greek alphabet—in order to denounce and disparage the emperor. For the year 1085, in which the death of Gregory VII sharpened many pens, Bernold of Constance wrote: "Eo tempore quidam ex Saxonibus a fidelitate sancti Petri apostatantes, et a rege Heremanno turpiter declinantes ͰΗΥΝΡΥΚΥΜ regem totiens abiuratum receperunt. . . . Episcopi autem Saxoniae et quidam ex principibus cum rege eorum Heremanno in fidelitate sancti Petri permanserunt. . . . Qui . . . postea a Saxonibus ad proprias sedes revocati sunt, postquam Saxones ͰΗΥΝΡΥΚΥΜ inde expulerunt. . . ."[4] ("At that time some of the Saxons who had fallen away from the faith of St. Peter and had shamefully turned from King Heremannus took Heinricus as their king. . . . The bishops of Saxony, however, and some of the princes remained with the king constant in the Christian faith. . . . Later they were recalled to their sees by the Saxons, after the Saxons had expelled Heinricus.")

In *Deutschlands Geschichtsquellen* Wattenbach and Holtzmann offer the comment on the passage that the use of Greek letters here has an "amusing" ("erheiternd") effect.[5] But Bernold's inspired idea demonstrates in all earnest that Ottonian Hellenism could literally be reversed in meaning. In 1085 ҺΗΥΝΡΥΚΥϹ (= *Heinricus*) did not call to the Swabian Gregorian's mind the successor of Constantine, the ecumenical kingdom, the second "sacred language," but rather perfidy, schism, heresy, apostasy. Bernold had used the Greek alphabet as if it were a death warrant.

2. Greek Studies North of the Alps

> und weiz niht war zuo daz sol:
> ich vernaeme kriechisch als wol.

[And I do not know what it means: I could as easily understand Greek.]

Hartmann von Aue, *Gregorius* 1629 f.

It is an open question whether it was the official schism (1054), the first crusade (1095)—in which the Greek Christians were often regarded as at least as foreign as the Moslems—or only the conquest of Constantinople by the Latins (1204) that opened the chasm that no attempts at reunification during the late Middle Ages and modern period have been able to bridge. The situation also differs in various geographical regions. In eleventh- and early twelfth-century Italy, there is no break to be seen in the relationship with Constantinople. The hostile posture which the reform papacy took against Constantinople was by no means the authoritative standard of the great Italian cities, especially the maritime cities, and ultimately not even the Roman attitude was consistently hostile; Pope Eugene III (1145–53) was a patron of literature on the *cathedra Petri* who was also particularly interested in Graecolatina. Thus the concept of a "Renaissance of the twelfth century" holds good for the translation literature of the twelfth century, which was primarily the work of Italians and which represents the third major Byzantine-Medieval Latin "batch" of transmitted texts (after the sixth and ninth centuries).

The relationship between the emperors of East and West were also hardly disturbed. Of course there were continual entanglements in Italy due to the claims of both to dominion in the region; but since a common enemy appeared in the Normans, there were also common interests.[6]

Pope Leo IX brought about a coalition of Greeks and Latins; in the critical moment, however, the pope was left with no resources beyond the German troops whom he had himself recruited and who were soundly defeated by the Normans in 1053. Emperor Lothar sent Bishop Anselm of Havelberg to Constantinople in 1136 in order to form an alliance with Emperor John II Comnenus (1118–43) against the Norman Roger of Sicily; the embassy became famous as an important event in intellectual and literary history, due to the disputation between the German bishop and Nicetas, metropolitan of Nicomedia. The first wife of Emperor Manuel I (1143–80) was a relative of the first Hohenstaufen emperor, Conrad III (Bertha of Sulzbach, Empress Eirene). Philip of Swabia married Irene, the daughter of the Byzantine emperor, in Augsburg on Pentecost 1197; she was called Maria in Germany, and Walther von der Vogelweide praised her as the "rose ane dorn, ein tube sunder gallen" ("rose without a thorn, a dove without rancor"). She died soon after Philip's murder (1208) and is buried in the Hohenstaufen monastery of Lorsch. In spite of occasional changes in the coalition, the Eastern and Western empires formed alliances again and again. Greco-Latin relations of the twelfth century, especially at the time of Emperor Manuel I, may be summed up in the phrase "Byzanz kehrt nach Italien zurück" ("The Byzantine Empire returns to Italy," P. Lamma).

The lack of a Greco-Latin translation literature in the crusader states is remarkable. Jerusalem was a Latin city for almost a century (from 15 July 1099 to October 1187); the Latins held Acre, recaptured during the third crusade, for another hundred years (1191–1291), and for a time (1229–44) Emperor Frederick II contractually safeguarded the Holy Sepulchre in Jerusalem (if not other sites as well) for Westerners.

The knightly orders developed prodigious building projects in the Latin kingdoms of the eastern Mediterranean coast. In the Kingdom of Jerusalem, there was a school of manuscript illumination beside the Church of the Holy Sepulchre; the Orient and Occident were probably most beautifully united in the "Riccardiana Psalter," from the last Latin period in Jerusalem, "the fascinating Teutonic interlude in the history of Outremer."[7] Latin Jerusalem had also produced an important historian in William of Tyre, who could probably orient himself somewhat in Greek, but of whom one cannot say he had "a good knowledge of the Greek language."[8] In the Latin Kingdom of Antioch, there were some translators from *Arabic* at work, among whom were the important native of Pisa Stephan of Antioch in the twelfth and Philip of Tripoli in the thirteenth century.[9]

Despite the strong presence of the Greek Church and liturgy in Syria and Palestine, it seems that there were no Greco-Latin translations there; only in the *tituli* of the church are Greek and Latin occasionally found together, as in the magnificent representation of the Word became visible (at the moment of the Annunciation) in a mosaic of the Church of the Holy Sepulchre: between Mary and the archangel Gabriel, Jesus appears as a child, encircled by the words of the Annunciation in Greek and Latin, the "sacred languages" of the ancient Christian ecumene.[10]

The situation in the crusader states here mirrors the intellectual life of the lands north of the Alps from which the crusaders primarily came. Almost all of the Carolingian monastic schools had declined. The Benedictine order was partially reorganized in new forms, such as the Cluniacs and Cistercians. Abbot Peter the Venerable of Cluny (1122–56) wrote a fine letter to Emperor John II in order to recover a lost Cluniac base near Constantinople;[11] Cluny did not make any great efforts to gain a footing in Greek—not even intellectually—in comparison with Peter the Venerable's commission of a Latin translation of the Koran from Arabic. Peter the Venerable was, however, not lacking in good will, openness to reconciliation, or tolerance for the Greek religious rites, all of which Bernard of Clairvaux did in fact lack to a great extent: for him, the preacher of the second crusade, the Greeks, heathens, and Jews were all alike.[12]

In the cathedral schools of the high Middle Ages, out of which the universities then grew, Greek played a remarkably unimportant role. The new translations from Greek executed during the high Middle Ages were, to be sure, of great and often even decisive importance in the intellectual history of the West: not only Aristotle's *Logica nova* but also John of Damascus' *De fide orthodoxa*, for instance, circulated with unprecedented speed and range. But this intellectual material was taken ready-made from the translators, in most cases Italians; it evoked no interest in the Greek original. North of the Alps, no one but Dionysius the Areopagite could entice one to study a Greek text. In the twelfth century, the West found its own great model: Rome became the ancestor of the new culture, and Greece receded into the distance of antiquity:

> Ce nos ont nostre livre apris
> Qu'an Grece ot de chevalrie
> Le premier los et de clergie.
> Puis vint chevalrie a Rome
> Et de la clergie la some,
> Qui or est an France venue.

(Chrétien de Troyes, Cligès 28–33)

[Our books teach us that Greece had the first and greatest renown for chivalry and also for learning. Then chivalry came to Rome, and the sum of learning did likewise, which thereafter came to France.]

No more than a certain slight interest in the meaning of a few Greek expressions is found among the great theologians of the high Middle Ages. Gerhoh of Reichersberg explained the difference between ΛΛΤΡΕΙΛ and ΔΟΥΛΕΙΛ to Bishop Eberhard of Bamberg: "These Greek expressions, *latria* and *dulia*, differ, as we have learned from Fathers of the Church who knew Greek, in this manner, that the service owed only to God is *latria*, while *dulia* is the service which men perform for each other. . . . They prove that this is so on the basis of the Greek manuscripts. For where our text of the Pauline epistles reads *spiritu ferventes*, *Domino servientes*, the Greek text has *latreuontes* [Rom. 12:11]. But where we read *per caritatem servite invicem*, the Greek manuscripts have *duleuite* [Gal. 5:13]. . . ."[13]

Are the *patres graecae linguae periti*, whom Gerhoh would like to thank for his information here, to be identified with the northern Italian translators in Constantinople (of whom Gerhoh incidentally mentions Moses of Bergamo and Hugh Etherianus; cf. Classen, *Gerhoh*, pp. 424 and 441), or is he referring to older authorities here, for instance, the commentary on Matthew by Christian of Stablo (see above, Chapter VIII, sec. 1; cf. the quotation from Galatians)?

It would be informative to follow via glossaries how Western scholarship groped its way toward the meaning of Greek theological terminology gloss by gloss. The way in which such a section of a glossary came together piece by piece is discernible in its composition. As an illustration of this point, one can take a passage from the "Glossarium Salomonis" (saec. IX), which was widely known in southern Germany and survives in printed form only in an incunabula (Augsburg, St. Ulrich and Afra 1475):

> Latreusis ˙ servitus
> Latria ˙ servitium vel servitus religionis, quae soli deo exhibetur; grecum est
> [from Aug. *De civ. dei* X 1]
> Latria divinitati vel si expressius dicendum est deitati debitus cultus dicitur
> [ibid.]

Westerners had even more difficulty with *dulia* than *latria*. The "Glossarium Ansileubi," finally compiled in Visigothic Spain, nevertheless did include *duleusis*; cf. W. M. Lindsay et al., eds., *Glossaria latina* (Paris 1926), I, 190. As noted above, Christian von Stablo made use of the quite uncommon terminological pair *duleusis/latreusis*. In the twelfth century the distinction between *latria* and *dulia* finally became common knowledge. Evidence is found not only in the quotation from Gerhoh, but also in a gloss from a still unpublished typological didactic poem (Inc. "Prima luce deum") in Heidelberg Sal. IX 15 (saec. XII), fol. 28[r]:

> Duobus nominibus utuntur greci ˙ ubi nos uno ˙ quia quod nos dicimus seruitus dei ˙ ipsi dicunt latria ˙ quod nos humana seruitus ˙ ipsi ˙ dulia ˙ Latria grece ˙ latine dicitur seruitus dei ˙ et inde ydolatria ˙ seruitus idolorum ˙ dulia ˙ seruitus humana.

[The Greeks use two words where we use one, for when we say "service to God," they say *latria*; when we say "service to men," they say *dulia*. Greek *latria* is called "service to God" in Latin; thence "idolatry" is the service to idols and *dulia* service to men.]

The gloss shows that the distinction between ΔΟΥΛΕΙΛ and ΛΛΤΡΕΙΛ was already a part of the scholastic knowledge of the time.

Research into the meanings of the concepts ΟΥϹΙΛ and ΥΠΟϹΤΛϹΙϹ proceeded with less success.[14] Many French scholars thought it best to eliminate Greek concepts from all discussions, since one could not come to terms with them anyway.[15]

We know of only one of the famous teachers of the eleventh and twelfth centuries who continued to cultivate Greek studies in the old, Carolingian style. Odo, who was bishop of Cambrai when he died in 1113 and had taught in the cathedral school in Tournai,[16] had a new, large-format *psalterium quadrupartitum* with supplements designed and executed. It was considered the memorial to his work in the new abbey of St. Martin in Tournai, founded by Odo.

Paris, BN nouv. acq. lat. 2195 contains the *psalterium quadrupartitum* of Salomo III, a 48-line format, with slight changes in the original arrangement: without the dedicatory poem, "Nongentis pariterque novem," but with the alphabetical table of the *tres linguae sacrae* (fol. 116ᵛ, with ꝏ and Ͻ for M and N in the Greek alphabet!). Cf. L. Delisle, *Mélanges de Paléographie et de Bibliographie* (Paris 1880), pp. 150–54. When Abbot Odo became bishop of Cambrai in 1105, it was noted in chancery hand that the codex was his memorial (fol. 119ʳ). A copy of the work is in Valenciennes, Bibliothèque Municipale 14 (old signatures are 7 and B. 1.37), saec. XII, from St. Amand; cf. J. Mangeart, *Catalogue descriptif et raisonné des manuscrits de la bibliothèque de Valenciennes* (Paris/Valenciennes 1860), no. 7, pp. 13–15; Cagin, *Te Deum*, pp. 529ff.

The *psalterium quadrupartitum* of Odo of Tournai (Cambrai) was a decidedly retrospective undertaking in his day; it is hardly by accident that the work was produced within the confines of the monastery founded by Odo and not in the cathedral school in Tournai.[17] In the high Middle Ages, bilinguals of the Psalter and Gospels were copied only in very rare cases; such editions of the Acts of the Apostles and Pauline epistles were no longer to be found. This reduction of the spectrum of bilingual texts is all the more remarkable, since it does not correspond to the general development of writing in the period. After the ninth century, the twelfth is again a century of prodigious quantitative accomplishments in the scriptoria. Obviously there was a lack of interest in these old works, prepared for study and display, on the part of those working in the scriptoria and libraries. There were other occupations for the intellect—for example (in rapidly growing numbers), Aristotle. The veneration of the *philosophus* did not, to be sure, go so far as to spawn bilingual editions of his works, but there are Aristotle manuscripts which are comparable to the multicolumn manuscripts of the Psalter. Just as the various versions of the Psalter had been arranged in parallel columns in the earlier Middle Ages in order to render the sense of the psalmist's words more accessible, so it happened that in the late Middle Ages a Latin translation of Aristotle from Arabic was copied in a column parallel to a translation of the same text from Greek, in order to better grasp the philosopher's ideas, which had often been obscured in the translations.[18]

The development of the old glossaries runs parallel to that of the bilinguals. Of course one can mention one of the more important figures of the twelfth century here as well—Wolfger of Prüfening, who passed on one more such glossary (Clm 13002). Wolfger was a monastic scholar, and it was in monasteries that his work survived. In the cathedral schools, it was the newly developed discipline of lexicography which took the place of these old reference works. The first of these lexicographical works appeared around the middle of the eleventh century—the *Elementarium doctrinae rudimentum* of the Italian Papias. Famous works which appeared later are the *Derivationes* of Hugh of Pisa (1190/1200) and the *Grecismus* of Eberhard of Béthune (d. 1212). Both of these last-named works indicate even in their titles the etymological manner, soon to become a mania, of these lexicographers, who refer to alleged Greek words and roots without hesitation; and since plagiarism is in the nature of the lexical genre, a depressing lineage of progressively deteriorating "lexicographical Greek" runs through the late Middle Ages to the Humanistic period.[19] Many of the malicious words of the Humanists about the medieval use of Greek refer to these works. The first to be annoyed by this "Greek," and to draw the conclusion from his anger that he should learn grammatical Greek, was however—it must be said in honor of the "Middle Ages"—a man of the thirteenth century, Roger Bacon.

3. Amalfi, Salerno, Benevento, Monte Cassino

> . . . adquisivit Amalfin.
> Urbs haec dives opum populoque referta videtur,
> Nulla magis locuples argento, vestibus, auro,
> Partibus innumeris. Hac plurimus urbe moratur
> Nauta maris coelique vias aperire peritus.
> Huc et Alexandri diversa feruntur ab urbe,
> Regis et Antiochi; haec freta plurima transit;
> His Arabes, Libi, Siculi noscuntur et Afri:
> Haec gens est totum notissima paene per orbem
> Et mercanda ferens et amans mercata referre.

[. . . he acquired Amalfi. This city seemed rich in resources and full of people; there is none richer in silver, vestments, gold, and innumerable other respects. Many a sailor, experienced in disclosing the ways of the seas and the heavens, stays in this city. Diverse things are brought hither from Alexandria and Antioch; this people crosses many seas. The Arabians, Libyans, Sicilians, and Africans know them: this people is practically the most famous in the entire world; they bear forth goods to be traded, and loving the business which they have transacted, they return.]

William of Apulia, *Gesta Roberti Wiscardi* 476–85, ed. M. Mathieu (Palermo 1961), p. 190

> und vuor engegen Salerne
> und suochte ouch dâ durch genist
> der wîsen arzâte list.

[And he went to Salerno and sought out the wise doctors' wisdom there, for the sake of a cure.]

Hartmann von Aue, *Der Arme Heinrich* 180–82.

In the late tenth and early eleventh centuries, the Campanian maritime cities Amalfi and Salerno became Naples' heirs as centers of the Greco-Latin reciprocal relations. The hagiographical and narrative traditions of translation were continued in Amalfi; in Salerno, medical studies flourished.

Before Venice began to extend its control into the eastern Mediterranean, Amalfi was the emporium of the Orient in the West. Ships from Amalfi supplied the colonies of Latins in Constantinople and on Mt. Athos, which already existed around the year 1000; in 1050 in Jerusalem they founded the hostel for pilgrims which was possibly the starting point of the Knights of St. John of Jerusalem.[20] Around the middle of the eleventh century, in the monastery on Mt. Athos that was associated with Amalfi,[21] a monk named Leo translated the famous *Miraculum a S. Michaele Chonis patratum* (Chonae in Asia Minor), the cult legend of the oldest shrine to St. Michael in all of Christendom;[22] the work was attributed to Patriarch Sisinnius of Constantinople (426–27). Perhaps it was the same Leo who, in 1048–49 in Constantinople, commissioned the Latin translations of the Greek Barlaam and Josaphat novel, the legend of Buddha in Christian guise; this work was the second novel translated from Greek during the Middle Ages, the first having been the adventures of Alexander, translated by Leo the archpriest.

Naples, Biblioteca Nazionale Cod. VIII. B. 10, not yet edited. On the question of authorship, see P. Peeters, "La première traduction latine de 'Barlaam et Joasaph' et son original grec," *AB* 49 (1931), 276–312; Siegmund, *Die Überlieferung*, pp. 257 f.; F. Dölger, *Der griechische Barlaam-Roman* (Ettal 1953), esp. p. 24, n. 1; H. Peri (Pflaum), "La plus ancienne traduction du roman grec de Barlaam et Josaphat," *Studi Mediolatini e Volgari* 6/7 (1959), 169–89. The novel was received with no less favor in the West than in the East; cf. J. Sonet, *Le roman de Barlaam et Josaphat*, I/2 (Louvain 1949–52). The translations into European vernaculars were most often from the Latin text; the German translation was by Rudolf von Ems. In one case, however, the translation was made directly from Greek into the vernacular: in an illuminated codex of the Barlaam and Josaphat novel from Mt. Athos (Iviron Cod. 69), an Old French translation has been entered in the margin; ed. P. Meyer, "Fragments d'une ancienne traduction française de Barlaam et Josaph, faite sur le grec au commencement du treizième siècle," *Bibliothèque de l'École des Chartes* VI/2 (1886), 313–30 (with plates).

A clan with the surname "Comiti⟨s⟩ Mauronis" was especially important in promoting Amalfi's cultural relations with the Byzantine Empire.[23] Maurus and his son Pantaleon donated the bronze gates of Amalfi (1065), Monte Cassino (around 1066), Rome (S. Paulo fuori le Mura, 1070), and St. Michael in Gargano (1076), all of which were cast in Constantinople. Another Pantaleon from the same Amalfi clan donated the Byzantine bronze doors of Atrani (1087).[24] But these "royal merchants" of Amalfi also attended to literary exports from East to West. A priest and monk named John, living in the monastery *Panagiotum* in Constantinople, relates the following story in the prologue to the *Vita vel passio S. Herinis virginis et martiris* (Irene) which he translated:[25]

> One day when I entered the house of the very noble man Lord Lupinus, the son of Lord Sergius, with the surname Comiti Mauronis, in order to pay him a visit, several others from Amalfi were there. While we were talking of one thing or another, whatever one customarily talks about as a comfort to a sick person, the conversation turned to the holy virgin and the blessed martyr of Christ Irene: That we neglected to investigate and find out who she was for all those years while the church of Amalfi was under her rule and also her protection, since there were in fact many noble, wise, and very rich men in this royal city and several interpreters of both languages. . . .

Pantaleon "exhorted" this same translator, John, "often to translate something into Latin which one finds in Greek but not in Latin books or narratives." John complied with this wish in his *Liber de miraculis*, which contains Greek narratives of asceticism, especially from the ΛΕΙΜΩΝ, the *Pratum spirituale* of John Moschus from the early seventh century. In the preface to this translation the garrulous translator, John, describes or rather apologizes for his method:[26]

> . . . if one wishes to write a letter to someone, then one drafts it, thereafter revises it, and finally writes out the revised version [*primum exemplat, postea emendat et iam emendata conscribit*]. I did not have this opportunity, however, for, as I have already noted, I have reached an advanced age, my eyes are growing dim and my kidneys are causing me pain; I could do no more. If I had the opportunity to write a second time, I would certainly find harmonious words and seek out a pleasing style in the order of words. But I leave that to you, you who are holier and wiser: stylize the material and the faithful translation of this little work as you deem fitting. But we would do better to leave this topic; for we read that Jerome worked in this manner: first he wrote with the help of a notary, then he revised that which had been dictated, and then he gave that to the book scribes. I did not have the opportunity to do that, for in the place where I live, there is not only no notary or scribe to be found, but not even anyone who understands a single Latin word.

In a third hagiographical work, John refers back to a Neapolitan translation:[27]

> Here begins the preface to the passion of the blessed Archbishop Nicholas. To be read on the day of his funeral. And, dear brothers, since the late subdeacon John, who translated the life of the holy father Nicholas, reported to the church in Naples that he could not find [the account of his] death, he omitted it. And that is not surpris-

ing, since he translated in Italy. Therefore, I, the most humble priest
and monk John, led by my love for [this] holy father, sought and
found the work while I was in Constantinople—and not on just any
scraps, but in records from the archives and revised codices. And,
according to my own modest understanding, I have translated it as
well as I could.

According to more recent opinions, this rather garrulous translator
lived in the second half of the eleventh century. His translation of John
Moschus (*Liber de miraculis*) had a certain circulation in the southern
German monasteries of the high Middle Ages. Information concerning
this translator of Amalfi-Constantinople is otherwise to be found primarily
in a compilation from the monastery of St. Severin in Naples from the
year 1174; the scribe of the codex, Marinus of Sorrent, "ingeniously
named it *Marinulus*, as if it were his small son."[28] It may be possible to
identify other texts in this codex as the work of Amalfi translators—the
last of the "Lombard" translation schools.[29]

In the high Middle Ages, medicine and philosophy entered into a close
association which was not dissolved again until the late Middle Ages. In
that earlier era, even theology and practical politics were associated with
medical science: not only were there physicians who executed translations (Constantinus Africanus, Johannes Afflatius, Rusticus of Pisa,
perhaps even Stephan of Antioch, later on Nicholas of Reggio), but even
those who discharged the office of ambassador (Philippus to "Prester
John"),[30] abbot (Wilhelmus Medicus of St. Denis), and pope (Petrus His-
panus = John XXI, 1276–77). The most important schools of this urbane
medicine were in Salerno and Toledo. Both transmitted primarily Arabic
learning; in Salerno, however, Greek also played a role.

The school in Salerno developed out of a community of practicing
physicians; beginning in the eleventh century, this school published its
own medical literature.[31] The earliest medical author from Salerno known
by name is a certain Guarimpotus (or Gariopontus, not to be confused
with the Neapolitan translator Guarimpotus). He compiled the *Passiona-
rius Galeni* from old translations and commentaries. Archbishop Alfanus
of Salerno (d. 1085; trained in Monte Cassino) translated "latinorum co-
gente penuria" the anthropologico-medical work ΠЄΡΙ ΦΥϹЄѠϹ
ΑΝΘΡѠΠΟΥ of the Syrian Nemesius of Emesa; he published the work
under the title *Premnon physicon*.[32] Alfanus did not know the author of
the Greek text; Burgundio, who again translated the work a century later,
thought the author to be Gregory of Nyssa, just as did Johannes Cuno, the
third translator, in the sixteenth century. Alfanus was a friend and patron
of Constantinus Africanus, the translator from Arabic; a broad stream of
the Greek tradition of scholastic medical literature entered Italy via Constantinus and by way of Arabic. His major work is the *Liber Pantegni*

(probably modelled on ΠΑΝΤΕΧΝΗ), in which he translated in large part Ali ben Abbas' (d. 994) comprehensive treatment of Greco-Arabic medicine; he dedicated the work to Abbot Desiderius of Monte Cassino.[33] Constantinus Africanus died in 1087 as a monk in Monte Cassino. It is not certain whether he taught in Salerno; but his works were in any case used there for a long time as a basis of instruction. Around the middle of the twelfth century, medical commentaries were published in Salerno; medicine began to establish ties with philosophy. Urso of Salerno was the most important representative of this theoretical aspect of Salernian medicine, which also took part in the reception of the works of Aristotle. Thus, with Salerno as its center, an Italian variant of Aristotelianism developed; and it was one which, "in contrast to the Aristotelianism of the North, was defined not by theological but rather by medical interests."[34]

The school of Salerno is important for more than just medical history, since it was responsible for the first wave of reception of Arabic science, in the eleventh century. A century later, the second wave followed via Toledo and other Spanish schools. It is an undecided question what the relationship was in Salerno between translations from the Arabic and translations from the Greek. In other words: did Alfanus of Salerno restrict himself to a translation of Nemesius of Emesa, or did he also translate other, specifically medical, works? The *Articella*, the textbook of Salernian medicine that was widely known from the twelfth century on, seems to contain not just Arabo-Latin but also Greco-Latin translations.

Cf. Kristeller, *Italia Medioevale e Umanistica* 19 (1976), 66 f.: "The Aphorisms [of Hippocrates] appear in the *Articella* in a new translation ('*Vita brevis, ars vero longa*') which in some manuscripts is preceded by a prologue that is at times attributed to Oribasius. This prologue suggests that the translation was made from the Greek. If this is correct, the translation should be linked with Alfanus." According to B. Alexanderson, *Die hippokratische Schrift Prognosticon* (Göteborg 1963), the text of Hippocrates' *Prognosticon* included in the *Articella* is a Greco-Latin translation. It would thus be a further trace of Greek translation in Salerno. Additionally, Kristeller considers yet another text of the *Articella* a post-1100 translation from Greek—Theophilus, *De urinis*. It is also significant for our conception of the school of Salerno whether Marius' work of natural philosophy, *De elementis*, had its origin there. The last editor, R. C. Dales, *On the Elements* (Berkeley/Los Angeles/London 1976), is inclined to attribute it to the school of Chartres.

The southern Italian *Almagest* translator of the mid-twelfth century came from Salerno, as he himself notes; see below, sec. 7.

Just as was the case in Naples, Amalfi, and Salerno, the inland ducal city of Benevento had its Greco-Latin traditions which could be traced back to its Lombard period. The Beneventan liturgy has transmitted an eleventh-century bilingual liturgy for Good Friday, the "Adoratio crucis,"[35] and (together with the Ravenna rite) the troparion "Όταν τῷ σταυρῷ *O quan-*

do in cruce: a liturgical composition which not only is Grecistic, but even adopts its text and melody directly from the Greek (see figure).[36]

Monte Cassino was apparently the focal point of the Greco-Latin culture which had such a rich development in Campania during the eleventh century. There was a Greco-Latin liturgy in Monte Cassino by the time of Abbot Bertharius (856–84) at the latest;[37] in the tenth century, Greek monks associated with Nilus of Rossano lived near Monte Cassino at least occasionally. Emperors of both East and West granted special privileges and gave many valuable gifts to Monte Cassino, as the foundation of the father of Western monasticism.[38]

Under Abbot Desiderius (1058–87), Monte Cassino experienced its golden age. This abbot, from a Lombard family and, in his time, an *uomo universale*, was closely associated with Maurus of Amalfi (who was responsible for bringing the cast bronze gates from Constantinople to Monte Cassino), Constantinus Africanus (who dedicated his *Pantegni* to Desiderius), and Alfanus of Salerno (who celebrated in song Abbot Desiderius' new buildings and their ornamentation):[39]

> Ibi sardius et chrysoprassus
> nitet ac speciosa smaragdus,
> simul emicat his amethistus,
> radiat pretiosa iacynthus.
> Varias quoque Graecia vestes
> dedit artificesque scientes;
> tribuit sua marmora Roma
> quibus est domus ista decora.

[There sardian and chrysoprase glitter, as does the splendid emerald; at the same time an amethyst shines forth from among them, the precious jacinth gleams. Greece also gives diverse garments and knowledgeable experts. It grants its marble statues to Rome, with which this house is ornamented.]

Archbishop Alfanus came out of Monte Cassino: the physician Constantinus and the merchant Maurus died there as monks. At this period, one could find so many authorities on Greek art and science nowhere in the West except Monte Cassino. It has, however, not yet been determined whether translations were also made there from Greek directly into Latin.[40]

As is often the case in the cultural history of medieval monasteries, a historian stands at the close of the great era and compiles the traditions of his monastery. In Monte Cassino, it is Petrus Diaconus.[41] He continued the rich tradition of polemical treatises present in the library of Monte Cassino with a work of his own—*Altercatio contra Graecum quendam* (ca. 1140). Petrus Diaconus knew very little Greek, and such a knowledge

Ὅ-ταν τῷ σταυρῷ προσήλωσαν παρά-νομοι τὸν Κύρι-ον τῆς δόξης, ἐ-βό-α πρὸς αὐτούς
O-tin to stau-ron prosi-losan para-nomi ton Kyri-on tis doxis, e-vo-a pros aptus

Τί ὑμ-ᾶς ἠδί-κησα; ἢ ἐν τίνι παρώργισα; Πρὸ ἐμοῦ τίς ὑμᾶς ἐρρύσατο ἐκ θλί-ψε-ως; Καὶ νῦν τι
Ti yma ydikysan? i en tini parogi-so? Pro emu tis imas e-risate ec klipse-os? Ke ni ti

μοι ἀντ-απο-δί-δο-τε πονηρὰ ἀντὶ ἀγα-θῶν; Ἀντὶ στύλου πυρὸς σταυρῷ με προσηλώ-σα-τε
mi ant-apo-dydo-te ponira anti agotho? Anti stislu piros stau-ron mu prosi-lonsa-te

ἀντὶ νεφέλης τάφον μοι ὠρύ-ξα-τε· ἀντὶ τοῦ μάν-να χολήν μοι ἐ-πο-τί-σα-τε· ἀντὶ τοῦ
anti nefe-li tafon mi e-ri-sa-te; anti tu manna cho-lin mu epo-ti-sa-te; anti tu

ὕ-δα-τος ὄξος με ἐπο-τί-σα-τε; Λοιπὸν καλῶ τὰ ἔθνη κἀκεῖ-νά με δο-ξά-σουσι σὺν Πα
y-da-to osos mi epo-ti-sa-te? Lipon ka-la ta etni kekyna me doxa-susyn syn Pa

τρὶ καὶ Ἁγί-ῳ Πνεύ-ματι. Ἀ-μήν.
tri ke Agi-o Pneumati. Amin.

O quando in cruce confixerant in-iqui Dominum glo-ri-æ! A-it ad e-os : Quid vobi

molestus sum? a-ut 4 in quo ira-tus sum? Ante me quis vos libera-vit ex angusti-is? Et nu

quid mihi reddi-tis ma-la pro bo-nis? Pro co-lumna ignis in cruce me configi-tis; pro

nube sepulchrum mihi fodistis; pro manna fel me po-ta-tis; propter aquas acetu

mihi in poculum porri-gi-tis. Ergo vocabo gentes ut ipsi me glori-fi-cent una cum Patre

et cum Sancto Spi-ri-tu. Amen.

must have seemed to him in general superfluous, since he considered the Latins superior to the Greeks in all matters. A note in Codex Casinensis 220 on the close of Petrus Chrysolanus' disputation (in 1112), attributed to Petrus Diaconus, has the Greek emperor himself say as much:[42] "Once wisdom was taken from the East to the West, from the Greeks to the Latins; now, on the contrary, a Latin comes from the West to the East and deigns to associate with the Greeks. . . ."

4. Venice

The rise of Venice began around the turn of the millenium, when the city, under the doges Pietro and Otto Orseoli, extended its rule to Dalmatia. In the course of the eleventh century, the Venetians gradually took the place of Amalfi in the eastern Mediterranean; in 1082 they obtained trade privileges in Constantinople. The crusades, which due to the hardships of the land route always made part of the journey by sea, soon gave the Venetians a key position in the eastern Mediterranean which they then exploited to the point of villainy on a world scale, especially in diverting the fourth crusade to Constantinople (1204): *prima Veneziani poi cristiani* was, "from the very beginning, fundamental" in Venetian policy.[43] Compared with the enormous influx of Greek art into Venice, what was undertaken in literary studies seems rather modest. Important traces of the early reception of Aristotle nevertheless lead back to a Venetian of the early twelfth century who translated from Greek—Jacobus Veneticus Grecus, the first systematic translator of Aristotle since Boethius.[44] Boethius had made important works of Aristotelian logic available to the Latin world through his translations; this *Aristoteles logicus* was not, however, entirely complete.[45] It was primarily the *Analytica posteriora* which were lacking for the completion of the "Organon," as Aristotle's collection of epistemologico-logical works was called. This work was the fundamental text of the "new logic" that was of such great significance for the new scientific and scholastic direction of Western thought after the mid-twelfth century.

The *Analytica posteriora* are the most certain attribution to Jacobus and also his most successful work; his translation held its own against several later translations even up to the fifteenth century.

Robert of Torigny, Abbot of Mont Saint Michel in Normandy, reports that Jacobus translated and wrote commentaries on "certain of Aristotle's books . . . namely, the *Topica, Analytica priora et posteriora,* and *Sophistici elenchi,* although older translations of these works already existed" (*Migne PL* 160, cols. 443 f.). Thus is one to take Jacobus for the translator and commentator of the entire *Organon,* with the exception of the short works, the *Categoriae* and *De interpretatione?* Modern scholarship is inclined to accept all that and much more. B. G. Dod, one of Minio-Paluello's collaborators on the *Aristoteles latinus,* cites, in addition to the titles noted above, Aristotle, *De physica*, *De anima*, *De memoria*, *De longitudine*, *De iuventute*, *De respiratione*, *De morte*, *De intelligentia*, and the earliest translation of the *Metaphysica* (in the *Cambridge History of Later Medieval Philosophy* [Cambridge 1982], p. 55). The problems of authorship here are complicated in the same way as in the glossary literature that was amassing at the same time ("Glossa ordinaria"). These works were tools, which were copied and transmitted; but scarcely anyone was interested in their practical, although artless, originators.

Jacobus Veneticus Grecus styled himself *philosophus* once. This appellation is certainly also applicable to him in the sense that he was one element in the filiation of philosophers who taught in Constantinople. In 1045 Constantine IX Monomachus had reopened this school, founded in late antiquity. A new stage in the confrontation with ancient philosophy began with the philosopher Michael Psellus—first mainly with Plato's philosophy, then under Michael's successor, Johannes Italus, with Aristotle. Just as Boethius' translations of Aristotle are to be seen in the context of the Alexandrian Aristotelianism of his day, one might also regard the translation work of Jacobus of Venice—as does Minio-Paluello—as a distant effect of the Aristotle renaissance in Constantinople.

The enigmatic Cerbanus, who must have led an exciting life (if it is the case that only one person is to be sought behind this name), seems also to have been a Venetian. From around 1118 to 1123, he was at the imperial court in Constantinople, working on translations from Greek hagiographical literature.[46] In the monastery of St. Mary in Pásztó (Hungary), he found Maximus Homologetes' (the Confessor) ΚΕφΑΛΑΙΑ ΠΕΡΙ Α-ΓΑΠΗC (*Capita de caritate*), which he translated and dedicated to Abbot David of Pannonhalma (1131–50).[47] The manuscript tradition indicates that the same person also executed the first (partial) Latin translation of John of Damascus' ΕΚΘΕCIC ΑΚΡΙΒΗC ΤΗC ΟΡΘΟΔΟΖΟΥ ΠΙ-CΤΕUC (*De fide orthodoxa*); Gerhoh of Reichersberg used this translation in 1147.

Ed. by R. L. Szigeti, *Translatio latina Ioannis Damasceni [De orthodoxa fide III 1–8] saec. XII in Hungaria confecta*, Magyar-Görög Tanulmányok 13 (Budapest 1940); new edition by É. M. Buytaert (together with Burgundio's translation), *Saint John Damascene: De fide orthodoxa. Versions of Burgundio and Cerbanus* (Louvain/Paderborn 1955). On the method of translation, see J. de Ghellinck, "L'entrée littéraire de Jean de Damas dans le monde occidental," *BZ* 21 (1912), 448–57, and recently, I. Boronkai, "Übersetzungsfehler in Cerbanus' lateinischer Version von Johannes Damascenus und Maximus Confessor," *Philologus* 115 (1971) (Festschrift Johannes Schneider), 32–45. E. Hocedez deals with the translations by Cerbanus, Burgundio, and Grosseteste in "Les trois premières traductions du 'De orthodoxa fide,'" *Le Musée Belge* 17 (1913), 109–23. On the use of Cerbanus' translation by Gerhoh of Reichersberg, see P. Classen, "Der verkannte Damascenus," *BZ* 52 (1959), 297–303, and *Gerhoch von Reichersberg*, pp. 124 f.

5. The Metropolis Constantinople

More than once in the course of its history, the Byzantine Empire was so menaced that the emperor's domain consisted of little more than the capital. With Constantinople as the starting point, the Greeks repeatedly, and with varying borders, reconquered their empire. At the beginning of the reign of Emperor Alexius I (1081–1118), the imperial capital was again in danger; initially, the first crusade was to bring relief for Constantinople from the Turkish and Petcheneg threat. At that time an enthusiastic Italian praised New Rome, which was defying the onslaught of barbarian nations, as the "Middle Kingdom" which was delaying the coming of the Antichrist: "Even if old Rome does lie in our domain—we who pride ourselves on our piety—it serves the barbarians and does not make use of its own laws. Only the empire of New Rome, Constantinople, which lies in the middle and concerning which the Apostle said, 'whoever holds it now, hold on to it, until it is removed from the middle,' has thus far resisted Medes and Persians, barbarians and Scythians, Vaginatai and Massagetai, Huns and Hungarians, Goths and Normans, Saracens and Moors."[48]

Constantinople held its own, and the twelfth century became an especially important *saeculum* for the city and its expansion. The Latins now had their own districts, churches, and monasteries in the *urbs regia*;[49] soon there were also multilingual Latin scholars in the Greek metropolis. What the Irish *peregrini* were to the Carolingian period and the Greek monks were to the Ottonian, the Italians living in Constantinople were to the twelfth century.

Just as the Greeks in the West could attain to honors under the Ottonians, so it was also possible for the Latins at the imperial Greek court of the twelfth century to hold Greek offices—for instance, as a translator of the large imperial documents with which the maritime cities of Italy had their privileges chartered in Greek and Latin.[50] The revived university attracted interest, and the ecclesiastical dignitaries in and around Constantinople, some of whom were associated with the university, were prepared for disputations. The burning controversies between East and West in theology and ecclesiastical politics continued on into the twelfth century in a more conciliatory manner; the same was true with respect to the conflict between the Western emperor and the papacy; a "knightly" element was at work here as well. In 1112, the archbishop of Milan, Petrus Grosolanus, whom the Greeks called Chrysolanos, gave a speech before Emperor Alexius in Constantinople, *De processione spiritus sancti*.[51] The emperor is supposed to have been so dissatisfied with the responses of his seven court theologians that he returned their *libelli* to them for revision and condensation into *one* text. A source from Monte Cassino reports that the emperor did not even want to deliver this text to Grosolanus.[52] In 1136, Emperor Lothar's legate, Bishop Anselm of Havelberg, disputed with Nicetas of Nicomedia; in 1154, he did the same with Basil of Achrida in Thessalonica. Especially under Emperor Manuel I (1143–80), who was sympathetic toward the West, the most populous city of Christendom became the second home of many educated Latins.

In his account of the debate of 1136, Bishop Anselm of Havelberg includes a description of the scholarly colony of Latins in Constantinople. This report is contained in the second and third books of his *Dialogi*, written down around 1149.

The work is called *Dialogi* in the edition printed by Migne (still to be used today: *PL* 188, cols. 1139–1248). But it follows from Anselm's remarks that the book should have a Greek title: "Incipit prologus Anselmi Havelbergensis episcopi in Ἀντιχείμενον contrapositorum sub dialogo conscriptum ad venerabilem papam Eugenium" (Migne *PL* 188, col. 1139, n. 3); ". . . placuit sanctitati vestrae . . . quatenus . . . Ἀντινχειμένων, id est librum contrapositorum, sub dialogo conscriberem" (col. 1140); ". . . ea quae ego in hoc Ἀντιχειμένων sub dialogo contexui, non subito ab aliquibus indicentur superflua" (col. 1142). This Greek title occurs in the early Latin Middle Ages one other time; see above, Chapter II, sec. 4. According to J. W. Braun, there is no manuscript evidence ("keine Quellengrundlage") to support the Greek title Ἀντιχείμενον or Ἀντιχειμένων; "Studien zur Überlieferung der Werke Anselms von Havelberg I," *DA* 28 (1972), 133–209, here p. 137, n. 8. In the same article, Braun refers to an "Überlieferungslücke von zweieinhalb Jahrhunderten" ("lacuna of two and a half centuries in the tradition"). Classen (*Burgundio*, p. 70) introduces an entirely new title—*Diacimenon* (?). Since the problem of the accurate rendering of the title does not yet seem to have been solved, I retain in the following discussion the already established and unproblematic (although certainly not original) title *Dialogi*.

As Emperor Lothar's ambassador in Constantinople, the German bishop broached the points of conflict between East and West. The emperor and patriarch thought it appropriate to organize an official disputation, for which Archbishop Nicetas of Nicomedia, one of the twelve *didascali* of the university, was appointed as the Greek representative. The assembly came together on 10 April 1136 in the church of St. Irene in the Pisan quarter of Constantinople. "Not a few Latins took part, among them three wise men, who knew both languages and were learned in literary matters; one was named Jacobus, a Venetian; another Burgundio, a Pisan; and the third and most distinguished, who was famous among the peoples of both nations because of his knowledge of both Greek and Latin literature, was named Moses, an Italian from Bergamo; he was chosen by everyone to be a faithful interpreter for both sides."[53] Before the disputation began, an interesting question of form was posed: what was to be the nature of the "faithful" translation? The question is comprehensible only if one keeps in mind that there were two basic types of translations known to the Middle Ages: the close, literal translation, and the freer translation, which rendered the sense of the text. Nicetas was of the opinion that Moses should translate "word for word, faithfully," "for we can in this way understand each other better, and he himself can do this more easily." Anselm responded: "The translation should adopt a middle course; it should take up and interpret each speech as a contextual whole, reaching out from its middle course to both sides, rendering the full and collective meaning of the words; through this manner of speaking, or rather translating, we will seem to be not adherents of words, but investigators of ideas."[54] "Non . . . verborum observatores, sed sententiarum investigatores"—with this contrastive pair of concepts, Anselm elegantly alluded to the "blind obedience to the word" so little prized in the New Testament; his remark did not fail to have an effect; the cautious Nicetas, who knew (as did all the Greeks) from long theological experience that religious conflicts having to do with words and syllables were the most embittered, accepted this tenet, and thus from the very beginning the debate had a design of tolerance; philistine pedantry was avoided. According to Anselm, Nicetas conceded in the end that the Holy Spirit proceeded from the Father *and from the son* (*filioque*) and said that one of the ecumenical councils led by both emperors and the pope should define the doctrine of the Trinity once and for all.

The debate was continued in Hagia Sophia in the week thereafter. The azymes and other differences between the Eastern and Western rites were discussed. Once again it was agreed that there should be a general council, "where," as Nicetas said, "everything which separates us and you from a single rite should be led back to a state of harmony through a unified form, so that Greeks and Latins become one people under the Lord Jesus Christ, in one faith, in one baptism, in one rite of the sacraments."

Anselm assented and with great agitation expressed the wish that his adversary in the debate might also be the Greek spokesman at this council. Filled with inspiration, the audience celebrated this conclusion of the debate, which was great in both spiritual and human terms: "Doxa soi, o Theos, Doxa soi, o Theos, Doxa soi, o Theos, quod est Gloria sit Deo, Gloria sit Deo, Gloria sit Deo. Calos dialogos, quod est bonus dualis sermo. Holographi, holographi, quod est totum scribatur, totum scribatur" ("Glory be to God. . . . the dialogue is good. . . . let it all be written down. . . .").[55]

The historic moment passed. Anselm of Havelberg did not write down his account of the debate until thirteen years later, at the wish of Pope Eugenius III, the patron of Burgundio the translator. Anselm still held on to the hope that under this pope, who was quite open-minded toward the Greek world, the debate of Constantinople might still bear late fruit. But the rapprochement of 1136 was certainly due primarily to the fortunate circumstance that the conciliatory Nicetas of Nicomedia spoke for the East, and the German "symbolist," filled with a spiritual ecclesiology, for the West. In the first book of his *Dialogi*, Anselm of Havelberg sets forth his understanding of theology and therewith demonstrates that the debate was possible only in the context of his nonjuridical comprehension of ecclesiastical matters. A second disputation between Anselm and Basil of Achrida in Thessalonica (in 1154) came to nothing.[56] Upon his return from this journey, Anselm received the archbishop of Ravenna, and in 1158 he died in Frederick Barbarossa's retinue outside of Milan.

Of the "three wise men" of the debate in 1136, "who knew both languages and were learned in literary matters," Jacobus the Venetian has already been mentioned; moreover, the meticulous translator of Aristotle seemed to be the predestined choice to carry out the literal translation desired by Nicetas. Burgundio of Pisa must be dealt with in more detail; to judge by his other works, he also would have preferred to translate literally rather than by sentence and sense. Around 1136, Moses of Bergamo was more highly esteemed than either of them.[57] He was in the service of the court in Constantinople (most likely as a translator), lived on the edge of the Venetian district, and had deposited his property in this district. He is the first Westerner in Constantinople—of whom we have any knowledge—to have collected Greek manuscripts.[58] The brief *Expositio in graecas dictiones quae inveniuntur in prologis S. Hieronymi* became the best known of his works; it owes its existence to the inquiry by the English cleric Paganus about the significance of the *Homerocentonae* and *Virgiliocentonae* in Jerome's *epist.* 53 (*Ad Paulinum*).[59] Other works by Moses are the *Exceptio compendiosa de divinitus inspirata scriptura*,[60] translated from Greek, a didactic epistle on the oblique cases of ΧΑΡΑΚΤΗΡ and related topics,[61] and a great panegyric of his native city of Bergamo, the *Liber Pergaminus*.[62] Haskins remarks: "The literary reputation of Moses and the nature of his writings indicate that the works which have thus far come to light are only fragmentary remains of a many-sided activity. A Latin poet, a translator from Greek, a grammarian and a collector of Greek manuscripts, he might almost hold his own three hundred years later."[63]

Pascalis Romanus was a Western translator and author living in the environs of Constantinople; he is still not well known.[64] In 1158 or 1163, he translated the *Disputatio Iudaeorum contra sanctum Anastasium*, which has been attributed, no doubt erroneously, to Anastasius Sinaita; he dedicated the work to Patriarch Heinricus Dandalo of Grado (ca. 1130–86); his translation of the life of Mary by Epiphanius of Constantinople was also dedicated to Heinricus.[65] In 1169 he finished a translation of the Cyranides book on the medical and magical powers of animals, stones, and plants.[66] The dream book *Liber thesauri occulti* (1165), Pascalis' own composition, compiled in part from Greek sources, has the same occult tendency.[67] In this book, as also in Leo Tuscus' translation of Achmet, the occult note of Greek culture at the court of Emperor Manuel I resounds.

In the later twelfth century, two brothers from Pisa played an important role in the capital of the Eastern Empire: Hugh Etherianus and Leo Tuscus.[68] Hugh Etherianus, a layman, had studied in France during the fifth decade of the twelfth century; he emigrated to Constantinople probably around 1160, and there he immersed himself in Greek philosophy and theology; in his position as Latin advisor to Emperor Manuel I, he already exercised a decisive influence during the christological controversies at the Council of Constantinople in 1166.[69] Subsequently, Hugh was the great theologian in controversial matters among the Greeks. He published a work on the issuance of the Holy Spirit in the Greek and Latin languages and translated the tract ΠΕΡΙ ΤΩΝ ΦΡΑΓΓΩΝ ΚΑΙ ΤΩΝ ΛΟΙΠΩΝ ΛΑΤΙΝΩΝ, which stemmed from the period of conflict in the eleventh century, into Latin. His brother Leo was an interpreter in Byzantine service; he translated Achmet's book on dreams from Greek into Latin and dedicated the work to his brother (1176).[70]

Hugh and Leo became the addressees of Western requests in Constantinople, just as Moses of Bergamo had been in earlier times. In response to the request of a noble Western visitor in Constantinople, Count Raimund I of Tortosa, Leo Tuscus translated the liturgy of John Chrysostom.[71] At the request of the *Sacri Palatii diaconus* and *scholasticus* Hugh of Honau (an island in the Rhine, near Strasbourg) and the *scholasticus* Peter of Vienna, Hugh Etherianus collected and translated a compilation of Greek patristic texts on trinitarian theology; Hugh of Honau, while a legate of Frederick Barbarossa in Constantinople in 1171, suggested the work and took it back with him to Germany from his second embassy to the Eastern capital in 1179; *Liber de differentia naturae et personae*.[72] Hugh of Honau especially prized the work which he had brought from the *urbs regia* because he saw in it that the doctrine of Gilbert of Poitiers (d. 1154), who "knew neither the books nor the language of the Greeks," was fully in the mainstream of the Greek philosophical tradition, a tradition which Hugh of Honau esteemed as the source of all knowledge, "since all of the disciplines of the Latins derived from Greek sources." Hugh of Honau wrote these words in the preface to his *Liber de diversitate naturae et personae proprietatumque personalium non tam Latinorum quam ex Graecorum auctoritatibus extractus*;[73] the preface provides important information on the relations between East and West under Emperors Manuel I and Frederick I. In his compilation, Hugh of Honau used not only the *Liber* of Hugh of Etherianus, but also a compilation of patristic trinitarian theology which he had himself collected, the *Liber de homoysion et homoeysion*.[74]

Three years after Hugh of Honau had returned, filled with gratitude, as a pilgrim whose wish had been granted, from his visit in the city of Constantinople with the Emperor Manuel and Hugh of Pisa, a massacre of

Latins broke out in Constantinople (1182); Hugh Etherianus died in the same year. Emperor Manuel, who had opened wide the "imperial city" to Westerners, had already died in 1180. As the self-styled avengers of the pogrom of Constantinople, the Normans conquered Thessalonica, the second largest city of the empire (1185), and with this a mechanism of violence was set in motion, which culminated in the Latin conquest of Constantinople on 13 April 1204.

The crusaders carried off untold treasures at that time from Constantinople's treasuries: the knight Heinrich of Uelmen, for example, took the famous staurotheque of Emperor Constantine VII Porphyrogenitus, which he presented to the convent of Stuben on the Mosel in 1208;[75] Bishop Conrad (of Krosigk) of Halberstadt "stayed for some time in Greece with the emperor and received a treasure more dear than gold and topaz, namely, the relics of many saints, and in addition, a not at all trifling set of vestments; this he accomplished through familiar intercourse with the emperor and through his mercy, as well as through that of other princes, bishops, and abbots."[76] These treasures of Constantinople continued to exercise an influence, both artistically and liturgically; the staurotheque mentioned above was copied by German goldsmiths, and the triumphant entrance of Bishop Conrad with the Greek liturgical vestments on 16 August 1205 was long celebrated as a separate feast day in St. Stephan's cathedral in Halberstadt, which, due to the vestments, became a storehouse of Byzantine treasures.[77] But there was no longer any *translatio studii* associated with this *translatio* of artistic treasures and relics. The knights who conquered Constantinople may well have imagined the capital of the "emperor of Greece" more in the style of the epics "König Rother" and "Herzog Ernst" than of the translator's prologues and letters of the western scholars in Constantinople. With the plundering of this Christian metropolis by the crusader knights, an epoch of peaceful and fruitful relations between the Latins and Greeks was irrevocably brought to an end.

Those were the men with the brazen necks, the boastful wit, the raised eyebrows, the cheeks always clean-scraped like those of youths, the bloodthirsty right arms, the nostrils quivering with rage, the proud eye raised, the insatiable jawbone, with the unloving heart, the shrill, hurried babbling,—the only thing lacking was that the words dance on their lips!—yes, those were the intelligent, wise men, as they thought of themselves, the lovers of truth, who faithful to their oath hated all wickedness; those were the men who were so much more pious than we wretched Greeks, so much more just and precise in obeying the commandments of Christ; those were the men who—and this is even more important—wore the cross on their shoulders, who often falsely swore on this cross and the Holy Scriptures that they would pass through Christian lands without blood-

shed, not straying to the right, not swerving to the left, since they
had only taken up weapons against the Saracens and wished to stain
their swords with nothing else but the blood of the destroyers of
Jerusalem; those were the men who had vowed to touch no women
as long as they marched as God's anointed troop in the service of the
Most High! But they showed themselves in truth to be chatterers
and fabricators of empty words. They wanted vengeance for the Holy
Sepulchre and often raged against Christ! In the name of the Cross,
they impiously overturn the cross and do not shudder to trample that
same symbol, which they wear on their shoulders, for a handful of
gold and silver. They cram pearls into their pockets and discard
Christ, the most valuable of all pearls. This, the purest and most
holy, they cast to the filthy beasts.

The Ishmaelites are not like this! They behaved nothing short of
philanthropically and gently in comparison with the countrymen of
these Latins as they captured Zion. They did not attack Latin women
with lustful belly laughs; they did not turn the empty grave of Christ
into a mass grave; they did not turn the entrance of life-giving places
into a deadly gullet of Hades, or the resurrection of Christ to the
downfall of many; but rather they granted the Latins the opportunity
to depart, established a modest ransom for all men, and left everything else to the owners, even if it was numerous as the sands of the
sea. Thus did the enemies of Christ deal with the Latins! Without the
sword, without fire, hunger, persecution, robbery, beating, oppres-
sion, they generously came to meet them. But these good Christians
treated us, their fellow believers, as I just described, and they could
not even accuse us of any wrongdoing.

O my city, my dear city, city of all cities! World-famous super-
naturally beautiful, sublime city! Foster mother of the Church,
ancestress of the faith, sage of the true doctrine, caretaker of scholarship, homestead of beauty! You who had to drink the cup of anger
from the hand of the Lord, you who have become the booty of a
flame which was more destructive than that which once fell from
heaven on the Pentapolis. What should I say of you? With what
should I compare you? For your affliction has become as great as the
sea."[78]

6. Pisa

Interpreting and translating are associated with urban culture. In the
monastery, village, and citadel there was rarely if ever the need for someone who knew a language other than the native language or that of the
religion. On the other hand the large city provided the opportunity for
many languages to come into contact. It was not by chance that translating
and interpreting decreased drastically in late antiquity with the depopula-
tion of the great commercial urban centers. They revived when the cities

began to blossom—most rapidly among the firstborn of modern Europeans, the Italians.

The most important home of Western translators during the high Middle Ages—next to the Greek capital, Constantinople—was the city of Pisa. This city at the mouth of the Arno had built a sea empire for itself through daring expeditions against the Saracens in Sardinia and the Balearic Islands, and its horizons stretched from the empire in the north to Sicily, from the islands off the coast of Spain to Constantinople and Jerusalem. The translators of Pisa participated "in litteris" in the extension of the "ancient magnificence" of the Pisan generations that designed cathedrals, baptisteries, and city towers on the green plain before the old city in revived classical form as a new focal point of sovereign authority.[79]

The scholarly ambitions of Pisa seem to have been aroused by the school of Salerno and were initially concerned with Arabic. Valentin Rose drew the information from the manuscript tradition that Johannes Agarenus (Sarracenus) or Afflatius, the student of Constantinus Africanus, continued the translation of the *Liber Pantegni* with a Pisan physician named Rusticus. This translation is supposed to have been executed during the military expediton of the Pisans against Arabic Majorca in 1114–15.[80]

In 1127, a certain Stephanus, *philosophiae discipulus*, had begun working on a new translation of the *Liber Pantegni* in Syrian Antioch, which had become a Latin city as a result of the first crusade.[81] While the first section of the medical work of Ali ben Abbas, the *Theorica Pantegni*, was primarily circulated in Constantinus Africanus' translation, the second section became known in the translation by Stephan of Antioch: *Practica Pantegni et Stephanonis*.[82] Both men translated from the Arabic. According to a reliable tradition, this Stephan was a Pisan; the Pisan quarter of Antioch, which had existed since 1108, had the same causal relationship with this translator from Arabic as did the Pisan quarter in Constantinople with the later translators from Greek. Stephan added a trilingual (Arabic-Greek-Latin) list of technical terms to his *Liber Pantegni* or *Liber regalis* (after the Arabic al-Malaki), *Medicaminum omnium breviarium* or *Synonymus* according to Dioscorides, and noted that "there were experts in Greek and Arabic to be found in Sicily and Salerno (where one could especially find scholars of this discipline), whom anyone could consult who so desired."[83] This passage is usually interpreted as a reference to the years of apprenticeship served by Stephan the Pisan-Antiochian translator in Salerno and Sicily.[84]

With the triple star of Burgundio, Hugh Etherianus, and Leo Tuscus, Pisan translation turned from Arabic entirely to Greek. Burgundio of Pisa (d. 1193) served his native city as *iudex* his whole life—not as a legal scholar, as they appeared at that time in Bologna, but rather as "a practicing judge in an Italian commune."[85] He must have been a young man when he took part in the disputation in Constantinople in 1136, mentioned above. It is possible and even probable that he obtained his knowledge of Greek in the Greek capital; since 1111 there had been a Pisan quarter there, in the best possible location for foreigners. Merely in order to retain this important foothold (against the Genoese, for instance, who would gladly have appropriated it from the Pisans), Pisa required men who knew Greek and were experienced in legal matters, and Burgundio was obviously the first choice of his countrymen for this position.

Burgundio was one of the three Pisans who led the important embassy to Ragusa and Constantinople, which lasted for three years (1168–71). Burgundio's son died during the journey, which became the motivation for one last great work of translation. The small, but in the development of Roman law during the Middle Ages important, translation of the Greek passages in the *Digesta* of the *Corpus Iuris Civilis* is also related to Burgundio's career as *iudex*. Perhaps he finished it right after the famous codex of digests, even today simply called the "Codex Pisanus," a pandect written soon after the promulgation of the law code (16 Dec. 533), probably in Constantinople; the text fills more than nine hundred folios. In the early Middle Ages, this valuable book was in southern Italy, perhaps in Amalfi, from which the Pisans are supposed to have taken it as booty. From the twelfth century on it was in Pisa, where it was preserved as a treasure until Florence, as the victor over Pisa, seized the work in 1406. Florence, Biblioteca Laurenziana, "Codex Pisanus"; facsimile ed., *Iustiniani Augusti Digestorum seu Pandectorum codex Florentinus olim Pisanus* (Rome, 1902–10); *CLA*, III, 295. The most important codex for the Greek passages which Burgundio translated into Latin is Leiden, d'Ablaing 1; see H. Fitting, "Bernardus Cremonensis und die lateinische Übersetzung des Griechischen in den Digesten," SB Berlin (1894), pp. 813–20; Classen, *Burgundio*, pp. 45–50 (bibliog.).

Burgundio owed the impetus for his first great translation enterprise to his countryman Pope Eugenius III (Bernhard of Pisa, pope from 1145–1153), the same pope who prompted Anselm of Havelberg to write an account of his disputation. In 1148, he began to translate the ΕΚΘΕCΙC ΑΚΡΙΒΗC ΤΗC ΟΡΘΟΔΟΖΟΥ ΠΙCΤΕωC of John of Damascus, the third and most important part of the ΠΗΓΗ ΓΝωCΕωC, for the pope.[86]

In 1151, Burgundio translated John Chrysostom's ninety homilies on Matthew for Eugenius III. In the preface, he describes how he came to the translation:[87]

Since there were two versions of the commentary on the Gospel of St. Matthew by the blessed John Chrysostom, both of which go back to him and neither of which was completely finished, Pope Eugenius III, the most scrupulous man in all respects, mindful of his role as the father of all for the general benefit of the entire world, took pains to bring the aforementioned commentaries to a proper conclusion. But since this task was not to be accomplished on this side of the sea, due to a lack of copies of the text, he turned to lands across the sea. And so he wrote to the patriarch of Antioch so that he might urge some translator to finish that which was lacking in these commentaries. He did not comply with this wish, due either to the laziness or to the ignorance of the translator, and sent the pope the commentary on the Evangelist by this same blessed John in a Greek text. When the bishop [of Rome] received it, he entrusted it to me, his *iudex*, Burgundio the Pisan, so that my translation could complete the work. When he found out that my version differed in all respects from the two versions mentioned above, he commanded me to publish this third edition.

And since I thought that this far surpassed my capabilities—not only because of the enormous length of the volume, but also due to its level of style and the profundity of its thought [*sententiarum profunditate*]—I was at first hesitant to subject myself to this task and felt that my back was against the wall, until, trusting in the merit of his request and supported by his promise to go through the entire work critically, I undertook to obey his orders with my best efforts. And, more quickly than expected, in the space of seven months, I have faithfully translated this work from Greek into Latin.

In so doing, I did not think that it was appropriate to alter the order [of words] of such a man; I translated word for word and preserved not only the sense, but also the order of the words as far as I could without any change [*verbum de verbo reddidi, non sensum solum, sed et ordinem verborum, in quantum potui, sine alteritate conservans*], so that it might be believed without question, because of the gracefulness of his thoughts no less than because of the peculiarity of his wording of the text, that this is a work of the blessed John, and so that this third edition might be preferred to the other two in the judgment of the studious reader, since it presents the tradition of the orthodox faith in more complete form.

In one further section of the preface, Burgundio introduced John Chrysostom's work itself—its origin as a succession of Sunday sermons, its "serial" character, and its method of commentary, which aimed more at *moralitas* (not "moral," but rather more like "sens moral") than allegory; with this last observation, Burgundio associated John Chrysostom's homilies on Matthew with Gregory the Great's *Moralia in Iob*, the work which was read in the high Middle Ages in the West, as it had been during the previous five centuries, with undiminished zeal as a guide to human self-knowledge. With this indication that the reader could also hope to profit spiritually from the work, Burgundio had given Chrysostom's book a good recommendation, and thus he could conclude on a confident note:

I offer this sort of book, which was completed as a result of my efforts, to your Majesty, Holy Father, so that, harmonized by the revisions of your eminence and resting on your authority, it might spread through and illuminate the entire world. . . .

In the seventh decade of the twelfth century, Burgundio established relations with the Hohenstaufen court. "Since Milan had been defeated and Italy conquered," he dedicated and sent a new translation of the ΠЄΡΙ ΦΥСЄШС ΔΝΘΡШΠΟΥ (*De natura hominis*) of Nemesius of Emesa to Emperor Frederick I. Burgundio was seeking a new patron and protector of his translation work:[88]

> Your Highness, the Emperor, since I noted in conversation with you that Your Majesty wishes to understand the nature of things and know their causes, I took it upon myself to translate this book, of the blessed Bishop Gregory of Nyssa, brother of St. Basil, in your name, from Greek into Latin. It treats in a philosophical manner the subject of the nature of man, of body and soul, the union of the two, the powers of imagination, discrimination, and memory, and the irrational. . . . I have the feeling that you are training yourself in this subject, and thus I wish to translate something more advanced for you, on the substance of the firmament, its form and movement, and on all natural movements [*passionibus*] below the firmament, such as those of the Milky Way, the comets, winds, lightning, thunder, rainbows, rain, hail, frost, why the sea is salty and does not increase in volume through the inflow of so many rivers and does not turn into fresh water, and on the cause of earthquakes.
> If all this could be brought into the illumination of the Latin language, by your order and in your time, then Your Majesty would acquire infinite glory and eternal fame, and your state [*vestra res publica*] would have great profit. . . .

Did the scholarly judge from Pisa, which was constant in its Hohenstaufen sympathies, want to encourage the war hero to try to match the Normans with the weapons of the intellect as well? At precisely this time at the court school of William I (1154–66) in Palermo, exactly the same sort of scientifico-philosophical translations from Greek were being executed which Burgundio here suggested to Emperor Frederick. . . . But Barbarossa was not the *rex philosophus* which Burgundio wished him to be: nothing more is known of the translations which he offered.[89]

Burgundio undertook a great new work of translation in the years 1171–73: in two years of work, he translated the eighty-eight homilies of John Chrysostom on St. John. After he had served the pope and the emperor with his translations, now a personal and religious motive moved him to this translation:[90]

> When I was in Constantinople as a legate sent by my fellow citizens to deal with affairs of state with Emperor Manuel, and my son Hugolinus, whom I had taken along, died along the way, snatched away by a disease, I decided that for the salvation of his soul I would translate from Greek into Latin the commentary on the Gospel of John the

holy evangelist, which the blessed patriarch John Chrysostom of
Constantinople wondrously wrote—first of all because I had already
translated the commentary of this same holy father, John Chrysostom, on the Gospel of Matthew the holy evangelist and given it to the
late pope Eugenius III, and also because the Latins sorely needed
this commentary on the Gospel of John. I discovered, namely, that
no one besides St. Augustine had written a continuous commentary
on it.[91] When I could not do this there [in Constantinople] because of
pressing community business . . . and could nowhere find a copy of
the book to buy, which I could have then brought back to Pisa with
me, . . . I borrowed two copies from two monasteries and gave them
to two scribes to copy, one of whom began at the beginning, the
other in the middle, and thus I had [the work] in a short time and
faithfully revised it day and night in my free time by careful listening.
When the business affairs of my city had been brought to a conclusion, I received the emperor's permission to return home, came to
Messina, stayed on there, and began to translate the book, writing
with my own hand, and thus I translated continually along the whole
way, in Naples and Gaeta, and wherever I stayed and could salvage
some free time. And finally, against all hope and with the help of
God, I translated the entire book word for word from Greek into
Latin in the space of two full years.

Burgundio still had twenty years to live as he wrote these words; he
nevertheless wrote the prologue as if his life were ready to be summed
up; the death of his son may have admonished him to do so. In the course
of the long prologue, he dealt in great detail with the very literal method
of translation, which he thought the right one. Burgundio showed by
means of numerous examples, especially from theology (Jerome), jurisprudence (Justinian), philosophy (Boethius), and medicine, and also by
referring to John Scottus' *Areopagitica*, that his translation *de verbo ad
verbum* was the proper one for the subject.[92]

In recent years there have been two attempts to approach the phenomenon of
Burgundio by seeking out the working copies of his translations. M. Morani, "Il
manoscritto Chigiano di Nemesio," *Rendiconti dell'Istituto Lombardo* 105 (1871),
621–35, identified the glosses in the Vatican manuscript Chigi R.IV. 13 (Nemesius
of Emesa) as entries by Burgundio the translator. By means of paleographical expertise, N. G. Wilson illuminated the Greek background of Burgundio's translation work in "A Mysterious Byzantine Scriptorium: Ioannikios and His Colleagues," *Scrittura e Civiltà* 7 (1983), 161–76. It is a group of manuscripts that go
back to Ioannikios the grammarian, as the Florentine librarian Bandini had recognized in the eighteenth century. Byzantine studies earlier dated the group, to the
fourteenth century; Wilson places it in the twelfth. Ioannikios' primary collaborator is identified as a scribe who first learned the Roman script and sometimes
retained his Roman scribal habits, such as numbering signatures in Roman
numerals, in his Greek work. In addition, marginal notes in Latin occur in two of

Ioannikios' manuscripts: Florence, Laur. Plut. LXXIV 5 (Galen, *De complexionibus*) and LXXIV 18 (Galen, *De pulsibus*). Since we know that in the last years of his life, after about 1178, Burgundio translated nothing besides Galen and used the above-named Florentine manuscript or a closely related one for *De complexionibus* (R. J. Durling, *Galenus latinus*, vol. I: *Burgundio of Pisa's Translation of Galen's* ΠΕΡΙ ΚΡΑΣΕΩΝ *"De complexionibus"* [Berlin/New York 1976]), we have come full circle: the annotator is Burgundio, who made preparations for his translation by means of notes in his Greek source text.

One question is solved; others arise. Where was the scriptorium of Ioannikios, in Constantinople or southern Italy? Not just the existence of Ioannikios' collaborator, the trained Latin scribe, speaks for the location of the scriptorium in the West, but also the use of paper, some of which was produced in Spain (Wilson, p. 172). Who were Ioannikios' patrons? Remarkably, his collection of manuscripts has remained together and, since the Renaissance, has been in Florence. In the final analysis, is that which the Florentines snatched from the archenemy, Pisa (just as they did the "Codex Pisanus" of the *Digests*), also to be a legacy of Burgundio?

Burgundio died in 1193 at an advanced age and was buried by the Pisans in an ancient sarcophagus in the church of St. Paul on the bank of the Arno; they celebrated him in his epitaph, engraved in marble, as a translator, scholar, teacher and commentator of sacred texts.[93] He also remained in the memories of his fellow citizens as an authority on medical science,[94] and finally also as an irreproachable and indefatigable person, whose constitution so closely corresponded to that of the maritime city that they could condense the memory of him into the distich:

QVI LEGIS IN TITULO SI SIC CUPIS ESSE PROBANDUS ·
HUIUS AD EXEMPLVM CURRE PER ALTA MARIS ·

[If you who read this inscription wish so to be praised, go, take to his example on the high seas!]

7. Norman Sicily

The Sicily which the Normans had snatched from the Arabs in the eleventh century became an island of trilingual culture (Latin, Greek, Arabic) in the twelfth century. King Roger II (1130–54) had a new work on geography written by the Arab Edrisi (Ibn Idris)—"entertainment for him who would like to roam through the world"; the book was known to the Arabs simply as "King Roger's book." The Greek Nilus Doxapatres wrote a "History of the Five Patriarchates" for the Normans, with a sarcastic barb against Rome and the Western Imperium: "Since the time when Rome ceased to be an imperial capital, because it fell into slavery to foreign peoples, the barbarians and Goths, and is still in their power, it has fallen from the imperial dignity and thus also from its ecclesiastical preeminence."[95] The court in Palermo accepted this already historic trilingualism and identified with it: the *trias* of a Latin, Greek, and Arabic notary's office at the court and, for instance, also a Greco-Latino-Arabic Psalter demonstrate that the situation was in fact so.[96] But the cultural exchange did not function very well, especially in the early period of the Norman monarchy: neither Edrisi nor Nilus Doxopatres was translated into Latin.[97]

The Normans did not just tolerate the Greek element in their southern Kingdom, but even encouraged it; Greek monasticism,[98] which had been forced to retreat again and again to Calabria during the Arab domination of Sicily in the ninth through eleventh centuries, now gained a new focal point in 1131 when Roger II donated the Salvator monastery on the land spit near Messina (*in lingua fari*); the first archimandrite of the Salvator monastery came from the monastery founded in 1105 by Bartholomew of Simeri, the monastery of the "new, guiding" Virgin (H NЄΛ OΔHГHTPIΛ) in Rossano (later *S. Maria del Patire* or *Patirion*).[99] In his royal court at Palermo, the Norman had himself depicted in a mosaic as a monarch being crowned by Christ. The inscription at the head reads POГЄPIOC PHȤ.

Under Roger's successor, King William I ("the Bad," 1154–66), the court in Palermo became a focus of Greek studies of philosophico-scientific bent, which then, through translations, had an influence in the northern regions of Western Europe. A letter from Archdeacon Henricus Aristippus to an Englishman who was determined to return home from the Sicilian Kingdom is especially important in providing information about this Sicilian Hellenism in the middle of the twelfth century:[100]

> In Sicily you have the Syracusan and Argolian [Greek?] libraries; there is no lack of Latin philosophy. Theoridus of Brindisi, the great authority on Greek literature, is available; your Aristippus is here, whom you can use as a whetstone, if not as the cutting edge. You have the *mechanica* of Hero the philosopher . . . Euclid's *optica* . . . Aristotle's *apodictice* . . . at hand; the *philosophica* of Anaxagoras, Aristotle, Themistius, Plutarch, and the other famous philosophers are in your hands. . . . , and I offer you theological, mathematical, and meteorological *theoreumata*. . . .
>
> Of course, you can find texts in England which are comparable to all of these . . . ; but do you have a King William . . . , whose court is a school, whose retinue is a gymnasium, whose individual words are philosophical apophthegmata, whose questions are unanswerable, whose solutions leave nothing undiscussed and whose zeal leaves nothing untried [*cuius curia scola, comitatus cuius gignasium, cuius singula verba philosophica apofthegmata, cuius questiones inextricabiles, cuius soluciones nichil indicussum, cuius studium nil relinquit*

intemptatum] . . . ? If these exhortations of your Aristippus do not make an impression on you, and you do not renounce this intended journey, then go and farewell! Take heed that you do not cheat yourself. As a comfort on the long journey, you shall have as many provisions as I can provide: Plato's *Phaedo*, on the immortality of the soul, translated from Greek into Latin. I began this in camp as the aforementioned king besieged the Samnite city of Benevento [1156], and finished it in Palermo.

Out of this panorama of translation literature current at that time, one might call special attention to the translation of Aristotle's *Meteora*, the fourth book of which Aristippus himself probably translated.[101] The most astonishing of the translations mentioned in the letter is the one which is to accompany the letter—Plato's *Phaedo*. The Sicilian archdeacon and head of the chancery of Palermo (ca. 1160–62) also translated Plato's *Meno*. He is the first medieval translator of Plato, and strangely enough he translated precisely those two Platonic dialogues in which a speaker with Henricus Aristippus' surname ("Aristippos") appears. According to his preface, he was requested to translate the *Meno*; he gave priority to this task above all others.[102] "I do not wish to conceal from you which great tasks I have put aside for your sake; for by the order of my Lord William, the glorious king of the Two Sicilies, I was working on a translation of the *opuscula* of Gregory of Nazianzus . . . and in addition I was preparing to translate into Latin, at the request of Maius, admiral of the Sicilian fleet, and Hugh, archbishop of Palermo [d. 1161], Diogenes' book on the lives, habits, and doctrines of the philosophers."

Both of Aristippus' translations of Plato are extant. "Even if they, along with the *Timaeus*, were not accepted into Scholastic studies and the doctrinal system of the *magistri*—at the threshold of the Arabism and Aristotelianism which stifled all other points of departure, they had no time to be so accepted—they did not go unmentioned in the moral books, the collections of aphorisms, and *exempla* of the late Middle Ages."[103] The Latin Diogenes Laertius seems to have been lost, although Walter Burley (d. 1337) still used it in composing his *De vita et moribus philosophorum*; the translation certainly came from the Sicilian school of translators. The Sicilian translation was replaced in the fifteenth century by a new one by Ambrogio of Traversari (for Cosimo de' Medici).

Aristippus had direct relations with the Eastern imperial city. He brought Ptolemy's ΜΕΓΙϹΤΗ ϹΥΝΤΑΞΙϹ (called *Almagest* in the high and late Middle Ages, after the Arabic) from there to Sicily. That was an important step for the medieval conception of the world, for the geographical knowledge of antiquity was regained via Ptolemy. The Greek codex containing this knowledge came to William I in Sicily via Aristippus as the gift of Emperor Manuel II. The codex has survived; along with many other splendid manuscripts of Greek natural science, it belonged to the Normano-Staufen library, fell booty to Charles of Anjou, and thence came to the popes, who, to be sure, could not keep it among their holdings.[104]

Aristippus did not translate his Ptolemy himself, but entrusted the job, *nolens volens*, to someone else, the so-called *Almagest* translator. This anonymous translator describes in his preface how, during his medical studies in Salerno, he had heard that Aristippus had brought Ptolemy's great geocentric-astronomical work along with him from Constantinople; how he followed him and found him at Etna, engaging in the dangerous act of observing the volcano; how he trained himself with translations of Euclid and Proclus; how Admiral Eugenius of Palermo, "virum tam grece quam arabice linguae peritissimum, latine quoque non ignarum" ("a man who was as expert in the Greek as in the Arabic language, and not unacquainted with Latin"), explained the work to him and finally translated the ΜΕΓΙCΤΗ CΥΝΤΑΞΙC, "contra viri discoli voluntatem" ("against the will of surly men").[105] Boese has proven that this translator of Ptolemy also translated Proclus' *Elementatio physica*; this was the first translation of Proclus of the Latin Middle Ages, which up until that time had only an indirect access to the thought of Proclus, through the *Areopagitica*.[106]

Following a hypothesis by Björnbo,[107] Busard has identified "certain traits that are characteristic of the translation of the *Almagest* produced in Sicily around 1160"[108] in the brief tractate *De isoperimetris* ("On Figures of the Same Size"); he also determined that there were relations between this text and the translation of *De curvis superficiebus*,[109] one of the most popular Archimedian tractates of the late Middle Ages in the West. Finally, Murdoch brought to light a Euclid translated from Greek and attributed it to the *Almagest* translator as well,[110] who, if all of these attributions are correct, was one of the greatest and most productive translators of the twelfth century.

Admiral Eugenius of Palermo (d. ca. 1202) is the most impressive representative of the trilingual culture of the "three-horned" *Trinacria*.[111] His native language was Greek, the language in which he wrote poetry.[112] He is supposed to have translated the Prophecy of the Erythraean sibyl, "drawn from the treasure of Emperor Manuel," from Greek into Latin;[113] he translated Ptolemy's *Optics* from Arabic into Latin, and the text is preserved only in this form.[114] Finally, he had a Greek edition prepared of the CΤΕΦΑΝΙΤΗC ΚΑΙ ΙΧΝΗΛΑΤΗC, a *Fürstenspiegel* translated from Arabic.

This collection of narratives, which goes back to the Sanskrit Pañcatantra and from which princes and rulers were to learn practical wisdom, came via Arabic ("Kalilah and Dimnah") into Byzantine literature through Symeon Seth, who translated the work at the request of Emperor Alexius Comnenus (probably the

First, 1081–1118). On the basis of the following verses, Eugenius of Palermo is probably to be viewed only as the donator of a copy of the text:

Τοῦτο δέδωκε, πρὸς ἡμας τὸ βιβλίον
'Ὥσπερ δώρημα, διδασκαλίας πλέον
Εὐγενὴς Εὐγένιος, ὁ τῆς Πανόρμου.

[The noble-born Eugenius of Palermo gave us this book, full of instruction, as a gift.]

Recently his share in the Sicilian edition of the *Fürstenspiegel* has been estimated to have been rather modest; see L.-O. Sjöberg, *Stephanites und Ichnelates* (Stockholm 1962), esp. pp. 105 ff. The collection reached the Latin West by two routes: first, through a translation from Greek, probably from the late Middle Ages (ed. A Hilka, "Eine lateinische Übersetzung der griechischen Version des Kalila-Buchs," Abh. Göttingen, n.s., 21/3 [1928], 59–166; see also Sjöberg, pp. 114 ff.); further, through the converted Jew Johannes of Capua, who (between 1263 and 1278) translated it from Hebrew (see Steinschneider, *Die hebräischen Übersetzungen des Mittelalters und die Juden als Dolmetscher* [Berlin 1893], p. 981). In the prefaces which precede the Latin edition of John of Capua, there is, among other things, a description of the peculiar path travelled by this book through cultures and languages: Indian—Persian—Arabic—Hebrew—Latin (cf. Hertel, *Das Pañcatantra. Seine Geschichte und seine Verbreitung* [Leipzig/Berlin 1914]; F. Geissler, "Das Pañcatantra, ein altindisches 'Fabelbuch,'" *Wissenschaftliche Annalen zur Verbreitung neuer Forschungsergebnisse* 3 [1954], 657–68): "Hic est liber parabolarum antiquorum sapientum nationum mundi. Et vocatur Liber Kelile et Dimne, et prius quidem in lingua fuerat Indorum translatus, inde in linguam translatus Persarum. Postea vero reduxerunt illum Arabes in linguam suam; ultimo ex inde ad linguam fuit redactus hebraicam. Nunc autem nostri propositi est ipsum in linguam fund⟨e⟩re latinam" ("This is the book of parables, ancient customs, and wisdom of the peoples of the world. The book is called 'Kalilah and Dimnah,' and indeed it was earlier extant in translation in the language of the Indians; thence it was translated into Persian. Afterwards the Arabs turned it into their own language; finally, it was rendered from that language into Hebrew. Now it is our plan to cast the work in the Latin language"); ed. L. Hervieux, *Les fabulistes latins*, V (Paris 1899), p. 80; based on that ed., F. Geissler, *Beispiele der alten Weisen. Des Johann von Capua Übersetzung der hebräischen Bearbeitung des indischen Pañcatantra ins Lateinische* (Berlin 1960), p. 4. This *Fürstenspiegel* never become a popular book in the Latin West as it had been in the Indian-Arabic-Greek East.

8. Spain and the Arabism of the High Middle Ages—Dionysius the Areopagite in the West

The myth of the Dark Ages no longer determines the consideration of the epoch with which we are here concerned, the period between 1100 and 1150. It has, on the contrary, become the custom to speak of a "Renaissance of the twelfth century": the darkness has receded to more remote periods. In due course of time, however, it will appear that the attribute of darkness refers rather to the modern historian's lack of knowledge than to any lack of thought in those centuries.

Klibansky, "The School of Chartres," p. 3

Die Quelle für Ordnungs- und Schönheitsdenken des Mittelalters ist Ps.-Dionysius.
[The source of the concepts of order and beauty in the Middle Ages is Pseudo-
Dionysius.]

P. Wilpert, *Nikolaus von Kues: Die belehrte Unwissenheit* (Hamburg 1967), II, 134

From the early eighth century on, Spain was in large part under Arabic
rule. Latin literature declined sharply, but did not disappear.[115] It is quite
remarkable how Latin literature in Spain at first remained scrupulously
untouched by all things Arabic,[116] while it maintained the openness to
Greek that was characteristic of the "golden" age of Visigothic culture.
Paulus Albarus of Córdoba (d. ca. 860) once wrote the following sentence,
in the style of the *Hisperica famina*: "Engloge emperie vestrae sumentes
eufrasia, imo energiae percurrentes epitoma, iucunda facta est anima
. . . ," which translates approximately as "We were quite delighted to
have received your lovely letter, which conveys to us a notion of your
present state; and as we read the summary of your activity . . ."[117] In the
tenth century, parallel to the development in central Europe, "ornamental" Greek makes its appearance in Spanish manuscripts: ω ΒωΝΗ
ΛΗΚΤωℙ ΚΑℙICCIMH . . . (*O bone lector karissime* . . .),[118] ΦΥΝΥΤ
Λω ΓℙΑΤΙΑC CΗϽCΠΗℙ (*Finit˙ Λ ω ˙Gratias semper*).[119] Not until the Latins had turned back the wheel of history and faced the Arabs
more independently did the process of the assimilation of Arabic culture
begin. The relation of Arabic to Latin literature in Spain developed essentially in the same way as did that of Greek to Latin literature in Italy.
Direct rule by a foreign culture was not conducive to intellectual exchange; only from a certain distance were the Latins willing and able to
assimilate the foreign. In the twelfth century, Spain was fully oriented
toward Arabic science.[120] In the Arabic medium the West again encountered much material from the ancient Greeks, which had often wan-
dered along remarkable paths through diverse languages, countries, and
peoples.

Alphonse VI of Castile conquered Moorish Toledo in 1085 and again
made it the capital of Spain. According to a scholarly legend created by
Amable Jourdain and expanded by Moritz Steinschneider, by the time of
Archbishop Raimund of Toledo (1125–52) the reconquered capital was
supposed to have been a great intellectual center, in which baptized Jews
executed translations from Arabic. Modern scholarship sets the accents
differently:[121] the early translators from the Arabic in Spain—John of
Seville (Hispalensis), Dominicus Gundissalinus, Hugo of Santalla, Plato
"Tiburtinus," Robert of Chester, Herman "Sclavus"—worked in various
regions of Spain; the concentration in Toledo did not come about until
later. The Jewish element is traceable (for example, with Dominicus Gundissalinus, who collaborated with an enigmatic Jewish scholar, "Aven-
dauth"), but it is not as significant as was earlier assumed: that John of
Seville was a baptized Jew has been shown to be a false conjecture.[122] The

Spanish translator class was international from the very beginning: Plato "Tiburtinus" probably came from Italy, Robert of Chester from England, Herman "Sclavus" from Carinthia (Herman de Carinthia, Herman Dalmata; not to be confused with Herman Alemannus, the German, who worked in Toledo a century later). The first high point of the school was reached with Gerard of Cremona;[123] Gerard delivered a wealth of Arabo-Latin translations to Scholastic philosophy, theology, and medicine, primarily works of Aristotle. An excerpt from Proclus' ϹΤΟΙΧΕΙШϹΙϹ ΘΕΟΛΟΓΙΚΗ came into circulation among the Scholastics through Gerard of Cremona in Aristotelian guise under the title *De essentia puritatis* or *Liber de causis*. The work was thought to be a part of Aristotle's *Metaphysics* until William of Moerbeke translated it anew from Greek. After Gerard of Cremona, Michael Scot was the great translator from Arabic;[124] it was due to him that the West became acquainted with the Arabic commentator on Aristotle Averroes (d. 1196).

The early translators from Arabic in Spain were interested exclusively in the natural sciences; mathematics and astronomy (astrology) dominated. For many of the Latins, overfed on the science of revelation and opinion, Spain, the agent of Arabic science, was an important discovery. Around 1170 an English scholar described ebulliently his flight from the barren jurisprudence in Paris to the Arabic sciences in Toledo:[125]

Cum dudum ab Anglia me causa studii excepissem et Parisiis aliquamdiu moram fecissem, videbam quosdam bestiales in scolis gravi auctoritate sedes occupare, habentes coram se scamna duo vel tria et desuper codices inportabiles, aureis litteris Ulpiani traditiones representantes, necnon et tenentes stilos plumbeos in manibus, cum quibus asteriscos et obelos in libris suis quadam reverentia depingebant. Qui, dum propter inscitiam suam locum statue tenerent, tamen volebant sola taciturnitate videri sapientes; sed tales, cum aliquid dicere conabantur, infantissimos reperiebam.

Cum hoc, inquam, in hunc modum se habere deprehenderem, ne et ego simile damnum incurrerem, artes, que scripturas illuminant, non in transitu salutandas vel sub compendio pretereundas mecum sollicita deliberatione tractabam. Sed quoniam doctrina Arabum, que in quadruvio fere tota existit, maxime his diebus apud Tholetum celebratur, illuc, ut sapientiores mundi philosophos audirem, festinanter properavi. Vocatus vero tandem ab amicis et invitatus, ut ab Hyspania redirem, cum pretiosa multitudine librorum in Angliam veni.

[In the time since I left England a while ago to pursue my studies, and have been in Paris, I have seen certain bestial creatures with great authority who occupy chairs in the schools and have two or three benches before them, on which rest immovable codices that represent the Ulpian legal tradition in golden letters; into their books these creatures reverently mark asterisks and obelisks with the lead styli that they hold in their hands. While they are reduced to the position of statues by their ignorance, they nevertheless wish to appear wise in their very taciturnity; but whenever they tried to say anything, I found them quite inarticulate and infantile.

When, as I say, I found the situation to be such, and lest I too meet a similar fate, I began studying the arts that elucidate the Scriptures, not superficially or haphazardly, but carefully and systematically. But since Arabic science, which is for the most part contained in the quadrivium, was at this time greatly celebrated in Toledo, I quickly hurried there so that I could hear the wiser among the world's philosophers. But when I was entreated and summoned by friends to return from Spain, I came to England with a multitude of quite valuable books.]

Now a multitude of material entered the West in the form of translations from Greek and Arabic: the Sicilian "*Almagest* translator" made a Greco-Latin version of Ptolemy's ΜΕΓΙCΤΗ CΥΝΤΑϟΙC, the Toledan translator Gerard of Cremona an Arabo-Latin version. Then in the course of the twelfth century, Aristotle became the center of translators' attention. For more than a hundred years, from the second quarter of the twelfth century through the middle of the thirteenth century, the reception of Aristotelian science occupied Western schools and the emerging universities. The reception of Aristotle reached the critical point in 1210, when a group of bishops met in Paris and simply prohibited instruction in Aristotle's works of natural philosophy.[126] The bishops also took the opportunity to set deterrent examples. For literary history the most interesting of these examples was the burning of David of Dinant's notebooks (*quaternuli*).[127] Thus the first creative phase of medieval Aristotelianism immediately had its "martyr," from whom the mistrusting authorities demanded the *sacrificium mentis*.[128]

The advance of Aristotelianism was not to be halted in that manner, however. After the scholarly reception, Aristotle even found an audience, in the later Middle Ages, among those who knew no Latin, especially in France, where Nicholas of Oresme translated Aristotle's *Ethics* and *Politics* and the Pseudo-Aristotelian *Economics* for King Charles V (1364–80), all practically applicable texts.[129] During this period of reception, many translations of Aristotle's works from Arabic came into circulation: the "Arabism" of the high Middle Ages frequently goes hand in hand with Aristotelianism; Aristotle became "the Philosopher" and Averroes his "Commentator." There was no great need for Greek studies at the schools of logical and scientific orientation. Peter Abelard (d. 1142), the great dialectician and, as it were, a new Jerome, recommended the study of the "three sacred languages" to the nuns of the community of Paraclete (which he had founded) and held the Abbess Heloise up to them as a shining example: in her time Heloise alone acquired a knowledge of the three languages, as he praises his former beloved.[130] We do not know whether Abelard also spoke in this manner from the podium. Robert of Melun (d. 1167), one of Abelard's successors in Paris, considered a knowledge of Greek superfluous and dangerous; the use of Greek theological expressions by Latins disturbed him as a "confusa greci sermonis et latini mixtura" ("confused mixture of the Greek and Latin languages").[131] That became a characteristic attitude of Scholasticism.

This was not the opinion at all French schools. Gilbert Porretanus (bishop of Poitiers, 1142–54) and his German students were even interested in Greek theology, since one could find a confirmation of Gilbert's theology there. At the end of the twelfth century, in a Latin dialogue on Gilbert's theology, it is, significantly, a Greek who leads the defense of this controversial teacher.[132] In a broader sense, Gilbert belonged to the School of Chartres, the citadel of Platonism in the twelfth century,[133] where William of Conches (d. 1154) explained the major works of Western philosophy: the Latin *Timaeus*,[134] Boethius' *De Consolatione Philosophiae*, and Macrobius' commentary on the *Somnium Scipionis*. Texts were studied which were saturated with Greek concepts and in which some Greek words were also used; but even at the school of Chartres there were no exceptional efforts in the area of Greek studies.[135]

But some author who was closely associated with this school must have become conscious of the fact that a knowledge of Greek was lacking in the magnificently developed Latin cultural world in the West, and that this deficiency was of some significance. Our principal witness for this state of affairs is the Englishman John of Salisbury, the student of Abelard, Gilbert of Poitiers, and William of Conches; he was the great Humanist of his time and died as bishop of Chartres (1176–80). As many theologians of his time, he acquired some basic knowledge of Greek from Latin works, such as Isidore of Seville's *Etymologiae*.[136] The titles of his works indicate that he was drawn to Greek studies: *Metalogicon*, *Policraticus*, *Entheticus*. In the *Policraticus* and *Metalogicon*, he readily used Greek expressions. In the years 1155–56, he undertook a journey to Italy; he traveled from Rome to Benevento with Pope Hadrian IV, the Englishman, and stayed there some three months. While there he had Greek lessons from a Greek of southern Italy—in this respect, he was a consummate precursor of the Humanists of the fourteenth century. As a forerunner of the early Humanists, he also discovered even at this time that lessons from an interpreter were of little profit to the person who was interested in the intellectual world of the Greeks. Thus John of Salisbury's thanks to his southern Italian language teacher sounds somewhat forced: he wished at least to thank him for his good will.[137]

John of Salisbury never progressed so far that he could read an unfamiliar Greek text or decide on a controversial interpretation. His own ignorance of Greek, and the wish to be able to read and understand Dionysius the Areopagite (who must have been intolerable to someone like John of Salisbury in the barbaric and bizarre form which the Carolingian translator had given him) made him become the patron of a new translation—the Dionysian translation of John Sarracenus.

Very little is known of John, the most important translator north of the Alps in the twelfth century. The testimony to John Sarracenus' life consists of two brief letters to the chancellor of the bishop of Poitiers and four dedicatory epistles, one each for the translation of the *Celestial Hierarchy* (to John of Salisbury, 1166), the *Ecclesiastical Hierarchy* (to John of Salisbury, 1167), the *Divine Names* (to Abbot Odo of St. Denis, 1167 or later), and the *Mystical Theology* (to Abbot Odo, 1167 or later). In addition, there is a letter from John of Salisbury to John Sarracenus.[138]

At the summit of John Sarracenus' Dionysian studies is, according to Théry, a commentary on the *Hierarchia caelestis* or *angelica*, as John Sarracenus says. In the prologue to this commentary,[139] John writes that Dionysius' sentences are "so difficult that they are scarcely read by anyone, due to enormous problems in understanding them. The translator, who in my opinion was not as well educated as he should have been, also added not a few obscurities. I would have preferred to listen silently to more knowledgeable scholars explain these texts, if that had been possible. But since there is no explicator and no student among us who can explain these texts, their most fruitful wisdom is as a hidden treasure from which one's study profits nothing." John here unmistakably takes up Anastasius Bibliothecarius' criticism of John Scottus, where the latter is described as "interpres minus quam oportuisset . . . eruditus." The import of the commentary is in its elucidation of the Carolingian translation. It was from this annotated revision of John Scottus' work that the plan for a comprehensive new translation of the *Celestial Hierarchy* developed (still according to Théry). In 1166, he dedicated the work to John of Salisbury,[140] who immediately pressed him also to make a new translation of the *residuum hierarchiae*, that is, the *Ecclesiastical Hierarchy*. For this reason, John of Salisbury also addressed the chancellor and *magister scholarum* of Poitiers, under whom John Sarracenus was obviously working at the time, and he attained his goal.[141] Abbot Odo II of St. Denis (1151–69) thereafter brought about the remaining new translations: *De divinis nominibus*, *De mystica theologia*, and the ten letters of Dionysius.

The distinctive characteristic of Sarracenus' translations is the almost complete lack of Greek expressions in the Latin context. He took great pains to render Dionysius entirely into Latin; from translation to translation he consistently eliminated more and more of John Scottus' Grecisms that had now become incomprehensible. His reference works were John Scottus' translation, a Greek text, and probably also Anastasius Bibliothecarius' supplements.[142] He was well acquainted with the Greek language and the Greek territories:

In Greek one finds certain compounds by which things are designated elegantly and pertinently; the Latins must inelegantly, less
precisely, and occasionally quite unsatisfactorily paraphrase the one
word with two or more expressions. In order to designate a person or
object, they repeat the articles in the proper positions, and by means
of the same article many statements are joined smoothly. I do not
wish to speak of the excellent construction of the participle and the
articular infinitive: such linguistic elegance cannot be found in
Latin.[143]

The *Symbolic Theology* should have been translated before the *Mystical Theology*. For it is made known in the words of the blessed
Dionysius that he wrote this work after the book *On the Divine
Names*. But in the Greek lands, where I was for some time, I carefully sought the work and did not find it. If you should obtain this book
or others (of which I spoke with Brother William) from this monk of
ours who is said to be proficient in Greek, I beg of you to report it to
me, your cleric. In the meantime, receive the translation of the *Mystical Theology*, which I have translated. It is surely called 'mystical'
in the sense of 'hidden' and 'closed', for when one ascends to a knowledge of God according to this work, by subtraction, then [the ques-
tion] of what God is remains closed and hidden [*quia cum iuxta eam
per ablationem ad dei cognicionem ascenditur, tandem quid sit deus
clausum et occultum relinquitur*]. It can, however, also be called
'mystical' because one finds out so much about divine doctrine. For
myo, from which it is called 'mystical', is translated as 'I close', 'I
learn', or 'I teach'.[144]

John Sarracenus was a prodigy in the twelfth century; most aspects of
his life lie in total obscurity. Is his surname the key, or perhaps the place
he worked, Poitiers?[145] his connection to John of Salisbury (who learned
Greek in southern Italy) or to the Abbot of St. Denis? With respect to
literary history, the close ties to St. Denis, as they surface in the dedication of the *Mystical Theology* quoted above, are of especial importance.
St. Denis is also the only place in France during the high Middle Ages
where active relations to the literature of the Greek East can be identified
with certainty.[146] The royal abbey had at least two Greek authorities during the second half of the twelfth century; both were named William. William Medicus (Guillaume de Gap,[147] William of Gap, abbot of St. Denis,
1173–86) translated Greek texts on the Pauline epistles for the English
theologian Herbert of Bosham.[148] He had brought back *libros grecos a
Constantinopoli* in 1167, among them "The Life and Maxims of Secundus
the Silent," which he himself translated from Greek into Latin.[149] This
translation attained a wide circulation and was itself in turn translated into
many vernacular languages. Furthermore, William Medicus brought a
Greek *Corpus Dionysiacum* to St. Denis, which contained Michael Syn-

cellus' encomium of the Areopagite and the Greek panegyric to the city of Paris as the burial place of the saint.[150] As is made clear in the preface, the other William of St. Denis translated this work and dedicated it to Abbot Ivo (1169–72) as his first work.[151] The translation of the thirty-seven "laudes ieromartiris Ariopagitae Dionysii . . . de graeco in latinum translatae, quas Graeci graece decantant" certainly also stems from this second William.[152]

The Abbey of St. Victor in Paris produced two great commentators on Dionysius, Hugh of St. Victor (d. 1141), who interpreted the *Celestial Hierarchy*,[153] and Thomas Gallus (d. 1246), who prepared an *Extractio* from Dionysius' works and gave commentary on the individual works.[154] Hugh of St. Victor still worked with John Scottus' translation, which he, however, criticized sharply.[155] His mistrust of the Carolingian translator contributed to the twelfth-century demand for a new translator. John Sarracenus' translation was then added to the older one and, with the Western commentaries on Dionysius, was collected into a new *Corpus Areopagiticum* of the high Middle Ages.[156] Albert the Great did not need to be a Greek authority in order to interpret Dionysius; the twelfth century had already prepared everything that he needed for this task, in Latin.

XII

The Late Middle Ages and the Early Humanistic Period

Divine omnis inventionis fons et origo [The source and origin of all divine invention]

Petrarch (*Fam.* XVIII, 2) with Macrobius (*Somn. Scip.* II 10, 11) on Homer

Videmus autem per cuncta ingenia etiam studiosissimorum omnium liberalium ac mechanicarum artium vetera repeti, et avidissime quidem, ac si totius revolutionis circulus proximo compleri spectaretur, resumimus non tantum graves sententiosos auctores, verum et eloquio et stilo et forma litterarum antiqua videmus omnes delectari, maxime quidem Italos, qui non satiantur disertissimo, ut natura Latini sunt, huius generis litterali eloquio, sed primorum vestigia petentes Graecis litteris maximum etiam studium impendunt. [But we see that the ancient knowledge of all the liberal and technical arts is being sought out by people of every disposition, even the most diligent, and this is being done most eagerly indeed, as if the circle of a full revolution is seen to be soon completed; not only are we taking up the weighty, sententious authors again, but we also see that everyone is delighted by the eloquence, style, and ancient form of the literature, especially the Italians, who are not satisfied with the most expressive eloquence of their own literate race, because they are Latins by nature, but, seeking the traces of the most distinguished, they expend the greatest of efforts on Greek literature.]

Nicholas of Cusa, *De concordantia catholica*, praef.

The miracle of salvation, which had been repeated again and again in the history of the Byzantine Empire since 626, occurred once more when Michael VIII Palaeologus came from Asia Minor in 1261 to reconquer Constantinople. In the central Peloponnesus, the Greeks also began to rule their own territory again; the Byzantines still had enough power to build the new capital, Mistra, at the foot of Mt. Taygetos, near the ancient site of Sparta and under the protection of the conquered crusader castle of Villehardouin. The Palaeologan dynasty was able to hold Constantinople until 1453 and Mistra until 1460. It was now no more than a small and politically weak Christian empire, but it was a great power in terms of intellect and culture. Through the revived Hellenism of the "Palaeologan Renaissance," the "last Byzantine Renaissance," great influence was exercised once more on the West.

1. Southern Italy under Hohenstaufen Rule

During the critical period between 1204 and 1261, when a "Latin Imperium" had been established in Constantinople, southern Italy under

Hohenstaufen rule remained as the main bridge between Greeks and Latins.

In 1189, Frederick Barbarossa went on crusade (from which he would not return), Henry VI took over his father's kingdom, and at almost the same time (after the death of William II of Sicily), he inherited the Norman Kingdom of Sicily in southern Italy through his wife, Constance. In 1194, he was able to enter Palermo, the *urbs felix, populo dotata trilingui*.[1] The traditions of the southern kingdom remained unchanged; Eugenius, who had embodied the literary culture of trilingual Sicily, entered into the service of the Hohenstaufen rulers.

After the early death of Henry VI (1196), his heir was Frederick, later the second emperor of this name (1211–50). Under him and his son, King Manfred of Sicily (1258–66), the native Greek culture of the region blossomed for the last time.

Of course even during Sicily's Norman period, a decline of the Greek element can be observed. While the chancery documents under Roger II (1130–54) were 75 to 80 percent Greek,[2] the number of Greek documents declined rapidly under the last Norman kings. The text tradition is so desolate for Sicily's Hohenstaufen period that "the opinion could be advanced that under Frederick II the chancery no longer produced any Greek documents."[3] Nevertheless, the old trilingualism (Latin-Greek-Arabic) of the Sicilian chancery was still preserved in the first half of the thirteenth century, and it enabled the great Staufer emperor to correspond in Greek with his son-in-law (after 1241) John III Vatatzes, the Greek emperor in Nicaea.[4] No less than the Normans did the Staufers respect the right of their Greek subjects to their own language, and they too expressed the universality of their rule through the cultivation of Greek. The *Liber Augustalis* ("Decrees of Melfi") of 1231, the "the first governmental [*staatlich*] law book in the West," was issued in both Latin and Greek.[5]

There were a number of Greek officeholders in the *magna curia*. The most important among them was the ΒΑΣΙΛΙΚΟΣ ΓΡΑΜΜΑΤΙΚΟΣ John of Otranto, the "Greek Petrus de Vinea."[6] Together with the ΧΑΡΤΟΦΥΛΑΞ Georgios (George of Gallipoli), he championed the Hohenstaufen-Ghibelline cause in Greek verse. It is one of the phenomenal events in Western literary history that a Western monarch gathered a school of Greek poets around him. It was a novel and unique accomplishment in Italo-Greek poetry that this school—in a similar manner to that of contemporary Middle High German poetry—broke through into political poetry.

Without Codex Florence, Bibliotheca Laurenziana Plut. V 10, saec. XIV, from San Nicola di Casole, we would know almost nothing of this poetry. The editions by M. Gigante, *Poeti italo-bizantini del secolo XIII* (Naples 1953) and the second edition, published under the title *Poeti bizantini di terra d'Otranto nel secolo XIII* (Naples 1979), sketch the basic developments in the modern study of this school of poets. The high point of the political poetry is the poem on Rome (ed. Gigante, 2nd ed., pp. 175 ff.), in which Georgios, in answer to the pope's bull of excommunication, calls Emperor Frederick τὸ θαῦμα τῆς οἰκουμένης 'wonder of the world' and Βασιλεύς τῶν ὅλων 'king of the universe'.

The astonishing appearance of the Greek poets from the Terra d'Otranto represents only the creative upper crust of a broadly based Greek literary culture in the Staufer kingdom of Sicily. For unlike the writing of official documents, Greek book production did not suffer a substantial decline during the course of the twelfth/thirteenth century.[7] Italo-Greek manuscript production (of which more than one thousand five hundred manuscripts have been preserved) did not begin and achieve any appreciable volume until the tenth century; it experienced a substantial increase toward the end of the eleventh century under the Normans, and was maintained almost without interruption several decades after the fall of the Staufers. The parallelism of the Norman and Staufer periods is also confirmed, even if one considers only the topic of the transmission of ancient Greek literature: around fifty codices with ancient Greek texts have survived from each of the two dynastic periods. The differences are reducible to matters of origin, physical production, and intellectual orientation. Origin: while Sicily was the nucleus of the kingdom during the Norman period, Frederick II shifted the center northward to Apulia. Apulian Terra d'Otranto became the primary origin of approximately four hundred Italo-Greek manuscripts from the thirteenth to the sixteenth century. Physical production: the quality of the writing materials diminished noticeably: parchment of lower quality, palimpsests, and paper are characteristic of Otrantine manuscripts. Intellectual orientation: above the invariable Christian substrate, there was a shift in Italo-Hellenism around 1200 from texts in natural science (mathematics, astronomy) to humanistic works. Forerunners of Humanism's interests appear. Codex Heidelberg Pal. gr. 45, with Homer's *Odyssey* and the *Batrachomyomachia* ("The Battle of the Frogs and Mice"), written in 1201 by Palaganos of Otranto, illustrates the shift in literary taste.

In the Greek-speaking Terra d'Otranto, the focus of intellectual life was the monastery of St. Nicholas in Casole, which flourished most splendidly under Abbot Nicholas-Nectarius.[8] All evidence for the intellectual origin of the Greeks around Frederick II points to this monastery. The liveliest connection between Greek and Latin at the time was accomplished by a small group of friends on each side of the Strait of Otranto: Abbot Nicholas-Nectarius of Casole near Otranto, Metropolitan George Bardanes of Corfu, and John (Grassus), an imperial notary from Otranto. The finest material produced by this circle is certainly the letters that went back and forth between Otranto and Corfu, with books and small gifts; the Homer which Bardanes received from the notary John of Otranto is memorable; he read about the events on the island of the Phaeacians, which he and many others thought to be Corfu, with especial pleasure.

The letters are preserved for the most part only in Latin translation, executed lovingly and congenially by one of the last Italo-Greek translators of Otranto, Federigo Mezio (d. 1612). He worked as a Greek translator for the Roman ecclesiastical historian of the Counter-Reformation, Caesar Baronius. Since Baronius printed only a part of the collection of letters (which his *consuetus interpres* translated for him and thus saved from oblivion) in the twelfth volume of his *Annales Ecclesiastici*, it was reserved for R. J,. Loenertz to bring these pearls of Greco-Latin literature of the Hohenstaufen period to light, in the supplement to J. M. Hoeck, *Nikolaos-Nektarios von Otranto. Epist.* 7, 8, and 9 deal with the reading of Homer.

Nicholas—with his monk's name, Nectarius—of Otranto was the great defender of Greek in southern Italy and simultaneously a mediator between the two worlds which had been bitterly opposed since 1204. He was the interpreter for the papal legates in Constantinople in 1205–7 and 1214–15. As the abbot of the Greek monastery of Casole near Otranto (after 1220), he led a legation from Emperor Frederick II to the Greek emperor, who was residing in Nicaea. He reports, in Latin and Greek, on the debates of the first papal legation in his ΤΡΙΑ ϹΥΝΤΑΓΜΑΤΑ. Two copies of this novel type of bilingual, which were executed with the collaboration of the author in the scriptorium at Casole, have survived.[9]

In 1232, the aged abbot defended the baptismal rite of southern Italy and Greece before authorities in Rome; he returned "as an Olympian victor" (Bardanes). He translated St. Basil's liturgy for a Latin archbishop from Otranto, who had brought back from a journey Leo Tuscus' translation of John Chrysostom's liturgy and thereupon took an interest in St. Basil's liturgy. The other Greco-Latin translations by Nicholas-Nectarius were also primarily to render Greek liturgy accessible to Latins. Of these works another bilingual manuscript in two columns is preserved, one of the most graphic monuments of the Greco-Latin culture of the Hohenstaufen period.[10]

The bilinguals from Casole, which carry over the ancient form of the bilingual biblical manuscript to the literature and translations of the contemporary period, represent one of the peculiarities of literary life in Casole. The other is the cultivation of the profane Greek authors in the rich monastic library. There was a manuscript of Aristophanes' comedies and one of Aristotle's *Sophistici Elenchi* in the collection;[11] the *Odyssey*, which John the notary, who was the student and friend of Abbot Nicholas-Nectarius, had sent on loan to Corfu, may also be reckoned as part of the monastic library. John Grassus owned a manuscript of the Sicilian Greek universal historian Diodorus, which he annotated in Greek and Latin.[12] In a time when Hellenism in Italy was receding greatly and was losing its support in the Eastern Roman Empire, Casole became one of the last strongholds of Greek culture in the West. Around the middle of the fifteenth century, Cardinal Bessarion carried off the best part of the library of Casole; included among Bessarion's collection, part of the Casole library later came into the Marciana of Venice.[13]

When George Bardanes finally decided to carry out his plan to visit Casole, Nicholas-Nectarius died (1235). Bardanes nevertheless crossed the Strait of Otranto with a message from his Greek lord to Pope Gregory IX and Emperor Frederick II; he was shipwrecked and fell ill. When he arrived in Otranto, he had to do without the company of John Grassus as well, since he had gone to Germany with Frederick II as an imperial notary. While ailing in the land of his vanished friends, he debated in Casole with a Franciscan named Bartholomew about the most recent heresy of the Latins, the doctrine of purgatory; he reported with great shock to the patriarch of Nicaea about the course of the discussion, in which the Franciscan held his ears closed during the Greek's argumentation;[14] he then returned to Corfu without having carried out his mission.

The school of Otranto also had a link to the court of Frederick II by means of John the notary. This notary is certainly the ΒΑCΙΛΙΚΟC ΓΡΑΜΜΑΤΙΚΟC who, with the ΧΑΡΤΟΦΥΛΑΞ George, championed the Hohenstaufen-Ghibelline cause in Greek verse.

In addition to these contemporary and living relationships to the Greek world, the associates of Frederick II also took up the ancient threads of the Greco-Latin tradition anew—the novel of Alexander and the "Aratea."[15] Nevertheless, the dominant force at the court of this emperor with a penchant for experimentation[16] was the same as it was everywhere else at that time in the West—Arabism.[17] His most important court scholar was Michael Scot, "the leading intellectual in western Europe during the first third of the thirteenth century," as Lynn Thorndike designates him in his monograph from 1965.[18] We know little of his life.[19] The first certain information about him is that in Toledo in 1217 he translated a work of the astronomer Al-Bitrogi ("Alpetragius") from the Arabic with the help of the "Levite" Abuteus; the work then became known as Alpetragius, *De sphaera*. In 1224 Pope Honorius III wanted to make him archbishop of Cashel in Ireland. Three years later Pope Gregory IX recommended Michael Scot to Archbishop Stephan Langton of Canterbury as an expert in Latin, Hebrew, and Arabic. But it was not a pope, but rather Emperor Frederick II, the *stupor mundi*, who became the focus of Michael Scot's life and work. His position at Frederick's court was that of astrologer. Astronomy and astrology were not distinguished until far into the modern period. As a science that linked heaven and earth, man and cosmos, nature and history, astrology occupied a very important, if not the most important, place among the system of natural sciences in the thirteenth century.[20]

The epoch-making accomplishment of Michael Scot was, however, not in the field of astronomy-astrology, but rather in an extension of the Aristotelian horizon in general. He introduced Averroes to the West—the great Arab (b. 1126 in Córdoba, d. 1198 in Morocco) who wrote commentaries on almost all of Aristotle's works. Michael Scot translated Averroes' commentary on Aristotle's *De caelo et mundo* (as well as the Aristotelian text itself) from Arabic into Latin.[21] And with that he gave impetus to the special direction of the thirteenth-century Aristotelian reception which is characterized by the catchword "Averroism." Modern research has confirmed Ernest Renan's designation of Michael Scot as the "premier introducteur d'Averroès chez les latins." Michael Scot accomplished this pioneering work at the court of Frederick II. In the later Middle Ages, an attempt was made to explain the Arabism at the court with the tale that the sons of Averroes had lived there. Renan showed that Frederick's Arabism was the nucleus of the legend.[22]

In addition to Averroes, Michael also translated works of the older Arabic scholar Avicenna (d. 1037 in Persia),[23] for example, the *De animalibus* (an abridgment of Aristotle's *De animalibus* and Avicenna's commentary), which was naturally of burning interest to the Hohenstaufen emperor.

In the presentation copy of Michael Scot's translation of Avicenna's *De animalibus*, there is a polyglot acclamation to the emperor:

> *latinum · arabicum · sclauicum · teutonicum · arabicum ·*
> Felix elmelic · dober Friderich salemelich ·

[Fortunate ruler, glorious Frederick, peace to you!]

One word each of the hexameter is Latin, Slavic, and German, two are Arabic (*al Malik, Salam'alayka*). It is a kind of homage to the various languages of Frederick's territories. The absence of Greek is less striking than that of French, for it too was spoken within the borders of the empire. The text is in Cod. Vat. Chigi E.VIII.251, fol. 184[r]; see also M.-T. D'Alverny, "L'Explicit du 'De animalibus' d'Avicenne traduit par Michel Scot," *Bibliothèque de l'École des Chartes* 115 (1957), 32–43; and further, Schramm and Mütherich, *Denkmale*, no. 210, p. 194. It was either from this manuscript or from a parallel text that the emperor had the translation copied and distributed from 1232 on. A number of the copies bear the explicit notation that they were produced "ad exemplar magnifici imperatoris domini Frederici." In the scribal colophon, many of the manuscripts extol the work as an "imperial book":

> Frenata penna finito nunc Avicenna
>   Libro cesareo: Gloria summo deo!

[The pen has now been stopped, Avicenna now finished; by means of the imperial book: glory to God in the highest!]

Just as Charlemagne once had copies for the cathedral library and monastic schools made from especially good or old books, so too did the Staufer provide the youthful university scholarship of his time with translations.

King Manfred (1258–66) continued the philosophico-empirical style of his father's *magna curia* at his own court; the emphasis was, however, again shifted from Arabic to Greek. The prolific Greek translator Bartholomew of Messina[24] worked *de mandato suo* and translated the Aristotelian *Magna Moralia*, the Pseudo-Aristotelian *Problemata*,[25] *De principiis*, and *De signis*,[26] *De mirabilibus auscultationibus*, *Physiognomia*,[27] and *De mundo*;[28] in addition, he translated a work by Hierocles on veterinary medicine and a Hippocratic work. Just as Emperor Frederick II had sent translations from Arabic to Bologna, King Manfred sent translations from Greek from his court school to the university of Paris: "We did not want the venerable authority of so many works to be translated with a living voice only for our delight and without profit to others; thus we took great pains to have these works translated by chosen men who are experienced in the expression of both languages, with faithful preservation of the inviolability of the words [*verborum fideliter servata virginitate*]."[29]

2. Greek Studies in Thirteenth-Century England

Despite the transfer of power from the Norman to the Hohenstaufen dynasty, the old Norman relations between the "Kingdom of the Two Sicilies" and England were still alive. With Sicilian aid, England was able to carry out quite astonishing Greek studies during the thirteenth century.

A critical examination of the translations from Greek that were studied in the schools of the West and the adherence to the Bible as the foundation of all studies moved the Englishman Robert Grosseteste (ca. 1168–1253) later bishop of Lincoln, to immerse himself in the study of Greek. He became the most important patron of Greek studies in Northern Europe on the frontier between the high and late Middle Ages.[30]

Grosseteste came to Greek studies late in life but pursued them with unprecedented energy. From about 1230 on, one finds that in his exegetical works he increasingly takes into account the *graeca lectio* of the Holy Scriptures.[31] But it seems that it was not until he became bishop of Lincoln (1235), England's largest bishopric, that he began his translations from Greek. First he revised Burgundio's translation of *De fide orthodoxa*;[32] he supplemented this work with translations of further works of John of Damascus, such as the so-called *Dialectica*.[33] These translations are strictly literal, just as is the translation of the letters of Ignatius of Antioch.[34] By contrast, the translation of the *Testamenta XII patriar-*

charum, which was regarded as an old constituent part of the Hebrew Bible, exhibits a greater degree of freedom with respect to the original text; Grosseteste translated this work in 1242, with the help of Nicholas Grecus.[35]

Grosseteste took great pains with a new translation of the Dionysian writings (1239–43). He had an extremely comprehensive *Corpus Dionysiacum* (including the works, scholia, introductions, "vitae," etc.) compiled for himself from both of the famous Dionysian manuscripts of St. Denis, the one sent by Emperor Michael II in 827 and the one brought back by Wilhelmus Medicus from Constantinople in 1167,[36] and from another Greek manuscript, which he himself may have provided; he entered textual emendations, variants, and notes into this compilation.[37] While Grosseteste sought out the base texts for his translation with unusual discretion and care, he was no less scrupulous in finding the precise Latin expressions in the translation itself. He repeatedly tried to incorporate the linguistic peculiarities of Dionysius' style into his explanations of words and constructions; he reflected on the basic problems of translating from Greek; in the introduction to the *De divinis nominibus*, he presented a "kind of grammatical introduction to the Greek language," with observations on Greek phonetics and compound words.[38]

While the laborious work on the *Corpus Areopagiticum* never came to have much influence in comparison with the *Extractio* of Grosseteste's friend Thomas Gallus, the translation of Aristotle's *Nicomachean Ethics* (1245–47) was given great attention in the Western schools; Albertus Magnus was the first to use the work. Through his comprehensiveness Grosseteste surpassed the older translations from Aristotle's *Ethics*, as well as the contemporary one (by Herman Alemannus in Toledo). He added versions of four Greek commentaries on the *Nicomachean Ethics* to his text.[39] He completed his "Corpus ethicum Aristotelicum" by translating two tractates, *De virtutibus et vitiis* and Pseudo-Andronicus' *De passionibus*.[40] He did not finish the translation of the Aristotelian *De caelo* with the commentary by Simplicius.[41]

The Greek Suidas lexicon (Suda) was an important reference work used by Grosseteste in his explanations and translations; the copy which Grosseteste owned is probably that of MS Leiden, Voss. gr. F. 2. Grosseteste translated seventy-one important articles from this lexicon; the article ΙΗCΟΥC had a wide circulation under the title *De probacione virginitatis beate Marie*, and was even translated into Old French (Anglo-Norman).[42]

Hebrew also came within Grosseteste's intellectual purview. A new translation of the Psalms, which he supervised, ". . . shows that he realized the need for the study of both Biblical tongues; but Greek was his first love and the sphere where he made his most original contribution. Unlike most medieval scholars he never fell under the spell of Hebrew and rabbinics to the neglect of Greek."[43] In his Greek studies, Grosseteste was simultaneously a savant and an organizer, an author and a scholar. He was sensitive to the elegant expression and wanted to render not just the *mens auctoris* but also the *venustas sermonis*;[44] but in his efforts to omit nothing from his Latin version, he turned out an extremely intricate product.[45] According to the tendency of his own thought, he was a Platonist, but his aspiration toward an understanding of nature referred him to Aristotle; he dedicated a great part of his energy to the translation and commentary of the Aristotelian corpus. His interest in experimentation led him somewhat beyond Aristotle;[46] in this respect the English bishop was a "modern man," just as Emperor Frederick II had been.

A circle of assistants, friends, and students took part in Grosseteste's Greek studies: ". . . vocavit Graecos et fecit libros grammaticae graecae de Graecia et aliis ⟨regionibus⟩ congregari" (". . . he summoned Greeks, and had books of Greek grammar brought together from Greece and other regions").[47] John of Basingstoke, archdeacon of Leicester (d. 1252), is supposed to have studied in Athens and experienced quite interesting things there. According to Matthew Paris, he not only found the *Testamenta XII patriarcharum* in Greek, which Grosseteste and Nicholas Grecus then translated,[48] but also "translated a text from Greek into Latin, in which the whole essence of grammar is contained skillfully and briefly, and which the master called the Donatus of the Greeks."[49] Could this be a grammar translated from Greek?[50] The further information given by Matthew about the *figurae Graecorum numerales* which John of Basingstoke brought back incline one to skepticism. They appear thus:

and have nothing to do with Greek numerical symbols, but rather make use of a stenographic system developed in England in the twelfth century.[51] The Greek tales of Matthew Paris are, however, in all their improbability, yet another piece of historical evidence for the new dawn of the name of Athens, which had sunk into obscurity during the Western Middle Ages:[52]

> The wise men among the Greeks studied in that city. And since wisdom is immortal . . . [the city] is called Athens from *A*, that is, 'without', and *thanatos*, that is, 'death', as if: 'the immortal'. . . . A girl named Constantina, the daughter of the archbishop of Athens and not yet twenty years old, was so gifted that she knew all of the difficulties of the trivium and quadrivium, for which reason the aforementioned magister John jokingly called her a second Catherina be-

cause of the splendor of her knowledge. This was the instructress of the teacher John, and whatever good thing he knew in the scholarly field, he had begged it, as he often affirmed, from her, although he had studied and read for a long time in Paris. This girl predicted plagues, thunder, solar eclipses, and, what is even more astonishing, earthquakes, and unerringly warned all her students.

Together with John of Basingstoke, Gregory of Huntingdon (the prior of Ramsey) must be mentioned. A Latino-Greek Psalter (in transcribed Greek) with supplementary material, among which are found the "Greek numerals" of John of Basingstoke, comes from his estate.[53] By far the most important person in Grosseteste's circle was Nicholas Grecus, or Siculus. Grosseteste had attracted him from southern Italy to England in 1237; as already mentioned, he assisted Grosseteste in the translation of the *Testamenta XII patriarcharum*. He is probably also the *magister Nicholaus* who is mentioned as an authority in the *Parcionarium grecum* of the London College of Arms.[54]

Long after Grosseteste's death, around 1270, Nicholas Grecus translated the Pseudo-Aristotelian work *De mundo*; Minio-Paluello recognized the most important distinguishing mark of Grosseteste's school of translation in this work—the use of *seu* in the rendering of Greek words with two alternative Latin terms; and thus he affirmed the identity of this Nicholas Siculus with Grosseteste's assistant, Nicholas Grecus. Nicholas Grecus was more than merely one of Grosseteste's students. "*De mundo* reads like a Latin text; Grosseteste's translations read like Greek texts with Latin words. . . . Nicholas is the only one of the thirteenth-century translators from Greek into Latin who . . . knows Greek perfectly, so to speak. . . . Nicholas taught Greek in the West before Barlaam, before Chrysoloras; he enriched the West with Greek texts that were intellectually understood and expressed in good Latin of the period."[55] Minio-Paluello suggests that with his translation Nicholas Grecus perhaps provided a countercheck on the work of the famous translator Bartholomew of Messina, who had already translated this work at the court of King Manfred of Sicily. In his *Opus tertium* (1267), Grosseteste's student Roger Bacon criticized the *translator Meinfredi* for his poor translation. In his translation of *De mundo*, Nicholas exhibited precisely those characteristics which Bacon missed in the translations by his contemporaries: an excellent knowledge of both Greek and Latin, and scholarly acumen.

The Franciscan Roger Bacon (1215–92)[56] sketched a very critical picture of Western Greek studies in his time: "There are not four Latins who know the grammar of Hebrew, Greek, and Arabic: well I know them, for I have conducted diligent inquiries on this side of the sea and beyond and have labored much in these matters. . . . Just as the layman speaks the language which he has learned and does not know its grammatical rules, so it is with them."[57] Native Greeks without grammatical training could only transmit a knowledge of their language on a very low level. There was nothing sensible to be learned from the widely circulated lexicographical works: "Papias, Hugutio, and Brito are liars whose lies stifle the Latin people."[58] "I do not believe Hugutio and Papias in anything, unless they are corroborated by others, since they erred in very many things, because they knew no Greek."[59] Bacon frequently engaged in polemic against the bishops who were not capable of accurately writing the Greek alphabet prescribed for the church dedication ceremony. The "accusatore del mondo" (F. Alessio) spared only Oxford, and the scholars and translators associated with it, from his biting criticism.

In order to understand Roger Bacon's severity properly, one must recognize what position Greek held in the educational system of Northern Europe during the late Middle Ages. In his grammatical didactic poem, which was often memorized in the schools, Eberhard of Béthune included a section *De nominibus exortis a greco*, in which Greek and Hebrew are mixed in a remarkable fashion, with legitimate and false etymologies:[60]

> Bucolon est cultura boum, bucolica signant,
> Mittere sit baleron hocque balista probat . . .
> Materiamque baton dicas, fit hyperbaton inde,
> Basileos rex est, fit basiliscus ab hoc.
> Quod bar filius est probat illud Bartholomaeus . . .

[*Bucolon* is the tending of cattle, from which *bucolics* takes its meaning; *baleron* is 'to launch', and this explains *balista* . . . ; and you call matter *baton*, whence *hyperbaton* comes; *basileos* is a king, and *basiliscus* comes from it. That *bar* means 'son' is explained *Bartholomew*. . . .]

Eberhard's didactic poem received the name *Grecismus* on account of this chapter. In the second half of the thirteenth century, Guilelmus Brito surpassed him with a poem of over two thousand lines on Hebrew and Greek words in Latin (*Brito metricus*), often with quite obviously arbitrary etymologies:[61]

> Fanum dic templum cui fano (φαίνω) prebuit ortum
> Seu fone (φωνή) aut Faunus; fert hoc a fando Latinus.
> Dicas fantasma de fano iungeque fasma (φάσμα)
> Cum fantasia, tribus istis vis datur una.

[*Fanum* is a temple, for which *fano* offers the origin or *fone* or *Faunus*; the Latins derive it from *fari*. You may say *fantasma* comes from *fano* and join *fasma* with *fantasia*, all three words have the same meaning.]

The celebrated Parisian teacher John Garland wrote the *Cornutus*: twenty-one "distichs" in the same aged and timeless "glossary Latin" with which Abbo had filled the third book of his *Bella Parisiacae urbis* at the end of the ninth century. John Garland tried, not without a certain wit, to include a group of related and rare words in each "distich":[62]

> *cespitem petit ornamentis equus purpura   superbus*
> Cespitat in   phaleris   hippus blactaque supinus
>
> *lingua   bono vino labitur sermo   stulto*
> Glossa velut temeto   labat, hemus in fatuato
>
> *bonus   operatione   fidelis   sermone*
> Qui calus in praxi, simul est et pisticus hemo,
>
> *cantus   praedicat*
> Illius oda placet, hic recte theologizat.

[The horse stamps around in the ornaments, proud of his purple blanket; the tongue becomes lax as with good wine; the speech of the fool becomes lax; he who is good in deed and also faithful in speech, his song is pleasing, his sermon correct.]

A counterpart of this work, with the eloquent name *Exoticon*, is attributed to Alexander of Hales.[63]

All of these works belong to the history of *Latin* language instruction of the Middle Ages. Their purpose is not to teach Greek or Hebrew, but rather to expand the expressive capacity of Latin by means of "exotic" finesse. If scholars allowed themselves to be deterred from sensibly learning Greek as a foreign language, that was not alone the fault of the authors of these fantastic works. In practice, however, these factitious lexicographical books determined the image of Greek in the late Middle Ages, especially since the possibility of a control on these works by Greek grammatical treatises was lacking, and the old glossaries had fallen into obscurity.

Roger Bacon, the "Doctor mirabilis," did not stop at the criticism of his contemporaries' knowledge of Greek. He was not concerned with an empirical knowledge of the language, such as that possessed by interpreters, but rather with a deep and considered understanding of the language. In order to obtain such an understanding, one needed a textbook. Thus Roger Bacon wrote a Greek grammar for Latins which was especially appropriate for use as an introduction to reading Greek. Bacon dealt with the Greek alphabet, phonetics, and orthography in great detail; the morphology was presented briefly, but in easy-to-remember paradigms; he included versions of familiar Latin texts, such as the paternoster and cantica, as exercises. Bacon used one or more Greek grammatical treatises as models and sources, as his examples, which correspond to the Greek grammatical tradition, demonstrate. In addition, he had learned from the Greeks in the West, as one must conclude from his iotacistic description of Greek phonetics.[64] With this work, Bacon produced the best aid (relatively speaking, and of those known thus far) in learning Greek in the Middle Ages; it does not appear to have been a great success.[65] But the degree of success has little meaning in comparison with the significance of the work as a symbol and symptom. Almost three hundred years after the decline of the grammatical study of Greek, which had been initiated on the Continent by the Irish, this Englishman gave a signal that there was again an awakening interest in the systematic study of Greek. A fragment of Roger Bacon's Hebrew grammar has also been preserved.[66]

The Englishman William of Mara, who deals with the Greek alphabet in a brief treatise, and the Fleming Gerard of Huy, who wrote the *Triglossos*, a brief, metrical guide to the study of the three (sacred) languages, are among the Franciscans who, in the late thirteenth century, accepted Roger Bacon's challenge to study languages. To be sure, Gerard did not get beyond the alphabet, numerals, and a little orthography and phonetics in Greek. The book was "la grammatica greca del Petrarca"; Weiss, "Per la storia degli studi greci del Petrarca: Il 'Triglossos,'" *Annali della Scuola Normale Superiore di Pisa*, Classe di Lettere II/21 (1952), 252–64; repr. in *Medieval and Humanist Greek* (1977), pp. 136–49 (bibliog.). On William of Mara and his critical glosses on the Bible (*Correctorium*), "the most learned and scientific of the century," see Smalley, *The Study of the Bible*, 2nd ed. (1952), pp. 335 f. (bibliog.).

3. The Mendicant Orders, the Western Mission, and the Linguistic Canon of the Council of Vienne

The significance of Greek studies in thirteenth-century England lies in the fact that, in at least one of the educational centers north of the Alps, there was no longer a total dependence on that which the translators from the Mediterranean area delivered, and that in the North there was an attempt to make direct use of the traditional role of southern Italy as an intermediary and of the Western bases in the eastern Mediterranean; additionally, there was a systematic attempt to supply the resources necessary for the study of Greek: Greek manuscripts, lexicon, grammar, and last but not least trained interpreters. These were already the essential elements of the humanistic approach to Greek; the topics which interested the Englishmen of the thirteenth century were, however, thoroughly medieval: Dionysius the Areopagite, Aristotle, John of Damascus. The ancient Greek poets, dramatists, and historians were outside of the intellectual horizon of the West at that time.

In the thirteenth century there were hardly any translators from northern and central Italy, as there had been in such abundance in the twelfth century. Even so, Pisa still produced the great mathematician Leonardus, who drew on many eastern sources.[67] The astrologer, astronomer, and physician Peter of Abano (ca. 1250–1316) transmitted Greek natural science and medical texts. He studied for a long time in Constantinople and Paris; during the last years of his life, he taught in Padua. As a translator, he was primarily concerned with the Aristotelian "problemata" literature; he completed Burgundio's translation of Galen's ΠΡΟC ΓΛΑΥΚΩΝΑ ΘΕΡΑΠΕΥΤΙΚΑ and reedited with commentary a translation of Dioscorides, attributed to Constantinus Africanus.[68] The Spiritual Franciscan Angelo Clareno da Cingoli (d. 1337) spent a long time in the East, not as a missionary, as were many of his Franciscan brothers, but rather in order to escape the persecution directed against the Fraticelli. He once again transmitted Greek patristic writings to the Latin Middle Ages in the spirit of monasticism, just as Evagrius, Rufinus, Martin of Braga, and John of Amalfi had done; he translated John Climacus' *Scala paradisi*, ascetic writings of Basil the Great, and homilies of Macarius the Egyptian.[69] The translation of the *Scala paradisi* became a great success. Gentile da Foligno translated Angelo's Latin text into Italian. In the fifteenth century Ambrogio Traversari undertook a new translation from Greek into Latin; but his humanistic, free translation never fully replaced the literal translation by Angelo.[70]

By 1204, time had run out for Constantinople, the metropolis which had long served as an intermediary between East and West. Immediately after the establishment of the "Latin" Empire of Constantinople (1204–61), it is true, Pope Innocent III called upon the professors and scholars of Paris to accept the invitation of the new Latin emperor, Baldwin, to Constantinople in order to participate in the founding of a new university. But nothing came of this university.[71]

The new Western mendicant orders of the Franciscans and Dominicans went to the Greek lands and founded monasteries at many places along the coast of the eastern Mediterranean. They were even successful in persuading some prominent Greeks to join their orders.[72] At first, however, this mission bore no fruit in terms of intellectual life, quite clearly because the Westerners, in possession of Latin and the "lingua franca," thought it scarcely necessary to learn any other languages. Around the middle of the thirteenth century, a change of opinion was in the offing. Perhaps there is a connection between the steady decline in the political and military position of the West in the eastern Mediterranean and the growing awareness that an "oriental mission" without a knowledge of the oriental languages was not possible.

In 1248, Pope Innocent IV decreed that several young men, who were born in the East and knew Arabic or another of the Oriental languages, were to study theology in Paris with funds from French monasteries and then perform missionary work *in partibus ultramarinis*. On the basis of various types of evidence, among which is the protest of the monasteries which were required to pay, it seems that the arrangement lasted some forty years, or at least the plan was followed that long by the papacy. The institute planned in Paris seems not to have thrived;[73] but, in their own way, the Dominicans and Franciscans complied with the intent of the appeal. In any case, around the middle of the thirteenth century, a new period begins in theological disputation with the Greek world.

One authority for this linguistic consciousness, which was changing due to missionary motives, was, on the Franciscan side, Roger Bacon, who was discussed in the previous section.

Among the Dominicans there arose a new series of polemical treatises, "against the Greeks," in accordance with the dogmatic and bellicose spirit of the order. These works attempted to vanquish Greek theology with its own weapons, namely, Greek patristic writings. A Latin in the Dominican monastery in Constantinople wrote the tractate *Contra Graecos* (Inc. "Licet Graecorum ecclesiam") in 1252; the work continued to be one of the most important sources of information on disputational theology with the Greeks up until the Union of Florence in 1439.

Migne PG 140, cols. 487–574. The oldest editions of the treatise attribute it to a certain Pantaleon and thus follow the postscript found at the end of the work:

> Hec vero gesta sunt anno ab incarnatione Domini nostri Ihesu Christi MLV [!], indictione octava. Quod ego Pantaleon cum in Constantinopoli essem, ubi hoc actum est, rem veraciter cognoscens, hunc libellum exemplari feci, quo legentibus pateat latine serenitatis institutio et nemo audeat talia presumere.

> [And these things took place in the year 1055 from the incarnation of our Lord Jesus Christ, in the eighth indiction. I, Pantaleon, who truly knows this matter, had this little book copied while I was in Constantinople, where the action occurred; let the disposition of serenity thus be revealed to the reader in Latin, and let no one dare presume to take such things for granted.]

Ed. by Dondaine, "Contra Graecos," *Archivum Fratrum Praedicatorum* 21 (1951), 323; his text differs slightly from Clm 110, fols. 86ᵛ–87ʳ. As Dondaine has shown, the postscript does not belong to the whole work, but rather only to the last section, a report on the excommunication of Patriarch Michael by the papal ambassadors of 1054. Should one (with Dondaine) consider Pantaleon an unknown thirteenth-century reviser, or not rather regard him as the quite familiar merchant Pantaleon of Amalfi?

The second name which occurs in the manuscript tradition is that of a certain Bartholomew, whom Loenertz still held to be author of *Contra Graecos*, in "Autour du traité de fr. Barthélemy de Constantinople contre la Grecs," *Archivum Fratrum Praedicatorum* 6 (1936), 361–71 (the fundamental study of Dominican Graecolatina in the mid-thirteenth century). Dondaine (pp. 423 ff.) prefers to regard Bartholomew as a later editor and cites *Contra Graecos* as an anonymous work.

What significance was attributed to the work is shown in the manuscript Florence, Ashburnham 81, saec. XIV, which was designed as a bilingual; the column of the manuscript which was intended for the Greek translation remained empty, however. At the end of the thirteenth century, the Dominican Buonaccorsi of Bologna composed a *Thesaurus veritatis fidei* with the aid of *Contra Graecos*; there are Greco-Latin copies of this work preserved (Paris, BN gr. 1251 and 1252). Loenertz concludes on this basis that the bilingual version of *Contra Graecos* did not remain a plan alone, but in fact did exist.

A few years after *Contra Graecos*, Bishop Nicholas of Cotrone wrote a *Liber de processione spiritus sancti et fide trinitatis contra errores Graecorum*, which Pope Urban IV submitted to Thomas Aquinas in 1263 for his opinion. On the basis of this *Libellus*, Thomas wrote his *Contra errores Graecorum.*[74]

Most commonly, the work by Bishop Nicholas of Cotrone is simply called *Libellus*, as it was by Thomas. It is printed in P. A. Uccelli, *S . Thomae Aquinatis . . . In Isaiam . . .* (Rome 1880), pp. 359–442. Nicholas of Cotrone is one of the most colorful, perhaps even scintillating, figures of the time. He was a native Greek from Dyrrhachium (Durres) in Epirus, a bishop among the Latins in Hohenstaufen Calabria (Cotrone); he was as popular in the papal curia as at the court in Nicaea or Constantinople and served as an intermediary under Emperors Theodore II Lascaris and Michael VIII Palaeologus. He seems to have been at the high point of his influence around 1260–65. The *Libellus* does not, however, bear witness to his honesty; it has long been recognized as a source of diverse falsifications (F. H. Reusch, "Die Fälschungen in dem Tractat des Thomas von Aquin gegen die Griechen," Abh. München 18 [1889], 675–742; Dondaine, "Nicolas de Cotrone et les sources du 'Contra errores Graecorum' de Saint Thomas," *Divus Thomas* 28 [1950], 313–40). But he was one of the very few people of his time to have been educated in both Greek and Latin; see P. Sambin, *Il vescovo cotronese Niccolò da Durazzo e un inventario di suoi codici latini e greci [1276]* (Rome 1954); Roberg, *Die Union . . . auf dem II. Konzil von Lyon* (1964), pp. 45 ff.

The administration of the Dominican order also recognized the relation between "mission" and language study. The general of the order, Humbert of Romans (1254–63), brought up the following points in a reform treatise, *Opus tripartitum*, which was intended for use at a church council (not held until 1274 in Lyons): since God no longer grants the knowledge of languages necessary for the preaching of the Gospel, as he did for the original Church, one must learn the languages through laborious study. At this time, just as at the time of Augustine and Jerome, Greek is a language which is especially to be studied, particularly since the knowledge of Greek is so rare that there is almost no one in the Roman curia who can read the detailed Greek letters received there. The Roman legates to the Greeks have to rely on translators, of whom one is never certain that they have actually mastered the Greek language and are translating conscientiously. With a view toward a future union, the Latins should possess all theologically important works of the Greeks and be able to read them. Much too little Greek literature is available in translation; the West does not have original Greek works at all. The writings of the Latin masters should be translated into Greek. Unfortunately, much too little interest is shown for these necessary studies and much too much for philosophical things. . . .[75]

As it happened, the second Council of Lyon (1274) did not address these questions; the union under Latin supremacy seemed much more easily attainable, since the severely threatened Emperor Michael VIII was prepared to make almost any concession necessary in order to save the city of Constantinople (which had not been reconquered until 1261) from the impending attack of Charles of Anjou. Thus a theological dispute, for which Thomas Aquinas (who died en route) and Bonaventure hurried to Lyon, was not necessary. The logothete of Emperor Michael VIII, George Akropolites, swore to papal primacy, appellation to Rome, and the commemoration of the pope, and the union was solemnly sealed with a liturgy of the "missa graeca":[76] the epistle was first read in Latin, then in Greek; the Gospel was sung in the same order. Bonaventure preached. Then the credo was intoned: first the Latins, then the Greeks. The *filioque*, customary only for the Latins, was humbly sung three times by the Greeks, so that no one could fail to take note of the fact that the Greeks had accepted this hated addition. The *laudes* of the pope, sung by the Greeks, closed the mass.[77]

In accordance with the tradition established in the eleventh and twelfth centuries, the emperor also availed himself of Western legates to and interpreters for the Latins at the Union Council of 1274. They were a Franciscan and a Dominican: the native of Constantinople Johannes Parastron, O.F.M., and the "translator of Aristotle," William of Moerbeke, O.P.

John Parastron, the Greek become Franciscan, was probably the most important mediator between East and West at that time. Roncaglia notes: "Se noi leggiamo il capitolo in cui Giorgio Pachymeres parla delle negoziazioni perseguite da Gregorio X e da Michele VIII Paleologo, che condussero all'effimera unione proclamata nel concilio di Lyon nel 1274, noi constateremo che quasi tutto si fa a Costantinopoli mediante l'azione dei Francescani. Chi tiene tutte le fila nelle sue mani è Giovanni Parastron" ("If we read the chapter in which George Pachymeres speaks of the negotiations conducted between Gregory X and Michael VIII Palaeologus, which led to the establishment of the union proclaimed at the council of Lyons in 1274, we discover that the acts of the Franciscans mediated almost everything done by Constantinople. John Parastron is the one who holds all the threads in his hand"); in *Studi Francescani* III/25, 181. Cf. Roncaglia, *Les frères mineurs et l'église orthodoxe*, pp. 140 ff.; Geanakoplos, *Emperor Michael Palaeologus and the West*, pp. 267 f.; Roberg, *Die Union . . . auf dem II. Konzil von Lyon*, pp. 67 and 251; Matteucci, in *La chiesa greca in Italia*, pp. 971 ff. He must have been the *Johannes Parastrus* who wrote Latin annotations to the Greek New Testament, now found in Paris (BN Coisl. 200), and translated it in sections; see R. Devreesse, *Le fonds Coislin* [de la Bibliothèque Nationale] (Paris 1945), pp. 177–79; *Byzance et la France médiévale*, no. 47, pp. 30 f.

Although he was himself active in the "mission" (archbishop of Corinth,

1278; d. before 1286), William of Moerbeke hardly served his missionary brothers with his translations; their value was to Scholastic philosophy, which even at this time accounted for the actual fame of the order. Finally the Dominican order had a translator equal to its own intellectual ambition. Albert the Great (1193–1280) had still been accustomed to doing without a translator from within the order. He wrote commentaries on the complete works of Aristotle, and in so doing set a vast amount of Greek scholarship in motion. He had to rely on a number of translators, some of whom he criticized quite harshly.[78] Even so, he never drew the logical consequence—that he himself should undertake the study of Greek. If one is concerned with "influences," then one can write books on Albert's Greco-Latinity; if one is restricted to direct contacts, open to proof, then one can capsulize Albert's place in Greco-Latin literary history with the four-word phrase, coined by Nicholas of Cusa: "Non grecus fuit Albertus!"[79]

One could say the same of Thomas Aquinas, who profited from the intellectual achievement of his fellow Dominican William of Moerbeke. Moerbeke took advantage of the favorable conditions and furthered, via his translations, Western acquaintance with texts of Greek science.[80] His interest concentrated naturally on Aristotle. The most important of his works for Western literary history is that on Aristotle's *Poetics*. He translated the work in Viterbo in 1278.[81] Translating Aristotle also included translating the commentaries on his texts that were necessary for university study.[82]

In addition, Moerbeke also translated a number of Archimedes' tracts[83] and important works of the Neoplatonic philosopher Proclus—the *Elementatio theologica*,[84] the brief texts *De fata, De providentia, De malo*,[85] and his commentaries on the *Timaeus* and the *Parmenides*.[86] With Proclus' commentary on the *Parmenides*, William of Moerbeke also translated the first hypothesis of the Platonic dialogue itself, so that after Cicero's and Chalcidius' *Timaeus* and Aristippus' *Meno* and *Phaedo*, the West now had a fourth Platonic dialogue in at least partial translation. This last translation of Plato before Chrysoloras' *Republic* was of great significance for the thought of the late Middle Ages; the German mysticism of the fifteenth century, which was supported by the Dominicans, saw in Plato's *Parmenides* the philosophical foundation of its *theologia negativa*. The Platonism of Nicholas of Cusa had much to do with the *Parmenides* and Proclus' commentary on that work.[87]

Not quite forty years after the Council of Lyons, another council met which finally did deal with the language question. In the meantime it had become clear that neither the Greek people nor their clergy and episcopate had been won with the Greek emperor's signature on a document acknowledging the union. The strategic position of the Latins in the eastern Mediterranean had also worsened; the castle of the Templars in Acre, the last fortress of the crusaders in the Holy Land, fell in 1291. After Roger Bacon, the Franciscan tertiary Raimundus Lullus of Palma de Mallorca stepped forth as a champion of the need for language study in the mission; he was not satisfied with memoranda to propagate his views. He founded a language school in Mallorca, which was, however, to train missionaries to the Moslems, and for which he risked and lost his life (stoned in Tunis in 1316). This "Doctor illuminatus" is primarily responsible for the decision of the Council of Vienne in 1312, the so-called language canon, which established two professorial chairs each for Hebrew, Greek, Arabic, and Chaldean (= Syrian) at each of the four most important *studia generalia* in the West: Paris, Oxford, Bologna, and Salamanca. In addition, the same was to be done at the seat of the papal curia, wherever that might be. These forty professors were not just to teach, but also to translate into Latin.

> With the cares which weigh on our shoulders, we reflect constantly on how we can lead the erring to the way of truth and win them for God with the aid of his mercy. . . . We do not doubt that for the fulfillment of this wish the interpretation and preaching of the divine word is quite appropriate. But we do not fail to recognize that these words can resound and return empty if they strike the ears of those who do not understand the language of the person speaking. Therefore, we imitate the example of him whom we represent—even if unworthily—on Earth, who wanted the Apostles, who were to go into the whole world to preach the Gospel, to be learned in all forms of speech [*in omni linguarum genere fore voluit eruditos*]; and we wish that the holy Church might abound in Catholic men who have knowledge of languages, especially those which the heathen speak, so that the heathen might learn of the holy institution and be joined to the community of Christian believers through the doctrine of the Christian faith and the reception of the holy baptismal sacrament. Thus, so that this form of linguistic understanding might be effectively received through study, we have, with the sanction of this council, provided that schools in the languages mentioned below be established wherever the Roman curia resides and at the universities of Paris, Oxford, Bologna, and Salamanca. In each of these places, Catholic men who have a sufficient knowledge of Hebrew, Greek, Arabic, and Chaldean should teach, two for each language. They should administer the schools, faithfully translate books from the languages into Latin, carefully teach the languages to others and impart to them a knowledge of the languages through zealous instruction, so that when they are instructed and sufficiently taught in these languages, they might, with God as their motivation, bear the hoped-for fruit and spread the faith with beneficial effect among those heathen nations. The Apostolic See should provide an appropriate remuneration for those reading at the Roman curia; the king of France should

do the same for those in Paris; for those in Oxford, the prelates, monasteries, chapters, convents, and faculties, exempt and nonexempt, and the rectors of the churches of England, Scotland, Ireland, and Wales; for those in Bologna, the same Italian offices as those in England; for those in Salamanca, the same Spanish offices; and in this, we impose the burden of contribution on each individual according to his means. . . .

Council of Vienne (1312), can. 11, published in 1317 by Pope John XXII in the *Clementinae*, lib. 5, tit. I, 1, which he edited; ed. E. Friedberg, *Corpus Iuris Canonici* (Leipzig 1879), II, 1179. It is not altogether certain whether Greek was mentioned from the very beginning in the conciliar canons. Weiss advances arguments for the original mention of Greek as well in *Bibliothèque d'Humanisme et Renaissance* 14 (1952), p. 1, n. 2. On Raymond Lull's intellectual paternity, see Altaner, "Raymundus Lullus und der Sprachenkanon (can. 11) des Konzils von Vienne (1312)," *Historisches Jahrbuch* 53 (1933); E. Müller, *Das Konzil von Vienne* (Münster 1934), pp. 155 ff. and 636 ff.

Thus everything was well ordered, from the deduction of language study from the baptismal order of Christ to provisions for financial support, so that deeds would in fact follow this still somewhat tormented insight into the necessity of language instruction. (It was of course the fault of those who were to be missionized that they did not understand the Latin missionaries. But since this did not help matters along, the missionary had to learn the language of those whom he addressed!) The papal curia henceforth paid language teachers from time to time; and also in Paris there were some initial signs of instruction in the "oriental languages," especially after the Council of Basel (1434) readopted, essentially unchanged, the resolution of Vienne.[88] In England, the taxes agreed upon began to be collected (in the see of Lincoln, for example) for one of the professorships in Hebrew planned for Oxford.[89] Richard of Bury, the passionate book collector, educator, bishop of Durham (1333–45), and diplomat of King Edward III of England, supported the resolution of the council because it suited his own *amor ecstaticus* of the world of books; in his *Philobiblon* of 1344, this predecessor of humanistic bibliophilism announced that among other things, he wanted to leave a Hebrew and a Greek grammar (probably Roger Bacon's) for the use of the scholars (in Oxford).[90]

But none of these projects actually flourished; there were neither enough professors nor enough students for the decreed studies. The trust had simply been too great that the spirit would surely follow willingly when everything had already been decreed, planned and financed. Thus this early chapter of Western educational planning ends rather pitifully. For all that, Greek was taught for a short time both at the curia in Avignon, by Barlaam (1342), and in Rome, by Simon Atumanus (ca. 1380). But it was not the spirit of the mission, but rather that of the *studia huma-*

niora which brought about the first continuous instruction of Greek in the West, by Manuel Chrysoloras in Florence—later, at a different place, and with a different purpose from that intended by the members of the council in 1312.

4. Anjou, Catalonia, Aragon, and the Avignon Papacy— Italo-Greeks and Italian Humanists

In southern Italy the last epoch of the cultural mission that had begun on Italian soil in former times with Magna Graecia began with the decline of the Hohenstaufen dynasty. Southern Italy also became a "Latin" land when Charles of Anjou (d. 1285), the victor over the Hohenstaufen rulers Manfred (1266) and Conradin (1268), was called into the country by the papacy: the Arabs were exterminated, and the church in southern Italy was de-Hellenized without delay.[91] At least a part of the Greek manuscripts taken from Hohenstaufen possession as booty was presented by Charles of Anjou to his feudal lords, the popes, who, however, lost most of their part of the booty during the Avignon period.[92]

At the same time, Charles of Anjou began to build a court library in Naples,[93] and translations also continued to be executed at his court. It seems that he had nothing translated but Arabic medical literature.[94]

In 1301 his son and successor, Charles II, commissioned the bishop of Oppido (Stephan?) to translate two medical treatises from Greek into Latin; only the order of payment is preserved (Weiss, *Rinascimento*, I [1950], 206). Bilinguals continued to be cultivated in the monastery of St. Benedetto Ullano (Val di Crati) in the see of Bisignagno (Calabria). In 1291 and 1292, Abbot Romanus wrote a Greco-Latin Psalter and a Greco-Latin evangelary: Cod. Vat. gr. 1070 (cf. Follieri, *Codices graeci*, pl. 57, pp. 81 f. [awkward Latin minuscule!], and Schneider, in *Biblica* 30 [1949], 480 f.) and Cod. Vat. Barb. gr. 541 (cf. Devreesse, *Les manuscrits grecs*, p. 42). It is not certain whether Nicholas of Reggio in Calabria already worked for Charles II.

Under King Robert I (1309–43), theological interests were added to the medical interests which to some extent had been inherited; Dante pointedly apostrophizes the sermonizing king as *re da sermone*.[95] The names of an entire group of translators are known, who worked for a set fee in a scribes' and translators' house in order to enlarge the court library: Andalò di Negro from Otranto, Azzolino de Urbe, Leo de Scolis from Altamura. . . . Nothing is preserved of their translations. It is thought that the court library of the house of Anjou was taken to Hungary in 1347–48 and that it was for the most part lost as a result of this undertaking.[96] Only the work of Nicholas of Reggio, who did not directly belong to the translators' organization of Anjou, has survived.

Nicholas Theoprepos of Reggio, a physician who perhaps came from a family of notaries,[97] began to translate in 1308 and was demonstrably at work until 1345. He and his patrons were primarily interested in the works of Galen, of which he translated more than fifty.[98] In addition, he translated portions of the *Corpus Hippocraticum* and perhaps other Greek medical works as well. Through his translation of Sophronius, he demonstrated that he was not merely a technical translator.[99] His interest in epigraphy, to which his translation of a Greek inscription from the temple of the Dioscuri in Naples bears witness, strikes one as a presentiment of Humanism.[100]

As a translator, Nicholas' work was quite characteristically medieval, since literal: he was concerned with scholarly accuracy and not stylistic beauty. Nicholas was also scholarly in his attitude toward older translations: for the sake of accuracy, he again translated medical works from Greek which had already been translated from Arabic; he also completed older translations from Greek.[101]

He also had contacts with Constantinople; at least once, in 1331, he was there as King Robert's ambassador. It is difficult to prove any connections between him and the early Humanists. Even so, Boccaccio was in Naples between 1325 and 1340, and Barlaam of Seminara was there for some time in 1339. Three years later, Barlaam was teaching Greek in the papal residence in Avignon.

The question of the relations between the Angevin translators in Naples and the early Humanists in that city is an unsolved problem of literary and intellectual history. "Es kann nicht Zufall gewesen sein, daß Neapel so vielen Humanisten offenstand, und die enthusiastische Meinung der Humanisten über Robert wäre nicht erklärbar, wenn er nicht der neuen Wissenschaft die Wege bereiten wollte" ("It cannot have been an accident that Naples was open to so many Humanists, and the Humanists' enthusiastic opinion of Robert would be inexplicable if it were not the case that he wanted to prepare the way for the new science"); Goetz, *Robert von Neapel*, p. 38. On the other hand, Weiss argues that ". . . the fact that not one single scrap of evidence remains to point even indirectly to a mutual interest in their respective activities, can but suggest this: that their failure in influencing each other reciprocally was probably due to there being not many interests shared by the two groups: the translators probably cared little for polite letters, while it is unlikely that the Humanist had more than a superficial interest in Greek medicine. Their only link in common was probably the royal patronage and the library, but little else" (*Rinascimento*, I, 210). One must bear in mind, however, that from the very beginning it was a part of the Humanists' stylization of themselves that they wished to attribute nothing to the "Middle Ages," and everything to the elegance of "antiquity."

The role which the French had played during the thirteenth century in the Mediterranean was transferred increasingly to the Spanish in the century following. Even Charles of Anjou was able to hold on to no more than continental "Sicily" after the Sicilian Vespers had called in the house of

Aragon as the heir of the Hohenstaufen dynasty (1282). In 1311 Catalonians founded the Latin Duchy of Athens. After almost a thousand years, a Spaniard again spoke of the beauty of the Acropolis—King Peter IV of Aragon and Catalan (1336–87).[102] Peter's son John I (1387–95) was an insatiable book collector, particularly interested in ancient Greek history. His most important book supplier was the grand master of the Hospitallers, Juan Fernández de Heredia (d. 1396), who was one of the first of the Western magnates to take a serious interest in the historiography and literature of ancient and medieval Greece: Juan collected the books which were obtainable, and even had some of them translated into Aragonese[103]—portions of Thucydides, Josephus (*De bello Iudaico*), and the Byzantine historian John Zonaras; but above all he had Plutarch translated. Around 1384–88, a Dominican missionary bishop at the papal court in Avignon translated thirty-nine biographies from Plutarch into Aragonese at Juan's request; his source was not the ancient Greek Plutarch, but rather a Byzantine Greek version which had been produced not long before that time in Rhodes.[104] Thus Plutarch's major work journeyed to the West not by the royal path of the classical languages, Greek and Latin, but via the plebeian way—from *vernacular to vernacular*! That was a harbinger of the shift in literary languages from the ancient to the modern, although the renaissance of the classical languages by Humanism was, to be sure, still to precede the full fruition of that development.

The religious center of the Occident was Avignon, not Rome, during the fourteenth century. From 1309 to 1377, the popes resided in Avignon, and their policies were made and carried out under the auspices of the French. It is the most disreputable period in the history of the papacy; contemporaries discredited it with the epithet "Babylonian Captivity." Yet in recent decades scholars have been able to identify some positive cultural aspects of this scandal of ecclesiastical history. The "Linguistic Canon of the Council of Vienne," noted above, stems from the Avignon period. The papal curia tried to institute instruction in Greek as agreed upon in Vienne. The first known Greek teacher in Avignon was Barlaam, who came from the Greek monastery of Seminara in Calabria.[105] He later became a teacher and abbot in Constantinople and died as bishop of Gerace in Calabria (1342–48). In 1339 he was part of the Greek embassy to the unification deliberations at Avignon, and in 1342 and 1347 he was there again.[106] At the time of his second visit (1342), he gave eighty-one days of Greek instruction; we know the duration of his tenure so precisely because the curia settled its account with him down to the very penny. It was at that time that Petrarch also took Greek lessons from Barlaam in Avignon.[107]

Barlaam's successor as bishop of Gerace in Calabria was Simon Atumanus (1348).[108] He was born in Constantinople, the son of a Turkish father and a Greek mother, educated there in the famous Studiu monastery, and made his fortune as a language expert in the politically disordered Mediterranean world of his day. From the bishopric of Gerace (1348–66), he advanced to the archepiscopal see of Thebes (1366–ca. 1380), the capital of the Catalonian "Duchy of Athens." Here too he was the successor of a great intermediary between East and West, the southern Italian Paul of Smyrna, who was certainly the crucial mediator in the attempt at ecclesiastical reconciliation—through the personal conversion of Emperor John V.[109] When Thebes changed from Catalonian to Navarrese hands in 1379, Simon Atumanus left the city and returned to a standby post at the papal court, which in the meantime was no longer in Avignon, but again in Rome. Between 1383 and 1386, Simon died in Rome.

Both in Avignon and in Rome, Simon left traces of his knowledge of languages. Around 1372–73, at the request of Cardinal Corsini at the papal court in Avignon, he translated Plutarch's *De cohibenda ira*, and thus was the first person to introduce the geniune Plutarch into the literature of the West.[110] Up to that time, the West had known only the pseudo-Plutarchian *De institutione principum*, which was quoted almost simultaneously both in the letter (cited above) of Henry Aristippus to the anonymous Englishman (ca. 1160)[111] and in John of Salisbury's *Policraticus*.

John of Salisbury, *Policraticus* IV 8, ed. C. C. I. Webb (London 1909), I, 265: "De magistratuum moderatione librum fertur scripsisse Plutarcus, qui inscribitur *Archigramaton*." Somewhat further on John includes an *Epistola Plutarchi Traianum instruentis* and then quotes extensively from an *Institutio Traiani* and *Archigramaton*. From that point on, these titles lurked about in late medieval literary histories as works of Plutarch. But no manuscripts of these texts that contain more than what John of Salisbury quoted have ever been found. For this reason, H. Liebeschütz called the *Institutio Traiani* "a pseudoclassical invention of his [i.e., John of Salisbury's] own, and an invention which in its combination of clerical and classical features is characteristic of the author" ("John of Salisbury and Pseudo-Plutarch," *Journal of the Warburg and Courtauld Institutes* 6 [1943], 33–39, here p. 34). The question has, however, not yet been finally resolved; cf. A. Momigliano, "Notes on Petrarch, John of Salisbury and the *Institutio Traiani*," *Journal of the Warburg and Courtauld Institutes* 12 (1949), 189 f.; and yet again, Liebeschütz, in the same issue of the journal, p. 190, and in *Mediaeval Humanism in the Life and Writings of John of Salisbury* (London 1950), pp. 24 f. S. Desideri, *La "Institutio Traiani"* (Genoa 1958); M. Kerner, "Zur Entstehungsgeschichte der 'Institutio Traiani,'" *DA* 32 (1976), 558–71 (bibliog.); T. Struve, *Die Entwicklung der organologischen Staatsauffassung im Mittelalter* (Stuttgart 1978), pp. 127 ff.

The "quotations" of John of Salisbury from his Pseudo-Plutarch shaped the late medieval conception of Plutarch in the West. Even Petrarch, who intensively collected the works of ancient historians and biographers, knew only this Pseudo-Plutarch who had been put together from the "quotations." He did, however, know from Aulus Gellius' *Noctes Atticae* that Plutarch wrote a moral work, *De cohibenda ira*.[112] It was in fact precisely with the Latin translation of this work that, in 1373, a year before Petrarch's death, the rediscovery of the authentic Plutarch began in the West.

In Rome around 1380, Simon Atumanus was teaching Greek. According to the testimony of his student Radulf de Rivo, he translated the Old Testament from Hebrew into Greek and Latin and arranged it trilingually; his death prevented him from completing the work. According to reports from the sixteenth century, he even brought about a trilingual edition of the *New* Testament, by translating the texts from Greek into Hebrew.[113] Thus a "Biblia triglotta" was produced one and a half centuries before the Complutensian Polyglot Bible of Jiménez de Cisneros. Simon Atumanus' third noteworthy attribute was his collection of manuscripts of the Greek classics, among them Homer, Plato, and Euripides.[114] Although Radulf de Rivo praised Simon Atumanus as "comparable to St. Jerome in his knowledge of the three languages,"[115] his work had no great influence—perhaps because he did too little to satisfy the humanistic need for distinction and elegance. Coluccio Salutati derisively called his literal translation of Plutarch a *semigreca translatio*;[116] since he could not translate from Greek himself, he gave Atumanus' translation "classical" dress. This procedure is quite characteristic of the early humanistic period.

5. Petrarch, Boccaccio, and the Italo-Greek Leontius Pilatus

Francesco Petrarca (1304–74) represents a turning point in both Latin *and* Greek studies.[117] Just as all Westerners of the fourteenth century, he too held the Greeks of his time in contempt and thought little or nothing of their "Byzantine" literature. But in his intensive study of the Latin authors, with which he began early, he also came across the classical Greek authors; in Cicero, Seneca, Macrobius (*Saturnalia*), Servius, Valerius Maximus, Apuleius, Terence, Augustine, and Lactantius, he time and again came upon Greek passages and Greek authors. It is revealing to see how helpless Petrarch was—at least in the earlier period—in the face of these Graeca. His famous Vergil manuscript, the "Virgilius Ambrosianus," which in size and decoration was in some senses the flagship of his book fleet,[118] contains glosses entered by Petrarch at various times of his life; in the older parts, one often comes across quotations that abruptly stop with the laconic remark *Grece* (*Ut ait Homerus: Grece!*).[119] At the time, Petrarch still had no hope that he would ever be able to fill these gaps appropriately; otherwise he would have left space vacant for later entries. Later, however, he nevertheless did draw an occasional word into his Vergil in Greek uncial.[120] He had in the meantime acquired a rudimentary knowledge of Greek. One of the resources that he used in studying Greek was the *Triglossos* of Gerard of Huy.[121] Petrarch took advantage of a better opportunity to learn Greek when Barlaam of Seminara appeared in Avignon. Petrarch took lessons from him, as noted above, and in turn taught the Italo-Greek Latin. Plato became a subject of study.[122] The lessons seem to have been ultimately as unsatisfactory as those of John of Salisbury two centuries earlier with an Italo-Greek. Petrarch's enthusiasm for Plato is traceable to this episode in his life. In the middle of an Aristotelian age, Petrarch changed his allegiance from the "Philosopher" of the Scholastics to the elder philosopher, from Aristotle to Plato, who was "already the most esteemed author of the later Byzantines."[123] Most likely it dates from this period that Petrarch had a thick Greek Plato codex on his bookshelf, which Boccaccio envied him greatly.[124]

Petrarch also acquired yet another Greek codex—Homer. In 1348 in Verona he became acquainted with Nicholas Sigerus, an envoy from Constantinople. Around 1353–54 Nicholas sent him the longed-for Homeric codex.[125] Since his intermezzo with Barlaam in Avignon, Petrarch had given no more attention to his Greek, and thus he could not read the book that he accepted so joyfully. But he tearfully embraced it and said "with a sigh: O great man, how I wish to hear you!"[126]

He also sought to find codices of Hesiod, Euripides, and Sophocles;[127] most likely, however, his library, so rich in the Latin classics, never included more than the two Greek manuscripts, Plato and Homer. For his knowledge of Greek literature, Petrarch remained—as did most Latins—dependent on the existing Latin translations, of which he possessed a considerable number. Since there was as yet no Latin translation of Homer, it had to be seen to, so that Petrarch and his friends could finally become better acquainted with him.

In 1359 in Padua, Petrarch met the Calabrian Leontius Pilatus,[128] who, as a student of Barlaam, seemed the right man to execute this translation, which for Petrarch was the most urgent of all. As a trial, Petrarch had him translate the first five books of the *Iliad* and seemed to be pleased with the results. Nevertheless he did not want to retain the Calabrian; he found him disagreeable. On the other hand, Leontius did not want to stay in Italy; he was drawn to the "Western Babylon,"[129] Avignon, so that he too might gain a bishopric, as had Barlaam and Simon Atumanus before him. Boccaccio solved the problem by moving the Signoria of Florence to set up a Greek lectorate for Leontius. By 1361 at the latest, Leontius was teaching Greek in Florence. Boccaccio learned the language somewhat more thoroughly from him than had Petrarch from Barlaam. At the same time Leontius translated Homer, as well as Euripides' *Hecuba*. Doubtless he did so with a view to his Greek lessons in Florence, for it was precisely with *Hecuba* that the reading of Euripides began according to Byzantine educational tradition.[130] Without question further incidental translations by Leontius will be identified.[131] The major portion of the translation of Homer was finished by 1362; he gave up the remainder of the work, because he did not want to stay in Florence any longer. In 1365 he was killed by lightning during a seastorm.[132]

The research of Agostino Pertusi has brought to light a number of Leontius' manuscripts. First Pertusi was able to identify Leontius' hand in the Euripides manuscripts, Florence, Laur. Plut. XXXI 10 and Florence, Laur. S. Marco 226 (A. Pertusi, "La scoperta di Euripide"). Laur. XXXI 10 is one of the "Ioannikios manuscripts," whose relations with Burgundio Wilson recently demonstrated (Wilson, in Scrittura e Civiltà 7 [1983], 163 f.). An interlinear translation of Euripides' Hecuba vv. 1–466 has been entered in this twelfth-century Greek manuscript of Sophocles and Euripides; in addition, diverse Latin glosses have been noted in the margin of the same section. There is a kind of copy of this manuscript in Laur. S. Marco 226; here the Greek text is also written in the hand of the translator and glossator. The translator, glossator, and scribe could be identified as Leontius Pilatus. Thereafter, Venice, Marc. gr. IX 2 (Iliad) and Venice, Marc. gr. IX 29 (Odyssey) were recognized as autographs of Leontius (Pertusi, Leonzio Pilato [1964]; with facsimile plates from the noted manuscripts). Leontius always worked according to the same plan: he copied the Greek text with wide spacing, wrote the translation interlinearly, and used the margins for glosses.

Leontius' translations were ultimately disappointing for his patron. In texts in which scientific precision was of prime importance, the literal method of translation characteristic of the Middle Ages was useful; in poetical works it was disastrous. When the word order of the Greek original paralleled the rules of Latin word order, a passable version resulted (beginning of the Iliad):[133]

> Iram cane deo Pelidis Achillis
> pestiferam, que innumerabiles Grecis dolores inposuit

Beware, however, if the Greek syntax differed from the Latin (beginning of the Hecuba):[134]

> Venio mortuorum profundidatem et obscuritatis ianuas
> linquens, ubi infernus sine habitatur deis,
> ego Polydorus . . . !

One need only refer back to Jerome to discover what was to be expected of a literal translation of Homer.[135] The results corresponded to his prognosis.[136] But the spirits had been awakened: Homer had returned to Western consciousness. Now it was clear that there was no way to avoid a systematic study of Greek if one wished to find "the source and origin of all divine invention" (Petrarch, with Macrobius, on Homer) among the Greeks.

After he had brought Leontius to Florence, Petrarch stepped into the background of the history of Homeric translation. In fact it was years before he saw the translation by the Calabrian. Without Petrarch, however, this work would scarcely have come about at this time. Petrarch thought of himself as a Janus figure, and that he certainly was in his Greek interests. They are typically medieval in several senses: he lacked the necessary élan to make use of the (few) aids and opportunities for the grammatical acquisition of the language. Greek remained a kind of ornament to Latin. In other ways, however, he also went beyond the Middle Ages: the Greek books that Petrarch embraces are no longer the Psalter, the Gospels, and theological works, but rather Plato and Homer. Ecclesiastical Greek recedes; antiquity stands in the foreground. The humanistic shift of axes has begun in Western consciousness—away from theology and philosophy, toward poetry, history, the epistolary art, rhetoric; away from all despicable Scholastic scholarship, toward the artistic freedom of the individual; away from the "Middle Ages," toward antiquity!

Petrarch was understood best in Florence. In his *Genealogiae deorum gentilium*, Boccaccio (1313–1375) again took up the old practice of inserting Greek quotations directly into his Latin text; after Liudprand of Cremona in the tenth century, he was the first Westerner to be an expert at this technique. In his copy of the *Genealogiae*[137] he wrote a number of lengthy citations from Homer in Greek letters; in the margin he noted the translation of Leontius Pilatus, which he occasionally corrected.[138] Boccaccio used a Greek minuscule that was mixed with several majuscule letters.[139] He was not yet able to work without error and sometimes had difficulty understanding the text. He took great pains to reacquire that fluid transition from Greek to Latin which was so admired in the ancients. The character of the book was, however, as was also the case with Liudprand of Cremona, altered by the copyists, who inserted the translations into the text.[140] But ultimately, Boccaccio's work was successful. One of the characteristics of the humanistic style goes back to him: a regained openness to original Greek citations.

When Boccaccio died, Coluccio Salutati acceded to his state office in Florence (1375–1406). Thereafter he was the strongest supporter of Greek studies in Florence. Salutati understood little Greek, but he took great pains with translations. When the opportunity again arose to bring a Greek teacher to Florence, he seized it. His name is connected with the recovery of Plutarch. In 1394 he revised the Latin style of the literal translation by Simon Atumanus of Plutarch's treatise on anger.[141] Salutati had to overcome great difficulties before he could gain possession of Plutarch's major work, the *Parallel Lives*. Juan Fernández de Heredia, who had acquired the work in 1384–88 at Avignon in an Aragonese translation, did not want to allow a translation. Not until Salutati offered the Latin *Odissea* of Leontius Pilatus (ca. 1395) did an exchange come about. The Florentine immediately translated the Aragonese Plutarch into Latin. But before he could finish the project, this circuitous route via the vernacular became superfluous, since in 1397 Manuel Chrysoloras began to teach Greek in Florence. Now the original Greek Plutarch was available in Florence, soon in several copies.

The translation of Plutarch was among the most urgent tasks of the first generation of humanistic translators gathered around Chrysoloras. Jacopo Angeli da Scarperia[142] in particular devoted himself to this task. The new translations had already crossed the Alps by the early fifteenth century. One should note here that during the Council of Constance (1416) four of Plutarch's *Vitae* in the translation of Leonardo Bruni were copied in Constance and taken to Reims, where they were immediately chained, as was the custom there.[143] Thus the biography of Plutarch began its grand march of triumph.[144] Suetonius had just reached the pinnacle of his fame, due to Petrarch. A generation later the Roman biographer had already been replaced by the Greek.[145] The fifteenth century found in Plutarch the confirmation of the notion that *virtus* and *fortuna* determine the fortune of men; Italian society of the time "recognized itself in Plutarch's figures, just as the nineteenth-century French bourgeoisie found itself again in the novels of Flaubert."[146] In the sixteenth century Jacques Amyot (d. 1593) eclipsed all other translations with his French version translated from the Greek; in its role as a "heroic Bible," Plutarch's *Lives* left its imprint on the modern Western conception of man.[147] Jean Paul called Plutarch the biographical Shakespeare of world history and thus characterized his enormous influence.[148] The return of the authentic Plutarch to the West is—along with that of Homer—the Greco-Latin *translatio studii* of the early humanistic period that had the most far-reaching consequences.

6. Constantinopolis Agonistes and the West— Manuel Chrysoloras—The Councils of the Fifteenth Century

The Byzantine Empire which had been miraculously restored in Constantinople in 1261 was again threatened by destruction, due to the expansionist greed of Charles of Anjou. Emperor Michael took refuge in the union of 1274, and thus won the papacy, if not as his ally, then at least as an adversary of an Angevin "crusade" against Constantinople. When the union dissolved in 1281, the Sicilian Vespers (1282) saved Constantinople from an invasion (to the benefit of Peter III of Aragon, a relative of the Hohenstaufen dynasty), since Anjou was then forced to use his arms in the South and West. Thus the fallen Hohenstaufen Empire, with its last movement, indirectly supported the unsteady Greek Empire.

Emperor John V (1341–91) embarked on a new course in the union with the West. In 1355, he sent an extensive bilingual chrysobull, in which he made arrangements for his personal conversion to Catholicism and promised to bring about the conversion of his subjects in return for military assistance.[149] Fourteen years later, he did in fact go to Italy and carry out his change of faith before Pope Urban V; but this act had no effect on the Greek Empire and the Orthodox Church. The emperor's weakness was clearly demonstrated by the fact that the Venetian bankers even dared to take him captive on his return journey in order to force him to pay his debts.

After having long been lost, the chrysobull of the union of 1369 has again come to the surface in the Vatican archives (A.A.Arm.I–XVIII, no. 401; old signature, Arm. II, Caps. II, no. 7), ed. S. Lampros, in *Neos Hellenomnemon* 11 (1914), 241–53. The chrysobull begins with the emperor's confession of faith, in two columns (Greek and Latin). Underneath these texts, the emperor's signature, in purple ink, stretches across almost the entire width of the parchment (facsimile in Lampros). The official attestation follows, with the naming of the six witnesses, who were proficient in both languages and attested to the identity of the Greek and Latin texts. There were three on each side: at the head of the Western interpreters stood Paul of Smyrna, who was at that time already the Latin archbishop of Constantinople and who, from 1355 on, carried out the negotiations between Emperor John V and the popes on the meticulous, "if"- and "but"-filled, treaties and drafts of treaties. The first of the Greek interpreters was the translator of Thomas Aquinas, Demetrios Kydones, who had personally converted to Catholicism even before his emperor. The chrysobull still bears the original gold bulla. On the Catalonian origin of the two other translators who are named on the Latin side in addition to Paul of Smyrna, see Setton, in *Proceedings of the American Philosophical Society* 100 (1956), 46 f.

The emperor's son, Manuel, who ransomed his father in Venice, became the second Greek emperor (Manuel II, 1391–1425) not afraid to seek Western help for the city which was almost permanently besieged by the Turks.[150] In the years 1399–1403, he traveled through Venice, Padua, Vicenza, and Pavia to Paris and London, then back to Paris, where he waited patiently for two years for the auxiliary troops which had been promised to him. The Abbey of St. Denis was an especially important stop for the Greek emperor (25 February 1401); in memory of his visit, he later sent via Manuel Chrysoloras a manuscript of the *Areopagitica*, decorated with a portrait of the imperial family.[151] The news of the Mongolian victory over the Turks ended his stay. Constantinople had again won a respite of almost two generations.

The journey of Manuel II through the capitals of the West—a journey as glorious as it was ineffectual—is the focal point of a series of East-West encounters which were of great importance for the humanistic movement. Coluccio Salutati's young friend Jacopo Angeli da Scarperia went to Constantinople in 1395 during a Turkish siege in order to learn the Greek language and acquire Greek manuscripts there. Most of Scarperia's translations are of Plutarch. At first he worked for Salutati, then for Petrus Philargis of Crete and then for the Greek Franciscan, cardinal, and later Pope Alexander V (1409–10).

On his return trip to Italy in 1396, Scarperia was accompanied by the Greek scholar Manuel Chrysoloras and Manuel's teacher, Demetrios Kydones. Chrysoloras[152] brought Emperor Manuel II's request for Western aid; but the West proved to be more interested in the Greek intellect than in the continued existence of the Greek state. In 1397 at the invitation of Salutati, Chrysoloras began to teach Greek in Florence. Statesmen and Humanists, among them Leonardo Bruni,[153] Palla Strozzi, and Pier Paolo Vergerio, congregated around the new teacher. Chrysoloras had Lucian's *Timon* and *Charon* translated and prompted a translation of Ptolemy's *Geography*, which Scarperia completed for Petrus Philargis/ Alexander V. As an aid in his teaching of Greek, Chrysoloras wrote a textbook in Greek, ЄΡШΘΜΑΤΑ, after Dionysius Thrax, which was later adapted into Latin by Guarino da Verona. In 1400, Chrysoloras went to the court of Gian Galeazzo Visconti in Lombardy, where he translated Plato's ΠΟΛΙΤΕΙΑ; Uberto Decembrio and later his son Pier Candido Decembrio polished the Latin style of the translation.[154] In 1406, Chrysoloras embraced Catholicism; he died in 1415 in Constance, during the council at which he was considered a candidate for pope.[155]

Chrysoloras' influential student Guarino da Verona (d. 1460) never tired of praising his teacher as the founder of a new era of scholarship; he became the standard-bearer of Greek studies, which were in fact beginning to blossom at that time. His name overshadowed those of the Italo-Greek teachers of the fourteenth century who had prepared the way for him.

Manuel Chrysoloras represents an exordium of the Greek school tradition in the West, of the "discovery" of Greek authors and their large-scale translation into Latin. All that had already existed, but on such a small scale that the Humanists could easily overlook it. The line of Italian manuscript hunters in Greece begins with Angeli da Scarperia; Guarino da Verona, Giovanni Aurispa, Francesco Filelfo, and Cyriacus of Ancona followed him; in addition to these five Italians who were most important in the "caccia ai manoscritti greci," there was yet another group of "esploratori minori."[156] The East-West migration of manuscripts that these people set in motion became still more intensified by means of the emigration of learned Greeks, driven by the threat to and fall of Constantinople. Large Greek book collections were now brought together in the West. The first Westerner to own a hundred or more Greek manuscripts was the Florentine Humanist Nicolò Niccoli (d. 1437). Cardinal Bessarion (d. 1472), who also sought Greek manuscripts in southern Italy, had five hundred Greek manuscripts; the thousand mark was first reached by the Vatican collection at the death of Sixtus IV (1484). These approximate numbers are meant only to illustrate how precipitously the strength of the Greek *presence* increased.[157]

It would go beyond the scope of the present work to give even a selective list of the tremendous number of teachers, translators, and commentators of Greek texts. In the course of one or two generations, the entire field changed: where once deficiency reigned supreme, now there was overabundance; where theology, philosophy, and the natural sciences were determinative, now the old and new arts (poetry, rhetoric, drama, historiography) were preeminent; what had been the affair of outsiders was now the passion of princes and prelates.

The councils of the first half of the fifteenth century play an important role in the meeting between Greek and Latin: in Pisa (1409), Constance (1414–18), Basel (begun in 1431 and never officially closed), and Ferrara-Florence (1438–39). Increasingly more frequently, Latins met with learned Greeks, who never ceased seeking Western aid for the hard-pressed imperial city.

In January of 1443, the council city of Basel received the magnificent Greek book collection of the Dominican and cardinal John Stojković of Ragusa (Dubrovnik), as his bequest to the city. The collection was placed in the Dominican monastery in Basel, was extensively used by the German Humanists, but remained intact only up until 1525, as a result of the Reformation and secularization. On this cardinal (who has received much attention in recent research on Humanism) and his library, see A. Krchňák, "De vita et operibus Joannis de Ragusio" (diss., Rome 1960); A. Vernet, "Les manuscrits grecs de Jean de Raguse († 1443)," *Basler Zeitschrift für Geschichte und Altertumskunde* 61 (1961), 75–108; R. W. Hunt, "Greek Manuscripts in the Bodleian Library from the Collection of John Stojković of Ragusa," *Studia Patristica* 7, TU 92 (1966), 75–82. The collector's interests of the Dalmatian cardinals was still decidedly prehumanistic: "John's collection was built up to gain a better understanding of the Greek church, its traditions and its writers" (Hunt). It was the first substantial collection of Greek manuscripts *north* of the Alps.

The Council of Ferrara-Florence represents the high point of Greco-Latin encounters.[158] A Western embassy including Cardinal Nicholas of Cusa went to Constantinople in 1437 and effected the dispatch of a historically unique delegation from Greek Christendom to the Western council: Emperor John VIII Palaeologus, Patriarch Joseph II of Constantinople, many bishops—among them Bessarion, metropolitan of Nicaea, and Isidore, metropolitan of Kiev—Georgios Gemisthos Plethon, the head of the Platonic revival in Mistra, and the grammatician, John Argyropoulos; they came to the council with several hundred other Greeks. Among the Latins who met the embassy in Venice was the Humanist, translator of the Greek Fathers, and minister general of the Camaldolese Ambrogio

Traversari, who in 1436 had published a new translation of the *Corpus Dionysiacum* that was intended for the council.[159] The Humanists Leonardo Bruni and Guarino da Verona also participated in the council. Under the effect of Plethon's discourses in Florence, Cosimo de' Medici founded a Platonic academy at which Plethon (d. 1451) taught for several years following the council. His intellectual heir was Marsilio Ficino (d. 1499), who published the first complete translation of Plato's works.[160] John Argyropoulos founded Greek philology in Italy (d. 1487).[161] Bessarion, "Latinorum graecissimus, Graecorum latinissimus" (L. Valla), remained behind in the West as a Roman cardinal and "Greek prince of the Italian Renaissance"; his house on the Roman Quirinal became the rendezvous of learned Greeks in Italy, and his Greek book collection the treasury of Greek literature.[162] At the time of the most severe threat to Constantinople and also after the fall of the city in 1453, there were hopes of new Hellenistic activity in the West, and these hopes attached to Bessarion. The city of Venice, the first to have shaken Constantinople to its very foundations, in the end became its richest heir through the free choice of the Greek emigrants; Bessarion's library was there even before his death (1472), and for many Greeks this city on the lagoon, which had such a wealth of Byzantine qualities, was still the most bearable place of exile.[163]

7. Medieval and Humanistic Translation: *transferre* and *traducere*—Nicholas of Cusa

The Humanists considered their Greek studies something completely new in comparison with those of the Middle Ages. Chrysoloras' student Leonardo Bruni wrote: "No one in Italy has known Greek literature for the past seven hundred years, and still we all acknowledge that all knowledge comes from Greek."[164] The medieval and often even the late antique translations from Greek were denounced as barbaric and replaced by new ones which were more in harmony with the rhetorical sensibilities of the time, although they were not always better translations. Translation became a matter of aesthetics. "The Humanist had in mind a stylistic correspondence between the Greek original and the Latin translation, which was achieved when the translation could be placed in the same rhetorical class as the original":[165] thus the Latin translations of the *Iliad* and *Odyssey* were successful if they sounded like Virgil's *Aeneid*.[166] This tendency went even further: Aristotle himself had to be read in an elegant Latin version: Petrarch had said that it was only through the crudity or envy of barbaric translators that Aristotle became *durus scaberque*; this became the credo of the humanistic translators of Aristotle. "To render Aristotle into an elegant Latin form meant to reawaken the true Aristotle."[167] In 1440, King Alphonse of Aragon and Sicily wrote to Leonardo Bruni: "Aristotelem

quicumque prius transtulit potius abstulit, quem tu tua ista suavi loquen-
cia et singulari pietate nobis restituis ac prope extinctum in lucem evocas"
("Earlier translators of Aristotle in fact made off with him; you have restored him to us with this sweet discourse of yours and with your extraordinary dutifulness, and you have called him forth into the light when he
was almost dead").[168]

In humanistic Latin, a new and revealing form for the word "translate"
prevailed—*traducere*. *Transferre* was the customary older term, in addition to *transvertere*, *interpretari*, and other similar words. The Humanists were not satisfied with these forms of expression; a new term had to
be found as well, to express the new form of humanistic translation. The
same Leonardi Bruni who had formulated the humanistic legend that the
Italian Middle Ages had "not known Greek literature" was the first to use
the new word *traducere* for "translate"; its origin is probably due to a misunderstanding of a passage in Aulus Gellius.[169] The word quickly gained
currency and has even made its way into the Romance vernaculars.[170] It
simply corresponded to a pressing need of the Humanists, for *traducere*
was something quite different from *transferre*. The latter meant medieval
slavery, blind submission to the letter, offense against the spirit of the
classical Latin language. The new word, on the other hand, signified the
new freedom of the translator: "Tradurre significa abbellire abbellire abbellire e soprattutto mutare togliere aggiungere" ("*traducere* means to
embellish and embellish and embellish, and above all to change, delete,
and add").[171] After a Leonardo Bruni had used the word, it must have been
considered a good ancient word—just as the Carolingian minuscule and
the Romanesque round-arched windows were thought to be from antiquity, since they looked quite different from the corresponding phenomena
which were known from the (late) Middle Ages, and since they conformed
to the conception of classicism held at the time. Both Italian and French
have proverbial phrases with which they express a mistrust of the modern
form of translation that developed in the humanistic period: "traduttore—
traditore," "les belles infidèles"!

Italian Humanism disassociated itself absolutely from the "Middle
Ages"; in other countries there were scholars who were quite capable of
combining humanistic ideas with an appreciation of the accomplishments
of their medieval predecessors. The rock of unshaken continuity in characteristically medieval Greek studies was the German Cardinal Nicholas
of Cusa (1401–64). He was no "obscurantist" to whom humanistic activities would have been suspicious, but rather, even in his younger days, he
was considered by his Italian friends to be one of their correspondents
who performed excellent service to humanistic endeavors. In imitation of
the Italian Humanists who swarmed out from the council city of Constance, Nicolaus Trevirensis, as he was called at that time, searched for
lost ancient texts in the libraries of the Rhineland; after many a premature

announcement of a sensation (for instance, around 1427, the notion was circulating in Italy that Nicholas had found Cicero's *De re publica*)[172] he was successful in making a great find—a codex of Plautus. Nicholas always remained a collector, if not hunter, of manuscripts. But he also had other, "more medieval" interests than did the Italian Humanists: it obviously mattered little to him to take the splendid Plautus codex from his native land; and should evidence accumulate that a great part of the German manuscript tradition of Tacitus was transferred to Italy by way of Nicholas Trevirensis, then the nonhumanistic contour of his personality would thereby be even more strongly emphasized.[173] He was the friend of a great number of Italian Humanists, including Nicholas V and Pius II, the two most humanistic-minded popes of his century. His lifelong occupation with textual and historical criticism is typically humanistic.[174] On the other hand, his Latin is not at all humanistic; the old Scholastic Latin was more fitting for both his thought and his work. For him, unlike for his Italian friends, no chasms separated antiquity, the "Middle Ages," and the present. He acted with the same pragmatism with respect to Greek as to Latin. He did not embrace the incomprehensible Greek originals with tearful eyes, but rather studied the translations. He did not scorn medieval resource works. In his library one found, and in part still finds, two bilingual Psalters (Kues, Hospitalbibliothek Cod. 9 and 10), the famous uncial manuscript of the "Cyrillus" glossary (Greco-Latin, London, British Library Harl. 5792), and a manuscript of the "Servius" glossary (Latino-Greek, Harl. 2773).[175] He owned numerous manuscripts having to do with the works of Dionysius the Areopagite: the excerpts of Thomas Gallus, translations of Robert Grosseteste and Hugh of St. Victor's commentary on the *Hierarchia caelestis*, based on John Scottus' translation (Kues 45), the *Opera Dionysii Areopagitae cum commentario* [Grosseteste] *et glossa* (Kues 44), and Ambrogio Traversari's translation of Dionysius, which was new at that time (Kues 43). Everything which the Middle Ages had known in the way of translations of Plato was collected in his library: Chalcidius' *Timaeus* (Harl. 2652); the eleventh-century glosses on the *Timaeus*, with which the study of Plato in the high Middle Ages began;[176] Henry Aristippus' *Meno* and *Phaedo* (Kues 177); William of Moerbeke's translation of the *Parmenides* and Proclus' commentary on that work (no less than three copies: Kues 186, Vat. lat. 3074, and a fragment in Strasbourg Cod. 84). In addition, he had the new, humanistic translations of Plato: that of the ΠΟΛΙΤΕΙΑ by Chrysoloras and Decembrio (Kues 178), the translations by Leonardo Bruni and Rinuccio d'Arezzo (in Kues 177), and that of the ΝΟΜΟΙ by George of Trebizond (Harl. 3261). Moreover, he naturally also had Macrobius' *Somnium Scipionis* (in Kues 177 and Harl. 2652), Apuleius (Brussels Cod. 10056–74), Proclus' *Elementatio theologica* in the translation of William of Moerbeke (Kues 195), the *Theologia Platonis* (in two versions: Strasbourg Cod. 84, a fragment in

Nicholas' own hand; Kues 185, a translation by Petrus Balbus), and John Scottus' ΠΕΡΙ ΦΥCΕWC ΜΕΡΙCΜΟΥ (London, British Library Add. 11035). The cardinal had collected, studied, and annotated nothing less than a "Bibliotheca Platonica Medii Aevi."[177] Two of these works interested Nicholas of Cusa so much that he had them translated:[178] "Parmenidem Platonis, magna veluti ardens siti, de graeco in latinum fecit converti; item Platonis Theologiam a Proclo . . . scriptam" ("As if he were burning with a great thirst, he had Plato's *Parmenides* rendered from Greek into Latin; the same is true for the *Theology of Plato*, written by Proclus").

Nicholas' fundamental notion of *coincidentia oppositorum* (which is experienced in *docta ignorantia*) seems to be a modern synthesis of all these Neoplatonic texts: a rational variant of apophasis, in which the insight that our highest knowledge of God can be no more than a recognition of our lack of knowledge is presented not as "being struck dumb by the arcanum, but as the intellectual experience of the coincidence of contradictory statements" (". . . ein Verstummen vor dem Geheimnis, sondern die Denkerfahrung vom Zusammenfallen widersprechender Aussagen").[179] Nevertheless, according to Nicholas' own testimony, his famous thought *preceded* his passion for collecting Neoplatonic texts:[180]

[Nicholas:] "God, who is truth, is, as the object of understanding, comprehensible in the highest degree, and, because of his comprehensibility, which is elevated above all else, he is again incomprehensible. Thus only learned ignorance and comprehensible incomprehensibility remain as the true path on which to approach him."

And I [the student]: "Splendid, master. Although this observation, which you have disclosed in 'learned ignorance,' has resulted not from any study, but rather through God's gift, even so you have, no doubt, consulted many of the old sages, in order to find out if that same idea is reflected in them all. If you remember anything of that which you read, add it to this, I beg of you."

And he: "I confess, my friend, that I had not yet seen Dionysius nor a single one of the old theologians when I received this idea from above; rather, it was only then that I plunged into the writings of the scholars, compared and found nothing else, in different forms, than that which had been revealed to me."

Nicholas of Cusa had of course become acquainted with Dionysius' basic idea in its late medieval form—for example, in Gerson's *De mystica Theologia* and Bonaventure's *Itinerarium mentis ad deum*, which, with notes from the *Timaeus*, Proclus' *Theologia Platonis* and commentary on the *Parmenides*, are contained in a manuscript on which Nicholas had already worked even as a student in Heidelberg, Padua, or Cologne.[181] Dionysius himself came into his intellectual purview some time later. He even acquired a Greek manuscript of his works; but he worked not with it, but rather with the Latin translations, primarily with that of his Florentine friend Ambrogio Traversari.

One of the great fifteenth-century revivers of Platonic philosophical thought had not drunk deeply from the original Greek sources for which the Humanists thirsted so intensely. Despite his collection of Graecolatina and even Greek manuscripts, despite his friendship with Humanists and his participation in the embassy to Constantinople and in the Florentine unification council, Nicholas' knowledge of Greek remained insignificant.[182] Without question he had the ability and opportunity to become a distinguished authority not only on Greek philosophy, but also on the Greek language; but it apparently seemed more practical to him and, with respect to his philosophical and theological interests, also a more direct route to his goals, to take the Latin translations as the basis of his work. The consciousness of form and the aesthetics of the newly approaching age also seem to have passed him by without much effect. Even in the particulars of his dealings with Greek, he remained a man of the Middle Ages.

One of the great concerns of the Humanists was the representation of the Graeca of the Latin writers, especially those of late antiquity. When Niccoli made a copy of Aulus Gellius in Florence, Traversari had "to draw the Greek letters neatly in the text for him."[183] The gradual solution of this problem is a chapter in itself—also in the history of early printed works.[184] The great stylists of the time were also fond of ornamenting their own humanistic Latin with scattered Greek words, taking the practice of late antiquity as a model here: Traversari imitated his Lactantius, and Erasmus his Jerome. On the basis of the early editions of the works of Nicholas of Cusa, it seems that he also made use of the humanistic ornamentation. If one verifies the Graeca in the incunabula, however, they are found in their Latin form, which is certainly also their original form. The Greek terms were for Nicholas, as for the philosophers and theologians of the late Middle Ages in general, a terminological supplement to the Latin language, and not a display of the *utriusque linguae peritus*.

Like Augustine, Nicholas of Cusa did not need to be a Greek scholar in order to follow the path of Platonic philosophy. Although he already stood firmly in the world of Humanism, he still faced toward the philosophical spirit of the late Middle Ages. The new *philological* Zeitgeist, however, called more for the *vir trilinguis*, the new Jerome. And since he appeared in the double form of Erasmus and Reuchlin, only the one, religious, aspect of the Zeitgeist was satisfied. The perspectives had simply been shifted too far.

When Dionysius the Areopagite disappeared from the purview of Greek studies in the West, he was replaced not by the Bible, but rather by Homer, and the Greek Fathers saw their rank contested by the ancient

Greek epic poets, historians, and dramatists. Had the Greek of the "Paleologan Renaissance" not already devoted themselves to antiquity and styled themselves "Hellenes" and the Turks "Persians"! The Western Humanists studied under these Greeks and, when the generation of the Greek emigrants which had escaped to Italy after the catastrophe of 1453 had disappeared, they passed on their antiquarian spirit.

Now there was no longer a living Greek counterpart to the West; in its place appeared a classical Greece which was conjured up and which endured for several centuries. The study of Greco-Roman antiquity as a uniform, distant, and ideal cultural complex replaced the medieval traditions of the school and the translator. And Western eyes have grown so accustomed to the marble against the blue of a shadowless day—or to the plaster cast under museum light—that they see nothing in the mosaic of late antique and medieval Graecolatina—which certainly has its dark zones, but also its living trail of gold—nothing, that is, but the Dark Ages.

Sigla and Abbreviations

AB	*Analecta Bollandiana*
Abh.	Abhandlungen der Akademie (Gesellschaft der Wissenschaften, etc.), phil.-hist. Klasse
Acta SS	*Acta Sanctorum*
AHDL	*Archives d'Histoire Doctrinale et Littéraire du Moyen Âge*
BHG	*Bibliotheca Hagiographica Graeca*
BHL	*Bibliotheca Hagiographica Latina*
BN	Biblioteca Nazionale, Bibliothèque Nationale
BZ	*Byzantinische Zeitschrift*
CC	*Corpus Christianorum*, Series Latina
CLA	E. A. Lowe [and B. Bischoff], *Codices Latini Antiquiores*
Clavis PG	*Clavis Patrum Graecorum*
Clavis PL	*Clavis Patrum Latinorum*
Clm	Codex latinus monacensis
CSEL	*Corpus Scriptorum Ecclesiasticorum Latinorum*
DA	*Deutsches Archiv*
GCS	*Die griechischen christlichen Schriftsteller der ersten Jahrhunderte*
MBK	*Mittelalterliche Bibliothekskataloge Deutschlands und der Schweiz*
MGH	*Monumenta Germaniae Historica*
Migne PG	J. P. Migne, *Patrologia Graeco-Latina*
Migne PL	J. P. Migne, *Patrologia Latina*
NA	*Neues Archiv*
RB	*Revue Bénédictine*
SB	Sitzungsberichte der Akademie (Gesellschaft der Wissenschaften, etc.), phil.-hist. Klasse
TU	*Texte und Untersuchungen zur Geschichte der altchristlichen Literatur*
⟨ ⟩	to be added to the documented Latin or Greek text
/ / /	erased letters in manuscripts

Notes

Notes to Author's Preface

1. Cf. the various essay competitions of the Académie des Inscriptions et Belles-Lettres, reported on in Chapter I; I might also add that the Turin Academy proposed the topic "Hellenism in Italy" for such a competition in 1870, but received no entries; see Ambroise Firmin-Didot, *Alde Manuce et l'hellénisme à Venise* (Paris 1875), p. xxv.

2. Harald Weinrich, "Thirty Years after Ernst Robert Curtius' Book, *Europäische Literatur und lateinisches Mittelalter*," *The Romanic Review* 69 (1978), 266.

3. Walter Berschin, "Griechisches im lateinischen Mittelalter," in *Reallexikon der Byzantinistik*, ed. Peter Wirth (Amsterdam 1969/70), I, cols. 227–304.

Notes to Chapter I

1. Ludwig Traube, *Einleitung*, p. 135.

2. According to the famous words of Bernard of Chartres, which John of Salisbury passed on: "Dicebat Bernardus Carnotensis nos esse quasi nanos gigantium humeris insidentes, ut possimus plura eis et remotiora uidere, non utique proprii uisus acumine aut eminentia corporis, sed quia in altum subuehimur et extollimur magnitudine gigantea" ("Bernard of Chartres said that we are as dwarfs sitting upon the shoulders of giants, so that we can see more and farther than they, not at all because of the clarity of our own sight nor by our own height, but because we are borne up to the heights and elevated by the great size of the giants"); *Metalogicon* III 4, ed. C. C. I. Webb (Oxford 1929), p. 136 (*Migne PL* 199, col. 900).

3. Valentin Rose, *Anecdota Graeca et Graecolatina*, II, 163. Cf. the method still employed by G. Voigt in accounting for the medieval transmission of ancient literature: "Das Bücherabschreiben war gemeinhin nur ein dürres Handwerk, von der Ordensregel bald geboten, um durch friedliche Beschäftigung die rohe Sitte zu brechen, um die Musse schwächlicher Brüder zu füllen oder um dem Kloster einen Erwerb zuzuwenden, bald nur gestattet, in andern Fällen auch wieder verboten. Wurden dann in den berühmten Häusern der Benedictiner zu Monte Cassino, Cluny, St. Gallen oder Fulda neben den theologischen, Mess- und Gebetbüchern auch einmal klassische Werke copirt, so geschah es nach dem Gebote des Abtes oder es war vielleicht auch die spielende Liebhaberei des Bruders selbst. Immer aber blieb es bei dem todten Buchstaben. Oft auch, während der vornehme Abt mit dem Falken auf der Hand durch die Felder strich, zu Turnieren und Hoffesten zog oder beim schlemmerischen Mahle den Possenreissern zuschaute, während die Brüder umherschlenderten oder ein müssiges Gespräch durch Wein belebten, verstaubten und verrotteten die Bücher in der dunkelsten und feuchtesten Zelle . . ." ("The transcription of books was generally nothing more than a sterile task, sometimes required by monastic rule in order to break the raw habits [of monks] through peaceful occupation, in order to fill the leisure time of frail brothers, or to bring earnings to the monastery; sometimes it was no more than tolerated, in other cases even forbidden anew. If in addition to theological texts, mass and prayer books, an occasional classical work was copied at that time in the famous Benedictine houses of Monte Cassino, Cluny, St. Gall, or Fulda, this was done as a result of the abbot's orders, or it was perhaps even the playful fancy of one of the brothers himself. But they always remained no more than lifeless letters. And often, while the noble abbot strolled through the fields with a falcon on his hand, journeyed to tournaments or court fes-

tivals, or was entertained by jesters at his gourmet table, while the friars dawdled about or animated their idle chatter with wine, the books rotted and collected dust in the darkest and dampest of cells . . ."); *Die Wiederbelebung des classischen Alterthums*, I, 8 f. The fantasies of the first segment of this statement had been rendered inappropriate by the appearance of Wattenbach's *Schriftwesen im Mittelalter* (1871) at the latest. The second part reproduces the humanistic topos of justification for plundering sorties into the ancient libraries.

4. Cf. Sabbadini, *Il metodo degli umanisti*, pp. 17 ff.

5. Siegmund gives a concise survey of the bilinguals up to the twelfth century in *Die Überlieferung der griechischen christlichen Literatur*, pp. 24–32. The article "Bibeltext des NT" by C. v. Tischendorf and O. v. Gebhardt, *Realencyklopädie für protestantische Theologie und Kirche*, 3rd ed. (Leipzig 1897), II, 728 ff., presents information concerning the significance of the textual history of the New Testament bilinguals.

6. Cambridge, University Library Nn. II. 41.—F. H. Scrivener, *Bezae Codex Cantabrigiensis* (Cambridge 1864).—*Codex Bezae Cantabrigiensis . . . sumptibus academiae phototypice repraesentatus* (Cambridge 1899).—H. Quentin, "Le Codex Bezae à Lyon au IXe siècle. Les citations du nouveau testament dans le martyrologe d'Adon," *RB* 23 (1906), 1–25. E. A. Lowe, "The Codex Bezae at Lyons," *Palaeographical Papers*, pp. 182–86. *CLA*, II, 140 (2nd ed.).

7. Oxford, Bodleian Library Laud. gr. 35.—A. F. C. von Tischendorf, *Codex Laudianus sive Actus Apostolorum Graece et Latine* (Leipzig 1870). *CLA*, II, 251 (2nd ed.), with bibliographical references, pp. 54 and 60. See also B. Bischoff and J. Hofmann, *Libri Sancti Kyliani. Die Würzburger Schreibschule und die Dombibliothek im VIII. und IX. Jahrhundert* (Würzburg 1952), pp. 90 f.

8. Dresden, Sächsische Landesbibliothek A 145^b.—C. F. Matthaei, *XIII epistolarum Pauli codex Graecus cum versione Latina veteri vulgo antehieronymiana olim Boernerianus nunc bibliothecae electoralis Dresdensis* (Meißen 1791; editio minor, Meißen 1818).—*Der Codex Boernerianus . . . in Lichtdruck nachgebildet*, ed. the Königliche Öffentliche Bibliothek in Dresden (Leipzig 1909), with an excellent "Introduction" by Alexander Reichardt on the more recent history of the manuscript and the research concerning it.

9. Cambridge, Trinity College B. 17. 1.—F. H. Scrivener, *An Exact Transcript of the Codex Augiensis* (Cambridge/London 1859). A more recent description by M. R. James, *The Western Manuscripts in the Library of Trinity College* (Cambridge 1900), I, 544–46. Cf. A. Holder and K. Preisendanz, *Die Reichenauer Handschriften*, 2nd ed. (Wiesbaden 1973), III/2, pp. 21 f., 247, 272, 291 (the latter two pages with bibliog. refs.).

10. In the preface to his edition of the Psalter of the Septuagint, A. Rahlfs notes, concerning the bilingual Psalters: "Diese Hss. sind interessant, weil sie lehren, wie man sich im Abendlande um den griech. Psalter bemüht hat. Aber in vorliegender Ausgabe habe ich sie bis auf wenige Stellen . . . ganz beiseite gelassen, da ich mir von ihrer Benutzung einen die Mühe lohnenden Nutzen nicht versprechen kann. Denn sie sind nicht nur recht inkorrekt geschrieben, sondern oft ist auch ihr griech. Text durch den dabei stehenden lateinischen beeinflußt, zuweilen in höchst sonderbarer Weise" ("These manuscripts are interesting because they demonstrate how the Greek Psalter aroused interest even in the West. In the present edition, however, I have . . . omitted them entirely except for a few passages, since I could not hope to benefit from their use in proportion to the labor involved. For not only are they quite incorrectly written, but often the Greek text is also influenced by the adjacent Latin, occasionally in quite peculiar fashion"); *Psalmi cum Odis*, Septuaginta Societas Scientiarum Gottingensis 10 (Göttingen 1931), p. 32. H. J. Frede characterizes the bilinguals as a "museum" of textual history": "Sie sind nicht die Kanäle, in denen eine lebendige Textüberlieferung und -entwicklung stattfindet. Ihr griechischer Text wird wie ein Museumsstück von Handschrift zu Handschrift vererbt . . ." ("They are not the channels through which a living textual transmission and development flowed. Their Greek text is passed on from manuscript to manuscript as if a museum piece . . ."); *Altlateinische Paulus-Handschriften* (Freiburg 1964), p. 91; cf. also ibid., pp. 50 ff. and 80 ff., specifically on the "Codex Boernerianus" and "Codex Augiensis."

11. Montfaucon, *Palaeographia Graeca*, pp. 217 ff. and 235 ff. The "Sedulius Psalter" is now in Paris, Arsenal Cod. 8407; the "Glossarium Laudunense" is in Laon, Bibl. Municipale Cod. 444.

12. E. Martène and U. Durand, *Veterum Scriptorum et Monumentorum Historicorum, Dogmaticorum, Moralium Amplissima Collectio* (Paris 1724), I, cols. 817 ff. and 827 ff.

13. L. A. Muratori, Diss. XLIV: "De literarum fortuna in Italia post annum Christi MC," in *Antiquitates Italicae Medii Aevi* (Milan 1740), III, cols. 883–998, esp. cols. 918 and 938.

14. Cf. Minio-Paluello, *Opuscula*, p. 565. Gradenigo's *Lettera* were not accessible to me. The *Ragionamento*, a book of 176 pages in octavo, is also rare; C. Gidel gives a detailed review of the book in *Nouvelles études*, pp. 225–44. The Academy address of D. M. Manni, *Dell'antichità oltre ogni credere delle lettere greche in Firenze* (Florence 1762), should also be mentioned here. He offers sundry pieces of antiquarianism concerning Greek in the high Middle Ages in the West: he discusses (p. 9), for example, whether the Florentines mentioned in Dante's *Paradiso* XVI 88 f., and named *Greci* ("Io vidi gli Ughi, e vidi i Catellini / Filippi, Greci") "non fossero in origine dalla Grecia venuti" ("could not have originally come from Greece"). With reference to the Florentine librarian A. M. Bandini he also mentions, however, the testimony of the Greco-Latin manuscripts.

15. G. Tiraboschi, *Storia della Letteratura Italiana* (Florence 1806), III/1, 334 ff. (high Middle Ages).

16. The specific subtitle of the book is *Recherches critiques sur l'âge et l'origine des traductions latines d'Aristote et sur des commentaires grecs ou arabes employés par les docteurs scolastiques*. The *Göttingische gelehrte Anzeigen* hailed the book in a detailed review as "eine der interessantesten Erscheinungen in der Literatur des Tages" ("one of the most interesting publications in the literature of the day"), 1819, item 142, pp. 1409–24. The German translation of the first edition by Adolf Stahr (Halle 1831) is valuable in its own right. In 1843 Charles Jourdain published a revised second edition of the work of his prematurely deceased father.

17. Minio-Paluello, *Opuscula*, p. 573.

18. P. Courcelle, *Les lettres grecques*, p. xi, n. 3, was the first to give particulars concerning this work, from which he took Renan's less than fortunate dictum "Rome retira ses légions, *la Gréce retira sa langue*, et le Moyen-Âge commença" ("Rome withdrew her legions, *Greece withdrew its language*, and the Middle Ages began").

19. Previously Cramer had already given special attention to medieval Greek studies in his *Geschichte der Erziehung und des Unterrichts in den Niederlanden während des Mittelalters* (Stralsund 1843); the *dissertatio* had manifold connections to that work. The work of André-Joseph-Ghislain le Glay, *Lettres* (deux) *sur l'Étude du grec dans les Pays-Bas avant le quinzième siècle*, 2nd ed. (Cambrai 1828), was not accessible to me.

20. Cramer, pars altera, p. 60. M. Coens, "Utriusque linguae peritus," *AB* 76 (1958), 118 ff.

21. *Hodoeporicon* (*um*) was in common use for "account of a journey"—from Jerome's *epist.* 108 ("Vita Paulae"), 8: "neque enim hodoeporicon eius diposui scribere" ("for I have not planned to write an account of the journey"), and *De viris illustribus*, c. 80 (elogium of Lactantius).

22. Egger, *L'hellénisme*, p. 44. However, he comments pertinently (p. 48): "un seul auteur grec paraît avoir été vraiment connu, au moins dans les cloîtres: c'est Denys l'Aréopagite" ("a single Greek writer seems to have been truly known, at least in the monasteries: that is Dionysius the Areopagite").

23. *L'hellénisme*, p. 49. On this "Collegium Constantinopolitanum" see Altaner, *Zeitschrift für Missionswissenschaft* 18 (1928), 194 ff. (bibliog.).

24. Gidel, *Nouvelles études*, p. 100. The verses of Columban are quoted here according to the edition by G. S. M. Walker, *Sancti Columbani Opera* (Dublin 1957), p. 194.

25. Courcelle, *Les lettres grecques*, 2nd ed. (1948), p. xi, mentions Gidel in the same breath with Egger and Sandys ("livres vieillis ou trop généraux"), by which Gidel's work is indeed rated too low; in its wealth of material, it surpasses the corresponding pages in Egger; with respect to information concerning the medieval study of Greek, Gidel's work is not lacking as much in critique and criteria as Sandys' *History of Classical Scholarship*.

26. See also Gardthausen's posthumous article "Die griechische Schrift des Mittelalters im Westen Europas," in *Byzantinisch-neugriechische Jahrbücher* 8 (1931), whose errors and inaccuracies demand a word of caution here.

27. Traube, "O Roma nobilis," p. 361.

28. On Greek in the Latin Middle Ages, see *Einleitung*, pp. 83–91, in the section devoted to the medieval Latin language—an inappropriate placement, since for Traube the topic actually belonged to the history of philology, which of course did not and does not yet exist as a distinct discipline. A reference to Traube's important review of Sandys' *History of Classical Scholarship* (in *Deutsche Literaturzeitung* 25 [1904], cols. 133–36) is lacking in the cited passage from *Einleitung* (p. 83, n. 1).

29. Steinacker, "Die römische Kirche und die griechischen Sprachkenntnisse des Frühmittelalters," in *Festschrift für Theodor Gomperz* (Vienna 1902), pp. 324–41; repr. in *Mitteilungen des Österreichischen Instituts für Geschichtsforschung* 62 (1954), 28–66. Here Steinacker not only added to his 1902 publication, but also prefaced it with a valuable review of the research—"Die Griechischkenntnisse des Abendlandes im Frühmittelalter." Steinacker still based the second version of the article primarily on conciliar acts and papal letters and accorded translations from the ascetic-monastic and liturgical domains too little consideration. The translations from the *Vitas patrum* by Roman clergy, mentioned below in Chapter VI, had by this time decisively altered the overall picture traced by Steinacker.

30. *Reallexikon der Byzantinistik*, ed. P. Wirth (Amsterdam 1969/70), vol. I: "Abendland und Byzanz": I. "Das abendländische Kaisertum," by W. Ohnsorge, cols. 126–69; II. "Kirchenmusik," by E. Jammers, cols. 169–227; III. "Literatur und Sprache": A. "Literatur" and "Griechisches im lateinischen Mittelalter," by W. Berschin, cols. 227–304; "Abendländisches in Byzanz," by A. Lumpe, cols. 304–45; B. "Sprache," by H. and R. Kahane, cols. 345–640; IV. "Mönchtum" by J. L. van Dieten, cols. 641–.

Notes to Chapter II

1. Ekkehart IV, *Casus S. Galli*, c. 94, ed. G. Meyer von Knonau (St. Gall 1877), p. 344; ed. H. F. Haefele (Darmstadt 1980), p. 194.

2. Bischoff, "The Study of Foreign Languages in the Middle Ages," *Mittelalterliche Studien*, II, 227–245.

3. *Apc* 1, 8; 21, 6; 22, 13.

4. Hilarius of Poitiers, *Prologus in librum psalmorum* 15; Migne PL 9, col. 241. Cf. Augustine, *Ennarationes in psalmos* LVIII 1, 1 and *In Iohannis evangelium tractatus* CXVII 4.

5. Prudentius, *Apotheosis*, vv. 381–85.

6. Isidore, *Etymologiae* IX 1, 3; on this point see also Borst, *Der Turmbau*, II/1, 454.

7. Allgeier, in *Biblica* 24 (1943), 282.

8. R. E. McNally, "The 'Tres linguae sacrae' in Early Irish Bible Exegesis," *Theological Studies* 19 (New York 1958), 395–403.

9. On Andrew of St. Victor, see Smalley, *The Study of the Bible*, pp. 112 ff.

10. Cf. Pertusi in *Atti del Convegno di Studi "Dante e la cultura veneta"* (1966). Dante knew that Gregory the Great had occupied himself with Dionysius' theory of angels; since the great author-pope had a different conception of the hierarchy of angels than did Dionysius, Dante depicted him sympathetically as the saint [*der Selige*] who "had to smile at himself, as soon as he opened his eyes in this heaven":

> E Dionisio con tanto disio
> a contemplar questi ordini si mise
> che li nomò e distinse com'io.
> Ma Gregorio da lui poi si divise
> onde, si tosto come li occhi aperse
> in questo ciel, di sè medesmo rise.
>
> *Divina Commedia, Paradiso* XXVIII 130–35

On Dante's quotations from Aristotle and Ptolemy, see Groppi, *Dante traduttore*, pp. 48–92.

11. The transition from Greek to Latin as the liturgical language is discussed by T. Klauser in *Miscellanea G. Mercati* (Rome 1946), I, 467–82, and J. A. Jungmann, *Missarum Sollemnia*, 5th ed. (Vienna/Freiburg/Basel 1962), I, 65 (bibliog.). Caspari's excursus "Über den gottesdienstlichen Gebrauch des Griechischen im Abendlande während des früheren Mittelalters" is still the fundamental study of the subject; in *Quellen zur Geschichte des Taufsymbols* (1875). Brou briefly lists the liturgical Graeca in *Sacris Erudiri* 1 (1948) and 4 (1952).

12. On the liturgical *Kyrie eleison*, see Jungmann, *Missarum Sollemnia*, I, 430 ff.

13. Cf. the article "Trishagion" in Riemann, *Musiklexikon, Sachteil*, 12th ed. (Mainz 1967), p. 987 (bibliog.). "Trishagion" in the Greek liturgy is treated by H. J. Schulz, *Die byzantinische Liturgie* (Freiburg 1964), pp. 46 ff.

14. Caspari, "Über den gottesdienstlichen Gebrauch," pp. 466 ff. J. Brinktrine, *Die feierliche Papstmesse und die Zeremonien bei Selig- und Heiligsprechungen* (Freiburg 1925), pp. 14 ff.

15. *Sacramentarium Fuldense*, Universitätsbibliothek Göttingen, cod. theol. 231; ed. by A. Richter and A. Schönfelder (Fulda 1912), p. 339.

16. Milan, Biblioteca Ambrosiana Z 52 sup., according to Caspari, p. 483, n. 18.

17. Cf. G. Iversen, *Tropes de l'Agnus Dei*, Corpus Troporum 4 (Stockholm 1980), pp. 30, 59 ff., 293 f. and pls. 1–4; C. M. Atkinson, "'O amnos tu theu': The Greek Agnus dei in the Roman Liturgy from the Eighth to the Eleventh Century," *Kirchenmusikalisches Jahrbuch* 65 (1981), 7–30.

18. In the Latin liturgy for 6 January, there are two such *Hodie* antiphons, translated from Greek (or composed in CHMЄPON style), which function as synopses of the ancient threefold significance of the Epiphany:

> Ad Magnificat antiphona:
> Tribus miraculis ornatum diem sanctum colimus
> hodie stella magos duxit ad praesepium
> hodie vinum ex aqua factum est ad nuptias
> hodie a Ioanne Christus baptizari voluit
> ut salvaret nos.

[We honor the holy day, adorned by three miracles; today the star led the Magi to the manger; today water was turned into wine at the wedding; today Christ wished to be baptized by John, that we might be saved.]

While the *Magnificat* antiphon enumerates the three mysteries commemorated on this day in the form of a three-tiered illumination, the *Benedictus* antiphon unites the three motifs in a new "typological" interpretation. Through its magnificent rhythms, this antiphon also produced a new linguistic harmony:

> Ad Benedictus antiphona:
> Hodie caelesti sponso iuncta est ecclesia
> quoniam in Iordane lavit Christus eius crimina
> currunt cum muneribus magi ad regales nuptias
> et ex aqua facto vino laetantur convivae.

[Today the church is united with the heavenly bridegroom because Christ washed away its sins in the Jordan; the Magi hasten with gifts to the regal wedding; and the guests rejoice in the water made wine.]

Cf. Hesbert, *Corpus Antiphonalium Officii*, III, nos. 5184 and 3095; Baumstark, in *Die Kirchenmusik* 10 (1909), 153–60, and *Oriens Christianus* III/11 (1936), 163 ff.; Wellesz, *Eastern Elements*, pp. 141–49; W. Nyssen, *tribus miraculis* (privately printed, Cologne 1971).

19. Manchester, John Rylands Library Pap. 470; still described as a "Christian prayer" by C. H. Roberts, *Catalogue of the Greek and Latin Papyri in the John Rylands Library* (Manchester 1938), III, no. 470, pp. 46 f.; identified by F. Mercenier, "L'antienne Mariale Grecque la plus ancienne," *Le Muséon* 52 (1939), 229–35. A more recent bibliography in Barré, *Prières anciennes*, p. 20. Cf. Hesbert, *Corpus Antiphonalium Officii*, III, no. 5041.—On the Madonna of Mercy, see C. Belting-Ihm, "*Sub matris tutela*," Abh. Heidelberg (1976).

20. A.-G. Martimort, "Origine et signification de l'alléluia de la messe romaine," *Kyriakon*, Festschrift Johannes Quasten (Münster 1970), II, 811–34.

21. Hesbert, *Corpus Antiphonalium Officii*, IV, no. 6444.—L. Brou, "L'alléluia gréco-latin 'Dies sanctificatus,'" *Revue Grégorienne* 23 (1938) and 24 (1939), passim. Wellesz, *Eastern Elements*, pp. 36–44.

22. On the Latin translation of the *Hymnos Akathistos*, see Chapter VIII under St. Denis. On the *Grates nunc omnes* as a contrafactum of a stanza by Romanos Melodos see H.

Spanke, "Aus der Vorgeschichte und Frühgeschichte der Sequenz," *Zeitschrift für deutsches Altertum* 71 (1934), 1–39, here p. 23. See Chapter XI concerning Greek in the Beneventan liturgy.

23. "Ordo XLI," M. Andrieu, *Les Ordines Romani du Haut Moyen Âge* (Louvain 1956), IV, 319 f. (he proposes a Celtic origin for the rite).

24. *Migne PL* 131, cols. 850 f.

25. F. Dornseiff, *Das Alphabet in Mystik und Magie*, 2nd ed. (Leipzig/Berlin 1925), esp. pp. 19 f. and 74 f.

26. *Plato latinus*, IV, 28, line 12.

27. C. Vogel and R. Elze, *Le Pontifical Romano-Germanique du Xe siècle* (Rome 1963), I, 136.

28. Ostrogorsky, in *BZ* 46 (1953), 157 (rev. of Ohnsorge, *Das Zweikaiserproblem*).

29. *Registrum Gregorii* III 63, *MGH Epistolae*, I, 225.

30. Nicholas I, *epist.* 88 (to Emperor Michael III, in 865), ed. E. Perels, *MGH Epistolae*, VI, 459 f. According to Perels, Anastasius Bibliothecarius was the pope's secretary: *Papst Nikolaus I. und Anastasius Bibliothecarius* (Berlin 1920), pp. 248 f. and 307.

31. Classen, in *Karl der Große*, I, 606. Beck, *Kirche und theologische Literatur*, pp. 306 ff.; his summary of the history of the *filioque* dispute is brief and informative.

32. "Tercia ordinacio est quod quicunque plus quam unum filium habuerit, alterum ad scolas ponere teneatur, latinis litteris imbuendum; et nisi quod littera greca una de princip(al)ibus tribus extat, quibus tripliciter crucifixi domini nostri titulus est inscriptus, consulerem salubriter, prout estimo, et prudenter ut omnino illa littera deleretur." "Brocardus," *Directorium ad passagium faciendum*, *Recueil des Historiens des Croisades. Documents Arméniens* (Paris 1906), II, 471. According to the editors, the author was the archbishop of the Dominican Mission, William Adam, who also wrote the scarcely less chauvinistic and malicious *De modo Sarracenos extirpandi* (1316/18). On the author, see T. Kaeppeli, *Scriptores Ordines Praedicatorum Medii Aevi* (Rome 1975), II, 81 f.

33. Isidore, *Etymologiae* I 3, 8–9. See below, Chapter VI, sec. 2. On the symbol Υ, see W. Harms, *Homo viator in bivio. Studien zur Bildlichkeit des Weges* (Munich 1970).

34. Cf. the comprehensive eight-page primer which Johann Froben printed for his son Johann Erasmus Froben (Basel 1516): *ALPHABETUM GRAECUM. Oratio dominica, Angelica Salutatio, Symbolum Apostolorum, Christi Seruatoris apud Matthaeum evangeliographum decreta, cum hoc genus aliis, Graece et latine. In usum iuventutis Graecarum adyta literarum subingressurae*, with the father's beautiful preface (again repr. in A. Horawitz, "Beiträge zur Geschichte des Griechischen in Deutschland," *Berliner Studien für classische Philologie und Archaeologie* 1 [1884], 440). Numerous *Alphabeta Graeca* of the sixteenth century are mentioned by Wilhelm Meyer, *Henricus Stephanus und die Regii Typi Graeci*, Abh. Göttingen (1902).

35. Cf. Bischoff, *Mittelalterliche Studien*, II, 255 ff.

36. L. Traube, *Nomina Sacra. Versuch einer Geschichte der christlichen Kürzung* (Munich 1907), pp. 161–64. W. M. Lindsay, *Notae Latinae* (Cambridge 1915), p. 403. Concerning such Grecistic formulations, on the analogy of ΙHC and ΧϷC, as s̄p̄c and ēp̄c (*spiritus, episcopus*), see Traube, p. 166, and D. Bains, *A Supplement to Notae Latinae* (Cambridge 1938), pp. 6 f.

37. A representative example of writing Western names in Greek script is found in the document Wolfenbüttel, Niedersächsisches Staatsarchiv 6 Urk. 10, a copy from the high Middle Ages of a papyrus document of Pope John XII from 968, which the abbess from the Ottonian dynastic house had the pope issue to her as ΓHϷBHϷΓϵ *uenerabili abbatisse*. A facsimile in the exhibition catalogue *Die Heiratsurkunde der Kaiserin Theophanu*, p. 18.

38. A famous Western scribal inscription in Greek script is Ο ΚΥϷΙC CЄϷBΑΝΑΟC ΑΙΝΟΙHCЄΝ (the last word emended) in the "Codex Amiatinus," Florence, Biblioteca Laurenziana Amiat. 1, fol 86ᵛ; facsimile in K. Zangemeister and W. Wattenbach, *Exempla codicum latinorum litteris maiusculis scriptorum* (Heidelberg 1876), pl. 35. On the much-discussed CЄϷBΑΝΑΟC = *Servandus*, see most recently E. A. Lowe, *English Uncial* (Oxford 1960), pp. 10 ff.

39. In Codex Messina, Biblioteca Universitaria gr. 112, saec. XIV, the Gospel of Mark is written in Sicilian dialect, with the Greek alphabet; cf. C. Tagliavini, *Le origine delle lingue*

neolatine, 6th ed. (Bologna 1972), pp. 517 ff. (bibliog.). Reference from Helmut Berschin.

40. For examples of Greek quire signatures in Latin manuscripts of various periods, see: the "Codex Theodosianus," Vat. Reg. lat. 886, saec. VI (*CLA*, I, 110); the two oldest manuscripts of John Scottus' ΠΕΡΙ ΦΥϹΕΩϹ ΜΕΡΙϹΜΟΥ, Reims 875 and Bamberg Philos. 2/1 [H J. IV. 5], both saec. IX; the homilary Karlsruhe Aug. XVI, Reichenau saec. X¹ (A. Holder, *Die Reichenauer Handschriften* [Leipzig 1906], I, 46), whose quires probably received their Greek signatures on the model of the bilingual "Codex Paulinus Augiensis" (cf. M. R. James, *The Western Manuscripts in the Library of Trinity College* [Cambridge 1900], I, 35); the Augustinian manuscript Orléans 163 (140) from Fleury, saec. XI (*Catalogue Général, Départements* [Paris 1889], XII, 77).

41. Certainly too much significance is given the dedication rite when Dornseiff (*Das Alphabet in Mystik und Magie*, p. 74, n. 2) remarks: "At various times during the Middle Ages, this prescription prevented the Greek alphabet from being forgotten in the West." On the *epistola formata*, see Chapter IV.

42. Traube, *MGH Poetae*, III, 822 ff., and Bischoff, *Mittelalterliche Studien*, II, 253 ff., have collected the scattered traces of the Greek *minuscule* in the West up to the High Middle Ages. Addenda to that list are: a Greek minuscule alphabet of the eleventh century in the Piedmont school manuscript Milan, Bibl. Ambrosiana M 79 sup., fol. 26ʳ, and the most prominent example of Greek minuscule at this period, the *majestas titulus* of the "Codex Aureus Epternacensis" in the Germanisches Nationalmuseum, Nuremberg; see below, Chapter X, sec. 5.

43. For this reason Bischoff also calls this ⊃⊂ "abendländisches M." It also occurs bisected as ⊃⋅ or ⊂ for N. On ⊃⊂ in England, see Chapter VI.

44. Cf. Isidore, *Etymologiae* I 19, *De figuris accentuum*: ". . . ΔΑϹΕΙΑ quod interpretatur aspiratio, id est ubi *H* littera poni debet, tali figura notatur ⊢. ΨΙΛΗ quod interpretatur siccitas sive purum, id est ubi *H* littera esse non debet, tali nota ostenditur ⊣. Quorum duorum accentuum figuram Latini ex ipsa littera aspirationis [*H*] fecerunt" (". . .ΔΑϹΕΙΑ, which is understood as an aspiration, i.e., where one should place an *H*, is marked by the symbol ⊢. ΨΙΛΗ, which is understood as simple or plain, i.e., where no *H* ought to be, is shown by the symbol ⊣. The Latins derived the symbols for the two accents from the letter of aspiration [*H*]"). According to Bischoff (*Mittelalterliche Studien*, II, 256), ⊢ occurs until the twelfth century.—It is open to question whether the symbol ꙋ, which appears in the ninth century (frequently for the diphthong *uo* in southern German names), is borrowed from Greek script (ꙋ = OY). Cf. B. Bischoff, *Paläographie des römischen Altertums und des abendländischen Mittelalters* (Berlin 1979), p. 156. A very early example of ꙋ is found in Abbeville, Bibliothèque Municipale 4, fol. 102ʳ, where the ligature, however, represents *VO* in *QVONIAM QVIDEM*; W. Köhler, *Die karolingischen Miniaturen*, vol. II: *Die Hofschule Karls des Großen* (Berlin 1958), pl. 40.

45. Pseudo-Philoxenus, ed. G. Goetz and G. Gundermann, *Corpus Glossariorum Latinorum*, II, 3–212, from Paris, BN lat. 7651, saec. IX; see pp. vii–xix on this manuscript and the lost manuscript from St. Germain. The "Greek" order of this glossary is noteworthy: A B G D . . . (∾ Λ Β Γ Δ . . .).

46. On the "Hermeneumata," see Goetz in his article "Glossographie" in Pauly-Wissowa, *Realencyclopädie*, VII/1, cols. 1437 f., and Marrou's very graphic presentation in *Histoire de l'éducation*, pp. 386 f. On the survival of the "Hermeneumata" in the Middle Ages, see Bischoff, *Mittelalterliche Studien*, II, 261. The dialogue passages of the "Hermeneumata" were regularly leveled out to vocabulary lists by the medieval tradition; cf. *Corpus Glossariorum*, III, 635–59: "Colloquia Quattuor emendata" (bibliog.). The "Hermeneumata Vaticana," which unfold a colorful vocabulary, conforming to the order of creation, had a Christian author (*Corpus Glossariorum*, III, 421–38). According to Traube (in *BZ* 3 [1894], 604 ff.; repr. *Vorlesungen und Abhandlungen* [Munich 1920], III, 205 ff.), the author was "ein Spätling, ein Bücherwurm . . . ein Ire" ("a latecomer, a bookworm . . . an Irishman"). Yet his reasons for the attribution of the work to the early Middle Ages and especially to an Irishman are weak.

47. Bischoff, *Mittelalterliche Studien*, II, 271 ff.

48. A much-discussed passage in Venantius Fortunatus gives a brief list of such Greek *rhetorica*: "Nam ΕΠΙΧΕΙΡΗΜΑΤΑ, ΕΛΛΕΙΨΕΙϹ, ΔΙΑΙΡΕϹΕΙϹ, ΠΑΡΕΝΘΕϹΕΙϹ et

reliqua orationibus dialectici . . . satagentes suis affectare syrmatibus soliti sunt adsuere vel proferre"; *Vita S. Martini*, Epistola ad Gregorium, *MGH Auctores antiquissimi* (1881), IV/1, 293.

49. Cf. the impressive theological vocabulary of Greek origin which Nicolas du Mortier collected and explained in his *Etymologiae Sacrae Graeco-Latinae* (Rome 1703).

50. Cf. *Mittellateinisches Wörterbuch* (Munich 1967), I, s.v. "anthropus."

51. B. Schwineköper, *Der Handschuh im Recht, Ämterwesen, Brauch und Volksglauben* (Berlin 1938), pp. 13 f.

52. O. Prinz, "Zum Einfluß des Griechischen auf den Wortschatz des Mittelalters," *Festschrift Bischoff*, p. 3 and n. 9 (bibliog.)

53. J. Schneider, "Gesellschaft und Sprache im Spiegel des mittellateinischen Wortschatzes," in V. Gortan and J. Schneider, eds., *Zum Nachleben des Lateinischen in der Feudalgesellschaft* (Berlin 1969), pp. 17 f.

54. O. Prinz, "Mittelalterliches im Wortschatz der Annalen Bertholds von Reichenau," *DA* 30 (1974), 488–504, here p. 492.

55. Cf. P. Lehmann, "Mittelalterliche Büchertitel," in *Erforschung des Mittelalters* (Stuttgart 1962), V, 1–93 passim. On *Polypticum*, etc., see the beginning of G. Roth's "*Polyptychon* der Abtei des heiligen Remigius" (diss., Bonn 1917). There is no study which deals specifically with Greek book titles in the Middle Ages. For the ancient period, see K.-E. Henrikson, *Griechische Büchertitel in der römischen Literatur* (Helsinki 1956).

56. One may refer to the appropriate articles of the *Mittellateinisches Wörterbuch* in particular; in general, to the comprehensive new survey by Kahane in the section "Sprache—Byzantinische Einflüsse im Westen" of the article "Abendland und Byzanz" in *Reallexikon für Byzantinistik*, I, cols. 345–498, esp. the "Katalog der Byzantinismen," cols. 366 ff.

57. Prinz, *Festschrift Bischoff*, p. 13.

58. *De differentiis et societatibus graeci latinique verbi*, ed. H. Keil, *Grammatici Latini*, V, 595–655; cf. Bischoff, *Mittelalterliche Studien*, II, 259. Brunhölzl (*Geschichte der lateinischen Literatur des Mittelalters*, p. 468) ascribes the excerpt to John Scottus; the ascription is, however, only a speculation (cf. Traube, "O Roma nobilis," p. 355), which must still be proved.

59. Macrobius remarks at the end of the section "De figuris" that there were practically no prepositions in (classical) Latin which, when linked to the verb, did not alter the meaning; on the other hand, a Greek verb with a prepositional prefix often meant the same as the verb without a prefix; ed. Keil, *Grammatici Latini*, V, 601. The tendency toward verbs with redundant prefixes (*circum-ad-stare* in the old *Canon Missae*!) is a well known development in the Latin of late antiquity and the Middle Ages: does it reflect colloquial speech, or is it a Greek influence?

60. Paris, BN lat. 528, fol. 134^{rv}, ed. H. Omont, *Bibliothèque de l'École des Chartes* 42 (1881), 126 f. The repository of the manuscript was St. Martial's in Limoges. K. Neff (*Die Gedichte des Paulus Diaconus* [Munich 1908], p. 58) conjectures that the text is evidence for Paulus Diaconus' Greek instruction at the court of Charlemagne: "Since the text is in accord with a considerable number of Paulus' poems, specifically with those which were written at Charlemagne's court, one can assume that its source was Paulus and his teaching." Bischoff argues, on the contrary (*Mittelalterliche Studien*, II, 259): "Since the sole manuscript was written in St. Denis at the beginning of the ninth century, one might well consider the Greeks who were working for Hilduin to be its source." Which conjecture is the more daring?

61. From MS Laon 444, ed. Eckstein, *Analecten zur Geschichte der Pädagogik*, pp. 3–11; on the sources and further dissemination of this so-called Greek "grammatical primer" of the Irish, see Bischoff, *Mittelalterliche Studien*, II, 259 f. and n. 76.

62. From MS Vienna 114, ed. Krause, *Jahrbuch der Österreichischen Byzantinischen Gesellschaft* 5 (1956), 8–15.

63. W. O. Schmitt, "Lateinischer und griechischer 'Donatus,'" *Philologus* 123 (1979), 97–108.

64. "Quoniam uero compertum tibi dixisti me grecas litteras absque ⟨ad⟩miniculo preceptoris adsecutum . . . pandam tibi, quo pacto mediocrem huiusce lingue peritiam adeptus sum. Psalterium habui grecum mihi per religionis institutionem admodum familiare. Id igi-

tur cum latino conferre incepi atque notare [tum] singula tum uerba, tum nomina et reliquas orationis partes, quidque singula significarent mandare memorie ac uim uerborum omnium tenere, quantum fas erat. Ibi profectus inicium sumpsi. Transiui deinceps ad euangelia, epistulas Pauli actusque apostolorum hisque familiariter obversatus sum; habent enim satis magnam uerborum copiam suntque omnia translata fideliter ac diligenter nec inconcinne. Postmodum uero et gentilium libros uidere uolui, eosque [haud] facile intellexi . . ." (to Francesco Coppola, podestà and capitano in Bologna); ed. L. Bertalot, "Zwölf Briefe des Ambrogio Traversari," *Römische Quartalschrift* 29 (1915), *91–*106, here *102; later edited by Sabbadini (*Il metodo degli umanisti*, p. 19), who emends the text drastically. And, without consideration of Sabbadini's conjectures, the text appears again in Bertalot's *Studien zum italienischen und deutschen Humanismus* (Rome 1975), I, 262.

65. The fame of having brought out the first catalogue of Greek manuscripts (in fact the first printed catalogue of manuscripts of any kind) belongs to the imperial city of Augsburg. The city council published the *Catalogus graecorum manuscriptorum librorum Augustanae bibliothecae*, compiled by Hieronymus Wolf, in 1575.

66. See below, Chapter XI, n. 58.

67. I. Stone, "Libraries of the Greek Monasteries in Southern Italy," in J. W. Thompson, *The Medieval Library*, 2nd ed. (New York 1957), pp. 330–37. Borsari, *Il monachesimo bizantino nella Sicilia e nell'Italia meridionale prenormanne*, pp. 80–88.

68. P. Canart, "Le livre grec en Italie méridionale sous les règnes Normand et Souabe," *Scrittura e Civiltà* 2 (1978), 103–62. G. Cavallo, "La cultura italo-greca nella produzione libraria," in *I bizantini in Italia*, ed. B. Pugliese Carratelli (Milan 1982), pp. 497–612.

69. Montfaucon, *Palaeographia Graeca*, pp. 214 f. In 1934 Bischoff rediscovered the papyrus sheets which had disappeared into the library of the British collector Thomas Phillipps; cf. Bischoff, "Ein wiedergefundener Papyrus und die ältesten Handschriften der Schule von Tours," *Mittelalterliche Studien*, I, 6–16. After further wanderings through private collections, the papyri are now in Paris, BN suppl. gr. 1379. Cf. P. Gasnault and J. Vezin, *Documents comptables de Saint-Martin de Tours à l'époque mérovingienne* (Paris 1975), esp. pp. 20–22: "Les papyrus grecs" (rev. by F. Magistrale, *Studi Medievali* III/19 [1978], 1071–74).

70. M. R. James, *A Descriptive Catalogue of the Manuscripts in the Library of Corpus Christi College* (Cambridge 1912), no. 183, pp. 439 f.; idem, in *The Library* IV/7 (1927), 339. Bischoff, *Mittelalterliche Studien*, I, 209 (with new evidence).

71. Perhaps the now-fragmentary purple Psalter, written in gold and silver ink, Zurich, Zentralbibliothek RP 1; cf. K. Preisendanz, "Reginbert von der Reichenau," *Neue Heidelberger Jahrbücher* (1952–53), 4 f.

72. Paris, BN gr. 437; H. Omont, "Manuscrit des oeuvres de S. Denys l'Aréopagite envoyé de Constantinople à Louis le Débonnaire," *Revue des Études Grecques* 17 (1904), 230–36 (with plate).

73. Wilhelmus Medicus brought the Dionysius manuscript BN gr. 933, from Constantinople to Paris around 1167. In the high Middle Ages, the evangelary BN gr. 375, written around 1021 by a Greek in Cologne (?), also came to St. Denis (cf. below, n. 77). In 1408 Emperor Manuel II, in memory of his visit in 1401, had Manuel Chrysoloras present the monastery with a magnificent manuscript of the Areopagite's works (Paris, Musée du Louvre Ivoires A 53); cf. the exhibition catalogue *Byzance et la France médiévale*, no. 51, pp. 32 f. St. Denis also preserved the famous papyrus letter of a Greek emperor from the ninth century (see below, Chapter VII, n. 49).

74. The "Codex Simeonis," Trier Domschatz no. 72 (143. F), a Greek lectionary, "saec. X/XI mit lateinischen Beischriften, die zeigen daß es mindestens schon saec. XIII im Abendland war" ("of the tenth/eleventh century, with Latin annotations, which show that it was already in the West by the thirteenth century"); Siegmund, *Die Überlieferung*, p. 29, n. 1. Yet R. M. Steininger (*Codex S. Simeonis* [Trier 1834], p. xii) believed, on the basis of a dated entry, "circa finem saeculi XVI. codicem adhuc in Oriente fuisse" ("that the codex was still in the East around the end of the sixteenth century").

75. Vienna, theol. gr. 336. Siegmund (*Die Überlieferung*, p. 29) mistakenly lists the codex as bilingual. A detailed evaluation in *Beschreibendes Verzeichnis der illuminierten Handschriften in Österreich*, VIII/4: P. Buberl and H. Gerstinger, *Die byzantinischen Handschriften* (Leipzig 1938), II, 35–38 (bibliog.). In response to my inquiry, Professor

Mazal and Dr. Irblich confirm that ΓΕΙΕШΝ was not a later addition (for the name of another warrior-saint), and that the title page with the picture of St. Gereon was one of the original constituents of the manuscript.

76. The Greek Psalter Vat. Reg. gr. 13, which scholars have attributed to an Irishman of the tenth century (H. Stevenson, *Codices Manuscripti Graeci Reginae Svecorum*, p. 9, and Schneider, in *Biblica* 30 [1949], 489–91), in fact turns out to be a Greek manuscript of a provincial type, probably written in the West; it was also used by the Latins by the twelfth century at the latest, but it is by no means an Irish product.

77. Paris, BN gr. 375, fol. 193ʳ (διὰ χειρός Ἡλίου πρεσβυτέρου καὶ μοναχοῦ σπιλεότου). Various entries point to St. Denis as the repository, among them *Odo divina permissione abbas beati Dionysii in Francia* and *sanctus dionysius* in runic script! The manuscript has been described by Montfaucon, *Palaeographia Graeca*, pp. 292 f., and H. Omont, *Fac-similés des Manuscrits grecs datés de la Bibliothèque Nationale* (Paris 1890), pl. 14. Devreesse (*Les manuscrits grecs de l'Italie méridionale*, p. 33, n. 9) considers the scribe to have been an Italo-Greek of the "Campanian School" and wonders whether the identification of κάστρο δὲ Κολονίας with Cologne is necessary. On Italo-Greek ornamentation, see most recently Grabar, *Les manuscrits grecs*, pp. 46 f. The manuscript has been at St. Denis since the high Middle Ages.

78. M. R. James, *The Western Manuscripts in the Library of Emmanuel College* (Cambridge 1904), pp. 133 ff. James' dating of the manuscripts to the twelfth century is difficult to understand.

79. Barbour, in *The Bodleian Library Record* 6 (1958), 401 ff.

80. James, "Greek Manuscripts in England before the Renaissance," *The Library* IV/7 (1927), 337–53; Stephens, "Greek Manuscripts in England during the Middle Ages," in *The Knowledge of Greek in England in the Middle Ages* (1933), pp. 118–30.

81. On eight of the Latino-Greek Codices Virgiliani, see R. Seider, "Beiträge zur Geschichte und Paläographie der antiken Vergilhandschriften," in *Studien zur antiken Epos*, ed. H. Görgemanns and E. A. Schmidt (Meisenheim 1976), pp. 129–72, esp. 157 ff. Also taken into consideration are the editions which did not contain a running Vergil text, but rather only excerpted and glossed words and lexical groups bilingually. (On their significance in the history of education, see the remarks of V. Reichmann, *Römische Literatur in griechischer Übersetzung* [Leipzig 1943]). The corresponding numbers in *CLA* are: II, 137 (Cambridge); II, 227 and III, 367 and X, p. 38 (Manchester, Milan, Cairo); III, 290 (Florence); III, 306 (Milan); X, 1522 (Vienna); X, 1570 (Cairo); XI, 1651 (El Cerrito, Calif.); XI, 1652 (New York). A ninth Vergilius Latino-graecus from the Egyptian Museum of the Berlin Stiftung Preußischer Kulturbesitz is discussed by H. Maehler, "Zweisprachiger Aeneiscodex," *Actes du XVᵉ congrès international de Papyrologie* (Brussels 1979), II, 18–41 (bibliog.). Fragments of two bilingual papyrus codices of Cicero in *CLA*, II, 224 and 226 (both Manchester).

82. In making this statement, one must take into account the Eastern Empire's loss of Egypt, which was the home of most Latino-Greek books of late antiquity (cf. Bataille, "Les glossaires gréco-latins," *Recherches de papyrologie* 4, pp. 161 ff.). The southeastern corner of the Mediterranean basin retained its multilingual character: see, for example, the fourteenth-century pentaglott Psalter of the monastery of St. Macarius in the Desert of Sketis, which combines texts in Ethiopian, Syrian, Bohairic, Arabic, and Armenian, in five parallel columns, into a genuinely pentecostal page format (now Rome, Biblioteca Vaticana Barb. or. 2; facsimile in the exhibition catalogue *Il libro della Biblia* [Rome 1972], pl. 45). The Latin and Greek traditions were clearly ruptured in that geographical area by Islam.

83. Siegmund (*Die Überlieferung*, pp. 24–32) presents an overview of the bilingual biblical manuscripts up to the twelfth century; on the bilingual Psalters, see Allgeier, in *Biblica* 24 (1943), 263 f., and Schneider, in *Biblica* 30 (1949), 479 ff., who presents supplementary material. No comprehensive and reliable list exists. Rahlfs (*Verzeichnis der griechischen Handschriften des alten Testaments*) describes the Greco-Latin Psalters in the entries for their respective libraries. A historical study of the Pauline bilinguals is presented by Frede's *Altlateinische Paulus-Handschriften*. On Dionysius Exiguus' bilingual collection of canon law, see Chapter IV.

84. Up until now, however, the late medieval bilingual of the Acts of the Apostles in Cod. Vat. Ottobon. gr. 258 has not been taken into account; cf. E. Feron and F. Battaglini, *Codices manuscripti graeci Ottoboniani* (Rome 1893), p. 145.

85. The "Codex Claromontanus" is Paris, BN gr. 107 and 107 A and 107 B. A fragment is in the Stadtarchiv in Mengeringhausen (Waldeck), ed. V. Schultze, *Codex Waldeccensis* [Munich 1904]; cf. Frede, *Altlateinische Paulus-Handschriften*, pp. 47 f.

86. Vat. Ottobon. gr. 258; cf. Feron and Battaglini (as in n. 84). Allgeier (in *Biblica* 24 [1943], 263) dates it saec. XIV; likewise, the opinion of Professor Elze in Rome is "in keinem Fall humanistisch" (information supplied to me through the good offices of Dr. Goldbrunner).

87. On Florence, Biblioteca Laurenziana Cod. Plut. XVII 13, see Schneider, in *Biblica* 30 (1949), 486 f. In addition to the supplement containing the Cantica, the codex includes Greek translations of Latin prayers (such as *Ave Maria* and *Salve Regina*) from the high Middle Ages.

88. Vat. Urb. lat. 9, described by C. Stornajolo, *Codices Urbinates Latini* (Rome 1902), I, 16.

89. On the change of opinion concerning the bilinguals, see Allgeier, in *Biblica* 24 (1943), 264 f.: "The mere existence of these MSS, as well as their number and the fact that they extend from the sixth century up to the high Middle Ages and are distributed throughout Western Europe, tells an important story in itself. Their significance becomes clear, however, only when one examines their historical function. This question interested earlier scholars very little; their major interest was in the importance of the MSS for textual criticism. One tried to get as close to the oldest form of the sacred text as possible. . . . Paul de Lagarde undertook the collation of the Bamberg and later the Basel Psalter with high expectations. Indeed later, A. Rahlfs, while he was collating for the Göttingen Septuagint, finally acknowledged his resignation to the fact that the variants contributed so little to the objective envisioned for them that he omitted them from the apparatus. Precisely those characteristics of the bilinguals which render them of little value for the textual critic make them valuable for the textual historian and present a first-class source for the scholar who wishes to trace the distribution of the knowledge of Greek in the Latin West before the humanistic period. Yet one must try to judge the bilinguals with the standards of their times. There is no evidence that they aimed at a modern form of Septuagint scholarship. On the other hand, the bilinguals had their place in the schools, in theological studies, and in language study." One must add *and in their representational character*.

90. Vienna, Österreichische Nationalbibliothek theol. gr. 137, saec. XI, two columns: on the left the Greek translation by Pope Zacharias in Greek minuscule, on the right the Latin original of Gregory the Great in Beneventan script; according to G. Cavallo, from Dalmatia.

91. Cf. F. Dölger, *Facsimiles byzantinischer Kaiserurkunden* (Munich 1931).

Notes to Chapter III

1. ". . . hortor omnis, qui facere id possunt, ut huius quoque generis laudem iam languenti Graeciae eripiant et transferant in hanc urbem sicut reliquas omnis, quae quidem erant expetendae, studio atque industria sua maiores nostri transtulerunt"; *Tusc.* II 2, cited by Boethius, *In Topica Ciceronis* V (*Migne PL* 64, col. 1152).

2. "A sermone Graeco puerum incipere malo, quia Latinum, qui pluribus in usu est, vel nobis nolentibus perbibet, simul quia disciplinis quoque Graecis prius instituendus est, unde et nostrae fluxerunt" ("I would prefer a boy begin with Greek, because Latin, which has a wide usage, he acquires from us even without any effort on our part, and again because he is also to be instructed first in the Greek disciplines, from which ours derive"); Quintilian, *Institutio oratoria* I 1, 12. On Greco-Latin education in antiquity, see Marrou, *Histoire de l'education*, pp. 379 ff.

3. Cf. Horace's words to Maecenas: *Docte sermones utriusque linguae*; *Carm.* III 8, 5. During the Middle Ages, it was said of very many people that they were *utriusque linguae peritus*, most often incorrectly; cf. Coens, in *AB* 76 (1958), 118–50.

4. In his *Claudius*, Suetonius transmitted three such letters of Augustus; the Middle Ages also knew them from Suetonius. An instructive facsimile of a page from the best surviving manuscript of the *Vitae Caesarum*, with two of the three letters mentioned, is printed in the "Editio maior" of M. Ihm (Leipzig 1907), pl. 1: Paris, BN lat. 6115, fol. 72[r], saec. IX[1], from St. Martin's in Tours (Carolingian minuscule, Graeca in majuscule).

5. Apuleius translated Plato's ΦΑΙΔΩΝ and wrote, among other works, *De Platone et*

eius dogmate. The *Asclepius*, in which Hermes Trismegistus appears as a teacher, was ascribed to him.

6. Cf. O. Weise, *Die griechischen Wörter im Latein* (Leipzig 1882).

7. Cf. J. M. Heer, *Die versio latina des Barnabasbriefes und ihr Verhältnis zur altlateinischen Bibel* (Freiburg 1908), p. xlv. Efforts to translate ϹⲰⲦⲈⲢ go back to Cicero; J. B. Hofmann and A. Szantyr, *Lateinische Syntax und Stilistik*, 2nd ed. (Munich 1972), pp. 741 f. (bibliog.).

8. "*Salvare* et *Salvator* non fuerunt haec latina, antequam veniret Salvator; quando ad Latinos venit, et haec latina fecit"; Augustine, *sermo* 299, 6 (*Migne PL* 38, col. 1371).

9. J. Schrijnen, *Charakteristik des Altchristlichen Latein* (Nijmegen 1932). C. Mohrmann, *Die altchristliche Sondersprache in den Sermones des hl. Augustin* (Nijmegen 1932). The "Scandinavian school" prefers to subsume the phenomenon under the concept of "Late Latin"; cf. E. Löfstedt, *Late Latin* (Oslo 1959).

10. Cf. Courcelle, *Les lettres grecques en occident*, 2nd ed. (Paris 1948), pp. 3–36.

11. Minio-Paluello, *Aristoteles latinus*, I/1–5, pp. lxxvii ff.; edition of the Pseudo-Augustinian *Tractatus de categoriis Aristotelis*, ibid., pp. 133–75.

12. Courcelle, *Les lettres grecques*, pp. 198 ff.

13. Acts 17:28. On this "Hellenistic speech about true knowledge of God," see M. Dibelius, "Paulus auf dem Areopag," in *Aufsätze zur Apostelgeschichte*, 4th ed. (Göttingen 1961), pp. 29–70.

14. Jerome, *epist.* 70. On "Antike Zitate in der Bibel," cf. K. Borinski, *Die Antike in Poetik und Kunsttheorie* (Leipzig 1914), I, 117 f.

15. *Epistulae Senecae ad Paulum et Pauli ad Senecam [quae vocantur]*, ed. C. W. Barlow (Rome 1938). Jerome, *De viris illustribus*, c. 18.

16. Gidel, *Nouvelles études*, p. 36.

17. Marius Victorinus translated the ⲈⲒⲤⲀⲄⲰⲄⲎ of Porphyry. See Courcelle, *Les lettres grecques*, pp. 122 ff., on Manlius Theodorus.

18. Ed. Waszink, *Plato latinus*, vol. IV.

19. M. J. Le Guillou, "Hilaire entre l'Orient et l'Occident," in *Hilaire de Poitiers, évêque et docteur* (Paris 1968), pp. 39–58.

20. Jerome quotes Hilary (in addition to Evagrius' vita of Anthony) as an example of free, sense-oriented [*sinngemäßes*], not literal, translation: "Dies me deficiet, si omnium, qui ad sensum interpretati sunt, testimonia replicavero. Sufficit in praesenti nominasse Hilarium confessorem, qui homilias in Iob et in psalmos tractatus plurimos in latinum vertit e graeco nec adsedit litterae dormitanti et putida rusticorum interpretatione se torsit, sed quasi captivos sensus in suam linguam victoris iure transposuit" ("I could not recall in a day all the works translated according to the sense. At the moment, it suffices to mention Hilarius the Confessor, who translated homilies on Job and many treatises on the Psalms from Greek into Latin, and he did not adhere to the sleepy letter nor torment himself with the affected translation of boorish texts, but by right of the conqueror, he transferred the meaning, as if a captive, into his own language"); *epist.* 57, 6 (*CSEL* 54, 511 f.).

21. W. Bulst, *Hymni latini antiquissimi LXXV Psalmi III* (Heidelberg 1956), pp. 8 f. and 31 ff.

22. The translator's prologues of Rufinus and Jerome are the focus of H. Marti's *Übersetzer der Augustin-Zeit. Interpretation von Selbstzeugnissen* (Munich 1974).

23. Rufinus' translations are listed (with a full bibliography) by Winkelmann in *Kyriakon*, Festschrift Johannes Quasten, II, 532, n. 1. On the *Admonitio S. Basilii ad filium spiritualem*, there cited as one of Rufinus' translations, see above, sec. 4. The prefaces to the translations have been collected by M. Simonetti, *Tyranni Rufini opera*, CC 20 (Turnhout 1961), pp. 231–85. H. Görgemanns and H. Krapp have recently edited the translation of ⲠⲈⲢⲒ ⲀⲢⲬⲰⲚ (Darmstadt 1976).

24. Rufinus' translation of Eusebius' *Ecclesiastical History* is edited by T. Mommsen, *GCS* 9/2 (Leipzig 1908); Rufinus' continuation of the work is edited in *Migne PL* 21, cols. 463–540.

25. A recent edition by V. Buchheit, *Tyranni Rufini librorum Adamanti Origenis adversus haereticos interpretatio* (Munich 1966). Buchheit's judgment of "Rufin als Fälscher des Dialogs" ("Rufinus as a falsifier of the dialogue"), pp. xxxv ff., is qualified by Görgemanns in his review of the edition (in *Theologische Revue* 64 [1968], 406–8).

26. *Migne PL* 103, cols. 487–554; cf. F. Lau, "Die beiden Regeln des Basilius," *Zeitschrift für Kirchengeschichte* 44 (1925), 13–29. On the dissemination of the translated regulae, see J. Gribomont, *Histoire du texte des Ascétiques de S. Basile* (Louvain 1953), "La version latine de Rufin," pp. 95–107; and Leclercq, in *Le millénaire du mont Athos*, II, 72 ff. Cf. K. Zelzer, "Die Rufinusübersetzung der Basiliusregel im Spiegel ihrer ältesten Handschriften," in *Latinität und alte Kirche*, Festschrift Rudolf Hanslik (Vienna/Cologne/Graz 1977), pp. 341–50; and "Zur Überlieferung der lateinischen Fassung der Basiliusregel," in *TU* 125 (Berlin 1981), 625–35. Evagrius' (d. 399) *Sententiae* also belong to the instructions in monastic life translated by Rufinus; cf. A. Wilmart, "Les versions latines des Sentences d'Évagre pour les vierges," *RB* 28 (1911), 143–53.

27. *Migne PL* 21, cols. 387–462. It was long disputed whether the "History of the Egyptian Monks" was a Latin composition or a translation from Greek; nowadays the latter theory is generally accepted; cf. Altaner-Stuiber, *Patrologie*, pp. 238 f.

28. On the translation of Basil's homilies, see M. Huglo, in *RB* 64 (1954), 129–32; Altaner, *Kleine patristische Schriften*, pp. 409–15. Two of Basil's homilies not translated by Rufinus are edited by D. Amand, in *RB* 57 (1947), 12–81. The translation dates to late antiquity (Paris, BN lat. 10593, saec. VI; *CLA*, V, 603). On the translation of Gregory's homilies, see esp. M. M. Wagner, *Rufinus the Translator: A Study of His Theory and Practice as Illustrated in His Version of the Apologetica of St. Gregory Nazianzen* (Washington 1945), and A. C. Way, in *Catalogus Translationum et Commentariorum* (1971), II, 127–34.

29. Ed. B. Rehm and F. Paschke, *GCS* 51 (Berlin 1965).

30. The reference is to the *Praecepta Pachomii*, eleven letters of Pachomius, one letter of Pachomius' student, Theodore, and a *Liber S. Orsiesii* by one of Pachomius' successors; ed. A. Boon, *Pachomiana latina* (Louvain 1932).

31. On Jerome as a translator, see most recently Winkelmann in *Kyriakon*, II, 538 ff., and G. Q. A. Meershoek, *Le latin biblique d'après Saint Jérôme* (Nijmegen/Utrecht 1966); reviewed by B. Löfstedt, in *Gnomon* 41 (1969), 362 ff.

32. A. Penna, *Principi e carattere dell'esegesi di S. Girolamo* (Rome 1950), pp. 12–15.

33. Cf. Blatt, in *Classica et Mediaevalia* 1 (1938), 218.

34. W. Süss, "Das Problem der lateinischen Bibelsprache," *Historische Vierteljahrschrift* 27 (1932), 7.

35. Winkelmann gives an overview of the late antique translations of Greco-Christian literature in *Theologische Literaturzeitung* 92 (1967), cols. 229 ff.; see also M. Bogaert, "Fragment inédit de Didyme l'Aveugle," *RB* 73 (1963), 9 ff.

36. *Hermae Pastor*, Vetus latina interpretatio, ed. A. Hilgenfeld (Leipzig 1873). In addition to this older, widely circulated translation, there is a more recent one which is preserved only in Cod. Vat. Pal. lat. 150, saec. XIV; ed. O. v. Gebhardt and A. Harnack, *Hermae Pastor* (Leipzig 1877).

37. S. Lundström, *Irenäusübersetzung* (Lund 1943); idem, *Neue Studien zur lateinischen Irenäusübersetzung*, Lunds Univ. Årsskrift, n.s., I 44 (Lund 1948); idem, "Das Katenenfragment mit Irenäus, Adv. Haer. V 24, 2 f.," *Zeitschrift für Kirchengeschichte* 69 (1958), 111 f., and *Lexicon errorum interpretum Latinorum* (Uppsala 1983).

38. In Chalcidius, "la phrase . . . donne l'impression d'être écrite par un auteur médiéval plutôt qu'antique" ("the phraseology . . . gives the impression of having been written by a medieval rather than ancient writer"); Blatt, in *Classica et Mediaevalia* 1 (1938), 226.

39. A. Wilmart, "Une version latine inédite de la vie de saint Antoine," *RB* 31 (1914–19), 163–73. G. Garitte, *Un témoin important du texte de la Vie de S. Antoine* (Brussels/Rome 1939). H. Hoppenbrouwers, *La plus ancienne version latine de la vie de S. Antoine* (Nijmegen 1960). G. Bartelink, "Observations de critique textuelle sur la plus ancienne version latine de la vie de Saint Antoine par Saint Athanase," *RB* 81 (1971), 92–95.

40. H. Rosweyde, *Vitae Patrum*, 2nd ed. (Antwerp 1628), p. 35 (*Migne PL* 73, col. 125). The text tradition of the prologue in Jerome's epistolary deviates slightly (*epist*. 57, 6; *CSEL* 54, 511). Marti documents parallel passages (*Übersetzer*, p. 146).

41. H. Dörrie, *Passio SS. Machabaeorum* (Göttingen 1938), p. 124. Dörrie did not know G. Morin, "L'opuscule de soi-disant Hégésippe sur les Machabées," *RB* 31 (1914–19), 83–91, where arguments are adduced that the *Passio SS. Machabaeorum* and the excerpt from Josephus' *De bello Iudaico* known by the title *Hegesippus* could have the same author—according to Morin, possibly the Spaniard Dexter, a contemporary of Jerome; cf. *De viris illustribus*, prol. and c. 132.

42. Ed. E. Amand de Mendieta and S. Y. Rudberg, *TU* 66 (Berlin 1958); see also Altaner, *Kleine patristische Schriften*, pp. 437–47.

43. "Ego enim non solum fateor, sed libera voce profiteor me in interpretatione Graecorum absque scripturis sanctis, ubi et verborum ordo mysterium est, non verbum e verbo, sed sensum exprimere de sensu" ("For I not only confess but acknowledge openly and freely that, in my translations of Greek texts—except for the Holy Scriptures, where even the order of the words is a divine mystery—I translate sense for sense and not word for word"); *epist*. 57, 5 (*CSEL* 54, 508). Jerome invokes Cicero's principles of translation. After a comparison of Cicero's and Jerome's practical application of translation principles, Cuendet concludes: Cicero "a donné à la traduction l'éclat d'une oeuvre originale, l'autre a réalisé une copie fidèle" ("has given the translation the brilliance of an original work, the other has produced a faithful copy"); in *Revue des études latines* 11 (1933), 400. Cf. Meershoek, *Le latin biblique d'après Saint Jérôme*, pp. 4 ff. Cf. also Marti, *Übersetzer*, pp. 188 ff.

44. C. H. Turner [and A. Souter], *The Oldest Manuscript of the Vulgate Gospels* (Oxford 1931), p. xxx.

45. B. Bischoff, "Zur Rekonstruktion der ältesten Handschrift der Vulgata-Evangelien," *Mittelalterliche Studien*, I, 101 ff.

46. Traube, *Deutsche Literaturzeitung* 25 (1904), cols. 134 f., and (the second quotation) *Einleitung*, pp. 90 f.

47. *Adversus Pelagianos* I 14 and *epist*. 14, 11. Cf. Courcelle, *Les lettres grecques*, pp. 47–78. On the vacillation of Jerome's attitude toward pagan antiquity, in spite of this comment, see H. Hagendahl, *Latin Fathers and the Classics* (Göteborg 1958), pp. 309 ff.

48. *Epist*. 23, 3.

49. Cf. Courcelle, *Les lettres grecques*, esp. pp. 129 ff.; Altaner, *Kleine patristische Schriften*, esp. pp. 137 ff. (bibliog.); H.-I. Marrou, *Saint Augustin et la fin de la culture antique* (Paris 1938–49), pp. 27–46 and 631–37 (suppl.); G. Villa, "Osservazioni sulla cultura greca di S. Agostino," *Bolletino Storico Agostiniano* 28 (1952), 19–21. Cf. also Marti, *Übersetzer*, pp. 20–25: "Das Ende der Zweisprachigkeit und Augustin."

50. *Confessiones* VIII 6.

51. *In Iohannis evangelium tractatus* IX 14 (*CC* 36, 98).

52. *In Iohannis evangelium tractatus* X 12 (*CC* 36, 108).

53. *Enarrationes in psalmos* XCV 15 (*CC* 39, 1352 f.).

54. Bischoff, "Die lateinischen Übersetzungen und Bearbeitungen aus den Oracula Sibyllina," *Mittelalterliche Studien*, I, esp. 150 f. and 154 f. Lactantius' *Divinae Institutiones* are transmitted in a splendid fifth-century uncial codex (among others): Bologna, Biblioteca Universitaria 701 (*CLA*, III, 280). The medieval repository of the codex was the imperial monastery of Nonantola; cf. R. W. Hunt, "The Medieval Home of the Bologna Manuscript of Lactantius," *Medievalia et Humanistica* 14 (1962), 3–6.

55. *De civitate dei* XVIII 23 (*CSEL* 40/2, 297 f.). Augustine did not himself translate these verses from Greek. It was initially in a poor translation that he read the verses, which according to Bischoff are possibly still preserved in two early Carolingian manuscripts (*Mittelalterliche Studien*, I, 155 ff.). The translation inserted into *De civitate dei* is probably a revised version of this first translation. It is metrically better than the first and generally reproduces the acrostic of the Greek text. A third translation, whose origin in early medieval England Bulst has made plausible (*Zeitschrift für deutsches Altertum* 75 [1938], 105 ff.), improves on the translation further, in that it includes a translation of seven additional lines, resulting in the acrostic CTAΥΡΟC. Concerning these verses in medieval drama (such as the *Ludus de Antichristo*), see K. Young, *The Drama in the Medieval Church* (Oxford 1933), II, 125–71.

56. "Petimus ergo et nobiscum petit omnis Africanarum ecclesiarum studiosa societas, ut interpretandis eorum libris, qui graece scripturas nostras quam optime tractauerunt, curam atque operam inpendere non graueris. potes enim efficere, ut nos quoque habeamus tales illos uiros et unum potissimum, quem tu libentius in tuis litteris sonas. de uertendis autem in linguam latinam sanctis litteris canonicis laborare te nollem, nisi eo modo, quo Iob interpretatus es, ut signis adhibitis, quid inter hanc tuam et LXX, quorum est grauissima auctoritas, interpretationem distet, appareat." Augustine, *epist*. 28, 2 (*CSEL* 33, 105 f.).

57. Courcelle, *Les lettres grecques*, pp. 192 f.

58. Cf. *Contra Iulianum* I 6, 21 f. (*Migne PL* 44, cols. 654 ff.). In order to refute a passage

from John Chrysostom concerning original sin that Julian of Aeclanum cites in Latin translation, Augustine goes back to the original text and gives his own literal translation.

59. Augustine is "für uns der erste abendländische Denker, bei dem eine Benützung von Übersetzungen nicht-biblischer Werke faßbar wird" ("the first Western philosopher whose use of translations of nonbiblical works becomes tangible for us"; Marti, *Übersetzer*, p. 24).

60. E. von Ivánka, *Plato christianus. Übernahme und Umgestaltung des Platonismus durch die Väter* (Einsiedeln 1964), pp. 189 ff. and 309 ff.

61. *Missale Romanum*, "In commemoratione omnium fidelium defunctorum" (2 Nov.) and "In die obitus seu depositionis defuncti." G. M. Dreves and C. Blume, *Ein Jahrtausend lateinischer Hymnendichtung* (Leipzig 1909), I, 329.

Notes to Chapter IV

1. Von den Brincken, *Nationes Christianorum Orientalium*, pp. 287 ff. and 382 ff. (bibliog.). F. Zarncke, "Der Priester Johannes," Abh. Leipzig 7 (1879), 827–1028, and 8 (1883), 1–186.

2. On this matter, see the works by M. Steinschneider listed in the Bibliography; A. Baumstark, *Geschichte der syrischen Literatur* (Bonn 1923); Laiguel-Lavastine, "Le rôle de l'hérésie de Nestorius dans les relations médicales entre l'Orient et l'Occident," *Archives Internationales d'Histoire des Sciences* 4 (1951), 63–72; I. Opelt, *Griechische Philosophie bei den Arabern* (Munich 1970).

3. Athanasius, *Vita S. Antonii*, c. 44 (*Migne PG* 26, col. 908).

4. *Migne PG* 26, col. 835; Evagrius translated freely, "ad peregrinos fratres" (*Migne PL* 73, col. 125).

5. *Confessiones* VIII 6.

6. On the form *vitas* as subject case (nom. pl.), cf. Batlle, *Die "Adhortationes,"* pp. 7–9 (bibliog.).

7. ἀπόφθεγμα was transcribed *apophthegma* under the influence of Italian Humanists; the ancient and Medieval Latin transcription of φθ is *pth: apopthegma* (or simply *pt*); see Wilhelm Schulze, *Orthographica*, pp. 51 and 74. On the sixth-century Roman and Spanish translations of the *Apophthegmata*, see Chapter VI.

8. Sulpicius Severus, *Dialogi* I 23.

9. *Dialogi* III 17.

10. *Natione Scytha*, according to Gennadius, *De viris illustribus*, c. 62—that is, he most likely came from the area around the mouth of the Danube (*Scythia minor*). Cf. H.-I. Marrou, "La patrie de Jean Cassien," and "Jean Cassien à Marseille," *Patristique et humanisme* (Paris 1976), pp. 345–72; O. Chadwick, *John Cassian*, 2nd ed. (Cambridge 1968).

11. *Conlatio* XIII 5 (*CSEL* 13/2, 365 f.). The Graeca are quite corrupt in the tradition, "which did not begin until the Carolingian period." It is uncertain whether the interpretations introduced by *hoc est* and *id est* are the author's or were incorporated into the text from marginal and interlinear glosses.

12. "Scripsit, experientia magistrante, librato sermone et, ut apertius dicam, sensu verba inveniens et actione linguam movens, res omnium monachorum professioni necessarias . . ."; Gennadius, *De viris illustribus*, c. 62.

13. Courcelle, *Les lettres grecques*, pp. 216–21.

14. Gregory of Tours, *Historiae* VI 6 and VIII 15.

15. *Vita S. Eugendi*, c. 23, *MGH Scriptores rerum Merovingicarum*, III, 165. New edition by F. Martine, *Vie des pères du Jura* (Paris 1968), c. 174, p. 428.

16. *Benedicti regula* LXXIII 5–6.

17. After the model of these religious discussions, *collationes* were also delivered in monasteries; cf. Ekkehart IV, *Casus S. Galli*, c. 36: "Erat . . . consuetudo . . . in intervallo laudum nocturno convenire in scriptorio collationesque tali horae aptissimas de scripturis facere" ("It was . . . customary . . . to assemble in the scriptorium during a pause in nightly prayers and discuss the Scriptures, which was most appropriate for that particular time"); ed. G. Meyer von Knonau (St. Gall 1877), pp. 133 ff.; ed. H. F. Haefele (Darmstadt 1980), p. 80. It was due to Wilhelm Wattenbach (*Schriftwesen im Mittelalter*, 3rd ed. [Leipzig 1896], p. 332) that the inaccurate translation came into circulation that one was occupied there "mit der Collation von Handschriften" ("with the collation of manuscripts")!

18. On the other hand, all three of Jerome's biographies of monks were translated into Greek; cf. W. A. Oldfather, ed., *Studies in the Text Tradition of St. Jerome's "Vitae Patrum"* (Urbana 1943).

19. Bardy, *La question des langues dans l'église ancienne*, p. 18.

20. "Lectiones etiam, quaecumque in ecclesia leguntur, quia necesse est Grece legi, semper stat, qui Siriste interpretatur propter populum, ut semper discant. Sane quicumque hic Latini sunt, id est qui nec Siriste nec Grece noverunt, ne constristentur, et ipsis exponitur eis, quia sunt alii fratres et sorores graecolatini, qui Latine exponunt eis." *Itinerarium Egeriae* (Peregrinatio Aetheriae) XLVII 4, ed. O. Prinz, 5th ed (Heidelberg 1960), pp. 55 ff.; ed. E. Franceschini and R. Weber, *CC* 175 (1965), 89. E. Löfstedt (*Philologischer Kommentar zur Peregrinatio Aetheriae* [Uppsala/Leipzig 1911], p. 338) understands "fratres et sorores" as "monks and nuns."

21. ". . . Hieronymus, cuius eloquium universus occidens sicut ros in uellus expectat"; Orosius, *Liber apologeticus* IV 6 (*CSEL* 5, 608).

22. H. v. Campenhausen, "Die asketische Heimatlosigkeit im altkirchlichen und frühmittelalterlichen Mönchtum," cited here from the essay collection *Tradition und Leben* (Tübingen 1960), p. 300. The review by K. Heussi (*Theologische Literaturzeitung* 57 [1932], cols. 295–97) is an indispensable corrective for several of von Campenhausen's opinions.

23. Texts in M. Rampolla, *Santa Melania giuniore senatrice Romana* (Rome 1905). It is uncertain whether the Greek or the Latin text of the vita is the original.

24. The seminal treatment of Anianus' translation is C. Baur, "L'entrée littéraire de Saint Chrysostome dans le monde latin," *Revue d'Histoire Ecclésiastique* 8 (1906), 249–65; idem, *Saint Chrysostome et ses oeuvres dans l'histoire littéraire* (Louvain/Paris 1907); Siegmund, *Die Überlieferung*, pp. 91–101 (MSS); Altaner, "Altlateinische Übersetzungen von Chrysostomusschriften," *TU* 83, 416–36; cf. *Clavis PL*, 2nd ed., p. 174, nos. 771 f., and (less dependable) *Clavis PG*, pp. 491 ff., esp. p. 651, no. 5130, *Versiones latinae.*—H. Honigmann ("Annianus, Deacon of Celeda," *Patristic Studies* [Rome 1953], 54–58) conjectures that the enigmatic Celeda was in Cyrenaica.

25. Ed. S. Vanderlinden (exclusively from Belgian and Parisian MSS), *Revue des Études Byzantines* 4 (1946), 178–217. The text there labeled A is considered the translation of Avitus of Braga. Avitus' letter of explanation to Bishop Balchonius (Palconius) of Braga contains important information concerning the origin of the Greek and Latin *Revelatio* (ed. Vanderlinden, pp. 188 f.). More recent bibliography in Altaner-Stuiber, *Patrologie*, p. 244.

26. Altaner (*TU* 83, 450–66) favors the interpretation that Jerome refers to the same Avitus in *epist.* 79, 106 and 124; this Avitus can be identified with Avitus of Braga "mit einiger Wahrscheinlichkeit" ("with some measure of probability"). Cf. J. Martin, "Die revelatio S. Stephani und Verwandtes," *Historisches Jahrbuch* 77 (1958), 419–33.

27. *De civitate dei* XXII 8: *De miraculis, quae ut mundus in Christum crederet facta sunt et fieri mundo credente non desinunt* (*CSEL* 40/2, 595 ff., here pp. 607–12). Later the coffin of St. Stephen is supposed to have been transported by mistake from Jerusalem to Constantinople; the Greek account of this occurrence was translated ca. 875 by Anastasius Bibliothecarius; this text is also printed in the addendum to vol. VII of the Maurist edition of Augustine (= *Migne PL* 41 cols. 817–22).

28. Gennadius mentions the discovery of the relics of St. Stephen (or the text on the subject) in no less than three passages of his continuation of Jerome's *De viris illustribus*: under *Orosius* (c. 174), *Lucianus* (c. 181), and *Avitus* (c. 182). The rejection of the text by the so-called *Decretum Gelasianum de libris recipiendis et non recipiendis: Revelatio quae appellatur Stephani: apocrypha* (V 5, 3) did not disrupt the circulation of the text; see E. v. Dobschütz, *Das Decretum Gelasianum, TU* 38/4, pp. 12, 279, and 302 f.

29. *Corpus Iuris Civilis, Digesta*, Const. Tanta c. 21, ed. P. Krüger and T. Mommsen, 9th ed. (Berlin 1902), p. xxvii. "Es gilt den genuinen Wortlaut des Gesetzes zu schützen und zu verhindern, daß eine zweite Fassung entsteht, die mit dem Geltungsanspruch des Originals auftreten und das Original verdrängen könnte. Daher wird nur eine Übersetzung erlaubt, die so wörtlich ist, daß sie nur mit Hilfe der Vorlage brauchbar ist" ("The aim was to preserve the wording of the law and to prevent a second version, which could come forward with the authority of the original and displace it. Thus only one translation was allowed, which was so literal that it could be used only in conjunction with the original"); Allgeier, in *Biblica* 24 (1943), 287; A. Berger, "The Emperor Justinian's Ban upon Commentaries to the Digest," *Bulletino dell'istituto di Diritto Romano* 55/56 (1951), 124–69.

30. Schwartz, in *Philologus* 88 (1933), 245 f.

31. Siegmund (*Die Überlieferung*, pp. 139–61) gives an informative overview. Schwartz (*Acta Conciliorum Oecumenicorum*) and Turner (*Ecclesiae Occidentalis Monumenta Iuris Antiquissima*) have made the material available.

32. Maassen, *Geschichte der Quellen*, pp. 8 ff. Caspar, *Geschichte des Papsttums*, I, 366 f. Schwartz, in *Zeitschrift für Rechtsgeschichte*, Kan. Abt. 25 (1936), 48 ff. and 59 ff.

33. Caspar, *Geschichte des Papsttums*, I, 233.

34. *Acta Conciliorum* I 5, pp. ix–xiv and 5–70. J. Rucker (*Ephesinische Konzilsakten in lateinischer Überlieferung* (Oxenbronn bei Günzburg 1930) is almost impenetrable, but can illustrate the great interest of the Reformation and Counter-Reformation in Greek codices with conciliar acts; for instance, the interest in the codex from the Pforzheim Reuchlin Library, which, as an "anscheinend ständig wanderndes Leihexemplar" ("apparently constantly circulating loan copy"), reached Wilna and is now in Leningrad.

35. *Acta Conciliorum* I 3 and 4.

36. *Acta Conciliorum* II 2, 2.

37. *Acta Conciliorum* II 3.

38. Schwartz' article of the same title (*Zeitschrift für Rechtsgeschichte*, Kan. Abt. 25 [1936]) is the fundamental study of the subject.

39. The "Prisca" is preserved in a splendid uncial manuscript: Oxford, Bodleian Library Mus. 100 and 101 and 102, Italy, saec. VI–VII (*CLA*, II, 255). The manuscript, which was in Fleury during the Middle Ages, fell into the hands of the Huguenot Justel, who was so annoyed by the canons of the Synod of Sardica that he cut them out of the manuscript. The manuscript was also divided into three sections; cf. C. H. Turner, "The Version Called Prisca," *Journal of Theological Studies* 30 (1929), 337–46; Schwartz, in *Zeitschrift für Rechtsgeschichte*, Kan. Abt. 25, pp. 95–108.

40. Maassen, *Geschichte der Quellen*, pp. 425–36; Schwartz, in *Zeitschrift für Rechtsgeschichte*, Kan. Abt. 25, pp. 108–14. More recent research, esp. on Dionysius' *Codex decretalium*, is treated by H. Wurm, *Studien und Texte zur Dekretalensammlung des Dionysius Exiguus* (Bonn 1939); W. M. Peitz, *Dionysius Exiguus-Studien. Neue Wege der philologischen und historischen Text- und Quellenkritik*, ed. H. Foerster (Berlin 1960), traces the entire Latin canonistic tradition back to Dionysius' own draft of the text, which he continually polished and improved, and of which copies were made at various times. Cf. the detailed reviews by K. Schäferdiek, in *Zeitschrift für Kirchengeschichte* 74 (1963), 353–68, and C. Munier, in *Sacris Erudiri* 14 (1963), 236–50.

41. All four prefaces to the canonistic collections are included in Maassen, *Geschichte der Quellen*, pp. 960–65.

42. Novara, Biblioteca Capitolare Cod. XXX, ed. Maassen, *Geschichte der Quellen*, pp. 964 f., and A. Amelli, *Spicilegium Casinense* (Monte Cassino 1888), I, 198; here according to Maassen's edition. Only the preface is preserved. Peitz (*Dionysius Exiguus-Studien*, pp. 273 ff.) treats the preface under the heading "Die vermeintliche 'Dionysiana III.'"

43. Schwartz notes that this edition was to be "an instrument in the diplomatic conflict with Emperor Anastasius," and was "occasioned by the planned Council of Heraclea, which later miscarried, and intended primarily for the bilingual Illyrian bishops"; *Zeitschrift für Rechtsgeschichte*, Kan. Abt. 25, p. 113. Yet what is one to make of the notion that such a book, so difficult to produce, was intended for bilingual bishops, whose own ability was sufficient for working through the Latin translation of a Greek canon (and vice versa)? Thus one must accept the statements of the preface to the work and assume that the book was intended for the pope.

44. Caspar, *Geschichte des Papsttums*, II, 770 ff.

45. Gregorii M., "Synodica," *Registrum* I 24, ed. P. Ewald and L. M. Hartmann, *MGH Epistolae*, I, 36.

46. Turner, *Ecclesiae Occidentalis Monumenta* I 2, 581 ff. (Synod of Carthage, 419). Maassen, *Geschichte der Quellen*, p. 11.

47. Thus, for example, a table of the Greek numerals is appended to the *regula formatarum* in the manuscript of the canons, Würzburg, Univ. Bibl. M. p. th. f. 70, saec. IX (fol. 140ᵛ).

48. Here according to the St. Gall tradition, from the "book of formulae" collected by Notker Balbulus for Salomo III of Constance; from Vienna, Österreichische Nationalbibliothek Cod. 1609, ed. E. Dümmler, *Das Formelbuch des Bischofs Salomo III von Konstanz*

(Leipzig 1857), pp. 26 f., no. 24, *Qualiter debeat epistola formata fieri exemplar.* (In a less satisfactory edition: *MGH Formulae Merowingici et Karolini aevi* [1886], p. 409.) There is no edition based on a broader tradition—from which one would be able to decide whether the typical Western misunderstanding of the fourth initial, Π = ΠΝΕΥΜΑ for *Petrus*, was found through the entire tradition. C. Fabricius imprudently based her study of "Die Litterae Formatae im Frühmittelalter," *Archiv für Urkundenforschung* 9 (1926), 39–86 and 168–94, on the edition in *MGH*.

49. Cf. Fabricius, "Die Litterae Formatae," esp. pp. 190–93.

50. Gratian, *Decretum*, dist. 73, ed. E. Friedberg (Leipzig 1879), cols. 260–62.

Notes to Chapter V

1. "Gothi isti quid ni et Vandali existimandi sunt? Nam postquam hae gentes semel iterumque Italiae influentes Roman ceperunt, ut imperium eorum, ita linguam quoque (quemadmodum aliqui putant) accepimus, et plurimi forsan ex illis oriundi sumus. Argumento sunt codices Gothice scripti, quae magna multitudo est: quae gens si scripturam Romanam deprauare potuit, quid de lingua . . . putandum est? . . . En quo literatura Romana recidit. Veteres admiscebant linguae suae Graecam: isti admiscent Gothicam." Lorenzo Valla, *De linguae latinae elegantia*, lib. III, praef., cited according to the Cologne edition of 1543, p. 204.

2. Introduction by E. Stutz, *Gotische Literaturdenkmäler* (Stuttgart 1966) (bibliog.). See also the more recent, comprehensive study by P. Scardigli, *Lingua e storia dei Goti* (Florence 1964); German translation by B. Vollmann, *Die Goten: Sprache und Kultur* (Munich 1973), reviewed by E. Stutz, *Beiträge zur Namenforschung* 10 (1975), 184–91; and also the special study by K. Gamber, "Die Liturgie der Goten," in *Liturgie und Kirchenbau: Studien zur Geschichte der Meßfeier und des Gotteshauses in der Frühzeit* (Regensburg 1976), pp. 72–96.

3. *Epist.* 106, 1. Altaner (*TU* 83, 448 f.) dates the letter between 404 and 410. A number of articles deal with this letter, which is "eine Art authentische Einleitung in die hexaplarische Rezension" ("a kind of authentic guide to the hexaplarian recension"; Allgeier, *Die Psalmen*, p. 19) of the Psalter (i.e., the *Psalterium Gallicanum*); see also J. Zeiller, "Saint Jérôme et les Goths," *Miscellanea Geronimiana* (Rome 1920), 123–30; L. de Bruyne, "La lettre de Jérôme à Sunnia et Fretela sur le Psautier," *Zeitschrift für neutestamentliche Wissenschaft* 28 (1929), 1–13; de Bruyne maintains in "Lettres fictives de S. Jérôme" (pp. 229–34 of the same volume) that the letter's address to the Goths is fictive; Allgeier, "Der Brief an Sunnia und Fretela und seine Bedeutung für die Textherstellung der Vulgata," *Biblica* 11 (1930), 86–107; Zeiller, in *Comptes Rendus de l'Académie des Inscriptions et Belles-Lettres* (Paris 1935), 238–50, where he again defends the authenticity of the address in opposition to de Bruyne; M. Metlen, in *The Journal of English and Germanic Philology* 36 (1937), 515–42. Stutz, *Gotische Literaturdenkmäler*, pp. 43 ff., reviews the older research and the "unerledigten und vielleicht unlösbaren Probleme" ("unsolved and perhaps unsolvable problems") of Jerome's letter.

4. The author is now generally held to be the Arian bishop Maximin, who is known for his *Dissertatio contra Ambrosium*, which also contains the biography of Wulfila by Auxentius. Despite the close relations of Maximin to the Arian Goths, M. Meslin maintains that Maximin may not be referred to as a Goth, but rather that he belonged to the Latin bishops of the "communautés hétérodoxes d'Illyricum"; *Les ariens d'occident, 335–430* (Paris 1967), pp. 92 ff.

5. Meslin, *Les ariens*, p. 152. Meslin ascribes further disputed works to Maximin, "le personnage le plus attachant de ces chrétiens séparés" ("the most charming personality among these 'separate Christians,'" p. 96), among them a Latin excerpt from Origen's commentary on Matthew (pp. 183 ff.). See also M. Thiel, *Hebräischkenntnisse*, pp. 31–34.

6. "Et si nos curae officii consularis impediunt quo minus in his studiis omne otium plenamque operam consumimus, pertinere tamen videtur hoc ad aliquam reipublicae curam, elucubratae rei doctrina cives instruere. Nec male de civibus meis merear, si cum prisca hominum virtus urbium caeterarum ad hanc unam rempublicam, dominationem, imperiumque transtulerit, ego id saltem quod reliquum est, Graecae sapientiae artibus mores nostrae civitatis instruxero." Boethius, *In Categorias Aristotelis*, lib. II, prol. (*Migne PL* 64, col.

201). The Ciceronian passage from the *Tusculanae Disputationes*, with its exhortation "to snatch the glory [of philosophy] from the already ailing Greece," is cited by Boethius, *In Topica Ciceronis*, lib. V. (*Migne PL* 64, col. 1152).

7. In 1981, three new comprehensive studies of and collections of essays on Boethius appeared. In order of importance: M. Gibson, ed., *Boethius: His Life, Thought and Influence* (Oxford); M. Masi, ed., *Boethius and the Liberal Arts* (Bern/Frankfurt); H. Chadwick, *Boethius: The Consolations of Music, Logic, Theology and Philosophy* (Oxford) (bibliog.). The general summary by C. Leonardi, L. Minio-Paluello, U. Pizzani, and P. Courcelle, "Boezio," in *Dizionario biografico degli Italiani* (1970), XI, 142–65, is still useful.

8. *Aristoteles latinus*, I/6.

9. "Translationibus enim tuis Pythagoras musicus, Ptolemaeus astronomus leguntur Itali: Nicomachus arithmeticus, geometricus Euclides audiuntur Ausonii: Plato theologus, Aristoteles logicus Quirinali voce disceptant: mechanicum etiam Archimedem Latialem Siculis reddidisti. Et quascumque disciplinas vel artes facunda Graecia per singulos viros edidit, te uno auctore patrio sermone Roma suscepit." Cassiodorus, *Variae* I 45 (*MGH Auctores antiquissimi*, XII, 40).

10. Ed. Friedlein (Leipzig 1867); the volume also contains Boethius' *De musica*. Potiron shows Boethius to be "un fidèle représentant de la tradition grecque" ("a true representative of the Greek tradition"); *Boèce: Théoricien de la musique grecque* (Paris 1961). Most recently see J. Caldwell, "The 'De Institutione Arithmeticae' and the 'De Institutione Musicae,'" in *Boethius*, ed. Gibson, pp. 135–54.

11. M. Geymonat edited the fragments (Verona, Biblioteca Capitolare, Cod. XL [38]; *CLA*, IV, 497 and 501), of the fifth century and rescripted in the eighth, which were again seriously damaged through the use of chemicals by nineteenth-century scholars: ed. *Euclidis latine facti fragmenta Veronensia* (Milan/Varese 1964). The fragments were already ascribed to Boethius at their discovery in 1817; the fact, however, that none of the German or Italian scholars who worked with the pages prior to Geymonat produced an edition led scholars to numerous misdirected speculations and disputes about Boethius' geometry; see Manitius, *Geschichte der lateinischen Literatur des Mittelalters*, I, 27 f., and Krüger, *Geschichte der römischen Litteratur* IV/2, 153 f. Geymonat edited "Nuovi Frammenti della Geometria 'Boeziana' in un codice del IX secolo," in *Scriptorium* 21 (1967), 3–16; see also M. Folkerts, *"Boethius" Geometrie II. Ein mathematisches Lehrbuch des Mittelalters* (Wiesbaden 1970), esp. p. 72, and D. Pingree, "Boethius' Geometry and Astronomy," in *Boethius*, ed. Gibson, pp. 155–61.

12. Gerbert, *epist.* 8 (from Bobbio, anno 983), ed. E. Weigle, *Die Briefsammlung Gerberts von Reims* (Berlin/Zurich/Dublin 1966), p. 31.

13. *De figuris numerorum* (on Greek and Latin numerals, coins and weights), *De metris fabularum Terentii* (Greek and Latin prosody), *Praeexercitamina* (a rhetoric based on the ΠΡΟΓΥΜΝΑΣΜΑΤΑ of Hermogenes).

14. Ed. by P. van den Woestijne (Bruges 1953).

15. P. Courcelle, *La consolation de Philosophie dans la tradition littéraire: Antécédents et posterité de Boèce* (Paris 1967). See also J. Beaumont, "The Latin Tradition of the 'De consolatione Philosophiae,'" in *Boethius*, ed. Gibson, pp. 278–305; A. Minnis, "Aspects of the Medieval French and English Traditions of the 'De consolatione Philosophiae,'" ibid., pp. 312–61; N. F. Palmer, "Latin and Vernacular in the Northern European Tradition of the 'De consolatione Philosophiae,'" ibid., pp. 362–97.

16. B. Fischer, "Codex Amiatinus und Cassiodor," *Biblische Zeitschrift*, n.s., 6 (1962), 57–79, here p. 70. On the translators' school in Vivarium and the text transmission of its works, see P. Courcelle, *Les lettres grecques*, pp. 313–88.

17. "quod si aliquid in eisdem [sc. Latinis expositoribus] neglegenter dictum reperit, tunc quibus lingua nota est a Graecis explanatoribus quae sunt salubriter tractata perquirant, quatenus in schola Christi neglegentiae tepore sublato vitalis agnitio flammatis mentibus inquiratur." *Institutiones* I, praef. 3, ed. R. A. B. Mynors (Oxford 1937), p. 5.

18. "sed nos potius Latino scriptores Domino iuvante sectamur, ut quoniam Italis scribimus, Romanos quoque expositores commodissime indicasse videamur. dulcius enim ab unoquoque suscipitur quod patrio sermone narratur. . . ." *Institutiones* I, praef. 4, ed. Mynors, p. 5. Rohlfs understood this passage as proof that the native language of the monks at Vivarium was Greek (*Griechen und Romanen in Unteritalien* [Geneva 1924], pp. 81 f.). This un-

tenable position (cf. Blatt, in *Classica et Mediaevalia* 1 [1938], 235) is abandoned by Rohlfs in his new survey of Greek Italy, *Neue Beiträge zur unteritalienischen Gräzität*, SB Munich (1962).

19. *Institutiones* I 8, 3. I. Wilhelmsson has proposed a rhythmical method of translation here, "Studien zu Mutianus dem Chrysostomosübersetzer" (diss., Lund 1944).

20. This translation, under the title *Adumbrationes in epistulas catholicas*, made the study of early Alexandrine theology possible in some few places during the Middle Ages. Cf. Siegmund, *Die Überlieferung*, pp. 58 and 164. Cassiodorus was also a party to the widespread anti-Origen campaign when he argued that the theology of "Origen's teacher" might be transmitted to the Latin world only *exclusis quibusdam offendiculis* (*Institutiones* I 8, 4). Cf. A. Knauber, "Die patrologische Schätzung des Clemens von Alexandrien bis zu seinem neuerlichen Bekanntwerden durch die ersten Druckeditionen des 16. Jahrhunderts," *Kyriakon*, I, 289–308.

21. *Institutiones* I 9, 1. The comprehensive translation *in duobus codicibus* is considered lost.

22. *Institutiones* I 8, 14–15.

23. Ed. by W. Jacob and R. Hanslik (*CSEL* 71). See also the accompanying publication by Jacob, *Die handschriftliche Überlieferung der sogenannten Historia tripartita des Epiphanius-Cassiodor*, *TU* 59 (1954), and the textual and linguistic comments by Lundström, according to whom Epiphanius made a "metricized" translation, as did Mutianus (*Zur Historia tripartita*, p. 5), and strove for "akzentuierende Klauseln mit korrekten Zäsuren" ("accentuated clauses with proper caesurae"), in *Archivum Latinitatis Medii Aevi* 23 (1953), 25. F. Weissengruber has written an entire book on the translation errors of the Historia tripartita: *Epiphanius Scholasticus als Übersetzer*, SB Vienna (1972).

24. *Institutiones* I 17.

25. The late antique translations of *De bello Iudaico* may still be consulted in the Basel edition of 1524, *Flavii Iosephi . . . Opera quaedam Ruffino presbytero interprete* (later editions changed the Latin text to conform to the Greek edition of Josephus which appeared in 1544). A Latin excerpt from *De bello Iudaico* in five books had a wide circulation under the name *Hegesippus* (see Siegmund, *Die Überlieferung*, pp. 102–7); edited by V. Ussani and C. Mras, *Hegesippi qui dicitur Historiae libri V*, *CSEL* 66/1–2 (1932–60). Morin (in *RB* 31 [1914–19], 83 ff.) sees similarities between the translation of the *Hegesippus* and the *Passio SS. Machabaeorum*, and examines the possible authorship by Dexter, the Spaniard whom Jerome includes in his *De viris illustribus*; see above, Chapter III, n. 41.

26. Ed. by F. Blatt, *The Latin Josephus* (*Antiquitates* lib. I–V) (Aarhus/Copenhagen 1958).

27. Blatt, in *Classica et Mediaevalia* 1 (1938), 237.

28. A reliable list of his translations was first given by Schwartz in the context of his description of the Codex Novara XXX, *Acta Conciliorum* IV 2 (Strasbourg 1914), pp. xvii f. A new survey of Dionysius' life and work is given by M. Mähler, "Denys le Petit, traducteur de la vie de Saint Pachôme," in *La vie latine de saint Pachôme*, ed. H. van Cranenburgh (Brussels 1969), pp. 28–48. The survey by H. Wurm, *Studien und Texte zur Dekretalensammlung des Dionysius Exiguus* (Bonn 1939), pp. 10–30, remains useful also, due to its detailed discussion of the life and clear presentation of the canonistic work. W. Peitz argues against previous scholarship in his *Dionysius Exiguus-Studien* (Berlin 1960), where he presents a completely novel biography of Dionysius (without supporting evidence).

29. *Institutiones* I 23, 2.

30. Caspar, *Geschichte des Papsttums*, II, 306 ff.

31. Dionysius added the translation of the *Epistola S. Proterii Alexandrinae urbis episcopi ad . . . papam Leonem pro hac eadem paschali quaestione directa* to the *Liber de paschate*; a letter of 525 also contains an opinion on the subject. All relevant material is available in the edition by B. Hoffmann, *Migne PL* 67, cols. 453–520.

32. *Migne PL* 67, cols. 345–408.

33. Eugippius was the author of the *Commemoratorium vitae S. Severini* and the *Excerptum ex operibus S. Augustini*. Cassiodorus pays tribute to Dionysius Exiguus and Eugippius (and to no other contemporary Christian writers) in *Institutiones* I 23.

34. "In plurimis enim iuxta philosophorum sententias immoratus, opulentiam tantam suae eruditionis expressit, ut pene nihil omiserit eorum quae ab illis doctis et otiosis ingeniis in hac parte per inextricabiles digesta sunt quaestiones." *Migne PL* 67, col. 345.

35. In his splendid study, Levine praises Dionysius' translation of Gregory of Nyssa in comparison with those of John Scottus and two Humanists, in *Harvard Studies in Classical Philology* 63 (1958), 473–92. On the plan for a third humanistic translation of ΠΕΡΙ ΚΑΤΑϹΚΕΥΗϹ ΑΝΘΡШΠΟΥ by the Nuremburg Humanist Johannes Cuno, see Sicherl, *Johannes Cuno*, pp. 142 f. (with no mention of the earlier translations). Basil the Great's *Hexaemeron* had already been translated into Latin by Eustathius about A.D. 400.

36. Ed. by H. van Cranenburgh, *La vie latine*.

37. *Migne PL* 67, cols. 417–54.

38. *Acta SS*, Oct. (Brussels 1780), IV, 225; older edition by H. Rosweyde, *Vitae Patrum*, pp. 374 f. = *Migne PL* 73, cols. 661–64. Dionysius' preface is edited by A. Amelli, *Spicilegium Casinense* (Monte Cassino 1888), I, p. l, n. 2 (= *Migne PL*, suppl. 4, cols. 21–22), and *AB* 11 (1892), 298 f.

39. "Si après cela on examine les relations que Denys le Petit entretenait avec l'Église d'Alexandrie, on constate que les points de contact sont nombreux, si bien que, des quinze ouvrages que nous connaisson de Denys, au moins dix se rapportent à la situation de cette Église . . ." ("If one examines in this regard the relations which Dionysius Exiguus maintained with the Church of Alexandria, one confirms that the points of contact are numerous, to the extent that of the fifteen works which we know to be Dionysius', at least ten relate to the situation of that church . . ."); Mähler in van Cranenburgh's *La vie latine*, pp. 44 ff.

40. *Les lettres grecques*, pp. 268 ff. On this point, however, see the critical appraisal by H. Kirkby, "The Scholar and His Public," in *Boethius*, ed. Gibson, pp. 44–69, esp. p. 61.

41. A survey of the Latin translations of Greek Apocrypha is found in Siegmund, *Die Überlieferung*, pp. 33–48 (bibliog.).

42. F. Blatt, *Die lateinischen Bearbeitungen der Acta Andreae et Matthiae apud anthropophagos* (Gießen 1930).

43. Ed. K. v. Tischendorf, *Evangelia apocrypha*, 2nd ed. (Leipzig 1876), pp. 51–111.

44. See E. Cothenet, "Marie dans les apocryphes," in *Maria*, ed. H. du Manoir (Paris 1961), VI, 71–156, esp. pp. 136 ff., and also M. Haibach-Reinisch, *Ein neuer "Transitus Mariae" des Pseudo-Melito* (Rome 1962). On the literary merits, see H. Lausberg, "Zur literarischen Gestaltung des 'Transitus Beatae Mariae,'" *Historisches Jahrbuch* 72 (1953), 25–49.

45. Ed. by E. v. Dobschütz, *TU* 38/4 (Leipzig 1912).

46. Siegmund, *Die Überlieferung*, p. 49.

47. Ed. by L. de Coninck, *CC* 88A (Turnhout 1977). Bishop Julian of Aeclanum (near Benevento), whom Gennadius called *Graeca et Latina lingua scholasticus* (*De viris illustribus*, c. 46), was driven from his see in 418 or 419 as a "Pelagian" and stayed in the East with Theodore of Mopsuestia in Cilicia and with Nestorius in Constantinople; see Altaner-Stuiber, *Patrologie*, 7th ed., p. 377 (bibliog.). That the translation has survived is due to Irish scribes: Milan, Ambros. C 301 inf. (*CLA*, III, 326) and Turin F. IV. 1, fascs. 5 and 6 (*CLA*, IV, 452).

48. Laistner, in *Harvard Theological Review* 40 (1947), 19–31; Siegmund, *Die Überlieferung*, pp. 107 ff.

49. Smalley, *The Study of the Bible*, p. 14.

50. W. Levison, "Konstantinische Schenkung und Silvester-Legende," in *Aus rheinischer und fränkischer Frühzeit* (Düsseldorf 1948), pp. 390–465.

51. Emperor Otto III appears to have been the only Western ruler of the Middle Ages who was aware of the counterfeit character of the Donation; see M. Uhlirz, *Otto III* (Berlin 1954), pp. 355 ff.

52. K. Heitmann, "Orpheus im Mittelalter," *Archiv für Kulturgeschichte* 45 (1963), 253–94, and idem, "Typen der Deformierung antiker Mythen im Mittelalter. Am Beispiel der Orpheussage, "*Romanistisches Jahrbuch* 14 (1963), 45–77. Cf. J. B. Friedman, *Orpheus in the Middle Ages* (Cambridge, Mass., 1970).

53. Ferrandus, *Vita S. Fulgentii*, c. 1, ed. G.-G. Lapeyre (Paris 1929), pp. 11 f. (also *Migne PL* 65, col. 119).

54. Ed. by A. Riese, 2nd ed. (Leipzig 1893).

55. For example, E. Rohde, *Der griechische Roman und seine Vorläufer*, 3rd ed. (Leipzig 1914), who classifies the work under the rubric "sophistische Liebesromane" ("sophistical romantic novels"). Rohde assumes, however, that the (lost) Greek original underwent a Christian revision through the Latin translation.

56. N. Henkel, *Studien zum Physiologus im Mittelalter* (Tübingen 1976) (bibliog.).

57. Ed. by R. Foerster, *Scriptores Physiognomonici Graeci et Latini* (Leipzig 1893), II, 1–145, and I, cxxxi ff. Foerster's argument that the author of the *De physiognomonia liber* could not have been a Christian—because of his use of *deorum* (p. cxxxvi)—cannot be taken as certain. The manuscript tradition does not begin before Liège 77, a presentation copy for Bishop Marbod of Rennes (1096–1123). The dedicatory poem has been newly edited by W. Bulst, *Carmina Leodiensia*, SB Heidelberg (1975), p. 18. The work was long attributed to Apuleius; cf. Marti, *Übersetzer*, p. 314.

58. Thorndike, in *Janus* 51 (1964), 3 f.

59. Beccaria investigated the Ravenna school of medical translation in his unfinished series of articles "Sulla tracce d'un antico canone latino di Ippocrate de di Galeno," *Italia Medioevale e Umanistica* 2 (1959); 4 (1961); 14 (1971). Schanz-Hosius-Krüger's survey is still useful: *Geschichte der römischen Litteratur*, IV/2, 272–302.

60. H. Mørland, *Die lateinischen Oribasiusübersetzungen*, Symbolae Osloenses suppl. 5 (Oslo 1932), and idem, *Oribasius latinus*, Symbolae Osloenses fasc. suppl. 10 (Oslo 1940)—an edition of the *Synopsis*. According to Mørland, the *Rufus de podagra* belongs to the same "Ravenna circle" of medical translations; ed. by Mørland in Symbolae Osloenses fasc. suppl. 6 (Oslo 1933).

61. *Institutiones* I 31.

62. Cf. Thorndike, *Magic and Experimental Science*, I, 605–12.

Notes to Chapter VI

1. Duchesne, *Liber Pontificalis*, I, 292 f.

2. *Acta Conciliorum* I 3 and I 4. Cf. A. Grillmeier and H. Bacht, *Das Konzil von Chalkedon* (Würzburg 1953), II, 816–22.

3. Rosweyde, *Vitae Patrum*, lib. V. (*Migne PL* 73, cols. 855–988). Batlle (*Die Adhortationes*) describes the text tradition in detail.

4. Rosweyde, *Vitae Patrum*, lib. VI (*Migne PL* 73, cols. 993–1022). In many manuscripts, a group of *sententiae patrum* is attached to this text; published by A. Wilmart, "Le recueil latin des apophtegmes," *RB* 34 (1922), 185–98. Batlle, *Die Adhortationes*, pp. 10–15, and idem, "'Vetera Nova.' Vorläufige kritische Ausgabe bei Rosweyde fehlender Vätersprüche," *Festschrift Bischoff* (Stuttgart 1971), pp. 32–42.

5. "You were God's consul, now enjoy your triumphs"; thus Gregory's contemporary grave inscription honored him in the ancient manner as a conqueror; Bede, *Historia ecclesiastica gentis Anglorum* II 1; see also Caspar, *Geschichte des Papsttums*, II, 511. J. M. Peterson holds Gregory's declaration that he knew no Greek to be a topos of modesty; "Did Gregory the Great Know Greek?" in *The Orthodox Churches and the West*, ed. D. Baker (Oxford 1976), pp. 121–34.

6. R. Riedinger, "Die Lateransynode von 649 und Maximos der Bekenner," in *Maximus Confessor*, ed. F. Heinzer and C. Schönborn (Fribourg 1982), pp. 111–21, here p. 120. This lecture provides the best introduction to Riedinger's argumentation, by means of which Erich Caspar's interpretation (until recently the one generally accepted) was refuted. A new edition by Riedinger of the *Concilium Lateranense a. 649 celebratum* appeared in *Acta Conciliorum Oecumenicorum* II 1 (Berlin/New York 1984).

7. ". . . *natione Graecus, ex patre Theodoro episcopo de civitate Hierosolima* . . ."; Duchesne, *Liber Pontificalis*, I, 331.

8. J. Gay, "Quelques remarques sur les papes grecs et syriens avant la querelle des iconoclastes 678–715," *Mélanges Schlumberger* (Paris 1924), I, 40–54.

9. Cf. Caspar (*Geschichte des Papsttums*, II, 634 ff.), whose conventional opinion ("Müdigkeit und Schwunglosigkeit dieses griechischen Papsttums," p. 643; "lassitude and lack of imagination of this Greek papacy") derives last but not least from his biased evaluation of sources: liturgical history is left out of consideration, as if the liturgy could never be an important historical element.

10. Maassen, *Geschichte der Quellen*, p. 760 f. Siegmund, *Die Überlieferung*, pp. 158 f.

11. Caspar, *Geschichte des Papsttums*, II, 614.

12. It would be profitable to examine critically all references to this influential person in

seventh/eighth-century Rome. The most significant report in the present context is that Bonifatius Consiliarius translated a part of the *Miracula SS. Cyri et Johannis* by Sophronius of Jerusalem; *Migne PG* 87 (1865), cols. 3379–3675. The *Liber pontificalis* mentions *Bonifatius* in the *Vita Benedicti II* (683–85) and *Vita Sergii* (687–701). Eddius Stephanus (*Vita S. Wilfridi*, cc. 5 and 53) and Bede (*Historia ecclesiastica gentis Anglorum* V 19) both mention him as the friend and teacher of Wilfrid, the missionary to the Frisians.

13. A manuscript of the translation, written in Rome in 800, is preserved in Cod. Vat. gr. 1666; see below, Chapter IX, sec. 2, ad init.

14. St. Binon, *Essai sur le cycle de Saint Mercure*, Bibliothèque de l'École des Hautes Études, Sciences Religieuses 53 (Paris 1937). Siegmund, *Die Überlieferung*, p. 242. *BHL* nos. 5933–39 surveys the rich literature which arose in Benevento through the veneration of Mercurius.

15. P. Goubert, "L'Espagne Byzantine. Influences Byzantines sur l'Espagne Wisigothique," *Revue des Études Byzantines* 4 (1946), 111–33.

16. Rosweyde, *Vitae Patrum*, lib. VII (*Migne PL* 73, cols. 1025–62). New edition by J. G. Freire, *A versão latina por Pascásio de Dume dos Apophthegmata Patrum* (Coimbra 1971), I/2 (I, 159 ff.: *Liber Geronticon de octo principalibus vitiis*). Freire has edited a further translation of *apopthegmata* from the sixth century in *Commonitiones sanctorum patrum*. *Uma nova colecção de apotegmas* (Coimbra 1974). This collection is to a large extent identical to the one published by Rosweyde in the third book of his *Vitae Patrum* under the name Rufinus.

17. Rosweyde included this translation in the appendix in his *Vitae Patrum*. New edition by C. W. Barlow, *Martini episcopi Bracarensis opera omnia* (New Haven 1950), pp. 30–51; the collections of canons, ibid., pp. 123–44. Cf. K. Schäferdiek, *Die Kirche in den Reichen der Westgoten und Suewen* (Berlin 1967), pp. 120 ff.

18. D. de Bruyne, "L'héritage littéraire de l'abbé Saint Valère," *RB* 32 (1920), 1–10. On the *Vita S. Mariae Aegyptiacae* in the compilation, one of the old translations of "expressive character," see Kunze, *Studien zur Legende der heiligen Maria Aegyptiaca*, pp. 28 ff.; cf. W. Berschin, in *Mittellateinisches Jahrbuch* 10 (1975), 310.

19. "The Greek roots and etymologies in Isidore's work, which are corrected and printed in Greek in Lindsay's edition, are in very many cases written in the Latin alphabet in the manuscripts and generally transmitted in more or less garbled form, since they did not always exhibit the classical linguistic forms even in the original text"; Bischoff, in *Latin Script and Letters* A.D. *400–900*, Festschrift Bieler, p. 209. In the same passage, Bischoff shows how the Medieval Latin word *bannita* = *syllaba*, *littera* came about from the transcription of the Graeca in *Etym.* I 16, 1: "nam syllaba dicta est ΛΠΟ ΤΟΥ CΥΛΛΛΜ ΒΛΝΕΙΝ ΤΛ ΓΡΛΜΜΛΤΛ."

20. *Etym.* I 3.

21. *Etym.* IX 1.

22. J. Fontaine's *Isidore de Séville et la culture classique dans l'Espagne Wisigothique* (Paris 1959), I/2 (pp. 58–61 on the passage cited concerning the Greek alphabet) contains an extensive source analysis.

23. Borst, *Der Turmbau*, III, 455.

24. Such important Celticists as Arbois de Jubainville and Heinrich Zimmer (e.g., *Pelagius in Irland* [Berlin 1901], pp. 5 ff.) have formulated critically indefensible arguments on this point. E. Coccia has collected much of the evidence employed in such untenable arguments; "La cultura irlandese precarolingia. Miracolo o mito?" *Studi Medievali* III/8 (1967), 257–420.

25. Roger, *L'enseignement*, pp. 268–73. Esposito, "The Knowledge of Greek in Ireland," *Studies* (Dublin) 1 (1912), here p. 683. Esposito's article is a devastating analysis of an older method of evidence collection and interpolation, such as is practiced uncritically—though not without elegance—by Stokes, "The Knowledge of Greek in Ireland," *Proceedings of the Irish Academy* III/2 (1891–93).

26. Schaffhausen, Stadtbibliothek Gen. 1, pp. 103 and 137. The Graeca are those of Dorbbene, abbot of Iona (d. 713) and scribe of the manuscript; they are not added later, as Lowe (*CLA*, VII, 998) leads one to believe. The manuscript was in Reichenau during the Middle Ages. Although lying off the English coasts, Iona and Lindisfarne belong to the Irish cultural sphere in the early Middle Ages.

27. Durham, Cathedral Library A II 10, fol. 3ᵛ; a greatly reduced photograph in C. Nordenfalk, "Before the Book of Durrow," *Acta Archaeologica* 18 (1947), 161; *CLA*, II, 147.
28. Cf. the use of ϕ in *filii* (fol. 27ʳ). A facsimile edition of the "Book of Lindisfarne" (London, BL Cotton Nero D IV) has been published by T. E. Kendrick, T. J. Brown, et al., eds. (Olten/Lausanne 1956; commentary volume 1960); *CLA*, II, 187.
29. Dublin, Trinity College 52; partial facsimile ("The Patrician Documents"), ed. E. Gwynn (Dublin 1937); *CLA*, II, 270. L. Bieler, "The Book of Armagh," *Great Books of Ireland*, Thomas Davis Lectures (Dublin 1967), pp. 51–63.
30. F. E. Warren, *The Antiphonary of Bangor* (London 1893), I, xix.
31. Ed. by M. W. Herren (Toronto 1974), p. 74 (cf. pp. 191 ff: "Greek and Greek-derived words"). See also Bieler, "Ireland's Graeco-Latin Heritage," *Studia Patristica*, *TU* 116, vol. XIII, p. 5 (bibliog.).
32. *Auraicept na n-Éces: The Scholar's Primer*, ed. G. Calder (Edinburgh 1917), pp. 230 f. for the Greek alphabet.
33. Ed. by J. Huemer (Leipzig 1886). Bischoff observes that the "gesamte frühe Überlieferung über Irland gegangen ist" ("entire early tradition was transmitted via Ireland"); *Mittelalterliche Studien*, I, 215.
34. Bischoff, *Mittelalterliche Studien*, I, 205–73.
35. *Epist.* 5, ed. G. S. M. Walker, *S. Columbani opera* (Dublin 1957), p. 54.
36. ". . . usque hodie supersunt de eorum discipulis, qui Latinam Graecamque linguam aeque ut propriam in qua nati sunt norunt"; *Historia ecclesiastica* IV 2.
37. Is one to imagine the fruit of this trilingual education in the form of the remarkable prologue to Aldhelm's work, with a mixture of Anglo-Saxon, Latin, and Greek (transmitted in the school manuscript Cambridge, Corpus Christi College 326, saec. X; ed. R. Ehwald, *Aldhelmi opera* [Berlin 1919], pp. 219 f.)?
38. See above, Chapter II, n. 38.
39. This impressive double page is reproduced (in greatly reduced format) in R. L. S. Mitford, *The Art of the Codex Amiatinus*, Jarrow Lecture (1967), pl. D.
40. E. A. Lowe, *English Uncial* (Oxford 1960), pl. 11.
41. Thus Blatt comments (in *Classica et Mediaevalia* 1, p. 235), obviously led astray by the passage from Bede, cited above, n. 36.
42. *Aldhelmi opera*, ed. Ehwald, pp. 81 f.
43. Traube, *Einleitung*, p. 100.
44. On the Syro-Palestinian origin of the letter ꓛ, see the author's "Griechisches bei den Iren," in *Die Iren und Europa im früheren Mittelalter* (Stuttgart 1982), I, 501–10.
45. On Bede's Greek studies, see most recently J. Gribomont, "Saint Bède et ses dictionnaires grecs," *RB* 89 (1979), 271–80; A. C. Dionisotti, "On Bede, Grammars and Greek," *RB* 92 (1982), 111–41; and, uninformed about the current scholarly discussion, K. M. Lynch, "The Venerable Bede's Knowledge of Greek," *Traditio* 39 (1983), 432–39.
46. Ed. by Laistner, *Bedae Venerabilis Expositio Actuum Apostolorum et Retractatio* (Cambridge, Mass., 1939); idem, "Bede as a Classical and Patristic Scholar," *The Intellectual Heritage of the Early Middle Ages*, pp. 93–116.
47. Oxford, Bodleian Library Laud. gr. 35, Sardinia, saec. VI–VII; *CLA*, II, 251. Laistner, "The Latin Version of Acts Known to the Venerable Bede," *The Intellectual Heritage*, pp. 150–64. B. Bischoff and J. Hofmann (*Libri Sancti Kyliani* [Würzburg 1952], pp. 90 f. [bibliog.]) briefly outline the fate of this bilingual of Acts (except for the "Codex Bezae," Cambridge, Univ. Libr. Nn. II 41, the only ancient bilingual text of Acts): from Sardinia to Northumbria, to "insular Germany" and back to England from the Würzburg Dombibliothek during the Thirty Years' War. Diverse annotations indicate that this codex, like the Psalterium Verona I (1) was used as a textbook. The handwriting sample *iacobus presbyter grecus* (saec. IX) on fol. 226ᵛ deserves special attention; cf. Lowe, *Palaeographical Papers* (1971), I, pl. 30, and C. Mango, "La culture grecque et l'occident au VIIIᵉ siècle," in *I problemi dell'occidente nel secolo VIII*, Settimane di studio 20 (Spoleto 1973), II, 683–721, esp. pp. 689 f. and pls. 1–3.
48. *De temporum ratione*, c. 1, ed. C. W. Jones, *Bedae opera de temporibus* (Cambridge, Mass., 1943), p. 181. In c. 14, Bede lists the Greek names for the months (and in c. 15 the Old English names); ed. Jones, pp. 210 f. I intentionally cite the older U.S. edition

of 1943 and not the recent 2nd edition in *CC* 123B (1977), which offers no scholarly advance over the previous edition and which the editor justly calls "eclectic." The new edition does not take into account the newly discovered fragments of *De temporum ratione* in an English uncial manuscript from the year 746 (Münster, Staatsarchiv Msc. I 243, and Bückeburg, Niedersächsisches Staatsarchiv Dep. 3).

Notes to Chapter VII

1. Ausonius, *Epistulae* VIII 1–3, ed. R. Peiper (Leipzig 1886), p. 232; ed. S. Prete (Leipzig 1978), p. 241.

2. *Technopaegnion* XIII 9–12, ed. Peiper, p. 166; ed. Prete, p. 135.

3. *Commemoratio professorum Burdigalensium* VIII 5–8, ed. Peiper, p. 57; ed. Prete, p. 42. The restriction placed on the income of the Greek professor in Trier and established in 376 is well known: "Trevirorum vel clarissimae civitati uberius aliquid putavimus deferendum, rhetori ut triginta, item viginti grammatico Latino, Graeco etiam, si qui dignus repperiri potuerit, duodecim praebeantur annonae" ("We think that the distinguished city of Trier should give more generous allocations, so that a rhetor be compensated with thirty annual allotments, a Latin grammarian likewise with twenty, and a Greek grammarian, if anyone suitable be found, with twelve"); *Codex Theodosianus* XIII, tit. 3, 11, ed. Theodor Mommsen (Berlin 1895), p. 743.

4. Sidonius Apollinaris described the table setting at Theuderich's (453–66) West Gothic court in Toulouse as follows: "toreumatum peripetasmatumque modo conchyliata profertur supellex, modo byssina" ("sometimes the purple and sometimes the fine linen cloths and carpets were brought forth"); *epist*. 2, 6, ed. C. Luetjohann (1887), *MGH Auctores antiquissimi*, VIII, 3.

5. Pierre Courcelle, *Les lettres grecques*, pp. 221 ff. Courcelle also includes Gennadius of Marseille in the group, albeit less convincingly.

6. This point is stressed by Courcelle, *Les lettres grecques*, pp. 216 ff., in contrast to the older notion of a flourishing Greek culture in Lérins (Eucherius of Lyon, Vincentius of Lérins, Salvian of Marseille); Honoratus of Lérins, not mentioned by Courcelle, does not change the general picture.

7. "Adiecit etiam atque compulit, ut laicorum popularitas psalmos et hymnos pararet . . . alii Graece, alii Latine prosas antiphonasque cantarent, ut non haberent spatium in ecclesia fabulis occupari" ("And he instituted a new practice and compelled the lay congregation to learn Psalms and hymns . . . and to sing some recitations and antiphons in Greek and some in Latin, so that they had no opportunity to engage in conversation in church"); *Vita S. Caesarii* I 19, ed. B. Krusch, *MGH Scriptores rerum Merovingicarum*, III, 463 f.

8. "Igitur [Chlodovechus] ab Anastasio imperatore codecillos de consolato accepit, et in basilica beati Martini tunica blattea indutus et clamide, imponens vertice diadema" ("Then [Clovis] received the imperial order of consulship from Emperor Anastasius, and in the basilica of St. Martin, clothed in the purple tunic and military mantle, he placed the diadem on his head"); Gregory of Tours, *Historiae* II 38, ed. B. Krusch and W. Levison (Hannover 1951), pp. 88 f.

9. Anthimus, *De observatione ciborum ad Theodoricum regem Francorum epistula*, ed. E. Liechtenhan (Berlin 1963). Around the year 600 St. Radegundis of Poitiers had a personal physician (*archiater*) in her service who had procured relics in Jerusalem (Baudonivia, *Vita S. Radegundis* II 14 and 17) and learned a surgical technique in Constantinople (Gregory, *Historiae* X 15, ed. Krusch and Levison, p. 504).

10. Gregory, *Historiae* V 44, ed. Krusch and Levison, p. 254.

11. "Et quia tam in sede apostolica quam etiam per totas orientales atque Italiae provincias dulcis et nimium salutaris consuetudo est intromissa, ut 'Kyrie eleison' frequentius cum grandi affectu et compunctione dicatur, placuit etiam nobis, ut in omnibus ecclesiis nostris ista tam sancta consuetudo et ad matutinum et ad missas et ad vesperam Deo propitio intromittatur." J. D. Mansi, *Conciliorum Amplissima Collectio*, VIII (Florence 1762), col. 727.

12. "Quomodo solemnis ordo ecclesiae agitur, quibusve instructionibus kanon ecclesiasticus decoratur, Germanus episcopus Parisius scripsit de missa" ("In what manner the

solemn rite of the church is performed, and by what order the ecclesiastical canon is adorned, Germanus, bishop of Paris, writes concerning the mass"); J. Quasten, ed., *Expositio antiquae liturgiae Gallicanae Parisiensi ascripta* (Münster 1934), p. 10.

13. Quasten, "Oriental Influence in the Gallican Liturgy," *Traditio* 1 (1943), 55–78. K. Gamber nevertheless considers authorship by Germanus of Paris possible, in *Ordo antiquus Gallicanus. Der gallikanische Meßritus des 6. Jahrhunderts* (Regensburg 1965), p. 12.

14. "Aius vero ante prophetiam pro hoc cantatur in graeca lingua, quia praedicatio novi testamenti in mundo per graecam linguam processit. . . . Servato ergo honore linguae, quae prima evangelium Christi vel suo signo recepit vel suis litteris docuit, primum canticum incipiente praesule ecclesia 'Aius' psallit dicens latinum cum graeco, ⟨et⟩ ut ostendatur iunctum testamentum vetus et novum, dicit 'amen' ex hebraeo, instar tituli, quod in trinitate linguarum instigante deo Pilatus posuit super crucem. . . ." *Expositio*, ed. Quasten, pp. 11 f.

15. Quasten, "Oriental Influence," p. 61.

16. L. Brehier, "Les Colonies d'Orientaux en Occident au commencement du moyen-âge," *BZ* 12 (1903), 1–39, here p. 18. Cf. P. Scheffer-Boichorst, "Zur Geschichte der Syrer im Abendlande," *Mittheilungen des Instituts für österreichische Geschichtsforschung* 6 (1885), 521–50. Ebersolt, *Orient et Occident*, pp. 22 ff.

17. The most famous passage in this context is the account of King Guntram's entrance into Orléans in 585, related by Gregory of Tours: "Processitque in obviam eius immensa populi turba cum signis adque vixillis canentes laudes. Et hinc lingua Syrorum, hinc Latinorum, hinc etiam ipsorum Iudaeorum in diversis laudibus variae concrepabat, dicens: 'Vivat rex . . .'" ("And an immense crowd of people advanced to meet him with banners and flags, singing praises. And from this side resounded in various forms of praise the Syrian language, from that side Latin, and from over there even Hebrew, saying, 'Long live the king . . .'"); ed. Krusch and Levison, p. 370.

18. Ed. B. Krusch, *Gregorii episcopi Turonensis Miracula et Opera minora*, 2nd ed. (Hannover 1969), p. 102.

19. See Chapter VI.

20. See Chapter III. R. Le Bourdellès' "Connaissance du grec et méthodes de traduction dans le monde carolingien jusqu'à Scot Érigène," in *Jean Scot Érigène et l'histoire de la philosophie*, p. 118, has announced a study on this topic and the "Excerpta Barbari."

21. Paris, BN lat. 4884 (CLA, V, 560), saec. VIII², contains a translation of an Alexandrine chronicle of the world. The manuscript bears the heading *Cronica Georgii ambionensis episcopi*, in a later hand (Lowe, "saec. IX–X), and *uel sicut alii dicunt victoris turonensis episcopi* (Lowe, "another hand added soon after"). Cf. Siegmund, *Die Überlieferung*, p. 172.

22. H. Butzmann, *Die Weissenburger Handschriften* (Frankfurt/M 1964), pp. 248 ff. (bibliog.). Cf. the manuscript Épinal, Bibliothèque Municipale 149 (68), epistles of Jerome, written in 744–45 in Tours. Greeks letters used numerically occur on fol. 97ᵛ; Tironian notes passim (CLA, VI, 762).

23. Bernhard Bischoff, "Ein wiedergefundener Papyrus und die ältesten Handschriften der Schule von Tours," *Mittelalterliche Studien*, I, 6–16. Also the Greek papyrus codex in the early medieval library of St. Martin's in Tours, noted above, Chapter II, n. 69.

24. "Direximus itaque excellentissimae praecellentiae vestrae et libros, quantos reperire potuimus; id est antiphonale et responsale, insimul artem grammaticam Aristo⟨te⟩lis, Dionisii Ariopagitis, geometricam, orthographiam, grammaticam, omnes greco eloquio scriptos" ("Thus we sent as many books as we could find to your most eminent excellency: an antiphonary and responsorial, and at the same time the *ars grammatica* of Aristotle, works of Dionysius the Areopagite, and works on geometry, orthography, and grammar, all written in Greek"); *MGH Epistolae*, III, 529 (*Migne PL* 98, col. 159).

25. "Nec patrio tantum sermone contentus, etiam peregrinis linguis ediscendis operam impendit. In quibus Latinam ita didicit, ut aeque illa ac patria lingua orare sit solitus. Graecam vero melius intellegere quam pronuntiare poterat" ("Not content with his native language alone, he expended much effort in learning Latin so well that he was as accustomed to speaking it as his native language. Greek, however, he could understand better than speak"); *Vita Karoli* 25, ed. G. Waitz and O. Holder-Egger, 6th ed. (Hannover/Leipzig 1911), p. 30. Compare Jerome's formulation here, *Prologus in Danihele propheta* (*Vulgata,*

ed. R. Weber [Stuttgart 1969], p. 1341): ". . . usque ad praesentem diem magis possum sermonem chaldaeum legere et intellegere quam sonare" (". . . up to the present day, I can read and understand the Chaldean language better than I can speak it"). Jerome means Aramaic.

26. Cf. Suetonius' *Augustus* 89, *Tiberius* 70, *Claudius* 42, and especially *Titus* 3.

27. *Vita Hludowici* 7, *MGH Scriptores*, II, 592. Cf. Adamnan, *Vita S. Columbae*, ed. A. O. Anderson and M. O. Anderson (London 1961), pp. 524 ff. (on the last day of his life, Columba was working on a Psalter); Ionas, *Vita S. Columbani* II 5, ed. B. Krusch (Hannover/Leipzig 1905), p. 237 (Abbot Athala of Bobbio was repairing book bindings up to his death).

28. "Lingua graeca et latina valde eruditus, sed graecam melius intellegere poterat quam loqui . . ." ("He was well educated in both Greek and Latin, but could understand Greek better than speak it"); *Vita Hludowici* 18.

29. *MGH Epistolae*, V, 159 (*Migne PL* 122, col. 1031).

30. Heiric, *Vita S. Germani*, ed. Ludwig Traube, *MGH Poetae*, III, 429.

31. Traube, "O Roma nobilis," pp. 353 f.

32. K. Neff, *Die Gedichte des Paulus Diaconus* (Munich 1908), pp. 67 f.

33. Cf. M. Rubensohn, "Eine Übersetzung des Paulus Diaconus aus der griechischen Anthologie," *Neue Jahrbücher für Philologie und Pädagogik* 147 (1893), pp. 764 f.

34. Cf. Neff, *Die Gedichte des Paulus Diaconus*, p. 68. W. Speyer, "Der Tod der Salome," *Jahrbuch für Antike und Christentum* 10 (1967), 176–80, deals with more recent research literature and parallels.

35. Ed. H. Bastgen, *MGH Concilia*, II, Supplement (Hannover/Leipzig 1924).

36. W. von den Steinen, "Entstehungsgeschichte der Libri Carolini," *Quellen und Forschungen aus italienischen Archiven und Bibliotheken* 21 (1930), 1–93, and "Karl der Große und die Libri Carolini," *NA* 49 (1931), 207–80. The manuscript Vat. lat. 7207, produced at Charlemagne's court, originally bore the kings' marginal notes in minuscule; the precious words (*syllogistice, optime, valde bene, catholice*, and others of the same kind) were later erased and rewritten in Tironian notes; see A. Freeman, "Further Studies in the *Libri Carolini* III," *Speculum* 46 (1971), 597–612.

37. A. Freeman, "Studies in the *Libri Carolini*," *Speculum* 32 (1957), 663–705, and "Further Studies in the *Libri Carolini* I–II," *Speculum* 40 (1965), 203–89 (a new analysis of the manuscripts by Bernhard Bischoff, pp. 218 ff.), and "Further Studies in the *Libri Carolini* III" ("marginal notes"). The ascription of the "Libri Carolini" to Theodulf is, however, disputed by L. Wallach, "The Unknown Author of the Libri Carolini," *Didascaliae*, Festschrift A. M. Albareda (New York 1961), pp. 469–515, and *Diplomatic Studies in Latin and Greek Documents from the Carolingian Age* (Ithaca 1977), pp. 43–294. Paul Meyvaert has commented in detail on this last-named study, in defense of Freeman's position (in *Revue Bénédictine* 89 [1979], 29–57). Cardinal Bellarmine considered the "Libri Carolini" forgeries and put them on the *Index librorum prohibitorum* in 1586!

38. L. Wallach, "The Greek and Latin Versions of II Nicaea and the Synodica of Hadrian I," *Traditio* 22 (1966), 103–25; "The Libri Carolini and Patristics, Latin and Greek: Prolegomena to a Critical Edition," *The Classical Tradition*, Festschrift H. Caplan (Ithaca 1966), pp. 451–514; and "The Testimonia of Image-Worship in Hadrian I's Synodica of 785 (JE 2448)," in *Geschichte und Gesellschaft*, Festschrift Karl Bosl (Stuttgart 1974), pp. 409–35.

39. "Tu, qui fidei tuae puritatem in imaginibus conservare te dicis, supplex eis adstare memento cum timiamatibus; nos praecepta Domini solerti indagatione perquiramus in divinę legis codicibus! Tu luminaribus perlustra picturas; nos frequentemus divinas Scripturas! Tu fucatorum venerator esto colorum; nos veneratores et capaces simus sensuum archanorum! Tu depictis demulcere tabulis; nos divinis mulceamur alloquiis!" "Libri Carolini" II 30, ed. Bastgen, p. 98.

40. Cf. Haendler, *Epochen karolingischer Theologie*, pp. 76 ff.

41. On this point, see W. Schmandt, "Studien zu den Libri Carolini" (diss., Mainz 1966), pp. 114 f.

42. *MGH Concilia*, II/1, 165.

43. Ὁ ἀπερίγραπτος λόγος τοῦ Πατρός ἐκ σοῦ, Θεοτόκε, περιεγράφη σαρκούμενος, καὶ τὴν ῥυπωθεῖσαν εἰκόνα εἰς τὸ ἀρχαῖον ἀναμορφώσας, τῷ Θείῳ κάλλει

συγκατέμιζεν. Ἀλλ' ὁμολογοῦντες τὴν σωτηρίαν, ἔργῳ καὶ λόγῳ ταύτην ἀνιστοροῦμεν. Cf. W. Nyssen, *Das Zeugnis des Bildes im frühen Byzanz* (Freiburg 1962), p. 38; L. Ouspensky and W. Lossky, *Der Sinn der Ikonen* (Olten 1952), p. 31.

44. E. Boshof has recently argued that the *Liber de imaginibus*, preserved among Agobard's works, was written by his order, in *Archbishop Agobard of Lyon* (Cologne/Vienna 1968), p. 157. On the intellectual background, see H. Liebeschütz, "Wesen und Grenzen des karolingischen Rationalismus," *Archiv für Kulturgeschichte* 33 (1951), 17–44.

45. Haendler, *Epochen karolingischer Theologie*, pp. 113 ff.

46. ". . . wir kennen die Ideen des fränkischen Hofes und damit Karls gut genug, um mit Sicherheit sagen zu können, daß ein derart ausschweifender Plan dort niemals erwogen worden ist" (". . . we are well enough acquainted with the ideas of the Frankish court and thus with Charlemagne's to say with certainty that such an extravagant plan as this was never considered there"); Classen, in *Karl der Große*, I, 597.

47. Ohnsorge, *Das Zweikaiserproblem im frühen Mittelalter* (Hildesheim 1947).

48. *Migne PL* 107, col. 143.

49. London, British Museum Add. 37768, fol. 3ᵛ; W. Köhler and F. Mütherich, *Die karolingischen Miniaturen* (Berlin 1971), IV, pl. 3. Cf. *MGH Poetae*, VI 163. This embassy possibly also brought the famous papyrus letter to the West which was then preserved in St. Denis. In the letter, the Greek emperor summons the addressee to a joint expedition against the infidels; K. Brandi, "Der byzantinische Kaiserbrief aus St. Denis . . . ," *Archiv für Urkundenforschung* 1 (1908), 5–86; F. Dölger, "Der Pariser Papyrus von St. Denis als ältestes Kreuzzugsdokument," *Actes du VIᵉ Congrès International d'Études Byzantines* (Paris 1950), I, 93–102. The papyrus letter is now in Paris, Archives nationales K.17 n.6; it is "the oldest (by some centuries) and singular piece of evidence of the political correspondence between Constantinople and medieval Europe; for it is well known that it is not until the twelfth century that original 'foreign correspondence' from the Byzantine emperors to the popes is preserved in the Vatican archives" (W. Ohnsorge, "Das Kaiserbündnis von 842–844 gegen die Sarazenen. Datum, Inhalt und politische Bedeutung des Kaiserbriefes aus St. Denis," *Abendland und Byzanz* [1958], pp. 131–83, here p. 131).

50. Einhart, *Vita Karoli* 16.

51. Notker, *Gesta Karoli* II 6, ed. H. F. Haefele, 2nd ed. (Berlin 1962), pp. 53 ff. See also J. Schneider, "Die Geschichte vom gewendeten Fisch," *Festschrift Bischoff* (Stuttgart 1971), pp. 218–25.

52. The *odoporicum* (Hermannus Contractus, *Chronicon, MGH Scriptores*, V, 102) in which Heito reports on his embassy is lost. But Notker most likely took his particulars concerning this journey from the work (delay in reception, separation into different quarters, shipwreck); *Gesta Karoli* II 6, ed. Haefele, p. 55.

53. *MGH Poetae*, I, 426–28.

54. A. Prost, ed., "Caractère et signification de quatre pièces liturgiques composés à Metz en latin et en grec au IXᵉ siècle," *Mémoires de la Société Nationale des Antiquaires de France* 37 (1886), 149–320, esp. 248 ff. There is a cursory description of the manuscript in W. Lipphardt, *Der karolingische Tonar von Metz* [= Cod. 351] (Münster 1965), pp. 6 f. (bibliog.). In addition to the bilingual *laudes*, the manuscript contains the following Graeca: fol. 66ʳ *Trishagion*, Greek in the Roman alphabet, and Latin; fol. 117ᵛ four proverbs in Greek majuscules with a Latin interlinear version, Inc. "Ο ΜΗ ΑΚΟΥΟΝ ΙΕΡΟΝΤΩΝ . . . Qui non audit senes . . . "; fol. 118ʳ another proverb under a schematic map of the world ("T-map") with the names of the winds: "ΕΥΧΗ ΠΑΤΡΩϹ ΙΚΤΙΖΗ ΟΙΚΟΝ . . . benedictio [oratio] patris edificat domum . . ." Reference to the relations of this variously interesting manuscript to Laon thanks to J. H. Contreni, based on a more precise analysis and description of fols. 78ᵛ–101ʳ (Hincmar of Laon, *Pittaciolus*) and fols. 101ʳ–2ᵛ. Idem, *Epistola ad Hincmarum Remensem*. The following text was compared with photographs of the manuscript, courtesy of the Bibl. Munic. Metz.

55. F. Rädle, in *Anzeiger für deutsches Altertum und deutsche Literatur* 95 (1984), 4.

56. Paris, BN gr. 437; cf. H. Omont, in *Revue des Études Grecques* 17 (1904), 230–36.

57. Emperor Louis' letter and Hilduin's reply are in *MGH Epistolae*, V, 325–35.

58. Cf. Löwe, in Wattenbach and Levison, *Deutschlands Geschichtsquellen*, H. 3, pp. 319 ff. [bibliog.].

59. Théry, *Études dionysiennes*, III, 435 and 462. R. Roques, "Traduction ou interpréta-

tion? Brèves remarques sur Jean Scot traducteur de Denys," *Libres sentiers vers l'érigénisme* (Rome 1975), pp. 99–130, here p. 121 (originally in *The Mind of Eriugena,* p. 64).

60. R. R. Bezzola, *Les origines et la formation de la littérature courtoise en occident* (Paris 1958), I, 195 ff. Without taking cognizance of Bezzola, R. McKitterick mentions a significantly lower number in "Charles the Bald (823–877) and His Library: The Patronage of Learning," The *English Historical Review* 95 (1980), 28–47.

61. Ratramnus, *Contra Graecorum opposita* (*Migne PL* 121, cols. 225–346). Aeneas, *Liber adversus Graecos* (*Migne PL* 121, cols. 685–762; preface in *MGH Epistolae,* VI, 171 ff.). The two opinion tracts have been transmitted together and remain together even today: Paris, BN lat. 2863 (Ratramnus) and 2864 (Aeneas), saec. IX, from St. Denis; the latter codex also contains the relevant epistles 100 and 101 of Nicholas I; cf. *Catalogue Général,* BN, 3 (Paris 1952), 175 (bibliog.).

62. H. Hoesch, *Die kanonischen Quellen im Werk Humberts von Moyenmoutier* (Cologne/Vienna 1970), pp. 186 f.

63. Cappuyns, *Jean Scot Érigène.* Siegmund, *Die Überlieferung,* pp. 185–89; Bieler, *Irland,* pp. 132–39; *The Mind of Eriugena: Papers of a Colloquium,* ed. O'Meara/Bieler (Dublin 1973); R. Roques, *Libres sentiers;* Kristeller, in *Latin Script and Letters* A.D. 400–900, Festschrift Bieler, pp. 156–64. The best and most recent overview is given by E. Jeauneau, "Jean Scot Érigène et le grec," *Archivum Latinitatis Medii Aevii* 41 (1979), 5–50.

64. *Annotationes in Marcianum,* ed. C. E. Lutz (Cambridge, Mass., 1939). See also C. E. Lutz, "Martianus Capella," in *Catalogus Translationum et Commentariorum,* II, 367 ff.; G. Schrimpf, "Zur Frage der Authentizität unserer Texte von Johannes Scottus' 'Annotationes in Martianum,'" in *The Mind of Eriugena,* pp. 125–38.

65. J. Smits van Waesberghe, "Die besondere Stellung der ars musica im Zeitalter der Karolinger," in *Dia-Pason. De omnibus, Ausgewählte Aufsätze* (Buren, Netherlands, 1976), pp. 48–70, esp. p. 58.

66. *MGH Epistolae,* VI, 159 (*Migne PL* 122, col. 1031). Chevallier (in *Dionysiaca*) gives a synopsis of the various Dionysius translations.

67. *Iohannes Scottus, Expositiones in Ierarchiam coelestam,* ed. J. Barbet (Turnhout 1975), with "Index verborum graecorum," pp. 225–34; "Index verborum Scoti," pp. 236–328; and "Index verborum Dionysii," pp. 329–58. Cf. Barbet's articles in *The Mind of Eriugena* and *Jean Scot Érigène et l'histoire de la philosophie.*

68. *MGH Epistolae,* VI, 162 (*Migne PL* 122, col. 1195). On the translation, see Cappuyns, *Jean Scot Érigène,* pp. 162–72, and "La 'versio Ambiguorum Maximi' de Jean Scot Érigène," *Recherches de théologie ancienne et médiévale* 30 (1963), 324–29. On the manuscripts, again Cappuyns, "Les 'Bibli Vulfadi' et Jean Scot Érigène," *Recherches de théologie ancienne et médiévale* 33 (1966), 137–39; D. Lohrmann, in *Quellen und Forschungen aus italienischen Archiven und Bibliotheken* 50 (1971), 429–31; E. Jeauneau, in *Jean Scot Érigène et l'histoire de la philosophie,* pp. 135 ff.

69. The two poems on the Dionysius translation (*Hanc libam sacro . . . , Lumine sidereo . . .*) and three on the Maximus translation (*Kyrrie, caeligenae . . . , Quisquis rhetorico . . . , Quisquis amat formam . . .*) are edited by Traube, *MGH Poetae,* III, 547–50.

70. It is preserved as *Sermo gregorii episcopi nysae de (imagine) in ea que relicta sunt in examero a beato basilio suo fratre* only in Bamberg, Staatl. Bibliothek Patr. 78 (B.IV.13), ed. M. Cappuyns, "Le 'De imagine' de Grégoire de Nysse traduit par Jean Scot Érigène," *Recherches de théologie ancienne et médiévale* 32 (1965), 205–62. From the *De divisione naturae,* it is clear that John Scottus held Gregory of Nyssa and Gregory Nazianzus to be one and the same person (Cappuyns, *Jean Scot,* pp. 176 ff.); is the use of the correct surname in the Bamberg manuscript only accidental? Levine has instructively compared the translations of Dionysius Exiguus and John Scottus (in *Harvard Studies in Classical Philology* 63 [1958], 473 ff.).

71. P. Meyvaert, "The Exegetical Treatise of Peter the Deacon and Eriugena's Latin Rendering of the 'Ad Thalassium' of Maximus Confessor," *Sacris Erudiri* 14 (1963), 130–48, and "Eriugena's Translation of the 'Ad Thalassium' of Maximus: Preliminaries to an Edition of This Work," in *The Mind of Eriugena,* pp. 78–88.

72. Repeatedly cited in *De divisione naturae* as *Liber* or *Sermo de fide;* Cappuyns, *Jean Scot, Érigène,* pp. 178 f.

73. Among other material, Théry presents a lexicon of the most important concepts of the Areopagite's system ("Scot Érigène, traducteur," pp. 185 ff.)—"important since, as is well known, much of it was adopted into later Scholasticism and mysticism" (Siegmund, *Die Überlieferung*, p. 185, n. 3). See also Théry's "Esquisse d'un lexique comparé: La terminologie d'Hilduin et de Jean Scot," *Études dionysiennes*, II, 417–91.

74. According to *MGH Poetae*, III, 540 and Cod. Laon 444, fol. 297[r] (facsimile in *MGH Poetae*, III, pl. 5). The nomen sacrum X͞ω *Christo* seemed to the scribe to require interpretation, while X͞P͞E *Christe* did not. *ar* = *articulus*. On the Greco-Latin macaronic poetry of John Scottus and its later influence, see Lapidge, "L'influence stylistique de la poésie de Jean Scot," in *Jean Scot Érigène et l'histoire de la philosophie*, pp. 441–51.

75. Ed. Traube, *MGH Poetae*, III, 553. A comprehensive discussion of the text tradition is found in G. Bernt, *Das lateinische Epigramm in Übergang von der Spätantike zum frühen Mittelalter* (Munich 1968), pp. 282–85; Bernt was also the first to recognize that the pentameter comes from Ausonius' *Tetrasticha de Caesaribus* (Otho 8, 4). The Graecum is *cleptes*, κλέπτης 'thief'. Since the spelling of the victim's name is also Grecized in the tradition (Igcmarus), one can imagine the original form of the hexameter as "Hic iacet ϕΙΓΚΜΑΡΟС ΚΛΕΠΤΗС uehementer auarus." Traube identifies the subject of the malicious epitaph as Archbishop Hincmar of Reims (845–82), still alive at the time; it is the best interpretation offered thus far (despite Brunhölzl, *Geschichte der lateinischen Literatur des Mittelalters*, I, 474).

76. Edition of the commentary on the Gospel of St. John by E. Jeauneau (Paris 1972).

77. Ed. E. Jeauneau (Paris 1969).

78. Ed. I. P. Sheldon-Williams and L. Bieler (Dublin 1968 [vol. 1], 1972 [vol. 2]). The common title during the Middle Ages was ΠΕΡΙ ϕΥCΕΩΝ; cf. Sheldon-Williams, "The Title of Eriugena's *Periphyseon*," *Studia Patristica* 3, *TU* 78 (Berlin 1961), pp. 297–302.

79. Bieler, *Irland*, pp. 136 f.

80. *Geschichte der lateinischen Literatur des Mittelalters*, I, 331. See also Paul Lehmann, *Erforschung des Mittelalters* (Stuttgart 1959), II, 146 f.

81. Ed. P. Lucentini (Rome 1974), and also "La 'Clavis physicae' di Honorius Augustodunensis e la tradizione eriugeniana nel secolo XII," in *Jean Scot Érigène et l'histoire de la philosophie*, pp. 405–14.

82. Paris, BN lat. 6734, from the Maas region, saec. XII. The codex was used and annotated by the Dominican theologian Berthold von Moosburg—"quasi sicuramente . . . a Regensburg intorno al 1327" ("almost certainly . . . in Regensburg circa 1327"), according to L. Sturlese, *Bertoldo di Moosburg: Expositio super elementationem theologicam Procli, 184–211 De animabus* (Rome 1974), p. xlv. Misled by the frontispiece, Berthold cites the *Clavis physicae* of Honorius Augustodunensis as the work of a Theodore, as did Nicholas of Cusa in his *Apologia doctae ignorantiae*, ed. R. Klibansky (Leipzig 1932), p. 29. From this the conclusion has been drawn that Nicholas of Cusa also used the codex, and it has even been argued that his handwriting is identifiable in the marginal notes: M.-T. D'Alverny, "Le cosmos symbolique du XIIe siècle," *AHDL* 20 (1953), 31–81, esp. p. 37, n. 1. According to D'Alverny, the codex may be identical with the *Disputatio Theodori Graeci cum Johanne Scotto*, listed in the library catalogue of the monastery in Michelsberg near Bamberg. A new description of the codex is given by Lucentini in the introduction to his edition of *Clavis physicae*, pp. ix–xv.

83. D'Alverny, "Le cosmos," p. 38.

84. "Le grammarien Gautbert serait-il à identifier avec Gautbert de Fleury (fin Xe siècle) qui, au dire d'Aimoin, fut 'haud mediocriter studiis a pueritia liberaliter imbut⟨us⟩ artium'?" ("Is the grammarian Gautbert to be identified with Gautbert of Fleury (end of the tenth century), who, in the words of Aimoin, had been 'imbued from his youth with a more than moderate study of the arts'?"); Cappuyns, *Jean Scot Érigène*, p. 55, n. 5. This attempt at identification is even less well founded than Manitius', *Geschichte der lateinischen Literatur*, II, 673 ff. From the *Grammaticorum* διαδοχή itself, one can conclude no more than that Gautbert was especially well informed about the school of Auxerre. Moreover, the name Gautbert (Gozbert, etc.) was not unusual at that time in France.

85. Leiden, Voss. lat. o.15, fols. 147[v]–48[r]; see K. A. De Meyer, *Codices Vossiani latini* (Leiden 1977), III, 38 (bibliog.); and also R. Quadri, *I collectanea di Eirico di Auxerre* (Fribourg 1966), pp. 15 ff.

86. William of Malmesbury, *Gesta regum Anglorum* II 122, ed. W. Stubbs (London 1887), I, 131 f.; cf. William of Malmesbury, *Gesta pontificum Anglorum* V 240, ed. N. E. S. A. Hamilton (London 1870), pp. 392 ff.

87. Ludwig Bieler, "'Vindicta scholarium.' Beiträge zur Geschichte eines Motivs," *Serta Philologica Aenipontana* 7/8 (1962), 383–85.

Notes to Chapter VIII

1. *Der karolingische Klosterplan von St. Gallen* (facsimile), ed. the Historischer Verein St. Gallen (Rorschach 1952); see also *Studien zum St. Galler Klosterplan*, ed. J. Duft (St. Gall 1962).

2. J. Perez de Urbél, *Isidor von Sevilla* (Cologne 1962), pp. 56 f.

3. *MGH Poetae*, II, 846.

4. Cf. Verona, Bibl. Capitolare Cod. XXX (28), fol. 36^v, with Augustine, *Enarrationes in psalmos* XCV 15 (cf. above, Chapter III, sec. 5). Pacificus copied an excerpt from the text into the margin: "anathole disis arcton mesembria." In the Veronese codices II and LXXXV, there are marginal notes in Greek script, from the time (?) of Bishop Egino (772–99). Cf. E. Carusi and W. M. Lindsay, *Monumenta palaeographica Veronensia* (Rome 1931), II, 5.

5. Verona, Bibl. Capitolare Cod. I (1), fol. 1^v, *pater imon . . .* (Greek paternoster in Roman transcription); below that there is a Greek majuscule alphabet written first in one direction and then the other (by a Greek); fol. 2^v, *Doxa patri ce yo . . .* ("Glory to the Father and the Son"); corrections of and additions to the Greek. "It was apparently used as an aid to studying Greek and exhibited to visiting Greek scholars" (Lowe, *CLA*, IV, 472).

6. H. Quentin, "Le Codex Bezae à Lyon au IXe siècle. Les citations du nouveau testament dans le martyrologe d'Adon," *RB* 22 (1906), 1–25. Lowe, "The Codex Bezae and Lyons," *Palaeographical Papers*, I, 182–86.

7. Épinal, Bibliothèque Municipale 149 (68); see above, Chapter VII, n. 22.

8. London, BL Harley 2793; cf. E. K. Rand, *A Survey of the Manuscripts of Tours* (Cambridge, Mass., 1929), I, 106.

9. Paris, BN lat. 17227. A facsimile of this page in Rand, *A Survey of the Manuscripts of Tours*, II, pl. 43. On the date, see B. Fischer, "Bibeltext und Bibelreform unter Karl dem Großen," in *Karl der Große*, II, 170.

10. Paris, BN lat. 6115 ("Codex Memmianus"); cf. E. K. Rand, "On the History of the *De vita Caesarum* of Suetonius in the Early Middle Ages," *Harvard Studies in Classical Philology* 37 (1926), 1–48, and *A Survey of the Manuscripts of Tours*, I, 129. I. v. Severus, *Lupus of Ferrières* (Münster i. W. 1940), pp. 58–60.

11. Vienna, Österreichische Nationalbibliothek 795, fol. 19^r. On the back of the page are Greek syllables, diphthongs, and composite numerals from 11 to 910. A runic alphabet, Gothic alphabets, and script samples follow; cf. F. Unterkircher, *Alkuin-Briefe und andere Traktate. Im Auftrage des Salzburger Erzbischofs Arn um 799 zu einem Sammelband vereinigt* (Graz 1969) (facsimile; bibliog.). A new paleographical analysis of the manuscript has been published by B. Bischoff, *Die südostdeutschen Schreibschulen der Karolingerzeit* (Wiesbaden 1980), II, 115–19.

12. Hrabanus Maurus, *De laudibus sanctae crucis*, Migne *PL* 107, cols. 133–294. Photographs from the "vermeintlich verschollenen Fuldaer Klosterexemplar" ("copy from the monastery at Fulda, presumed lost"), Cod. Vat. Reg. Lat. 124, in H.-G. Müller, *Hrabanus Maurus—De laudibus sanctae crucis* (Ratingen 1973); rev. by R. Kottje in *DA* 31 (1975), 597 f. Facsimile of Cod. Vindob. 652, ed. K. Holter (Graz 1973).

13. *Migne PL* 107, col. 20. H. Klingenberg treats the "innere Buchstabenrechnung (Gematrie)" of this figural poem in "Hrabanus Maurus: In honorem sanctae crucis," *Festschrift Otto Höfler* (Vienna 1968), II, 272–300; cf. J. Rathofer, *Der Heliand* (Cologne/Graz 1962), pp. 537 f. and color pl. 3 (from Vat. Reg. lat. 124). Hrabanus knew the figure $\diamond\!\!\diamond$ = 1000 from Priscian, *De figuris numerorum*, ed. H. Keil, *Grammatici Latini* (Leipzig 1859), III, 407.

14. *De computo*, c. 7, ed. W. M. Stevens, *CC Continuatio Mediaevalis* 44 (1979), p. 213.

15. According to Bischoff, Kues Cod. 10 was most likely written "ca. saec. X in Fulda," *Mittelalterliche Studien*, II, 253, n. 35.

16. On the protective wrapper of the manuscript Cassel, Hess. Landesbibliothek 2°

astron. 2 (formerly in Fulda, early ninth century) one finds the invocation "ЄN TI ѾNO–ϽϹΛ ΠΛΤΡѠϹ ΚЄ ΟҮΟϹ . . . In nomine patris et filii . . ."; cf. E. Freise, "Die Anfänge der Geschichtsschreibung im Kloster Fulda" (diss., Münster i. W. 1979), pl. 20. The Basel Isidore manuscript F. III.15a, from Fulda ca. 800, contains names of the signs of the zodiac with Greek equivalents; (fol. 16ᵛ) cf. Youssouf Kamal, *Monumenta cartographica Africae et Aegypti* (1930), III, fasc. 1, fol. 511. ΟΡΙѠΝ is written on the famous Fulda calendar page Berlin Staatsbibliothek Preuß. Kulturbesitz theol. lat. fol. 192; cf. A. Boeckler, *Deutsche Buchmalerei vorgotischer Zeit* (Königstein i. Taunus 1976), p. 22. In the Ottonian period, the examples of the decorative use of Greek script in Fulda join together to form a small group; cf. Hannover 189 (on this point and on the copy of the lost codex of the lives of the Essen patron saints, see below, Chapter X, n. 69). The baptismal scrutiny in the "Fulda Sacramentary" of the Göttingen Universitätsbibliothek (see above, Chapter II, sec. 1) also belongs to this context.

17. Bruun Candidus calls the St. Michael's rotunda, built by Eigil, a "cimiterium . . . , quod graece dicitur ΚΟΙΜΗΤΗΡΙΟΝ, latine vero dormitorium"; *Vita Eigilis*, c. 17, *MGH Scriptores*, XV, 230. Bruun plays with the sacred languages in the metrical version of the vita, XIV 34 f.: "Omnia fac cum consilio, sic Idida [= Salomon] quondam / Basileos Solymae [= Jerusalem] repetens. . . ."

18. *MGH Scriptores*, XV, 163.

19. Ermenrich, *Epistola ad Grimaldum abbatem*, *MGH Epistolae*, V, 569; cf. *MGH Poetae*, III, 701. The Latin interpretation of the Greek verse-riddle is written in the margin of the manuscript St. Gall, Stiftsbibliothek 265, p. 72.

20. Walafrid, *De exordiis et incrementis* 7 (see below, section 7).

21. Einhard, *Vita Karoli* 16.

22. Lupus, *epist.* 5, ed. L. Levillain (Paris 1927), I, 46 and 50.

23. Vienna, Österreichische Nationalbibliothek 189.

24. *Migne PL* 120, cols. 31–994. Manitius, *Geschichte der lateinischen Literatur*, I, 408; E. Klostermann and E. Benz, *Zur Überlieferung der Matthäuserklärung des Origenes*, TU 47/2 (Leipzig 1931); *Clavis PG*, no. 1450.

25. A. E. Schönbach, "Über einige Evangelienkommentare des Mittelalters," SB Vienna 146 (1902–3), 4th Abh., pp. 142–74, esp. pp. 152 ff.; Manitius, *Geschichte der lateinischen Literatur*, I, 408; E. Klostermann and E. Benz, *Zur Überlieferung der Matthäuserklärung des Origenes*.—According to Bischoff (*Mittelalterliche Studien*, I, 59), the fragment of a splendid Latin-Greek glossary (*Corpus Glossariorum Latinorum*, III, xii) in Paris, BN lat. 6503, fols. 1–4, saec. IX, comes from Corbie (= "glossarium Grecum et Latinum," Becker, *Catalogi*, no. 136, 250?; and p. 247, "epistole Pauli Grece. epistole Pauli Latine").

26. *Migne PL* 106, cols. 1261–1504. E. Dümmler has again called attention to this author, previously discovered by Wimpfeling: "Über Christian von Stavelot und seine Auslegung zum Matthäus," SB Berlin 34/2 (1890), 2nd Abh., pp. 935–52. Laistner (*The Intellectual Heritage*, pp. 216 ff.) investigated Christian's Greek quotations and came to the conclusion "that he belonged to that very small band of ninth-century scholars who really had a practical knowledge of Greek and not merely a small vocabulary of Greek words derived from Isidore or from some glossary" (p. 232).

27. *Migne PL* 106, cols. 1299 f.

28. "Scribitur autem Iesus I et H et C et apice desuper apud nos. Nam in Graecorum libris solummodo per I et C et apice desuper invenitur scriptum, et sicut alia nomina dei comprehensive debent scribi, quia nomen dei non potest litteris explicari. Quando purum hominem significat per omnes litteras scribitur" ("And we write 'Jesus' with I and H and C with a macron over them. The Greeks write it with only I and C with a macron above, just as the other names of God ought to be written in abbreviated form, since the name of God cannot be expounded in letters. When a simple human is meant, all the letters are written"); *Migne PL* 106, col. 1278; cf. L. Traube, *Nomina Sacra. Versuch einer Geschichte der christlichen Kürzung* (Munich 1907), p. 6.

29. "Primum Matthaei Evangelium, quoniam tempore Caii factum est. Secundum Marci, quod Claudii tempore in Roma Graeco sermone scriptum fuit. Tertium Lucae in Achaia Graeco eloquio. Quartum Ioannis in Asia in civitate Epheso Graeco eloquio nihilominus tempore Nervae imperatoris. Quia Romani qui omni mundo dominibantur Graeca lingua loquebantur ... propterea illi tres Graece scripserunt. Ipsa quoque sonorior omnibus linguis

habetur. Potest ipse ordo evangeliorum ideo sic haberi ut unus apostolus si⟨t⟩ in capite, alter in fine. Et illi duo qui inter ipsos habentur, auctoritatem ab ipsis duobus habeant. Vidi tamen librum evangelii Graece scriptum, qui dicebatur sancti Hilarii fuisse, in quo primi erant Matthaeus et Ioannes et p⟨ost⟩ alii duo. Interrogavi enim Euphemium Graecum cur hoc ita esset: Dixit mihi: In similitudinem boni agricolae, qui quos fortiores habet boves primo iungit" ("The Gospel of Matthew is first, because it was written in the time of Caligula; the second is Mark, since it was written at Rome in the Greek language in Claudius' time; the third is Luke, written in Greece in the Greek language; the fourth is John, written in Greek in the Asian city of Ephesus in the time of Nerva. Since the Romans who ruled throughout the world spoke Greek, these three [authors] wrote in Greek. This language is also more resonant than all other languages. The order itself of the evangelists can therefore be regarded thus—that one apostle is at the beginning, another at the end; and those two which come between the others derive authority from them. But I saw a book of the Gospels written in Greek, which is said to have belonged to Hilary, in which Matthew and John came first and the other two thereafter. I then asked Euphemus the Greek why this was so; he said to me: 'On the model of the good farmer who yokes his stronger oxen in front'"); *Migne PL* 106, cols. 1265 f. Bishop Aeneas of Paris refers to a Greek named Euphemus at about the same time (*Liber adversus Graecos* 146, *Migne PL* 121, col. 738): "In Vita beati Basilii, Caesariensis archiepiscopi, quae de Graeco in Latinum a quodam Graeco vocabulo Euphemio est veraciter de verbo ad verbum translato, inter cetera sic legitur . . . " ("In the vita of the St. Basil [of Pseudo-Amphilochius of Iconium], archbishop of Caesarea, which was accurately translated word for word from Greek into Latin by a certain Greek named Euphemius, one reads among other things . . . "). Euphemius' translation is the oldest of the three Latin translations of the vita of Basil; cf. Siegmund, *Die Überlieferung*, pp. 259 f.

30. "'Blasphemus' graecum esse non dubitabit, nisi qui id per 'p' et 'h' scribi parum attendit. Itaque Graecus quidam Graecos 'blasphemus' dicere correpta paenultima mihi constanter asseruit et id ipsum Einhardus noster astruxit" ("No one will doubt that *blasphemus* is Greek, unless he pays too little attention to the fact that the word is written with *p* and *h*. And thus a certain Greek firmly declared to me that Greeks say 'blasphemus' with a short penultimate, and our Einhard supports this view"); Lupus, *epist.* 8, ed. Levillain, I, 64 and 66.

31. Laistner, *The Intellectual Heritage*, p. 230. The evidence adduced by Laistner (n. 49) for the interpretation *Graecus* 'a person who had some acquaintance with that language' is less than convincing. This interpretation is, however, confirmed by other evidence, e.g., in the epithet *Grecus* of Jacobus Veneticus Grecus or *magister Moyses graecus* (G. Cremaschi, *Mosè del Brolo* [Bergamo 1945], p. 163, app.) or Nicholas of Cusa's note on Albertus Magnus in Cod. 96 of the Hospitalbibliothek in Cusa: "Non grecus fuit Albertus." Laistner's restriction of the meaning to "*Irish* Greek scholars" is nevertheless untenable.

32. Laistner, *Thought and Letters*, p. 241.

33. "Wer in den Tagen Karl's des Kahlen Griechisch auf dem Kontinent kann, ist ein Ire, oder zuversichtlich: es ist ihm die Kenntnis durch einen Iren vermittelt worden, oder das Gerücht, das ihn mit diesem Ruhm umgibt, ist Schwindel. Den ganzen Fortschritt kennzeichnet es, daß das Exemplar des Dionysius Areopagites, das einst Pabst Paul I. an König Pippin geschenkt hat, erst jetzt der Ire Johannes verstehen und Karl dem Kahlen übersetzen kann"; Traube, "O Roma nobilis," p. 354.

34. Siegmund, *Die Überlieferung*, p. 30, on the "Codex Paulinus Augiensis" (Cambridge, Trinity College B 17.1).

35. Alcuin, *epist.* 307, *MGH Epistolae*, IV, 466 ff. Art historians suspect the presence of Greek manuscript illuminators at about the same time and in the same area. Thus the illustrations of the Evangelists in the Aachen (now Vienna) "Coronation Evangelary" are explained, since they are executed in the late antique style of illumination which was unfamiliar in the North at this period; the text contains the name DEMETRIVS PRESBYTER in a careless capitalis rustica; Vienna, Hofburg, Weltliche Schatzkammer, s.n., fol. 118^r (first page of the Gospel of Luke); cf. W. Koehler, *Die karolingischen Miniaturen* (Berlin 1960), III, pl. 23 and p. 51 n. Lowe and Bischoff date the entry to the Ottonian period, however; cf. *CLA*, X, 1469 and *Medieval Learning and Literature*, Festschrift Richard William Hunt (Oxford 1976), p. 4, n. 3.

36. *Translatio SS. Marcellini et Petri IV* 1, *MGH Scriptores*, XV, 256. The Bollandist

Papebroch wondered whether the *Graecus* could be understood as a native of Graz (*Acta SS Iuni.* [Antwerp 1695], I, 199)!

37. Löwe, in Wattenbach and Levison, *Deutschlands Geschichtsquellen*, H. 5, p. 607 (bibliog.).

38. In Paris, BN lat. 528; see Chapter II above.

39. Paul von Winterfeld, "Ein abendländisches Zeugnis über den ΥΜΝΟΣ ΑΚΑΘΙΣΤΟΣ der griechischen Kirche," *Zeitschrift für deutsches Altertum* 47 (1904), 81–88.

40. Huglo, "L'ancienne version latine de l'hymne acathiste," *Le Muséon* 64 (1951), 27–61.

41. Beck, *Kirche und theologische Literatur*, pp. 427 f. (bibliog.); cf. J. Szövérffy, *A Guide to Byzantine Hymnography* (Brookline/Leiden 1978), I, 116 ff.

42. Translation from the Latin text of Meersseman, *Der Hymnos Akathistos*, I, 101 ff. The editions by Huglo and von Winterfeld, not altogether superseded by Meersseman, were also consulted.

43. Von Winterfeld has also identified two adaptations of the prologue; "Ein abendländisches Zeugnis," pp. 86 ff. A new printing of the prologue in Meersseman, *Der Hymnos Akathistos*, pp. 128 f.

44. He mentions the Greek names of the sites of exile and burial. The use of *cata mane* in the first section, an ancient Grecism in Latin (e.g., *Vulgata*, Ezek. 46:14 and 15), is noteworthy.

45. Von Winterfeld claims to recognize traces of a Greek original of the prologue in the Latin text; "Ein abendländisches Zeugnis," p. 83, app. Huglo believes the prologue is the work of a Latin, in fact of the translator; "L'ancienne version," pp. 44 f. Meersseman does not take up the matter. Wallach takes the essays into account in his *Diplomatic Studies in Latin and Greek Documents* (1977).

46. The strict literalness of the translation of the hymn makes such statements possible; "L'ancienne version," pp. 55 f.

47. Usener, in *Jahrbücher für protestantische Theologie und Kirche* 13 (1887), 247 ff.; Beck, *Kirche und theologische Literatur*, pp. 496 ff.

48. Huglo, "L'ancienne version," p. 57.

49. By a purely speculative method, Meersseman (*Der Hymnos Akathistos*, I, 45 ff.) arrived at the conclusion that the hymn was translated in the Venetian territories by Bishop Christopher I of Olivolo (798–810; 813–27) during the conflict between the Franks and the Greeks. Since Meersseman saw this as no longer anything more than a "bold working hypothesis" ("kühne Arbeitshypothese") in his second volume (p. vii), it "probably no longer needs to be critically examined" ("braucht wohl nicht mehr kritisch darauf eingegangen werden"; Bulst, in *BZ* 55 [1962], 325). Pertusi also rejects Meersseman's hypothesis, in *Dante e la cultura Veneta* (1966), pp. 158 f.

50. See Chapter II above.

51. Jeauneau, "Les écoles de Laon et d'Auxerre au IX*e* siècle," in *La Scuola nell'Occidente latino dell'Alto Medioevo* (Spoleto 1972), pp. 495 ff. J. J. Contreni, "The Formation of Laon's Cathedral Library in the Ninth Century," *Studi Medievali* III/13 (1972), 919–39. B. Merlette, "Écoles et bibliothèques a Laon . . . ," *Actes du 95*e* Congrès national des Sociétés savantes, Reims 1970* (Paris 1975), I, 21–53. Contreni, "The Irish 'Colony' at Laon during the Time of John Scottus," in *Jean Scot Érigène et l'histoire de la philosophie; The Cathedral School of Laon* (Munich 1978); and "John Scottus, Martin Hibernensis, the Liberal Arts, and Teaching," in *Insular Latin Studies*, ed. M. Herren (Toronto 1981), pp. 23–44.

52. Hincmar of Reims, *Opusculum LV capitulorum* 43 (*Migne PL* 126, cols. 448 f.). The reprint in *MGH Poetae*, III, 408 n., is of no use.

53. Bischoff, *Mittelalterliche Studien*, II, 266. A detailed, even if somewhat obscured, description of the manuscript is given by Miller in *Notices et Extraits* 29/2 (1880). Contreni often refers to the manuscript in *The Cathedral School of Laon*, esp. pp. 69 f., just as does Jeauneau in "Jean Scot Érigène et le grec," *Archivum Latinitatis Medii Aevi* 41 (1979), 5 ff. A facsimile edition of the manuscript is a desideratum. A specimen facsimile (fol. 297r) is given in *MGH Poetae*, III, pl. 5, with Traube's commentary, p. 821.

54. Excerpts edited by Miller, pp. 25–112; the text of the Laudunensis was included in

Goetz' critical edition of the "Cyrillus glossary"; *Corpus Glossariorum Latinorum*, II, 215–483; pl. 3 of the same work presents an illustration of the beginning of the glossary, Cod. Laon 444, fol. 5ʳ.

55. Specimens, ed. Miller, pp. 112–18.

56. Ed. by Eckstein, *Programm der Lateinischen Hauptschule in Halle für das Schuljahr 1860–61*, pp. 3–11; excerpt ed. Miller, pp. 202–5. On the dissemination of the manuscripts of this Irish "elementary grammar," see Bischoff, *Mittelalterliche Studien*, II, 259, n. 76.

57. On this topic, see most recently Jeauneau, "Jean Scot Érigène," pp. 28 ff.

58. *Aristoteles latinus*, I, 133–75. Cf. above, Chapter III, n. 11 with the corresponding text. The *Graeca collecta* from the pseudo-Augustinian *Categoriae decem* are preserved in Paris, BN lat. 10307, in addition to Laon 444.

59. Ed. by C. du Cange, *Glossarium Mediae et Infimae Latinitatis* (Paris 1678), I, xxxv; Montfaucon, *Palaeographica Graeca*, p. 249; Contreni, *The Cathedral School of Laon*, p. 104. According to Contreni, the addressee, "S," was Lupus of Ferrières, who bore the nickname "Servatus."

60. Deciphered by W. Schmitz, "Tironisches und Kryptographisches," *NA* 15 (1890), 197 f. (*MGH Poetae*, III, 686). ⋏ ⌶ ∈ ⌈⁻ = AMEN stands at the end of the dedication, in the cipher used and explained by Dubthach, for example (see section 5). The resolution of the nominal siglum *H* will always be hypothetical. Here I mention only the two most plausible solutions: *H* = the addressee = Hincmaro = Hincmar of Laon (Traube, *MGH Poetae*, III, 686); *H* = the sender = Hartgarius, one of Bishop Hincmar's known collaborators (Contreni, *The Cathedral School of Laon*, p. 61).

61. Ed. by Laistner, "Notes on Greek from the Lectures of a Ninth Century Monastery Teacher," *The Bulletin of the John Rylands Library* 7 (1923), 446–49. Thiel, *Hebräischkenntnisse*, pp. 139 ff.

62. Ed. by Laistner, "Notes on Greek"; idem, "Rivipullensis and the Scholia of Martin of Laon," *Mélanges Mandonnet*, II (Paris 1930), 31–37; Bischoff, *Mittelalterliche Studien*, II, 266, n. 104; Thiel, *Hebräischkenntnisse*, pp. 152 f. See, however, Contreni's argument against the attribution to Martin in "Three Carolingian Texts Attributed to Laon: Reconsiderations," *Studi Medievali* III/17 (1976), 797–813. Cf. Lapidge, in *Jean Scot Érigène et l'histoire de la philosophie*, pp. 443 f.

63. *MGH Poetae*, III, 696 f.

64. C. E. Lutz, "Martianus Capella," in *Catalogus Translationum et Commentariorum*, III, 370 f. (bibliog.); Contreni opposes this thesis in "Three Carolingian Texts," pp. 797 ff. and *Catalogus Translationum*, III, 451 f.

65. C. Leonardi, "Nuove voci poetiche tra secolo IX e XI," *Studi Medievali* III/2 (1961), 141 ff., has found traces of the School of Laon in Vat. Reg. lat. 1625; they are *membra disiecta* from Paris, BN lat. 10307; cf. Contreni, in *Le Moyen Âge* 78 (1972), 31, and Jeauneau, in *La Scuola nell'Occidente*, p. 505.

66. John Scottus' commentary on the Gospel of John is preserved only in Cod. Laon 81. On the significance of this tradition for early Scholasticism, see Jeauneau in his edition of the commentary (Paris 1972), pp. 56 ff. and 369 ff.

67. "In a manuscript that has been traditionally attributed to the school of Heiric of Auxerre [Paris, BN lat. 12949], one finds a Roman transcription of a Greek text of one passage from the Epistle to the Ephesians (2:19–22) and of another from the gospel of St. John (21:19–20). The epistle is the one read on the common of the apostles; the gospel is the one read on the feast of St. John the Evangelist in the region of Auxerre. But—and this is the important point—the introductory formulae, in contrast to the former case, are precisely those of the Latin liturgy, translated into Greek." Jeauneau, "Jean Scot Érigène," pp. 29 f.

68. Traube, *MGH Poetae*, III, 421 f.

69. J. Mabillon, *De re diplomatica libri VI* (Paris 1681), pl. 57, p. 458.

70. *Bella Parisiacae urbis* III 30 f., ed. Paul von Winterfeld, *MGH Poetae*, IV, 117. H. Waquet arbitrarily omitted the third book from his new edition: *Abbon: Le siège de Paris par les Normands* (Paris 1942).

71. *Bella* III 4–6.

72. *Bella* III 50 f.

73. M. L. W. Laistner, "Abbo of St.-Germain-des-Prés," *Archivum Latinitatis Medii*

Aevi 1 (1924), 27–31, here p. 27; M. Arullani, "Un glossario in versi del IX secolo," *Atti dell'Accademia degli Arcadi*, n.s., 9/10 (1933), 23–85; B. Löfstedt, "Zu den Glossen von Abbos 'Bella Parisiacae urbis,'" *Studi Medievali* III/22 (1981), 261–66.

74. Löwe, in Wattenbach and Levison, *Deutschlands Geschichtsquellen*, H. 5, p. 581.

75. The concept goes back to Alistair Campbell. M. Lapidge understands it in a broad sense in "The Hermeneutic Style in Tenth-Century Anglo-Latin Literature," *Anglo-Saxon England* 4 (1975), 67: "a style whose most striking feature is the ostentatious parade of unusual, often very arcane and apparently learned vocabulary."

76. *Gesta Berengarii imperatoris, MGH Poetae*, IV, 355–401.

77. Lapidge, "L'influence stylistique de la poésie de Jean Scot," in *Jean Scot Érigène et l'histoire de la philosophie*, p. 451: "Ce qui reste sûr, c'est que la création de cette stylistique doit être attribuée à l'originalité de Jean Scot . . . " ("what remains certain is that the creation of this art of composition is to be attributed to the originality of John Scottus . . . ").

78. W. Koehler, *Buchmalerei des frühen Mittelalters. Fragmente und Entwürfe aus dem Nachlaß* (Munich 1972), pp. 179 f.

79. The point of departure for all modern research on Sedulius' works was Traube's chapter "Sedulius Scottus" in "O Roma nobilis," pp. 42–67. After Traube, Siegmund Hellmann examined in particular Sedulius' *Fürstenspiegel* and collection of excerpted passages, in *Sedulius Scottus* (Munich 1906). R. Düchting has written a critical commentary on Sedulius' poetic works: *Sedulius Scottus* (Munich 1968).

80. D. Brearley's edition, *Commentum Sedulii Scotti in maiorem Donatum grammaticum* (Toronto 1975), presents a commendable "Index Graecitatis," (pp. 284–86), but deals with the Graeca in a manner too far removed from the manuscript tradition "ad amussim optimorum scriptorum."

81. Stern notes in his description of the "Reichenau Notebook": "According to L. Traube . . . the Dresden and Paris codices were written by Sedulius. The excellent paleographer would have scarcely held this opinion had he been able to compare the hands of the two manuscripts"; in *Zeitschrift für celtische Philologie* 6 (1908), 551, n. 1. In all probability Traube was able to compare the hands of the two manuscripts: in the *Mélanges Graux* (1884), Omont published a photograph from the "Sedulius Psalter"; in 1902 photographs from the Codex Boernerianus were made for Traube, as Reichardt notes in his facsimile of the Codex Boernerianus (1909). Traube tacitly withdrew his earlier interpretation (see Chapter I above).

82. Cf. the facsimile edition of Codex Bernensis 363 (Leiden 1897), in the preface to which Hermann Hagen printed the annotations identified by name (pp. xliii–lxviii). A great number of the marginal notes refer to *ioh⟨annes⟩*. Contreni confirms the old assumption that this reference is to John Scottus in "The Irish in the Western Carolingian Empire (according to James F. Kenney and Bern, Burgerbibliothek 363)," in *Die Iren und Europa im früheren Mittelalter*, ed. H. Löwe (Stuttgart 1982), pp. 758–98. The medieval repository of the codex was probably Strasbourg; cf. Bischoff, "Irische Schreiber," *Mittelalterliche Studien*, III, 46.

83. *Carm*. 34, *MGH Poetae*, III, 199. See Düchting, *Sedulius*, pp. 120 f. Clark wanted to identify Fergus with Moengal-Marcellus of St. Gall, just so that he could interpret from the Marcus of Sedulius' verses that the Irish bishop had been in St. Gall (*The Abbey of St. Gall* [Cambridge 1926], p. 37). But the name Marcus itself will not lend itself to any quick identification. Heiric of Auxerre, for example, knew a Bishop Marcus, a Brythonic (i.e., probably Welsh) anchorite, living in Soissons and educated in Ireland (*Miracula S. Germani* I 6, cited in *MGH Poetae*, III, 422, n. 3).

84. From Valenciennes 81 (74), ed. Bischoff, *Mittelalterliche Studien*, II, 267, n. 109. This Fergus is probably the *grammaticus* and authority on the use of a Greek medication who is mentioned in the note from Bishop Pardulus of Lyon to Johannes (Scottus?), *MGH Poetae*, III, 518 n. In Codex Bernensis 363 there are also a few notes marked *fergus* and *fér*; cf. facsimile, ed. Hagen, p. xlvi. Cf. J. J. Contreni, "Masters and Medicine in Northern France during the Reign of Charles the Bald," in *Charles the Bald: Court and Kingdom*, ed. M. Gibson and J. Nelson (Oxford 1981), pp. 333–50.

85. J. L. Heiberg, "Et lille Bidrag til Belysning af Middelalderens Kendskab til Graesk," *Oversigt over det Kong. Danske Videnskabernes Selskabs Forhandlinger* (1889), pp. 198–204. R. Derolez, "Dubthach's Cryptogram," *L'Antiquité Classique* 21 (1952), 359–75. The Boethius manuscript Bamberg Class. 6 [HJ.IV.11], saec. XI, contains the entire explanation; Brussels 9565–66 (from St. Laurentius' in Liège) contains excerpts.

86. On Concen, see Derolez, "Dubthach's Cryptogram," p. 370. On the "Leiden Priscian" (Leiden, BPL 67, written in 838), see J. F. Kenney, *The Sources for the Early History of Ireland*, 2nd ed. (Shannon 1967), pp. 556 f. (In the "corrigenda" to the 2nd ed., the catalogue signature is incorrectly changed to "Voss. lat. 67"; this latter is also a Priscian manuscript, but not the famous Irish "Leiden Priscian"; Bischoff, "Irische Schreiber," pp. 50 f. and 56, n. 4.

87. Traube, "O Roma nobilis," p. 351, and the facsimile of Cod. Bern. 363, ed. Hagen, p. lxvii: *dub.*

88. "Greek Psalter with Latin interlinear version (up to Ps. 12; Pss. 13–16 only scattered words; from Ps. 17 on, only Greek) in Greek uncial" (Siegmund, *Die Überlieferung*, p. 27). A reproduction of fol. 3ᵛ (with appended Greek minuscule alphabet) in *MGH Poetae*, III, pl. 7. Traube's promise "fata codicis scitu sane dignissima alio loco enarrabo" (p. 823) was kept in the essay published with R. Ehwald, "Jean-Baptiste Maugérard. Ein Beitrag zur Bibliotheksgeschichte," Abh. Munich 23 (1906), 301–88. The codex motivated the bibliophile abbot in Murbach Bartholomew of Andlau or his assistant to make a Grecistic entry in the codex (Traube and Ehwald, pl. 1):

GRECIS ˙ LITTERIS ˙ AFFATIM ˙ ERUDITUS
DOMINUS ˙ BARTOLOMEUS ˙ / / / / / / / / / / / / / /
/ / / / ˙ HUNC LIBRUM ΛΘΗΧΛ ϤϷΛΣΗ
CONSCRIPTUM ˙ RESTITVIT ˙
˙ ШϷΛΤΕ ˙ ΠϷΟΕШ ˙
˙ M ˙ C ˙ C ˙ C ˙ C ˙ LXIIII ˙

ΛΘΗΧΛ ϤϷΛΣΗ = ἀττικῇ φράσει? ШϷΛΤΕ ΠϷΟΕШ = ORATE PRO EO.
/ / / are Maugérard's erasures.

89. *MGH Poetae*, III, 698–700.

90. Ed. by E. Baehrens, *Poetae Latini Minores* (Leipzig 1883), v, 375–78; *CC* 133A, 729–40.

91. Bischoff, in *Latin Script and Letters*, pp. 207 ff.

92. Ekkehart, *Casus S. Galli* 2.

93. The grammatical manuscript St. Gall, Stiftsbibliothek 877, saec. IX in., may be regarded as evidence for Greek studies in St. Gall before the Irish; it includes two *epistolae formatae*, "Greek numerals, alphabet, and Greco-Latin vocabulary (entirely in Roman script)" (G. Scherrer, *Verzeichniss der Handschriften der Stiftsbibliothek von St. Gallen* [Halle 1875], p. 305); A. Bruckner, *Scriptoria Medii Aevi Helvetica* (Geneva 1936), II, 81; rev. by B. Bischoff, in *Historisches Jahrbuch* 57 (1937), 695, according to whom the manuscript is from northern France.

94. All three manuscripts are available in facsimile editions: the evangelary in Rettig's epoch-making tracing (1836), the Pauline Epistles in the edition introduced by Reichardt (1909), and the Psalter in the edition introduced by Bieler (1960); see Bibliography and Chapter I. Most recently on the manuscript group see Barré, *Prières anciennes*, p. 93; Frede, *Altlateinische Paulus-Handschriften*, pp. 50–77; and N. Daniel, *Handschriften des zehnten Jahrhunderts aus der Freisinger Dombibliothek* (Munich 1973), pp. 36–38; they all refer to Bischoff, who published his view of the relationships in "Irische Schreiber," pp. 51 ff.: "It is probable that the [Bernese] Horace and the three bilinguals were copied from source texts out of the circle of Sedulius' students."

95. St. Gall, Stiftsbibliothek 48, p. 129. The best text, relatively speaking, is still that by S. Berger, "De la tradition de l'art grec dans les manuscrits latin des évangiles," *Mémoires de la Société Nationale des Antiquaires de France* 52 (1891), 144–54.

96. St. Gall, Stiftsbibliothek 17, saec. IX ex., Pss. 101–50 with bilingual supplementary material (alphabet, cantica, paternoster, credo, litany). On the cantica, see Schneider, in *Biblica* 30 (1949), 483. The facsimile in A. Bruckner's *Scriptoria Medii Aevi Helvetica* (Geneva 1938), III, pl. 26, makes possible a critical comparison with Frede's comment (*Altlateinische Paulus-Handschriften*, p. 79) that the Greek text "was copied from a minuscule source manuscript," that the source manuscript "probably came directly from Constantinople," and that it was thus proved "that there was a knowledge of Greek in St. Gall around the middle of the ninth century that was even independent in all respects of Irish influence." Can one draw all these conclusions from the use of a minuscule cross for ψ ? For otherwise the Greek alphabet used is majuscule.

97. Only remnants of this bilingual are preserved in St. Gall, Stiftsbibliothek 1395, pp. 336–61, described by Rahlfs, *Verzeichnis der griechischen Handschriften*, p. 70.

98. Ekkehard, *Casus S. Galli* 46.

99. Dositheus' grammar: Stiftsbibliothek 902; the "elementary grammar" of the Irish from Laon was entered on pp. 61–68 "with diverse variants . . . saec. X in." (Bischoff, *Mittelalterliche Studien*, II, 260, n. 76). The Priscian, with Old Irish glosses, is in Stiftsbibliothek 904.

100. The dialogue *En carissime* ΛΔΗΛϕΟC of MS Zurich C 129 (saec. IX², from St. Gall), offers a good example of how Graeca were adopted into the classroom in the later ninth century;, ed. Paul von Winterfeld and J. Schwalm, in *NA* 27 (1902), 742–43.

101. In his *Notatio*, Notker Balbulus called upon his student Salomo III to repay him at some later time for all his pains and efforts by commissioning a translation of Origen's commentary on the Song of Songs ("si aliquando sumptibus abundaveris et alicuius hominis latina et greca lingua eruditi amicitia usus fueris"); Notker certainly knew Jerome's translation of Origen's two homilies on the Song of Songs, but not Rufinus' translation of the commentary. E. Dümmler, *Das Formelbuch des Bischofs Salomo III von Konstanz* (Leipzig 1857), p. 66.

102. St. Gall, Stiftsbibliothek 17, 23 ("Folchart's Psalter") and 899.

103. St. Gall, Stiftsbibliothek 294 and 295.

104. Göttweig, Stiftsbibliothek 30, fol. 71; A. Merton's statements in *Die Buchmalerei in St. Gallen vom 9. zum 11. Jahrhundert* (Leipzig 1912), p. 32, are silently corrected by Bischoff, *Mittelalterliche Studien*, II, 255, n. 46. The bilingual litany from Sangall. 17 is printed in Cagin, *Te Deum*, pp. 501–5.

105. J. Duft and P. Meyer, *Die irischen Miniaturen der Stiftsbibliothek* (Olten/Bern/Lausanne 1953).

106. This much-discussed expression is found in the manuscript of a text on the significance of tone letters (St. Gall 381); the same manuscript (and no other) attributes the work to Notker. The text has been printed often, e.g., by A. Schubiger, *Die Sängerschule St. Gallens vom 8. bis ins 12. Jahrhundert* (Einsiedeln/New York 1858), p. 10; most recently, R. van Doren, "Étude sur l'influence musicale de l'abbaye de Saint-Gall," *Académie R. de Belgique, Beaux-Arts, Mémoires* II/3 (Brussels 1923), 105–13. According to van Doren, both the identification of the author and the closing phrase, with mention of the *ellinici fratres*, were additions originating in St. Gall. Opposing views had been expressed by von den Steinen, *Notker*, I, 495, and Laistner, in *History* 13 (1928), 143 f., and *Thought and Letters*, 2nd ed., p. 243, n. 3.

107. A detailed description by H. Husmann, *Tropen- und Sequenzenhandschriften* (Munich/Duisburg 1964), pp. 42–44.

108. Cod. 381, p. 35. Paul von Winterfeld (*MGH Poetae*, IV, 321) reconstructs, in Greek majuscules, a written form worth consideration (in Sangall. 381, only the "nomina sacra" are written in majuscules: ΚΥΡΡΙΕ ΧΡΙCΤΕ). Dreves prints the text in Greek minuscules, which the original certainly did not have, and emends the manuscript reading *sodisse*, which Ekkehard IV imitated and glossed with *salva* in the eleventh century (Dreves, in *Analecta Hymnica* 50 [1907], 255; Ekkehard IV, *Liber Benedictionum* XXXII 52). On a sixteenth-century transmission of the processional hymn from Utrecht, see Pralle, in *Theologische Quartalschrift* 128 (1948), 395.

109. Von den Steinen (*Notker*, I, 526 ff.) has identified the poet Hartmann: not Abbot Hartmann of St. Gall (ca. 922–25), but rather an earlier Hartmann, who appeared around 883 as a young poet.

110. Troper and sequence manuscripts (in chronological order): Stiftsbibliothek 484, saec. X; 382, saec. X/XI; 378, saec. XI; 380, saec. XI²; descriptions by Husmann, *Tropen- und Sequenzenhandschriften*, pp. 35 ff. Further Graecolatina are in the gradual and sacramentary MS 338, saec. XI¹, and in the gradual MS 376, saec. XI¹; cf. G. Scherrer, *Verzeichniss der Handschriften der Stiftsbibliothek von St. Gallen*, under the numbers mentioned. The indices to Scherrer's *Verzeichniss* are reliable guides to the Graecolatina of the Stiftsbibliothek: subject index, s.vv. "Agios," "Glossae," "Paternoster graece," "Symbolum apostolicum," "Symbolum Nicaeno-Ctinopolit," and especially the index of scripts, s.v. "Griechische Schrift." "A descriptive catalogue, in five parts, of Greek texts contained in the St. Gall manuscripts" is found in B. M. Kaczynski, "Learning in the Medieval West" (diss., Yale 1975), pp. 272–303.

111. Berlin, theol. qu. 11; V. Rose, *Verzeichniss der lateinischen Handschriften* [der Kgl. Bibliothek zu Berlin], II/2 (Berlin 1903), 685 f. (no. 694). The ivory binding, unique in design, was already lost after the transfer of the codex from the Minden Cathedral treasury to the Prussian state. The manuscript was among the Berlin manuscripts taken to Grüssau in Silesia for storage during World War II. The manuscript was long thought to be lost, but in 1983 it was discovered in the Cracow Biblioteka Jagiellonska, where it is preserved under its old Berlin shelf mark.

112. The passages quoted from Ekkehard I's sequences on Benedict, John the Baptist, and Paul are from *Analecta Hymnica* 50, 272 ff.

113. J. Egli gives a good overview of the Graeca of Ekkehard IV in *Der Liber Benedictionum Ekkeharts IV. nebst den kleineren Dichtungen aus dem Codex Sangallensis 393* (St. Gall 1909), pp. xxxvi f. The cited passages are *Lib. Ben.* XXXII 52, V 9, and XXVI 26.

114. *Casus S. Galli* 94, ed. G. Meyer von Knonau (St. Gall 1877), pp. 344 ff. The antiphon *Maria et flumina* in Hesbert, *Corpus Antiphonalium*, III, no. 3700 (for Epiphany).

115. St. Gallen, Stiftsbibliothek 560, p. 374. Cf. W. Berschin, *Vitae sanctae Wiboradae* (St. Gall 1983), p. 20.

116. K. Preisendanz, "Reginbert von der Reichenau," *Neue Heidelberger Jahrbücher* (1952–53), pp. 4 f.

117. Karlsruhe, Aug. XXXVIII, fols. 1^r–8^r.

118. Würzburg, M.p.th.f. 75, written under Abbot Ruadhelm of Reichenau (838–42); cf. B. Bischoff and J. Hofmann, *Libri Sancti Kyliani* (Würzburg 1952), p. 126 (bibliog.). The manuscript from which the text was directly copied for Otgar, archbishop of Mainz, is still extant in Karlsruhe, Aug. XCIV: this follows not only from the comparison of the system of decoration and layout found in both manuscripts, but also from the name entered on the back flyleaf of the manuscript remaining in the Reichenau collection—*Otgar*; this is not the scribe's name (as Preisendanz conjectures in *Die Kultur der Abtei Reichenau*, p. 676), but rather a note that the volume was copied for Otgar.

119. Walafrid, in the work on the liturgy dedicated to Reginbert of Reichenau, *De exordiis et incrementis* 7, "Quomodo theotisce domus dei dicitur," ed. A. Knoepfler (Munich 1890), pp. 18 ff. In Walafrid's miscellany manuscript (St. Gall 878, p. 320), a runic alphabet is found together with Hebrew and Greek material; see Derolez, *Runica Manuscripta*, p. 75; Bischoff, *Mittelalterliche Studien*, II, 40.

120. The manuscript discovered by Mone in the Stiftsbibliothek of St. Paul in Lavanttal has since been recatalogued so often that it has become a serious obstacle to the use of the research literature on the subject. The manuscript is best known under the catalogue number 25.2.31b (former XXV d 86). K. Preisendanz described it under this number in *Die Reichenauer Handschriften*, 2nd ed., III/2 (Wiesbaden 1973), 124–27 and pl. 2 (Greek articles). In his supplement to the bibliography (p. 282), the currently valid number is, however, given as "Cod. 86b/1 (ehem. 25.2.31b)"; and in the *Jahrbuch der Österr. Byzantinischen Gesellschaft* 5 (1956), 7–25, W. Krause compared the manuscript with Vienna MS 114 of Froumund under the number "St. Paul XXV D/65." Thus it is not surprising—although it does detract from the scholarly relevance of this work—that Krause was unacquainted with important older research on the "Reichenau Notebook," especially Stern's description in *Zeitschrift für celtische Philologie* 6 (1908), which is indispensable even now. According to Bischoff, the "Reichenau Notebook" must "have come from the West Frankish Kingdom, where the scholarly Irish element had its center in the area of Laon-Soissons," (*Mittelalterliche Studien*, III, 48 f.), just as had other important Irish manuscripts of Reichenau (e.g., Priscian, Aug. CXXXII). According to information from the St. Paul Stiftsbibliothek, the valid catalogue number is 86b/1.

121. Frede, *Altlateinische Paulus-Handschriften*, pp. 80–87; Preisendanz, *Die Reichenauer Handschriften*, III/2, 21 f. and 272 (bibliog.).

122. Zurich, Zentralbibliothek Rh. hist. 27, p. ciii; facsimile ed. J. Autenrieth, D. Geuenich, and K. Schmid (Hannover 1979); M. Borgolte, *Der Gesandtentausch der Karolinger mit den Abbasiden und mit den Patriarchen von Jerusalem* (Munich 1976), pp. 114 ff.

123. Zurich, Rh. hist. 27, p. liii; F. V. Mareš has corrected the name, incorrectly read in other research, in "Die Namen des Sklavenapostels Methodius von Saloniki und seiner Gefährten im Verbrüderungsbuch des Reichenauer Klosters," *Cyrillomethodianum* (Thessaloníki 1971), I, 107–12; cf. J. Schütz, "Methods Widersacher Wiching und dessen pannonisch-mährische Gefährten," in *Marburger Abhandlungen zur Geschichte und Kultur*

Osteuropas 14 (1977), 390–94; A. Zettler, "Cyrill und Method im Reichenauer Verbrüderungsbuch," *Frühmittelalterliche Studien* 17 (1983), 280–98.

124. The names of both the Greek Constantine and Symeon of Jerusalem were entered into the Reichenau confraternal book by a Western hand in Grecistic letters: Zurich Rh. hist. 27, pp. iii and lxxxiii. A new edition of the *Vita Symeonis Achivi* by T. Klüppel and W. Berschin, in *Die Abtei Reichenau* (Sigmaringen 1974), pp. 115–24.

125. Zurich, Zentralbibliothek Rh. hist. 27, p. clxi.

126. "Formulae Augienses, Collectio C," no. 21, ed. K. Zeumer, *MGH Formulae* (1886), p. 374. The collection is considered to be "Walafrid's collection of letters"; cf. K. Beyerle, ed., *Die Kultur der Abtei Reichenau*, I, 100 f.

127. I.e., the letter *Cogitis me*, ascribed to Jerome, which, according to the now prevalent opinion, was written by Paschasius Radbertus of Corbie; cf. A. Ripberger, *Der Pseudo-Hieronymus-Brief IX 'Cogitis me'. Ein erster marianischer Traktat des Mittelalters von Paschasius Radbert* (Fribourg 1962) (edition and bibliog.). Radbert of Corbie attributed a sermon for Paula and Eustochium and their monastery to Jerome: "novo loquendi genere sanctis, quae vobiscum degunt, virginibus, latino utens eloquio, exhortationis gratia sermonem faciam de assumptione beatae et gloriosae semper virginis Mariae, more eorum qui declamatorie in ecclesiis solent loqui ad populum, quod utique genus docendi necdum attigeram" ("In a new way of speaking to the holy virgins who live with you, I will compose a sermon in Latin on the assumption of the blessed and glorious eternal virgin Mary, in the manner of those who are accustomed to speak to the people in churches by declamation, a method of teaching that I have not yet practiced"; c. 1); this was done in order to suppress the reading of an "apocryphal book on the assumption of the Virgin" on holy days: "ne forte si venerit vestris in manibus illud apocryphum de transitu eiusdem virginis dubia pro certis recipiatis" ("lest if by chance that apocryphal book on the assumption of this same Virgin come into your hands, you admit doubts for certainties"; c. 7). Perhaps the late antique disguise of the letter was originally only an imitation of the popular pastime of Charlemagne's court (Ripberger, pp. 15 f.). Yet the vigor with which Hincmar of Reims silenced Ratramnus, the monk of Corbie, who knew and named the author as his confrater, and with which he promoted the liturgical use of the work (through the preparation of a deluxe manuscript), ultimately transformed the letter into a falsification. The *apocryphum de transitu . . . virginis* is to be understood as one of the Latin versions of the *Transitus Mariae*.

128. Gerhoh was mistaken, however, when he supposed that he saw evidence that *De assumptione beatae Mariae* was translated from Greek: "Sermo quoque ipse, ut in modo dictaminis apparet, Grece primo editus et postea in Latinum translatus . . . " ("This discourse was also first published in Greek and afterwards translated into Latin, as the mode of speech demonstrates . . . "); ed. P. Classen, in *Gerhohi opera inedita* (Rome 1955), I, 375 f.

129. *Analecta Hymnica* 44, 204.

130. *Analecta Hymnica* 50, 310.

Notes to Chapter IX

1. Gay, *L'Italie méridionale et l'empire byzantine*, p. 25.

2. Einhard also found Charles' lack of interest in Rome and Italy remarkable: "Quam [sc. urbem Romam] cum tanti penderet, tamen intra XLVII annorum, quibus regnaverat, spatium quater tantum illo votorum solvendorum ac supplicandi causa profectus est" ("although he valued it [i.e., Rome] so highly, he nevertheless went there only four times during the forty-seven years of his reign in order to fulfill his vows and pray"), namely, in 774, 781, 787, and 800; *Vita Karoli* 27.

3. Ed. by E. Dümmler, *MGH Epistolae*, VI, 201–5, here pp. 204 f.

4. A. Rahlfs, *Septuaginta-Studien* (Göttingen 1907), II, 92.

5. According to Schneider (*Cantica*, p. 103), the scholarly work contained a criticism of the "Symeon Psalter." Allgeier (in *Biblica* 24 [1943], 275) conjectures somewhat differently with regard to the motifs: "Es handelt sich . . . nicht um einen revidierten Mailänder Psalter, sondern um die Rechtfertigung desselben gegenüber der hexaplarischen Rezension des hl. Hieronymus. . . . Es liegt nahe . . . an die karolingischen Bestrebungen zu denken, das Psalterium Gallicanum auch in der Lombardei durchzuführen. Dabei scheint auch der Vorwurf gefallen zu sein, die Mailänder Rezension stimme nicht zur Septuaginta" ("It is a ques-

tion not of a revised Milanese Psalter, but rather of a justification thereof against St. Jerome's hexaplarian recension. It is natural to think of the Carolingian efforts to make the 'Psalterium Gallicanum' the standard in Lombardy. At that time it also seems that the Milanese recension was reproached for not conforming to the Septuagint").

6. G. Morin, in *RB* 10 (1893), 193–97.

7. Rahlfs, *Septuaginta-Studien*, II, 94.

8. Schneider, *Cantica*, pp. 106 f.

9. Cf. Löwe, in Wattenbach and Levison, *Deutschlands Geschichtsquellen*, H. 4, pp. 408 f., on an "Iro-Scottish group associated with St. Ambrose," to which Symeon "was closely connected" and the author of the *Litterae de psalterio transferendo* "presumably belonged."

10. For example, Vat. Pal. lat. 846, fols. 115ʳ–16ʳ, Lorsch, saec. IX¹ (B. Bischoff, *Lorsch im Spiegel seiner Handschriften* [Munich 1974], p. 32); Siegmund, *Die Überlieferung*, pp. 233 f.

11. On Arichis, see Chapter VI above. Bishop Aio of Benevento received a translation from Anastasius Bibliothecarius of Theodore Studites' homily on the Apostle Bartholomew. Ademar of Benevento translated a *Vita Gregorii Nazianzeni* in 903 (*BHL* 3667); Siegmund, *Die Überlieferung*, p. 264; *Catalogus Translationum*, II, 173 f. A second translation of Theodore Studites' homily on the Apostle Bartholomew, attributed to Abbot Bertharius of Monte Cassino (856–84; *BHL* 1005; Siegmund, *Die Überlieferung*, pp. 258 f.) is only a modified version of Anastasius' translation; in addition, Siegmund's misgivings about the tradition of Abbot Bertharius as the author of this version have also been confirmed; cf. Westerbergh, *Anastasius Bibliothecarius: Sermo Theodori Studitae* (Stockholm 1963), pp. 51 and 93. Nevertheless, the text tradition of an *ordo* for the Tuesday after Easter, which provides for a Greco-Latin antiphony, goes back to Abbot Bertharius of Monte Cassino (Cagin, *Te Deum*, pp. 161 ff.).

12. V. Falkenhausen, *Untersuchungen über die byzantinische Herrschaft in Süditalien*, pp. 29 ff. E. Eickhoff, *Seekrieg und Seepolitik zwischen Islam und Abendland. Das Mittelmeer unter byzantinischer und arabischer Hegemonie (650–1040)* (Berlin 1966).

13. The most conspicuous evidence of the Greco-Latin culture of the city of Bari is the Exultet-Rotulus I of the cathedral in Bari (saec. XI): while the text of the Exultet is Latin, the series of saints which frame the text band is Greek in both the style of illustration and inscription. On Easter night in Bari, prayers were offered for the pope (first noted for Alexander [II, 1061–73]), the archbishop, the Greek emperor (first noted for Constantine [IX, 1042–55]) and the empress; after 1071 one also took pains to make mention of "lucidissimi ducis nostri domni Rubberti [Robert Guiscard]," whose name immediately replaced the emperor's; G. Cavallo, *Rotoli di Exultet dell'Italia meridionale* (Bari 1973), pp. 47–80, esp. pp. 48 f.

14. K. Meisen, *Nikolauskult und Nikolausbrauch im Abendlande* (Düsseldorf 1931).

15. Ferrari, *Early Roman Monasteries*, pp. 419 ff. and under the names of the individual monasteries.

16. Cod. Vat. gr. 1666, fol. 41ᵛ. Batiffol, "Librairies byzantines à Rome," *Mélanges d'Archéologie et d'Histoire* 8 (1888), 297 ff., has given a description of this cimelia of Italo-Hellenism, which is not fully replaced by C. Giannelli, *Codices Vaticani Graeci 1485–1683* (Rome 1950), pp. 408 f., and Follieri, *Codices graeci*, pl. 11 and pp. 20 f. On the ornamentation, see most recently Grabar, *Les manuscrits grecs*, pp. 30 f. The subscription belongs to the later additions to the codex, just as does the Easter table next to it, written in Beneventan script and including a key to the Greek numerals.

17. Usener, in *Jahrbücher für protestantische Theologie* 13 (1887), 244–59. Beck, *Kirche und theologische Literatur*, pp. 496 f.

18. Batiffol, "Librairies byzantines à Rome," p. 300.

19. Rosweyde included the *Vita S. Iohannis Eleemosynarii* in his *Vitae Patrum* (Migne *PL* 73, cols. 337–91). In the first words of Anastasius' prologue, Laehr sees "ein unmißverständliches Bekenntnis des ehemaligen Gegenpapstes" ("an unambiguous acknowledgement of the former antipope"; in *NA* 47 [1927/28], 418): "Cogitante me ac diu tacite solliciteque mecum considerante, quid in domo Dei commodius ac dignius operari possem . . ." ("I deliberated and for a long time silently and anxiously considered what I might appropriately and more suitably do in the house of God"; Migne *PL* 73, col. 337; cf. *MGH*

Epistolae, VII, 396). The prologue is famous for its postulation of a papal right of judgment in literary matters: "Sed licet membranas inciderim, scedulas praeparaverim, non tamen hunc in codicem conficere ausus sum, antequam a dominatione vestra, o millies beate, licentiam adipisci promerui. Neque enim fas est ut absque vicario Dei, absque clavigero caeli . . . absque te omnium arbitro aliquid consummetur aut divulgetur" ("But although I might have cut the parchment and prepared the small pages, I did not, nevertheless, dare to write in the codex until I could obtain permission from your lordship, O thousand times blessed one. For it is not fit that anything be completed and published without the vicar of God, without the bearer of the keys to heaven . . . without you, the judge of all"); *MGH Epistolae*, VII, 397.

20. H. Gelzer, *Leontios von Neapolis Leben des Heiligen Johannes des Barmherzigen* (Freiburg/Leipzig 1893), p. xxxvi.

21. Sigebert of Gembloux, *Catalogus de viris illustribus*, c. 103, Migne PL 160, col. 570 (in the edition by R. Witte [Frankfurt 1974], c. 104).

22. The *Vita S. Basilii* is also included in Rosweyde's *Vitae Patrum*, Migne PL 73, cols. 293–320, although the author is incorrectly identified, since Rosweyde held the addressee of the prologue, Ursus, to be the translator. On a later translation by the priest Ursus of Naples see section 3 below.

23. The remarkably crude translation has been edited in *AB* 15 (1896), 257–67, from Codex Mantua, Biblioteca Comunale C.IV.13 (a. 1446), originally from Polirone; *MGH Epistolae*, VII, 402 includes the prologue only. The story of "St. John the Cottager," who lived near his father's house as an unrecognized pauper, is related to the legend of St. Alexius.

24. John the Merciful had fostered the cult of the two Egyptian martyrs Cyrus and Johannes. Anastasius' poorly transmitted prologue is edited in *MGH Epistolae*, VII, 426 f., according to Chartres 63, "saec. IX/X." The addressee is unknown. The text of the passion is in *Migne PL* 129, cols. 705–14; the *miracula* is in *Migne PG* 87 (1865), cols. 3423–3675. In his translation of the *miracula*, Anastasius continued the work of the ancient Roman translator Bonifatius Consiliarius; Anastasius mentions his predecessor in the prologue. On the Greek source, see T. Nissen, "De SS. Cyri et Iohannis vitae formis," *AB* 57 (1939), 65 ff.

25. The text is in *Migne PL* 41, cols. 817–22; the prologue is in *MGH Epistolae*, VII, 427 f. The dedication to Bishop Landulf of Capua (*MGH Epistolae*, VII, 427 f.) is also important for its mention of a translation of a *sermo* by Amphilochius of Iconium, which could be contained in the "Reichenauer Corpus der Marienpredigten" (Aug. LXXX); see Chapter VIII above.

26. The dedicatory epistle is in *MGH Epistolae*, VII, 429 f. While the translation of the *passio* of the 1,480 martyrs of Mt. Ararat (Acacius and his companions) is clearly identifiable (*BHL* 20), it has not yet been finally determined which of the extant translations of the passion of Bishop Peter of Alexandria is to be ascribed to Anastasius (even after P. Devos' "Une passion grecque inédite de S. Pierre d'Alexandrie et sa traduction par Anastase le Bibliothécaire," *AB* 83 [1965], 157–87).

27. The dedicatory epistle to Bishop Gauderich is in *MGH Epistolae*, VII, 436–38. The translation itself is lost; cf. Wattenbach and Levison, *Deutschlands Geschichtsquellen*, H. 4, p. 472 and n. 340 (bibliog.).

28. Ed. by Westerbergh, *Anastasius Bibliothecarius*.

29. The prologue has been transmitted in various versions; cf. *MGH Epistolae*, VII, 438 f. The text of the *Passio et miracula S. Demetrii* is in *Migne PL* 129, cols. 715–26.

30. Translation of the Latin text of the preface, *MGH Epistolae*, VII, 440 f. The Graeca are explained in the editor's notes. On the various ninth-century Dionysian passions, see Wattenbach and Levison, *Deutschlands Geschichtsquellen*, H. 3, p. 320 and n. 90, and H. 4, p. 466 and n. 319 (biblioig.). The complete text of the *Passio S. Dionysii* translated by Anastasius is edited only in P. F. Chiffletius, *Dissertationes tres* (Paris 1676), pp. 7–35.

31. Ed. by C. de Boor, *Theophanis Chronographia* (Leipzig 1885), II, 31–346; see also D. Tabachowitz, "Sprachliches zur lateinischen Theophanes-Übersetzung des Anastasius Bibliothecarius," *BZ* 38 (1938), 16–22. The translation of Nicephorus' *Chronography* which Migne prints (*Migne PL* 129, cols. 129 ff.) is not Anastasius', as Lapôtre has noted (p. 337). The dedication to Johannes Diaconus is edited in *MGH Epistolae*, VII, 419–21.

32. *Migne PL* 129, cols. 557–690. The dedication to Johannes Diaconus is edited in *MGH Epistolae* VII, 423–26.

33. *Commemoratio* (Inc. "Afflictionum maeores . . . "), *Migne PL* 129, cols. 591–604. The dedication to Bishop Martin of Narni is in *MGH Epistolae*, VII, 426 f. P. Peeters, who found the Greek text in a manuscript in Patmos and published it, holds that the Greek vita was "écrite ou revisée après 726, début du conflit iconoclaste" ("written or revised after 726, the beginning of the iconoclastic conflict"); "Une vie grecque du pape S. Martin I," *AB* 51 (1933), 225–62, here p. 252. The Greek vita is considered to be one of the works of the Greek colony in Rome.

34. *Epist.* 130, *MGH Epistolae*, VI, 651. When Pope Nicholas writes that Charles the Bald should submit the translation for examination *iuxta morem*, he adopts the same view of a right to censorship which Anastasius propagates in the prologue to the *Vita S. Iohannis Eleemosynarii* (see above, n. 19). Johannes takes up the idea in the dedication of the *Vita S. Gregorii M.* to Pope John VIII (*Migne PL* 75, col. 61). According to Cappuyns (*Jean Scot Érigène*, pp. 155 f.), the letter in which Pope Nicholas I requested the translation of John Scottus for examination was a forgery. Cappuyns' arguments are considerable, and many have assented to his view, among them Siegmund, *Die Überlieferung*, p. 191, n. 2. The main argument, however, that *iuxta morem* "eût été inouï au IXe siècle" ("would have been unprecedented in the ninth century"), is not to the point. In the "Roman renaissance" of the later ninth century, the idea of a papal right to censorship was in fact to be found—unless *all three* passages cited above were forgeries.

35. *MGH Epistolae*, VII, 431 f.—". . . sa traduction est illisible . . . "; Blatt, in *Classica et Mediaevalia* 1 (1938), 240.

36. Cf. Siegmund, *Die Überlieferung*, p. 191; Dondaine, *Le Corpus dionysien*, pp. 50 ff.

37. S. Pétridès, ed., "Traités liturgiques de saint Maxime et de saint Germain traduits par Anastase le Bibliothécaire," *Revue de l'Orient Chrétien* 10 (1905), 289–309 and 350–64.

38. *MGH Epistolae*, VII, 434 f.

39. One may well consider *Leo humilis interpres latinorum ac ellenicorum* a continuator of Anastasius' work; he translated the *Gesta SS. Samonae, Guriae et Abibi* from Greek for a certain *Stephanus Romanae sedis secundicerius*; cf. Siegmund, *Die Überlieferung* pp. 255, 272, and addendum, p. 283. In addition, Bishop John of Arezzo, recently identified as the author of *De assumptione*, must also be mentioned (Philippart, *AB* 92 [1974], 345 f.). According to current information, he was certainly not a translator, but he did work with contemporaneous translation literature; cf. above, Chapter VIII, sec. 7.

40. New surveys: Löwe, in Wattenbach and Levison, *Deutschlands Geschichtsquellen*, H. 4, pp. 439–47, esp. pp. 443 f. (bibliog.); Pertusi, "Bisanzio e l'irradiazione della sua civiltà in occidente nell'alto medioevo," in *Centri e vie di irradiazione della civiltà* (Spoleto 1964), pp. 75–133, here pp. 110 ff.; Kuss, in *Geschichte in Wissenschaft und Unterricht* 18 (1967), 129–46; N. Cilento, "L'agiografia e la traduzione dal greco," in *Civiltà napoletana del Medioevo* (Naples 1969), pp. 31–54. F. Luzzati-Laganà, "Le firme greche nei documenti de Ducato di Napoli," *Studi Medievali* III/23 (1982), 729–52.

41. *Monumenta Epigraphica Christiana saec. XIII antiquiora*, ed. A. Silvagni, vol. IV, fasc. 1: *Neapolis* (Rome 1943), pls. 1–6. H. Delehaye, "Hagiographie Napolitaine," *AB* 57 (1939), 5–64.

42. In the Neapolitan historical works of the ninth/tenth century, the Greco-Latin mode of clerical and lay singing of Psalms is repeatedly mentioned: *Vita Athanasii episcopi* [Athanasius I, d. 872], c. 1, *MGH Scriptores rerum Langobardicarum* (Hannover 1878), p. 440; *Translatio S. Athanasii* 1 [in 877], ibid., p. 451; *Translatio S. Severini* 6, ibid., p. 456.

43. *MGH Epistolae*, VI, 193 f.: Deacon Paul's dedication for the *Vitae S. Mariae Aegyptiacae*, which he presented "cum tomulo de cuiusdam vicedomini paenitentia." It is very easy to suppose that the translator was also the *donator*. On Paul, see M. Fuiano, "I rapporti tra oriente ed occidente nell'attività culturale di Paulo diacono della chiesa napoletana nel sec. IX," *Atti del 3° Congresso Internazionale di Studi sull'Alto Medioevo* (Spoleto 1959), pp. 397–435; repr. in Fuiano, *La cultura a Napoli nell'alto medioevo* (Naples 1961), pp. 131–52.

44. *Vita S. Mariae Aegyptiacae*, in Rosweyde's *Vitae Patrum*, *Migne PL* 73, cols. 671–90.

45. *Paenitentia Theophili*, Acta SS Feb. (Antwerp 1658), I, 483–87; new edition by G. G. Meersseman, *Kritische glossen op de griekse Theophilus-Legende (7^e eeuw) en haar latijnse vertaling*, Mededelingen von de K. Vlaamse Academie voor Wetenschappen (Brussels 1963), pp. 17–32. A. Gier, *Der Sünder als Beispiel. Zu Gestalt und Funktion hagiographischer Gebrauchstexte anhand der Theophiluslegende* (Frankfurt 1977), pp. 39–46.

46. Kunze, *Studien zur Legende der heiligen Maria Aegyptiaca*, p. 40.

47. D. Mallardo, "Giovanni Diacono napoletana," *Rivista di storia della Chiesa in Italia* 2 (1948), 317–37, and 4 (1950), 325–58.

48. *Methodius ad Theodorum*, ed. G. Anrich, *Hagios Nikolaos* (Leipzig/Berlin 1913), I, 140 ff.; see vol. II, p. 84.

49. *Vita S. Nicolai*, ed. B. Mombritius, *Sanctuarium* (Paris 1910), II, 292–309. In the prologue, the translator (Johannes) says that he is "quintum percurrens lustrum."

50. *Acta SS* Mart. (Antwerp 1668), II, 22–25. Johannes Diaconus translated with the aid of a Greek: "accito Graeco peritissimo" (prol.).

51. Partially edited from Naples, BN VIII.B.9, fols. 199ᵛ–209ᵛ, saec. XV (according to *AB* 30 [1911], 172), by F. Dolbeau, "La vie latine de saint Euthyme," *Mélanges de l'École Française de Rome* (1982), 315–335.

52. The *Passio Arethae* is only partially preserved, in a Baroque copy, and printed in *Acta SS* Oct. (Brussels 1861), X, 761 f. Athanasius adapted it freely: "serie commutata ad dilucidandas sententias nonnulla ingerimus nostra" (c. 2).

53. Prologue in A. Mai, *Spicilegium Romanum* (Rome 1840), IV, 283–85; the *Passio* text is in *Bibliotheca Casinensis* (Monte Cassino 1877), III, Florilegium, pp. 102–9. The work is dedicated "Athanasio gratia dei venerabilissimo Christi famulo," not "Anastasio abbati," as Mai prints; cf. Siegmund, *Die Überlieferung*, p. 228; *AB* 100 (1983), 377, n. 13. This author too gives much more of an adaptation than a translation. He says that he was asked "ut B. Anastasii martyrium, quod quidam grammaticae artis expertissimus de graeco in latinum confuso transtulerat ⟨sermone⟩, urbanius regulari digestu componerem." This predecessor who was an "expert in grammar" was either the (probably Roman) translator, who was the first to translate the *Passio S. Anastasii* (between 630 and 730), or the Venerable Bede, who, according to his own testimony, corrected this translation.

54. The *Vita S. Basilii* is printed in *Bibliotheca Casinensis* (1877), III, Florilegium, pp. 205–19. Cf. Siegmund, *Die Überlieferung*, pp. 259 f.

55. ". . . Gregorius Parthenopensis loci seruator . . . ceu quorundam passiones sanctorum Martyrum, rustico Achiuorum stylo digestas, legi in ecclesia comperisset, et ex his populus audiens ridiculum potius quam imitationem acquireret, Christi aemulatione permotus non est passus Dei opus ludibrium fieri populorum" (". . . Gregory of Naples, servator of the place . . . discovered that when the passions of certain of the holy martyrs, composed in the rustic style of the Greeks, were read in church, and the people heard them, they found in them a cause more of laughter than of emulation; moved by the emulation of Christ, he did not suffer that God's work be ridiculed by the people"; *Acta SS* Feb. (Antwerp 1658), II, 30. Siegmund remarks on the passage: "Dadurch fällt doch ein interessantes Licht auf den Sprachenkampf in Neapel" ("Thus an interesting light is cast on the linguistic conflicts in Naples"); *Die Überlieferung*, p. 273. Yet it is not certain that "the Greek language" is the meaning of "rustico Achivorum stylo": it can also be "the Greek style of composition" of an all-too-literal Latin translation, and this would have provoked the scorn of the Neapolitans more readily than a rustic Greek, however boorish it might have been. One might compare this interpretation with the opening of the prologue, with its invective against hagiographical writers who have filled the lives of the saints with "absurd words" and "obscure meanings": ". . . tanta eas [sc. martyrum passiones] absurditate faminum, tantaque obscuritate sensuum repleuere . . ."

56. F. Savio, "Pietro suddiacono napoletano," *Atti della R. Accademia di Scienze di Torino* 36 (1900/1901), 665–79; P. Devos, "Deux oeuvres méconnues de Pierre sous-diacre de Naples au Xᵉ siècle," *AB* 76 (1958), 336–53. According to the cited studies, the oeuvre of Petrus Subdiaconus comprises some dozen translations and adaptations of hagiographical material. Many of the attributions are, however, unproven. It is not even certain whether there was one or many translators by the name of Petrus in Naples in the ninth/tenth century.

57. From the large Bamberg manuscript Hist. 3 (E.III.14), northern Italy, saec. X–XI, ed. F. Pfister, *Der Alexanderroman des Archipresbyters Leo* (Heidelberg 1913). On the prologue, see W. Bulst, in *Studien zur lateinischen Dichtung des Mittelalters*, Festschrift Karl Strecker (Dresden 1931), pp. 12–17; cf. the rejoinder by Pfister, "Zum Prolog des Archipresbyter Leo und zu den alten Drucken der 'Historia de Preliis,'" *Rheinisches Museum* 90 (1941), 273 ff. D. J. A. Ross has reported on a new (incomplete) manuscript

tradition: "A New Manuscript of Archpriest Leo of Naples' Nativitas et Victoria Alexandri Magni," *Classica et Mediaevalia* 20 (1959), 98–158.

58. An overview is given by D. J. A. Ross, *Alexander Historiatus: A Guide to Medieval Illustrated Alexander Literature* (London 1963), and F. Pfister, "Studien zum Alexanderroman," in a revised version by R. Merkelbach, in Pfister, *Kleine Schriften zum Alexanderroman* (Meisenheim 1976), pp. 17–52, here p. 23 (bibliog.).

59. H.-J. Bergemeister, *Die Historia de Preliis Alexandri Magni, Synoptische Edition der Rezensionen des Leo Presbyter und der interpolierten Fassungen J¹, J² und J³ (Buch I und II)* (Meisenheim 1975). K. Steffens, *Die Historia de preliis Alexandri Magni Rezension J³* (Meisenheim 1975). A. Hilka and H.-J. Bergemeister, *Historia Alexandri Magni (Historia de Preliis) Rezension J²* (Meisenheim 1976). On the entire complex of medieval Alexander literature, see G. Cary and D. J. A. Ross, *The Medieval Alexander* (Cambridge 1956).

Notes to Chapter x

1. H. Jantzen, *Ottonische Kunst*, 2nd ed. (Hamburg 1959), pp. 58 f.

2. The best analysis of the problem of a tenth-century Latin epochal style is given by Erich Auerbach, *Literatursprache und Publikum* (Bern 1958), pp. 99–133.

3. Rather, *Qualitatis coniectura cuiusdam* 2 (Migne PL 136, col. 523); in his literary portrait of Rather (*Literatursprache und Publikum*, pp. 99 ff.), Auerbach translates "und bildet sich etwas auf das griechische Wort ein, wo er doch kaum Latein kann" (p. 110). Obviously Rather's dictum is the model for Ekkehard IV's famous verse "Esse velim Grecus, cum sim vix, domna, Latinus" (*Casus S. Galli* 94), which is itself related to the letter of a pupil in the cathedral school of Mainz around 1032, "Eximię iuventuti Wormatiensium, insudanti studiis et artibus Atheniensium, R. Mogontinus non Grecus, sed vix effectus Latinus . . . " (ed. W. Bulst, *Die ältere Wormser Briefsammlung* [Weimar 1949], no. 26, p. 48, n. 2).

4. Von den Steinen, *Notker*, II, 118.

5. A Latino-Greek Agnes sequence, composed before 1071 and unfortunately rather poorly transmitted, is printed in *Analecta Hymnica* 51, 99 f.

6. Of the modern historiographical literature on East-West relations in the tenth century, one might mention only Leyser, "The Tenth Century in Byzantine-Western Relationship," in *Relations between East and West in the Middle Ages* (Edinburgh 1973), pp. 29 ff.

7. "Quid dicam, quam facile doctrinas ebibet Grecas, qui tam puerilibus in annis epotavit Latinas?" Liudprand, ΛΝΤΛΠΟΔΟCΙC VI 2, ed. J. Becker, *Die Werke Liudprands von Cremona* (Hannover/Leipzig 1915), p. 153. Liudprand's works are complemented by an Easter sermon found in Clm 6426, which characteristically bears a Greek title (in majuscule, with minuscule mixed in): OMIΛEIA TOY λιOYTZIOY ITαΛIKOY διAKONOY; cf. B. Bischoff, *Anecdota novissima* (Stuttgart 1984), pl. 1.

8. ΛΝΤΛΠΟΔΟCΙC VI 5. Cf. O. Treitinger, *Die oströmische Kaiser- und Reichsidee nach ihrer Gestaltung im höfischen Zeremoniell* (Jena 1938), pp. 199 ff.

9. ΛΝΤΛΠΟΔΟCΙC I 1 and especially III 1.

10. From Abbot John of Gorze, for example, who took part in an embassy to Cordova in 953–55. Abbot John of St. Arnulf in Metz described his experiences in the unusual *Hystoria de vita domni Ioannis Gorzie coenobii abbatis*, esp. cc. 118 ff., ed. G. H. Pertz, *MGH Scriptores*, IV, 371 ff.

11. Auerbach, *Literatursprache und Publikum*, p. 114.

12. ΛΝΤΛΠΟΔΟCΙC III 25, ed. Becker, pp. 83–85, here with a modified representation of the Graeca; cf. the remarks on the text tradition later in sec. 2. The accents, which occur irregularly in the manuscript, are ignored; cf. the facsimiles of this chapter from Clm 6388 in J. Koder and T. Weber, *Liutprand von Cremona in Konstantinopel* (Vienna 1980), pls. 2–5.

13. Cf. the exhibition catalogues *Rhein und Maas* (Cologne 1972), I, p. 171, and *Monumenta Annonis* (Cologne 1975), p. 180. H. Wentzel presents other fabric motifs of athletes battling lions ("Simson cloth") in ancient Western possession: "Das byzantinische Erbe der ottonischen Kaiser. Hypothesen über den Brautschatz der Theophano," *Aachener Kunstblätter* 43 (1972), pp. 11–96, here pp. 21 ff.

14. E. v. Ivánka, in the introduction to F. Loretto's translation of *Nikephoros Phokas*,

'*der bleiche Tod der Sarazenen*,' *und Johannes Tzimiskes. Die Zeit von 959 bis 976 in der Darstellung des Leon Diakonos* (Graz/Vienna/Cologne 1961), pp. 5 f.

15. ΛΝΤΛΠΟΔΟCΙC III 41. Cf. Ovid, *Metam*. III 316–38. Koder and Weber include a facsimile of this passage too, in *Liutprand*, pls. 6–7 (from Clm. 6388). Koder speculates on its origin from scholia on the *Odyssey* (pp. 32 f.). This suggestion is all the more important since Koder has been able to identify a number of Liudprand's Graeca as citations from Homer.

16. Becker included a photograph of the "Metz Excerpts" (Metz, Cod. 145, fol. 204ʳ) with the textual history on pl. 1; the photograph is now of great value, since the manuscript burned during World War II.

17. Liudprand, *Relatio de legatione Constantinopolitana*, cc. 11, 12, 51, 21.

18. *Relatio* 10, ed. Becker, *Die Werke Liudprands*, p. 181. The text is presented here in the same manner as the text from the ΛΝΤΛΠΟΔΟCΙC quoted above.

19. M. de Ferdinandy, *Der heilige Kaiser. Otto III. und seine Ahnen* (Tübingen 1969); G. Schlumberger, *Un empereur byzantin au dixième siècle: Nicéphore Phocas* (Paris 1890).

20. According to a later tradition, with which M. Uhlirz concurs, this monk named Gregory was Empress Theophano's brother ("Studien über Theophano," *DA* 6 [1943], 442–74, esp. pp. 462 ff.). In opposition to this opinion, see F. Dölger, "Wer war Theophano?" *Historisches Jahrbuch* 62/69 (1942/49), 646–58, esp. p. 657. Hamilton does not take either article into account: "The City of Rome and the Eastern Churches in the Tenth Century," *Orientalia Christiana Periodica* 27 (1961), 18.

21. Peter Damian, *De abdicatione episcopatus* 10 (*Migne PL* 145, 440). Greco-Latin monastic life in tenth-century Rome is described by Hamilton, "The City of Rome," pp. 5 ff.; Ferrari gives detailed information concerning the individual monasteries in *Early Roman Monasteries*, pp. 78 ff., on SS. Boniface and Alexius.

22. "Ubi nescio, quid divinum exprimitur, cum homo genere Grecus, imperio Romanus quasi hereditario iure thesauros sibi Grecę ac Romanę repetit sapientię"; *epist*. 187, ed. F. Weigle (Berlin 1966), p. 225 (Weigle's *Grecię* must be emended).

23. "Nunc secunda valitudine reddita, inter rei publicae ac privatae curas, in hoc ipso itinere Italico positus, comesque individuus, quoad vita superfuerit, in omni obsequio futurus, quae de hac quaestione concepi, breviter describo, ne sacrum palatium torpuisse putet Italia, et ne se solam iactet Grecia in imperiali philosophia et Romana potentia. Nostrum, nostrum est Romanum imperium . . . "; ed. J. Havet, *Lettres de Gerbert* (Paris 1889), p. 237.

24. *MGH Poetae*, V, 475 f. See also the literature listed by D. Schaller and E. Könsgen, *Initia carminum Latinorum saeculo undecimo antiquiorum* (Göttingen 1977), no. 14362.

25. On Otto III's palace in Rome and the Byzantine titulature, see M. Uhlirz, *Otto III.*, Jahrbücher des deutschen Reichs unter Otto II. und Otto III., 2 (Berlin 1954), 272 ff. The work of Mathilde Uhlirz is in general to be consulted on the historical data concerning Otto III.

26. *MGH Poetae*, V, 467; cf. the description of the procession, which introduces the poem in the majority of the manuscripts, and is thus inaptly transferred to the apparatus of the edition. On the origin of the procession, see Chapter VI.

27. Especially in the *Graphia aureae urbis Romae*, ed. P. E. Schramm, *Kaiser, Rom und Renovatio* (Leipzig/Berlin 1929), II, 73–104.

28. Wipo, *Gesta Chuonradi* 22, ed. H. Bresslau, 3rd ed. (Hannover 1915), p. 41.

29. El Escorial, Cod. Vitrinas 17, fol. 2ᵛ. The head of the Virgin on the facing page, fol. 3ʳ, is also painted by a Greek artist. A. Boeckler uncertainly formulated the nature of the problem in his monumental publication *Das goldene Evangelienbuch Heinrichs III* (Berlin 1933), p. 17: "Ob diese byzantinischen Teile als Restaurationen zu betrachten sind . . . oder ob sie dem Wunsch entsprangen, wenigstens Christus, Maria und den Matthäusengel entsprechend dem veränderten Schönheitsideal einer anderen Geschmacksrichtung und späteren Zeit (am ehesten saec. XIV) darzustellen, wird sich kaum entscheiden lassen" ("It can scarcely be determined whether these Byzantine components are to be regarded as restorations . . . or if they arise from the wish to portray at least Christ, Mary, and the angel of Matthew in a style corresponding to the modified ideal of beauty of another taste and a later time [most likely saec. XIV]"). On the other hand, P. Schweinfurth has now clarified the problem of dating the Byzantine portion of the codex ("mittelbyzantinisch") and quite cor-

rectly inferred "eine Tendenz nach der Seite des byzantinischen Kulturkreises bereits bei der Entstehung dieser großen salischen Handschrift" ("a tendency toward the side of Byzantine culture, even at the time when this great Salian manuscript was being produced") from the Grecizing text of the *majestas*, and the four instances of the inscription ΚШΝϹΘΛΝΘΙΝΥϹ around the heads in profile on the square, medallions of fol. 23ʳ (cf. Boeckler, pl. 41), in "Das goldene Evangelienbuch Heinrichs III und Byzanz," *Zeitschrift für Kunstgeschichte* 10 (1941/42), 42–66. At the end of the Gospel of St. Matthew (fol. 55ᵛ), one finds the terminal sign Ш.

30. "[Noster Caesar] Constantinopolitano [sc. imperatori] rescribens iactavit se inter alia descendere a Grecorum prosapia, Theophanu et fortissimo Ottone sui generis auctoribus. Ideoque nec mirum esse, si Grecos diligeret, quos vellet etiam habitu et moribus imitari; quod et fecit"; thus Adam of Bremen reports in a rather reserved manner in the year 1049, at the beginning of the Investiture Controversy, in *Gesta Hammaburgensis ecclesiae* III 32, ed. B. Schmeidler (Hannover/Leipzig 1917), p. 174.

31. Facsimile in F. Steffens, *Lateinische Paläographie*, 2nd ed. (Berlin/Leipzig 1929), pl. 72.

32. Johannes of St. Arnulf, *Hystoria de vita domni Ioannis Gorzie coenobii abbatis* 25 and 34, *MGH Scriptores*, IV, 344 and 346.

33. ". . . dominus virtutum omnium conversus respexit de caelo et vidit et visitavit vineam istam atque de omnibus saeculis istuc congregavit, de Graecia videlicet, Burgundia, ac de penitus totis divisis orbe Britannis . . ." (". . . turning around, the lord of all virtues looked back from heaven, perceived and saw this vineyard and assembled them there from all nations—of course from Greece, from Burgundy, and from the British, who are isolated from the whole world . . ."); John of Gorze, *Miracula S. Gorgonii* 26 (written ca. 964), *MGH Scriptores*, IV, 246. The last part of the passage is a quotation from Virgil (*Ecl.* I 66)—"et penitus toto divisos orbe Britannicos"—and thus the line should be emended to "toto divisos orbe Britannis." Graecia sounded so improbable to the editor, G. H. Pertz, that he added the conjecture "an Rhaetia?" in a footnote.

34. "Coetum quoque Grecorum ac Scottorum agglomerans non modicum, propriis alebat stipendiis commixtum diversae linguae populum. Quibus etiam cotidie congregari statuerat divisis altariis in oratorio, ubi deo supplices laudes persolverent more patrio"; Widrich von Toul, *Vita S. Gerhardi episcopi (963–994)* 19, *MGH Scriptores*, IV, 501. McNulty and Hamilton comment: "His solution resembled that which Pope Benedict VII implemented at St. Bonifatius, Rome, and may have been inspired by it"; in *Le Millénaire du Mont Athos*, I, 199.

35. *Annales S. Bavonis Gandensis*, *MGH Scriptores* (Hannover 1829), II, 189.

36. *Acta SS* Iul. (Antwerp 1729), VI, 324–37. Margrave Boniface of Tuscany requested the pope's permission to build a church in honor of Symeon the Armenian in the same year as he died. This must be taken as the second case (after that of St. Ulrich of Augsburg, in 993) of papal canonization; see J. Schlafke, *De competentia in causis sanctorum decernendi* (Rome 1961), pp. 22 ff.; cf. also Leclercq, in *Le Millénaire du Mont Athos*, II, 66 f.

37. *Migne PL* 133, col. 881. Manitius, *Geschichte der lateinischen Literatur*, II, 531 ff.

38. William of Malmesbury, *Gesta pontificum Anglorum* V 260, ed. N. E. S. A. Hamilton (London 1870), p. 415.

39. See Chapter VIII.

40. *Vita Meinwerci episcopi Patherbrunnensis* 155, ed. F. Tenckhoff (Hannover 1921), p. 82.

41. *Gesta S. Servatii* VI, ed. F. Wilhelm, *Sanct Servatius* (Munich 1910), pp. 19 ff. Greek legates to the Mainz Synod of 1049 are supposed to have confirmed the genealogy of St. Servatius in the presence of Emperor Henry III (*Sanct Servatius*, pp. 24 f.). In Iocundus' *Vita S. Servatii*, the corresponding passages are in cc. 7 and 8, ed. P. C. Boeren, *Jocundus, biographe de Saint Servais* (The Hague 1972), pp. 139 ff. Despite Boeren's positive judgment of the Alagrecus episode (pp. 56 ff.), an ambiguous impression remains: either a cleric from the Greek East did in fact take advantage of the Western mania for miracles and glory in relics, or someone in Maastricht simply invented this farfetched witness to the importance of St. Servatius. Had Reichenau not undermined its own claim to possess the relics of St. Mark the Evangelist with the narrative of the dream of a Greek bishop, to whom the Reichenau Mark is supposed to have revealed his identity with the following Greek

words: ЄΓO HYMH MΛPKOC ΘЄOΛOΓOC ? (Karlsruhe, Bad. Landesbibliothek Aug. LXXXIV, fol. 143ʳ, F. J. Mone, *Quellensammlung zur badischen Landesgeschichte* [Karlsruhe 1848], I, 66.)

42. H. Dauphin, *Le Bienheureux Richard, abbé de Saint-Vanne de Verdun* (Louvain/ Paris 1946).

43. *Carmina Cantabrigiensia*, no. 25, ed. W. Bulst (Heidelberg 1950), p. 51; K. Stecker, *Die Cambridger Lieder* (Berlin 1926), p. 68.

44. *Vita et conversatio et obitus viri dei Symeonis*, ed. G. Henschen, *Acta SS Iuni.* (Antwerp 1695), I, 89–95; on p. 99, an engraving by Caspar Merian of the Porta Nigra as it was modified into a Romanesque basilica. This Symeon was canonized in Rome soon after his death, just as was St. Symeon of Polirone. Scholars in this field regard the pope's canonization of the former Symeon, initially proposed by Archbishop Poppo in Trier, as the third such papal procedure; cf. Schlafke, *De competentia*, pp. 23 ff.; A. Heintz, "Der heilige Symeon von Trier. Seine Kanonisation und seine Reliquien," *Festschrift Alois Thomas* (Trier 1967), pp. 163–73.

45. *Vita S. Nili abbatis* 73–74, *Acta SS* Sept. (Antwerp 1760), VII, 326 f. On Nilus of Rossano, see Borsari, *Il Monachesimo Bizantino*, pp. 265 ff. E. Follieri lists Greek manuscripts that stem from the time of the coexistence of Latin and Greek monks in Monte Cassino in "Due codici greci già Cassinesi oggi alla Biblioteca Vaticana: gli Ottob. gr. 250 e 251," in *Palaeographica, Diplomatica et Archivistica*, Studi in onore di Giulio Battelli (Rome 1979), I, 159–221.

46. De Ferdinandy, *Der heilige Kaiser*, pp. 265 ff.

47. G. Giovannelli, "I fondatori di Grottaferrata ed il mondo bizantino nell'alto medioevo nell'Italia meridionale," *Atti del 3° Congresso Internazionale di Studi sull'Alto Medioevo* (Spoleto 1959), pp. 421–35. The library at Grottaferrata preserves a few manuscripts which the calligrapher Nilus of Rossano himself wrote, and some on which he worked with others; S. Gassisi, "I manoscritti autografi di S. Nilo Iuniore, fondatore del monastero di S. M. di Grottaferrata," *Oriens Christianus* 4 (1904), pp. 308–70; Devreesse, *Les manuscrits grecs*, pp. 27 f.

48. A. Schulte, "Deutsche Könige, Kaiser, Päpste als Kanoniker an deutschen und römischen Kirchen," *Historiches Jahrbuch* 54 (1934), 137–77 (published separately, Darmstadt 1960). J. Fleckenstein, *Die Hofkapelle der deutschen Könige* (Stuttgart 1966), II, 151 ff. and 230 ff.

49. The annual entries in Flodoard's "Annals" are provided with Greek numerals, whose enigmatic meaning has been explained by H. Foerster in *Schweiz. Beiträge zur Allgemeinen Geschichte* 2 (1944), 143 ff.: the author encoded his own age in each such entry! Cf. P. C. Jacobsen, *Flodoard von Reims. Sein Leben und seine Dichtung De triumphis Christi* (Leiden/Cologne 1978), pp. 22 f.

50. Bischoff, *Mittelalterliche Studien*, I, 205. This Israel is probably the same one mentioned in the *Grammaticorum* διαδοχή (see the end of Chapter VII). His didactic poem on the prosody of final syllables is edited in *MGH Poetae*, V, 501 f.; and an account of his life is given by Manitius, *Geschichte der lateinischen Literatur*, II, 178. Israel the Irishman was also the author of "Scripturę finem sibi quęrunt hic Ysagoge" in Traube's "Carmina Scottorum Latina et Graecanica," *MGH Poetae*, III, 685. In the well-known practice of the Grecistic alienation of one's own name, the author identified himself as ICPΛ, to be completed as ICPΛ⟨HΛ⟩ (not ICPΛ⟨EL⟩, as in *MGH Poetae*, V/3 [1979], p. 648). With this resolution disappears that mysterious "Jepa" from the history of medieval philosophy, and into his place steps the Irishman Israel of Trier, as the author of a glossary on Porphyry (ed. B. S. v. Waltershausen, *Frühmittelalterliche Glossen des angeblichen Jepa zur Isagoge des Porphyrius* [Münster 1924]). It has been claimed that the kernel of the late medieval debate on universals is to be found here; cf. O. Lewry, "Boethian Logic in the Medieval West," in M. Gibson, ed., *Boethius* (Oxford 1981), pp. 90–134, here p. 93. Israel additionally revised the commentary by Remigius of Auxerre on Donatus' *Ars minor*; cf. C. Jeudy, "Isräel le grammarien et la tradition manuscrite du commentaire de Remi d'Auxerre à l'*Ars minor* de Donat," *Studi Medievali* III/18, 2 (1977), 185–205. Thus the *Grammaticorum* διαδοχή, which numbers Israel among the students of Remigius, is confirmed.

51. Ruotger, *Vita Domni Brunonis* 7, ed. I. Ott (Cologne/Graz 1952), p. 8.

52. Trier, Stadtbibliothek Cod. 7. The book obviously had some association with an artistic school, seen in both the prologue in golden uncials on a purple background (*MGH Poetae*, V, 390) and the decorative letters; cf. M. Keuffer, *Verzeichnis der Handschriften der Stadtbibliothek zu Trier* (Trier 1888), I, 7–9; C. Nordenfalk, "Der Meister des Registrum Gregorii," *Münchner Jahrbuch der bildenden Kunst* III/1 (1950), 61–77, here p. 64. B. Nitschke opposes the attribution of the work to the "Master of the Registrum" in *Die Handschriftengruppe um den Meister des Registrum Gregorii* (Recklinghausen 1966), pp. 20 ff.

53. Allgeier, in *Biblica* 24 (1943), 269.—On the "Codex Simeonis" in Trier, see Chapter II.

54. Allgeier, in *Oriens Christianus* III/10 (1935), 139–60.

55. The following example from Ps. 127 is taken from the diplomatic edition by C. Hamann, *De psalterio triplici Cusano* [Schulprogram] (Hamburg 1891), p. 14.

56. For example, in the "Greco-Egyptian Schoolbook," Cambridge, University Library Add. 5896 (P. Oxy. 1099), which lists the difficult vocabulary of a portion of *Aeneid* IV in a Latin column and translates these words in the Greek column. Cf. R. Seider, *Paläographie der lateinischen Papyri* (Stuttgart 1978), II/1, no. 57; *CLA*, II, 137.

57. The incipit page to Luke (fol. 80ʳ) contains four medallions with the legends [ΚѠΝΘΛΝΘΙΝѴϹ] (three times) and [ΚѠΝΘΘΛΝΤΙѴϹ] (once). Here the Graeca exhibit the awkwardness that is common in Western manuscripts.

58. London, British Library Add. 11035. I. P. Sheldon-Williams and L. Bieler, *Iohannis Scotti Eriugenae Periphyseon* (Dublin 1968), I, 17 f. (the bibliography does not mention the detailed description found in *Mitteilungen und Forschungsbeiträge der Cusanus-Gesellschaft* 3 [1963]). Bischoff, *Mittelalterliche Studien*, II, 254, dates the hand "saec. XI ex."

59. The Hague, Museum Meermanno-Westreenianum Fol. 6, reported on by P. Lehmann, "Holländische Reisefrüchte," SB Munich (1920), pp. 16 f.

60. "Here was a philologist at work who frequently made use of minuscule for Graeca and could write Hebrew names in the formal, unvocalized square script, to which he added transcriptions or interpretations in mirror writing, running from right to left [!]"; Bischoff, *Mittelalterliche Studien*, II, 254 f.

61. Formerly Maihingen, Fürstlich. Öttingen-Wallersteinische Bibliothek I 2 4°3; sold in 1935 to the Preußische Staatsbibliothek, Berlin and there given the signature lat. 4°939; disappeared after 1945 only to be rediscovered in 1985 in the Biblioteka Jagiellonska in Cracow under the Berlin signature. The best description is by G. Schepß, *Handschriftliche Studien zu Boethius De consolatione philosophiae*, Programm der K. Studienanstalt Würzburg für 1880/81 (Würzburg 1881), pp. 5–29.

62. Ed. by K. Strecker, *Die Tegernseer Briefsammlung* (Berlin 1925), p. xii.

63. G. Schepß, "Funde und Studien zu Apollonius Tyrius . . . ," NA 9 (1883), 173 ff.

64. *Gesta Apollonii, MGH Poetae*, II, 484–506; cf. Manitius, *Geschichte der lateinischen Literatur des Mittelalters*, I, 614–16.

65. Ed. by Krause, in *Jahrbuch der Österr. Byzantinischen Gesellschaft* 5 (1956), 7–25, from Vienna, Österreichische Nationalbibliothek Cod. 114. On the manuscript, see Strecker, *Die Tegernseer Briefsammlung*, p. xiii (bibliog.).

66. Paris, BN lat. 817; facsimile reproductions in Bloch and Schnitzler, *Die ottonische Kölner Malerschule*, I (Düsseldorf 1967), pls. 84, 86, 96, 104.

67. These neologisms are a peculiarity of John Scottus' translator's language in contrast with Hilduin's, as one may infer from Théry's tables, "Terminologie d'Hilduin et de Scot," in *Études Dionysiennes*, II, 422–91.

68. Darmstadt, Hessische Landes- und Hochschulbibliothek 1640, fol. 6ᵛ. Facsimile edition in *Der Darmstädter Hitda-Codex* (Berlin 1968), pl. 5. Eastern elements in the theological plan of the Hitda Codex are treated by W. Nyssen, *Der heilende Christus* (Mainz 1977), esp. p. 38: baptism in the Jordan as "Photismos."

69. The Baroque copies of the illustrations in this lost codex were not discovered until a few years ago; see T. Rensing, "Zwei ottonische Kunstwerke des Essener Münsterschatzes," *Westfalen* 40 (1962), 44–58; and further on the subject, T. Schnitzler, in *Studien zur Buchmalerei und Goldschmiedekunst des Mittelalters*, Festschrift Karl Hermann Use-

ner (Marburg 1967), pp. 115–18. The copy is so exact that one can prove that the originals came from Fulda. The mistake in ΘΕΟΤΕΚΟC also seems to be characteristic for Fulda; cf. the coronation illustration in Hannover 189, painted in Fulda: ϽΣΑΡΙΛ ΘΕШΔΕΚШC.

70. *MGH Poetae*, V, 303 f. On further Graeca in Essen inscriptions, see Drögereit, "Griechisch-Byzantinisches aus Essen," *BZ* 46 (1953), 110–15.

71. Düsseldorf D1, fol. 216ʳ, Greek paternoster in Greek majuscules, with interlinear Latin version, and a Hebrew paternoster in Roman script in addition; cf. H. Dausend, *Das älteste Sakramentar der Münsterkirche zu Essen* (Cologne 1920), p. 58.

72. Ed. I. Opelt, "Die Essener 'Missa greca' der liturgischen Handschrift Düsseldorf D2," *Jahrbuch der Österr. Byzantinistik* 23 (1974), 77–88. According to Opelt, the text was probably written "by dictation." According to Jammers, *Die Essener Neumenhandschriften* (1952), p. 20, the melodies are "a new composition, insofar as it was not adopted from Byzantine material." Empress Theophano and her retinue are proposed by many scholars. However, the "Byzantine canonesses" Anteconia, Antephona, and Sophia who "probably went to the convent in Essen after the death of Theophano" (Jammers, p. 20) are "based on an error" (Drögereit, in *BZ* 46, 113).

73. A. Gelenius, *Colonia supplex* (Cologne 1639), p. 49.

74. W. Ohnsorge, "Eine Rotulus-Bulle des Kaisers Michael VI. Stratiotikos von 1056," *Abendland und Byzanz. Gesammelte Aufsätze* (Darmstadt 1958), pp. 333–41.

75. The epistles de luxe of the Byzantines were in fact treated in this manner. The *Chronicon SS. Simonis et Iudae* tell that around 1049 Emperor Henry III presented his convent in Goslar with an example of Byzantine foreign correspondence: from the heavy golden seal ("sigillo aureo satis ponderoso") a chalice was made; from the letter itself (probably a *rotulus* on purple parchment with gold ink), an ornament for the public side of the altar ("de littera vero fiebat palla altaris"); cf. W. Ohnsorge, "Das nach Goslar gelangte Auslandsschreiben des Konstantinos IX. Monomachos für Kaiser Heinrich III. von 1049," *Abendland und Byzanz* (1958), pp. 317–32, esp. p. 320.

76. Manchester, John Rylands Library lat. 110, fol. 17ʳ. R. Kahsnitz, *The Gospel Book of Abbess Svanhild of Essen in the John Rylands Library* (Manchester 1971).

77. Clm 14137; Chroust, *Monumenta Palaeographica*, Ser. 1, Lief. 3, 7.—Cf. A. Kraus, *Die Translatio S. Dionysii Areopagitae von St. Emmeram in Regensburg*, SB Munich (1972).

78. Clm 14322; Chroust, *Monumenta Palaeographica*, Ser. 1, Lief. 3, 5; von den Steinen, *Notker*, II, 211 f. H. Spanke (in *Zeitschrift für deutsches Altertum* 71 [1934], 1–39) discovered that the famous "uni-choral" Christmas sequence *Grates nunc omnes*, which prefaces many sequence collections, is a contrafactum of an Ἀγγελικαί song of Romanos Melodos; and, without any valid reason, he conjectures that the translation was made in Regensburg.

79. It is uncertain whether a "journey to Hungary" must be adduced (as has been confirmed for Arnold) in order to explain the "extraordinarily strong Greek element in his language"; see B. Bischoff, "Literarisches und künstlerisches Leben in St. Emmeram," *Studien und Mitteilungen zur Geschichte des Benediktinerordens* 51 (1933), 122. Arnold most likely came upon a Greek glossary in the monastery: *MBK*, IV/1 (Munich 1977), p. 145, 71 *Glosa Greca*.

80. Otto II is supposed to have received the *psalterium quadrupartitum* as a gift, while on a visit to St. Gall with Otto I and Theophano in 972. At least this is the account given by F. Leitschuh, *Katalog der Handschriften der K. Bibliothek Bamberg* (Bamberg 1895/1906), I, 39. The legend is connected with the final sentences of Ekkehard IV's *Casus S. Galli*: "Otto filius armarium sibi aperiri rogat. Quod ille [sc. abbas] renuere non ausus, condicto tamen risibili, ne tantus praedo locum et fratres spoliaret, aperiri iubet. Ille autem libris optimis illectus, plures abstulit . . ." ("Otto asked that the chest be opened for him, which the abbot could not refuse; but rather he ordered it opened, with the facetious remark that such a robber would not despoil the place and the brothers. But he was enticed by the best books and took many of them away . . ."); ed. G. Meyer v. Knonau (St. Gall 1877), p. 450; ed. Haefele (Darmstadt 1980), p. 285.

81. Bamberg, Staatliche Bibliothek Class. 5, 6, 7, 8, described by Leitschuh, *Katalog der Handschriften der K. Bibliothek Bamberg*, I, 6–11.

82. Chroust, *Monumenta Palaeographica*, Ser. 1, Lief. 18, 7 and 8. Schramm and Mütherich, *Denkmale der deutschen Könige und Kaiser*, p. 129, no. 41 (bibliog.), and on p.

246, a photograph of fol. 9ᵛ with four female figures which bear the names of the four arts of the quadrivium.

83. Bamberg, Staatliche Bibliothek Philos. 2/1 (HJ.IV.5). Traube considered the manuscript an autograph. On the problem of John Scottus' autographs, see most recently the articles by Bishop and Vezin in *Jean Scot Érigène et l'histoire de la philosophie* (1977).

84. Probably identical with Paris, BN lat. 6734; see above, Chapter VII, sec. 6.

85. *MBK* III/3 (Munich 1939), p. 367, 35.

86. H. v. Fichtenau, "Wolfger von Prüfening," *Mitteilungen des Österreichischen Instituts für Geschichtsforschung* 51 (1937), 313–57. B. Bischoff, "Wolfger von Prüfening," in Stammler and Langosch, *Verfasserlexikon* (Berlin 1953), IV, 1051–56. The *hermeneumata*, combined with the "Glossarium Salomonis" in Clm 13002, are now called "Hermeneumata Monacensia," after the present repository; ed. Goetz, *Corpus Glossariorum Latinorum*, III, 119–220. A new description of Clm 13002 is given by H.-G. Schmitz, *Kloster Prüfening im 12. Jahrhundert* (Munich 1975), pp. 111–17.

Notes to Chapter XI

1. On the liturgy and the law, see E. Kantorowicz, *The King's Two Bodies* (Princeton 1957), pp. 87 ff. According to Troje, there is "reason to suspect that the Greek element in all its manifestations somehow went against the nature of the Bolognese type of lawyer that prevailed in Italy" (*Graeca leguntur*, p. 289). Another of his interpretations is clearly untenable: "It was the Bolognese teachers who first eliminated the Greek element from their education without making a secret of it" (*Graeca leguntur*, pp. 291 f.); for Bologna was never a place where Greek played any important role, and thus it could not be "eliminated" here. Probability and improbabilities are similarly close together in Troje's work *Europa und griechisches Recht*, which has the merit of calling attention to many an implication of basic legal understanding—for instance, the initial sentence of Justinian's *Digests*, where lawyers are compared with priests ("sacerdotes . . . veram nisi fallor philosophiam . . . affectantes"; D. 1, 1, 1).

2. Thus the title to the translation of Leo of Achrida's letter does not say more than that Humbert *applied himself* to the translation: "Haec quidem calumnia graeco sermone edita . . . cum fuisset Trani exhibita fratri Humberto . . . episcopo in latinum est translata eius studio et delata domino papae Leoni nono" (Hoesch, *Die kanonischen Quellen im Werk Humberts*, p. 13; Hagen, *Catalogus Codicum Bernensium*, p. 312). Here one might compare the tenor of such a title when it introduces one of Humbert's own works (dialogue between a Roman and a Constantinopolitan: "responsio . . . instar dialogi ab ipso latine conscripta." The title to Humbert's response to Nicetas Stethatus in Cod. Bern. 292 is similar.

3. "Illud etiam erat in eo admirandum quod ultra quinquagenarius tanto fervebat studio, ut divinarum lectionem scripturarum Graeco addisceret eloquio" ("And this was to be admired in him, that even beyond the age of fifty he burned with such zeal that he learned to read the Holy Scriptures in Greek"); *Vita Leonis Papae* 6 (28), *Acta SS* April. (Antwerp 1685), II, 664. According to the comprehensive examination of the manuscripts by H. Tritz, the vita is to be ascribed to Humbert of Silva Candida, in "Die hagiographischen Quellen zur Geschichte Papst Leos IX," *Studi Gregoriani* 4 (1952), 191–364, esp. 229 f.; in opposition, see H.-G. Krause, "Über den Verfasser der Vita Leonis IX papae," *DA* 32 (1976), pp. 49–77.

4. Bernold, *Chronicon* ad a. 1085, *MGH Scriptores*, V, 444. In his tenth polemical treatise, Bernold gives interesting advice on the comparison of various translations of conciliar acts: *De excommunicatis vitandis*, c. 43, *MGH Libelli de lite* (1892), II, 131.

5. Wattenbach and Holtzmann, *Deutschlands Geschichtsquellen*, 2nd ed. (1948), fasc. 3, 528.

6. Lamma, *Comneni e Staufer*, 2 vols. (Rome 1955–57). Cf. P. Classen, "La politica di Manuele Comneno tra Federico Barbarossa e le città italiane," in *Popolo e Stato in Italia nell'età di Federico Barbarossa. Relazioni e communicazioni al XXXIII Congresso Storico Subalpino Alessandria 1968* (Turin 1970), pp. 265–79.

7. On the Psalter, Florence, Biblioteca Riccardiana 323, see H. Buchthal, *Miniature Painting in the Latin Kingdom of Jerusalem* (Oxford 1957), pp. 39–46 and 143 f., here p. 46. "The most likely person to have commissioned it is of course the Emperor Frederick him-

self, . . . intended as a wedding present, to be sent to Worms, to remind the Emperor's English bride [Isabella, m. 1235] as well as his German subjects, of his outstanding success as the protector of the Holy Sepulchre" (p. 41). A kind of French "colonial style" was dominant in Acre, on the other hand, especially in the last phase; cf. J. Folda, *Crusader Manuscript Illumination at Saint-Jean d'Acre, 1275–1291* (Princeton 1976).

8. H. Prutz, "Studien über Wilhelm von Tyrus," *NA* 8 (1883), 93–132, here p. 96.

9. Haskins, "Translators in Syria during the Crusades," *Mediaeval Science*, pp. 130–40 and p. xii. On Stephan of Antioch see also below, p. (ooo) and (n. 84.) On Philip of Tripoli see most recently M. A. Manzalaoui, "Philip of Tripoli and His Textual Methods," in W. F. Ryan and C. B. Schmitt, eds., *Pseudo-Aristotle, The 'Secret of Secrets': Sources and Influences* (London 1982), pp. 55–72.

10. ". . . gratissimo vultu puer Ihesus refulgens umbilicotenus cernitur esse depictus, ad sinistram vero ipsius mater, ad dextram autem Gabriel archangelus illam notam depromens salutationem: Ave, Maria, gratia plena, Dominus tecum, benedicta in mulieribus et benedictus fructus ventris tui. Hec salutatio tam Latine quam Grece circa ipsum Dominum Christum descripta est" (". . . the boy Jesus, shining in his most pleasing face, was seen to be depicted in a bust-portrait, his mother on his right, the archangel Gabriel on his left, saying the famous salutation: 'Hail Mary, full of grace, the Lord is with you, blessed are you among women and blessed the fruit of your womb.' This salutation was written in Latin and Greek around our Lord Christ himself"); *Libellus de locis sanctis* 6, ed. M. L. and W. Bulst (Heidelberg 1976), p. 15.

11. Ed. by G. Constable, *The Letters of Peter the Venerable* (Cambridge, Mass., 1967), I, no. 75, pp. 208 f.; and also the letter to the patriarch of Constantinople, no. 76, pp. 209 f. L. Gay deals with nothing beyond these two letters in "L'abbaye de Cluny et Byzance au début du XIIIe siècle," *Échos d'Orient* 30 (1931), 84–90.

12. Von den Brincken, *Nationes Christianorum Orientalium*, p. 27.

13. *Migne PL* 193, col. 547.

14. Théry, *Studia Medievalia in honorem R. J. Martin* (Bruges 1948), p. 366.

15. Robert of Melun, *Sententiae*, ed. R. M. Martin, *Œuvres de Robert de Melun* (Louvain 1947, III/1, 36 ff. Hugh of Folietum (Fouilloy), *De claustro animae* IV, prol. (*Migne PL* 176, col. 1131).

16. Manitius, *Geschichte der lateinischen Literatur*, III, 239 f. and 533 f. T. Gregory, *Platonismo medievale* (Rome 1958), pp. 31 ff.: "La dottrina del peccato originale e il realismo platonico: Oddone di Tournai" (bibliog.).

17. One monk was a contemporary of Odo of Tournai, Hugo of Flavigny (1065–ca. 1114), who left traces of an interest in Greek in the autograph of his chronicle. At his time and in his geographical area (the general vicinity of Verdun), they are surprising: the Greek alphabet, the Greek paternoster in majuscules, with a *minuscule* version underneath; in Berlin, Deutsche Staatsbibliothek Phill. 1870, fol. 1^r and 1^v; cf. V. Rose, *Verzeichniss der lateinischen Handschriften* I, 321.

18. For example, Vienna, Österreichische Nationalbibliothek, Cod. 2318, with Aristotle's *Physica, De caelo*, and *De generatione* in Gerard of Cremona's *Arabo*-Latin translation, to which the corresponding *Greco*-Latin translation is added, page for page, in place of a commentary; *Aristoteles latinus*, Codices, I, 286 f. See also the exhibition catalogue *Wissenschaft im Mittelalter*, pp. 214 f.

19. On the Latin lexicographical tradition, see Manitius, *Geschichte der lateinischen Literatur*, II, 717 ff. (Papias), and III, 187 ff. (Osbern, Hugutio); K. Grubmüller, *Vocabularius Ex quo* (Munich 1967), pp. 13–44 (bibliog.; see also R. W. Hunt, "Studies on Priscian in the Eleventh and Twelfth Centuries, I–II," *Mediaeval and Renaissance Studies* 1 [1943], 194–231, and 2 [1950], 1–56, and "Hugutio and Petrus Helias," *Mediaeval and Renaissance Studies* 2 [1950], 174–78).

20. Hofmeister, "Der Übersetzer Johannes und das Geschlecht Comitis Mauronis in Amalfi," *Historische Vierteljahrschrift* 27 (1932); A. Michel, *Amalfi und Jerusalem im griechischen Kirchenstreit (1054–1090)* (Rome 1939); H. M. Willard, *Abbot Desiderius and the Ties between Montecassino and Amalfi in the Eleventh Century* (Monte Cassino 1973); U. Schwarz, *Amalfi im frühen Mittelalter* (Tübingen 1978).

21. A. Pertusi, "Nuovi documenti sui Benedettini Amalfitani dell'Athos," *Aevum* 27

(1953), 400–429; in expanded form: "Monasteri e monaci italiani all'Athos nell'alto medioevo," in *Le Millénaire du Mont Athos*, I, 217–51.

22. Only the prologue has been edited: *AB* 9 (1890), 202 f. Cf. Siegmund, *Die Überlieferung*, pp. 270 ff.; see also W. von Rintelen, *Kultgeographische Studien in der Italia Byzantina* (Meisenheim 1968), p. 45.

23. The motivation for the discovery of the translators' school in Amalfi came from M. Hoferer's "Schulprogramm": *Ioannis Monachi Liber de Miraculis*, (Aschaffenburg 1884; printed in Würzburg). To be sure, Hoferer was in doubt about the provenance of the text which he was editing and erred *toto caelo* in dating it. Only the remarks concerning the translator-Latin are still of some value in Hoferer's "Schulprogramm." Otherwise, his work has been replaced by Huber, *Johannes Monachus: Liber de Miraculis* (Heidelberg 1913), whose conclusions are further refined in a historical and genealogical sense by Hofmeister, in *Historische Vierteljahrschrift* 27 (1932).

24. G. Matthiae, *Le porte bronzee bizantine in Italia* (Rome 1971). H. Belting, "Byzantine Art among Greeks and Latins in Southern Italy," *Dumbarton Oaks Papers* 28 (1974).

25. Prologue, ed. Hofmeister, in *Münchener Museum* 4 (1924), 138 ff.; also in Huber, *Johannes Monachus*, p. xviii. Huber extracts from the prologue (p. xix) the "following points for our Johannes Monachus: by birth he most certainly came from Amalfi, and most probably from one of the monasteries in the area of this city, which was of such great importance at that time: it matters little whether one prefers the somewhat closer monastery of the Holy Trinity in Cava (founded ca. 990) or the monastery of St. Severin in Naples." According to Huber, the monastery, *Panagiotum*, was "the monastery of Panagia near Constantinople" (p. xxii). On the dating of the text, see Schwarz, *Amalfi*, p. 69, n. 4.

26. Johannes Monachus, *Liber de Miraculis*, ed. Huber, pp. 1 f.

27. Hofmeister, in *Münchener Museum*, 4, pp. 135 f. Also in Huber, *Johannes Monachus*, p. xvii.

28. In 1718, Emperor Charles VI transferred the manuscript from the monastery of St. Severin in Naples to the Vienna Hofbibliothek (Signature, lat. 739); in 1919 it was transferred back to Naples (Naples, Biblioteca Nazionale Ex Vindobonense lat. 15). Against the objection of the Greifswald professor (Hofmeister, in *Münchener Museum*, 4, p. 148, n. 1), the opinion of the Bohemian Benedictine (Huber, *Johannes Monachus*, p. xiv) is to be maintained, that *Marinulus* is the name of the codex. One might compare here the ancient name *Martinellus* for the collection of works on Martin. On the manuscript, see most recently Schwarz, *Amalfi*, pp. 80 f.

29. Hofmeister (in *Münchener Museum* 4, pp. 133 f. and 141 f.) refers to a *Vita S. Iohannis Calybitae*, which is not identical with Anastasius Bibliothecarius' translation, and to Anastasius Bibliothecarius' revision of a translation of the *Vita S. Iohannis Eleemosynarii*. Both texts are in Naples, Biblioteca Nazionale Ex Vindobonense lat. 15.

30. In 1177, Pope Alexander III sent his physician, Philippus, on a journey to the legendary priest-king with a letter full of papal aplomb (ed. F. Zarncke, "Der Priester Johannes," Abh. Leipzig 7 [1879], 115–18. A physician by the name of Nicholas delivered the bilingual epistle (from 1199) of Emperor Alexius III to the commune of Genoa; preserved in the city archive of Genoa, Mat. Polit. N. g. 2727, Parte I, C.; cf. Dölger, *Facsimiles byzantinischer Kaiserurkunden* (1931), no. 8.

31. Kristeller, "The School of Salerno," in *Studies in Renaissance Thought and Letters* (Rome 1956), 495–551; "Nuove fonti per la medicina salernitana del secolo XII," *Rassegna storica Salernitana* 18 (1957), 61–75; "Bartholomaeus, Musandinus and Maurus of Salerno and Other Early Commentators of the 'Articella,' with a Tentative List of Texts and Manuscripts," *Italia Medioevale e Umanistica* 19 (1976), 57–87; "Philosophy and Medicine in Medieval and Renaissance Italy," in *Organism, Medicine, and Metaphysics*, ed. S. F. Spicker (Dordrecht 1978), pp. 29–40. G. Baader, "Die Anfänge der medizinischen Ausbildung im Abendland bis 1100," in *La Scuola nell'Occidente latino dell'Alto Medioevo* (Spoleto 1972), pp. 669–718.

32. C. Holzinger still edited the Nemesius translation as the work of an anonymous translator (Leipzig/Prague 1887). Several reviews of this edition promoted the matter so effectively (for instance, by referring to a tradition with the name of the translator) that a new edition became justifiable: C. Burkhard, *Nemesii episcopi Premnon Physicon . . . a N. Alfa-*

no archiepiscopo Salerni in latinum translatus (Leipzig 1917); the necessary bibliographical references are found on pp. x f.; only one is absent—the one who first recognized and appreciated Alfanus' full significance: Ernest Renan, *Mélanges religieux et historiques* (Paris 1904), esp. p. 348 (originally, *Journal des Savants* [April 1851]). G. Verbeke and J. R. Moncho make several observations on Alfanus in their new edition of Burgundio's translation (Leiden 1975), pp. lxxxvi–viii (without complete bibliographical information). Alfanus is not mentioned in Sicherl's analysis of the third, humanistic translation of Nemesius, in *Johannes Cuno*, pp. 139–42. A novelettish biography may be found in the *Dizionario biografico degli Italiani* (1960), II. 253–57. A thorough monographic study is a desideratum.

33. Schipperges, *Die Assimilation der arabischen Medizin*, pp. 17–49; G. Baader, "Zur Terminologie des Constantinus Africanus," *Medizinhistorisches Journal* 2 (1967), 36–53.

34. P. O. Kristeller, "Beitrag der Schule von Salerno zur Entwicklung der scholastischen Wissenschaft im 12. Jh.," in *Artes liberales*, ed. J. Koch (Leiden/Cologne 1959), pp. 84–90, here p. 88. Birkenmajer, "Le rôle joué par les médecins et les naturalistes dans la réception d'Aristote au XIIᵉ et XIIIᵉ siècles," in *La Pologne au VIᵉ Congrès International des Sciences Historiques* (Warsaw/Lemberg 1930), pp. 1–15. This rather inaccessible publication has been reprinted in Birkenmajer, *Études d'histoire des sciences et de la philosophie du moyen âge* (Breslau/Warsaw/Cracow 1970), pp. 73–87.

35. *Paléographie Musicale*, XIV, 296 ff.; Wellesz, *Eastern Elements*, pp. 25 f. On the history of the "Adoratio crucis," see J. Drumbl, "Zweisprachige Antiphonen zur Kreuzverehrung," *Italia Medioevale e Umanistica* 19 (1976), 41–55. On the older Beneventan Graecolatina, see Chapters VI and IX.

36. *Paléographie Musicale*, XIV, 306 f; cf. Wellesz, *Eastern Elements*, pp. 68–77, here pp. 72 f. The Greek text is transmitted (in Latin transcription) only in MS Benevento VI.38; on the other hand, the Latin translation is transmitted in a small group of graduals from Benevento and two missals from elsewhere. The text and notation here are from Hesbert's standard publication in the *Paléographie Musicale*.

37. Cagin, *Te Deum*, pp. 161 ff.

38. Bloch, "Monte Cassino, Byzantium and the West in the Earlier Middle Ages," *Dumbarton Oaks Papers* 3 (1946), 163–224. The most important source is the chronicle of Monte Cassino, *MGH Scriptores*, XXXIV (1980). See also H. Hoffmann, "Studien zur Chronik von Montecassino," *DA* 29 (1973), 59–162; idem, "Stilistische Tradition in der Klosterchronik von Montecassino," in *Mittelalterliche Textüberlieferung und ihre kritische Aufarbeitung. Beiträge der MGH zum 31. Deutschen Historikertag* (Munich 1976); p. 32 of this work includes a facsimile of one page from the autograph of the chronicle, where one can also see how the Graeca were inserted: "Hic arichis intra menia beneventi templum domino opulentissimum ac decentissimum condidit quod greco uocabulo ΑΓΗΑΝ ϹΩϕΗΑΝ · id est sanctam sapientiam nominauit '" ("Within the walls of Benevento, this Arichis built a most sumptious and handsome church for the Lord which was given the Greek name 'Hagia Sophia,' that is, 'Holy Wisdom'").

39. *Carm.* 54, 29–36, ed. A. Lentini and F. Avagliano, *I Carmi di Alfano I, Arcivescovo di Salerno* (Monte Cassino 1974), p. 218.

40. Siegmund (*Die Überlieferung*, p. 263, n. 1) speaks of a "Passio Eustathii, die von Joh. Subd. Cassin. übersetzt wurde, ex praecepto abbatis Desiderii, wie in Benev. III s. XI steht."

41. E. Caspar, *Petrus Diaconus und die Monte Cassineser Fälschungen* (Berlin 1909). Manitius, *Geschichte der lateinischen Literatur*, III, 546 ff.; Bloch, in *Dumbarton Oaks Papers* 3 (1946), 192 f. and 223 f.

42. "Cum ergo perfecto libello legisset Grosolanus illum ante imperatorem, affuerunt etiam Graeci cum septem suis libellis. Quibus imperator perspectis coepit conquerendo dicere: Olim sapientia deducta est de Oriente in Occidentem a Graecis ad Latinos. Nunc e contrario de Occidente in Orientem Latinus veniens descendit ad Graecos." A. Amelli, *Due sermoni inediti di Pietro Grosolano*, Fontes Ambrosiani 6 (Florence 1933), pp. 35 f.

43. H. Kretschmayr, *Geschichte von Venedig* (Gotha 1905), I, 154.

44. Minio-Paluello, *Opuscula*, pp. 178–88, 189–228, 383–87, 565–86; Pertusi, in *Dante e la Cultura Veneta* (Florence 1966), p. 173; *Aristoteles latinus* (1968), IV/1 and (1970), XXV/1.

45. See the survey of Boethius' translations from the *Organon* above in Chapter V.

46. A. Pelzer, in *Revue d'Histoire Ecclésiastique* 43 (1948), 384 f. On the adventurous life of Cerbanus, see Pertusi, in *Dante e la Cultura Veneta*, pp. 166–72.

47. Ed. by A. Terebessy, *Translatio latina S. Maximi Confessoris [De caritate ad Elpidium lib. I–IV] saec. XII in Hungaria confecta*, Magyar-Görög Tanulmáyok 25 (Budapest 1944). On Greek monasteries in Hungary and their Latinization since the end of the twelfth century (Pásztó was, for example, already Cistercian by 1190), see G. Moravcsik, *Byzantium and the Magyars* (Amsterdam 1970), pp. 109 ff.

48. Bonizo of Sutri, *Liber de vita christiana* VII 1, ed. E. Perels (Berlin 1930), p. 233; W. Berschin, *Bonizo von Sutri* (Berlin/New York 1972), p. 113, n. 511.

49. R. Janin, *La Géographie Ecclésiastique de l'Empire Byzantin*, I/3, 2nd ed. (Paris 1969), pp. 569–93.

50. In the state archives of Pisa, one of these impressive documents is preserved: a Greek chrysobull of Emperor Isaac Angelus for Pisa in the year 1192 and including a Latin *authenticum*, ed. G. Müller, *Documenti sulle Relazioni delle Città Toscane coll'Oriente Cristiano e coi Turchi* (Florence 1879), pp. 40–58. On "Scambi diplomatici, commerciali e culturali tra Bisanzio e le repubbliche marinare italiane," see Lamma, *Comneni e Staufer*, II, 184 ff.

51. *De processione spiritus sancti contra Graecos*, ed. A. Amelli, *Due sermoni*, pp. 14–35; Beck, *Kirche und theologische Literatur*, pp. 312 f.; Haskins, *Mediaeval Culture*, pp. 163–65.

52. Amelli, *Due sermoni*, p. 35, n. 1.

53. *Dialogi* II 1 (*Migne PL* 188, col. 1163).

54. *Migne PL* 188, col. 1164.

55. *Dialogi* III 22 (*Migne PL* 188, col. 1248).

56. Beck, *Kirche und theologische Literatur*, p. 626 (bibliog.).

57. G. Cremaschi, *Mosè del Brolo e la cultura a Bergamo nei secoli XI–XII* (Bergamo 1945); Manitius, *Geschichte der lateinischen Literatur*, III, 683–87.

58. This information is found, along with many other important details in cultural history, in Moses' letter (preserved in the original, probably a. 1130) to his brother, Prior Peter of St. Alexander near Bergamo, ed. Cremaschi, *Mosè del Brolo*, pp. 142–47 (with a facsimile). The passage about the Greek books reads (according to the facsimile): ". . . contigit in hoc anno . . . regionem Ueneticorum nobis uicinam penitus incendio deflagrari, ubi cuncta mea preter equitaturas et indumenta deposita fuerant. Combusti sunt igitur omnes libri greci quos multo dudum labore quesiueram precii xi [!] librarum auri . . ." (". . . it happened in this year . . . that the Venetian territory bordering on ours was completely destroyed by fire; all my possessions were deposited there except for my mounts and my clothing. Thus all the Greek books, which I bought some time ago at the price of eleven pounds of gold, have been consumed by the flames . . .").

59. Edited in Pitra's *Analecta Sacra*, V (1888)—as the work of an anonymous Irishman from the school of John Scottus!—then by Gustavson in the *Acta Societas Fennicae* 22 (1897), as an anonymous work of the twelfth century, and finally, after Haskins had restored the work to its author (in *Mediaeval Science*, pp. 197 ff.), by Cremaschi, *Mosè*, pp. 163–95.

60. Found by Haskins in MS Nîmes 52; only the prologue has been edited, in *Mediaeval Science*, pp. 201 f.

61. Ed. by Haskins, *Mediaeval Science*, pp. 203–6; Cremaschi, *Mosè*, pp. 197–200. The letter was written *ex Datia*; on this point, Haskins: "The mention of Dacia would seem to point to the Danubian campaigns of John Comnenus in 1128, on which Moses may have accompanied him in some secretarial position such as he seems to have held at the court."

62. The most recent edition by G. Gorni, "Il 'Liber Pergaminus' di Mosè de Brolo," *Studi Medievali* III/11 (1970), pp. 409–60.

63. Haskins, *Mediaeval Science*, p. 206.

64. Haskins, *Mediaeval Science*, pp. 218–21; Haskins, "Pascalis Romanus," *Byzantion* 2 (1925), 231–36.

65. Ed. by Franceschini, in *Studi e Note di Filologia Latina Medievale* (Milan 1938).

66. Ed. by L. Delatte, *Textes latins et vieux français relatifs aux Cyranides* (Liège/Paris 1942), pp. 1–206. The author is designated *PA*, which is generally resolved as Pascalis. D. Kaimakis, *Die Kyraniden (Cyranides)* (Meisenheim 1976).

67. Ed. by S. Collin-Roset, *AHDL* 30 (1963), 111–98.

68. Fundamental information on the life and work is found in A. Dondaine, *AHDL* 19 (1952), 67–134.

69. P. Classen, "Das Konzil von Konstantinopel 1166 und dei Lateiner," *BZ* 48 (1955), 339–68; see also A. Dondaine, "Hugues Éthérien et le concile de Constantinople de 1166," *Historisches Jahrbuch* 77 (1958), 473–83.

70. The text of the dedication is edited by Haskins, *Mediaeval Science*, p. 217. On the date, see Dondaine, *AHDL* 19 (1952), p. 122.

71. A. Strittmatter, "Notes on Leo Tuscus' Translation of the Liturgy of St. John Chrysostom," *Didascaliae*, Festschrift A. M. Albareda (New York 1961), pp. 409–24. Strittmatter edited an older translation of both the Chrysostoman and the Basilian liturgy from the "Cistercian manuscript" Paris, BN nouv. acq. lat. 1791, in *Traditio* 1 (1943), 79–137.

72. Ed. by N. Häring, "The 'Liber de Differentia naturae et personae' by Hugh Etherian and the Letters Addressed to Him by Peter of Vienna and Hugh of Honau," *Mediaeval Studies* 24 (1962), 1–34; on Peter of Vienna, see H. Fichtenau, "Magister Petrus von Wien," *Beiträge zur Mediävistik. Ausgewählte Aufsätze* (Stuttgart 1975), I, 218–38.

73. Ed. by N. Häring, in *AHDL* 29 (1962), 103–216.

74. Ed. by N. Häring, in *AHDL* 34 (1967), 129–253, and 35 (1968), 211–95.

75. It has been in the cathedral treasury in Limburg an der Lahn since 1827. J. Rauch, Schenk zu Schweinsberg, and J. M. Wilm, "Die Limberger Staurothek," *Das Münster* 8 (1955), 201–40. The staurotheque of St. Matthias (St. Eucharius) in Trier is a replica of the staurotheque formerly from Stuben, now in Limburg; cf. the exhibition catalogue *Rhein und Maas* (Cologne 1972), p. 346 (bibliog.).

76. Thus Bishop Conrad describes in his donation to the Halberstadt Cathedral (16 August 1208) his acquisitions in Constantinople; ed. G. Schmidt, *Urkundenbuch des Hochstifts Halberstadt und seiner Bischöfe* (Leipzig 1883), I, 400–403, here p. 401 (B. Bischoff includes only an excerpt in *Mittelalterliche Schatzverzeichnisse* [Munich 1967], I, 150–52). The tragically entangled episcopate of Bishop Conrad, who remained loyal to the Hohenstaufen dynasty, resigned after the murder of Philip of Swabia, and withdrew into a Cistercian monastery, is described in *Gesta episcoporum Halberstadensium*, MGH *Scriptores*, XXIII, 78–123.

77. The celebration of the translation was established in the document of the year 1208 cited in note 76. On the preserved treasure, see J. Fleming, E. Lehmann, and E. Schubert, *Dom und Domschatz zu Halberstadt* (Berlin 1973); also see the exhibition catalogue *Byzantinische Kostbarkeiten* (Berlin 1977), pp. 23 f. and passim.

78. The passage is taken from the chronicle by Nicetas of Chonae (Choniates), ed. I. A. van Dieten, *Corpus Fontium Historiae Byzantinae*, XI, 575–76 (*Migne PG* 139). A new Greek edition by J.-L. van Dieten, *Nicetae Choniatae Historia* (Berlin/New York 1975), vol. I.

79. Rudolf Borchardt, "Pisa," *Prosa* (Stuttgart 1960), III, 114 ff.

80. V. Rose, *Verzeichniss*, II/3, no. 898, p. 1061, at the description of Cod. lat. fol. 74. Cf. also Schipperges, *Die Assimilation der arabischen Medizin*, pp. 35–37.

81. Rose, *Verzeichniss*, II/3, 1059 ff. Haskins, *Mediaeval Science*, pp. 131–35.

82. It seems that Constantinus Africanus left the *Practica* incomplete. According to Rose (p. 1064), when Stephan of Pisa began to work on the text, he did not know the conclusion of the work by Johannes Agarenus. But is that a probable notion when the Pisan Rusticus worked together with Johannes Agarenus, and Stephan and Rusticus were both Pisans?

83. Rose, *Verzeichniss*, II/3, 1063.

84. Two years before the appearance of Rose's description of Berol. lat. fol. 74, which was fundamental with respect to the Pisan translator of Aristotle, Remigio Sabbadini had pointed out a manuscript of the *Rhetorica ad Herennium* in the Milanese Biblioteca Ambrosiana (E 7 sup.), which a certain *Stephanus thesaurarius Antioche* wrote in 1121; the numbers which he uses are of the Greek numerical system, although written in Roman letters ("Spogli ambrosiani latini," *Studi italiani di filologia classica* 11 [1903], 272 f.; cf. F. Steffens, *Lateinische Paläographie*, 2nd ed. [Berlin 1929], pl. 83ᶜ). According to R. W. Hunt, this system also attests to the writing of the *Liber Mamonis in astronomia a Stephano philosopho translatus* (cf. Haskins, *Mediaeval Science*, pp. 98–103) by Stephan of Antioch; in "Stephan of Antioch," *Mediaeval and Renaissance Studies* 2 (1950), pp. 172 f.

85. Classen, *Burgundio*, p. 5. Older surveys of the life and work are found in F. Buonamici, *Burgundio Pisano*, in *Annali delle Università Toscane* 28 (Pisa 1908); R. Mols, "Bur-

gundio de Pise," *Dictionnaire d'Histoire et de Géographie Ecclésiastiques* (Paris 1938), X, 1363–69; and F. Liotta, "Burgundione," *Dizionario biografico degli Italiani* (1972), XV, 423–28.

86. On a somewhat older partial translation, see the remarks in section 4 above on Cerbanus, and the literature cited there. On Burgundio's translation, see also L. Callari, "Contributo allo studio della versione di Burgundio Pisano del 'De orthodoxa fide' di Giovanni Damasceno," *Atti del R. Istituto Veneto di Scienze, Lettere ed Arti, Classe di Scienze Morale e Lettere* 100 (1940–41), 197–246.

87. Burgundio, *Prologus super opus beati Johannis Chrysostomi archiepiscopi CP. super Matthaeum*, ed. E. Martène and M. Durand, in *Veterum Scriptorum . . . Amplissima Collectio* (Paris 1724), I, 817–19; also in S. M. Bandini, *Catalogus codicum Latinorum Bibliothecae Mediceae Laurentianae* (Florence 1777), IV, 450. On the translation, see M. Flecchia, in *Aevum* 26 (1952), p. 113–30. On Burgundio's translation of Basil the Great's commentary on Isaiah for Pope Eugenius III and on a possible translation of Basil's homilies on the hexaemeron, see Classen, *Burgundio*, pp. 36 f. One would do well to take the old Latin translation by Eustathius into account in further discussions.

88. *Némésius d'Émèse, De Natura Hominis. Traduction de Burgundio de Pise*, ed. G. Verbeke and J. R. Moncho (Leiden 1975), pp. 1 f. Before Burgundio, Alfanus of Salerno had translated it; Johannes Cuno worked on the translation after him (1511–12). The humanistic translation is stylistically better, but less faithful than Burgundio's; cf. Sicherl, *Johannes Cuno*, pp. 141 f. According to Hugh of Honau, *Liber de ignorantia* X 30 (ed. N. M. Häring, in *Mediaeval Studies* 25 [1963], 220), Burgundio dedicated and presented his translation to Emperor Frederick, *victo Mediolano et subacta Italia*; cf. Classen, *Burgundio*, pp. 28 ff. and 74.

89. Burgundio translated some sections concerning wine-growing from the early Byzantine "Geoponica"; Buonamici edits copies of two codices with this *Liber de vindemiis* in the appendix to his treatise in *Annali delle Università Toscane* 28 (1908). On the source and further manuscripts, see Classen, *Burgundio*, p. 35, n. 7.

90. Classen has edited the prologue to this translation, with detailed commentary, in *Burgundio*, pp. 84–102.

91. Burgundio did not know the commentary on John which Rupert of Deutz published around 1115. The works of the great German symbolist hardly became well known in Italy, however; cf. H. Haacke, "Die Überlieferung der Schriften Ruperts von Deutz," *DA* 16 (1960), 397–436, with "Nachlese," *DA* 26 (1970), 528–40.

92. H. Dausend, "Zur Übersetzungsweise Burgundios von Pisa," *Wiener Studien* 35 (1913), 353–69; Classen, *Burgundio*, pp. 54 ff. and 89 ff.

93. Most recently described by Classen, *Burgundio*, pp. 7 f. and pl. 1.

94. There is no critically certified list of Burgundio's translations. Haskins (*Mediaeval Science*, p. 208) speaks of ten translations of Galen, among them *De sectis medicorum* in 1185, dedicated to Barbarossa's son Henry, later Emperor Henry VI. Burgundio's translation *De complexionibus* has been edited for the first time as vol. I of *Galenus latinus* by R. Durling. We may expect that with the continuation of the *Galenus latinus* there will be some clarification of the last period of Burgundio's work as a translator.

95. E. Caspar, *Roger II. (1101–1154) und die Gründung der normannisch-sicilischen Monarchie* (Innsbruck 1904), pp. 346 ff. (Nilus Doxapatres) and pp. 448 ff.

96. On the ministerial trilingualism and on the noteworthy recession of Greek (and Arabic) as a language of the chancery in the course of the twelfth century, see K. A. Kehr, *Die Urkunden der normannisch-sicilischen Könige* (Innsbruck 1902), pp. 239 ff. On the chancery, see also Niese, in *Historische Zeitschrift* 108 (1912), 490 ff. The manuscript London, British Library Harl. 5786, contains in its three columns the Greek, Latin, and Arabic texts, and is considered a presentation copy of the court in Palermo (at the latest, 1153). *Facsimiles of the Palaeographical Society*, ser. 1 (London 1873–83), pl. 132; A. Watson, *Catalogue of Dated and Datable Manuscripts* (London 1979), no. 383, pl. 84 a–e.

97. A. de Stefano emphasizes the eclectic character of this culture, which did not attain to unity until the rule of Frederick II, in *La cultura in Sicilia nel periodo normanno*, 2nd ed. (Bologna 1954), pp. 84 ff.

98. Scaduto, *Il monachesimo basiliano nella Sicilia medievale* (1947); Borsari, *Il monachesimo bizantino nella Sicilia e nell'Italia meridionale prenormanne* (1963).

99. Batiffol, *L'abbaye de Rossano*, pp. 2 ff.

100. The famous dedicatory epistle was most recently reedited by Minio-Paluello and Drossaert Lulofs, *Plato latinus*, II: *Phaedo*, pp. 89 f. On the addressee, see Haskins, *Mediaeval Science*, pp. 169 ff. The first editor, Rose, understood Hero's *mechanica* to mean pneumatic system (in *Hermes* 1 [1866], 380 f.); E. Grant has opposed this interpretation, up until now the generally accepted one, in "Henricus Aristippus, William of Moerbeke and Two Alleged Mediaeval Translations of Hero's 'Pneumatica,'" *Speculum* 46 (1971), 656–69. Hugh Falcandus gives some information about the rise and fall of Henry Aristippus in *Liber de regno Siciliae*. Aristippus died, probably already in 1162, in the prison in Palermo: "captus fuerat et Panormum reductus . . . in carcere post non multum temporis miserie simul et vivendi modum sortitus est"; Hugh Falcandus, ed. G. B. Siragusa (Rome 1897), p. 81. On Aristippus, see E. Franceschini's summary in *Dizionario biografico degli Italiani* (1962), IV, 201–6.

101. Minio-Paluello has proved this on the basis of comparisons of other translations by Aristippus in *Opuscula*, pp. 62–71. The great Toledan translator of Aristotle from the Arabic, Gerard of Cremona, translated all four books of the *Meteora* (Minio-Paluello, *Opuscula*, p. 135, n. 2); his translation of the fourth book did not, however, supplant Aristippus'. In a combination of translations which was significant for the reception of Aristotle's works in the high Middle Ages, the *Meteora* had a wide circulation—in Gerard's translation of books I–III from Arabic and Aristippus' translation of book IV from Greek—until William of Moerbeke again translated the whole work from Greek around 1260.

102. Kordeuter and Labowsky, *Plato latinus*, II: *Meno*, p. 6.

103. "[Haben sie] auch nicht, wie der Timaeus, in die Schulstudien und in die Lehrgebäude der Magister Eingang gefunden—an der Schwelle des alle anderen Ansätze erdrückenden Arabismus und Aristotelismus hatten sie nicht die Zeit dazu—, so werden sie doch in den Moralbüchern, den Spruch- und Beispielsammlungen des späten Mittelalters nicht unerwähnt gelassen"; Rose, "Die Lücke im Diogenes Laërtius und der alte Übersetzer," *Hermes* 1, p. 374.

104. It is Codex Venice, Marc. gr. 313; cf. Canart, *Scrittura e Civiltà* 2 (1978), p. 149. On the history of the collection, see above in Chapter II.

105. Foreword, ed. Haskins, *Mediaeval Science*, pp. 191–93.

106. Boese, *Die mittelalterliche Übersetzung der* ΣΤΟΙΧΕΙΩΣΙΣ ΦΥΣΙΚΗ *des Proclus* (Berlin 1958).

107. A. A. Björnbo, "Die mittelalterlichen lateinischen Übersetzungen aus dem Griechischen auf dem Gebiete der mathematischen Wissenschaften," *Archiv für die Geschichte der Naturwissenschaften und Technik* 1 (1909), 385–94.

108. H. L. L. Busard, "Der Traktat 'De isoperimetris,' der unmittelbar aus dem Griechischen ins Lateinische übersetzt worden ist" (with an edition), *Mediaeval Studies* 42 (1980), 61–88, here p. 63.

109. On *De curvis superficiebus*, see M. Clagett, *Archimedes in the Middle Ages* (Madison 1964), I, 439 ff., esp. p. 442.

110. J. E. Murdoch, "Euclides graeco-latinus: A Hitherto Unknown Medieval Latin Translation of the 'Elements' Made Directly from the Greek," *Harvard Studies in Classical Philology* 71 (1966), 249–302.

111. E. Jamison, *Admiral Eugenius of Sicily* (London 1957).

112. Ed. L. Sternbach, in *BZ* 11 (1902), 406–51.; ed. M. Gigante, *Eugenio da Palermo: Versus iambici* (Palermo 1964).

113. Ed. by O. Holder-Egger, "Italienische Prophetien des 13. Jahrhunderts," *NA* 15 (1890), 151–73; see also, more recently, Jamison, *Eugenius*, pp. 21–32. The papal prophecies (*Papalisto*) which were famous in the late Middle Ages derived from the Byzantine oracle on emperors; in the oldest form of these prophecies, fifteen popes are characterized, beginning with Nicholas III (Orsini, 1277–80), of whom it is said, "Genus nequam, ursa catulos pascens" ("a worthless family, a bear which nourishes her whelps"), which Dante took up again in the *Divina Commedia* (*Inferno* XIX); cf. H. Grundmann, "Die Papstprophetien des Mittelalters," *Archiv für Kulturgeschichte* 19 (1929), 77–138, and "Boniface VIII. und Dante," in *Dante und die Mächtigen seiner Zeit* (Munich 1960), pp. 16 f.

114. A. Lejeune, *L'Optique de Claude Ptolémée dans la version latine* (Louvain 1956).

115. M. C. Díaz y Díaz has provided an almost complete survey in *Index Scriptorum Latinorum Medii Aevi Hispanorum* (Madrid 1959).

116. M. C. Díaz y Díaz, "Le latin du haut moyen âge espagnol," in *La lexicographie du latin médiéval et ses rapports avec les recherches actuelles sur la civilisation du moyen âge* (Paris 1981), pp. 105–14.

117. Paulus Albarus, *epist.* 4, 1 (*Migne PL* 121, col. 427).

118. Manchester, John Rylands Library 89, Spanish Cassiodorus manuscript from the year 949, fol. 4ʳ; cf. M. R. James, *A Descriptive Catalogue of the Latin Manuscripts in the John Rylands University Library* (London 1921), I, 162, and II, pl. 120.

119. Madrid, Biblioteca de la R. Academia de la Historia 8, Cassiodorus manuscript from San Millán de la Cogolla, saec. X, fol. 341; cited from M. C. Díaz y Díaz, *Libros y librerías en la Rioja altomedieval* (Logroño 1979), p. 142. ⋏⋃⋃ should probably be resolved as the symbol of history, "the beginning and the end," as above, Chapter II, sec. 3, ad init.

120. C. Haskins, "Translators from the Arabic in Spain," *Mediaeval Science*, pp. 3–19; Sarton, *Introduction*, II/1, 114 f. and 169–79; Franceschini, "Il contributo dell'Italia alla trasmissione del pensiero greco in occidente nei secoli XII–XIII," in *Scritti di Filologia Latina Medievale* (1976); and especially Jourdain's still classic *Recherches sur les anciennes traductions d'Aristote*.

121. See the definitive survey by M.-T. d'Alverny, "Translations and Translators," in *Renaissance and Renewal in the Twelfth Century*, ed. R. L. Benson and G. Constable (Oxford 1982), pp. 421–62, here pp. 444 ff.: "Translations in Spain" (bibliog.).

122. D'Alverny, "Translations and Translators," p. 444, n. 97.

123. D. 1187; on Gerard, see I. Opelt, "Zur Übersetzungstechnik Gerhards von Cremona," *Glotta* 38 (1960), 135–70.

124. D. 1135; L. Thorndike, *Michael Scot* (London 1965).

125. Daniel of Morley, *Philosophia (Liber de naturis inferiorum et superiorum)*, praef., ed. G. Maurach, *Mittellateinisches Jahrbuch* 14 (1979), 212–45, here p. 212.

126. "nec libri Aristotelis de naturali philosophia nec commenta legantur"; H. Denifle and E. Chatelain, *Chartularium Universitatis Parisiensis* (Paris 1889), I, 70.

127. Cf. Friedrich Überweg's *Grundriß der Geschichte der Philosophie*, vol. II: *Die patristische und scholastische Philosophie*, 13th ed., ed. B. Geyer (Basel/Stuttgart 1956), pp. 251 f. and 706 f. (bibliog.). Book burnings have often had exactly the opposite effect to that intended. Despite the campaign of 1210, David's teachings were still quite well known (from Albertus Magnus and Thomas); and in the end A. Birkenmajer has recovered a part of the texts: "Découverte de fragments manuscrits de David de Dinant," *Revue néoscolastique de Philosophie* 35 (1933), 220–29 (repr. in Birkenmajer's *Études d'histoire des sciences et de la philosophie du moyen âge*, pp. 11–20. M. Kurdziałek has edited the fragments: *Davidis de Dinanto Quaternulorum fragmenta*, Studia Mediewistyczne 3 (Warsaw 1963).

128. According to a report by Albertus Magnus, David translated a work of natural science (*De problematibus quibusdam*) from Greek for Emperor Frederick II; it begins thus: "Cum essem in Graecia, venit ad manus meas liber de problematibus meteorum"; cf. Birkenmajer, "Découverte," pp. 221 ff. This translation has, however, not yet been rediscovered. Thus despite Birkenmajer's fine discovery, this David of Dinant, who traveled in Greece, translated for Frederick II, and was condemned in Paris, remains an enigma. The most recent work on the subject is M.-T. d'Alverny's "Les nouveaux apports dans les domaines de la science et de la pensée au temps de Philippe Auguste: La philosophie," in *La France de Philippe Auguste* (Paris 1982), pp. 863–80.

129. J. Monfrin, "Humanisme et traductions au moyen âge," in *L'humanisme médiéval dans les littératures romanes du XIIᵉ au XIVᵉ siècle*, ed. A. Fourrier (Paris 1964), 217–46, and "Les traducteurs et leur public en France au moyen âge," ibid., pp. 247–62; Goldbrunner, in *Archiv für Kulturgeschichte* 50 (1968), 200–239.

130. Abelard, *epist.* 9, "Ad virgines Paraclitenses de studio litterarum" (*Migne PL* 178, cols. 332 f.).

131. *Sententiae*, praef., ed. R. M. Martin, *Œuvres de Robert de Melun*, III/1, 36 ff. See also M. V. Anastos, in *Twelfth Century Europe*, ed. Clagett, Post, and Reynolds, 2nd ed. (Madison 1966), pp. 132 ff.

132. *Dialogus Ratii et Everardi*, ed. N. M. Häring, in *Mediaeval Studies* 15 (1953), 243–89. One presentation manuscript, with Gilbert's commentaries on Boethius' *Opuscula sacra*, closes with a Greek alphabetic table: Valenciennes 189 (B.4.63); J. Mangeart, *Catalogue . . . des manuscrits de la bibliothèque de Valenciennes*, no. 189, p. 178.

133. Klibansky, "The School of Chartres," in *Twelfth Century Europe*, pp. 3 ff. Châtillon, "Les écoles de Chartres et de Saint-Victor," in *La Scuola nell'Occidente latino dell'Alto Medioevo* (1972), pp. 795–839.

134. M. Gibson, "The Study of the 'Timaeus' in the Eleventh and Twelfth Centuries," *Pensamiento* 25 (1969), 183–94.

135. Greek mythology, for instance, which played an important role in the School of Chartres as it did elsewhere, was obtained not from Greek but from Latin sources, especially Ovid's *Metamorphoses*.

136. For the following, cf. Théry, in *AHDL* 18 (1950–51), 55 f.

137. ". . . non pigebit referre nec forte audire displicebit quod a Greco interprete et qui Latinam linguam commode nouerat, dum in Apulia morarer, accepi; nam et ipsi uolo referre gratiam, etsi non utilitatis (que tamen in his aliqua est), saltem bone uoluntatis, qua auditoribus prodesse cupiebat" (". . . it will cause no shame to report and will not be displeasing to hear that while I was in Apulia I took lessons from a Greek translator who knew Latin rather well, and I would like to thank him, if not for any gain [although there was also some of this], at least for the good will with which he wanted to help his students"); John of Salisbury, *Metalogicon* I 15, ed. C. C. I. Webb (Oxford 1929), p. 37.

138. Théry's essay "Documents concernant Jean Sarrazin," *AHDL* 18 (1950–51), is incomplete; thus one must also consult the *Histoire littéraire de la France*, 2nd ed. (Paris 1869), XIV, 191–94, and Grabmann, *Mittelalterliches Geistesleben* (Munich 1926), I, 454–60 (dedicatory epistle to Abbot Odo of St. Denis).

139. Théry, in *AHDL* 18, 45 f.; Grabmann, p. 459.

140. The dedication of Johannes Sarracenus is to be found in John of Salisbury's collection of letters, *epist.* 149 (*Migne PL* 199, cols. 143 f.). Cf. Théry, in *AHDL* 18, 51 ff. John of Salisbury's answer is in *epist.* 169 (*Migne PL* 199, cols. 161 ff.).

141. Cf. John of Salisbury, *epist.* 229 and 230 (*Migne PL* 199, cols. 259 ff.). In the new edition by W. J. Millor and C. N. L. Brooke, *The Letters of John of Salisbury*, vol. II (Oxford 1979), unfortunately, only half of the correspondence is present. The letters of Johannes Sarracenus were not included.

142. Théry, "Jean Sarrazin, 'traducteur' de Scot Érigène," *Studia Medievalia in honorem R. J. Martin*, pp. 359 ff.

143. Written to John of Salisbury (*Migne PL* 199, col. 143).

144. Written to Odo of St. Denis; Grabmann, *Mittelalterliches Geistesleben*, I, 456 f. The *frater* William of St. Denis was already mentioned in the first letter to Odo of St. Denis as a Greek authority (dedicatory epistle to *De divinis nominibus*): "Ceterum si in aliquo forte deliqui, vestre sit oro et fratris Wilhelmi diligentie emendare" ("If by chance I am lacking in something, I pray that your diligence and that of brother William will emend it"); ed. Grabmann, p. 456. It can scarcely be determined which of the two Williams of St. Denis who worked with Greek was meant here.

145. The bishop of Poitiers from 1152–54 was Gilbert, whose theology, at least in his students' eyes, was closely akin to the Greek. During the time when Johannes Sarracenus was translating the *Hierarchies* (1166–67), an Englishman had the episcopal throne of this city, which was also ruled by the English.

146. Fundamental information is found in Delisle, in *Journal des Savants* (1900), 725–39; a new survey is given by Weiss, "Lo studio del greco all'abbazia di San Dionigi durante il medioevo," *Medieval and Humanist Greek* (1977), pp. 44–59.

147. E. Wickersheimer, *Dictionnaire biographique des médecins en France au moyen âge* (Paris 1936), s.v. "Guillaume de Gap"; Wickersheimer supports the identification of the two Williams of St. Denis. Under "Guillaume de Harcigny," Wickersheimer's *Dictionnaire* mentions a French physician who traveled in the East (d. 1393). ". . . les médecins des vieux âges ont souvent arpenté l'Europe et l'Asie en tous sens, que ce fût pour parfaire leurs études en se mettant à l'école des maîtres les plus rèputés ou pour voler au secours d'un souverain se trouvant mal à l'autre bout de la chrétienté" ("Physicians of earlier times often literally had to roam up and down Europe and Asia, in order to complete their studies by enrolling in the schools of the most famous masters, or to fly to the aid of a monarch who had fallen ill at the other end of Christendom"); T. d'Angomont, *Revue du mouen âge latin* 38 (1982), 199 f.

148. Delisle, in *Journal des Savants* (1900); On Herbert of Bosham as an **exegete, see** Smalley, *The Study of the Bible*, passim.

149. Ed. by A. Hilka, *88. Jahresbericht der schlesischen Gesellschaft für vaterländische Cultur (1910), IV. Abteilung, c. Sektion für neuere Philologie,* pp. 5–23. A new edition by W. Suchier, in L. W. Daly and W. Suchier, *Altercatio Hadriani Augusti et Epicteti Philosophi* (Urbana, Ill., 1939), pp. 147 ff. Weiss remarks pertinently: "La caccia ai codici greci in oriente per conto dell'abbazia . . . è un fatto che si può dir unico nella storia della cultura occidentale prima dei tempi di Guarino da Verona e dell'Aurispa" ("The search for Greek codices in the East on behalf of the abbacy . . . is a fact which can be termed unique in the history of Western culture before the time of Guarino da Verona and Aurispa" (*Rivista di Storia della Chiesa in Italia* 6 [1952], 429). One could of course also mention Moses of Bergamo.

150. Loenertz, "Le Panégyrique de S. Denys l'Aréopagite par S. Michel le Syncelle," in *Byzantina et Franco-Graeca* (1970).

151. Only the dedication has been printed, in Delisle, in *Journal des Savants* (1900), p. 727 f. On the manuscript, Paris, BN grec 933, from which William most likely translated, see ibid., p. 730.

152. Weiss, *Medieval and Humanist Greek,* pp. 58 f. (excerpt, based on two manuscripts); Handschin, *Annales Musicologiques* 2 (1954), 48 f. (additional manuscript: Paris BN nouv. acq. 1509). Handschin suggested, without knowing the essays by Delisle and Weiss, that Wilhelmus Medicus was the translator.

153. On the importance of Dionysius for Hugh of St. Victor, see Châtillon, in *La Scuola nell'Occidente latino dell'Alto Medioevo,* pp. 834 f. R. Javelet, *Image et ressemblance au XIIᵉ siècle. De saint Anselme à Alain de Lille,* I/2 (Paris 1967).

154. G. Théry, "Thomas Gallus. Aperçu Biographique," *AHDL* 12 (1939), 141–208. On a commentary by Thomas Gallus on the *Mystical Theology,* see Théry, "Les oeuvres dionysiennes de Thomas Gallus," *La vie spirituelle, Supplément* 33 (1932), 129–54. J. Walsh has published newly found comments on the letters of Dionysius in "The 'Expositions' of Thomas Gallus on the Pseudo-Dionysian Letters," *AHDL* 30 (1963), 199–220.

155. Châtillon, "Hugues de Saint-Victor critique de Jean Scot," in *Jean Scot Érigène et l'histoire de la philosophie,* pp. 415 ff.

156. Dondaine, *Le Corpus dionysien de l'Université de Paris,* esp. pp. 122 ff.

Notes to Chapter XII

1. Peter of Eboli, *Liber ad honorem Augusti* (for Emperor Henry VI), line 36, ed. G. B. Siragusa (Rome 1906), p. 9. See also the picture of the *Notarii Greci, Notarii Saraceni,* and *Notarii Latini* of the old chancery in Palermo in Siragusa, p. 124 (Cod. Bern 120).

2. C. Brühl, *Urkunden und Kanzlei König Rogers II. von Sizilien* (Cologne/Vienna 1978).

3. M. B. Wellas, *Griechisches aus dem Umkreis Kaiser Friedrichs II.* (Munich 1983), pp. 2 f.

4. "In the palimpsest Laurent. Conv. Soppr. 152, saec. XIII, of Basilian origin, four Greek letters of Friedrich II to the Byzantine ruler are preserved" (Wellas, p. 18). I take the reference to the trilingual Bible manuscript Venice, Marc. gr. 11, "saec. XIII, de provenance sicilienne, Actes et épîtres en grec-latin-arabe," from Canart's article "Le livre grec . . . ," *Scrittura e Civiltà* 2 (1978), 144, n. 93.

5. *Constitutiones regum regni utriusque Siciliae mandante Friderico II Imperatore . . . concinnatae* (Naples 1786); H. Conrad, T. von der Lieck-Buyken, and W. Wagner, *Die Konstitutionen Friedrichs II. von Hohenstaufen für sein Königreich Sizilien. Nach einer lateinischen Handschrift des 13. Jahrhunderts hrsg. und übersetzt* (Cologne/Vienna 1973). On the "official" character of the translation, see Wellas, *Griechisches,* p. 33.

6. Wellas, *Griechisches,* p. 56.

7. For the following, see Canart, "Le livre grec . . . ," 103–62; G. Cavallo, "La trasmissione scritta della cultura greca antica in Calabria e in Sicilia tra i secoli X–XV," *Scrittura e Civiltà* 4 (1980), 157–245; Cavallo, "La cultura italo-greca nella produzione libraria," in *I bizantini in Italia,* ed. G. Pugliese Carratelli (Milan 1982), pp. 497–612 (bibliog.). At the same time, Cavallo's exemplary essay "Libri greci e resistenza etnica in terra d'Otranto" appeared in the paperback collection *Libri e letturi nel mondo bizantino* (Bari 1982), pp. 157–78, edited by Cavallo.

8. The fundamental study is J. M. Hoeck and R. J. Loenertz, *Nikolaos-Nektarios von Otranto, Abt von Casole* (Ettal 1965).

9. Rome, Vat. Pal. gr. 232 and Paris, BN suppl. gr. 1232. Both place the Greek and Latin in two facing columns; cf. Devreesse, *Les manuscrits grecs*, pp. 46 f., and Hoeck and Loenertz, *Nikolaos-Nektarios*, p. 98, pls. 1 and 3. Both manuscripts are palimpsests.

10. Karlsruhe, Badische Landesbibliothek Cod. Ettenheimmünster 6. Despite the splendid presentation in Franz Joseph Mone's *Lateinische und Griechische Messen* (1850), the codex has hardly become well known. See also Hoeck and Loenertz, *Nikolaos-Nektarios*, pp. 74–82. Paris, BN lat. 1002, saec. XII–XIV, is related to the Karlsruhe manuscript; cf. A. Strittmatter, "Missa Grecorum . . . ," *Traditio* 1 (1943), 79–137, here pp. 136 ff., and Strittmatter, "Notes on Leo Tuscus' Translation of the Liturgy of St. John Chrysostom," in *Didascaliae*, Festschrift A. M. Albareda (New York 1961). pp. 411–24, here p. 416; Hoeck and Loenertz, *Nikolaos-Nektarios*, p. 48, n. 49. The counterpart of the Latin translations of the Greek liturgy is a Greek translation of the Latin mass, ed. by A. Heisenberg, "Neue Quellen zur Geschichte des lateinischen Kaisertums und der Kirchenunion II," SB Munich (1923), no. 2, pp. 46 ff. (repr. in Heisenberg, *Quellen und Studien zur spätbyzantinischen Geschichte* [London 1973]). It is one of the works of Nikolaos Mesarites, but is generally attributed to Nicholas-Nectarius of Otranto; cf. Hoeck and Loenertz, *Nikolaos-Nektarios*, p. 82.

11. According to the typicon of Casole, the *Sophistici Elenchi* and the Aristophanes were lent out to a notary; H. Omont, "Le Typicon de Saint-Nicolas di Casole près d'Otrante. Notice du Ms. C. III. 17 de Turin," *Revue des études grecques* 3 (1890), 381–91, here p. 390. There is also a considerable medieval tradition from southern Italy of the works of Sophocles and especially Euripides; cf. Pertusi, "La scoperta di Euripide nel primo Umanesimo," *Italia Medioevale e Umanistica* 3 (1960), 102 ff. (bibliog.). The interest expressed in the Greek dramatists by late medieval Greek circles in southern Italy is striking. Who would think it possible that a Psalter was erased during the Middle Ages so that a Sophocles could be written on the parchment: Florence, Laur. Conv. Soppr. 152, written in 1282 (Otranto?)! And this is not a unique case.

12. Paris, BN gr. 1665. On this manuscript, see the informative notice by A. Diller, "Diodorus in Terra d'Otranto," *Classical Philology* 48 (1953), 257 f.

13. Thus the Aristophanes codex from Casole, mentioned above, is supposed to be identical with Cod. Venet. Marc. gr. 474; cr. Antonius Galateus [A. Ferrari from Galatina], *De situ Japygiae*, in J. G. Graevius, *Thesaurus Antiquitatum et Historiarum Italiae* (Leiden 1723), IX/5, 11. Ultimately, however, Bessarion's removal of the books most probably saved them from the Turks, who laid waste to Casole in 1480; cf. L. Labowsky, *Bessarion's Library and the Biblioteca Marciana: Six Early Inventories* (Rome 1979).

14. M. Roncaglia, *Georges Bardanes, métropolite de Corfu, et Barthélémy, de l'ordre franciscain*, Studi e Testi Francescani 4 (Rome 1953), and "Il primo incontro dei Francescani con i greci: Fra Bartolomeo O.F.M. e Georgios Bardanes a Casole (Otranto)," *Atti dello VIII Congresso Internazionale di Studi Bizantini*, (Rome 1953), I, 448–52: "Da questo primo colloquio dei Francescani con i Greci nacque tutta la controversia sulla beatitudine dei Santi e sul Purgatorio. . . . La cosa sembra aver avuto non sola una certa ripercussione nel mondo greco ma anche in quello latino. . . . Il malinteso su questo punto teologico interruppe per il momento le trattative per l'unione delle Chiese" ("All of the controversy on the beatitude of the saints and on purgatory arose from this first conversation between the Franciscans and the Greeks. . . . This matter seems to have had certain repercussions not only in the Greek world, but also in the Latin. . . . The misunderstanding of this theological point momentarily interrupted the negotiations for the unification of the Church"). I follow Hoeck and Loenertz (pp. 166 ff.) on the dating of Bardanes' journey to Otranto.

15. F. Mütherich, "Handschriften im Umkreis Friedrichs II.," in *Probleme um Friedrich II.*, ed. J. Fleckenstein (Sigmaringen 1974), pp. 9–12. The southern Italian manuscript Leipzig, Universitätsbibliothek Rep. II 4° 143, saec. XIII ex., contains an Alexander romance (*Historia de preliis*) with illustrations that go back to a Greek source; cf. D. J. A. Ross, *Alexander historiatus* (London 1963), pp. 53 f. With the aid of the ancient series of illustrations of Aratus, the *Liber introductorius*, a compendium on spheres and stars, planets and zodiacal signs that Michael Scot was commissioned to compile by Emperor Frederick II, was illustrated; cf. M. Bauer, "Der Liber Introductorius des Michael Scottus in der Abschrift clm 10268" (diss., Munich 1983).

16. Among the many tales concerning Frederick II's experiments in natural science, the following is connected with a tradition concerning the knowledge of Greek at his court. In 1497 an enormous pike was caught in a lake near the imperial city of Heilbronn; it bore a copper ring with the *Greek* inscription: "I am the fish that Emperor Frederick II placed in this lake with his own hand on 5 October 1230." The widely known story obviously goes back to Conrad Celtis and Bishop Johannes Dalberg of Worms. The ring is allegedly preserved in the treasury of the Heidelberg castle; cf. A. Hauber, "Kaiser Friedrich II der Staufer und der langlebige Fisch," *Archiv für die Geschichte der Naturwissenschaften und der Technik* 3 (1912), 315–29. The oldest preserved text of the Greek inscription on the ring appears to be that on an inserted page (fol. 28 bis) in Codex Vat. Pal. lat. 1368. The manuscript, formerly in Heidelberg, came from the collection of the scholar Sebastian Münster (d. 1552).

17. Haskins, "Science at the Court of the Emperor Frederick II," *Mediaeval Science*, pp. 242 ff.; Niese, "Zur Geschichte des geistigen Lebens," *Historische Zeitschrift* 108 (1912).

18. L. Thorndike, *Michael Scot* (London 1965), p. 1.

19. Haskins' *Mediaeval Science*, pp. 272 ff., is still fundamental in the critique of the accounts of Michael Scot's life.

20. L. Thorndike, "The Place of Astrology in the History of Science," *Isis* 46 (1955), 273–78.

21. R. de Vaux, "La première entrée d'Averroës chez les latins," *Revue des sciences philosophiques et théologiques* 22 (1933), 193–245; M. Grabmann, *Mittelalterliches Geistesleben* (1936), II, 109 ff.

22. E. Renan, *Averroès et l'Averroïsme* (Paris 1852), pp. 162 and 230 f. M. Gorce (*L'essor de la pensée au moyen âge* [Paris 1933], p. 52), following Renan, notes: "le fils d'Averroès à la cour de Frédéric, c'est Michel Scot"!

23. "Le saint Augustin de l'Islam" is the description of Avicenna given by Gorce, *L'essor*, p. 21.

24. S. Impellizzeri, "Bartolomeo da Messina," *Dizionario Biografico degli Italiani* 6 (1964), 729 f. (bibliog.). The most important manuscript is Padua, Bibl. Antoniana Scaff. XVII 370, described by E. Franceschini, *Aevum* 9 (1935), 3–26.

25. Ed. by R. Seligsohn, "Die Übersetzung der ps. aristotelischen Problemata durch Bartholomäus von Messina" (diss., Berlin 1934).

26. Ed. by W. Kley, *Theophrasts metaphysisches Bruchstück und die Schrift Περὶ σημείων in der lateinischen Übersetzung des Bartholomäus von Messina*, diss., Berlin (Würzburg 1936).

27. Ed. by R. Foerster, *Scriptores physiognomonici graeci et latini* (Leipzig 1893), pp. 5–91. Foerster characterizes Bartholomew's method of translation thus: ". . . id egit ut verbum verbo redderet et sensum loci non assequi quam mutatione verborum extricare mallet" ("The matter is such that he translated word for word and preferred not to follow the sense of the passage, rather than to make it clear by changing words"); prologue, p. l.

28. Ed. by W. L. Lorimer and L. Minio-Paluello, *Aristoteles latinus*, XI/1–2.

29. H. Denifle and E. Chatelain, *Chartularium Universitatis Parisiensis* (Paris 1889), I, 436. The letter which contains the name of Emperor Frederick II is included in J.-L.-A. Huillard-Bréholles, *Historia diplomatica Friderici secundi*, (Paris 1854), IV/1, 383–85.

30. E. Franceschini, *Roberto Grossatesta, vescovo di Lincoln, e le sue traduzioni latine* (Venice 1933); S. H. Thomson, *The Writings of Robert Grosseteste* (Cambridge 1940); D. A. Callus, ed., *Robert Grosseteste, Scholar and Bishop* (Oxford 1955) (bibliog.); see in the latter volume esp. Callus, "Robert Grosseteste as Scholar," pp. 1–69, B. Smalley, "The Biblical Scholar," pp. 70–97; R. W. Hunt, "The Library of Robert Grosseteste," pp. 121–45. A summary of older research in K. D. Hill, "Robert Grosseteste and His Work of Greek Translation," in *The Orthodox Churches and the West*, ed. D. Baker (Oxford 1976), pp. 213–22.

31. Cf. the Greek manuscript of the gospels from Grosseteste's own collection: Cambridge, Gonville and Caius College MS 403; Hunt, in *Robert Grosseteste*, p. 135.

32. His achievement is precisely characterized in a rubric: "Correxit autem dominus R. Grosseteste lincolniensis episcopus veterem translationem et inseruit multa que transtulit ex greco exemplario quae in veteri translatione non habentur" ("Lord R. Grosseteste, Bishop of Lincoln, corrected the old translation and inserted many things which he translated from the Greek copy that were not in the old translation"); Hocedez, in *Le Musée Belge* 17 (1913), 110, according to MS Cambridge, Pembroke College 20, fol. 1ʳ.

33. Cf. Thomson, *The Writings*, pp. 45 ff.; Callus, in *Robert Grosseteste*, pp. 53 f.; *St. John Damascene: Dialectica. Version of Robert Grosseteste*, ed. O. A. Colligan (Louvain/Paderborn 1953).

34. It is certain that Grosseteste translated the apocryphal letters of Ignatius; whether he also translated the authentic letters is still disputed; cf. Callus, in *Robert Grosseteste*, pp. 54 f.

35. The manuscript used for the translation is Cambridge, University Library Ff.1.24 (saec. X); Hunt, in *Robert Grosseteste*, p. 134.

36. Paris, BN gr. 437 and gr. 933.

37. Oxford, Bodleian Library MS Canonici gr. 97; Barbour identified the work as coming from Grosseteste's circle and described the manuscript in *The Bodleian Library Record* 6 (1957/61), 401–16.

38. L. Baur, *Die philosophischen Werke des Robert Grosseteste* (Münster 1912), pp. 40 f.

39. F. M. Powicke, "Robert Grosseteste and the Nicomachean Ethics," *Proceedings of the British Academy* 16 (1930), 85–104; J. Dunbabin, "Robert Grosseteste as Translator, Transmitter and Commentator: The 'Nicomachean Ethics,'" *Traditio* 28 (1972), 460–72; H. P. F. Mercken, ed., *The Greek Commentaries on the Nicomachean Ethics of Aristotle in the Latin Translation of R. Grosseteste. I. Eustratius on Book I and the Anonymous Scholia on Books II, III, IV, Corpus Latinum Commentariorum in Aristotelem Graecorum*, VI (Leiden 1973).

40. Callus, in *Robert Grosseteste*, p. 64; L. Tropia, "La versione latina medievale del ΠΕΡΙ ΠΑΘΩΝ dello Pseudoandronico," *Aevum* 26 (1952), 97–112 (with an edition of *De passionibus*, pp. 106–12). A new edition by A. Glibert-Thirry, *Pseudo-Andronicus de Rhodes ΠΕΡΙ ΠΑΘΩΝ, Corpus Latinum Commentariorum in Aristotelem Graecorum*, suppl. 2 (Leiden 1977).

41. D. J. Allan, "Medieval Versions of Aristotle, De Caelo, and the Commentary of Simplicius," *Mediaeval and Renaissance Studies* 2 (1950), 82–120.

42. Thomson, *The Writings*, pp. 64 f.

43. Smalley, in *Robert Grosseteste*, pp. 96 f.

44. Callus, in *Robert Grosseteste*, pp. 58 f.

45. "Even the Greek μέν and δέ were always rendered by *quidem* and *autem*"; Hill, in *The Orthodox Churches*, p. 219.

46. A. C. Crombie, *Robert Grosseteste and the Origins of Experimental Science*, 2nd ed. (Oxford 1961).

47. Roger Bacon, *Opus tertium* 25, ed. J. S. Brewer, *Fr. Rogeri Bacon opera quaedam hactenus inedita* (London 1859), p. 91.

48. Matthew Paris, *Chronica maiora* ad a. 1252, ed. H. R. Luard (London 1880), V, 284 f.

49. "Memoratus insuper magister J(ohannes) quoddam scriptum transtulit de Graeco in Latinum, in quo artificiose et compendiose tota vis grammaticae continetur; quod idem magister Donatum Graecorum appellavit"; Matthew Paris, ed. Luard, V, 286.

50. W. O. Schmitt ("Lateinischer und griechischer 'Donatus,'" *Philologus* 123 [1979], 97–108) has rendered certain the meaning *Donatus* = *ars grammatica*: "'Donatus' is used metonymically; it is an *appellativum* with a discipline-specific signification"; p. 99. He points out that a *Donatus graece* is listed in a book list from Christ Church, Canterbury, from 1170 (p. 101)—a precursor of Basingstoke's work? Nevertheless, no English attempts at a Greek grammar before Roger Bacon have survived.

51. Cf. Bischoff, "Die sogenannten 'griechischen' und 'chaldäischen' Zahlzeichen des abendländischen Mittelalters," *Mittelalterliche Studien*, I, 67 ff. (bibliog.).

52. Matthew Paris, ed. Luard, V, 286 f.

53. Cambridge, Corpus Christi College Cod. 468; cf. M. R. James, *A Descriptive Catalogue of the Manuscripts of the Library of Corpus Christi College* (Cambridge 1912), II, 399 ff., and *The Sources of Archbishop Parker's Collection of MSS*, (Cambridge 1899), p. 10. Cf. also Schneider, *Cantica*, pp. 118 f.

54. London, College of Arms Arundel 9, Greco-Latin lexicon containing sixteen thousand words, with declensional and conjugational data; cf. M. R. James, "A Graeco-Latin Lexicon of the Thirteenth Century," *Mélanges É. Chatelain* (Paris 1910), pp. 396–411, and Thomson, *The Writings*, pp. 251 f.

55. Minio-Paluello, "I due traduttori medievali del *De mundo*," *Opuscula*, pp. 108–13, here p. 111. See here also the introduction to the second edition of *Aristoteles latinus*, XI/ 1–2.

56. A. G. Little, ed., *Roger Bacon: Essays Contributed by Various Writers on the Occasion of the Commemoration of the Seventh Century of His Birth* (Oxford 1914); here see esp. L. Baur, "Der Einfluß des Robert Grosseteste auf die wissenschaftliche Richtung des Roger Bacon," pp. 33–54; S. A. Hirsch, "Roger Bacon and Philology," pp. 101–51. More recent work on the subject is treated in F. Alessio, "Un secolo di studi su Ruggero Bacone (1848– 1957)," *Rivista Critica di Storia della Filosofia* 14 (1959), 81–102.

57. ". . . non sunt quatuor Latini, qui sciant grammaticam Hebraeorum et Graecorum et Arabum: bene enim cognosco eos, quia et citra mare et ultra diligenter feci inquiri, et multum in his laboravi. Multi vero inveniuntur qui sciunt loqui Graecum et Arabicum et Hebraeum inter Latinos, sed paucissimi sunt, qui sciunt rationem grammaticae ipsius, nec sciunt docere eam: tentavi enim permultos. Sicut enim laici loquuntur linguas quas addiscunt et nesciunt rationem grammaticae, sic est de istis. Vidimus enim multos laicos, qui optime loquebantur Latinum, et tamen nihil sciverunt de regulis grammaticae; et sic est modo de omnibus Hebraeis fere, et similiter de Graecis veris, non solum de Latinis qui sciunt Graecum et Hebraeum"; *Opus tertium* 10, ed. J. S. Brewer, *Fr. Rogeri Bacon opera*, pp. 33 f.

58. "Vulgus Latinorum cum capitibus suis multipliciter oberrat; primo quia aestimat esse Latina vel Graeca vel Hebraea, et e converso, quae non sunt; secundo quia derivationes falsas et interpretationes facit et etymologias in his; tertio, quia falsa pronuntiat et scribit, et praecipue illi qui primi sunt in expositionibus vocabulorum linguae Latinae, ut sunt Papias et Hugutio et Brito, mendaces, quorum mendaciis vulgus opprimitur Latinorum" ("The Latin people and their leaders blunder about in various ways; first of all, because they think that certain words are Latin or Greek or Hebrew, and vice versa, which are not; secondly, because they give false derivations, interpretations, and etymologies of them; thirdly, because they pronounce and write incorrectly, especially those who are the most distinguished in the exposition of Latin terms, just as Papias and Hugutio and Brito are liars, whose lies stifle the Latin people"); *Compendium studii philosophiae* 7, ed. Brewer, *Fr. Rogeri Bacon opera*, pp. 446 f. In the *Compendium*, Bacon presents numerous examples in support of his drastic judgment. John Garland (d. 1272) provided the key word for this critique when he called the *Grecismus* of Eberhard of Béthune "mendax," in *Morale scolarium* 359, ed. L. J. Paetow (Berkeley 1927), pp. 103 and 223.

59. *Grammatica*, ed. Nolan (Cambridge 1902), p. 37.

60. Eberhard of Béthune, *Grecismus* VIII 40–41 and 44–46, ed. I. Wrobel (Breslau 1887), p. 29.

61. *Brito metricus* 686–89, ed. L. W. Daly (Philadelphia 1968), p. 34.

62. *Cornutus*, the first and second "distichs" here from H. Liebl, *Die Disticha Cornuti*, Schulprogramm (Straubing 1888), p. 16. In his new edition, E. Habel omits the glosses, which are, however, an essential part of this kind of work and as a rule are traceable to the author of such a "versificierten Fremdwörterbuchs für Vorgeschrittene" ("versified dictionary of foreign borrowings, for advanced students," Liebl); see Habel, ed., *Der deutsche Cornutus. I. Teil: Der Cornutus des Johannes de Garlandia* (Berlin 1908).

63. Bischoff (*Mittelalterliche Studien*, II, 274 f.) supports the view that the work was written by the Franciscan theologian.

64. M. R. James ("Greek Manuscripts in England before the Renaissance," *The Library* IV/7 [1927], 345) and W. O. Schmitt ("Lateinischer und griechischer 'Donatus,'" 106) both assume that Bacon made use of earlier English work in his Greek grammar.

65. Cf. Heiberg, in *BZ* 9 (1900), 479–91, the edition by Nolan (Cambridge 1902), and also Heiberg's review, in *BZ* 12 (1903), 343–47.

66. Edited by S. A. Hirsch and also by Nolan, in his edition of Bacon's Greek grammar.

67. M. Cantor, *Vorlesungen über Geschichte der Mathematik* (Leipzig 1982), II, 3–48; A. P. Juschkewitsch, *Geschichte der Mathematik im Mittelalter* (Leipzig 1964), pp. 371–87.

68. Sarton, *Introduction*, III/1, 439–46.

69. L. Oliger, *Expositio Regulae Fratrum Minorum Auctore Angelo Clareno* (Quaracchi 1912), pp. xxxiv–lv; J. Gribomont, *Histoire du texte des Ascétiques de S. Basile* (Louvain 1953), pp. 91–94; L. von Auw, "Angelo Clareno et les spirituels franciscains" (diss., Lausanne 1948), pp. 31–35: "Les traductions"; von Auw, *Angeli Clareni opera*, vol. I: *Epistolae*

(Rome 1980). On the whole, Angelo's translations have not yet been precisely identified. The revisor of the Byzantine Emperors' Oracle, who turned it into the famous papal prophecies (*Papalisto*), has been sought among the Franciscan Spirituals; H. Grundmann, "Die Papstprophetien des Mittelalters," *Ausgewählte Aufsätze* (Stuttgart 1977), II, 1–57.

70. A. Sottili has published a methodologically exemplary and fruitful comparison of the translations of Clareno and Traversari: "Humanistische Neuverwendung mittelalterlicher Übersetzungen. Zum mittelalterlichen und humanistischen Fortleben des Johannes Climacus," in *Die Rezeption der Antike*, ed. A. Buck (Hamburg 1981), pp. 165–85.

71. F. Fuchs, *Die Höheren Schulen von Konstantinopel im Mittelalter* (Leipzig/Berlin 1926), pp. 53 f.

72. Altaner identifies several of them in *Zeitschrift für Missionswissenschaft* 18 (1928), 201 ff.

73. On this "Oriental Institute" in Paris, see Altaner, in *Zeitschrift für Missionswissenschaft* 18 (1928), 195 f. Historically, the project also came to nothing: "We know nothing of the personalities or the possible results of the Oriental missionaries who were trained at the papal institute" (p. 195).

74. Ed. by P. Glorieux, S. Thomas *d'Aquin, Contra errores Graecorum* (Tournai/Paris/Rome/New York 1957).

75. Summary based on Altaner, in *Zeitschrift für Missionswissenschaft* 21 (1931), 115 f.

76. C. J. v. Hefele, *Conciliengeschichte*, 2nd ed. (Frieburg 1890), VI, 137 ff.; W. Norden, *Das Papsttum und Byzanz* (Berlin 1903), 533 ff.; Roberg, *Die Union . . . auf dem II. Konzil von Lyon*, pp. 135 ff. D. J. Geanakoplos, "Bonaventura, the Two Mendicant Orders and the Greeks at the Council of Lyons," in *The Orthodox Churches and the West*, pp. 183–211.

77. "Et quando ventum est ad articulum illud: Qui a Patre Filioque procedit, sollempniter et devote ter cantaverunt"; *Ordinato concilii generalis Lugdunensis*, ed. A. Franchi, *Il Concilio II di Lione (1274) secondo la Ordinatio Concilii Generalis Lugdunensis* (Rome 1965), pp. 82 f.

78. Albertus Magnus' *Zoology* depends in large part on Michael Scot's translation, *De animalibus*; cf. H. Stadler, Albertus Magnus, De animalibus, vols. I–II (Münster 1916–21); but Michael Scot is criticized by Albert thus: "in rei veritate nescivit naturas bene, nec bene intellexit libros Aristotelis" ("in actuality he did not know nature well, nor did he well understand the books of Aristotle"; *De meteoris* III 4, c. 26, ed. A. Borgnet, *B. Alberti Magni . . . Opera omnia* [Paris 1890], IV, 697).

79. This dictum is found, written in the hand of Nicholas of Cusa, in the margin of a manuscript of Albertus Magnus' commentary on Dionysius the Areopagite: *De divinis nominibus*, Cusa, Hospitalbibliothek Cod. 96. Grabmann, "Der Einfluß Alberts des Großen auf das mittelalterliche Geistesleben," *Mittelalterliches Geistesleben*, II, 324–412, here p. 390.

80. Grabmann, *Guglielmo di Moerbeke* (1946). On the method of translation, see Minio-Paluello, "Guglielmo di Moerbeke traduttore della Poetica di Aristotele," *Opuscula*, pp. 40 ff. G. Verbeke, "Guillaume de Moerbeke, traducteur de Jean Philopon," *Revue Philosophique de Louvain* 49 (1951), 222–35; "Guillaume de Moerbeke, traducteur de Proclus," *Revue Philosophique de Louvain* 51 (1953), 349–73; and "Guillaume de Moerbeke et sa méthode de traduction," in *Medioevo e Rinascimento*, Festschrift Bruno Nardi (Florence 1955), pp. 779–800. R. Thillet, *Alexandre d'Aphrodise: De fato ad imperatores, Version de Guillaume de Moerbeke* (Paris 1963), esp. pp. 29–35 (a list of forty-nine translations of William of Moerbeke). B. Schneider, *Die mittelalterlichen griechisch-lateinischen Übersetzungen der aristotelischen Rhetorik* (Berlin/New York 1971). E. Grant argues against the postulation of a translation of Hero's *Pneumatics* by William of Moerbeke in *Speculum* 46 (1971), 656–69.

81. Ed. by L. Minio-Paluello, *Aristoteles latinus*, 2nd ed. (Brussels/Paris 1968), vol. XXXIII. Hermannus Alemannus undertook an Arabic-Latin translation already in 1250, but found the text so difficult that he preferred to translate Averroes' commentary for the *viri studiosi*; *Aristoteles latinus*, 2nd ed. (1968), XXXIII, 41 ff.

82. New editions of the translations by William of Moerbeke are found in *Corpus Latinum Commentariorum in Aristotelem Graecorum*, I: *Thémistius: Commentaire sur le traité de l'âme d'Aristote*, ed. G. Verbeke (Louvain 1957); II: *Ammonius: Commentaire sur le Peri Hermeneias d'Aristote*, ed. G. Verbeke (Louvain 1961); III: *Jean Philopon: Commentarius in Aristotelis De anima*, ed. G. Verbeke (Louvain 1966); IV: *Alexandre d'Aphrodisias: Com-*

mentaire sur les Météores d'Aristote, ed. J. Smet (Leiden 1968); V/1–2: *Simplicius: Commentaire sur les Catégories d'Aristote*, ed. A. Pattin (Leiden 1971–75).

83. M. Clagett, *Archimedes in the Middle Ages*, vol. II: *The Translations from the Greek by William of Moerbeke* (Philadelphia 1976). The manuscript Rome, Vat. Ottobon. lat. 1850 is "the autograph copy of William of Moerbeke's Archimedean translations"; Clagett, II, 60.

84. Ed. by C. Vansteenkiste, in *Tijdschrift voor Filosofie* 13 (1951), 263–302 and 491–531.

85. Ed. by Boese, *Procli Diadochi Tria Opuscula* (1960).

86. Klibansky and Labowsky, *Plato latinus*, III (London 1953). The works of Proclus are in part preserved only in the Latin translation of William of Moerbeke; cf. H. Boese, "Über die Bedeutung der mittelalterlichen Proclusübersetzungen im Rahmen der Textüberlieferung," *Colloques internationaux du Centre de la Recherche Scientifique. Sciences Humaines. Le Néoplatonisme, Royaumont 1969* (Paris 1971), pp. 395–402.

87. Klibansky, *Ein Proklos-Fund und seine Bedeutung* (1929), and "Plato's Parmenides in the Middle Ages and the Renaissance," *Mediaeval and Renaissance Studies* 1 (1943), 281–330. Cf. also Grabmann, "Die Proklosübersetzungen des Wilhelm von Moerbeke und ihre Verwertung in der lateinischen Literatur des Mittelalters," *Mittelalterliches Geistesleben*, II, 413–23.

88. Altaner, "Die Durchführung des Wiener Konzilsbeschlusses . . . ," *Zeitschrift für Kirchengeschichte* 52 (1933), 226–36.

89. Weiss, "England and the Decree of the Council of Vienne," in *Medieval and Humanist Greek*, pp. 68–79.

90. ". . . dampnosa nimis est hodie studio Latinorum greci sermonis inscitia, sine quo scriptorum veterum dogmata sive christianorum sive gentilium nequeunt comprehendi . . . quibus defectibus proinde Clemens V. occurrit, si tamen prelati que faciliter statuunt, fideliter observarent. Quamobrem grammaticam, tam hebraicam quam grecam, nostris scholaribus providere curavimus . . ." (". . . the ignorance of the Greek language is a great hindrance to the study of the Latins nowadays, since the doctrines of the ancient writings, whether Christian or pagan, cannot be understood without a knowledge of Greek. . . . Clement V is now opposing these defects—if only the prelates would faithfully hold to that which they so carelessly stipulate. For this reason we have taken care to provide our scholars with grammars, both Hebrew and Greek . . ."); Richard of Bury, *Philobiblon* 10, ed. A. Altamura (Naples 1954), pp. 110 f.

91. Scaduto, *Il monachesimo basiliano nella Sicilia medievale*, pp. 291 ff. (Dominicans and Franciscans as visitors in Basilian monasteries) and pp. 324 f. (prohibition of leavened bread and beards).

92. R. Devreesse, *Le fonds grec de la Bibliothèque Vaticane des origines à Paul V* (Rome 1965), pp. 2–4 (bibliog.). See also above, Chapter II.

93. C. G. Coulter, "The Library of the Angevin Kings," *Transactions and Proceedings of the American Philological Association* 75 (1944), 141–55.

94. Weiss, "The Greek Culture of South Italy in the Later Middle Ages," in *Medieval and Humanist Greek*, pp. 13–43, and "The Translators from the Greek of the Angevin Court of Naples," ibid., pp. 108–33.

95. "Re da sermone," *Paradiso* VIII 147. W. Goetz, *König Robert von Neapel (1309–1343). Seine Persönlichkeit und sein Verhältnis zum Humanismus* (Tübingen 1910).

96. Weiss, *Medieval and Humanist Greek*, p. 121.

97. Weiss, ibid., pp. 125 ff. F. Lo Parco, "Niccolò da Reggio antesignano del risorgimento ellenico nel secolo XIV," *Atti della R. Accademia di archeologia, lettere e belle arti di Napoli*, n.s., II/2 (1913), 241–317.

98. R. Sabbadini, "Le opere di Galeno tradotte da Nicola de Deoprepio di Reggio," *Studi storici e giuridici dedicati ed offerti a Federico Ciccaglione* (Catania 1910), II, 15–24; L. Thorndike, "Translations of Works of Galen from the Greek by Niccolò da Reggio (c. 1308–1345)," *Byzantina Metabyzantina* 1 (1946), 213–45. The dedication of the translation of the *Liber Galieni de passionibus uniuscuiusque particule et cura ipsarum* in Paris, BN nouv. acq. lat 1365 indicates that the Greek source was given to King Robert as a present from Emperor Andronicus (II, 1282–1328, or III, 1332–41?); see L. Delisle, in *Mélanges de Paléographie et de Bibliographie* (Paris 1880), pp. 432 f. According to Delisle, the Paris codex is the original presentation copy of the translator, Nicholas Theoprepos.

99. Lo Parco, in *Atti della R. Accademia . . . di Napoli*, n.s., II/2, 284 f.

100. On this matter, see Lo Parco, *Niccolò da Reggio grecista italiota del sec. XIV* (Naples 1909).

101. For example, Burgundio's translation of Galen's commentary on the "Aphorisms" of Hippocrates; cf. Thorndike, in *Byzantina Metabyzantina* 1, 225.

102. F. Gregorovius, *Geschichte der Stadt Athen im Mittelalter* (Stuttgart 1889), II, 192; A. Rubió y Lluch, "Significació de l'elogi de l'Acròpolis d'Atenes pel Rei Pere'l Ceremoniós," *Homenaje ofrecido a Menéndez Pidal* (Madrid 1925), III, 37–56; Setton, *Catalan Domination of Athens*, pp. 187 f. Of course King Peter did not call the mountain "Acropolis," but rather used its medieval name, *Castell de Cetines* (= εἰς τας Ἀθήνας).

103. Setton, *Catalan Domination*, pp. 119 f., and "The Byzantine Background to the Italian Renaissance," *Proceedings of the American Philosophical Society* 100 (1956), 65 f.; A. Luttrell, "Greek Histories Translated and Compiled for Juan Fernández de Heredia, Master of Rhodes, 1377–1396," *Speculum* 35 (1960), 401–7.

104. G. Di Stefano, *La découverte de Plutarque en occident. Aspects de la vie intellectuelle en Avignon au XIVᵉ siècle* (Turin 1968); Weiss, "Lo studio di Plutarco nel Trecento," in *Medieval and Humanist Greek*, pp. 204–26.

105. On Barlaam, see Beck, *Kirche und theologische Literatur*, pp. 717–19; Weiss, *Medieval and Humanist Greek*, p. 197 (bibliog.).

106. K. H. Schäfer, *Die Ausgaben der apostolischen Kammer unter Benedikt XII.* (Paderborn 1914), p. 91.

107. Petrarch reports on this in his letter of thanks to Nicholas Sigeros, *Familiarium rerum*, lib. XVIII 2, 9, ed. V. Rossi, *Francesco Petrarca: Le Familiari* (Florence 1937), III, 277.

108. G. Mercati, *Se la versione dall'ebraico del codice veneto greco VII sia di Simone Atumano arcivescovo di Tebe* (Rome 1916); Fedalto, *Simone Atumano* (Brescia 1968).

109. On Paul of Smyrna, see Halecki, *Un Empereur de Byzance à Rome* (1930), esp. pp. 36–39, and Setton, in *Proceedings of the American Philosophical Society* 100, 45 f.

110. Di Stefano, *La découverte de Plutarque*, pp. 25 ff.: "Simon Atumano, premier traducteur de Plutarque," with an edition of the translation *De furoris ireque abstinentia*, pp. 91–129, according to the codex unicus, Seville, Biblioteca Colombina 85-5-34.

111. See above, p. 232.

112. Aulus Gellius, *Noctes Atticae* I 26, 7 is the source of Petrarch's *Familiarum rerum* XII 14, 3, ed. V. Rossi, III, 39.

113. The documents are collected in Mercati, *Se la versione dall'ebraico*, pp. 15 ff. According to Mercati, Cod. Mar. gr. VII is a remnant of Atumanus' work on the Bible. Radulf de Rivo (d. 1403) took a magnificently illuminated twelfth-century Greek New Testament with him from Grottaferrata to his Flemish homeland, where Erasmus used it a century later in an edition of the Greek New Testament; now Vienna, Suppl. gr. 52; cf. the exhibition catalogue *Wissenschaft im Mittelalter*, p. 144 (bibliog.; but see also C. Mohlberg, *Radulf de Rivo* [Louvain/Paris/Brussels 1911], pp. 25 ff.).

114. The Platonic codex Vienna, Österreichische Nationalbibliothek phil. gr. 21, the Homeric codex Vienna, phil. gr. 56 (from Terra d'Otranto, ca. 1300; cf. Cavallo, in *I bizantini in Italia*, p. 604, pl 537), and Laur. XXXII 2 (Florence), famous as a Euripidean codex (cf. Pertusi, "La scoperta di Euripide," pp. 104 ff.), come from Simon Atumano' collection.

115. From a note in Codex Vienna, Suppl. gr. 52; Mohlberg, *Radulf de Rivo*, p. 20.

116. *Epist.* VIII 23, ed. F. Novati, *Epistolario di Coluccio Salutati* (Rome 1893), II, 483.

117. P. de Nolhac, *Pétrarque et l'humanisme* (Paris 1907), II, 126–88; "Pétrarque et les auteurs grecs." R. Weiss, "Petrarca e il mondo greco," in *Medieval and Humanist Greek*, pp. 166–92.

118. Milan, Biblioteca Ambrosiana S. P. 10, 27 (olim A 49 inf.), facs. ed. G. Galbiati (Milan 1930).

119. Cf. de Nolhac, *Pétrarque et l'humanisme*, I, 159. The reproduction from the "Virgilius Ambrosianus" in Steffens, *Lateinische Paläographie*, 2nd ed. (1929), pl. 101, shows such notes by Petrarch.

120. Weiss, *Medieval and Humanist Greek*, p. 178.

121. Weiss, "Per la storia degli studi greci del Petrarca: Il 'Triglossos,'" in *Medieval and Humanist Greek*, pp. 136–47.

122. Weiss, *Medieval and Humanist Greek*, p. 176.

123. R. Hirzel, *Plutarch* (Leipzig 1912), p. 103.

124. Weiss, *Medieval and Humanist Greek*, p. 176.

125. Loenertz, "Ambassadeurs grecs auprès du pape Clément VI 1348," in *Byzantina et Franco-Graeca*, pp. 285 ff. The Homer which Sigerus sent to Petrarch is preserved in Ambros. gr. I.98 inf.; cf. A. Pertusi, "L'Omero inviato al Petrarca da Nicola Sigero," in *Mélanges Tisserant* (Rome 1964), III, 113–39.

126. ". . . Homerus tuus apud me mutus, imo vero ego apud illum surdus sum. Gaudeo tamen vel aspectu solo et sepe illum amplexus ac suspirans dico: O magne vir, quam cupide te audirem! sed aurium mearum alteram mors obstruxit, alteram longiquitas invisa terrarum"; *Familiarium rerum* XVIII, 2, ed. V. Rossi, *Francesco Petrarca: Le Familiari*, III, 277. The two "Greek ears" which Petrarch misses are (the deceased) Barlaam and (the distant) Nicholas Sigerus.

127. Petrarch requested Hesiod and Euripides from Nicholas Sigerus in the letter of thanks cited in the previous note; he then attempted to acquire Euripides and Sophocles from Leontius Pilatus (*Rerum senilium*, lib. VI 1).

128. A. Pertusi, *Leonzio Pilato fra Petrarca e Boccaccio* (Venice/Rome 1964); Pertusi, "Leonzio Pilato e la tradizione di cultura italo-greca," *Byzantino-Sicula* 2 (1966), 66–84.

129. "Nonne ego fui, qui Leontium Pylatum a Venetiis occiduam Babilonem querentem a longa peregrinatione meis flexi consiliis, et in patria tenui, qui illum in propriam domum suscepi et diu hospitem habui, et maximo labore meo curavi, ut inter doctores Florentini studii susciperetur, ei ex publico mercede apposita? Fui equidem! Ipse insuper fui, qui primus meis sumptibus Homeri libros et alios quosdam Grecos in Etruriam revocavi, ex qua multis ante seculis abierant non redituri? Nec in Etruriam tantum, sed in patriam deduxi. Ipse ego fui, qui primus ex Latinis a Leontio in privato Yliadem audivi. Ipse insuper fui, qui, ut legerentur publici Homeri libri, operatus sum" ("Was I not the one who turned Leontius Pilatus, who was seeking the Western Babylon from Venice, from his wanderings, and held him in our city? I, who took him into my own home and long had him as a guest, and took great pains that he be accepted among the learned of Florentine intellectual life, that he receive an appointment funded by public monies? Indeed it was I! Moreover was it not I who, at my own expense, first restored the works of Homer and certain other Greeks to Etruria, from which they departed centuries ago unwilling to return? I introduced them not only to Etruria, but even to our native city. It was I who was first among the Latins to hear the *Iliad* from Leontius in private. And it was I who labored so that the public might read Homer's works"); Boccacio, *Genealogiae deorum gentilium* XV 7, ed. V. Romano (Bari 1951), p. 766.

130. Cf. P. O. Kristeller, *Renaissance Concepts of Man and Other Essays* (New York 1972), p. 75.

131. In a methodologically interesting study, G. Martellotti has treated Leontius' translation of two verses from the *Anthologia Palatina*: "Osservazioni sul carattere orale del primo insegnamento del greco nell'Italia umanistica," *Annali dell'Istituto Universitario Orientale*, Sezione Linguistica (Naples 1959), I, 59–64. Leontius used this epigram (XVI 297) on the seven Homeric sites in class, and both Domenico Silvestri and Boccaccio noted it. On the basis of their transcriptions, some conclusions regarding Leontius' pronunciation of Greek may be drawn: it had, not unexpectedly, the character of vulgar Greek ('Επτά = *Ephta*, etc.). According to G. Billanovich, the Pseudo-Aristotelian work *De mirabilibus auscultationibus* (a second translation, based on Bartholomaeus of Messina) may also be attributed to Leontius ("Il Petrarca e i retori latini minori," *Italia Medioevale e Umanistica* 5 [1962], 103–64, here pp. 118 ff.).

132. The account is found in Petrarch's *Rerum senilium* lib. VI 1. On the date, see Pertusi, *Leonzio Pilato*, p. 35.

133. Pertusi, *Leonzio Pilato*, p. 205.

134. Pertusi, *Leonzio Pilato*, p. 114.

135. "Quodsi cui non uidetur linguae gratiam interpretatione mutari, Homerum ad uerbum exprimat in Latinum . . . uidebit ordinem ridiculum et poetam eloquentissimum uix loquentem" ("And whoever does not think that a translator changes the beauties of a language, let him translate Homer literally into Latin . . . he will find the word order absurd and the most eloquent of poets scarcely articulate"); Jerome, preface to the translation of Eusebius' *Chronicle*, ed. R. Helm, *GCS* 47 (Berlin 1956), p. 4. Jerome also includes the dictum in *epist.* 57 ("Ad Pammachium de optimo genere interpretandi"). Petrarch naturally knew the passage, and cited it in a letter to Boccaccio, *Variae* 25.

136. It is, however, a matter of debate whether Leontius intended to isolate the Latin interlinear gloss from the Greek original, or whether he did not rather have bilingual texts in mind, such as bilingual editions of classical literature, for the purpose of facilitating the study of the original. The autographs of Leontius thus far discovered indicate that the Calabrian translator did not aspire to the composition of Latin texts that were themselves worth reading. Using Leontius' Latin translation, Johannes Sophianos wrote a bilingual of the *Odyssey*, with Latin and Greek columns, in Stuttgart, Württ. Landesbibliothek cod. poet. et philol. 2°5. On this manuscript, see most recently P. O. Kristeller, in *Nicolò Cusano agli Inizi del Mondo Moderno* (Florence 1970), pp. 178 and 193.

137. Florence, Laur. Plut. LII 9, identified as Boccaccio's own working copy by O. Hecker, *Boccaccio-Funde* (Braunschweig 1902).

138. Hecker, *Boccaccio-Funde*, pp. 137–57: "Das Griechische in dem Original"; see also pl. 22.

139. "It is worthy of note that majuscules are always used for γ, η, μ, τ, and φ"; Hecker, p. 138.

140. Later manuscripts placed the translation gloss in the text itself, as does also the most recent edition, by V. Romano.

141. *De remediis et medicina ire*, ed. Di Stefano, *La découverte de Plutarque*, pp. 132–71. This treatise of Plutarch was then translated from the Latin text into French by Nicolas de Gonesse in 1400–1401. Although the French translator says that he used Simon Atumanus' Latin text, it was, according to the determinations by Di Stefano, Salutati's text that was its basis.

142. Weiss, "Jacopo Angeli da Scarperia (ca. 1360–1410/11)," *Medieval and Humanist Greek*, pp. 255–77.

143. Weiss, "Lo studio di Plutarco nel Trecento," *Medieval and Humanist Greek*, pp. 204–26, here p. 225.

144. V. R. Giustiniani, "Sulle traduzioni delle 'Vite' du Plutarco nel Quattrocento," *Rinascimento* II/1 (1961), 3–62.

145. W. Berschin, "Sueton und Plutarch im 14. Jahrhundert," in *Biographie und Autobiographie in der Renaissance*, ed. A. Buck (Wiesbaden 1983), pp. 35–43.

146. V. R. Giustiniani, "Plutarch und die humanistische Ethik," in *Ethik im Humanismus*, ed. W. Ruegg and D. Wuttke (Boppard 1979), pp. 45–62.

147. The term "heroic bible" ("Heroenbibel") comes from R. W. Emerson; cf. R. Hirzel, *Plutarch*, p. 131.

148. R. Hirzel, *Plutarch*, p. 174.

149. Rome Archivio Segreto Vaticano A. A. Arm. I–XVIII no. 396. See Halecki, *Un Empereur de Byzance à Rome*, p. 31; "Among the chrysobulls of the Byzantine emperors preserved in the archives of the Holy See, none is more curious. . . . This striking parchment . . . divided into two parallel columns, one of which contains the Greek text and the other the Latin translation, has aroused the interest of historians for centuries."

150. M. Jugie, "Le voyage de l'Empereur Manuel Paléologue en Occident (1399–1403)," *Échos d'Orient* 15 (1912), 322–32. G. Schlumberger's essay ("Un Empereur de Byzance à Paris et à Londres," *Byzance et croisades* [Paris 1927], pp. 87–147) seems almost to be a doublet of Jugie's.

151. Paris, Louvre Ivoires A 53, described briefly in the exhibition catalogue *Byzance et la France médiévale*, pp. 32 f., and in detail (with photographs) by G. Théry, "Recherches pour une édition grecque historique du Pseudo-Denys," *The New Scholasticism* 3 (1929), 353–442, here pp. 425 ff.

152. The basic study is G. Cammelli, *I dotti bizantini e le origini dell'Umanesimo*, vol. I: *Manuele Crisolora* (Florence 1941).

153. H. Baron, *Leonardo Bruni Aretino: Humanistisch-philosophische Schriften. Mit einer Chronologie seiner Werke und Briefe* (Leipzig/Berlin 1928); rev. by L. Bertalot, *Archivum Romanicum* 15 (1931), 284–323, and *Historische Vierteljahrschrift* 29 (1934), 385–400; both reviews are reprinted in abridged form in L. Bertalot, *Studien zum italienischen und deutschen Humanismus*, ed. P. O. Kristeller (Rome 1975), II, 375–420 and 425–38. Baron, *Humanistic Political Literature in Florence and Venice* (Cambridge, Mass., 1955), pp. 114 ff.: "Bruni's Development as a Translator from the Greek"; Baron, *From Petrarch to Leonardo Bruni* (Chicago/London 1968).

154. Cammelli, *I dotti bizantini*, I, 122 ff. The bilingual Greco-Latin gravestone of Uberto Decembrio (d. 1427) is in the vestibule of St. Ambrogio in Milan.

155. His grave inscription in a chapel of the Dominican monastery in Constance (today the Inselhotel) boasts of him that he died "EA EXISTIMATIONE UT AB OMNIBUS SUMMO SACERDOTIO DIGNUS HABERETUR" (Cammelli, *Manuele Crisolora*, pp. 168 f.); cf. I. Thomson, "Manuel Chrysoloras and the Early Italian Renaissance," *Greek, Roman and Byzantine Studies* 7 (1966), 63–82.

156. R. Sabbadini, *Le scoperte dei codici latini e greci ne' secoli XIV e XV* (Florence 1905), I. 43 ff.

157. According to P. Kibre, "The Intellectual Interests Reflected in Libraries of the Fourteenth and Fifteenth Centuries," *Journal of the History of Ideas* 7 (1946), 257–97; repr. in Kibre, *Studies in Medieval Science* (London 1984).

158. Gill, *The Council of Florence* (bibliog.).

159. C. L. Stinger, *Humanism and the Church Fathers: Ambrogio Traversari (1386–1439) and Christian Antiquity in the Italian Renaissance* (Albany 1977). On Traversari's free, humanistic method of translation, see A. Sottili, "Humanistische Neuverwendung mittelalterlicher Übersetzungen," pp. 165–85.

160. P. O. Kristeller, "Marsilio Ficino as a Beginning Student of Plato," *Scriptorium* 20 (1966), 41–54; Kristeller, "Byzantine and Western Platonism in the Fifteenth Century," *Renaissance Concepts of Man*, pp. 86 ff.; Kristeller, *Die Philosophie des Marsilio Ficino* (Frankfurt 1972).

161. Cammelli, *I dotti bizantini*, vol. II: *Giovanni Argiropulo*.

162. Mohler, *Bessarion*, I, 408 ff.: "Bessarions Bibliothek." See also *Miscellanea marciana di studi bessarionei (a coronamento del V Centenario della donazione nicena)* (Padua 1976). Labowsky, *Bessarion's Library and the Biblioteca Marciana*.

163. Geanakoplos, *Greek Scholars in Venice* and "The Greco-Byzantine Colony in Venice and Its Significance in the Renaissance," *Byzantine East and Latin West*, pp. 112–37.

164. Cammelli, *Manuele Crisolora*, p. 51.

165. Sottili, "Humanistische Neuverwendung," pp. 168 f.

166. Sabbadini, *Il metodo degli umanisti*, pp. 25 ff.

167. Garin, "Le traduzioni umanistiche di Aristotele nel secolo XV," *Atti dell'Accademia Fiorentina di scienze morali 'La Colombaria'* 16 (1951), 57 f.

168. T. de Marinis, *La Biblioteca Napoletana dei Re d'Aragona* (Milan 1947), II, 15. On Bruni as translator, see J. Soudek, "Leonardo Bruni and His Public," *Studies in Medieval and Renaissance History* 5 (1968), 49 ff., and Goldbrunner, in *Archiv für Kulturgeschichte* 50 (1968), 200–239.

169. R. Sabbadini, "'Maccheroni'" 'Traddurre,'" *Rendiconti del R. Istituto Lombardo di Scienze e Lettere* II/49 (1916), 219–24.

170. L. Wolf, "Fr. *traduire*, lat. *traducere* und die kulturelle Hegemonie Italiens zur Zeit der Renaissance," *Zeitschrift für romanische Philologie* 87 (1971), 99–105.

171. Sabbadini, *Il metodo degli umanisti*, p. 26.

172. The supposed discovery turned out to be the generally familiar excerpt from the *De re publica*: the *Somnium Scipionis* with Macrobius' commentary; E. Vansteenberghe, *Le Cardinal Nicolas de Cues* (Paris 1920), pp. 18 f. As is generally known, the great discovery did not come until the nineteenth century, in a palimpsest from Bobbio; cf. G. Mercati, *Ciceronis de re publica libri e codice rescripto Vat. lat. 5757. Prolegomena* (Rome 1934).

173. Nicholas presented the codex to Cardinal Orsini, his superior at that time; now Cod. Vat. lat. 3870. On Nicholas and the Tacitus manuscripts, see L. Pralle, *Die Wiederentdeckung des Tacitus* (Fulda 1952).

174. P. O. Kristeller, "A Latin Translation of Gemistos Plethon's 'De fato' by Johannes Sophianos Dedicated to Nicholas of Cusa," in *Nicolò Cusano agli Inizi del Mondo Moderno*, pp. 175–93, here p. 183. The essay deals with the entire subject of Nicholas' Greek interests.

175. Harleianus 2773 belongs to a well-known group of school manuscripts from Trier, St. Eucharius (St. Matthias); cf. K. Manitius, *Forschungen und Fortschritte* 29 (1955), 319.

176. Gibson, "The Study of the 'Timaeus' in the Eleventh and Twelfth Centuries," *Pensamiento* 25 (1969), 191.

177. Cf. Honecker, *Nikolaus von Cues und die griechische Sprache* (1938), pp. 53 ff. and 62 ff.; Klibansky, *The Continuity of the Platonic Tradition*, pp. 30 f. See also "Kritisches Verzeichnis der Londoner Handschriften aus dem Besitz des Nikolaus von Kues," *Mitteilungen und Forschungsbeiträge der Cusanus-Gesellschaft* 3 (1963); 5 (1965); 8 (1970); 10 (1973); 12 (1977).

178. Giovanni Andrea dei Bussi's oration on Nicholas of Cusa, appended to the edition of Apuleius, Rome: Sweynheym and Pannartz, 1469; here from the reprint by Honecker, *Nikolaus von Cues*, p. 72. Both translations have now been identified by Klibansky's research: the translation of Parmenides is by George of Trebizond (preface in Klibansky, in *Mediaeval and Renaissance Studies* 1 [1943], 291 f.). Nicholas first presented a Greek text of the *Theologia Platonis* to Ambrogio Traversari (Vansteenberghe, *Nicolas de Cues*, p. 30, n. 2); the translation, however, was then executed by Petrus Balbus Pisanus, bishop of Tropea; see Klibansky, *Ein Proklos-Fund*, p. 26, n. 2. Further translations dedicated to Nicholas are Johannes Sophianos' translation of Plethon, edited by Kristeller (cf. above, n. 174), and Athanasius Constantinopolitanus' translation of Plato's *Lysis*; Athanasius was later bishop of Gerace: in Brussels Cod. 9142–45; cf. Vansteenberghe, *Nicolas de Cues*, pp. 29 f.

179. G. v. Bredow, *Platonismus im Mittelalter* (Frieburg 1972), 49.

180. *Apologia doctae ignorantiae*, Basel edition 1565, p. 67; ed. R. Klibansky (Leipzig 1932), p. 12.

181. Strasbourg Cod. 84, with the important interpretation of manuscript evidence by E. Vansteenberghe, "Quelques lectures de jeunesse de Nicolas de Cues d'après un manuscrit inconnu de sa bibliothèque," *AHDL* 3 (1928), 275–84. A new description, with a somewhat different evaluation, is found in R. Haubst, "Die Thomas- und Proklos-Exzerpte des 'Nicolaus Trevirensis' im Codicillus Straßburg 84," *Mitteilungen . . . der Cusanus-Gesellschaft* 1 (1961), 17–51.

182. Honecker (*Nikolaus von Cues*, p. 22) has shown how appropriately Nicholas' knowledge of Greek was periphrastically described by the words of the Humanist Francesco Pizolpasso: "Vir siquidem aliquando introductus linguae graecae, ceterum alias eruditissimus . . ." ("A man who had only an introduction to the Greek language, but who was otherwise most erudite"). In his investigations, Honecker was able to take into account only a very few of the numerous, valuable codices (as has been ascertained in recent years) which were sold out of the Hospitalbibliothek of Cusa in the eighteenth century to Harley in England and are now found in the British Library; cf. "Kritisches Verzeichnis der Londoner Handschriften aus dem Besitz des Nikolaus von Kues," in *Mitteilungen . . . der Cusanus-Gesellschaft* 3 (1963), etc. A. Krchňák prefaces that series of publications with a summary of Nicholas' Greek interests: "Neue Handschriftenfunde in London und Oxford," *Mitteilungen . . . der Cusanus-Gesellschaft* 3 (1963), 101–8, here p. 106. Krchňák takes a Greek codex which Nicholas of Cusa is supposed to have borrowed from John of Ragusa in Constantinople and then— although not his property—annotated as "clear evidence against Martin Honecker that Cusanus knew Greek well and that he had no difficulty in reading Greek manuscripts. This argument is supported by the results of an investigation of the London manuscripts. Nicholas of Cusa wrote glosses into several manuscripts with his own hand . . ." ("gegen Martin Honecker eindeutig erwiesen, daß Cusanus die griechische Sprache gut beherrschte und daß ihm das Lesen griechischer Handschriften keine Schwierigkeiten machte. Diese Feststellung wird durch die Ergebnisse der Untersuchung der Londoner Hss. bestätigt. Nikolaus von Kues versah mehrere Hss. mit eigenhändigen griechischen Glossen . . ."). One of the manuscripts cited in this context is described in more detail in the same volume, but the author, R. Haubst, comes to a more discriminating conclusion: "Diese Indizien ergänzen in beachtenswerte Weise das Bild, das M. Honecker . . . zeichnete; sie zeigen deutlich, daß Nikolaus sich zum mindesten in seinen letzten Lebensjahren auch selbst um den griechischen Originaltext *bemühte*" ("These pieces of evidence complement, in remarkable fashion, the picture sketched out by M. Honecker; they show quite clearly that at least in the last years of his life, Nicholas himself *took some pains* with the Greek original"; p. 31). He could, for example, study the Greek *Hexaemeron* homilies of Basil the Great (Harl. 5576, described by M. Sicherl in *Mitteilungen . . . der Cusanus-Gesellschaft* 10 [1973], esp. pp. 84 f.)—perhaps with the aid of the old, literal translation of Eustathius?

183. Voigt, *Die Wiederbelebung des classischen Altertums*, I, 318. The Humanists were fond of setting off the Graeca in a Latin text with red ink—perhaps in imitation of models such as the Bolognese Lactantius codex of the fifth century ("at the beginning of the MS. the Greek citations are in red"; *CLA* III, 280).

184. R. Proctor, *The Printing of Greek in the Fifteenth Century* (Oxford 1900), pp. 24–48.

Bibliography

Acta Conciliorum Oecumenicorum. Ed. E. Schwartz et al. T. I: *Concilium Universale Ephesinum A. 431*, 5 vols. Berlin/Leipzig 1922–30; t. II: *Concilium Universale Chalcedonense*, 6 vols. 1932–38; t. III: *Collectio Sabbaitica* . . . , 1940; t. IV: *Concilium Universale Constantinopolitanum sub Iustiniano habitum*: vol. 1: *Concilii actiones VIII*, 1971; vol. 2: *Johannis Maxentii libelli, Collectio Codicis Novariensis XXX . . . Procli tomus ad Armenios* . . . , Strasbourg 1914; vol. 3: *Indices Generales*, 1974–84. Series secunda, vol. 1: *Concilium Lateranense a. 649 celebratum.* Ed. R. Riedinger. 1984.

Alexanderson, B. "Die hippokratische Schrift Prognostikon. Überlieferung und Text." Diss. Göteborg 1963.

Allgeier, A. "Zwei griechisch-lateinische Bibelhandschriften aus Cues und ihre Bedeutung für die Frage der abendländischen Septuaginta-Überlieferung," *Oriens Christianus* III/10 (1935), 139–60.

———. "Das Psalmenbuch des Konstanzer Bischofs Salomon III. in Bamberg. Eine Untersuchung zur Frage der mehrspaltigen Psalterien," *Jahresbericht der Görres-Gesellschaft 1938* (Cologne 1939), 102–21.

———. *Die Psalmen der Vulgata. Ihre Eigenart, sprachliche Grundlage und geschichtliche Stellung.* Paderborn 1940.

———. "Exegetische Beiträge zur Geschichte des Griechischen vor dem Humanismus," *Biblica* 24 (1943), 261–88.

Altamura, A. *La letteratura dell'età Angioina.* Naples 1952.

Altaner, B. "Die Heranbildung eines einheimischen Klerus in der Mission des 13. und 14. Jahrhunderts," *Zeitschrift für Missionswissenschaft* 18 (1928), 193–208.

———. "Sprachstudien und Sprachkenntnisse im Dienste der Mission des 13. und 14. Jahrhunderts," *Zeitschrift für Missionswissenschaft* 21 (1931), 113–36.

———. "Die Durchführung des Vienner Konzilsbeschlusses über die Errichtung von Lehrstühlen für orientalische Sprachen," *Zeitschrift für Kirchengeschichte* 52 (1933), 226–36.

———. "Raymundus Lullus und der Sprachenkanon (can. 11) des Konzils von Vienne (1312)," *Historisches Jahrbuch* 53 (1933), 190–219.

———. "Die Kenntnis des Griechischen in den Missionsorden während des 13. und 14. Jahrhunderts," *Zeitschrift für Kirchengeschichte* 53 (1934), 436–93.

———. "Sprachkenntnisse und Dolmetscherwesen im missionarischen und diplomatischen Verkehr zwischen Abendland (Päpstliche Kurie) und Orient im 13. und 14. Jahrhundert," *Zeitschrift für Kirchengeschichte* 55 (1936), 83–126.

———. *Kleine patristische Schriften.* Ed. G. Glockmann. *TU* 83. Berlin 1967: "Augustinus und die griechische Sprache," 129–53 [originally in *Festschrift Dölger*, 1939]; "Altlateinische Übersetzungen von Schriften des Athanasios von Alexandreia," 392–408 [originally in *BZ* 41 (1941)]; "Altlateinische Übersetzungen von Basiliusschriften," 409–15 [originally in *Historisches Jahrbuch* 61 (1941)]; "Altlateinische Übersetzungen von Chrysostomusschriften," 416–36 [originally in *Historisches Jahrbuch* 61 (1941)]; "Eustathius, der lateinische Übersetzer der Hexaëmeron-Homilien Basilius' des Großen," 437–47 [originally in *Zeitschrift für Neutestamentliche Wissenschaft* 39 (1940)].

———. and A. Stuiber. *Patrologie. Leben, Schriften und Lehre der Kirchenväter.* 7th ed. Freiburg/Basel/Vienna 1966.

d'Alverny, M.-T. "Les traductions d'Avicenne (Moyen Âge et Renaissance)," in *Avicenna nella Storia della Cultura Medioevale.* Rome 1957, pp. 71–87.

———. "Les nouveaux apports dans les domaines de la science et de la pensée au temps de Philippe Auguste: La philosophie," in *La France de Philippe Auguste*. Paris 1982, pp. 863–80.

―――. "Translations and Translators," in *Renaissance and Renewal in the Twelfth Century*. Oxford 1982, pp. 421–62.

Amand de Mendieta, E. "Les deux homélies sur la création de l'homme que les manuscrits attribuent à Basile de Césarée ou à Grégoire de Nysse," in *Zetesis*. Festschrift E. de Strycker. Antwerp/Utrecht 1973, pp. 695–716.

Analecta Hymnica medii aevi. Ed. G. M. Dreves, C. Blume, H. M. Bannister, vols. 1–55, Leipzig 1886–1922; Index, vols. 1–2, ed. M. Lütolf, Bern/Munich 1978. Rev. [of the Index] by W. Lipphardt, *Jahrbuch für Liturgie und Hymnologie* 24 (1980), 129–32.

Anastos, M. V. "Some Aspects of Byzantine Influence on Latin Thought," in *Twelfth-Century Europe and the Foundations of Modern Society*, 2nd ed. Ed. M. Clagett, G. Post, and R. Reynolds. Madison 1966, pp. 131–88.

Aristoteles latinus. *Codices* descripserunt G. Lacombe et al. *Pars prior*, 1937; *Pars posterior et Supplementa*, 1955; *Supplementa altera*, 1961.—*Opera*. Ed. L. Minio-Paluello et al. Vol. I: *Categoriae vel Praedicamenta*, 1961–66; vol. II: *De Interpretatione vel Periermenias*, 1965; vol. III: *Analytica Priora*, 1962; vol. IV: *Analytica Posteriora*, 2nd ed., 1968; vol. V: *Topica*, 1969; vol. VI: *De Sophisticis Elenchis*, 1975; vol. VII: *Physica*, 1957; vol. XI: *De Mundo*, 2nd ed., 1965; vol. XVII: *De Generatione Animalium*, 1966; vol. XXV: *Metyaphysica*, 1970–76; vol. XXVI: *Ethica Nicomachea*, 1972–74; vol. XXIX: *Politica*, 1961; vol XXXI: *Rhetorica*, 1978; vol. XXXIII: *De Arte Poetica*, 2nd ed., 1968.

Arnaldi, G. "Giovanni Immonide e la cultura a Roma al tempo di Giovanni VIII," *Bullettino dell'Istituto storico italiano per il medio evo* 68 (1956), 33–83.

Atkinson, C. M. "'O amnos tu theu': The Greek Agnus dei in the Roman Liturgy from the Eighth to the Eleventh Century," *Kirchenmusikalisches Jahrbuch* 65 (1981), 7–30.

―――. "Zur Entstehung und Überlieferung der 'Missa Graeca,'" *Archiv für Musikwissenschaft* 39 (1982), 113–45. Rev. by M. Huglo, *Scriptorium* 37 (1983), 4*f.

Auw, L. von. "Angelo Clareno et les spirituels franciscains." Diss. Lausanne 1948.

Baader, G. See *La Scuola nell'Occidente*.

Baebler, J. J. *Beiträge zu einer Geschichte der lateinischen Grammatik im Mittelalter*. Halle 1885.

Badawi, A. *La transmission de la philosophie grecque au monde arabe*. Paris 1968.

Baehr, R. "Rolle und Bild der Übersetzung im Spiegel literarischer Texte des 12. und 13. Jahrhunderts in Frankreich," *Europäische Mehrsprachigkeit*. Festschrift Mario Wandruszka. Tübingen 1981, pp. 329–48.

Baeumker, C. *Der Platonismus im Mittelalter*, *Festrede der K. Akademie der Wissenschaften*. Munich 1916.

Baker, D. See *Orthodox Churches* . . .

Balard, M. *La Romanie Génoise*. Vols. I–II. Rome 1978.

Ball, H. *Byzantinisches Christentum*. *Drei Heiligenleben* [: Joannes Climax, Dionysius Areopagita, Symeon the Stylite.] Munich/Leipzig 1923 [repr. with foreword by W. Gurian, Munich 1931]; 2nd ed., Einsiedeln/Zurich/Cologne 1958.

Barbour, "A Manuscript of Ps.-Dionysius Areopagita Copied for Robert Grosseteste," *The Bodleian Library Record* 6 (1957/61), 401–16.

Bardy, G. *La question des langues dans l'église ancienne*. Vol. I. Paris 1948.

Barnes, J. See *Boethius: His Life* . . .

Barré, H. *Prières anciennes de l'occident à la Mère du Sauveur. Des origines à saint Anselme*. Paris 1963.

Bartelink, G. J. M. *Hieronymus: Liber de optimo genere interpretandi (Epistula 57)*. *Ein Kommentar*. Leiden 1980.

Barwick, K. *Remmius Palaemon und die römische Ars Grammatica*. Leipzig 1922.

Bataille, A. "Les glossaires gréco-latins sur papyrus," *Recherches de papyrologie* 4 (1967), 161–69.

Batiffol, P. "Librairies byzantines à Rome," *Mélanges d'Archéologie et d'Histoire* 8 (1888), 297–308.

―――. "Das Archiv des griechischen Colleg's in Rom," *Römische Quartalschrift* 2 (1888), 217–21.

Bibliography 357

—. "Vier Bibliotheken von alten basilianischen Klöstern in Unteritalien," *Römische Quartalschrift* 3 (1889), 31–41.
Batlle, C. M. *Die 'Adhortationes sanctorum patrum' ('Verba seniorum') im lateinischen Mittelalter. Überlieferung, Fortleben und Wirkung.* Münster 1972.
Baumgartner, A. *Die lateinische und griechische Literatur der christlichen Völker.* 3rd and 4th ed. Freiburg 1905.
Baumstark, A. "Die Hodie-Antiphonen des römischen Breviers und der Kreis ihrer griechischen Parallelen," *Die Kirchenmusik* 10 (1909), 153–60.
—. "Byzantinisches in den Weihnachtstexten des römischen Antiphonarius Officii," *Oriens Christianus* III/11 (1936), 163–87.
—. *Liturgie comparée.* 3rd ed. Chevetogne/Paris 1953.
Beccaria, A. *I Codici di Medicina del Periodo Presalernitano.* Rome 1956.
—. "Sulle tracce d'un antico canone latino di Ippocrate e di Galeno I–III," *Italia Medioevale e Umanistica* 2 (1959), 1–56, 4 (1961), 1–75; 14 (1971), 1–23.
Beck, H. G. *Kirche und theologische Literatur im byzantinischen Reich.* Munich 1959.
—. *Ideen und Realitäten in Byzanz. Gesammelte Aufsätze.* London 1972.
Becker, G. *Catalogi Bibliothecarum antiqui.* 2nd ed. Hildesheim 1973.
Berger, S. *Histoire de la Vulgate.* Paris 1893.
Bernstein, E. *Die Literatur des deutschen Frühhumanismus.* Stuttgart 1978. Rev. by W. Maaz, *Mittellateinisches Jahrbuch* 15 (1980), 221 f.
Berschin, W. "Griechisches im lateinischen Mittelalter," *Reallexikon der Byzantinistik.* Vol. I, cols. 227–304. Amsterdam 1969–70.
—. "Drei griechische Majestas-Tituli in der Trier-Echternacher Buchmalerei," *Frühmittelalterliche Studien* 14 (1980), 299–309.
—. "Griechisches bei den Iren," in *Die Iren und Europa im früheren Mittelalter.* Ed. H. Löwe. Stuttgart 1982, I, 501–10.
—. "Sueton und Plutarch im 14. Jahrhundert," in *Biographie und Autobiographie in der Renaissance.* Ed. A. Buck. Wiesbaden 1983, pp. 35–43.
—. "Traduzioni in latino nel secolo XIII." in *Aspetti della letteratura latina nel secolo XIII. Atti del I° Convegno dell'Associazione per il Medioevo e l'Umanesimo latini, Perugia 1983.* Perugia/Florence 1986, pp. 229–242..
Bickel, E. *Lehrbuch der Geschichte der römischen Literatur.* 2nd ed. Heidelberg 1961.
Bieler, L. *Psalterium Graeco-Latinum. Codex Basiliensis A. VII. 3.* Amsterdam 1960.
—. *Irland, Wegbereiter des Mittelalters.* Olten/Lausanne/Freiburg 1961.
—. "Christian Ireland's Graeco-Latin Heritage," *Studia Patristica* 13. TU 116. Berlin 1975, pp. 3–8.
Billanovich, G. "Il Petrarca e i retori latini minori," *Italia Medioevale e Umanistica* 5 (1962), 103–64.
Birkenmajer, A. "Découverte de fragments manuscrits de David de Dinant," *Revue néoscolastique de Philosophie* 35 (1933), 220–29.
—. *Études d'histoire des sciences et de la philosophie du moyen âge.* Breslau/Warsaw/Cracow 1970: "Découverte de fragments manuscrits de David de Dinant," 11–20 [originally in *Revue néoscolastique de Philosophie* 35 (1933)]; "Le rôle joué par les médecins et les naturalistes dans la réception d'Aristote au XIIe et XIIIe siècles," 73–87 [originally in *La Pologne au VIe Congrès International des Sciences Historiques, Oslo 1928,* Warsaw/Lemberg 1930].
Bischoff, B. *Mittelalterliche Studien.* Vol. I. Stuttgart 1966: "Die sogenannten 'griechischen' und 'chaldäischen' Zahlzeichen des abendländischen Mittelalters," 67–73 [originally in *Scritti in onore di Vincenzo Federici,* Florence 1945]; "Zur Rekonstruktion der ältesten Handschrift der Vulgata-Evangelien und der Vorlage ihrer Marginalien," 101–11 [originally in *Biblica* 22 (1941)]; "Die lateinischen Übersetzungen und Bearbeitungen aus den Oracula Sibyllina," 150–71 [originally in *Mélanges Joseph de Ghellinck,* Gembloux 1951]; "Il Monachesimo Irlandese nei suoi rapporti col continente," 195–205 [originally in Settimane di studio 4 (Spoleto 1957)]; "Wendepunkte in der Geschichte der lateinischen Exegese im Frühmittelalter," 205–73 [originally in *Sacris Erudiri* 6 (1954)]. Vol. II (1967): "The Study of Foreign Languages in the Middle Ages," 227–45 [originally in *Speculum* 36 (1961)]; "Das griechische Element in der abendländischen Bildung des Mittelalters," 246–75 [originally in *BZ* 44 (1951)]. Vol. III (1981): "Irische Schreiber im Karolin-

gerreich," 39–54 [originally in *Jean Scot Érigène et l'histoire de la philosophie*]; "Bannita: 1. Syllaba, 2. Littera," 243–47 [originally in *Festschrift Ludwig Bieler*]; "Ein lateinisches Gegenstück zur Inschrift der Santissima Icone des Doms von Spoleto," 271–76 [originally in *Miscellanea Giorgio Cencetti*].

———. *Sammelhandschrift Diez. B. Sant. 66. Grammatici latini et Catalogus librorum*. Graz 1973.

———. *Paläographie des römischen Altertums und des abendländischen Mittelalters*. Berlin 1979.

———. *Anecdota novissima*. Stuttgart 1984: "Eine Osterpredigt Liudprands von Cremona (um 960)," 20–34; "Sibylla Theodola, eine Beschreibung des Paradieses (Achtes Jahrhundert?)," 57–79; "Vulgärgriechisch-lateinisches Glossar (Zehntes bis elftes Jahrhundert)," 248 f.

———. "Italienische Handschriften des neunten bis elften Jahrhunderts in frühmittelalterlichen Bibliotheken außerhalb Italiens," in *Atti del Convegno Internazionale Il libro e il testo*. Ed. C. Questa and R. Raffaelli. Urbino 1984, pp. 171–94.

Bishop, E. *Liturgica Historica: Papers on the Liturgy and Religious Life of the Western Church*. Oxford 1918.

I bizantini in Italia. Ed. G. Pugliese Carratelli. [privately printed] Milan 1982: G. Cavallo, "La cultura italo-greca nella produzione libraria," 497–612; M. Gigante, "La civiltà letteraria," 615–51.

Björnbo, A. A. "Die mittelalterlichen lateinischen Übersetzungen aus dem Griechischen auf dem Gebiete der mathematischen Wissenschaften," *Archiv für die Geschichte der Naturwissenschaften und der Technik* 1 (1909), 385–94.

Blatt, F. *Die lateinischen Bearbeitungen der Acta Andreae et Matthiae apud anthropophagos*. Gießen 1930.

———. "Sprachwandel im Latein des Mittelalters," *Historische Vierteljahrschrift* 28 (1934), 22–52 [also published separately, Darmstadt 1970].

———. "Remarques sur l'histoire des traductions latines," *Classica et Mediaevalia* 1 (1938), 217–42.

———. *The Latin Josephus*. Vol. I. Copenhagen 1958.

Bloch, H. "Monte Cassino, Byzantium and the West in the Earlier Middle Ages," *Dumbarton Oaks Papers* 3 (1946), 163–224.

———. See *La Scuola nell'Occidente*.

Bodnar, E. W. *Cyriacus of Ancona and Athens*. Brussels/Berchem 1960.

Boese, H. *Die mittelalterliche Übersetzung der ΣΤΟΙΧΕΙΩΣΙΣ ΦΥΣΙΚΗ des Proclus. Procli Diadochi Lycii Elementatio Physica*. Berlin 1958.

———, ed. *Procli Diadochi Tria Opuscula (De Providentia, Libertate, Malo) Latine Guilelmo de Moerbeka vertente et Graece*. Berlin 1960.

Boethius and the Liberal Arts. Ed. M. Masi. Bern/Frankfurt/Las Vegas 1981: P. Kibre, "The Boethian 'De Institutione Arithmetica' and the 'Quadrivium' in the Thirteenth Century University Milieu at Paris," 67–80; M. Masi, "The Influence of Boethius' 'De Arithmetica' on Late Medieval Mathematics," 81–95; U. Pizzani, "The Influence of the 'De Institutione Musica' of Boethius up to Gerbert D'Aurillac: A Tentative Contribution," 97–156; C. M. Bower, "The Role of Boethius' 'De Institutione Musica' in the Speculative Tradition of Western Musical Thought," 157–74; M. Folkerts, "The Importance of the Pseudo-Boethian 'Geometria' during the Middle Ages," 187–209; P. Courcelle, "Boethius, Lady Philosophy, and the Representations of the Muses," 211–18.

Boethius: His Life, Thought and Influence. Ed. M. Gibson, Oxford 1981: J. Matthews, "Anicius Manlius Severinus Boethius," 15–43; H. Kirkby, "The Scholar and his Public," 44–69; J. Barnes, "Boethius and the Study of Logic," 73–89; O. Lewry, "Boethian Logic in the Medieval West," 90–134; J. Caldwell, "The 'De Institutione Arithmetica' and the 'De Institutione Musica,'" 135–54; D. Pingree, "Boethius' Geometry and Astronomy," 155–61; A. White, "Boethius in the Medieval Quadrivium," 162–205; A. Grafton, "Boethius in the Renaissance," 410–15.

Bogaert, P. M. "Un manuscrit de Lérins. Contribution à l'histoire de la vieille version latine du livre de Judith," *RB* 84 (1974), 301–12.

Bolgar, R. R. *The Classical Heritage and Its Beneficiaries*. Cambridge 1954.

Bolton, B. M. See *Orthodox Churches . . .*

Borgolte, M. "Papst Leo III., Karl der Große und der Filioque-Streit von Jerusalem," *Byzantina* 10 (1980), 403–27.

Borsari, S. *Il monachesimo bizantino nella Sicilia e nell'Italia meridionale prenormanne*. Naples 1963. Rev. by E. Patlagean, *Studi Medievali* III/6 (1965), 300–305.

Borst, A. *Der Turmbau von Babel. Geschichte der Meinungen über Ursprung und Vielfalt der Sprachen und Völker*. Vols. I–IV. Stuttgart 1957–63.

Bouhot, J.-P. "Ancienne version latine d'un sermon 'De Ioseph et de castitate' d'un Pseudo-Jean Chrysostome," in ΑΝΤΙΔΩΡΟΝ. *Festschrift Maurits Geerard*. Wetteren 1984, I, 47–56.

Bower, C. M. See *Boethius and the Liberal Arts*.

Brandes, H. *Visio S. Pauli*. Halle 1885.

Brandi, K. "Der byzantinische Kaiserbrief aus St. Denis und die Schrift der frühmittelalterlichen Kanzleien. Diplomatisch-paläographische Untersuchungen zur Geschichte der Beziehungen zwischen Byzanz und dem Abendland, vornehmlich in fränkischer Zeit," *Archiv für Urkundenforschung* 1 (1908), 5–85.

Broccia, G. *Enchiridion. Per la Storia di una denominazione libraria*. Rome 1979.

Brou, L. "L'alléluia gréco-latin 'Dies sanctificatus' de la messe du jour de Noël. Origine et évolution d'un chant bilingue et protéiforme," *Revue Grégorienne* 23 (1938), 170–76; 24 (1939), 1–8, 81–89, 202–13.

———. "Les chants en langue grecque dans les liturgies latines," *Sacris Erudiri* 1 (1948), 165–80; 4 (1952), 226–38.

———. "Restes de l'homélie sur la Dormition de l'archevêque Jean de Thessalonique dans le plus ancien antiphonaire connu, et le dernier Magnificat de la Vierge," *Archiv für Liturgiewissenschaft* 2 (1952), 84–93.

Brown, E. A. R. "The Cistercians in the Latin Empire of Constantinople and Greece, 1204–1276," *Traditio* 14 (1958), 63–120.

Brühl, C. "Das Archiv der Stadt Messina in Sevilla," *DA* 34 (1978), 560–66.

Brunhölzl, F. *Geschichte der lateinischen Literatur des Mittelalters*. Vol. 1. Munich 1975.

Burgmann, L. "Eine griechische Fassung der 'Assisen von Ariano,'" in *Fontes minores*. Ed. D. Simon. Frankfurt 1982, V, 179–92.

Busard, H. L. L. "Der Traktat *De isoperimetris*, der unmittelbar aus dem Griechischen ins Lateinische übersetzt worden ist," *Mediaeval Studies* 42 (1980), 61–88.

———, ed. *The First Latin Translation of Euclid's Elements Commonly Ascribed to Adelard of Bath*. Leiden 1983.

———, ed. *The Latin Translation of the Arabic Version of Euclid's Elements Commonly Ascribed to Gerard of Cremona*. Leiden 1984.

Butzer, P. L. "Die Mathematiker des Aachen-Lütticher Raumes von der karoling'schen bis zur spätottonischen Epoche," *Annalen des Historischen Vereins für den Niederrhein* 178 (1976), pp. 7–30.

Buytaert, E. M. *L'héritage littéraire d'Eusèbe d'Emèse*. Louvain 1949.

Byzance et la France médiévale. Manuscrits à peintures du IIe au XVIe siècle [exhibition catalogue]. Paris 1958.

Byzantinische Kostbarkeiten aus Museen, Kirchenschätzen und Bibliotheken [exhibition catalogue]. Berlin 1977.

Cagin, P. *Te Deum ou Illatio? Contribution à l'histoire de l'Euchologie latine*. Solesmes 1906.

Caldwell, J. See *Boethius: His Life . . .*

Callus, C. A., and R. W. Hunt, eds. *Iohannes Blund. Tractatus de anima*. London 1970.

The Cambridge History of Later Medieval Philosophy. Ed. N. Kretzmann, A. Kenny, J. Pinborg, E. Stump. Cambridge 1982: A. Kenny and J. Pinborg, "Medieval Philosophical Literature," 11–42; B. G. Dod, "Aristoteles latinus," 45–79; C. H. Lohr, "The Medieval Interpretation of Aristotle," 80–98.

Cammelli, G. *I dotti bizantini e le origini dell'Umanesimo*. Vol. I: *Manuele Crisolora* and vol. II: *Giovanni Argiropulo*, Florence 1941; vol. III: *Demetrio Calcondila*, Florence 1954.

Canart, P. "Le livre grec en Italie méridionale sous les règnes Normand et Souabe: Aspects matériels et sociaux," *Scrittura e Civiltà* 2 (1978), 103–62.

————. "Le patriarche Méthode de Constantinople copiste à Rome," in *Palaeographica, Diplomatica et Archivistica*. Festschrift Giulio Battelli. Vol. I. Rome 1979, pp. 343–53.

Cappuyns, M. *Jean Scot Érigène, sa vie, son oeuvre, sa pensée*. Louvain/Paris 1933.

Carey, G., and D. J. A. Ross. *The Medieval Alexander*. Cambridge 1956.

Caspar, E. "Die Lateransynode von 649," *Zeitschrift für Kirchengeschichte* 51 (1932), 75–137.

————. *Geschichte des Papsttums*. Vol. II: *Das Papsttum unter byzantinischer Herrschaft*. Tübingen 1933.

Caspari, C. P. "Über den gottesdienstlichen Gebrauch des Griechischen im Abendlande während des früheren Mittelalters," *Ungedruckte, unbeachtete und wenig beachtete Quellen zur Geschichte des Taufsymbols und der Glaubensregel*. Vol. III. Christiania [Oslo] 1875, pp. 466–510.

Catalogus Translationum et Commentariorum. Mediaeval and Renaissance Latin Translations and Commentaries. Annotated Lists and Guides. Ed. P. O. Kristeller et al. Vol. I. Washington 1960: "Alexander Aphrodisiensis," 77–135; "Autolycus," 167–72; "Hypsicles," 173. Vol. II (1971): "Vita Secundi," 1–3; "S. Gregorius Nazianzenus (with Gregorius Presbyter, Vita Gregorii Nazianzeni)," 43–192; "Martianus Capella," 367–81. Vol III (1976); "Dionysius Periegetes," 21–61; "Musici scriptores Graeci," 63–73; "Priscianus Lydus," 75–82; "Thessalus Astrologus," 83–86. Vol. IV (1980): "Dioscorides," 1–143; "Paulus Aegineta," 145–91.

Cavallera, F. *Saint Jérôme. Sa vie et son oeuvre*. Vols. I–II. Louvain/Paris 1922.

Cavallo, G. "La produzione di manoscritti greci in Occidente tra età tardoantica e alto medioevo. Note ed ipotesi," *Scrittura e Civiltà* 1 (1977), 111–31.

————. "Interazione tra scrittura greca e scrittura latina a Roma tra VIII e IX secolo," in *Miscellanea codicologica F. Masai dicata*. Ghent 1979, pp. 23–29.

————. "La trasmissione scritta della cultura greca antica in Calabria e in Sicilia tra i secoli X–XV. Consistenza, tipologia, fruizione," *Scrittura e Civiltà* 4 (1980), 157–245.

————, ed. *Libri e lettori nel mondo bizantino*. Bari 1982: "Libri greci e resistenza etnica in terra d'Otranto," 157–78.

————. "Manoscritti italo-greci e cultura benedittina (secoli X–XII)," in *L'esperienza monastica benedittina e la Puglia*. Galatina, I, 169–95.

————. See *I bizantini in Italia*.

————. "La cultura a Ravenna tra Corte e Chiesa," in *Le sedi della cultura nell'Emilia Romagna. L'alto Medioevo*. [privately printed] Milan 1983, pp. 29–51.

Chadwick, H. *The Sentences of Sextus*. Cambridge 1959.

————. *Boethius: The Consolations of Music, Logic, Theology and Philosophy*. Oxford 1981.

Châtillon, J. "Les écoles de Chartres et de Saint-Victor." See *La Scuola nell'Occidente*.

————. "Hugues de Saint-Victor critique de Jean Scot." See *Jean Scot Érigène et l'histoire de la philosophie*.

Chevallier, P. See *Dionysiaca*.

La Chiesa greca in Italia dall'VIII dal XVI secolo. Vols. I–III. Padua 1972–73: D. Girgensohn, "Dall'episcopato greco all'episcopato latino nell'Italia meridionale," 25–43; E. Theodoru, "Ἑλληνοϊταλικαὶ σχέσεις καὶ ἐπαφαὶ ἐπὶ λειτουργικῶν ζητημάτων περὶ τὸν Θαιῶνα," 257–69; A. Pertusi, "Rapporti tra il monachesimo italogreco ed il monachesimo bizantino nell'alto Medio Evo," 437–520; E. Follieri, "Il culto dei santi nell'Italia greca," 533–77; E. E. Anastasiou, "Αἱ προσπάθειαι τοῦ Βαρλαὰμ τοῦ Καλαβροῦ διὰ τὴν ἕνωσιν τῶν Ἐκκλησιῶν," 663–84; F. Russo, "La partecipazione dei vescovi calabrogreci ai concili (sec. VI–XIV)," 781–92; F. Zagiba, "Die Italogriechen und die Slavenmission im 9. Jahrhundert im östlichen Mitteleuropa," 919–26; G. Matteucci, "Una lettera del 7 aprile 1274 da Leuca (Lecce) ed un nascosto unionista costantinopolitano: Giovanni Parastron O.F.M.," 971–1000; J. A. Brundage, "The Decretalists and the Greek Church of South Italy," 1075–84; O. Rousseau, "La visite de Nil de Rossano au Mont-Cassin," 1111–38; K. Gamber, "Die griechisch-lateinischen Mess-Libelli in Süditalien," 1299–1306.

Chroust, A. *Monumenta Palaeographica. Denkmäler der Schreibkunst des Mittelalters*. Ser. 1, vols. 1–3, Munich 1902–6; ser. 2, vols. 1–3, 1911–17; ser. 3, vols. 1–3, Leipzig 1931–40.

Cilento, N. *Civiltà napoletana del Medioevo*. N.p. [Naples] 1969: "L'agiografia e le traduzioni dal greco," 31–54.

Clagett, M. *Archimedes in the Middle Ages*. Vol. I: *The Arabo-Latin Tradition*. Madison 1964.

Classen, P. *Gerhoch von Reichersberg*. Wiesbaden 1960.

———. "Karl der Große, das Papsttum und Byzanz," in *Karl der Große*. Vol. I. Düsseldorf 1965, pp. 537–608.

———. *Burgundio von Pisa*. SB Heidelberg 1974.

Clavis Patrum Graecorum. Ed. M. Geerard. Vol. I: *Patres Antenicaeni*, Turnhout 1983; vol. II: *Ab Athanasio ad Chrysostomum*, Turnhout 1974; vol. III: *A Cyrillo Alexandrino ad Iohannem Damascenum*, 1979; vol. IV: *Concilia, Catenae*, 1980.

Clavis Patrum Latinorum. 2nd ed. Ed. E. Dekkers and A. Gaar. Steenbrugge 1961.

Codices Latini Antiquiores: A Palaeographical Guide to Latin Manuscripts Prior to the Ninth Century. Ed. E. A. Lowe [and B. Bischoff]. Pts. I–XI. Oxford 1934–66. *Supplement*. Oxford 1971.

Coens, M. "Utriusque linguae peritus," *AB* 76 (1958), 118–50.

Compagna, A. M., Perrone Capano, and A. Varvaro, "Capitoli per la storia linguistica dell'-Italia meridionale e della Sicilia. II. Annotazioni volgari di S. Elia di Carbone (Secoli XV–XVI)," *Medioevo Romanzo* 8 (1981/83), 91–132.

Contreni, J. J. *The Cathedral School of Laon from 850–930*. Munich 1978.

———. "A propos de quelques manuscrits de l'école de Laon au IXe siècle: Découvertes et problèmes," *Le Moyen Âge* 78 (1972), 5–39.

———. "John Scottus, Martin Hibernensis, the Liberal Arts, and Teaching," in *Insular Latin Studies*. Ed. M. W. Herren. Toronto 1981, pp. 23–44.

———. "The Irish in the Western Carolingian Empire (according to James F. Kenney and Bern, Burgerbibliothek 363)," in *Die Iren und Europa im früheren Mittelalter*. Ed. H. Löwe. Stuttgart 1982, pp. 758–98.

———. "Masters and Medicine in Northern France during the Reign of Charles the Bald," in *Charles the Bald: Court and Kingdom*. Ed. M. Gibson and J. Nelson. Oxford 1981, pp. 333–50.

Corpus Christianorum. Series Apocryphorum. Vols. I–II: *Acta Iohannis*. Ed. E. Junod and J.-D. Kaestli. Turnhout 1983.

Corpus Glossariorum Latinorum. Ed. G. Goetz. Vols. I–VII. Leipzig 1888–1923.

Corpus Latinum Commentariorum in Aristotelem Graecorum. Ed. G. Verbeke et al. Louvain/Paris/Leiden 1957 ff.

Cortesi, M. "Il 'Vocabularium' greco di Giovanni Tortelli," *Italia Medioevale e Umanistica* 22 (1979), 449–83.

Corti, M. *Studi sulla latinità merovingia in testi agiografici minori*. Messina/Milan 1939: "La tradizione letteraria come tramite di grecismi," 126–42.

Coseriu, E. "Das Problem des griechischen Einflusses auf das Vulgärlatein," in *Sprache und Geschichte*. Festschrift Harri Meier. Munich 1971, pp. 135–47.

Courcelle, P. *Les lettres grecques en occident. De Macrobe à Cassiodore*. 2nd ed. Paris 1948. Rev. [1st ed.] by G. Bardy, *Revue du Moyen Âge Latin* 1 (1945), 312–19.

———. See *Boethius and the Liberal Arts*.

Cramer, F. *De Graecis per occidentem studiis*. Pars prior: *Inde a primo medio aevo usque ad Carolum Magnum*. Stralsund 1849. Pars altera: *Inde a Carolo Magno usque ad expeditiones in terram sanctam susceptas*. Stralsund 1853.

Cuendet, G. "Cicéron et Jérôme traducteurs," *Revue des études latines* 11 (1933), 380–400.

Cuissard, C. "L'étude du grec à Orléans depuis le IXe siècle jusqu'au milieu du XVIIIe siècle," *Memoires de la Société archéologique de Orléanais* 19 (1883), 645–839 [also published separately].

Curtius, E. R. *Europäische Literatur und lateinisches Mittelalter*. 2nd ed. Bern 1954.

Dales, R. C., ed. *Marius: On the Elements*. Berkeley/Los Angeles/London 1976.

Deér, J. *Byzanz und das abendländische Herrschertum. Ausgewählte Aufsätze*. Sigmaringen 1977.

De Ghellinck, J. *L'essor de la littérature latine au XIIe siècle*. 2nd ed. Brussels 1955.

Delaruelle, É. "La connaissance du grec en occident du Ve au IXe siècle," *Mélanges de la Société Toulousiane d'études classiques* 1 (1946), 207–26.

Delaruelle, L. "Le dictionnaire grec-latin de Crastone," *Studi Italiani di filologia classica*, n.s., 8 (1930), 221–46.

Delisle, L. "Mémoire sur d'anciens sacramentaires," *Mémoires de l'Institut National de France, Académie des Inscriptions et Belles-Lettres* 32/1 (Paris 1886), 57–423.

――――. "Traductions de textes grecs faites par des religieux de Saint-Denis au XIIe siècle," *Journal des Savants* (1900), 725–32, 738 f.

Della Torre, A. *Storia dell'Accademia Platonica di Firenze*. Florence 1902.

Derenzini, G. "All'origine della tradizione di opere scientifiche classiche: vicende di testi e codici tra Bisanzio e Palermo," *Physis* 18 (1976), 87–103.

Derolez, R. *Runica Manuscripta: The English Tradition*. Bruges 1954.

Devreesse, R. *Les manuscrits grecs de l'Italie méridionale*. Rome 1955.

Di Benedetto, F. "Leonzio, Omero e le Pandette," *Italia Medioevale e Umanistica* 12 (1969), 53–112.

Di Camillo, O. *El Humanismo Castellano del Siglo XV*. Valencia 1976.

Diehl, C. *Études sur l'administration byzantine dans l'exarchat de Ravenne (568–751)*. Paris 1888.

Diels, H. *Die Handschriften der antiken Ärzte*. Vol. I: *Hippokrates und Galenos*, Abh. Berlin 1905; vol. II: *Die übrigen griechischen Ärzte*, Abh. Berlin 1906.

Diem, G. "Traductions gréco-latines de la Métaphysique," *Archiv für Geschichte der Philosophie* 49 (1967), 7–71.

Diller, A. "Diodorus in Terra d'Otranto," *Classical Philology* 48 (1953), 257 f.

Dionisotti, A. C. "On Bede, Grammars, and Greek," *RB* 92 (1982), 111–41.

Dionysiaca. Recueil donnant l'ensemble des traductions latines des ouvrages attribués au Denys de l'Aréopage. Ed. P. Chevallier. Vols. I–II. N.p./n.d. [Bruges 1937/50]. Rev. by Y. Ricaud, *Revue d'Histoire Ecclésiastique* 45 (1950), 234–40.

Di Stefano, G. *La découverte de Plutarque en occident. Aspects de la vie intellectuelle en Avignon au XIVe siècle*. Turin 1968.

Dod, B. G. See *Cambridge History of Later Medieval Philosophy*.

Dold, A. *Das Geheimnis einer byzantinischen Staatsurkunde aus dem Jahre 1351*. Beuron 1958.

Dölger, F. See *Le Millénaire du Mont Athos*.

――――. *Facsimiles byzantinischer Kaiserurkunden*. Munich 1931.

Döllinger, I. von. "Einfluß der griechischen Literatur und Cultur auf die abendländischen Welt," in *Akademische Vorträge*. Vol. I. Nördlingen 1888, pp. 163–86.

Dondaine, A. "Nicolas de Cotrone et les sources du 'Contra errores Graecorum' de Saint Thomas," *Divus Thomas* 28 (Fribourg 1950), 313–40.

――――. "'Contra Graecos.' Premiers écrits polémiques des dominicains d'Orient," *Archivum Fratrum Praedicatorum* 21 (1951), 320–446.

――――. "Hugues Éthérien et Léon Toscan," *AHDL* 19 (1953), 67–134.

Dondaine, H. F. *Le Corpus dionysien de l'Université de Paris au XIIIe siècle*. Rome 1953.

Dörrie, H. *Passio SS. Machabaeorum, die antike lateinische Übersetzung des IV. Makkabäerbuches*. Abh. Göttingen 1938.

Drögereit, R. "Griechisch-Byzantinisches aus Essen," *BZ* 46 (1953), 110–15.

Dronke, P. *Fabula: Explorations into the Uses of Myth in Medieval Platonism*. Leiden/Cologne 1974.

Duchesne, L. *Le Liber pontificalis*. Vol. I. Paris 1886. Vol. II. 1892. Vol. III. Ed. C. Vogel. 1957.

Duft, J. "Über Irland und den irischen Einfluß auf das Festland," *Zeitschrift für Schweiz. Kirchengeschichte* 51 (1957), 147–50.

――――. "Irische Handsschriftenüberlieferung in St. Gallen," in *Die Iren und Europa im früheren Mittelalter*. Ed. H. Löwe. Stuttgart 1982, II, 916–37.

――――. "Die Griechisch-Kenntnisse im mittelalterlichen Abendland," *Innsbrucker Historische Studien* 5 (1982), 169–74.

Durling, R. J. "Corrigenda and Addenda to Diels' Galenica I," *Traditio* 23 (1967), 461–76; "II": 37 (1981), 373–81.

Ebersolt, J. *Orient et Occident. Recherches sur les influences byzantines et orientales en France avant et pendant les croisades*. 2nd ed. Paris 1954.

Eckstein, F. A. "Analecten zur Geschichte der Pädagogik. I. Ein griechisches Elementarbuch aus dem Mittelalter," in *Programm der Lateinischen Hauptschule in Halle für das Schuljahr 1860–1861*. Halle 1861, pp. 1–11.

————. *Lateinischer und griechischer Unterricht*. [Posth.] Ed. H. Heyden. Leipzig 1887.

Egger, E. *L'hellénisme en France*. *Leçons sur l'influence des études grecques dans le développement de la langue et de la littérature françaises*. Vol. I. Paris 1869.

Ehrhard, A. *Überlieferung und Bestand der hagiographischen und homiletischen Literatur der griechischen Kirche*. Vols. I–III. *TU* 50–52. Leipzig 1937–43.

Ehrle, F. "Zur Geschichte des Schatzes, der Bibliothek und des Archivs der Päpste im vierzehnten Jahrhundert," *Archiv für Literatur und Kirchengeschichte des Mittelalters* 1 (1885), 1–364.

Esposito, M. "The Knowledge of Greek in Ireland during the Middle Ages," *Studies* 1 (Dublin 1912), 665–83.

Evans, G. R. "Anselm of Canterbury and Anselm of Havelberg. The Controversy with the Greeks," *Analecta Praemonstratensia* 53 (1977), 158–75.

Exhibition catalogues. See *Byzance et la France médiévale*; *Byzantinische Kostbarkeiten*; *Die Heiratsurkunde der Kaiserin Theophanu*; *Venezia e Bisanzio*; *Wissenschaft im Mittelalter*.

Faes de Mottoni, B. *Il 'Corpus Dionysianum' nel Medioevo. Rassegna di studi 1900–1972*. Bologna 1977.

Falkenhausen, V. von. *Untersuchungen über die byzantinische Herrschaft in Süditalien vom 9. bis 11. Jahrhundert*. Wiesbaden 1967.

————. "Taranto in epoca bizantina," *Studi Medievali* III/9 (1968), 133–66.

————. "Il monachesimo greco e i suoi rapporti con il monachesimo benedittino." In *L'esperienza monastica benedittina e la Puglia*. Lecce 1983, I, 119–35.

Fedalto, G. *Simone Atumano. Monaco di Studio, arcivescovo latino di Tebe. Secolo XIV*. Brescia n.d. [1968].

————. *La chiesa latina in Oriente*. Vol. I. [Verona] 1973, 2nd ed., 1981; vol. II: *Hierarchia latina Orientis*, 1976; vol. III: *Documenti Veneziani*, 1978.

Fenster, E. *Laudes Constantinopolitanae*. Munich 1968.

Ferrari, G. *Early Roman Monasteries: Notes for the History of the Monasteries and Convents at Rome from the V through the X Century*. Rome 1957.

Fichtner, G. *Corpus Hippocraticum. Verzeichnis des hippokratischen und pseudohippokratischen Schriften*. Tübingen: Institut für Geschichte der Medizin, 1985.

————. *Corpus Galenicum. Verzeichnis der galenischen und pseudogalenischen Schriften*. Tübingen: Institut für Geschichte de Medizin, 1985.

Firmin-Didot, A. *Alde Manuce et l'Hellénisme à Venise*. Paris 1875.

Fischer, B. "Die Lesungen der römischen Ostervigil unter Gregor d. Gr.," in *Colligere fragmenta*. Festschrift Alban Dold. Beuron 1952, pp. 144–59.

————. "Bibelausgaben des frühen Mittelalters," in *La bibbia nell'alto medioevo*. Spoleto 1963, pp. 519–600.

Fischer, E. H. *Gregor der Große und Byzanz. Ein Beitrag zur Geschichte der päpstl. Politik*. Sonderdruck aus Zeitschrift der Savigny-Stiftung für Rechtsgeschichte, vol. 67. Weimar 1950.

Folkerts, M. See *Boethius and the Liberal Arts*.

Follieri, E. "I rapporti fra Bisanzio e l'Occidente nel campo dell'agiografia," *Proceedings of the XIIIth International Congress of Byzantine Studies, Oxford 1966*. London 1967, pp. 355–62.

————. *Codices Graeci Bibliothecae Vaticanae selecti*. Rome 1969.

————. "Due codici greci già Cassinesi oggi alla Biblioteca Vaticana: Gli Ottob. gr. 250 e 251," in *Palaeographica, Diplomatica et Archivistica*. Festschrift Giulio Battelli. Vol. I. Rome 1979, pp. 159–221.

————. See *La Chiesa greca in Italia*.

Frakes, J. C. "The Knowledge of Greek in the Early Middle Ages: The Commentaries on Boethius' *Consolatio*," *Studii Medievali* 111/27 (1986), 23–43.

————. "Griechisches im frühmittelalterlichen St. Gallen: Ein methodologischer Beitrag zu Notker Labeos Griechischkenntnissen," *Zeitschrift für deutsche Philologie* 106 (1987), 25–34.

Franceschini, E. *Studi e Note di Filologia Latina Medievale*. Milan 1938: "Il ΠΕΡΙ ΤΟΥ ΒΙΟΥ ΤΗΣ ΥΠΕΡΑΓΙΑΣ ΘΕΟΤΟΚΟΥ di Epifanio nella versione latina medievale di Pasquale Romano," 107–28.

————. *Scritti di Filologia Latina Medievale.* Vols. I–II. Padua 1976: "Ricerche e studi su Aristotele nel Medioevo latino," 377–408 [originally in *Rivista di Filosofia Neo-Scolastica,* Supplemento al vol. 48 (1956)]; "Roberto Grossatesta, vescovo di Lincoln, e le sue traduzioni latine," 409–544 [originally in *Atti del R. Istituto Veneto di Scienze, Lettere ed Arti* 93 (1933)]; "Il contributo dell'Italia alla trasmissione del pensiero greco in Occidente nei secoli XII–XIII e la questione di Giacomo Chierico di Venezia," 560–88 [originally in *Atti della XXVI Riunione della Società Italiana per il Progresso delle Scienze* (Rome 1938)]; "La 'Poetica' di Aristotele nel secolo XIII," 589–614 [originally in *Atti del R. Istituto Veneto di Scienze, Lettere ed Arti* 94 (1934)]; "La revisione moerbekana della 'Translatio Lincolniensis' dell'Etica Nicomachea," 637–53 [originally in *Rivista di Filosofia Neo-Scolastica* 30 (1938)]; "Sulle versioni latine medievali del ΠΕΡΙ ΧΡΩΜΑΤΩΝ," 654–73 [originally in *Festschrift Augustin Mansion,* Louvain 1955]; "Leonardo Bruni e il 'vetus interpres' dell'Etica a Nicomaco," 674–92 [originally in *Medioevo e Rinascimento,* Festschrift Bruno Nardi, Florence 1955].

————. "Le traduzioni latine aristoteliche e pseudo-aristoteliche del cod. Antoniano XVII 370," *Aevum* 9 (1935), 3–26.

Franchi, A. "La svolta politico-ecclesiastica fra Roma e Bisanzio (1249–1254). La legazione di Giovanni de Parma. Il ruolo di Federigo II," *Picenum Seraphicum* 14 (1977/1978), 7–288.

Frasca, S. "Glosse siciliane in scrittura greca," *Bollettino del Centro di studi filologici e linguistici siciliani* 3 (1955), 314–16.

Frede, H. J. *Altlateinische Paulus-Handschriften.* Freiburg 1964.

Frenaud, G. "Le culte de Notre Dame dans l'ancienne liturgie latine," in *Maria. Études sur la sainte Vierge.* Ed. H. du Manoir. Vol. VI. Paris 1961, pp. 157–211.

Frova, C. "Le opere aritmetiche di Gerberto d'Aurillac," *Studi sul medioevo cristiano.* Festschrift Raffaello Morghen. Rome 1974, I, 323–53.

Gamillschegg, E. See *Repertorium der griechischen Kopisten.*

Gandillac, M. de. *La philosophie de Nicolas de Cues.* Paris [1941].

Gardthausen, V. *Griechische Paläographie.* Vol. I. 2nd ed. Leipzig 1911. Vol. II. 1913.

————. "Die griechische Schrift des Mittelalters im Westen Europas," *Byzantinisch-neugriechische Jahrbücher* 8 (1931), 114–35.

Garin, E. "Le traduzioni umanistiche di Aristotele nel secolo XV," *Atti e Memorie dell'Accademia Fiorentina di Scienze Morali 'La Colombaria'* 16 [n.s., 2] (Florence 1951), 55–104.

————. "Ricerche sulle traduzioni di Platone nella prima metà del secolo XV," *Medioevo e Rinascimento.* Festschrift Bruno Nardi. Florence 1955, pp. 339–74.

————. *Studi sul platonismo medievale.* Florence 1958.

Gavinelli, S. "Per un'enciclopedia carolingia (Codice Bernese 363)," *Italia Medioevale e Umanistica* 26 (1983), 1–25.

Gay, J. *L'Italie méridionale et l'empire byzantin depuis l'avènement de Basile Ier jusqu'à la prise de Bari par les Normands (867–1071).* Paris 1904.

Geanakoplos, D. J. *Emperor Michael Palaeologus and the West 1258–1282: A Study in Byzantine-Latin Relations.* Cambridge, Mass., 1959.

————. *Greek Scholars in Venice: Studies in the Dissemination of Greek Learning from Byzantium to Western Europe.* Cambridge, Mass. 1962 [repr. as *Byzantium and the Renaissance* (1973)].

————. *Byzantine East and Latin West: Two Worlds of Christendom in Middle Ages and Renaissance.* Oxford 1966.

————. *Interaction of the "Sibling" Byzantine and Western Cultures in the Middle Ages and Italian Renaissance (330–1600)* [collected papers]. New Haven/London 1976. Rev. by G. Cavallo, *Rivista di Filologia e di Istruzione Classica* 108 (1980), pp. 362–65.

————. See *Orthodox Churches . . .*

Gianola, G. M. *Il Greco di Dante.* Venice 1980.

Gibson, M. "The Study of the 'Timaeus' in the Eleventh and Twelfth Centuries," *Pensiamento* 25 (Madrid 1969), 183–94.

————. See *Boethius: His Life . . .*

Gidel, C. "Les études grecques en Europe depuis le quatrième siècle après J.-C. jusqu'à la chute de Constantinople (1453)," in *Nouvelles études sur la littérature grecque moderne.* Paris 1878, pp. 1–289.

Gigante, M., ed. *Poeti bizantini di terra d'Otranto nel secolo XIII*. 2nd ed. Naples 1979.

———. See *I bizantini in Italia*.

Gill, J. *The Council of Florence*. Cambridge 1959.

———. *Byantium and the Papacy 1198–1400*. New Brunswick, N.J., 1979.

Giunta, F. *Bizantini e Bizantinismo nella Sicilia normanna*. 2nd ed. Palermo 1974.

Giustiniani, V. R. "Sulle traduzioni latine delle 'Vita' di Plutarco nel Quattrocento," *Rinascimento* II/1 (1961), 3–62.

———. "Plutarch und die humanistische Ethik," in *Ethik im Humanismus*. Ed. W. Rüegg and D. Wuttke. Boppard 1979, pp. 45–62.

Glässer, E. "Dolmetschen im Mittelalter. Ein Beitrag zur Entwicklung des Völkergedankens," in *Beiträge zur Geschichte des Dolmetschens*. Schriften des Auslands- und Dolmetscherinstituts Germersheim I. Munich 1956, pp. 61–79.

Goetz, G. "Glossographie," in Pauly-Wissowa, *Real-Encyclopädie der Classischen Altertumswissenschaften*. Vol. VII/1. Stuttgart 1910, cols. 1433–66.

———. See *Corpus Glossariorum Latinorum*.

Goldbrunner, H. "Durandus de Alvernia, Nicolaus von Oresme und Leonardo Bruni. Zu den Übersetzungen der pseudo-aristotelischen Ökonomik," *Archiv für Kulturgeschichte* 50 (1968), 200–239.

Golubovich, G. *Biblioteca Bio-Bibliografica della Terra Santa e dell'Oriente Francescano*. Vol. I: *1215–1300*. Quaracchi 1906. Vol. II: *Addenda al Sec. XIII, e Fonti pel Sec. XIV*. 1913. Vol. III: *1300–1332*. 1919.

Grabar, A. *Les manuscrits grecs enluminés de provenance italienne (IXe–XIe siècles)*. Paris 1972.

Grabmann, M. *Forschungen über die lateinischen Aristoteles-Übersetzungen des 13. Jahrhunderts*. Münster 1916.

———. *Mittelalterliches Geistesleben*. Vol. I. Munich 1926: "Die mittelalterlichen lateinischen Übersetzungen der Schriften des Pseudo-Dionysius Areopagita," 449–68. Vol. II. Munich 1936: "Die Proklosübersetzungen des Wilhelm von Moerbeke und ihre Verwertung in der lateinischen Literatur des Mittelalters," 413–23.

———. *Guglielmo di Moerbeke*. Rome 1946.

Grafton, A. See *Boethius: His Life* . . .

Grégoire, H., and R. Keyser, "La chanson de Roland et Byzance (ou de l'utilité du grec pour les romanistes)," *Byzantion* 14 (1939), 265–316.

Gregory, T. *Platonismo medievale. Studi e ricerche*. Rome 1958.

Gribomont, J. "Saint Bède et ses dictionnaires grecs," *RB* 89 (1979), 271–80.

———. See *Richesses et déficiences des anciens psautiers latins*.

Groppi, F. *Dante traduttore*. 2nd ed. Rome 1962.

Grundmann, H. "Die Papstprophetien des Mittelalters," *Ausgewählte Aufsätze*. Vol. II. Stuttgart 1977, pp. 1–57.

Guillou, A. "Grecs d'Italie du Sud et de Sicile au Moyen Âge: les moines," *Mélanges de l'École Française de Rome* 75 (1963), 79–110.

———. See *La Scuola nell'Occidente*.

Hadot, P. *Marius Victorinus. Recherches sur sa vie et ses oeuvres*. Paris 1971.

Haendler, G. *Epochen karolingischer Theologie. Eine Untersuchung über die karolingischen Gutachten zum byzantinischen Bilderstreit*. Berlin 1958.

Hagen, H. [Introduction to the facsimile ed.] *Codex Bernensis 363*. Leiden 1897. Rev. by L. C. Stern, *Zeitschrift für celtische Philologie* 4 (1903), 178–86.

Hahn, L. "Zum Sprachenkampf im römischen Reich bis auf die Zeit Justinians," *Philologus*, Supplement 10 (1907), 675–718.

Hahnloser, H. R. "Magistra Latinitas und Peritia Greca." In *Festschrift für Herbert von Einem*. Berlin 1965, pp. 77–93.

Halecki, O. *Un Empereur de Byzance à Rome. Vingt ans de travail pour l'union des églises et pour la défense de l'Empire d'Orient 1355–1375*. Warsaw 1930.

Halkin, F. "Sainte Tatiana. Légende grecque d'une 'martyre romaine,'" *AB* 89 (1971), 265–309.

Hamilton, B. "The City of Rome and the Eastern Churches in the Tenth Century," *Orientalia Christiana Periodica* 27 (1961), 5–26.

————. *The Latin Church in the Crusader States*. London 1980.

————. See *Le Millénaire du Mont Athos*.

Hammond-Bammel, C. P. *Der Römerbrieftext des Rufin und seine Origenes-Übersetzung*. Freiburg 1985.

Handschin, J. *Das Zeremonienwerk Kaiser Konstantins und die sangbare Dichtung*. Basel 1942.

————. "Sur quelques tropaires grecs, traduits en latin," *Annales musicologiques* 2 (1954), 27–60.

Harlfinger, D. See *Repertorium der griechischen Kopisten*.

Harth, H. "Leonardo Brunis Selbstverständnis als Übersetzer," *Archiv für Kulturgeschichte* 50 (1968), 41–63.

Hartmann, G. M. "Die Bedeutung des Griechentums für die Entwicklung des italienischen Humanismus," in *Probleme der neugriechischen Literatur*. Vol. II. Berliner Byzantinische Arbeiten 15. Berlin 1960, pp. 3–36.

Hartmann, L. M. "Johannicius von Ravenna," in *Festschrift Theodor Gomperz*. Vienna 1902, pp. 319–23.

Hartwig, O. "Die Übersetzungsliteratur Unteritaliens in der normannisch-staufischen Epoche," *Zentralblatt für Bibliothekswesen* 3 (1886), 161–90, 223–25, 505 f.

Haskins, C. H. *Studies in the History of Mediaeval Science*. 2nd ed. Cambridge, Mass., 1927: "The Greek Element in the Renaissance of the Twelfth Century," 141–54 [originally in *The American Historical Review* 25 (1920)]; "The Sicilian Translators of the Twelfth Century," 155–93 [originally in *Harvard Studies in Classical Philology* 21 (1910)]; "North-Italian Translators of the Twelfth Century," 194–222; "Science at the Court of the Emperor Frederick II," 242–71 [originally in *The American Historical Review* 27 (1922)].

————. *Studies in Mediaeval Culture*. Cambridge, Mass., 1929: "Contacts with Byzantium: A Canterbury Monk at Constantinople, c. 1090; Chrysolanus of Milan; Paschal the Roman," 160–69 [originally in *English Historical Review* 25 (1910), and *Byzantion* 2 (1926)].

————. *The Renaissance of the Twelfth Century*. 2nd ed. New York 1957.

Heath, R. G. "The Western Schism of the Franks and the 'Filioque,'" *The Journal of Ecclesiastical History* 23 (1972), 97–113.

Hecker, O. *Boccaccio-Funde*. Braunschweig 1902: "Das Griechische in dem Original," pp. 137 ff.

Heer, J. M. *Die versio latina des Barnabasbriefes und ihr Verhältnis zur altlateinischen Bibel*. Freiburg 1908.

Heiberg, J. L. "Die griechische Grammatik Roger Bacons," *BZ* 9 (1900), 479–91.

————. "Les sciences grecques et leur transmission," *Scientia* 31 (1922), 1–10 and 97–104.

————. "Les premiers manuscrits grecs de la bibliothèque papale," *Bulletin de l'Académie R. Danoise des Sciences et des Lettres pour l'année 1891*. Copenhagen 1892, pp. 305–18.

Heilig, K. J. "Ostrom und das Deutsche Reich um die Mitte des 12. Jahrhunderts," in *Kaisertum und Herzogsgewalt im Zeitalters Friedrichs I*. Leipzig 1944.

Heinzer, F. "Zu einem unbeachteten Maximuszitat im Periphyseon des Johannes Scottus Eriugena," *Traditio* 40 (1984), 300–306.

Die Heiratsurkunde der Kaiserin Theophanu 972 April 14 Rom [exhibition catalogue, Wolfenbüttel]. Göttingen 1972.

Heisenberg. A. *Quellen und Studien zur spätbyzantinischen Geschichte*. London 1973.

Hemmerdinger, B. "Les lettres latines à Constantinople jusqu'à Justinien," *Byzantinische Forschungen* (1966), 174–78.

————. "Le *De plantis*, de Nicolas de Damas à Planude," *Philologus* 111 (1967), 56–65.

Henss, W. *Leitbilder der Bibelübersetzung im 5. Jahrhundert. Die Praefatio im Evangelienkodex Brixianus (f) und das Problem der gotisch-lateinischen Bibelbilinguen*. Abh. Heidelberg 1973.

Heppell, M. See *Orthodox Churches* . . .

Herde, P. "Das Papsttum und die griechische Kirche in Süditalien vom 11. bis zum 13. Jahrhundert," *DA* 26 (1960), 1–46.

Hermann, A. "Dolmetscher," in *Reallexikon für Antike und Christentum*. Vol. IV. Stuttgart 1959, pp. 24–49.

Herrin, J. "Aspects of the Process of Hellenization in the Early Middle Ages," *The Annual of the British School at Athens* 68 (1973), 113–26.

Hesbert, R.-J. *Corpus Antiphonalium Officii.* Vol. I: *Manuscripti* [sic] *'Cursus Romanus.'* Rome 1963. Vol. II: *Manuscripti 'Cursus Monasticus.'* 1965. Vol. III: *Invitatoria et Antiphonae.* 1968. Vol. IV: *Responsoria, Versus, Hymni et Varia.* 1970. Vol. V: *Fontes.* 1975. Vol. VI: *Fontes.* 1979.

Hiestand, R. *Byzanz und das Regnum Italicum im 10. Jahrhundert.* Zurich 1964.

Hill, K. D. See *Orthodox Churches . . .*

Hiltbrunner, O. *Latina Graeca. Semasiologische Studien über lateinische Wörter im Hinblick auf ihr Verhältnis zu griechischen Vorbildern.* Bern 1958.

Hirzel, R. *Plutarch.* Das Erbe der Alten 4. Leipzig 1912.

Hoeck, J. M., and R. J. Loenertz. *Nikolaos-Nektarios von Otranto, Abt von Casole. Beiträge zur Geschichte der ost-westlichen Beziehungen unter Innozenz III. und Friedrich II.* Ettal 1965.

Hoffmann, E. *Platonismus und christliche Philosophie.* Zurich/Stuttgart 1960: "Platonismus und Mittelalter," pp. 230–311.

Hofmeister, A. "Zur griechisch-lateinischen Übersetzungsliteratur des früheren Mittelalters. Die frühere Wiener Handschrift lat. 739," *Münchner Museum für Philologie des Mittelalters und der Renaissance* 4 (1924), 129–53.

———. "Der Übersetzer Johannes und das Geschlecht Comitis Mauronis in Amalfi," *Historische Vierteljahrschrift* 27 (1932), 225–84, 493–508, 831–33.

Holzberg, N. *Willibald Pirckheimer. Griechischer Humanismus in Deutschland.* Munich 1981.

Homeyer, H. "Zur *Synkrisis* des Manuel Chrysoloras, einem Vergleich zwischen Rom und Konstantinopel. Ein Beitrag zum italienischen Frühhumanismus," *Klio* 62 (1980), 525–34.

Honecker, M. *Nikolaus von Cues und die griechische Sprache.* SB Heidelberg 1938.

Hoßfeld, P. "Der Gebrauch der aristotelischen Übersetzung in den 'Meteora' des Albertus Magnus," *Mediaeval Studies* 42 (1980), 395–406.

Huber, M. *Johannes Monachus: Liber de Miraculis.* Sammlung mittellateinischer Texte 7. Heidelberg 1913. Rev. by Van de Vorst, *AB* 33 (1914), 363–65; A. Hofmeister, *Literarisches Zentralblatt* 67 (1916), cols. 995–97.

Huglo, M. "L'ancienne version latine de l'hymne acathiste," *Le Muséon* 64 (1951), 27–61.

———. "Les anciennes versions latines des homélies de saint Basile," *RB* 64 (1954), 129–32.

———. "Les chants de la missa graeca de Saint-Denis," in *Essays Presented to Egon Wellesz.* Oxford 1966, pp. 74–83.

———. "Relations musicales entre Byzance et l'Occident," in *Proceedings of the XIIIth International Congress of Byzantine Studies, Oxford 1966.* London 1967, pp. 267–80.

Hunger, H. *Die hochsprachliche profane Literatur der Byzantiner.* Vols. I–II. Munich 1978.

———. See *Repertorium der griechischen Kopisten.*

Hunt, R. W. *The History of Grammar in the Middle Ages: Collected Papers.* Amsterdam 1980.

Images et signes de l'Orient dans l'Occident médiévale (littérature et civilisation). Marseille 1982.

Immisch, O. "Sprach- und stilgeschichtliche Parallelen zwischen Griechisch und Lateinisch," *Neue Jahrbücher für das klassische Altertum* 15 (1912), 27–49.

Irigoin, J. "La culture grecque dans l'occident latin du VIIe au XIe siècle," in *La cultura antica nell'occidente latino dal VII all'XI secolo.* Vol. I. Spoleto 1975, pp. 425–46.

———. "L'Italie méridionale et la tradition des textes antiques," *Jahrbuch der österr. Byzantinistik* 18 (1969), 37–55.

Irmscher, J. "Latein und Griechisch im Cinquecento" [read "Quattrocento"!], in *Corona Gratiarum.* Festschrift Eligius Dekkers. Vol. II. Bruges/The Hague 1975, pp. 389–402.

Ising, E. *Die Herausbildung der Volkssprachen in Mittel- und Osteuropa. Studien über den Einfluß der lateinischen Elementargrammatik des Aelius Donatus "De octo partibus orationis ars minor."* Berlin 1970.

Ito, S. *The Medieval Latin Translation of the Data of Euclid.* Tokyo/Boston/Basel/Stuttgart 1980.

Ivánka, E. von. "Abendland und Byzanz," *Wissenschaft und Weltbild* 1 (1948), 205–19.

Jacob, A. "Les écritures de Terre d'Otranto," in *La paléographie grecque et byzantine*. Paris 1977, pp. 269–81.

Jakobs, H. "St. Pantaleon und der Griechenmarkt zu Köln," *Annalen des Historischen Vereins für den Niederrhein* 164 (1962), 5–55.

James, M. R. "A Graeco-Latin Lexicon of the Thirteenth Century," *Mélanges É. Chatelain*. Paris 1910, pp. 396–411.

———. "Greek Manuscripts in England before the Renaissance," *The Library* IV/7 (1927), 337–53.

———. *Apocrypha anecdota*. Cambridge 1893.

Jamison, E. *Admiral Eugenius of Sicily*. London 1957.

Jammers, E. *Musik in Byzanz, im päpstlichen Rom und im Frankenreich*. Abh. Heidelberg 1962.

———. *Die Essener Neumenhandschriften der Landes- und Stadtbibliothek Düsseldorf*. Ratingen 1952. Rev. by B. Bischoff, *Annalen des Hist. Vereins für den Niederrhein* 157 (1954), 191–94.

Jean Scot Érigène et l'histoire de la philosophie. Colloques Internationaux du Centre de la Recherche Scientifique. Paris 1977: B. Bischoff, "Irische Schreiber im Karolingerreich," 47–58; J. J. Contreni, "The Irish 'Colony' at Laon during the Time of John Scottus," 59–67; T. A. M. Bishop, "Autographa of John the Scot," 89–94; J. Vezin, "A propos des manuscrits de Jean Scot. Quelques remarques sur les manuscrits autographes du haut moyen âge," 95–99; B. Bischoff and É. Jeauneau, "Ein neuer Text aus der Gedankenwelt des Johannes Scottus," 109–16; R. Le Bourdellès, "Connaissance du grec et méthodes de traduction dans le monde carolingien jusqu'à Scot Érigène," 117–22; J. Barbet, "Le traitement des 'Expositiones in Ierarchiam caelestem' de Jean Scot par le compilateur du 'Corpus' dionysien du XIIIᵉ siècle," 125–34; É. Jeauneau, "La traduction érigénienne des 'Ambigua' de Maxime le Confesseur: Thomas Gale (1636–1702) et le 'Codex Remensis,'" 135–44; M.-T. d'Alverny, "Les 'Solutiones ad Chosroem' de Priscianus Lydus et Jean Scot," 145–60; J. Préaux, "Jean Scot et Martin de Laon en face du 'De Nuptiis' de Martianus Capella," 161–70; C. Leonardi, "Glosse Eriugeniane a Marziano Capella in un codice Leidense," 171–82; L. Bieler, "Observations on Eriugena's Commentary on the Gospel of John: A Second Harvest," 235–41; P. Lucentini, "La 'Clavis physicae' di Honorius Augustodunensis e la tradizione eriugeniana nel secolo XII," 405–14; J. Châtillon, "Hugues de Saint-Victor critique de Jean Scot," 415–31; P. Vignaux, "Jean de Ripa, Hugues de Saint-Victor et Jean Scot sur les théophanies," 433–39; M. Lapidge, "L'influence stylistique de la poésie de Jean Scot," 441–51.

Jeauneau, É. "Les écoles de Laon et d'Auxerre au IXᵉ siècle," in *La Scuola nell'Occidente*.

———. "Guillaume de Malmesbury, premier éditeur anglais du 'Periphyseon.'" In *Sapientiae doctrinae*. Mélanges Hildebrand Bascour. Louvain 1980, pp. 148–179.

———. "Pour le dossier d'Israël Scot," *AHDL* 60 (1985), 7–72.

———. "Jean Scot Érigène et le grec," *Archivum Latinitatis Medii Aevi* 41 (1979), 5–50.

———. See *Jean Scot Érigène et l'histoire de la philosophie*.

Junod. E. See *Corpus Christianorum. Series Apocryphorum*.

Kaczynski, B. M. "Greek Learning in the Medieval West: A Study of St. Gall 816–1022." Diss. Yale 1975.

———. *The Study of Greek at the Monastery of St. Gall, 816–1022*. Cambridge: Medieval Academy of America, forthcoming.

Kaeppeli, T. *Scriptores ordinis praedicatorum medii aevi*. Vols. I–. Rome 1970–.

Kaestli, J.-D. See *Corpus Christianorum. Series Apocryphorum*.

Kahane, H. and R. "Abendland und Byzanz: Sprache. Byzantinische Einflüsse im Westen," *Reallexikon der Byzantinistik*. Vol. I, cols. 345–498. Amsterdam 1970–72.

Kamp, N. *Kirche und Monarchie im staufischen Königreich Sizilien*. Munich 1975.

Kappelmacher, A. "Der schriftstellerische Plan des Boethius," *Wiener Studien* 46 (1928), 215–25.

Kaulen, F. *Sprachliches Handbuch zur biblischen Vulgata. Eine systematische Darstellung ihres lateinischen Sprachcharakters*. 2nd ed. Freiburg 1904.

Kenny, A. See *Cambridge History of Later Medieval Philosophy*.

Kibre, P. "Hippocrates Latinus: Repertorium of Hippocratic Writings in the Latin Middle Ages," *Traditio* 31 ff. (1975 ff.), passim.

————. "The Intellectual Interests Reflected in Libraries of the Fourteenth and Fifteenth Centuries," *Journal of the History of Ideas* 7 (1946), 257–97.

————. *Studies in Medieval Science: Alchemy, Astrology, Mathematics and Medicine* [collected papers]. London 1984.

————. See *Boethius and the Liberal Arts.*

Kirkby, H. See *Boethius: His Life . . .*

Klibansky, R. *Ein Proklos-Fund und seine Bedeutung.* SB Heidelberg 1929.

————. *The Continuity of the Platonic Tradition during the Middle Ages.* London 1939. Rev. by E. H. Kantorowicz, *The Philosophical Review* 51 (1942), 312–23.

————. "Plato's Parmenides in the Middle Ages and the Renaissance," *Mediaeval and Renaissance Studies* 1 (1943), 281–330.

————. "The School of Chartres," in *Twelfth-Century Europe and the Foundations of Modern Society.* Ed. M. Clagett, G. Post, R. Reynolds. 2nd ed. Madison 1966, pp. 3–14.

————. "Zur Geschichte der Überlieferung der Docta Ignorantia des Nikolaus von Kues," in *Nikolaus von Kues: Die belehrte Unwissenheit. Buch III, lateinisch-deutsch.* Schriften des Nikolaus von Kues in deutscher Übersetzung 15c. Hamburg 1977, pp. 205–36.

————. See *Plato latinus.*

Kloepfer, R. *Die Theorie der literarischen Übersetzung. Romanisch-deutscher Sprachbereich.* Munich 1967.

Klostermann, E., and E. Benz. *Die Überlieferung der Matthäuserklärung des Origenes. TU* 47/2. Leipzig 1931.

————. *Origenes Matthäuserklärung.* Vol. I. GCS 40. Leipzig 1935. Vol. II. GCS 38. 1933.

Kluge, O. "Die griechischen Studien in Renaissance und Humanismus," *Zeitschrift für Geschichte der Erziehung und des Unterrichts* 24 (1934), 1–54.

Koch, J. *Platonismus im Mittelalter.* Kölner Universitätsreden 4. Krefeld 1951.

Koder, J., and T. Weber. *Liutprand von Cremona in Konstantinopel. Untersuchungen zum griechischen Sprachschatz und zu realienkundlichen Aussagen in seinen Werken.* Vienna 1980.

Koffmane, G. *Geschichte des Kirchenlateins. Entstehung und Entwickelung des Kirchenlateins bis auf Augustinus–Hieronymus.* Vol. I/1–2. Breslau 1879–81; repr. Hildesheim 1966.

Köhler, E. "Byzanz und die Literatur der Romania," in *Grundriß der romanischen Literaturen des Mittelalters.* Vol. I. Heidelberg 1972, pp. 396–407.

Krause, W. "Das Fragment einer griechischen Grammatik des Cod. Vindob. 114 und das griech.-lat. Glossar der St. Pauler Handschrift XXV D/65" [read "St. Paul 86b/1"!], *Jahrbuch der Österr. Byzantinischen Gesellschaft* 5 (1956), 7–25.

Krchňák, A. *De vita et operibus Ioannis de Ragusio.* Rome 1960.

Kresten, O. "Pallida mors Sarracenorum. Zur Wanderung eines literarischen Topos von Liutprand von Cremona bis Otto von Freising und zu seiner byzantinischen Vorlage," *Römische Historische Mitteilungen* 17 (1975), 23–75.

Kretzmann, N. See *Cambridge History of Later Medieval Philosophy.*

Kreuzer, G. *Die Honoriusfrage im Mittelalter und in der Neuzeit.* Stuttgart 1975.

Kristeller, P. O. *Studies in Renaissance Thought and Letters.* Rome 1956: "The School of Salerno," 495–551 [originally in *Bulletin of the History of Medicine* 17 (1945)].

————. "The Historical Position of Johannes Scottus Eriugena," in *Latin Script and Letters A.D. 400–900.* Festschrift Ludwig Bieler. Leiden 1976, pp. 156–64.

————. "Marsilio Ficino as a Beginning Student of Plato," *Scriptorium* 20 (1966), 41–54.

————. "A Latin Translation of Gemistos Plethon's 'De fato' by Johannes Sophianos Dedicated to Nicholas of Cusa," in *Nicolò Cusano agli Inizi del Mondo Moderno.* Florence 1970, pp. 175–93.

————. *Die Philosophie des Marsilio Ficino.* Frankfurt 1972.

————. *Renaissance Concepts of Man.* New York/Evanston/San Francisco/London 1972: "Italian Humanism and Byzantium," 64–85; "Byzantine and Western Platonism in the Fifteenth Century," 86–109.

————. "Bartholomaeus, Musandinus and Maurus of Salerno and Other Early Commentators of the 'Articella,' with a Tentative List of Texts and Manuscripts," *Italia Medioevale e Umanistica* 19 (1976), 57–87.

———. "Philosophy and Medicine in Medieval and Renaissance Italy," in *Organism, Medicine, and Metaphysics.* Ed. S. F. Spicker. Dordrecht 1978, pp. 29–40.

———. See *Catalogus Translationum et Commentariorum.*

Krumbacher, K. *Geschichte der byzantinischen Litteratur.* 2nd ed. Munich 1897.

Kuev, M. M. "Zur Geschichte der 'Dreisprachendoktrin,'" *Byzantinobulgarica* 2 (1966), 53–65.

Die Kultur der Abtei Reichenau. Erinnerungsschrift zur zwölfhundertsten Wiederkehr des Gründungsjahres des Inselklosters 724–1924. Vols. I–II. Munich 1925: K. Preisendanz, "Aus Bücherei und Schreibstube der Reichenau," 657–83; K. Beyerle, "Das Reichenauer Verbrüderungsbuch als Quelle der Klostergeschichte," 1107–1217.

Kunze, K. *Studien zur Legende der heiligen Maria Aegyptiaca im deutschen Sprachgebiet.* Berlin 1969.

Kürbis, B. "Studia nad Kodeksem Matyldy. I. Sekwencja 'Ad celebres rex cęlice,'" *Studia Źródłoznawcze* 27 (1983), 97–112.

Kusch, H. "Die Beuroner Vetus Latina und ihre Bedeutung für die Altertumswissenschaft," *Forschungen und Fortschritte* 29 (1955), 46–57.

Kuss, H. "Orient und Okzident im geistigen Leben des mittelalterlichen Süditalien," *Geschichte in Wissenschaft und Unterricht* 18 (1967), 129–46.

Labowsky, L. *Bessarion's Library and the Biblioteca Marciana: Six Early Inventories.* Rome 1979.

Laehr, G. "Die Briefe und Prologe des Bibliothekars Anastasius, *NA* 47 (1927/28), 416–68.

Laistner, M. L. W. "Notes on Greek from the Lectures of a Ninth Century Monastery Teacher," *The Bulletin of the John Rylands Library* 7 (1923), 421–56 [also published separately].

———. "The Revival of Greek in Western Europe in the Carolingian Age," *History* 9 (1924), 177–87.

———. *Bedae Venerabilis Expositio Actuum Apostolorum et Retractio.* Cambridge, Mass., 1939.

———. "Antiochene Exegesis in Western Europe during the Middle Ages," *Harvard Theological Review* 40 (1947), 19–31.

———. *Thought and Letters in Western Europe,* A.D. 500–900. 2nd ed. London 1957.

———. *The Intellectual Heritage of the Early Middle Ages.* Ithaca 1957: "Bede as a Classical and a Patristic Scholar," 93–116 [originally in *Transactions of the Royal Historical Society* IV/16 (London 1933)]; "The Library of the Venerable Bede," 117–49 [originally in *Bede: His Life, Times, and Writings,* ed. A. H. Thompson (Oxford 1935)]; "A Ninth-Century Commentator on the Gospel according to Matthew," 216–36 [originally in *Harvard Theological Review* 20 (1927)].

Lamma, P. *Comneni e Staufer.* Vols. I–II. Rome 1955–57.

———. *Oriente e Occidente nell'alto medioevo.* Padua 1968: "Il problema dei due Imperi e dell'Italia meridionale nel giudizio delle fonti letterarie dei secoli IX e X," 231–37.

———. "Byzanz kehrt nach Italien zurück," in *Beiträge zur Geschichte Italiens im 12. Jahrhundert. Vorträge und Forschungen* Sonderband 9. Sigmaringen 1971.

Lampros, S. "'Αὐτοκρατόρων τοῦ Βυζαντίου χρυσόβουλλα καὶ χρυσᾶ γράμματα ἀναφερόμενα εἰς τὴν ἕνωσιν τῶν ἐκκλησιῶν," *Neos Hellenomnemon* 11 (1914), 94–128, 241–54, and pls. 1–6.

Lapidge, M. "The Hermeneutic Style in Tenth-Century Anglo-Latin Literature," *Anglo-Saxon England* 4 (1975), 67–111.

Lehmann, P. *Erforschung des Mittelalters.* Vol. III. Stuttgart 1960: "Von Quellen und Autoritäten irisch-lateinischer Texte," 143–48.

Lemerle, P. *Le premier humanisme byzantin. Notes et remarques sur enseignement et culture à Byzance des origines au Xᵉ siècle.* Paris 1971.

Leonardi, C. "Anastasio Bibliotecario e l'ottavo concilio ecumenico," *Studi Medievali* III/8 (1967), 59–192. Rev. by D. Lohrmann, *Quellen und Forschungen aus italienischen Archiven und Bibliotheken* 50 (1971), 420–31.

———. "L'agiografia romana nel secolo IX," in *Hagiographie, cultures et sociétés.* Paris 1981, pp. 471–89.

Levine, P. "Two Early Latin Versions of St. Gregory of Nyssa's Περὶ κατασκευῆς ἀνθρώπου," *Harvard Studies in Classical Philology* 63 (1958), 473–92.

Lewry, O. See *Boethius: His Life* . . .

Leyser, K. "The Tenth Century in Byzantine-Western Relationship," in *Relations between East and West in the Middle Ages*. Ed. D. Baker. Edinburgh 1973, pp. 29–63.

Liber Pontificalis. See L. Duchesne.

Lindberg, C. "The Transmission of Greek and Arabic Learning to the West," *Science in the Middle Ages* (1978), 52–90.

Loenertz, R.-J. "Autour du traité de fr. Barthélemy de Constantinople contre les Grecs," *Archivum Fratrum Praedicatorum* 6 (1936), 361–71.

———. "Athènes et Néopatras. Regestes et notices pour servir à l'histoire des duchés catalans (1311–1394)," *Archivum Fratrum Praedicatorum* 25 (1955), 100–212 and 428–31; 28 (1958), 5–91.

———. *Byzantina et Franco-Graeca*. Rome 1970: "Le panégyrique de S. Denys l'Aréopagite par S. Michel le Syncelle," 149–62 [originally in *AB* 68 (1950)]; "La légende parisienne de S. Denys l'Aréopagite. Sa genèse et son premier témoin," 163–83 [originally in *AB* 69 (1951)]; "Ambassadeurs grecs auprès du pape Clément VI 1348," 285–302 [originally in *Orientalis Christiana Periodica* 10 (1953)].

———. See J. M. Hoeck.

Löfstedt, B. "Zu den Glossen von Abbos 'Bella Parisiacae Urbis,'" *Studi Medievali* III/22 (1981), 261–66.

Löhneysen, W. von. *Mistra. Griechenlands Schicksal im Mittelalter*. Munich 1977.

Lohr, C. H. "Medieval Latin Aristotle Commentaries," *Traditio* 23 (1967); 24 (1968); 26–30 (1970–74), passim.

———. See *Cambridge History of Later Medieval Philosophy*.

Loomis, L. R. *Medieval Hellenism*. Lancaster, Pa. 1906.

Lo Parco, F. "Scolario-Saba. Bibliofilo Italiota, vissuto tra l'XI e il XII secolo e la Biblioteca del Monastero basiliano del SS. Salvatore di Bordonaro, presso Messina," *Atti della R. Accademia di Archeologie, Lettere e Belle Arti*, n.s., I/2 (1910).

Lowe, E. A. *Palaeographical Papers*. Ed. L. Bieler. Vols. I–II. Oxford 1972: "The Codex Bezae and Lyons," 182–86 [originally in *Journal of Theological Studies* 25 (1924)]; "A Note on the Codex Bezae," 224–28 [originally in *Bulletin of the Bezan Club* 4 (1927)]; "An Eighth-Century List of Books in a Bodleian Manuscript from Würzburg and Its Probable Relation to the Laudian Acts," 239–50; "Codex Bezae: The Date of Corrector G," 275 f. [originally in *Bulletin of the Bezan Club* 5 (1928)]; "Greek Symptoms in a Sixth-Century Manuscript of St. Augustine and in a Group of Latin Legal Manuscripts," 466–74 [originally in *Didascaliae*, Festschrift A. M. Albareda (New York 1961)].

———. See *Codices Latini Antiquiores*.

Löwe, H. "Cyrill und Methodius zwischen Byzanz und Rom," in *Gli Slavi occidentali e meridionali nell'alto medioevo*, Settimane di studio 30. Spoleto 1983, pp. 631–99.

Lundström, S. "Studien zur lateinischen Irenaeus-Übersetzung." Diss. Lund 1943.

———. *Zur Historia tripartita des Cassiodor*. Lunds Universitets Årsskrift, n.s., I/49. Lund 1952.

———. "Sprachliche Bemerkungen zur Historia tripartita des Cassiodor," *Archivum Latinitatis Medii Aevi* 23 (1953), 19–34.

———. *Übersetzungstechnische Untersuchungen auf dem Gebiete der christlichen Latinität*. Lunds Universitets Årsskrift, n.s., I/55. Lund 1955.

———. *Lexicon errorum interpretum Latinorum*. Uppsala 1983.

Luscombe, D. "Some Examples of the Use Made of the Works of the Pseudo-Dionysius by University Teachers in the Later Middle Ages," in *Les Universités à la fin du moyen âge*. Ed. J. Paquet and J. Ijsewijn. Louvain 1978, pp. 228–41.

Luzzati-Laganà, F. "Le firme greche nei documenti del Ducato di Napoli," *Studi Medievali* III/23 (1982), 729–52.

Lynch, K. M. "The Venerable Bede's Knowledge of Greek," *Traditio* 39 (1983), 432–39.

Maassen, F. *Geschichte der Quellen und der Literatur des canonischen Rechts im Abendlande*. Graz 1870.

McNally, R. E. "The 'Tres linguae sacrae' in Early Irish Bible Exegesis," *Theological Studies* 19 (New York 1958), 395–403.

McNulty, P. M. See *Le Millénaire du Mont Athos*.

Malingrey, A. M., ed. *Jean Chrysostome, Lettre d'exil à Olympias et à tous les fidèles (Quod nemo laeditur . . .)*. Paris 1964.

———. "Une ancienne version latine du texte de Jean Chrysostome *Quod nemo laeditur* . . . ," *Sacris Erudiri* 16 (1965), 320–54.

———. "La traduction latine d'un texte de Jean Chrysostome (*Quod nemo laeditur*)," *TU* 92 (1966), 248–54.

———. "La tradition manuscrite du 'De sacerdotio' de saint Jean Chrysostome à la lumière du 'vetus interpres latinus,'" in ΑΝΤΙΔΩΡΟΝ. Festschrift Maurits Geerard. Wetteren 1984, I, 27–32.

Mallardo, D. "Giovanni Diacono napoletano," *Rivista di Storia della Chiesa in Italia* 2 (1948), 317–37, and 4 (1950), 325–58.

Mango, C. "La culture grecque et l'occident au VIII⁰ siècle," in *I problemi dell'occidente nel secolo VIII*. Settimane di studio 20. Vol. II. Spoleto 1973, pp. 683–721.

Manitius, M. *Geschichte der lateinischen Literatur des Mittelalters*. Vols. I–III. Munich 1911–31.

Manselli, R. "The Legend of Barlaam and Joasaph in Byzantium in the Romance Empire," in *East and West*, n.s., 7 (1956/57), 331–40.

Marrou, H.-I. *Saint Augustin et la fin de la culture antique*. 4th ed. Paris 1958.

———. *Histoire de l'éducation dans l'antiquité*. 6th ed. Paris 1965. 1st ed. rev. by M. L. W. Laistner, *Gnomon* 21 (1949), 97–101.

Martellotti, G. "Osservazioni sul carattere orale del primo insegnamento del greco nell'Italia umanistica," *Annali dell'Istituto Universitario Orientale di Napoli*, Sez. Linguistica 1 (1959), 59–64.

Marti, H. *Übersetzer der Augustin-Zeit. Interpretation von Selbstzeugnissen*. Munich 1974.

Masai, F. *Pléthon et le Platonisme de Mistra*. Paris 1956.

Masi, M., ed. See *Boethius and the Liberal Arts*.

Matrod, H. "Les Frères Mineurs et l'étude du grec au XIII⁰ siècle," *Études franciscaines* 35 (1923), 474–98.

Matthews, J. See *Boethius: His Life . . .*

Mazal, O. "Spuren einer 'Missa graeca' im Benediktinerstift Kremsmünster," *Biblos* 29 (1980), 159–65.

———. *Byzanz und das Abendland* [exhibition catalogue, Vienna]. Graz 1981. Rev. by W. Berschin, *Mittellateinisches Jahrbuch* 18 (1983), 293 f.

Meersseman, G. G. *Der Hymnos Akathistos im Abendland*. Vols. I–II. Fribourg 1958–60. Rev. by W. Bulst, *BZ* 55 (1962), 324–26.

Meier, Gabriel. "Geschichte der Schule von St. Gallen im Mittelalter," *Jahrbuch für Schweiz. Geschichte* 10 (1885), 35–127.

Meisen, K. *Nikolauskult und Nikolausbrauch im Abendlande*. Düsseldorf 1931.

Mercati, G. *Notizie di Procoro e Demetrio Cidone, Manuele Caleca e Teodoro Meliteniota ed altri appunti per la storia della teologie e della letteratura bizantina del secolo XIV*. Rome 1931.

———. *Ultimi Contributi alla Storia degli Umanisti*. Vols. I–II. Rome 1939.

———. *Se la versione dall'ebraico del codice veneto greco VII sia di Simone Atumano arcivescovo di Tebe*. Rome 1916.

Merlette, B. "Écoles et bibliothèques, à Laon, du déclin de l'antiquité au développement de l'Université," *Actes du 95⁰ Congrès national des sociétés savantes (Reims 1970), Section de philologie et d'histoire jusqu'à 1610*. Vol. I. Paris 1975, pp. 21–53.

Messerer, W. *Der Bamberger Domschatz in seinem Bestande bis zum Ende der Hohenstaufen-Zeit*. Munich 1952.

Michel, A. *Humbert und Kerullarios*. Vols. I–II. Paderborn 1924–30.

———. "Sprache und Schisma," in *Festschrift Kardinal Faulhaber*. Munich 1949, pp. 37–69.

———. "Die griechischen Klostersiedlungen zu Rom bis zur Mitte des 11. Jahrhunderts," *Ostkirchliche Studien* 1 (1952), 145–73.

Miklosich, F., and I. Müller. *Acta et diplomata graeca medii aevi*, vol. 3: *Acta et diplomata graeca res graecas italasque illustrantia*. Vienna 1865.

Le Millénaire du Mont Athos 963–1963. Vol. I. Chevetogne 1963: F. Dölger, "Kaiser und Mönch auf dem Athos," 145–48; J. Leclercq, "L'érémitisme en occident jusqu'à l'an mil," 161–80; P. M. McNulty and B. Hamilton, "Orientale Lumen et Magistra Latinitas: Greek Influences on Western Monasticism (900–1100), 181–216; A. Pertusi, "Monasteri e monaci italiani all'Athos nell'alto medioevo," 217–51. Vol. II. Chevetogne/Venice 1964: J. Leclercq, "Les relations entre le monachisme oriental et le monachisme occidental dans le haut moyen âge," 49–80.

Miller, M. E. "Glossaire grec-latin de la Bibliothéque de Laon," *Notices et Extraits de la Bibliothèque Nationale* 29/2 (Paris 1880), 1–230.

The Mind of Eriugena: Papers of a Colloquium. Ed. J. J. O'Meara and L. Bieler. Dublin 1973: I. P. Sheldon-Williams, "Eriugena's Greek Sources," 1–14; R. Roques, "Traduction ou interprétation? Brèves remarques sur Jean Scot traducteur de Denys," 59–76; P. Meyvaert, "Eriugena's Translation of the *Ad Thalassium* of Maximus: Preliminaries to an Edition of this Work," 78–88; J. Barbet, "La Tradition du texte latin de la Hiérarchie céleste dans les manuscrits des *Expositiones in Hierarchiam caelestem*," 89–97; G. Schrimpf, "Zur Frage der Authentizität unserer Texte von Johannes Scottus' 'Annotationes in Martianum'" 125–38.

Minio-Paluello, L. *Opuscula*. Amsterdam 1972: "Guglielmo di Moerbeke traduttore della *Poetica* di Aristotele (1278)," 40–56 [originally in *Rivista di Filosofia Neo-Scolastica* 39 (1947)]; "Henri Aristippe, Guillaume de Moerbeke et les traductions latines médiévales des 'Météorologiques' et du 'De Generatione et Corruptione' d'Aristote," 57–86 [originally in *Revue Philosophique de Louvain* 45 (1947)]; "Iacobus Veneticus Grecus: Canonist and Translator of Aristotle," 189–228 [originally in *Traditio* 8 (1952)]; "A Latin Commentary (? translated by Boethius) on the 'Prior Analytics,' and Its Greek Sources," 347–56 [originally in *Journal of Historical Studies* 77 (1957)]; "Giacomo Veneto e l'Aristotelismo Latino," 565–86 [originally in *Venezia e l'Oriente fra tardo Medioevo e Rinascimento*, Florence 1966].

———. See *Aristoteles latinus*.

———. See *La Scuola nell'Occidente*.

Mioni, E. "Le 'Vitae Patrum' nella traduzione di Ambrogio Traversari," *Aevum* 24 (1950), 319–31.

Mohler, L. *Kardinal Bessarion als Theologe, Humanist und Staatsmann*. Vols. I–III. Paderborn 1923–42.

Mohrmann, C. "Les emprunts grecs dans la latinité chrétienne," *Vigiliae Christianae* 4 (1950), 193–211.

Mone, F. J. *Lateinische und griechische Messen*. Frankfurt 1850.

Montfaucon, B. de. *Palaeographia Graeca*. Paris 1708.

Morano, M. "Il manoscritto Chigiano di Nemesio," *Rendiconti dell'Istituto Lombardo* 105 (1971), 621–35.

Morin, G. "L'opuscule perdu du soi-disant Hégésippe sur les Machabées," *RB* 31 (1914/19), 83–91.

Muckle, J. T. "Greek Works Translated Directly into Latin before 1350," *Mediaeval Studies* 4 (1942), 33–42; 5 (1943), 102–14.

Mühmelt, M. *Griechische Grammatik in der Vergilerklärung*. Munich 1965.

Muller, J.-C. "Linguistisches aus der Echternacher Klosterbibliothek," *Hémecht* 3 (Luxembourg 1983), 381–403.

Murdoch, J. E. "Euclides graeco-latinus: A Hitherto Unknown Mediaeval Latin Translation of the 'Elements' Made Directly from the Greek," *Harvard Studies in Classical Philology* 71 (1966), 249–302.

Nardi, B. *Saggi sull'aristotelismo padovano dal secolo XIV al XVI*. Florence 1958.

Narr, G., ed. *Griechisch und Romanisch*. Tübingen 1971: E. Coseriu, "Das Problem des griechischen Einflusses auf das Vulgärlatein," 1–15; W. Schulze, "Graeca Latina," 17–52 [originally separately printed, Göttingen 1901]; F. Pfister, "Vulgärlatein und Vulgärgriechisch," 151–164 [originally in *Rheinisches Museum*, n.s., 67 (1912)].

Newald, R. *Nachleben des antiken Geistes im Abendland bis zum Beginn des Humanismus*. Tübingen 1960.

Nicol, D. M. See *Orthodox Churches* . . .

Nida, E. A. Toward a Science of Translating, with Special Reference to Principles and Procedures Involved in Bible Translating. Leiden 1964.

Niese, H. "Zur Geschichte des geistigen Lebens am Hofe Kaiser Friedrichs II.," *Historische Zeitschrift* 108 (1912), 473–540 [also published separately, Darmstadt 1967].

Nolan, E., and S. A. Hirsch. *The Greek Grammar of Roger Bacon and a Fragment of His Hebrew Grammar.* Cambridge 1902. Rev. by J. L. Heiberg, *BZ* 12 (1903), 343–47.

Nolhac, P. de. *Les études grecques de Pétrarque.* Comptes rendus de l'Académie des Inscriptions et Belles Lettres. Paris 1888.

———. *Pétrarque et l'humanisme.* Vols. I–II. Paris 1907.

Norden, E. *Die antike Kunstprosa.* 2nd ed. Vols. I–II. Leipzig 1909.

Nyssen, W. *Das Zeugnis des Bildes im frühen Byzanz.* Freiburg 1962.

Occidente et Orient au Xe siècle. Actes du IXe congrès de la société des Historiens médiévistes de l'Enseignement Supérieur Public. Paris 1979.

Ohnsorge, W. *Das Zweikaiserproblem im früheren Mittelalter.* Hildesheim 1947. Rev. by G. Ostrogorsky, *BZ* 46 (1953), 153–58.

———. *Abendland und Byzanz. Gesammelte Aufsätze* [I] *zur Geschichte der byzantinisch-abendländischen Beziehungen und des Kaisertums.* Darmstadt 1958: "Das Kaiserbündnis von 842–844 gegen die Sarazenen. Datum, Inhalt und politische Bedeutung des 'Kaiserbriefes aus St. Denis,'" 131–83 [originally in *Archiv für Diplomatik* 1 (1955)]; "Drei Deperdita der byzantinischen Kaiserkanzlei und die Frankenadressen im Zeremonienbuch des Konstantinos Porphyrogennetos," 227–54 [originally in *BZ* 45 (1952)]; "Das nach Goslar gelangte Auslandsschreiben des Konstantinos IX. Monomachos für Kaiser Heinrich III. von 1049," 317–32 [originally in *Braunschweigisches Jahrbuch* 32 (1951)]; "Eine Rotulus-Bulle des Kaisers Michael VI. Stratiotikos von 1056," 333–41 [originally in *BZ* 46 (1953)]; "Die Byzanzreise des Erzbischofs Gebhard von Salzburg und das päpstliche Schisma im Jahre 1062," 342–63 [originally in *Historisches Jahrbuch* 75 (1956)].

———. *Konstantinopel und der Okzident. Gesammelte Aufsätze* [II]. Darmstadt 1966.

———. *Ost-Rom und der Westen. Gesammelte Aufsätze* [III] *zur Geschichte der byzantinisch-abendländischen Beziehungen und des Kaisertums.* Darmstadt 1983.

———. "Der griechische Papstpapyrus aus Erfurt," in ΧΑΛΙΚΕΣ. *Festgabe für die Teilnehmer am XI. Internationalen Byzantinistenkongreß.* Ed. H. G. Beck. Munich 1958, pp. 9–37.

Olivieri, L. "L'aristotelismo veneto tra Aristotele arabo-latino e greco-latino," *Scrivium* 5 (1984), 52–73.

Omont, G. "La messe grecque de Saint Denys au moyen-âge," *Études d'histoire du moyen âge dédiées à G. Monod.* Paris 1896, pp. 177–85.

Omont, H. "Le Typicon de Saint-Nicolas di Casole près d'Otrante. Notice du Ms. C.III.17 de Turin," *Revue des études grecques* 3 (1890), 381–91.

Opelt, I. "Zur Übersetzungstechnik Gerhards von Cremona," *Glotta* 38 (1960), 135–70.

———. "Die Essener 'Missa greca' der liturgischen Handschrift Düsseldorf D2," *Jahrbuch der Österr. Byzantinistik* 23 (1974), 77–88.

The Orthodox Churches and the West. Ed. D. Baker. Oxford 1976: J. M. Petersen, "Did Gregory the Great Know Greek?" 121–34; D. M. Nichol, "The Papal Scandal," 141–68; B. M. Bolton, "A Mission to the Orthodox? The Cistercians in Romania," 169–81; D. J. Geanakoplos, "Bonaventura, the Two Mendicant Orders and the Greeks at the Council of Lyons," 183–211; K. D. Hill, "Robert Grosseteste and His Work of Greek Translation," 213–22; M. Heppell, "New Light on the Visit of Grigori Tsamblak to the Council of Constance," 223–29.

Paléographie Musicale. Vol. XIV: *Le Codex 10673 de la Bibliothèque Vaticane, Fonds latin (XIe siècle). Graduel bénéventain.* Ed. J. Gajard [and R.-J. Hesbert]. Tournai 1931.

Palma, M. "Antigrafo/apografo. La formazione del testo latino degli Atti del Concilio costantinopolitano dell'869–70," in *Atti del Convegno Internazionale Il libro e il testo.* Ed. C. Questa and R. Raffaelli. Urbino 1984, pp. 171–94.

Paravicini Bagliani, A. "La provenienza 'angioina' dei codici greci della biblioteca di Bonifacio VIII," *Italia Medioevale e Umanistica* 26 (1983), 27–69.

Parlangèli, O. "Testi siciliani in caratteri greci," *Bolletino del Centro di Studi Filologici e Linguistici Siciliani* 7 [Saggi Li Gotti 2] (1962), 464–68.

———. "La predica salentina in caratteri greci," in *Romanica*. Festschrift Gerhard Rohlfs. Halle/Saale 1958, pp. 336–60.

Peeters, P. "Une vie grecque du pape S. Martin I.," *AB* 51 (1933), 225–62.

———. *Recherches d'histoire et de philologie orientales* 2. Brussels 1951: "Erudits et polyglottes d'autrefois," 5–22 [originally in *Bulletin de la Classe des Lettres de l'Académie R. de Belgique* V/21 (1935)].

Perels, E. *Papst Nikolaus I. und Anastasius Bibliothecarius*. Berlin 1920.

Peri, V. "Βιργύλιος = Sapientissimus. Riflessi culturali latino-greci nell'agiografia bizantina," *Italia Medioevale e Umanistica* 19 (1976), 29–40.

Pertusi, A. "La scoperta di Euripide nel primo Umanesimo," *Italia Medioevale e Umanistica* 3 (1960), 101–52.

———. "Bisanzio e l'irradiazione della sua civiltà in occidente nell'alto medioevo," in *Centri e vie di irradiazione della civiltà nell'alto medievo*. Spoleto 1964, pp. 75–133.

———. *Leonzio Pilato fra Petrarca e Bocaccio. Le sue versioni omeriche negli autografi di Venezia e la cultura greca del primo Umanesimo*. Venice/Rome 1964.

———. "Leonzio Pilato e la tradizione di cultura italo-greca," *Byzantino-Sicula* 2 (Palermo 1966), 66–84.

———. "Cultura greco-bizantina nel trado medioevo nelle Venezie e suoi echi in Dante," *Atti del Convegno di Studi 'Dante e la cultura veneta.'* Florence 1966, pp. 157–97.

———. "ΕΡΩΤΗΜΑΤΑ. Per la storia e le fonti delle prime grammatiche greche a stampa," *Italia Medioevale e Umanistica* 5 (1962), 321–51.

———. "Venezia e Bisanzio: 1000–1204," *Dumbarton Oaks Papers* 33 (1979), 1–22.

———. "L'umanesimo greco dalla fine del secolo XIV agli inizi del secolo XVI," in *Storia della cultura veneta*. Vol. III/1. Vicenza 1980, pp. 177–264.

———. See *La Chiesa greca in Italia*.

Pesenti, G. "La scuola di greco a Firenze nel primo Rinascimento," *Atene e Roma* 12 (1931), 84–89.

Petersen, J. M. See *Orthodox Churches . . .*

Petitmengin, P., et al. *Pélagie la pénitente. Métamorphoses d'une légende*. Vol. I. Paris 1981.

Petrucci, A. "Virgilio nella cultura scritta romana," in *Virgilio e noi*, Pubblicazioni dell'Istituto di Filologia Classica e Medievale 74. Genoa 1981, pp. 51–72.

Petschenig, M. "Ein griechisch-lateinisches Glossar des achten Jahrhunderts, (St. Paul i. Lavanttal, Stiftsbibliothek)," *Wiener Studien* 5 (1883), 159–163.

Pfeiffer, R. *History of Classical Scholarship*. Vol. I: *From the Beginnings to the End of the Hellenistic Age*. Oxford 1968. Vol. II: *From 1300 to 1850*. Oxford 1976.

Philippart, G. "Jean èvêque d'Arezzo (IXᵉ s.), auteur du 'De Assumptione' de Reichenau," *AB* 92 (1974), 345 f.

Pinborg, J. See *Cambridge History of Later Medieval Philosophy*.

Pingree, D. See *Boethius: His Life . . .*

Pintaudi, R., ed. *Marsilio Ficino, Lessico greco-latino. Laur. Ashb. 1439*. Rome 1977.

Pizzani, U. See *Boethius and the Liberal Arts*.

Plato latinus. Vol. I: *Meno interprete Henrico Aristippo*. Ed. V. Kordeuter and C. Labowsky. London 1940. Vol. II: *Phaedo interprete Henrico Aristippo*. Ed. L. Minio-Paluello and H. J. Drossaart Lulofs. 1950. Vol. III: *Parmenides . . . necnon Procli Commentarium in Parmenidem . . . interprete Guillelmo de Moerbeka*. Ed. R. Klibansky and C. Labowsky. 1953. Vol. IV: *Timaeus a Calcidio translatus commentarioque instructus*. Ed. J. H. Waszink. London/Leiden 1962.

Plezia, M., ed. "Aristotelis qui ferebatur Liver De Pomo. Versio latina vetusta interprete Manfredo duce," *Eos* 47 (Breslau 1954), 191–217.

Pralle, L. "Der Gebrauch griechischer Texte in der römischen Liturgie. Nach Mitteilungen von Liturgikern des 16. Jahrhunderts," *Theologische Quartalschrift* 128 (1948), 385–97.

———. "Ein griechischer Gottesdienst in mittelalterlichen Würzburg," *Würzburger Diözesangeschichtsblätter* 16/17 (1955), 359–67.

Preisendanz, K. "Die Reichenauer Kreuzreliquie," *Die Pyramide* 15 (1926), 201.

Pricocco, S. "Sidonio Apollinare traduttore della Vita di Apollonio di Tiana di Filostrato," *Nuovo Didaskaleion* 15 (1965), 73–98.

Pringsheim, F. "Griechischer Einfluß auf das römische Recht," *Bolletino dell'Istituto di Diritto Romano* 63 (1960), 1–17.

Prinz, O. "Zum Einfluß des Griechischen auf den Wortschatz des Mittellateins," *Festschrift Bernhard Bischoff*. Stuttgart 1971, pp. 1–15.

——. "Mittellateinische Wortneubildungen, ihre Entwicklungstendenzen und ihre Triebkräfte," *Philologus* 122 (1978), 249–75.

——. "Bemerkungen zum Wortschatz der lateinischen Übersetzung des Pseudo-Methodios," in *Variorum munera florum*. Festschrift Hans F. Haefele. Sigmaringen 1985, pp. 17–22.

——. "Eine frühe abendländische Aktualisierung der lateinischen Übersetzung des Pseudo-Methodios," *DA* 41 (1985), 1–23.

Pritchet, C. D., ed. *Iohannis Alexandrini Commentaria in librum De sectis Galeni*. Leiden 1982 (rev. by M. Th. d'Alverny, in *Scriptorium* 38 [1984], 361–70.

Puccioni, G. *La fortuna medievale della origo gentis Romanae*. Messina/Florence 1958.

——. "A proposito di cultura greca nell'occidente latino in epoca medievale," *Atene e Roma* (1978), 93–100.

Puniet, P. de. "Formulaire grec de l'épiphanie dans une traduction latine ancienne," *RB* 29 (1912), 29–46.

Rabbow, P. "Zur Geschichte des urkundlichen Sinns," *Historische Zeitschrift* 126 (1922), 58–79.

Rahlfs, A. *Verzeichnis der griechischen Handschriften des Alten Testaments*. Nachrichten Göttingen, Beiheft 1914.

Reichardt, A. *Der Codex Boernerianus der Briefe des Apostels Paulus (Msc. Dresd. A 145^b) in Lichtdruck nachgebildet*. Leipzig 1909.

Reichenkron, G. "Zu den ersten Beziehungen zwischen Byzanz und den ältesten französischen Chanson de Geste," *Südostforschungen* 15 (1956), 160–66.

Reisdoerfer, J. "Graecum est, non legitur?" *Nos Cahiers* 2 (Luxembourg 1982), 71–77.

Rentschler, M. "Griechische Kultur und Byzanz im Urteil westlicher Autoren des 10. Jahrhunderts," *Saeculum* 29 (1978), 324–455.

——. *Liudprand von Cremona. Eine Studie zum ost-westlichen Kulturgefälle im Mittelalter*. Frankfurt 1981.

Renucci, P. *Dante disciple et juge du monde gréco-latin*. Paris 1954.

Repertorium der griechischen Kopisten 800–1600. Vol. I: E. Gamillschegg, H. Hunger, and D. Harlfinger, *Handschriften aus den Bibliotheken Großbritanniens*. Vienna 1981.

Rettig, H. C. M. *Antiquissimus Quatuor Evangeliorum Canonicorum Codex Sangallensis Graeco-Latinus interlinearis*. Zurich 1836.

Ricci, P. G. "La prima cattedra di greco in Firenze," *Rinascimento* 3 (1952), 159–65.

Richard, J. "La vogue de l'Orient dans la littérature occidentale du moyen âge," *Mélanges René Crozet*. Vol. I. Poitiers 1966, pp. 557–61.

——. *La Papauté et les missions d'Orient au Moyen Âge (XIIIe–XVe)*. Rome 1977.

Riché, P. *Éducation et culture dans l'occident barbare, VIe–VIIIe*. Paris 1962.

Richesses et déficiences des anciens psautiers latins. Collectanea Biblica Latina 13. Rome 1959: J. Gribomont and A. Thibaut, "Méthode et esprit des traducteurs du psautier grec," 51–105; A. Thibaut, "La révision hexaplaire de Saint Jérôme," 107–49.

Richter, H. E. *Übersetzer und Übersetzungen in der römischen Literatur*. Diss. Erlangen. Coburg 1938.

Riedinger, R. "Aus den Akten der Lateran-Synode von 649," *BZ* 69 (1976), 17–38.

——. "Grammatiker-Gelehrsamkeit in den Akten der Lateran-Synode von 649," *Jahrbuch der Österr. Byzantinistik* 25 (1976), 57–61.

——. "Griechische Konzilsakten auf dem Wege ins lateinische Mittelalter," *Annuarium Historiae Conciliorum* 9 (1977), 253–301.

——. *Lateinische Übersetzungen griechischer Häretikertexte des siebenten Jahrhunderts*. SB Vienna 1979.

——. *Die Präsenz- und Subskriptionslisten des VI. oekumenischen Konzils (680/81) und der Papyrus Vind.G.3*. Abh. Munich, n.s., 85 (1979).

——. "Die Epistula synodica des Sophronios von Jerusalem im Codex Parisinus BN Graecus 1115," *Byzantiaka* 2 (1982), 143–54.

——. "Kuriale und Unziale in der lateinischen Überlieferung der Akten des VI.

oekumenischen Konzils (680/81) (CPG 9416–9442)," in ANTIΔΩPON. Festschrift Maurits Geerard. Wetteren 1984, I, 145–67.

———. "Die Lateranakten von 649. Ein Werk der Byzantiner um Maximos Homologetes," in *Byzantina* 13. Festschrift Johannes Karayannopulos. Thessalonike 1985, pp. 519–34.

———. See *Acta Conciliorum Oecumenicorum.*

Roberg, B. *Die Union zwischen der griechischen und der lateinischen Kirche auf dem II. Konzil von Lyon (1274).* Bonn 1964.

———. "Die Tartaren auf dem 2. Konzil von Lyon 1274," *Annuarium Historiae Conciliorum* 5 (1973), 241–302.

———. "Das 'orientalische Problem' auf dem Lugdunense II," *Annuarium Historiae Conciliorum* 9 (1977), 43–66.

Robert Grosseteste, Scholar and Bishop: Essays in Commemoration of the Seventh Centenary of His Death. Ed. D. A. Callus. Oxford 1955: D. A. Callus, "Robert Grosseteste as Scholar," 1–69; B. Smalley, "The Biblical Scholar," 70–97; R. W. Hunt, "The Library of Robert Grosseteste," 121–45.

Roger, M. *L'enseignement des lettres classiques d'Ausone à Alcuin.* Paris 1905.

Rohlfs, G. *Scavi linguistici nella Magna Grecia.* Halle/Rome 1933.

———. *Romanische Sprachgeographie.* Munich 1971: "Griechische Einflüsse," 89–96.

Roncaglia, M. "Il fratri minori e lo studio delle lingue orientali nel secolo XIII," *Studi Francescani* III/25 (1953), 169–84.

———. *Georges Bardanes, métropolite de Corfou, et Barthélémy de l'Ordre franciscain.* Studi e Testi Francescani 4. Rome 1953.

———. *Les frères mineurs et l'église grecque orthodoxe au XIIIe siècle (1231–1274).* Biblioteca Bio-Bibliografica della Terra Santa e dell'Oriente Francescano IV/2. Cairo 1954.

Rönsch, H. *Itala und Vulgata. Das Sprachidiom der urchristlichen Vulgata unter Berücksichtigung der römischen Volkssprache.* 2nd ed. Marburg/Lahn 1985.

Rose, V. *Anecdota Graeca et Graecolatina.* Vols. I–II. Berlin 1864–70.

———. "Die Lücke im Diogenes Laërtius und der alte Übersetzer," *Hermes* 1 (1866), 367–97.

———. "Über die griechischen Commentare zur Ethik des Aristoteles," *Hermes,* 5 (1871), 61–113.

———. "Über die Medicina Plinii," *Hermes* 8 (1874), 18–66.

———. "Ptolemaeus und die Schule von Toledo," *Hermes* 8 (1874), 327–49.

Rüdiger, H. "Die Wiederentdeckung der antiken Literatur im Zeitalter der Renaissance," in *Geschichte der Textüberlieferung der antiken und mittelalterlichen Literatur,* Vol. I. Zurich 1961, pp. 511–90.

Runciman, S. *The Last Byzantine Renaissance.* Cambridge 1970.

Russo, F. "Relazioni Culturali tra la Calabria e l'Oriente Bizantino nel Medioevo," *Bolletino della Badia greca di Grottaferrata,* n.s., 7 (1953), 49–64.

———. "Attività artistico-culturale del monachismo calabro-greco anteriormente all'epoca normanna," *Atti dello VIII Congresso Internazionale di Studi Bizantini Palermo 1951.* Vol. I. Rome 1953, pp. 463–75.

———. See *La Chiesa greca in Italia.*

Saalfeld, A. *Index graecorum vocabulorum in linguam latinam translatorum.* Berlin 1874.

Sabbadini, R. *Le scoperte dei codici latini e greci ne'secoli XIV e XV.* Vols. I–II. Florence 1905–14.

———. *Il metodo degli umanisti.* Florence 1920.

———. *Guariniana.* Ed. M. Sancipriano. Turin 1964.

Salonius, A. H. *Passio S. Perpetuae. Kritische Bemerkungen mit besonderer Berücksichtigung der griechisch-lateinischen Überlieferung des Textes.* Översikt av Finska Vetenskaps-Societetens Förhandlingar 63, 1920–21. Helsinki 1921.

Sandys, J. E. *A History of Classical Scholarship.* Vol. I. 3rd ed. Cambridge 1921. 1st ed rev. by L. Traube, *Deutsche Literaturzeitung* 25 (1904), cols. 133–36.

Sansterre, J.-M. *Les moines grecs et orientaux à Rome aux époques byzantines et caroligiennes (milieu du VIe siècle–fin du IXe siècle).* Vols. I–II. Brussels 1983.

Sarton, G. *Introduction to the History of Science.* Vols. I–V. 2nd ed. Baltimore 1947–50.

Scaduto, M. *Il monachesimo basiliano nella Sicilia medievale.* Rome 1947.

Schanz, M., C. Hosius, and G. Krüger. *Geschichte der römischen Litteratur.* Vol. IV/1 (2nd ed.)–2. Munich 1914–20.

Schermann, T. *Propheten- und Apostellegenden nebst Jüngerkatalogen des Dorotheus und verwandter Texte.* TU 31/3. Leipzig 1907.

Schipperges, H. *Die Assimilation der arabischen Medizin durch das lateinische Mittelalter.* Wiesbaden 1964.

Schlumberger, G. *Un empereur byzantin au dixième siècle, Nicéphore Phocas.* Paris 1890.

Schmitt, C. B. "Theophrastus in the Middle Ages," *Viator* 2 (1971), 251–70.

Schmitt, W. O. "Lateinischer und griechischer 'Donatus.' Ein Beitrag zur Geschichte der Griechischstudien im lateinischen Mittelalter," *Philologus* 123 (1979), 97–108.

———. "Donati Graeci. Zum Griechischstudium der italienischen Humanisten," *Actes de la XIIe conférence internationale d'études classiques . . . 1972.* Bucharest/Amsterdam 1975, pp. 205–13.

Schneider, B. *Die mittelalterlichen griechisch-lateinischen Übersetzungen der aristotelischen Rhetorik.* Berlin/New York 1971.

Schneider, H. *Die altlateinischen biblischen Cantica.* Beuron 1938.

———. "Die biblischen Oden im Mittelalter," *Biblica* 30 (1949), 479–500.

Schneider, J. "Graecizare, latinizare und verwandte Verben im mittelalterlichen Latein," in *Griechenland-Byzanz-Europa.* Ed. J. Herrmann, H. Köpstein, and R. Müller. Berlin 1985, pp. 142–52.

Schramm, P. E., and F. Mütherich. *Denkmale der deutschen Könige und Kaiser.* Munich 1962.

Schreiner, P. "Eine griechische Grabinschrift aus dem Jahre 1186 in Corridonia," *Jahrbuch der österr. Byzantinistik* 20 (1971), 149–60.

Schrimpf, G. *Die Axiomenschrift des Boethius (De hebdomadibus) als philosophisches Lehrbuch des Mittelalters.* Leiden 1966.

Schulze, G. [W.]. *Orthographica et Graeca Latina.* 2nd ed. Rome 1958.

Schwartz, E. "Zweisprachigkeit in den Konzilsakten," *Philologus* 88 (1933), 245–53.

———. "Die Kanonessammlungen der alten Reichskirche," *Zeitschrift für Rechtsgeschichte,* Kan. Abt. 25 (1936), 1–114.

———. See *Acta Conciliorum Oecumenicorum.*

Schwarz, W. *Principles and Problems of Biblical Translation: Some Reformation Controversies and Their Background.* Cambridge 1955.

Schweinfurth, P. *Die byzantinische Form.* Berlin 1943.

La Scuola nell'Occidente latino dell'Alto Medioevo. Spoleto 1972: A. Guillou, "L'école dans l'Italie byzantine," 291–311; É. Jeauneau, "Les écoles de Laon et d'Auxerre au IXe siècle," 495–522; H. Bloch, "Monte Cassino's Teachers and Library in the High Middle Ages," 563–605; G. Baader, "Die Anfänge der medizinischen Ausbildung im Abendland bis 1100," 669–718; L. Minio-Paluello, "Nuovi impulsi allo studio della logica: la seconda fase della riscoperta di Aristotele e di Boezio," 743–66; J. Châtillon, "Les écoles de Chartres et de Saint-Victor," 795–839.

Seidel, I. *Byzanz im Spiegel der literarischen Entwicklung Frankreichs im 12. Jahrhundert.* Diss. Freiburg 1976. Frankfurt/Bern/Las Vegas 1977.

Seigel, E. *Rhetoric and Philosophy in Renaissance Humanism.* Princeton 1969.

Setton, K. M. *Catalan Domination of Athens 1311–1388.* Cambridge, Mass., 1948.

———. "The Byzantine Background to the Italian Renaissance," *Proceedings of the American Philosophical Society* 100 (1956), 1–76.

———. *The Papacy and the Levant (1204–1571).* Vol. I. Philadelphia 1976.

Shanzer, D. R. "'Me quoque excellentior': Boethius' 'De consolatione' 4, 6, 38," *Classical Quarterly* 33 (1983), 277–83.

Sherrard, P. *The Greek East and the Latin West: A Study in the Christian Tradition.* London 1959.

———. *Athos.* Olten/Lausanne/Freiburg 1959.

Shiel, J. "Boethius' Commentaries on Aristotle," *Mediaeval and Renaissance Studies* 4 (1958), 217–44.

———. "Boethius the Hellenist," *History Today* 14 (1964), 478–86.

———. "A Recent Discovery: Boethius' Notes on the Prior Analytics," *Vivarium* 20 (1982), 128–41.

————. "A Set of Greek Reference Signs in the Florentine Ms. of Boethius' Translation of the Prior Analytics (B.N. Conv. Soppr. J. VI. 34)," *Scriptorium* 38 (1984), 327–42.

Sicherl, M. "Platonismus und Textüberlieferung," *Jahrbuch der Österr. Byzantinischen Gesellschaft* 15 (1966), 201–29.

————. *Johannes Cuno. Ein Wegbereiter des Griechischen in Deutschland.* Heidelberg 1978.

Sieben, H.-J. "Die früh- und hochmittelalterliche Konzilsidee im Kontext der *filioque*-Kontroverse," *Traditio* 35 (1979), 173–207.

Siegmund, A. *Die Überlieferung der griechischen christlichen Literatur in der lateinischen Kirche bis zum zwölften Jahrhundert.* Munich-Pasing 1949. Rev. by F. Dölger, *DA* 8 (1950–51), 522–24.

Silverstein, T. "Hermann of Carinthia and Greek: A Problem of the 'New Science' of the Twelfth Century," in *Medioevo e Rinascimento.* Festschrift Bruno Nardi. Florence 1955, pp. 681–99.

————. *Visio Sancti Pauli: The History of the Apocalypse in Latin together with Nine Texts.* London 1935.

————. *Visiones et revelaciones Sancti Pauli. Una nuova tradizione di testi latini nel Medio Evo,* Accademia Nazionale dei Lincei anno 371, 1974, quaderno 188. Rome 1974.

————. "The Vision of Saint Paul: New Links and Patterns in the Western Tradition," *AHDL* 26 (1959), 199–248. Rev. by J. van der Straeten, *AB* 78 (1960), 453 f.

Smalley, B. *The Study of the Bible in the Middle Ages.* 2nd ed. Oxford 1952.

Sottili, A. "Humanistische Neuverwendung mittelalterlicher Übersetzungen. Zum mittelalterlichen und humanistischen Fortleben des Johannes Climacus," in *Die Rezeption der Antike.* Ed. A. Buck. Hamburg 1981, pp. 165–85.

Soudek, J. "Leonardo Bruni and His Public: A Statistical and Interpretive Study of His Annotated Latin Version of the (Pseudo-)Aristotelian Economics," *Studies in Medieval and Renaissance History* 5 (1968), 49–136.

Souter, A. "The Anonymous Latin Translation of Origen on St. Matthew . . . ," *Journal of Theological Studies* 35 (1934), 63–66.

Soyter, G. "Die byzantinischen Einflüsse auf die Kultur des mittelalterlichen Deutschland," *Vierteljahresschrift für Südosteuropa* 5 (1941), 153–72.

Speyer, W. "Angebliche Übersetzungen des heidnischen und christlichen Altertums," *Jahrbuch für Antike und Christentum* 11/12 (1968/69), 26–41.

Staats, R. *Theologie der Reichskrone. Ottonische "Renovatio imperii" im Spiegel einer Insignie.* Stuttgart 1976: "Politische und kulturelle Beziehungen der Ottonen zu Byzanz," pp. 114 f.

Stammler, W., and K. Langosch. *Die deutsche Literatur des Mittelalters. Verfasserlexikon.* Vols. I–V. Berlin/Leipzig 1933–55. 2nd ed. by K. Ruh. Berlin/New York 1978 ff.

Steel, C., ed. *Proclus. Commentaire sur le Parménide de Platon. Traduction de Guillaume de Moerbeke.* Vol. I. Louvain 1982.

Steenberghen, F. van. *Aristotle in the West: The Origins of Latin Aristotelianism.* Louvain 1955.

Steffens, F. *Lateinische Paläographie.* 2nd ed. Berlin/Leipzig 1929.

Steinacker, H. "Die römische Kirche und die griechischen Sprachkenntnisse des Frümittelalters," *Mitteilungen des österr. Instituts für Geschichtsforschung* 62 (1954), 28–66.

Steinschneider, M. *Die hebräischen Übersetzungen des Mittelalters und die Juden als Dolmetscher.* Berlin 1893.

————. *Die arabischen Übersetzungen aus dem Griechischen.* Leipzig 1897.

————. *Die europäischen Übersetzungen aus dem Arabischen bis Mitte des 17. Jahrhunderts I–II.* SB Vienna 149–51 (1905–6).

Stephens, G. R. "The Knowledge of Greek in England in the Middle Ages." Diss. Philadelphia 1933.

Stern, L. C. "Über die irische Handschrift in St. Paul," *Zeitschrift für celtische Philologie* 6 (1908), 546–55.

Stichel, R. "To EYPMAION. Ein süditalienisches Zeugnis zur Terminologie der griechischen Schrift," *Jahrbuch der österr. Byzantinistik* 26 (1977), 185–92.

Stinger, C. L. *Humanism and the Church Fathers: Ambrogio Traversari (1386–1439) and Christian Antiquity in the Italian Renaissance.* Albany, N.Y., 1977.

Stokes, G. T. "Greek in Gaul and Western Europe down to A.D. 700," *Proceedings of the R. Irish Academy* III/2 (1891–93), 177–86.

———. "The Knowledge of Greek in Ireland between A.D. 500 and 900," *Proceedings of the R. Irish Academy* III/2 (1891–93), 187–202.

Strittmatter, A. "'Missa Grecorum,' 'Missa Sancti Iohannis Crisostomi': The Oldest Latin Version Known of the Byzantine Liturgies of St. Basil and St. John Chrysostom," *Traditio* 1 (1943), 79–137.

———. "Notes on Leo Tuscus' Translation of the Liturgy of St. John Chrysostom," in *Didascaliae*. Festschrift A. M. Albareda. New York 1961, pp. 409–24.

Stump, E. See *Cambridge History of Later Medieval Philosophy*.

Szklenar, H. *Studien zum Bild des Orients in vorhöfischen deutschen Epen*. Göttingen 1966.

Tagliavini, C. *Le origini delle lingue neolatine*. 6th ed. Bologna 1972.

Theiler, W. *Die Vorbereitung des Neuplatonismus*. Berlin 1930.

Theiner, A., and F. Miklosich. *Monumenta spectantia ad unionem ecclesiarum graecae et romanae*. Vienna 1872.

Theisen, W. R. "*Liber de visu*: The Greco-Latin Translation of Euclid's Optics," *Mediaeval Studies* 41 (1979), 44–105.

Théry, G. "Scot Érigène, traducteur de Denys," *Archivum Latinitatis Medii Aevi* 6 (1931), 185–278.

———. *Études dionysiennes*. Vol. I: *Hilduin, traducteur de Denys*. Vol. II: *Hilduin, traducteur de Denys* [edition]. Études de philosophie médiévale 16 and 19. Paris 1932–37.

———. "Catalogue des manuscrits dionysiens des bibliothèques d'Autriche," *AHDL* 10 (1936), 163–264; 11 (1938), 87–131.

———. "Jean Sarrazin, 'traducteur' de Scot Érigène," in *Studia Mediaevalia in honorem R. J. Martin*. Bruges n.d. [1948], 359–81.

———. "Documents concernant Jean Sarrazin," *AHDL* 18 (1951), 45–87.

———. *Autour du décret de 1210: I. David de Dinant*. Kain, Belgium, 1925.

———. "Essai sur David de Dinant d'après Albert le Grand et Saint Thomas," in *Mélanges Thomistes*. Kain 1923, pp. 361–408.

Thibaut, A. See *Richesses et déficiences des anciens psautiers latins*.

Thiel, M. *Grundlagen und Gestalt der Hebräischkenntnisse des frühen Mittelalters*. Biblioteca degli 'Studi Medievali' 4. Spoleto 1973, [pp. 3–211 = *Studi Medievali* III 10/3 (1969), 4–212].

Thorndike, L. A. *A History of Magic and Experimental Science*. Vols. I–IV. New York 1923–34.

———. "Relation between Byzantine and Western Science and Pseudo-Science before 1350," *Janus* 51 (1964), 1–48.

Thurot, C. "Notices et extraits de divers manuscrits latins pour servir à l'histoire des doctrines grammaticales au moyen âge," *Notices et Extraits de la Bibliothèque Nationale* 22/2. Paris 1869.

Tisserant, E. *Ascension d'Isaïe. Traduction de la version éthiopienne avec les principales variantes des versions grecque, latines et slave*. Paris 1909.

Toubert, H. "Le bréviaire d'Oderisius (Paris, Bibliothèque Mazarine, MS 364) et les influences byzantines au Mont-Cassin," *Mélanges de l'École française de Rome* 83 (1971), 187–261.

Tougard, A. *L'hellénisme dans les écrivains du moyen-âge du septième au douzième siècle*. Paris 1886.

Tournoy, G. "De transmissie van griekse teksten uit de Oudheid," *School en Omroep* (Jan. 1979), 13–17.

Traube, L. "O Roma nobilis. Philologische Untersuchungen aus dem Mittelalter," Abh. Munich 19 (1891), 299–395.

———. *Einleitung in die lateinische Philologie des Mittelalters* [transcription of lectures]. Ed. P. Lehmann. Munich 1911.

Troje, H. E. *Europa und griechisches Recht* [inaugural lecture]. Frankfurt 1971.

———. *Graeca leguntur. Die Aneignung des byzantinisches Rechts und die Entstehung eines humanistischen Corpus iuris civilis in der Jurisprudenz des 16. Jahrhunderts*. Cologne/Vienna 1971.

Turner, C. H. *Ecclesiae Occidentalis Monumenta Iuris Antiquissima*. *Canonum et Conciliorum Graecorum Interpretationes Latinae*. Vols. I/1, I/2, and II/1. Oxford 1899/1913/1907.

Ullendorff, E., and C. F. Beckingham. *The Hebrew Letters of Prester John*. Oxford 1982.
Ullman, B. L. *The Humanism of Coluccio Salutati*. Padua 1963.
———. "Geometry in the Mediaeval Quadrivium," *Studi di Bibliografia e di Storia in onore di R. de Marinis*. Verona 1964, IV, 263–85.
Usener, H. "Legendenaustausch der griechischen und römischen Kirche, *Jahrbücher für prot. Theologie* 13 (1887), 240–59.

Vaccari, A. "La Grecia nell'Italia meridionale," *Orientalia Christiana Analecta* 3 (1925), 273–323.
Van de Vyver, A. "Les étapes du développement philosophique du haut moyen-âge," *Revue Belge de Philologie et d'Histoire* 7 (1929), 425–52.
———. "Les plus anciennes traductions latines médiévales (X^e–XIe siècles) de traités d'astronomie et d'astrologie," *Osiris* 1 (1936), 658–91.
Veloudis, G. *Der neugriechische Alexander*. Munich 1968.
Venezia e Bisanzio [exhibition catalogue]. Ed. I. Furlan et al. Venice 1974.
Verbraken, P.-P. "Deux anciennes versions latines de l'Homélie sur l'Aumône CPG 4618 attribuée à Jean Chrysostome," in ANTIΔΩPON. Festschrift Maurits Geerard. Wetteren 1984, I, 33–45.
Voigt, G. *Die Wiederbelebung des classischen Alterthums oder das erste Jahrhundert des Humanismus*. Vols. I–II. 3rd ed. Berlin 1893.
Von den Brincken, A.-D. *Die "Nationes Christianorum Orientalium" im Verständnis der lateinischen Historiographie von der Mitte des 12. bis in die zweite Hälfte des 14. Jahrhunderts*. Cologne/Vienna 1973.
Von den Steinen, W. *Notker der Dichter und seine geistige Welt*. Vols. I–II. Bern 1948.
Vuillemin-Diem, G. "Untersuchungen zu Wilhelm von Moerbekes Metaphysikübersetzung," in *Studien zur mittelalterlichen Geistesgeschichte und ihren Quellen*. Ed. A. Zimmermann. Berlin/New York 1982, pp. 102–208.

Walker, G. S. M. "On the Use of Greek Words in the Writings of Columbanus of Luxeuil," *Archivum Latinitatis Medii Aevi* 21 (1951), 117–31.
Wallach, L. *Diplomatic Studies in Latin and Greek Documents from the Carolingian Age*. Ithaca, N.Y., 1977.
Walzer, R. *Greek into Arabic*. Oxford 1962.
Wattenbach, W., and W. Levison [and H. Löwe]. *Deutschlands Geschichtsquellen im Mittelalter: Vorzeit und Karolinger*. H. 1–5. Weimar 1952–73.
Wattenbach, W., and R. Holtzmann. *Deutschlands Geschichtsquellen im Mittelalter: Deutsche Kaiserzeit*. H. 1. 3rd ed. Tübingen 1948. H. 2–4. 2nd ed. Tübingen 1948.
Wattenbach, W., and R. Holtzmann [and F.-J. Schmale]. *Deutschlands Geschichtsquellen im Mittelalter: Die Zeit der Sachsen und Salier, "Dritter Teil."* Darmstadt 1971.
Wattenbach, W., and F.-J. Schmale. *Deutschlands Geschichtsquellen im Mittelalter: Vom Tode Kaiser Heinrichs V. bis zum Ende des Interregnum*. Vol. I Darmstadt 1976.
Weise, O. *Die griechischen Wörter im Latein*. Leipzig 1882.
Weiss, R. *Humanism in England during the Fifteenth Century*. 3rd ed. Oxford 1967.
———. *Medieval and Humanist Greek*. Padua 1977: "Greek in Western Europe at the End of the Middle Ages," 3–12 [originally in *Dublin Review* 119 (1955)]; "The Greek Culture of South Italy in the Later Middle Ages," 13–43 [originally in *Proceedings of the Brit. Academy* 37 (1953)]; "Lo studio del greco all'abbazia di San Dionigi durante il medioevo," 44–59 [originally in *Rivista di Storia della Chiesa in Italia* 6 (1952)]; "Lo studio del greco all'università di Parigi alla fine del Medioevo," 60–64 [originally in *Convivium* 23 (1955)]; "Per una lettera di Lorenzo d'Aquileia sullo studio del greco e delle lingue orientali a Parigi alla fine del Duecento," 65–67 [originally in *Rivista di Storia della Chiesa in Italia* 5 (1951)]; "England and the Decree of the Council of Vienne on the Teaching of Greek, Arabic, Hebrew and Syriac," 68–79 [originally in *Bibliothèque d'Humanisme et Renaissance* 14 (1952)]; "The Study of Greek in England during the Fourteenth Century," 80–107 [originally in *Rinascimento* 2 (1951)]; "The Translators from the Greek of the Angevin

Court of Naples," 108–33 [originally in *Rinascimento* 1 (1950)]; "Per la storia degli studi greci del Petrarca: Il 'Triglossos,'" 136–49 [originally in *Annali della Scuola Normale Superiore di Pisa*, Classe di Lettere II/21 (1952)]; "Petrarca e il mondo greco," 166–92 [originally in *Atti e Memorie dell'Accademia Petrarca di Lettere, Arti e Scienze di Arezzo* II/36 (1952–1953)]; "Per la storia degli studi greci alla Curia papale nel tardo Duecento e nel Trecento," 193–203; "Lo studio di Plutarco nel Trecento," 204–26 [originally in *La Parola del Passato* 8 (1953)]; "Gli inizi dello studio del greco a Firenze," 227–54; "Iacopo Angeli da Scarperia (c. 1360–1410/11)," 255–77 [originally in *Medioevo e Rinascimento*, Festschrift Bruno Nardi, Florence 1955]; "Ciriaco d'Ancona in Oriente," 284–99 [originally in *Venezia e l'Oriente fra tardo Medioevo e Rinascimento*, Florence 1966].

————. *The Renaissance Discovery of Classical Antiquity*. Oxford 1969.

————. "Biondo Flavio archeologo," *Studi Romagnoli* 14 (1963), 335–41.

Weitzmann, K. "Various Aspects of Byzantine Influence on the Latin Countries from the Sixth to the Twelfth Centuries," *Dumbarton Oaks Papers* 30 (1966), 3–24.

Wellas, M. B. *Griechisches aus dem Umkreis Kaiser Friedrichs II*. Munich 1983.

Wellesz, E. *Eastern Elements in Western Chant: Studies in the Early History of Ecclesiastical Music*. Oxford/Boston 1947. Rev. by M. F. Bukofzer, *Speculum* 23 (1948), 520–23; B. Stäblein, *Die Musikforschung* 5 (1952), 60–63 [with a reply by Wellesz, pp. 131–37]; J. Handschin, *Acta Musicologica* 24 (1952), 199–202.

Wenger, A. *L'Assomption de la T. S. Vierge dans la tradition byzantine du VIe au Xe siècle. Études et documents*. Paris 1955.

Westerbergh, U. *Anastasius Bibliothecarius: Sermo Theodori Studitae de sancto Bartholomeo apostolo*. Stockholm 1963.

White, A. See *Boethius: His Life . . .*

Wickersheimer, E. *Dictionnaire biographique des médecins en France au moyen âge*. Vols. I–II. Paris 1936. Supplement. Genf/Paris 1979.

————. *Les manuscrits latins de médecine du haut moyen âge dans les bibliothèques de France*. Paris 1966.

Wilpert, P. "Philon bei Nikolaus von Kues," in *Antike und Orient im Mittelalter*. Berlin 1962, pp. 69–79.

Wilson, N. G. "A Mysterious Byzantine Scriptorium: Ioannikios and His Colleagues," *Scrittura e Civiltà* 7 (1983), 161–76.

————. "Litera Neritina," *Scriptorium* 21 (1967), 73 f.

————. "New Light on Burgundio of Pisa," *Studi Italiani di filologia classica* III/3 (1986), 113–18.

Wingate, S. D. "The Mediaeval Latin Versions of the Aristotelian Scientific Corpus, with Special Reference to the Biological Works." Diss. London 1931.

Winkelmann, F. "Spätantike lateinische Übersetzungen christlicher griechischer Literatur," *Theologische Literaturzeitung* 92 (1967), cols. 229–40.

————. "Einige Bemerkungen zu den Aussagen des Rufinus von Aquileia und des Hieronymus über ihre Übersetzungstheorie und -methode," in *Kyriakon*. Festschrift Johannes Quasten. Vol. II. Münster 1970, pp. 532–47.

Wissenschaft im Mittelalter [exhibition catalogue]. Ed. O. Mazal, E. Irblich, and I. Németh. Vienna 1975.

Yates, F. A. "Ramon Lull and John Scotus Eriugena," in *Lull and Bruno: Collected Essays*. Vol. I. London/Boston/Henley 1982, pp. 78–125.

Zaccaria, V. "Pier Candido Decembrio e Leonardo Bruni," *Studi Medievali* III/8 (1967), 529–54.

————. "Pier Candido Decembrio, Michele Pizolpasso e Ugolino Pisani," *Atti dell'Istituto Veneto di scienze lettere ed arti* 133 (1974/75), 187–212.

————. "Pier Candido Decembrio traduttore della 'Repubblica' di Platone," *Italia Medioevale e Umanistica* 2 (1959), 179–206.

Zagiba, F. *Musikgeschichte Mitteleuropas von den Anfängen bis zum Ende des 10. Jahrhunderts*. Vol. 1. Vienna 1976.

Zanetti, P. S. "Sul criterio e il valore della traduzione per Cicerone e S. Girolamo," in *Atti del I congresso internazionale di Studi Ciceroniani*. Vol. II. Rome 1961, pp. 355–405.

Zgusta, L. "Die Rolle des Griechischen im Römischen Kaiserreich," in *Die Sprachen im Römischen Reich der Kaiserzeit*. Ed. G. Neumann and J. Mutermann. Cologne 1980, pp. 121–45.

Zilliacus, H. *Zum Kampf der Weltsprachen im oströmischen Reich*. Helsinki 1935.

Zimmer, F. "Der Codex Augiensis (Cambridge, Trinity College B.17.1), eine Abschrift des Boernerianus (Dresden, Sächs. Landesbibliothek A 145ᵇ)," *Zeitschrift für wissenschaftliche Theologie* 30 (1887), 76–91.

Chronological Table

(Abbreviations as in Index of Names; Cpl. = Constantinople)

from 200	Oldest Latin Bible translation: "Vetus latina"
ca. 207–32	Origen teaches the allegorical exegesis of the Bible in Alexandria
245–70	Plotinus revives Platonism in Rome
254	D. Origen in Caesarea
325	I Ecumenical Council in Nicaea (I)
356	D. St. Anthony, monastic father
364	Greco-Latin–educated Ausonius teaches the future emperor Gratian in Trier
ca. 365	1st anonymous translation of Athanasius' *Life of St. Anthony*
ca. 370	Evagrius of Antioch, 2nd translation of the *Life of St. Anthony*
ca. 378	Jerome translates Eusebius' *Chronicle* and completes it up to 378
ca. 380	P. Damasus I commissions Jerome to revise the Latin Bible
	Praetextatus translates Themistius' Aristotle commentary
	Avienus translates Aratus' *Phainomena*
381	II Ecumenical Council in Cpl. (I)
386	Jerome emigrates to Bethlehem. Palestine becomes a center of Greco-Latin literature
ca. 390	Rufinus translates Origen, *Peri archon*
393	Jerome, *De viris illustribus*
from 394	Jerome translates *Peri archon* (as counter-translation to Rufinus')
395	Rufinus translates Eusebius' *Ecclesiastical History* and completes it up to the death of Theodosius the Great (395)
ca. 400	Macrobius writes the *Saturnalia* and a commentary on the *Somnium Scipionis*
	Itinerarium Egeriae (*Peregrinatio Aetheriae*)
	Eustathius translates Basil's *Hexaemeron Homilies*
	Rufinus translates the Adamantius Dialogue
	Rufinus, *Historia monachorum in Aegypto*
after 400	Chalcidius translates the *Timaeus*
405	John Cassian founds the monastery of St. Victor at Marseille
410	D. Rufinus
415/20	Anianus of Celeda translates John Chrysostom's homilies on Matthew and *De laudibus S. Pauli*
after 415	Avitus of Braga translates the *Revelatio S. Stephani*
after 419	The *Regula formatarum* of the Council of Nicaea arrives in the West via P. Atticus of Cpl.

420	D. Jerome
ca. 420	John Cassian, *Collationes patrum*
ca. 428	In his *De haeresibus* Augustine translates parts of Epiphanius' *Panarion*
430	D. Augustine
431	III Ecumenical Council in Ephesus; Marius Mercator translates the conciliar acts into Latin
ca. 439	Martianus Capella, *De nuptiis Mercurii et Philologiae*
440	*Vita S. Melaniae*; end of Palestine's Greco-Latin literary epoch
451	IV Ecumenical Council in Chalcedon
467–72	The Greek Anthemius is emperor in the West
485	D. Proclus
496–545	Dionysius Exiguus works as a translator in the service of the Church in Rome
ca. 500	Dionysius Areopagita
	Gennadius of Marseille, *De viris illustribus*
after 500	Translation of works of Oribasius the physician, in Gothic Ravenna
514–23	Dionysius Exiguus dedicates a bilingual (Greco-Latin) collection of conciliar canons to P. Hormisdas
524	Boethius, *De consolatione Philosophiae*
ca. 525	With his *Liber de Paschate* Dionysius Exiguus introduces the Alexandrine calculation of the date of Easter; he translates the *Vita Pachomii* and Gregory of Nyssa, *De conditione hominis*
526–27	Priscian, *Institutiones artis grammaticae*
529	The Synod of Vienne introduces the *kyrie* in Gaul
ca. 529	*Benedicti regula*
533	E. Justinian promulgates the *Digests* of the *Corpus Iuris Civilis*
after 537	Cassiodorus founds Vivarium and writes the *Institutiones*; translators of Vivarium: Epiphanius, Bellator, Mutianus; most significant translations: *Historia tripartita* and Flavius Josephus, *Antiquitates*
537–751	Byzantine epoch of the papacy
ca. 550	*Opus imperfectum in Matthaeum*
	Rusticus revises the translation of the conciliar acts of Ephesus and Chalcedon
553	V Ecumenical Council at Cpl. (II)
	Byzantine victory over the remaining Goths on Mt. Vesuvius
before 555	The Roman deacon Pelagius (after 555, P. Pelagius I) translates *Verba seniorum*
568	The Lombards in Italy
ca. 570	B. Germanus of Paris, *Expositio Brevis Antiquae Liturgiae Gallicanae*
before 580	Paschasius of Dumio translates the *Liber Geronticon*
593	Gregory the Great, *Dialogi*
619	D. Johannes Moschus, author of *Leimon*, in Rome
626	Siege of Cpl. by the Persian King Chosroes II
ca. 629	Isidore of Seville, *Etymologiae*
before 649	1st Greek monastery in Rome: SS. Vincentius and Anastasius (Tre Fontane)

649	The Lateran Synod, led by Maximus Confessor and the Greeks of Rome, rejects Monothelitism
655	P. Martin I dies in exile in the Crimea
662	D. Maximus Confessor
668	P. Vitalian I sends the Greek monks Hadrian and Theodore to England
680–81	VI Ecumenical Council in Cpl. (III)
682–83	The bilingual Sicilian P. Leo II begins a translation of the acts of the 6th Council
687–701	P. Sergius I introduces the Greek Feasts of the Virgin in Rome
ca. 690	Aldhelm of Malmesbury, *De metris, aenigmatibus ac pedum regulis*
before 700	Book of Lindisfarne: "ornamental Greek"
725	Beda Venerabilis, *De temporum ratione*
725–31	Bede writes the *Retractatio in actus apostolorum* with the aid of a bilingual manuscript of the Acts of the Apostles (Oxford, Laud. gr. 35)
741–52	P. Zacharias I translates Gregory's *Dialogi* into Greek
758–87	Duke Arichis II of Benevento
771–814	Charlemagne
774	Charlemagne conquers the Lombard Kingdom; the Frankish domains border on the Greek
781	Hruodtrud, Charlemagne's oldest daughter, betrothed to Basileus Constantine VI
782–86	A. Petrus of Reichenau brings a Greek psalterium from Rome
783	Paulus Diaconus is to teach Greek at the Carolingian court
787	VII Ecumenical Council in Nicaea (II); Empress Eirene ends the first phase of iconoclasm; Byzantine icono-theology formulated
after 787	B. Theodulf of Orleans writes the "Libri Carolini" in response to the Council
789	The Carolingians found the monastery of S. Ambrogio outside of Milan
ca. 799	*Formae litterarum secundum Graecos* (Vienna, Österreichische Nationalbibliothek 795)
800	Charlemagne becomes emperor; the "Zweikaiserproblem" arises
811	A. Heito of Reichenau envoy in Cpl.
812	Greek legation in Aachen; Greek *laudes* for Charlemagne; antiphons translated from Greek: *Veterem hominem*
813	AB. Amalar of Trier and Petrus of Nonantola in Cpl.: *Versus marini*
813–20	Iconoclasm of E. Leo V, the Armenian; Methodius in exile in Rome
before 817	Hrabanus Maurus, *De laudibus sanctae crucis*
825	Synod of Paris: reinstatement of iconolatry in the West
827	Byzantine legation presents the Greek text of Dionysius Areopagita to Louis the Pious in Compiègne (Paris BN gr. 437)
835	Hilduin of St. Denis completes his translation of Dionysius Areopagita; translation of *Hymnos Akathistos* (in St. Denis?)
ca. 837	Envoys of Patriarchs Basil of Jerusalem and Christopher of Alexandria in Reichenau
840–77	Charles the Bald, most important literary patron of the early Middle Ages

ca. 841	Walahfrid Strabo, *De exordiis et incrementis*
842	Greek legation to K. Lothar in Trier
843	Synod of Cpl. finally concludes iconoclastic controversy
845–ca. 880	Johannes Scottus Eriugena at the West Frankish court; Greek poems for Charles the Bald
ca. 850	With the arrival of the Irishmen Marcus and Marcellus, the study of Graeca in St. Gall begins
	Dubthach's cryptogram
	Greco-Latin psalter studies in S. Ambrogio at Milan
	Marble calendar of S. Giovanni Maggiore in Naples
	Paschasius Radbertus, *Expositio in Matthaeum*
ca. 854	Ermenrich of Ellwangen, *Epistola ad Grimaldum*
after 856	Bertharius, a. of Monte Cassino, introduces Greek *liturgica*
before 858	Sedulian Psalter (Paris, Arsenal 8407)
858–67	P. Nicholas I; Anastasius Bibliothecarius begins his Greco-Latin translations: *Vita S. Iohannis Eleemosynarii, Vita Basilii*
858–78	B. Hincmar of Laon, patron of the Irish colony at Laon and of the Greek studies of the Irishman Martinus
ca. 858	John Scottus begins his new translation of the works of Dionysius Areopagita
ca. 863	John Scottus translates the *Ambigua* of Maximus Confessor
ca. 865	Christian of Stablo, *Expositio in Matthaeum*
ca. 867	John Scottus, *De divisione naturae*
ca. 868	B. Aeneas of Paris, *Adversus Graecos*
	Ratramnus of Corbie, *Contra Graecorum opposita*
	Anastasius Bibliothecarius translates the *Vita S. Iohannis Calybitae*
869–70	VIII Ecumenical Council in Cpl. (IV); among the Roman legates is Anastasius Bibliothecarius, who brings the acts to Rome and translates them
ca. 870	Codex Laudunensis 444, the "Thesaurus linguae graecae" of the Carolingian period
	Hincmar of Reims, *Opusculum LV capitulorum*
875–77	Anastasius Bibliothecarius translates on a grand scale, compiles the *Chronica tripartita*, revises John Scottus' Dionysian translation and the translation of the acts of the VII Ecumenical Council (Cpl. III)
875	Paulus Diaconus of Naples dedicates the *Vita S. Mariae Aegyptiacae* and the *Paenitentia Theophili* to Charles the Bald
ca. 875	Johannes of Naples translates the *Vita S. Nicolai*
after 875	Anastasius Bibliothecarius translates Methodius' *Passio S. Dionysii*, Maximus Confessor's *Mystagogia*, and the *Historia ecclesiastica*, attributed to Germanus of Cpl., for Charles the Bald
after 876	Guarimpotus of Naples translates the *Passio S. Eustratii et VI sociorum in Armenia*
ca. 876–98	B. Athanasius II of Naples, translator of the *Passio Arethae* and patron of the translators Guarimpotus and Gregorius
889–97	Abbo of St.-Germain-des-Prés, *Bella Parisiacae urbis*
ca. 900	Johannes Diaconus of Naples, translator of Greek hagiography and the *Passio XL martyrum Sebastenorum*

908	D. Remigius of Auxerre
909	B. Salomo III of Constance, *Psalterium quadrupartitum*
ca. 910	Duke Gregory II of Naples, patron of the translators Ursus and Bonitus
915–24	*Gesta Berengarii imperatoris*
933	John of Gorze, pilgrimage to Mt. Gargano
942	Archipresbyter Leo of Naples brings a copy of the Alexander romance from Cpl. to the Campanian ducal court
ca. 947	D. Israel of St. Maximin at Trier
949	Liudprand envoy of Berengar of Ivrea in Cpl.
before 950	Bonitus, subdeacon of Naples, translates the *Vita S. Theodori*
after 950	John of Amalfi translates the *Liber de miraculis* and *Vita vel passio S. Herinis virginis et martiris*
951	Otto I king of Italy
ca. 953	Leo Archipresbyter translates the *Vita Alexandri Magni*
955	Battle of Lechfeld; end of Hungarian raids
958	Liudprand begins the *Antapodosis* in Frankfurt
ca. 960	D. Subdeacon Petrus of Naples, reviser of numerous translations of Greek saints' lives
962	Otto I emperor
963	The monk Athanasius Athonites founds the first monastery on Mt. Athos
963–94	B. Gerard of Toul assembles Greeks and Irish
after 966	B. Reginold of Eichstätt writes the Latino-Greco-Hebrew *Historia de S. Willibaldo*
968	Liudprand of Cremona leads a legation to Cpl.: *Relatio de legatione Constantinopolitana*
971	AB. Gero of Cologne leads a legation to Cpl.
972	Otto II and Theophano married in Rome
973	D. Ekkehart I of St. Gall
	D. Otto (I) the Great
977	Sergius of Damascus becomes abbot of St. Boniface and Alexius on the Aventine
980	Birth of Otto III, son of Theophano and Otto II
ca. 980	Nilus of Rossano in the Duchy of Benevento
after 980	The Greek monk Gregory becomes abbot of Burtscheid
982	Battle of Cotrone
983–1002	Otto III
ca. 984	Master of the *Registrum Gregorii*
991	D. Empress Theophano, buried in St. Pantaleon at Cologne
997	Gerbert of Reims (d'Aurillac) tutor of Otto III
	Johannes Philagathos, antipope
997–1038	K. Stephan I of Hungary
998	Gerbert of Reims, *De rationali et ratione uti*
999–1003	As Silvester II, Gerbert reigns over the Western Church
999–1021	AB. Heribert of Cologne; Grecistic style in the Ottonian school of painting in Cologne
ca. 1000	The Doges Pietro and Otto Orseoli extend Venetian rule to Dalmatia

	Amalfian settlements in Cpl. and on Mt. Athos
1004	Nilus of Rossano founds the last Greek monastery in the vicinity of Rome: Grottaferrata
1007	E. Henry II establishes the see of Bamberg
1009–36	B. Meinwerk of Paderborn employs *greci operarii*
1016	D. The Armenian Symeon in Polirone
1018	E. Basil II of Cpl. subjugates the Bulgarians: opening of the land route to Cpl.
ca. 1020	E. Henry II's constellation mantle
1020–30	*Codex aureus Epternacensis*
1026–27	Pilgrimage to Palestine under the leadership of Richard of St. Vanne at Verdun
1027–28	Legation of B. Werner of Strasbourg in Cpl.
1034	D. Ademar of Chabannes in St. Martial at Limoges; he transmits the *Grammaticorum diadoche*
1035	D. Symeon, recluse in the Porta Nigra at Trier
1037	D. Avicenna
ca. 1050	Amalfian pilgrim hospice in Jerusalem
	In the Amalfian monastery on Mt. Athos, the monk Leo translates the *Miraculum a S. Michaele Chonis patratum* and occasions a translation of the romance of Barlaam and Josaphat
	Papias, *Elementarium doctrinae rudimentum*
1053	German troops, enlisted by P. Leo IX, defeated by Normans in southern Italy
1054	Humbert of Silva Candida places the bull of excommunication for the patriarch of Cpl. on the high altar of Hagia Sophia
	D. Hermannus Contractus of Reichenau, composer of sequences in Greco-Latin macaronic style
1058–87	A. Desiderius of Monte Cassino: the golden age of the monastery
after 1058	B. Alfanus of Salerno translates *Peri physeos anthropou* of Nemesius of Emesa
ca. 1060	D. Ekkehart IV of St. Gall
1064	Mass pilgrimage to Palestine
1065	Maurus of Amalfi and his son Pantaleon donate the bronze doors of Amalfi, which were cast in Cpl. The family Comitis Mauronis employs Johannes, a translator living in Cpl.
1082	Venetian trade privilege in Cpl.
1085	Alphonse VI of Castile conquers Moorish Toledo
1087	Constantinus Africanus, translator of Arabic medical treatises (*Liber Pantegni*), dies as a monk in Monte Cassino
1095–99	First Crusade ends with conquest of Jerusalem
1105	Bartholomaeus of Simeri founds the Patirion of Rosanno
after 1105	*Psalterium quadrupartitum* of Odo of Tournai
from 1108	Pisan quarter in Antioch; Stephan the Pisan translates there from Arabic
from 1111	Pisan quarter in Cpl.
1112	Petrus Grosolanus (Chrysolanus) disputes in Cpl.: *De processione spiritus sancti contra Graecos*
ca. 1120	Cerbanus (the Venetian?) translates at the imperial court in Cpl.

1122–56	A. Peter the Venerable of Cluny commissions the translation of the Koran from Arabic into Latin
1127	In Antioch, Stephan of Pisa executes a new translation of the *Liber Pantegni* and adds Dioscorides' *Medicaminum omnium breviarium*
1128	Jacobus Veneticus Graecus translates Aristotle's *Analytica posteriora*
1130–54	Roger II of Sicily
1131	Foundation of the Greek Salvator monastery "in lingua fari" at Messina
after 1131	Cerbanus translates Maximus Confessor's *Capita de caritate* for A. David of Pannonhalma (Hungary)
1136	Legation of B. Anselm of Havelberg and disputation with Nicetas of Nicomedia in Cpl.; translators: Jacobus Veneticus, Moses of Bergamo, Burgundio of Pisa
ca. 1140	Petrus Diaconus of Monte Cassino, *Altercatio contra Graecum quendam*
	Moses of Bergamo translates *Expositio in graecas dictiones quae inveniuntur in prologis S. Hieronymi* and *Exceptio compendiosa de divinitus inspirata scriptura*; he writes the *Liber Pergaminus*. First Western collector of Greek manuscripts during the Middle Ages
1141	D. Hugh of St. Victor, commentator on Dionysius, *De caelesti hierarchia*
1143–80	E. Manuel I
1145–53	P. Eugenius III, literary patron
1146	Bernard of Clairvaux preaches the second Crusade
before 1147	Cerbanus translates John of Damascus' *De fide orthodoxa*
1148	Burgundio of Pisa begins to translate John of Damascus' *De fide orthodoxa*
1149	Anselm of Havelberg, *Dialogi*
1151	Burgundio translates John Chrysostom's ninety homilies on Matthew
1154	Eugenius of Palermo translates Ptolemy's *Optica* from Arabic
	Anselm of Havelberg disputes with Basil of Achrida in Thessalonica
	D. Gilbertus Porretanus [Gilbert of Poitiers]
	D. William of Conches, commentator on the *Timaeus*, *De consolatione Philosophiae*, and Macrobius' commentary on the *Somnium Scipionis*
1154–66	William I of Sicily
1155–56	John of Salisbury has Greek lessons from a southern Italian
1156	Archdeacon Henricus Aristippus translates Plato's *Phaedo* and Aristotle's *Meteora* IV at the court of William I of Sicily
ca. 1157	John of Salisbury, *Entheticus*
1158	Henricus Aristippus brings the *Almagest* (Ptolemy) from Cpl.
	Wolfger of Prüfening, collector of glossaries (Clm 13002)
1159	John of Salisbury, *Metalogicon* and *Policraticus*
ca. 1160	Pascalis Romanus dedicates the *Disputatio Iudaeorum contra S. Anastasium*, translated from Greek, to P. Henricus Dandalo of Grado

	John of Salisbury (in the *Policraticus*) and Henricus Aristippus mention Pseudo-Plutarch, *De institutione principum*
1161	Henricus Aristippus translates Plato's *Meno*
after 1162	Burgundio presents Frederick Barbarossa with a new translation of Nemesius of Emesa's *De natura hominis*
1165	Pascalis Romanus, *Liber thesauri occulti*
1166	Synod of Cpl.; the Pisan Hugh Etherianus is adivsor to Manuel I
1166–69	Johannes Sarracenus executes a new translation of the works of Dionysius Areopagita and writes a commentary on *De caelesti hierarchia*
after 1166	Hugh Etherianus translates *Peri ton Francon kai ton loipon Latinon*
1167	Wilhelmus Medicus brings a second Dionysian manuscript to St. Denis from Cpl. (Paris BN gr. 933); from 1173 to 1186 he is abbot of St. Denis and translates from Greek
after 1167	Gerard of Cremona translates Proclus' *De essentia puritatis* from Arabic
1171	Hugh of Honau as envoy of E. Frederick I in Cpl.
1171–73	Burgundio translates John Chrysostom's eighty-eight homilies on the Gospel of St. John
1175	Hugh Etherianus collects Greek patristic texts and translates them in the *Liber de differentia naturae et personae*
	An unidentified Sicilian translator of Ptolemy's *Almagest* and Proclus' *Elementatio physicae*
1176	Leo Tuscus translates Achmet's work on dream interpretation and dedicates it to his brother, Hugh Etherianus
1179	Hugh of Honau brings back to Germany the *Liber de differentia naturae et personae* from his second embassy to Cpl.
1182	Massacre of Latins in Cpl.
1185	Norman conquest of Thessalonica
1187	Latin loss of Jerusalem
1189–91	Third Crusade; reconquest of Acre in 1191
1190–95	Eugenius of Palermo translates the prophecy of the Erythraean Sibyl
1190/1200	Hugutio of Pisa, *Derivationes*
1191–97	E. Henry VI
1193	D. Burgundio of Pisa
1193–1280	Albertus Magnus
1196	D. Averroes
1197	Philip of Swabia marries Irene (Maria), daughter of the Byzantine emperor
1201	Palaganos of Otranto copies Homer's *Odyssey* and the *Batrachomyomachia* ("The Battle of the Frogs and Mice," Heidelberg, Pal. gr. 45)
1202	D. Admiral Eugenius of Palermo, patron of Greco-Latin and Arabo-Latin translations
1204	Under Venetian leadership, Latin conquest of Cpl.
1205	B. Conrad of Halberstadt presents his cathedral with the Greek liturgical vestments

1205–7	Nicholas-Nectarius of Otranto interprets for the papal legates in Cpl. and publishes in Greek and Latin *Tria Syntagmata*
before 1210	Eberhard of Béthune, *Grecismus*
1211–50	E. Frederick II, final flowering of Greek culture in southern Italy
1212	D. Eberhard of Béthune
1217	Michael Scot translates Al-Bitrogi's (Alpetragius') *De sphaera* from Arabic, with the aid of the "Levite" Aebuteus
after 1217	Michael Scot translates Avicenna, *Abbreviationes*
1220	Nicholas-Nectarius leads a legation of E. Frederick II to the Greek imperial residence in Nicaea
1229	E. Frederick II contractually secures for the Latins access to the Holy Sepulchre for 15 years
1229–32	John Garland, *Cornutus*
1231	*Liber augustalis* ("Decrees of Melfi")
1232	Nicholas-Nectarius defends the southern Italian–Greek baptismal rite
1235	D. Nicholas-Nectarius of Casole, collector of Greek manuscripts: Aristophanes' comedies, Aristotle's *Sophistici Elenchi*, Homer's *Odyssey*; writer of the bilinguals of Casole; translator of the Basilian litgurgy
	B. Robert Grosseteste of Lincoln revises Burgundio's translation of John of Damascus' *De fide orthodoxa*
	D. Michael Scot, translator from Arabic
after 1235	Metropolitan George Bardanes debates the doctrine of purgatory with a Franciscan
1237	Nicholas Grecus (Siculus) in England
1239–43	Robert Grosseteste executes a new translation of the works of Dionysius Areopagita
1242	Robert Grosseteste translates *Testamenta XII patriarcharum*
1245	D. Alexander of Hales, probable author of *Exoticon*
1245–47	Robert Grosseteste translates Aristotle's *Nicomachean Ethics*
1246	D. Thomas Gallus, author of an *Extractio* from the works of Dionysius Areopagita
1248	P. Innocent IV wishes to have young men born in the "Orient" study theology in Paris
after 1250	*Brito metricus*
1252	D. John of Basingstoke, archdeacon of Leicester; probable translator of a Greek grammar (*Donatus grecus*)
	A Dominican in Cpl. writes *Contra Graecos*
1253	D. Robert Grosseteste
1254–63	Humbert of Romans, general of the Dominican Order, *Opus tripartitum*
1258–66	K. Manfred of Sicily, under whom Bartholomaeus of Messina translates Aristotle's *Magna moralia* and the Pseudo-Aristotelian *Problemata*, *De principiis*, *De signis*, and *De mundo*, among others, as well as a veterinary medical treatise by Hierocles
ca. 1260	Nicholas of Durazzo, b. of Cotrone, *Liber de processione spiritus sancti et fide trinitatis contra errores Graecorum*
1260–67	William of Moerbeke translates Aristotle

1261	Reconquest of Cpl. by E. Michael VIII
1264	Thomas Aquinas, *Contra errores Graecorum*
1266–68	Roger Bacon, "Doctor mirabilis," writes *Opus maius* and *Opus tertium*
1268	William of Moerbeke translates Proclus' *Elementatio theologica*
1268–72	William of Moerbeke translates the *Timaeus* and Proclus' commentary on the *Parmenides*
ca. 1270	Nicholas Grecus executes a new translation of Pseudo-Aristotle, *De mundo*
1274	XIV Ecumenical Council in Lyon (II); union with the Greek Church; Greek emperor's interpreters are Johannes Parastron (O.F.M.) and William of Moerbeke (O.P.)
ca. 1275	William of Mara, tract on the Greek alphabet
1276	Raimundus Lullus, "Doctor illuminatus," founds language and missionary school in Mallorca
1276–77	Petrus Hispanus reigns over the Western Church as P. Johannes XXI
1278	William of Moerbeke translates Aristotle's *Poetics* in Viterbo
1281	The ecclesiastical union dissolves
1282	The Sicilian Vespers
1285	D. Charles of Anjou; expelled the Arabs from and "de-Hellenized" southern Italy; founded court library in Naples; translations there of Arabic medical literature
1286	D. William of Moerbeke
ca. 1290	The Dominican Buonaccorsi of Bologna compiles the *Thesaurus veritatis fidei*
1291	Acre, the last Latin bastion in the Holy Land, falls
1291–92	A. Romanus of S. Benedetto Ullano in Calabria copies bilinguals (Psalter and evangelary)
ca. 1300	Petrus of Abano reedits Dioscorides' *De materia medica* and completes Burgundio's translation of Galen
1301	Charles II of Anjou commissions B. Stephan (?) of Oppido to translate two medical tracts from Greek into Latin
1308–45	In Naples, by commission of K. Robert I, Nicholas Theoprepos of Reggio translates medical works, esp. Galen and Hippocrates, but also Sophronius
1309–77	The popes reside in Avignon: "Babylonian Captivity"
1311	Catalonian founding of the Athenian Duchy
1312	XV Ecumenical Council in Vienne: "Linguistic Canon"
1316	Raimundus Lullus stoned to death in Tunis
1325–40	Boccaccio in Naples
1331	Nicholas Theoprepos envoy of K. Robert in Cpl.
1337	D. Angelo Clareno de Cingoli, Minorite and translator of Johannes Climacus' *Scala paradisi* and other ascetic works
1339–42	The Calabrese Barlaam envoy of the Greek emperor to the papal curia in Avignon; he occasionally teaches Greek; Petrarch studies under him
1344	Richard of Bury, *Philobiblon*
1347–48	Disappearance of the court library in Naples

ca. 1353	Nicholas Sigerus sends Petrarch a Homer codex from Cpl.: "beginning and typological example of a literary migration of incalculable consequence" (Georg Voigt)
1355	Chrysobull of E. John V to P. Innocent VI
ca. 1359–62	Boccaccio takes the southern Italian Leontius Pilatus into his house in Florence; Leontius translates the first five books of the *Iliad*
1360	Petrarch, "Letter to Homer" (XXIV 12)
1361	Leontius Pilatus teaches Greek in Florence and translates Euripides, *Hecuba*
1365	Boccaccio, *Genealogia deorum gentilium*
	D. Leontius Pilatus
1369	E. John V converts in the presence of P. Urban V; six translators assist with the preparation of the document: among others, Paul of Smyrna, Latin ab. of Cpl., and Demetrius Kydones (Rome, Arch. Vat., A.A.Arm.I–XVIII no. 401)
1372–73	Simon Atumanus translates Plutarch's *De cohibenda ira*
1374	D. Petrarch
1375	D. Boccaccio
1375–1406	Coluccio Salutati Florentine chancellor of state
ca. 1380	Simon Atumanus teaches Greek at the Roman curia
1384–88	Juan Fernández de Heredia commissions a translation of Plutarch's *Lives* into Aragonese
1387–95	K. John I of Aragon/Catalonia, collector of works on the history of Greek antiquity
ca. 1392	Coluccio Salutati revises Simon Atumanus' translation of Plutarch
1395	Jacopo Angeli da Scarperia travels to Cpl., under Turkish siege, learns Greek and collects manuscripts
	Coluccio Salutati receives the Aragonese translation of Plutarch's *Lives*
1396	D. Juan Fernández de Heredia
	Manuel Chrysoloras and Demetrios Kydones in Italy
1397	Manuel Chrysoloras teaches Greek in Florence, writes the textbook *Erotemata*, and inspires a translation of Lucian; through the work of his students (e.g., Bruni, Poggio, Filelfo), Florence becomes the leading city of Greco-Latin translations
1399–1403	E. Manuel II travels through the West, seeking aid, and visits St. Denis in 1401; later sends the monastery a manuscript of the *Areopagitica* (Paris, Louvre Ivoires A 53)
ca. 1400	Jacopo Angeli da Scarperia translates Plutarch's *Lives*
after 1400	In Milan, Manuel Chrysoloras translates Plato's *Politeia*
1403	D. Radulf of Rivo; brought from Grottaferrata to Flanders the Greek New Testament which Erasmus later used for his second edition of the Greek NT (Vienna, Österreichische Nationalbibliothek Suppl. graec. 52)
1406	Leonardo Bruni translates Demosthenes' *Orations* and Plutarch's *Lives* into elegant Latin and plans to translate Plato's works
	Florence defeats Pisa and takes the "Codex Pisanus" of the Justinian *Digests*
1409	Council of Pisa

1409–10	The Greek Franciscan (from Crete) Petrus Philargis rules Western Church as Alexander V
1410	Scarperia completes the translation of Ptolemy's *Cosmography*
ca. 1414	Bruni translates the Aristotelian *Economics*
1414–18	XVI Ecumenical Council in Constance; Agapito Cenci translates Aristeides; Pietro Paolo Vergerio, secretary of K. Sigismund, translates Arrianus' *Anabasis*; Chrysoloras is candidate for the papacy
1415	Manuel Chrysoloras, first important Greek teacher in the West since antiquity, dies in Constance and is buried in the Dominican monastery (now the Inselhotel)
1421–23	Aurispa brings 238 Greek manuscripts to Italy from his journey to Cpl.
1421–58	K. Alphonse of Naples and Sicily
ca. 1423	Bruni translates Plato's *Phaedrus*
1425	Aurispa teaches Greek in Florence
1427	D. Uberto Decembrio; revised the Latin style of Chrysoloras' translation of Plato's *Politeia*
	Bruni Florentine chancellor of state
1429	Francesco Filelfo teaches Greek in Florence
from 1431	Council of Basil; in 1434 confirms the "Linguistic Canon" of the Council of Vienne
1432	Ambrogio Traversari in Grottaferrata
1436	Traversari executes a new translation of the *Corpus Dionysiacum*
1437	Bruni completes the translation of Aristotle's *Ethics*
	Western embassy to Cpl., including Nicholas of Cusa
1438–39	XVII Ecumenical Council in Ferrara/Florence; revived union with the Greek Church; many Greek scholars remain in Italy, among them Georgios Gemisthos Plethon
before 1439	Pier Candido Decembrio completes the revision of Chrysoloras' translation of Plato's *Politeia*, begun by his father
1439	Bessarion converts and becomes the "cardinal of Nicaea"; his court of literati in Rome becomes the intellectual focal point of Greeks in Italy
	D. Ambrogio Traversari
1440	Nicholas of Cusa, *De docta ignorantia*
	Decembrio translates portions of the *Iliad* into Latin verse
ca. 1440	Under the influence of Plethon's orations, Cosimo de' Medici supports Platonic studies in Florence
1442	Lorenzo Valla, *De elegantiis linguae latinae*
1443	Basel receives the Greek book collection of Johannes of Ragusa
1444	D. Leonardo Bruni Aretino
1446	Bessarion assumes supervision of Italy's Greek monasteries; he procures valuable parts of the library of Casole; in the course of time his Greek library becomes the largest in the West (ca. 500 volumes)
1447	Poggio translates Xenophon's *Kyrou paideia*
1447–55	P. Nicholas V, the first and best of the Renaissance popes, patron of literature and the "graeculi esurientes"; many translation commissions for George of Trebizond and many others

1449   Nicholas of Cusa, *Apologia doctae ignorantiae*
1450   Theodore of Gaza assumes a chair of philosophy in Rome and trans-
        lates Aristotle

        Niccolo Perotti enters the service of Bessarion; P. Nicholas V com-
        missions him to translate Polybius and regales him with princely
        honors
1451   D. Plethon, intellectual father of the Platonic Academy
1452   Lorenzo Valla translates Thucydides for P. Nicholas V and receives
        500 scudi and the commission to translate Herodotus

        George of Trebizond botches a translation of the *Almagest* (Ptol-
        emy) and falls into papal disfavor
1453   Decembrio translates Appianos; Guarino translates Strabo's *Geog-
        raphy*

        Cpl. falls to the Turks; Isidore of Kiev estimates the number of
        manuscripts destroyed at 120,000; Nicholas V seeks Greek manu-
        scripts for sale
1454   Enea Silvio Piccolomini presents K. Alfonse of Naples with Verger-
        io's translation of Arrianus; Bartholomaeus Facius revises the
        translation
1455   Bessarion is candidate for the papacy; the papal library contains 353
        Greek manuscripts at the death of Nicholas V
from 1456   Johannes Argyropoulos teaches at the Florentine Academy
1457   D. Lorenzo Valla
1459   D. Aurispa, teacher of Greek in Bologna, Florence, and Ferrara
1460   D. Guarino of Verona, teacher of Greek in Venice, Verona, Flor-
        ence, and Ferrara; reviser of Chrysoloras' Greek grammar

        Mistra falls to the Turks
1463   Marsilio Ficino receives a commission from Cosimo de' Medici to
        translate and write commentaries on Hermes Trismegistus and
        Plato
1464   D. Nicholas of Cusa, collector of important Greco-Latin codices,
        mediator between Middle Ages and modern times

Index of Manuscripts Cited

(+ = lost or destroyed)

PAPYRI AND ARCHIVAL
DOCUMENTS

Index of Names [to 1800]

[a. = abbot/abbess; ab. = archbishop; ap. = apostle; b. = bishop; c. = cardinal; d. = duke/duchess; e. = emperor/empress; g. = grammarian; k. = king; m. = metropolitan; mk. = monk; p. = pope/patriarch; ph. = physician; q. = queen; St. = Saint; tr. = translator]

402